Women in Behavior Science

Women in Behavior Science is a unique text that showcases the perspectives, stories, and lessons of notable female behavior scientists at all stages of their careers, with relevance for the field's many women pursuing careers in academia today.

With the insights of esteemed female behavior scientists from diverse backgrounds, the book brings together their challenges and successes to include their own distinct perspectives on their professional and personal development. The book includes three sections that span the different phases of the academic lifespan from graduate school to retirement and post-retirement. Each section covers a wide range of topics such as expanding one's work in new and diverse areas; deciding when and how to make transitions; making something out of nothing or very little; navigating relationships with family, children, and life partners both inside and outside of academy; values-based living; how to thrive in competitive environments; and building values-consistent repertoires in settings that may be gender-marginalizing. Presenting a behind-the-scenes view of academia, the authors also provide open and vulnerable narratives about their psychological and socio-cultural experiences, their stories of marginalization, their difficulties with mental and physical health challenges, grief and loss, and caring for others with chronic health conditions.

Reframing the cultural-level recognition of female behavior scientists today, this book is essential reading for graduate and postgraduate students of Behavioral Science, especially for those focusing on diversity and cultural issues. It is also a must-read for professionals interested in understanding the experiences of diverse groups in this field.

Ruth Anne Rehfeldt is currently Dean at Waubonsee Community College. She has a 20+ year history of mentoring graduate students in behavior analysis, and has won a number of awards for her teaching and research while a faculty member at Southern Illinois University. Ruth Anne served as Editor for The Psychological Record, President for the Association for Behavior Analysis International (ABAI), and is Fellow of both the Association for Behavior Analysis International and the Association for Contextual Behavior Science. Her research has focused on interventions for teaching language and cognitive skills in a variety of populations and settings.

Traci M. Cihon was an associate professor at the University of North Texas while this volume was completed. She is the current editor of *Behavior and Social Issues*, an active member of the Behaviorists for Social Responsibility Special Interest Group of ABAI, and maintains an active research agenda related to include culturo behavior science and behavioral systems analysis, social behavior and social action, behavioral approaches to education (e.g., language acquisition, reading instruction, Precision Teaching), and interdisciplinary collaboration.

Erin B. Rasmussen is Professor of Experimental Psychology at Idaho State University. Her research interests are broadly in the area of behavioral economics and behavioral pharmacology. Her specific work, which has been funded by the National Institutes of Health, focuses on behavioral economic factors that influence food-based choice related to obesity in both humans and rats.

Behavior Science: Theory, Research and Practice
Series Editor: The Association for Behavior Analysis International

Behavior Science Perspectives on Culture and Community
Edited by Traci M. Cihon and Mark A. Mattaini

Applied Behavior Science in Organizations
Consilience of Historical and Emerging Trends in Organizational Behavior Management
Edited by Ramona A. Houmanfar, Mitch Fryling & Mark P. Alavosius

A Programming Contingency Analysis of Mental Health
Israel Goldiamond

Acceptance and Commitment for Behavior Analysts
A Practice Guide from Theory to Treatment
Edited by Mark R. Dixon, Steven C. Hayes and Jordan Belisle

Women in Behavior Science
Observations of Life Inside and Outside the Academy
Edited by Ruth Anne Rehfeldt, Traci M. Cihon and Erin B. Rasmussen

For more information about this series, please visit: www.routledge.com/Behavior-Science/book-series/ABAI

Women in Behavior Science

Observations of Life Inside and Outside the Academy

Edited by Ruth Anne Rehfeldt, Traci M. Cihon and Erin B. Rasmussen

Routledge
Taylor & Francis Group
NEW YORK AND LONDON

Designed cover image: Getty

First published 2023
by Routledge
605 Third Avenue, New York, NY 10158

and by Routledge
4 Park Square, Milton Park, Abingdon, Oxon, OX14 4RN

Routledge is an imprint of the Taylor & Francis Group, an informa business

Library of Congress Cataloging-in-Publication Data
Names: Rehfeldt, Ruth Anne, editor. | Cihon, Traci, editor. | Rasmussen, Erin Brooke, 1971– editor.
Title: Women in behavior science : observations of life inside and outside of the academy / edited by Ruth Anne Rehfeldt, Traci Cihon & Erin B. Rasmussen.
Description: 1 Edition. | New York, NY : Routledge, 2023. | Series: Behaviour science ABAI | Includes bibliographical references and index. | Summary: "Women in Behavior Science is a unique text that showcases the perspectives, stories, and lessons of notable female behavior scientists at all stages of their careers, with relevance for the field's many women pursuing careers in academia today"— Provided by publisher.
Identifiers: LCCN 2022043799 (print) | LCCN 2022043800 (ebook) | ISBN 9781032107318 (hardcover) | ISBN 9781032107301 (paperback) | ISBN 9781003216773 (ebook)
Subjects: LCSH: Women psychologists. | Women in science.
Classification: LCC BF109.A1 .W645 2023 (print) | LCC BF109.A1 (ebook) | DDC 150.82—dc23/eng/20221212
LC record available at https://lccn.loc.gov/2022043799
LC ebook record available at https://lccn.loc.gov/2022043800

ISBN: 978-1-032-10731-8 (hbk)
ISBN: 978-1-032-10730-1 (pbk)
ISBN: 978-1-003-21677-3 (ebk)

DOI: 10.4324/9781003216773

Typeset in Bembo
by Apex CoVantage, LLC

Contents

Contributors

Cynthia M. Anderson The May Institute

Sierra Baca-Zeff Idaho State University

Kelly M. Banna Department of Psychology, Millersville University of Pennsylvania

Jade Campbell Louisiana Contextual Science Research Group, University of Louisiana at Lafayette

Traci M. Cihon University of North Texas

Ariana D'Arms Western Connecticut State University

Paula Danquah-Brobby, PhD, BCBA, LBA, IBA George Mason University, College of Science

Karola Dillenburger Queens University—Belfast

Jovonnie Esquierdo-Leal University of Nevada, Reno

Lynn Farrell National College of Ireland

Casey Irwin Helvey Department of Psychology, University of North Carolina Wilmington

Luiza Hübner Director of Behavior Analysis Hübner Center (BAHC), in São Paulo, Brazil

Martha Hübner Full professor at University of São Paulo, Brazil, Psychology Institute and researcher at the National Institute of Science and Technology, Instituto Nacional de Ciência e Psicologia (INCT), Estudos sobre Comportamento, Cognição e Ensino (ECCE), FAPESP #2014/50909–8 CNPq #564686/2014–1 CAPES #8887.136407/2017–00

Amoy Kito Hugh-Pennie The Children's Institute of Hong Kong

Corina Jimenez-Gomez Auburn University

Karen Kate Kellum University of Mississippi

Louise McHugh University College Dublin

Morgan Musquez Idaho State University

Adel C. Najdowski Pepperdine University

Amy L. Odum Department of Psychology, Utah State University

Stephanie M. Peterson Western Michigan University

Erin B. Rasmussen Idaho State University

Ruth Anne Rehfeldt The Chicago School of Professional Psychology, Chicago

Sarah M. Richling Auburn University

Lise Roll-Pettersson Stockholm University

Kathryn M. Roose University of Nevada, Reno

Rocío Rosales University of Massachusetts Lowell

Denise Ross-Page University of Wisconsin-Milwaukee, Institute for Urban Education

Allyson R. Salzer University of Kansas

Emily K. Sandoz Louisiana Contextual Science Research Group, University of Louisiana at Lafayette

Zuilma Gabriela Sigurðardóttir University of Iceland

Julie M. Slowiak, Ph.D., BCBA-D University of Minnesota Duluth

Brooke M. Smith Western Michigan University

Shrinidhi Subramaniam Department of Psychology and Child Development, California State University, Stanislaus

Beth Sulzer-Azaroff Professor Emerita, University of Massachusetts, Amherst

Eric C. Thompson School of Education and Human Sciences, University of Kansas

Janani Vaidya Louisiana Contextual Science Research Group, University of Louisiana at Lafayette and National Louis University

Wendy Donlin Washington Department of Psychology, University of North Carolina Wilmington

Jomella Watson-Thompson Department of Applied Behavioral Science, University of Kansas

Jennifer R. Wolgemuth University of South Florida

Introduction

Behavior analysis is a powerful science of behavior change. It has the potential to remediate suffering, shift systemic and structural contingencies that create barriers to justice, equity, and inclusion, and prevent the worsening of a wide variety of conditions. Embracing diverse views and perspectives can increase the variability that is cultivated when the voices of those who have been traditionally marginalized and oppressed are lifted, heard, and included. Although women behavior scientists have advanced relevant and valuable perspectives on behavior analysis as a science and practice, cultural-level contingencies have not always been recognized in their contributions.

In fact, the discipline has benefited from the contributions of many scholars with diverse, underrepresented, and intersectional identities over the course of decades, not all of which have been appropriately recognized. There is no doubt that the field of behavior analysis would not be the thriving discipline that it is today without the contributions of these individuals, many of whom identify as women. These women have held successful careers in academia; yet, their stories may not be familiar to you. There are many reasons why this may be the case. Perhaps it is because they have not yet told their stories, or perhaps it is because there has not been a platform for them to do so, or otherwise.

Several female academicians in behavior analysis were invited to contribute a chapter to this volume, *Women in Behavior Science: Observations on Life Inside and Outside the Academy*. This book showcases the perspectives, stories, and lessons of these prominent female behavior scientists. It is a volume that highlights the challenges and successes these women have experienced and it includes their unique perspectives on their professional and personal development. One purpose of this volume is to provide you, the audience, with a collection of insights, experiences, and wisdom acquired and told from the perspectives of female academicians in behavior analysis.

We specifically organized the book to reflect three stages of one's career in the academy, beginning with graduate school (Chapter 1) and the job search (Chapter 2) and ending with retirement (Chapter 23). It covers a wide range of topics such as expanding one's work in new and diverse areas (Chapter 17); deciding when and how to make transitions (Chapter 13); making something out of nothing or very little (Chapter 16); navigating relationships with family, children, and life partners both inside and outside of academy (Chapters 6, 10, and 19); loss and grief (Chapter 22); values-based living (Chapter 20); how to thrive in competitive environments (Chapter 21); and building values-consistent repertoires in settings that may be gender-marginalizing (Chapter 4). The collection also focuses on aspects of one's job such as mentoring and scholarship (Chapters 5, 6, and 7), as well as on the nuances of life outside of the academy (Chapters 3, 8, 12, 14, 15, and 18). It represents a contextual portrayal of the experiences of women scientists, intended to be shared with the field's many females pursuing careers in academia today. Our hope was not to provide a

DOI: 10.4324/9781003216773-1

recipe-like book or a set of how-tos, but rather, to reveal how one's experiences as an academician are colored by such life factors as parenting, changing jobs, enduring health issues, and more. Indeed, being a woman itself is an experience, one worth highlighting through the experiences some of our field's most talented and prolific scientists.

The co-editors of this book were in graduate school in the mid-1990s and early 2000s—a time when the demographic makeup of the field of behavior analysis was predominately white, male, cis-gender, and heterosexual. Though there were efforts to draw attention to issues related to diversity, they were often met with some resistance. For example, the *Women Behaving Boldly* panels in the late 1990s at the ABAI conventions were well-attended events that detailed some of the issues related to being a female (though, mostly through the lens of the white, cis-gendered identity) behavior analyst. One of the panelists showed the audience some data she had collected highlighting the lower percentage of women (as compared to men) whose work was published in our flagship journals and who were selected for editorial boards (see McSweeney et al., 2000; McSweeney & Swindell, 1998). As audience members who chose to earn a PhD in behavior analysis (or a PhD with an emphasis in behavior analysis), this lack of representativeness was difficult to witness. The presentation seemed to generate occasionally defensive and downright hostile responses from some of those attending (and not only women). Nonetheless, some were listening because there were subsequent cracks placed in the "glass ceiling." For example, we have seen a substantial rise in women publishing more in our flagship journals since, along with an increase in the percentage of women on editorial boards (see Rotta et al., 2022 for a comprehensive history and review of these factors). This is also happening in other fields (e.g., Mauleón et al., 2013).

Ironically, part of the resistance to diversity efforts in the field could also be attributed to a foundational tenet to our field: that the science of behavior analysis seeks to understand principles of behavior that underlie all people, organisms, and settings. In other words, according to the science, we are *all the same* in terms of general principles (e.g., responsiveness to reinforcement and punishment); so why the fuss about the details of differences? (We have heard this same argument, incidentally, by those in fields like behavioral neuroscience, a discipline that seeks to find underlying principles of the nervous system.) For behavior analysts, factors related to diversity fell under the umbrella of "behavioral history," in terms of important variables that helped explain, predict, and control behavior, and were therefore minimized and, in some cases, dismissed as "just more variables" to test (see also Hayes & Toarmino, 1995). Nevertheless, behavior analysis is late to the game of cultural change related to diversity and inclusion. Behavior analysis is still very homogenous—mostly white, now male and female, cis-gender, and heterosexual, especially in the sociodemographic characteristics of those holding certification in behavior analysis (Behavior Analysis Certification Board, n.d.).

Fast forward to the present time, in the wake of: the #metoo movement; challenges to reproductive rights; continued racial injustice against Black, Indigenous, People of Color individuals (BIPoC); politics intended to harm those in lesbian, gay, bisexual, transgender, queer and/or questioning, intersexed, asexual, and two-spirit (LGBTQIA2S+) communities; and a pandemic. The zeitgeist is changing. Many individuals in the discipline are now poised to more carefully and intentionally examine diversity in all of its forms. There are the beginnings of better characterization, acknowledgement, awareness, acceptance, and inclusion of diversity. We are finally starting the work of creating and cultivating a culture of behavior analysis in which access, justice, diversity, equity, and inclusion are present, deliberately sought, and celebrated.

When we planned this book, inclusion was what we had in mind. But we also wanted this volume to be different from other books on academia—we wanted the female perspective, broadly defined. The contributors of this book are indeed academics, though in various developmental stages. Some are graduate students or have just graduated. Some are early in their careers, and some are more seasoned. Some are retired and some have left academia. The contributors come from different types of colleges and universities—from smaller, private liberal arts colleges to larger research-intensive public universities. They reside in different parts of the world—places like Brazil, Iceland, Ireland, Sweden, and the United States. Some are immigrants to their current country of residence. Our contributors have different ethnicities and races. Some are gender-marginalized members of our academic community. Some are able-bodied. Some of these identities intersect. We wanted the authors of this book to represent a wide array of these factors, yet we acknowledge upfront that we could still do better. We are open and humble as we examine who may have been left out.

Even though we are delighted to share this volume with you, we recognize that this book is just the beginning of a much longer journey. We see that there is a need for additional volumes that amplify the voices of many more behavior analysts, particularly those who are members of other marginalized and oppressed populations and identities. It is our hope that this volume can stimulate and support further actions and momentum toward that outcome. We will do what behavior analysts do best: examine the data and keep changing the conditions until we better meet our target—fully representative inclusion.

As you read this collection of narratives, you will see these contributors are not just academics—they are also real people. They are beloved family members and friends. Some have partners and some have children; some do not. All seem to have had a hand in mentoring and teaching others about behavior analysis and have developed a passion for that part of academic work. They all have stories to tell about their perspectives of academia. Some of these stories will make you cry; others will make you smile widely. Two themes in particular emerged from our contributors' reflections. The first is that being a successful, engaged, and above all, happy academician is contextually influenced; one's job is not confined to one's place of work. Each contributor explores how specific variables inside and outside of the workplace interact, including the rich, multilayered contingencies at work, at home, and in their respective communities and cultures, as well as the private psychological experiences and unique learning histories that accompany. The second is that our contributors' career pursuits were guided by their own personal values. Values without a doubt change over the course of one's adult life, and it is easy to lose touch as one gets caught up in the demands of daily routine. We applaud the holistic, organic approach the authors adopted in telling their stories. We appreciate the perspectives that they lend in terms of how they have worked to sustain their values over time, how those values may have shifted, and how, despite challenges or obstacles, they managed to stay true to their values as best they could and offer strategies for how the rest of us might do the same (see Chapter 20).

This is a different kind of book, as you will see. What makes this book special is a behind-the-scenes look at academia told by some of the women in behavior analysis. What makes this book unique compared to other books on academia is what the authors divulge. Sure, there is typical information every academic should know, such as information on the job search and the "holy trifecta" of teaching, research, and service, and of tenure and promotion. But something magical happened with this book. The authors provided open, honest narratives—divulging parts of their lives that academics do not typically talk about—the emotionally fulfilling and challenging aspects of this career path. They also shared difficult parts of their lives, such as their stories of marginalization, their difficulties with mental and physical health challenges, grief and loss, and caring for others with chronic health conditions. We asked the authors to be vulnerable, even when being vulnerable has not always resulted in reinforcement; and they did so, when being vulnerable also meant being uncomfortable and putting themselves at risk for leaner schedules of reinforcement, loss of reinforcement, or otherwise.

While this book focuses only on a segment of behavior analysts—those in academia, some of whom identify as women—it needs to be stated that other areas of behavior analysis and demographics of behavior analysts could benefit from the broad perspective of women's voices. We recommend a valuable book on mentoring entitled *Building and Sustaining Meaningful and Effective Relationships as a Supervisor and Mentor* (2020) by Linda LeBlanc, Tyra Sellers, and Shahla Ala'i. But more is still needed on the other aspects of the applied field as well. The voices of authors who have experienced marginalization in areas such as gender, race, ethnicity, sexuality, able-bodiedness, neurodiversity, as well as unmentioned and/or intersecting identities, are critical. These narratives provide compelling perspectives that help increase openness and understanding and are the foundations for cultural change. We are hopeful that the future of behavior analysis will be an inclusive and welcoming one.

So, here we have a record, or a permanent product, if you will, delineating the insights, perspectives, and experiences of a number of strong, balanced, and foremost, honest female academicians in the science of behavior analysis. We hope future generations of scientists of all genders, colors, and backgrounds can learn from the accounts of our contributors as society in general, and higher education specifically, continue to evolve (see Chapter 4).

In closing, we share with you that on February 26, 2022, the contributor of our final chapter, Beth Sulzer-Azaroff, passed away. Beth worked earnestly on her chapter during the long months of the pandemic, and she eagerly anticipated the publication of this book. We regret that she could not see the final product. As conveyed by Alavosius (2022), Beth was a pioneer in many areas of behavior analysis, including education, organizational behavior management, personalized systems of instruction, and best practices in behavior analytic services for persons with developmental disabilities and their families. Importantly, humane values guided her work throughout her career, which she also helped to shape in those she mentored (Alavosius, 2022). We thus dedicate this book to Beth's memory, and believe it is fitting that her words, late in life, resonate as the closing, but not final, words of this book.

The Editors

References

Alavosius, M. P. (2022). Remembering Beth Sulzer-Azaroff. *Journal of Organizational Behavior Management*, 1–7. https://doi.org/10.1080/01608061.2022.2070574

Behavior Analyst Certification Board. (n.d). *BACB certificant data*. www.bacb.com/BACB-certificant-data

Hayes, S. C., & Toarmino, D. (1995). If behavioral principles are generally applicable, why is it necessary to understand cultural diversity? *The Behavior Therapist*, *18*, 21–23.

Leblanc, L., Sellars, T., & Ala'I, S. (2020). *Building and sustaining meaningful and effective relationships as a supervisor and mentor*. Sloan.

Mauleón, E., Hillán, L., Moreno, L., et al. (2013). Assessing gender balance among journal authors and editorial board members. *Scientometrics, 95*, 87–114. https://doi.org/10.1007/s11192-012-0824-4

McSweeney, F. K., Donahoe, P., & Swindell, S. (2000). Women in applied behavior analysis. *The Behavior Analyst*, *23*(2), 267–277. https://doi.org/10.1007/BF03392015

McSweeney, F. K., & Swindell, S. (1998). Women in the experimental analysis of behavior. *The Behavior Analyst*, *21*(2), 193–202. https://doi.org/10.1007/BF03391963

Rotta, K., Li, A., Curiel, E. S., Curiel, H., & Poling, A. (2022). Women in behavior analysis: A review of the literature. *Behavior Analysis in Practice*, *15*(2), 592–607. https://doi:10.1007/s40617-021-00642-z

Part I

Beginning

1 Planting Seeds

Learning, Growing, and Thriving in Graduate School

Allyson R. Salzer, Jovonnie Esquierdo-Leal, and Kathryn M. Roose

Planting Seeds: Learning, Growing, and Thriving in Graduate School

Historically, men have earned more advanced academic degrees than women; however, the trend has changed over the last 50 years. According to the National Center for Education Statistics, in the United States, women earned a majority of the associate's, bachelor's, master's, and doctoral degrees awarded in the 2020–2021 academic year. The change in trend began in the 1977–1978 academic year when women began earning the majority of associate's degrees. The trend continued into 1981–1982 with women earning the majority of bachelor's degrees, and into 1986–1987 and 2005–2006 with master's and doctoral degrees, respectively. Indeed, in 2020–2021, women earned over 61% of master's degrees and 53% of doctoral degrees (U.S. Department of Education, National Center for Education Statistics [NCES], 2020a).

The difference and trend between the number of degrees earned by men or women are more pronounced in psychology. For example, 5,600 men and over 23,500 women received master's degrees in psychology in the 2018–2019 academic year (NCES, 2020d, 2020e), and approximately 1,600 men and 4,600 women received doctoral degrees in the same year (NCES, 2020b, 2020c). Although not all behaviorally focused degree programs are embedded in psychology departments (others may be in education, special education, behavioral sciences, or other fields), these statistics may apply to behavior analysis as well, especially given the recent growth in the field.

The Behavior Analysis Certification Board (BACB) noted that the number of newly certified Board Certified Behavior Analysts (BCBAs) has been increasing annually, with over 6,000 newly certified BCBAs in 2020 alone (BACB, 2020). Additionally, since the Registered Behavior Technician (RBT) credential was introduced in 2014, the BACB has certified over 89,000 RBTs, some of whom may pursue bachelor's or master's degrees to further their careers in behavior analysis. The demand for BCBAs and BCBA-Ds increased by 4,209% from 2010–2020 as indicated by BCBA job postings, which dramatically rose from 789 in 2010 to 33,996 in 2020 (BACB, 2021). Moreover, 86.2% of BCBAs and BCBA-Ds (doctoral) are women, proportions similarly noted for Board Certified assistant Behavior Analysts (BCaBAs; 84.6%) and RBTs (85.0%; BACB, 2020).

This growing demand for BACB certification has resulted in the proliferation of behavior analysis programs across the world—both online and in person. For example, the number of institutions with Association for Behavior Analysis International (ABAI) Verified Course Sequences (VCS) relating to certification grew from 81 in 2005 to 293 in 2015 (Pastrana et al., 2018) and to 374 in 2021 (ABAI, 2021). Other areas of behavior analysis are also growing and thriving, including organizational behavior management,

DOI: 10.4324/9781003216773-3

behavior-based safety, culturo-behavior science, and applied animal behavior. For example, there are now six institutions worldwide with an ABAI VCS in culturo-behavior science in alignment with a growing interest in the use of behavior science to address large-scale societal issues.

The expansion of the field of behavior analysis, along with the increasing number of behavior analytic graduate programs, can add to the already daunting nature of considering the variables that contribute to a student's choice of attending graduate school. These steps often require a decision between working full-time, working part-time, or not working at all and focusing solely on furthering one's education, each of which may be correlated with the potential to accrue debt. Research suggests that women of color experience even greater disparities in the academy (Ramos & Yi, 2020; Walkington, 2017). Sexism and discrimination are some of the factors that influence one's decision to pursue graduate school, and even more so, contribute to the leaky pipeline—a metaphor that is used to describe the attrition of women in academia at each rank of professor (Ysseldyk et al., 2019). With fewer women in academic roles (i.e., professors, deans, chairs, and more), there are fewer opportunities for women in graduate school to access meaningful mentorship from other women. Using proactive strategies to create support systems that combat the effects of gender bias and sexism will be a critical part of one's journey prior to, throughout, and after graduate school. This chapter explores the preparation and experiences of women pursuing graduate degrees, including interviews, relationships with mentors, and finding their way to their career goals.

Selecting a Potential Advisor or Program

Choosing an advisor is one of the first steps on the journey to graduate school. An advisor will be a mentor in graduate school (and beyond) and it is important to consider the areas of research you would like to pursue as well as whether your advisor has the background and mentoring skills to support you. Before searching faculty profiles online, it might be helpful to reflect on your academic and career goals and the qualities of a mentor that are important to you. Some graduate students prefer highly structured mentorship while others prefer to work more independently (see Rasmussen et al., Chapter 6 of this book). Some advisors have very distinct lines of research and are easily able to give prospective graduate students a preview of the kinds of research they will engage in during their graduate studies, while others supervise students with a wide variety of interests which may offer more options for students who have not yet selected a specialty or are interested in a research topic that is not yet well established in behavior analysis (e.g., social justice, public policy). Some advisors may be more amenable to pursuing these underrepresented topics, and prospective students will need to evaluate their options if contributing to this line of work is important to them. Students should also consider how their personal values align with a prospective advisor's values. Though the advisor–advisee relationship will center on research and/or academic work, the culture of a laboratory or program may be influenced, even unintentionally, by personal or sociopolitical factors (e.g., political climate, religion).

Despite the best intentions of proactive students researching programs, there may be some challenges in finding the best fit. One such challenge is that honest discussions about dissatisfaction with mentorship styles are sometimes hidden under equivocal statements. For example, a colleague who knows a particular mentor is not active with students might say that a faculty member "encourages independence" instead of using direct language describing an advisor's limitation. When faced with such vague statements, prospective students may consider asking more direct questions to evoke specific information important to that student such as:

Will I be able to pick my own research topic?
What is the expectation of students in lab meetings?
Can you describe the writing process and the quality and timeliness of feedback you receive from your advisor?
What is your experience as a woman/woman of color/parent in your lab?

To learn about prospective advisors and universities, programs, and laboratory culture prior to committing to a program and mentor, it can be helpful to reach out to current or past students to inquire about their experiences with the culture and climate of the lab or the program. Current undergraduate advisors might also be a good resource to consult.

Mentoring students and early-career professionals is a separate skill set from being a professor (see Rasmussen et al., Chapter 6 in this book). Advisors provide feedback and serve as role models for their students, which lends itself to the saying "pick the mentor and then the project" (Marino, 2020, p. 4). One survey suggests that qualities of effective mentors include active listening, professional experience in the area of interest of the advisee, and characteristics relating to relatability, compassion, and availability (Straus et al., 2013). Furthermore, in behavior analysis specifically, qualities in which behavior analytic studies have been conducted such as providing effective feedback and creating opportunities for advisees is important (LeBlanc, 2015; Sleiman et al., 2020; Taylor, 2015). A good advisor should also be cognizant of the current climate for women, Black, Indigenous, and People of Color (BIPOC), and other marginalized and excluded identities. They should be familiar with issues such as attending to salary inequities or limited opportunities for women and BIPOC women. A good mentor should also be able to work with the advisee to support their personal and professional endeavors (Taylor, 2015).

Although the task of choosing a graduate-student mentor is daunting, it is important to note that your primary mentor does not need to fulfill every role if you have access to other sources of mentorship (formal or informal). For women specifically, having other role models or mentors of the same gender may help fill in gaps that a primary mentor may not be able to provide. Indeed, LeBlanc (2015) describes how multiple role models are a benefit for students. More importantly, according to Taylor (2015), finding an advisor who matches the same enthusiasm for a subject and can help a mentee reach their long-term goals is more important than choosing an advisor based on gender.

In addition to the options for advisors, mentors, and coursework, the availability of practicum and research experiences may be just as crucial in selecting a graduate program. Different programs offer vastly different practical and research experiences. For example, programs accredited by ABAI may offer up to 11 different practical training opportunities (with an added option for "other") ranging from autism and developmental disabilities to alcohol/drug abuse, business, education, health, mental health, and more. Programs may also offer up to 12 different research-training opportunities (with an added option for "other") with some examples including autism and developmental disabilities, behavioral pharmacology, experimental analysis of behavior, organizational behavior management, conceptual issues, and verbal behavior. While some experiences are plentiful, others are scarcer. For example, out of the 19 master's programs that were reaccredited in recent years, practical experiences in autism, developmental disabilities, and special education are available at most programs, while practical experience in other areas such as mental health, business/industry/government, and alcohol and drug abuse are more difficult to find. Prospective graduate students may want to research all opportunities that are available at each university if they are interested in a variety of experiences.

Graduate School Application

If you have not done so already, applying to graduate school is the perfect time to create your curriculum vitae (commonly abbreviated as CV or vita). A CV is different from a resume that you might have already created to obtain employment. A CV is a compilation of your academic credentials or "a record of what you have done and a ticket allowing you to do more" (Hayes & Hayes, 1989, p. 15). A prospective graduate student may not have many entries on their CV as they are just embarking on their career. For instance, early in graduate school, many students include conference attendance and academic courses completed to track progress and participation in the absence of conference presentations and completed degrees. However, once students begin to fill their CV with conference presentations, it is no longer necessary to include conference attendance. Similarly, once a student completes a master's degree, listing the individual courses is no longer necessary. However, Hayes and Hayes (1989) suggest, "Write up your vita now. No matter how puny. From acorns giant oaks grow, and you might as well begin. It will also get you thinking about your career development" (p. 17). Your CV will grow throughout your graduate school career and will serve as a valuable record of your accomplishments.

Typically, CVs include the following information: personal information (e.g., contact information), educational history (degree[s]), professional positions (paid and unpaid), membership in professional associations (including membership type and years of active membership), professional activities (e.g., committee memberships/leadership, guest lectures, webinar presentations), editorial activities (e.g., reviewer for a journal), grants received, conference presentations (papers and posters, invited or accepted), publications, current projects, a statement of professional interests, and professional references. You should provide sufficient detail for each item such that its importance and relevance to your academic and professional experiences are conveyed in a way that readers will understand your history and interests.

Women may want to pay particular attention to their CVs as there is some evidence that the applications of prospective women graduate students may be judged more critically than the applications of prospective men graduate students. Franco et al. (2021) conducted a randomized controlled trial that examined the impact of gender on the evaluation of CVs. They provided external reviewers with identical CVs that were given names traditionally associated with men or women (i.e., the same CV was used for the man and the woman). The external reviewers rated the CVs in four categories: scientific contribution, leadership potential, ability to work in groups, and international experience. The men received higher scores than the women in all four categories. Women reviewers gave men higher scores than women on scientific contribution, and men reviewers gave men higher scores than women on scientific contribution and leadership potential (Franco et al., 2021).

Other types of documentation that support a CV or graduate school application may also be subject to gender bias. Lerchenmueller and colleagues (2019) compared publications in clinical research and found articles written by men were more likely to use positive words in their titles and abstracts than women, suggesting that women were more likely to be cautious in asserting the importance or significance of their work. In addition, Schmader and colleagues (2007) found gender differences in letters of recommendation for men and women. Specifically, letters of recommendation for men were found to be longer than letters of recommendation for women. Men were more likely to be described with words related to ability, research, and stand-out adjectives (e.g., excellent, amazing, outstanding);

women were more likely to be associated with their teaching experience and grindstone adjectives (e.g., hardworking, diligent). Therefore, when preparing a CV, women may benefit from reviewing the language used to highlight experiences and achievements, to ensure the use of stand-out adjectives to draw the readers' attention to the importance and relevance of their work (Schmader et al., 2007).

The Interview

Interviews for graduate school often include meetings with members of the graduate community, interviews with prospective mentors, and opportunities to explore the community in which you may live. Although the requirement to attend in-person interviews for graduate positions varies by school, some components are consistent. Students should expect to meet with faculty and their laboratories and to tour the lab space. Some interview weekends will have students interview with multiple faculty members and laboratories rather than a single professor. During this time, both the faculty and current students will conduct interviews to gauge how well the prospective student may fit into a particular laboratory or program. This is also a time for the interviewee to ask questions and determine to what extent the program will move them toward their career goals. The interview may include interactions with the student host or other students during "down-time" as well as conversations during dinners or other informal gatherings. Essentially, the interview starts the moment interviewees step off the plane and does not end until take-off back home. Even then, a short email of thanks can leave a lasting positive impression.

Feeling confident and making a good first impression are considerations one will need to make prior to an interview. Implicit bias is prevalent and those in hiring positions have been made aware of these concerns (Dasgupta & Asgari, 2004). However, even with acknowledgment of these concerns, first impressions potentially can make or break an offer. To help aid first impressions, preparation is key. From your professional appearance to the look of your application packet, consider how to form a lasting impression. Seek advice from your colleagues, practice interview questions with a trusted source, and prepare a one-minute elevator pitch that highlights research interests and what you bring to the table. Prepare an "Interview Toolkit" including a flash drive, laptop cable, phone charger, extra copies of application materials (e.g., CV), and other helpful items such as snacks, mints, tissues or wipes, a Tide® pen, and any other comforts or solutions for emergencies. Being prepared can help make interviews go smoothly and help you get through the day. Finally, remember that interviews go both ways: the final decision to matriculate into a program is always yours and should align with your personal and professional goals and values.

You Got in—Now What? Orientation and the First Year

During the initial orientation process, a high volume of information is conveyed to prepare students for expectations while attending graduate school and to set students up for success. In some instances, the program director has meetings with the new cohort to outline department-level expectations such as the number of credit hours students are expected to take, the number of hours that should be allocated to research each week, and other university or program requirements.

The broad-level information provided to students is meant to aid in the transition to the intense training requirements within the program. However, there may be undertones of expectations or policies that disproportionately impact women. The time requirements to which students need to commit can directly conflict with other personal goals (e.g., familial obligations). If students are in relationships, they may be warned that these relationships will likely have times of difficulty. Students are sometimes advised to seriously consider waiting on extracurricular activities or personal milestones such as getting married or having children while in school, either directly or through insinuations.[1] Though traditional approaches to personal or familial obligations are changing, one should never feel pressured into accepting others' views of how a professional career should unfold. If faced with such challenges, they should look to others for guidance—this may include trusted mentors in the field, administrators at their university, colleagues, or even close friends and family that understand the student's values (see also Rasmussen et al., Chapter 6 in this book).

Despite the potential for overwhelming feelings during the first few days in a program, there are a number of exciting events as well. For new students, it is especially important to take part in department activities and welcome events to meet faculty and students. Often departments set up get-togethers prior to the school year which allows new and returning students to interact. These gatherings can be a great way to break the ice and meet new colleagues.

Relationships With Mentors

Establishing and maintaining relationships with advisors and other mentors is an important part of graduate school. These relationships often remain well after graduation. You may see these individuals at conferences, have similar research lines, or even collaborate on projects. At this point, you have already met with, and may have even started working on, projects with your graduate advisor. Even though research projects might be underway, mentorship expands beyond the scope of research. Mentors can help shape students into researchers, professionals, and leaders in the field. With whom you surround yourself in graduate school matters. In fact, time to graduation and other metrics are correlated with advisor support (Litalien & Guay, 2015). Those in psychology programs who do not have a mentoring figure have historically expressed regret at the decision when surveyed at the end of their programs, and those who are mentored express a generally positive experience (Clark et al., 2000).

Mentoring is a process by which a person, usually of superior rank, guides the development of another individual (Savage et al., 2004). Specifically, a hierarchical relationship forms which is most successful when both parties put forth the effort to create a mutually beneficial relationship (Lechuga, 2011; Rasmussen et al., Chapter 6 in this book). To have a successful relationship within this unequal power dynamic, open communication and mutual understanding are imperative. Having an effective mentor leads the student to become an independent researcher (Lin & Cranton, 2005) and contributes positively to a student's wellness and performance (Kutsyuruba et al., 2019). Being authentic is an essential part of building relationships between mentor and mentee (Makhamreh & Stockley, 2019).

Mentors also play a contributing factor to the mental health of their mentees. In the general population, women are consistently more likely to suffer from mental health disorders than men (Eaton et al., 2012). This trend is also observed in graduate-student populations such that women are more likely to experience anxiety and depression than men (Evans et al., 2018). Those with positive mentorship experiences report feeling supported while those with negative mentorship experiences report feeling hopeless and depressed (Makhamreh & Stockley, 2019). As mentioned, it is possible to have multiple mentors to fulfill the different types of support students might need—from research experience to cultivating work-life balance and everything in between. Mentorship does not need to come from only your advisor.

Women may face specific challenges in their relationships with mentors. The indication of a gender gap may disproportionately impact women in graduate school, and the opportunity to be mentored by women is critically important to their success. For example, women in the fields of science, technology, engineering, and math (STEM) who are advised by women tend to publish more than women in STEM who are advised by men (Gaule & Piacentini, 2018; Pezzoni et al., 2016). However, when the ratio of faculty to students is higher, time to degree completion is reduced for women in the program when compared to men in the program, which may be viewed as a benefit for women (Neumark & Gardecki, 1998). The struggles women face in STEM are also present in behavior analysis. LeBlanc (2015) remarks that actively creating opportunities for students to take on leadership roles not only benefits them in terms of networking experiences, but also can make them effective mentors for others, providing long-term benefits to students of behavior analysis. However, mentors must actively create an environment in which women feel supported and encouraged to take on leadership and mentoring roles. Traditionally, men are offered and assume more leadership roles than women, perhaps due to the intimidation women face in graduate school (Taylor, 2015).

Finding a Support System

When students begin graduate school, their social life is often de-prioritized. Nonetheless, a support system is essential to one's success in graduate school. Jairam and Kahl (2012) suggest that social support can help reduce stress and feelings of isolation among graduate students. They state, "social support stems from people to whom one is socially tied (e.g., family members and friends) and is defined as what they say and do regarding stressful events" (Jairam & Kahl, 2012, p. 312). Students who have made it through one of the most competitive processes (i.e., admissions) will find themselves surrounded by talented and motivated peers. This can create competition and influence one's confidence and perceived competence (Jairam & Kahl, 2012; Litalien & Guay, 2015). Confidence may also impact one's decision to continue their degree, and completion rates among doctoral students are already of concern in some disciplines (Council of Graduate Schools [CGS], 2021).

Colleagues and peers in the program can provide social support. Finding peers with similar backgrounds or interests can create opportunities to obtain valuable input and/or feedback, share honest opinions and experiences, and learn about other faculty members' or students' work. Additionally, maintaining solid relationships with one's family and friends outside of the university setting will also contribute to one's success, and, for some, serve as a constant source of motivation (Baker & Pifer, 2011; Gardner & Gopaul, 2012), reminding them why they pursued graduate school in the first place.

Maintaining relationships and creating new ones while balancing other commitments may require some creativity, especially as a BIPOC woman attending a predominantly white university. Students should find a community—in person or virtual—that can lift them and create a space in which they feel empowered. There are several sources one can turn to including conferences (e.g., Black Applied Behavior Analysts [BABA]), special interest groups [SIGs], and social media pages (see Louise McHugh, Chapter 12 in this book).

Practica and Research

Graduate school is some students' first close contact with experience in the field. This work experience may be paid or unpaid. It may take place in the university or in the community. It may also involve clinical work, research, or teaching. Some students may have simultaneous access to different opportunities (e.g., teaching assistant and clinical work, basic laboratory, and philosophical work), while others may participate in one activity at a time or accumulate several different experiences throughout graduate school. As previously noted, the types of experiences available to students may factor into program selection.

Once students have started a program, it is important to make the most of the opportunities available in their program.

For students interested in pursuing a clinical career, BCBA supervision may be available in their program and students may be eligible to take the BCBA exam shortly after completing their master's degree. BCBA supervision can be quite expensive (an informal internet search reveals uncovered supervision rates up to $125/hr) and students may wish to take advantage of free or less expensive opportunities offered through their graduate school programs. If your laboratory does not offer BCBA supervision, you may be able to request practical training in a different laboratory to fulfill this goal while maintaining membership in your own laboratory. Practical training obtained in graduate school will factor into a competitive job market; maintaining detailed records of your experiences and milestones will be helpful to prospective employers (e.g., direct service provided, supervision experience, assessments/curricula used).

For students with different career goals, programs and universities offer varying research opportunities. Some laboratories focus on conceptual and philosophical activities, conducting basic or applied research, developing scientific writing skills, and participating in lengthy discussions and debates. Students may have an opportunity to work on a grant-funded project, which also may include learning valuable skills relating to grant management, reporting outcomes, and participating in writing more grants. Each activity has the potential to impact student career trajectories, with some students maintaining focus on the same goal throughout graduate school, and others finding their focus shift. In short, students should be aware of and take the opportunities of varied experiences while in graduate school as these prospects may not be as available after graduation.

While accruing practical and/or research experience, there may be opportunities for students to participate in conference presentations and/or publishing activities. Some laboratories are very structured in their activities, with junior students being assigned to projects by their advisors. Other labs are structured differently, with senior students mentoring junior students in the laboratory by including them on projects, or the other way around, with students requesting to participate in the projects of others. This is a critical time for students to begin building their CVs. Volunteering to assist with a research project is not only a great learning experience, but it may result in an opportunity to present data at a conference or authorship on a publication, both of which will enhance applications to PhD programs for master's students, and CVs for those entering the job market.

Finally, should students find that they do not have access to certain experiences within their own program or university, they may find those opportunities in the broader scientific community. Students may get involved with their local behavior analysis organizations, ABAI, ABAI SIGs, or other behavior analytic organizations and find opportunities to participate in writing, research, and other projects.

Teaching Experience

Teaching experience can increase one's chances of being accepted to graduate school (especially in the case of doctoral programs). It can also serve as a source of income and experience and may provide insight into whether pursuing an academic position is desirable. Finally, it can increase the likelihood of being offered an academic faculty position (Varga, 2011) and can boost one's resume for nonacademic positions. Yet, teaching experience is not available to every student, and the likelihood of obtaining a paid teaching position (i.e., a teaching graduate assistantship) varies from program to program, and sometimes, advisor to advisor. In this section, we aim to explore teaching in four ways: obtaining a teaching assistantship, building an effective teaching repertoire, managing challenges, and leveraging experience to transition into a career.

Obtaining a Teaching Assistantship

The possibility of obtaining a teaching assistantship will depend on several factors. In the same manner one researches advisors and potential research opportunities, they should also consider whether the college/university, department, and program they are applying to offers Graduate Teaching Assistantships (GTAs) to students. What complicates this search is the fact that colleges and universities can provide departments and programs varying opportunities for GTAs based on factors that are less visible to students and faculty, such as department size, budget constraints, and enrollments. Further, even when GTAs are offered, they can be competitive and dependent on the number of students the program is able to fund. Prospective students should inquire about the number of available GTA positions and the average duration of these positions. Additionally, they should review the courses typically assigned to graduate students to teach and determine whether those topics align with their career goals, keeping in mind that their interests may change over the course of their graduate careers.

With growing competition in graduate admissions, prospective graduate students should bolster their application in a way that maximizes the likelihood of obtaining funded teaching opportunities. Though prior experience is helpful, programs recognize undergraduate students have fewer opportunities to gain formal teaching experience. When formal teaching experience is not possible, highlight teaching skills or other related experiences that make up a teaching repertoire: leading or training for student and community clubs and organizations, peer-tutoring opportunities, undergraduate research on related content, special projects, conference presentations, writing abilities, public speaking, and ability to build rapport or strong social networks.

Although we have focused our attention thus far on GTAs, this does not mean the opportunity to gain teaching experience is limited solely to assistantships. Building social capital (Szreter, 2000) is a crucial part of graduate school. Students should find opportunities to work with multiple faculty members within and outside of the program or department as this may provide new opportunities such as volunteering as an unpaid teaching assistant or guest lecturing. By getting to know a faculty member in class or by working in their lab, students may be able to arrange a day to cover a class, proctor an exam, or assist with other course-related activities such as grading. Students should also look for opportunities outside of their program; this may include tutoring, working in a writing or career center, teaching at a community college (Varga, 2011), or offering community lectures and training on content relevant to one's research or practica. Finally, even though many teaching opportunities are offered to doctoral students, master's students are encouraged to seek the same opportunities. Teaching may be in their future even if they do not plan on becoming a professor. In fact, many institutions rely heavily on part-time instructors to meet their educational needs.

Expanding the Teaching Repertoire and Making a Lasting Impact

If there is one piece of advice you should take from this section, it can be captured by the following quote, "Who dares to teach must never cease to learn" (Cotton Dana, 1967, p. 55; see also Rehfeldt, Chapter 18 of this book). In an environment plagued by imposter phenomenon (Hutchins, 2015), we must all remember that learning is constant, and one should never hold themselves to unrealistic standards. A teaching repertoire is always evolving, and as long as one stays humble and values-focused, their efforts will not go unnoticed.

Nevertheless, there are ways to ensure the teaching opportunities offered in graduate school set students up for success in their teaching careers later.

First, students should find ways to familiarize themselves with pedagogy through mentorship, university workshops and programs, and research. They should identify best practices and techniques for each course and find the one that works for them and the class. There are numerous teaching resources available to students as well as early and seasoned faculty members. From research on behavioral approaches to college teaching (e.g., Binder, 1996; Hurtado-Parrado et al., 2021) to assistantships that are specifically designed to provide experience in instructional design (Chase & Houmanfar, 2009; Chase et al., 2013; Cihon et al., 2017), students will find that there is a wealth of behavior analytic evidence to draw upon. Instructors should also consider universal design for learning (Burgstahler, 2015), implementing a variety of teaching methods their students benefit from most (Al-Azawei et al., 2016; Wu, 2010). Studying and implementing various approaches not only permits a better understanding of teaching effectiveness, it also permits the identification of strengths and opportunities for growth. Relatedly, regularly create evaluation opportunities for students; this will allow for a better understanding of how the content is received—this feedback can be used to update content, incorporate examples that align with student interests, and ultimately influence instructional design. Finally, find a support network. While a mentor or advisor is an invaluable resource, finding teaching peers may also prove just as valuable. Connect with other students who share similar interests or experiences. Offer each other support by collaborating on course development, practicing lectures, offering feedback, and sharing experiences (Varga, 2011). Having a trusted colleague to listen to problems and offer advice goes a long way. Lastly, many institutions have teaching and learning centers that offer seminars and workshops for graduate students and postdoctoral researchers (postdocs); inquire about these opportunities early on so that you can take advantage of as many as possible.

By taking the time to hone teaching skills while university resources are available, students will find that those resources paired with hands-on practice and exposure will shape an effective teaching repertoire. This will benefit students in many ways, as we will discuss. At the same time, teaching as a graduate student (and beyond) comes with challenges, and one should be well equipped to address those challenges so that they and their students get the most of their time together. Remember, teaching and the learning that ensues is always a two-way street.

Dual Role of Student and Instructor

Graduate students face many challenges, and the tendency to question their skills may increase, especially in a competitive and elitist academic environment (hooks, 1994). There are many factors that contribute to one's success as an instructor and it is important to be privy to as many of these challenges as possible. First, graduate students are in a unique situation in which they are both students and instructors. Therefore, they may find that relating to students is easy but establishing themselves as credible sources instead of peers is difficult. Second, as GTAs navigate the dual role of student and instructor, they will learn that they are evaluated differently by different groups of individuals (e.g., students, faculty, community members). These evaluations can be both helpful and harmful, especially for those who identify with marginalized or historically excluded identities.

Though research is limited, there are a few studies that speak to the experience of GTAs. For instance, Nasser-Abu Alhija and Fresko (2018) report that GTA ratings vary from field to field. That is, ratings tend to be lower for GTAs in basic sciences and engineering than for GTAs in social sciences and business. Additionally, the study found that larger classes were correlated with lower ratings; GTAs teaching more courses (larger teaching loads) received higher ratings; and student attendance rates were positively correlated with ratings.

Studies with other student-related roles also point to possible gender bias with students. For instance, Moss-Racusin et al. (2012) found that faculty ratings for men and women who applied for a student-lab-manager position showed gender bias toward men. Specifically, participants (academic faculty members), regardless of gender, rated women as less competent and less hirable than men, offering lower salaries and fewer mentoring opportunities, even when they were rated as likable. These findings coincide with those from a plethora of other studies indicating participants tend to emphasize qualities consistent with gender stereotypes and evaluate women less favorably when they do not meet those expectations (Anderson, 2010; Bacon, 2015). These perceptions also are especially challenging for women of color, whose intersecting marginalized identities are the target of varying forms of inequities and operate together resulting in exacerbated effects (Crenshaw, 1989). This can contribute to imposter phenomenon, where self-doubt about one's accomplishments and abilities negatively impact one's health (Bernard et al., 2002; Thompson et al., 1998), confidence, social relationships, and professional goals (Leary et al., 2000).

The findings shared previously are not meant to discourage GTAs. In fact, there are also some studies that demonstrate the benefits of teaching as a graduate student. For example, it has been suggested that both undergraduate and graduate teaching assistants mutually benefit from this experience. Bettinger et al. (2016) report that undergraduates are more likely to major in a subject if their introductory course is taught by a graduate student. This may speak to relatability and representation. Additionally, it has been argued that graduate students who teach more frequently establish stronger faculty connections (Landrum & Nelsen, 2002), graduate earlier, and are more likely to be hired into an academic faculty position (Bettinger et al., 2016). Finally, regardless of whether teaching is a long-term plan or not, save all course content in a folder so that it can be accessed easily in the future. Even if teaching is not part of the plan now, one never knows what the future holds, and you may find an opportunity to teach the course again without having to reinvent the wheel.

Conferences and Networking

Conferences can be an exciting time for students—they permit one to travel to new cities, catch up with friends and colleagues, and explore research that they might not otherwise contact within their own departments. Conference attendance is a luxury, with many associated costs. Students may be able to find financial support from their university or program and explore other ways to reduce costs including sharing hotel rooms, bringing their own food, and seeking out student awards or support from the conference organizers (and students should continue advocating for this financial support).

Conference activities include networking, presenting research, and listening to researchers in the field talk about their recent work. Many students strive to meet "big names" in the field. To do so, it is best to actively participate in the conference and save nonconference-related sightseeing for after the closing remarks. Examples of invaluable opportunities include attending presentations delivered by speakers whom students wish to meet, attending book signings or "meet-and-greets," or even saying hello at the convention bar, coffee shop, or reception area after the day's events. In most cases, these researchers will be honored to meet students interested in their work. Preparation is essential to elevate the meeting from "I love your work" to "I just read your recent article in (journal name) and I'm interested in the intervention you used. Do you mind if I ask you a couple of questions about your research?"

Within the conference atmosphere and the opportunity to network with other professionals, women are not immune to uncomfortable circumstances. Women report higher levels of gender bias than men, including being made to feel inferior and being a target of condescending behavior (Heaton et al., 2020; Sapiro & Campbell, 2018). This bias does not come solely from men; women may be intimidating or combative toward new arrivals to the field. Rivalry among women may stem from internalized misogyny and sexism (Kiner, 2020)—where women's relational networks result in bias, sexism, or discrimination (Dixon et al., 2018) toward other women. Additionally, the underrepresentation of women in certain spaces or roles contributes to the generation of rules (Dixon et al., 2018; Houmanfar et al., 2009), such as the idea that there is only "one seat at the table" (Kiner, 2020). These negative interactions can be exacerbated at conferences where numerous bright individuals may compete for reinforcers such as face time with distinguished members of the field, partaking in discussions of upcoming leaders, and other networking opportunities.

Beyond this type of unwelcoming and uncomfortable experience, women may face even more difficult circumstances at conferences. Sexual advances toward women, primarily students, from established members of the field are another unfortunate reality at conferences within the field of behavior analysis and in the broader community. LeBlanc (2015) describes her experience observing more senior men interacting with younger women in which "relatively prolific behavior analysts . . . behave inappropriately towards female students and young professionals at conferences" (p. 243). A variety of articles from different professional and academic fields have addressed harassment at professional conferences (e.g., Flores, 2019; Heaton et al., 2020; Marts, 2017; Sapiro & Campbell, 2018). Survey research shows varying rates from around 20% (Heaton et al., 2020; Sapiro & Campbell, 2018) to up to 60% (Marts, 2017) of reported sexual harassment. As expected, women report harassment at higher rates than men, including being called a term of endearment (e.g., honey, sweetie); being leered or stared at; being asked for sex; being touched, groped, or grabbed; and other uncomfortable and inappropriate behaviors. While it is difficult to estimate what proportion of these events are reported, workplace research has shown generally low rates of reporting similar types of behavior. For example, one study estimates that around 5 million employees are sexually harassed at work every year, and 99.8% of those people never file formal charges (McCann et al., 2018). It is reasonable to assume reporting rates are similar in other types of professional environments. Indeed, one small survey study found that 82% of individuals who experienced harassment at a professional conference did not report the harassment. Reasons varied from thinking that the harassment was not serious enough to report, not knowing how or to whom to report the incident, or thinking that they would be blamed for the incident, among other reasons (Marts, 2017).

Women students are in a particularly vulnerable position at conferences due to the discrepancies in power dynamics and the pressures they face to make good impressions (Flores, 2019). Because of this power imbalance, many women fear approaching others about their experiences (LeBlanc, 2015). These negative experiences can in turn create aversive contexts in which conferences are no longer rewarding. To best prevent putting themselves in those situations, many women travel and attend events together, especially during evening events. LeBlanc (2015) mentioned how she "directly and immediately" stepped in during situations of power imbalance to aid women. Many other female leaders report the same (see Nosik & Grow, 2015). If you or someone you know experiences unwelcome or unwanted behavior at a professional conference, please speak to your advisor or a trusted colleague.

Apart from the concerns noted previously, conference attendance and participation are invaluable experiences in graduate school. Women have a strong presence at ABAI conferences. According to 75% of respondents to a poll conducted by ABAI (2020), 65% identified as cisgender women, 16% identifying as cisgender men, 1% androgynous, less than 1% transgender and gender-fluid, and 2% other; an additional 16% preferred not to answer (ABAI, 2020). This suggests that ABAI conferences are opportunities for women to meet other women in the field, and to build a network to share experiences and provide support. More generally, conferences provide an opportunity for students (and others) to stay in contact with current research, explore a variety of program areas, network, and collaborate. Students may want to explore their local ABAI affiliated chapters (regional chapters of ABAI) and ABAI SIGs to meet other students and more senior behavior analysts who are interested in partnering or collaborating on projects. Local chapters are a great place to meet people in your community as there may be opportunities to advocate for the work of behavior analysts locally. ABAI is a melting pot of behavior analysts and other scientists from around the world who meet annually to speak about important issues in the field and discuss innovative research. SIGs specialize in discrete topics (e.g., autism, health and fitness, social issues) and provide a supportive environment for projects and publications relating to their relevant topic.

ABAI also has a Student Committee with the mission to provide organizational support for ABAI student members. The Student Committee promotes student participation as well as professional growth and enables members to contribute to the science of behavior analysis. The Student Committee engages in activities throughout the year, but most activities are concentrated around the annual convention. The Committee coordinates panels dedicated to the professional development of students and coordinates student activities at the conference. Student members of ABAI are also eligible for a variety of student research awards from the Society for the Advancement of Behavior Analysis. Student awards can also be available from ABAI's affiliated chapters and SIGs. Opportunities may be found on the ABAI website.[2]

Troubleshooting

Throughout the graduate school experience, university settings and graduate programs may change. Graduate students, colleagues, and faculty come and go, and students themselves grow and evolve. During this time, students may find lean schedules of reinforcement or aversive conditions temporarily, or longer-term. For example, once the excitement of the interview process has waned, students may find that their advisor, mentors, and colleagues are not as supportive as they expected. Additionally, students are likely to experience an evolution in their perspectives, interests, and goals as they contact more experiences in the scientific world. Should you find yourself in such a position, there are many paths you can take. First, pinpoint the presumed problem and operationally define your current situation and how it differs from what you hoped to experience and achieve in graduate school. Next, identify whether the issue is something you have any control over. We cannot control retirement dates of trusted mentors or the graduation dates of supportive colleagues. But you may have the ability to advocate for other types of change within your graduate school experience. Students may be able to have candid conversations with their advisor regarding their needs and whether those needs can be met. If not, students may be able to switch to a new advisor and laboratory more in line with their interests after careful and candid conversations with their advisor and the program director. In some situations, students may prefer to move to a different university entirely. This does not have to be an aversive experience, and students should not be afraid to respectfully voice their reasons for being unable to continue with the present variables. If switching mentors or labs is not a possibility due to the size of the program, or lack of space in other laboratories, students may be successful by expanding their support system outside of their current advisor and lab, or even outside of their university. Finding support is critical to one's success in graduate school.

Beyond the mentor and laboratory experience, students may experience challenges related to other aspects of their graduate school experience. While some arrive at graduate school with clear goals for practical experience and specialization, others may experience a change in preference when presented with a variety of practical and research opportunities. For example, many students enter graduate programs in behavior analysis to work with children with autism/autistic children as that may be their only previous contact with the science of behavior. They may find once they enter a program that there are a variety of other specializations such as basic science, organizational behavior management, applied animal behavior, community, social, and ethical issues. Thus, graduate students may encounter a situation in which they would prefer to change specializations, move to a different practicum, switch from clinical work to research, or otherwise be in a position in which they must approach their advisor and request a change in assignment. This is a delicate situation as experiences may be limited, and advisors may be in a situation in which a certain number of graduate students are required for a particular purpose (e.g., clinical operation). Research has indicated that women are less likely to negotiate or advocate for themselves (e.g., Bowles et al., 2007; Bowles & McGinn, 2005), which in this case could result in continuing in a practicum not in alignment with future goals. Each situation will certainly be subject to unique contingencies, but in the absence of resistance, students may benefit by candid conversations with their mentors and direct requests to participate in experiences consistent with their future goals. Universities may offer negotiating and conflict-resolution workshops for those who may need some guidance on how to address these situations; senior colleagues, peers, and/or other mentors may also offer advice.

Conclusion

As a graduate student, it is easy to become overwhelmed by coursework, research, graduate assistantships, and internships. However, many students will find that these areas provide the early grounding for a successful career. As a graduate student—whether through GTAs, leadership, research positions, and other opportunities—there are several things that can be done to prepare for a future position. Take advantage of as many prospects as possible: attend conferences, collaborate with others to publish, interact with groups active in the field (e.g., SIGs, university clubs, Facebook professional groups). As you do this, update your CV regularly to document your accomplishments and to watch your career grow.

Graduate school is a pivotal moment in academic life. You can expect to work hard, grow towards your goals and career, and meet people who may be in your life indefinitely. You can expect to face a variety of challenges including balancing coursework, practica, research, teaching, and valued activities outside of graduate school (e.g., social life, family, health). Women face additional challenges as described throughout this chapter. Despite these challenges, women are earning advanced degrees at higher rates than men. By effectively navigating your graduate school career, you may find that you make lifelong friends, solidify your footing in the field, and set a course for your next steps in life as described in the chapters that follow.

Notes

1. Based on personal correspondence with current and former graduate students.
2. www.abainternational.org/about-us/organizational-chart/membership/student-committee/details.aspx

References

Al-Azawei, A., Serenelli, F., & Lundqvist, K. (2016). Universal design for learning (UDL): A content analysis of peer-reviewed journal papers from 2021–2015. *Journal of the Scholarship of Teaching and Learning, 16*(3), 39–56. https://doi.org/10.14434/josotl.v16i3.19295

Anderson, K. J. (2010). Students' stereotypes of professors: An exploration of the double violations of ethnicity and gender. *Social Psychology of Education, 13*(4), 459–472. https://doi.org/10.1007/s11218-010-9121-3
Association for Behavior Analysis International. (2020). *ABAI diversity data: Membership: 2020 members.* Presented at the 2020 Annual Conference. Online: May 2020. https://media.abainternational.org/dei/DEI%20Data%202019-2020%20Membership.pdf
Association for Behavior Analysis International. (2021). *ABAI verified course sequence directory*. Retrieved October 26, 2021, from www.abainternational.org/vcs/directory.aspx
Bacon, P. L. (2015). *He's sarcastic and she's caring: Students' stereotypes of the typical male and female professor.* Poster presented at the Annual Meeting of the Society for Personality and Social Psychology.
Baker, V. L., & Pifer, M. J. (2011). The role of relationships in the transition from doctoral student to independent scholar. *Studies in Continuing Education, 33*(1), 5–17. https://doi.org/10.1080/0158037X.2010.515569
Behavior Analysis Certification Board. (2020). *BACB certificant data.* www.bacb.com/bacb-certificant-data/
Behavior Analyst Certification Board. (2021). *US employment demand for behavior analysts: 2010–2020.* Author.
Bernard, N. S., Dollinger, S. J., & Ramaniah, N. V. (2002). Applying the big five personality factors to the impostor phenomenon. *Journal of Personality Assessment, 78*(2), 321–333. https://doi.org/10.1207/S15327752JPA7802_07
Bettinger, E. P., Long, B. T., & Taylor, E. S. (2016). When inputs are outputs: The case of graduate student instructors. *Economics of Education Review, 52*, 63–76. https://doi.org/10.1016/j.econedurev.2016.01.005
Binder, C. (1996). Behavioral fluency: Evolution of a new paradigm. *The Behavior Analyst, 19*(2), 163–197. https://doi.org/10.1007/BF03393163
Bowles, H. R., Babcock, L., & Lai, L. (2007). Social incentives for gender differences in the propensity to initiate negotiations: Sometimes it does hurt to ask. *Organizational Behavior and Human Decision Processes, 103*(1), 84–103. https://doi.org/10.1016/j.obhdp.2006.09.001
Bowles, H. R., & McGinn, K. L. (2005). Claiming authority: Negotiating challenges for women leaders. In D. M. Messick & R. M. Kramer (Eds.), *The psychology of leadership: New perspectives and research* (pp. 191–208). Lawrence Erlbaum Associates Publishers.
Burgstahler, S. E. (2015). *Universal design in higher education: From principles to practice.* Harvard Education Press.
Chase, J. A., & Houmanfar, R. (2009). The differential effects of elaborate feedback and basic feedback on student performance in a modified, personalized system of instruction course. *Journal of Behavioral Education, 18*, 245–265. https://doi.org/10.1007/s10864-009-9089-2
Chase, J. A., Houmanfar, R., Hayes, S. C., Ward, T. A., Vilardaga, J. P., & Follette, V. (2013). Values are not just goals: Online ACT-based values training adds to goal setting in improving undergraduate college student performance. *Journal of Contextual Behavioral Science, 2*(3–4), 79–84. https://doi.org/10.1016/j.jcbs.2013.08.002
Cihon, T. M., White, R., Zimmerman, V. L., Gesick, J., Stordahl, S., & Eshleman, J. (2017). The effects of precision teaching with textual or tact relations on intraverbal relations. *Behavioral Development Bulletin, 22*(1), 129. https://doi.org/10.1037/bdb0000056
Clark, R. A., Harden, S. L., & Johnson, W. B. (2000). Mentor relationships in clinical psychology doctoral training: Results of a national survey. *Teaching of Psychology, 27*(4), 262–268. https://doi.org/10.1207/S15328023TOP2704_04
Cotton Dana, J. (1967). In *The New York Time Book Review*, March 5, p. 55.
Council of Graduate Schools (CGS). (2021). *Ph.D. completion project.* https://cgsnet.org/phd-completion-project
Crenshaw, K. (1989). Demarginalizing the intersection of race and sex: A black feminist critique of antidiscrimination doctrine, Feminist theory and antiracist politics. *University of Chicago Legal Forum, 1989*, 139–167. https://chicagounbound.uchicago.edu/uclf/vol1989/iss1/8/
Dasgupta, N., & Asgari, S. (2004). Seeing is believing: Exposure to counterstereotypic women leaders and its effect on the malleability of automatic gender stereotyping. *Journal of Experimental Social Psychology, 40*(5), 642–658. https://doi.org/10.1016/j.jesp.2004.02.003
Dixon, M. R., Belisle, J., Rehfeldt, R. A., & Root, W. B. (2018). Why we are still not acting to save the world: The upward challenge of a post-Skinnerian behavior science. *Perspectives on Behavior Science, 41*(1), 241–267. https://doi.org/10.1007/s40614-018-0162-9

Eaton, N. R., Keyes, K. M., Krueger, R. F., Balsis, S., Skodol, A. E., Markon, K. E., Grant, B. F., & Hasin, D. S. (2012). An invariant dimensional liability model of gender differences in mental disorder prevalence: Evidence from a national sample. *Journal of Abnormal Psychology, 121*(1), 282–288. https://doi.org/10.1037/A0024780
Evans, T. M., Bira, L., Gastelum, J. B., Weiss, L. T., & Vanderford, N. L. (2018). Evidence for a mental health crisis in graduate education. *Nature Biotechnology, 36*(3), 282–284. https://doi.org/10.1038/nbt.4089
Flores, N. M. (2019). Harassment at conferences: Will #MeToo momentum translate to real change? *Gender and Education, 32*(1), 137–144. https://doi.org/10.1080/09540253.2019.1633462
Franco, M. C., Helal, L., Cenci, M. S., & Moher, D. (2021). The impact of gender on researchers' assessment: A randomized controlled trial. *Journal of Clinical Epidemiology, 138*, 95–101. https://doi.org/10.1016/j.jclinepi.2021.05.026
Gardner, S. K., & Gopaul, B. (2012). The part-time doctoral student experience. *International Journal of Doctoral Studies*, 7, 63–78. https://doi.org/10.28945/1561
Gaule, P., & Piacentini, M. (2018). An advisor like me? Advisor gender and post-graduate careers in science. *Research Policy, 47*(4), 805–813. https://doi.org/10.1016/J.RESPOL.2018.02.011
Hayes, S. C., & Hayes, L. J. (1989). Writing your vita. *APS Observer, 2*(3), 15–17.
Heaton, B., Streszoff, D., Fox, C. H., Kaye, E. A., Gebel, C. M., Quintiliani, L. M., & Garcia, R. I. (2020). Survey of dental researchers' perceptions of sexual harassment at AADR conferences: 2015 to 2018. *Journal of Dental Research, 99*(5), 488–497. https://doi.org/10.1177/0022034520908504
hooks, b. (1994). *Teaching to transgress: Education as the practice of freedom*. Routledge. https://doi.org/10.3366/para.1994.17.3.270
Houmanfar, R., Rodrigues, N. J., & Smith, G. S. (2009). Role of communication networks in behavioral systems analysis. *Journal of Organizational Behavior Management, 29*(3–4), 257–275. https://doi.org/10.1080/01608060903092102
Hurtado-Parrado, C., Pfaller-Sadovsky, N., Medina, L., Gayman, C. M., Rost, K. A., & Schofill, D. (2021). A systematic review and quantitative analysis of interteaching. *Journal of Behavioral Education*. https://doi.org/10.1007/s10864-021-09452-3
Hutchins, H. M. (2015). Outing the imposter: A study exploring imposter phenomenon among higher education faculty. *New Horizons in Adult Education and Human Resource Development, 27*(2), 3–12. https://doi.org/10.1002/nha3.20098
Jairam, D., & Kahl, D. H. (2012). Navigating the doctoral experience: The role of social support in successful degree completion. *International Journal of Doctoral Studies*, 7, 311–329. https://doi.org/10.28945/1700
Kiner, M. (2020). *It's time to break the cycle of female rivalry*. https://hbr.org/2020/04/its-time-to-break-the-cycle-of-female-rivalry
Kutsyuruba, B., & Godden, L. (2019). The role of mentoring and coaching as a means of supporting the well-being of educators and students. *International Journal of Mentoring and Coaching in Education, 8*(4), 229–234. https://doi.org/10.1108/IJMCE-12-2019-081
Landrum, R. E., & Nelsen, L. R. (2002). The undergraduate research assistantship: An analysis of the benefits. *Teaching of Psychology, 29*(1), 15–19. https://doi.org/10.1207/S15328023TOP2901_04
Leary, M. R., Patton, K. M., Orlando, A. E., & Wagoner Funk, W. (2000). The impostor phenomenon: Self-perceptions, reflected appraisals, and interpersonal strategies. *Journal of Personality, 68*(4), 725–756. https://doi.org/10.1111/1467-6494.00114
LeBlanc, L. A. (2015). My mentors and their influences on my career. *The Behavior Analyst, 38*(2), 237–245. https://doi.org/10.1007/s40614-015-0035-4
Lechuga, V. M. (2011). Faculty-graduate student mentoring relationship: Mentors' perceived roles and responsibilities. *Higher Education, 62*(6), 757–771. https://doi.org/10.1007/s10734-011-9416-0
Lerchenmueller, M. J., Sorenson, O., & Jena, A. B. (2019). Gender differences in how scientists present the importance of their research: Observational study. *BMJ (Clinical research ed.), 367*, l6573. https://doi.org/10.1136/bmj.l6573
Lin, L., & Cranton, P. (2005). From scholarship student to responsible scholar: A transformative process. *Teaching in Higher Education, 10*(4), 447–459. https://doi.org/10.1080/13562510500239026
Litalien, D., & Guay, F. (2015). Dropout intentions in PhD studies: A comprehensive model based on interpersonal relationships and motivational resources. *Contemporary Educational Psychology, 41*, 218–231. https://doi.org/10.1016/j.cedpsych.2015.03.004

Makhamreh, M., & Stockley, D. (2019). Mentorship and well-being: Examining doctoral students' lived experiences in doctoral supervision context. *International Journal of Mentoring and Coaching in Education, 9*(1), 1–20. https://doi.org/10.1108/IJMCE-02-2019-0013

Marino, F. E. (2020). Mentoring gone wrong: What is happening to mentorship in academia? *Policy Futures in Education*. https://doi.org/10.1177/1478210320972199

Marts, S. (2017). Open secrets and missing stairs: Sexual and gender based harassment at scientific meetings. *Smarts Consulting*. https://static1.squarespace.com/static/51a662bde4b06440a1627b96/t/58b067e846c3c4cf659bd4e3/1487955946386/Open+Secrets+and+Missing+Stairs.pdf

McCann, C., Tomaskovic-Devey, D., & Badgett, L. (2018). Employers' responses to sexual harassment. *SSRN*. https://doi.org/10.2139/ssrn.3407960

Moss-Racusin, C. A., Dovidio, J. F., Brescoll, V. L., Graham, M. J., & Handelsman, J. (2012). Science faculty's subtle gender biases favor male students. *Proceedings of the National Academy of Sciences, 109*(41), 16474–16479. https://doi.org/10.1073/pnas.1211286109

Nasser-Abu Alhija, F., & Fresko, B. (2018). Graduate teaching assistants: How well do their students think they do? *Assessment & Evaluation in Higher Education, 43*(6), 943–954. https://doi.org/10.1080/02602938.2018.1423673

Neumark, D., & Gardecki, R. (1998). Women helping women? Role model and mentoring effects on female Ph.D. students in economics. *Journal of Human Resources, 33*(1), 220–246. https://doi.org/10.2307/146320

Nosik, M. R., & Grow, L. L. (2015). Prominent women in behavior analysis: An introduction. *The Behavior Analyst, 38*(2), 225–227. https://doi.org/10.1007/s40614-015-0032-7

Pastrana, S. J., Frewing, T. M., Grow, L. L., Nosik, M. R., Turner, M., & Carr, J. E. (2018). Frequently assigned readings in behavior analysis graduate training programs. *Behavior Analysis in Practice, 11*(3), 267–273. https://doi.org/10.1007/s40617-016-0137-9

Pezzoni, M., Mairesse, J., Stephan, P., & Lane, J. (2016). Gender and the publication output of graduate students: A case study. *PLoS One, 11*(1), e0145146. https://doi.org/10.1371/JOURNAL.PONE.0145146

Ramos, D., & Yi, V. (2020). Doctoral women of color coping with racism and sexism in the academy. *International Journal of Doctoral Studies, 15*, 135–158. https://doi.org/10.28945/4508

Sapiro, V., & Campbell, D. (2018). Report on the 2017 APSA survey on sexual harassment at annual meetings. *PS: Political Science & Politics, 51*(1), 197–206. https://doi.org/10.1017/S1049096517002104

Savage, H. E., Karp, R. S., & Logue, R. (2004). Faculty mentorship at colleges and universities. *College Teaching, 52*(1), 21–24. https://doi.org/10.3200/CTCH.52.1.21-24

Schmader, T., Whitehead, J., & Wysocki, V. H. (2007). A linguistic comparison of letters of recommendation for male and female chemistry and biochemistry job applicants. *Sex Roles, 57*(7–8), 509–514. https://doi.org/10.1007/s11199-007-9291-4

Sleiman, A. A., Sigurjonsdottir, S., Elnes, A., Gage, N. A., & Gravina, N. G. (2020). A quantitative review of performance feedback in organizational settings (1998–2018). *Journal of Organizational Behavior Management, 40*(3–4), 303–332. https://doi.org/10.1080/01608061.2020.1823300

Straus, S. E., Johnson, M. O., Marquez, C., & Feldman, M. D. (2013). Characteristics of successful and failed mentoring relationships: A qualitative study across two academic health centers. *Academic Medicine: Journal of the Association of American Medical Colleges, 88*(1), 82–89. https://doi.org/10.1097/ACM.0B013E31827647A0

Szreter, S. (2000). Social capital, the economy, and education in historical perspective. In S. Baron, J. Field, & T. Schuller (Eds.), *Social capital: Critical perspectives* (pp. 56–77). Oxford University Press.

Taylor, B. A. (2015). Stereo knobs and swing sets: Falling in love with the science of behavior. *The Behavior Analyst, 38*(2), 283–292. https://doi.org/10.1007/s40614-015-0041-6

Thompson, T., Davis, H., & Davidson, J. (1998). Attributional and affective responses of impostors to academic success and failure outcomes. *Personality and Individual Differences, 25*(2), 381–396. https://doi.org/10.1016/S0191-8869(98)00065-8

U.S. Department of Education, National Center for Education Statistics, Integrated Postsecondary Education Data System (IPEDS). (2020a). *Degrees conferred by postsecondary institutions, by level of degree and sex of student: Selected years, 1869–70 through 2027–28*. https://nces.ed.gov/programs/digest/d17/tables/dt17_318.10.asp?current=yes

U.S. Department of Education, National Center for Education Statistics, Integrated Postsecondary Education Data System (IPEDS). (2020b). *Doctor's degrees conferred to females by postsecondary institutions, by*

race/ethnicity and field of study: 2017–18 and 2018–19. https://nces.ed.gov/programs/digest/d20/tables/dt20_324.35.asp
U.S. Department of Education, National Center for Education Statistics, Integrated Postsecondary Education Data System (IPEDS). (2020c). *Doctor's degrees conferred to males by postsecondary institutions, by race/ethnicity and field of study: 2017–18 and 2018–19*. https://nces.ed.gov/programs/digest/d20/tables/dt20_324.30.asp
U.S. Department of Education, National Center for Education Statistics, Integrated Postsecondary Education Data System (IPEDS). (2020d). *Master's degrees conferred to females by postsecondary institutions, by race/ethnicity and field of study: 2017–18 and 2018–19*. https://nces.ed.gov/programs/digest/d20/tables/dt20_323.50.asp
U.S. Department of Education, National Center for Education Statistics, Integrated Postsecondary Education Data System (IPEDS). (2020e). *Master's degrees conferred to males by postsecondary institutions, by race/ethnicity and field of study: 2017–18 and 2018–19*. https://nces.ed.gov/programs/digest/d20/tables/dt20_323.40.asp
Varga, K. (2011, February 28). Gaining teaching experience in graduate school. *Association for Psychological Science*. www.psychologicalscience.org/observer/gaining-teaching-experience-in-graduate-school
Walkington, L. (2017). How far have we really come? Black women faculty and graduate students' experiences in higher education. *Humboldt Journal of Social Relations*, *39*, 51–65. www.jstor.org/stable/90007871
Wu, X. (2010). Universal design for learning: A collaborative framework for designing inclusive curriculum. *i.e.: Inquiry in Education*, *1*(6). https://digitalcommons.nl.edu/ie/vol1/iss2/6
Ysseldyk., R., Greenaway, K H., Hassinger, E., Zutrauen, S., Linz, J., Bhatia, M. P., Frye, M., Starkenburg, E., & Tai, V. (2019). A leak in the academic pipeline: Identity and health among postdoctoral women. *Frontiers*, *10*, 1297. https://doi.org/10.3389/fpsyg.2019.01297

2 The Job Search

Corina Jimenez-Gomez and Sarah M. Richling

The Job Search

There are many ways to navigate the challenges and opportunities faced by early-career academics. This chapter is not intended to be a how-to guide for everyone. Nor is it a guide on "how to be a woman and have it all." What we describe in this chapter is informed by our individual histories and how we have experienced life's events, which are neither perfect nor representative of all women. Therefore, we see it fitting to provide some context describing who we are and how we arrived at our current role before providing suggestions for readers. We also would like to relay some relevant dialogue we engaged in, as collaborative authors, while preparing to write this chapter which we believe will help lay the groundwork and tone for the remainder of its contents.

In the planning stage for the current chapter, we both found ourselves taking an impersonal, academic tone toward our outline development. Although the initial request asked us to include a personal narrative, neither of us naturally did so. During a conversation, we each reflected on what in our histories might be suppressing our behavior related to sharing personal information about ourselves or adopting a personal tone in our writing. We immediately agreed these behaviors were likely not initially evoked given our formal training as scientific writers and behavioral scientists. Our learning histories involved adopting rules regarding removing our personal perspectives or values and incorporating as much factual information and as many references as possible. As that applied to the topic of the current chapter—the job search—each of us immediately started considering which empirical sources would provide the reader with the best evidence-based strategy for effectively navigating the job market. We did not immediately consider our own experiences as a reputable source of information.

In addition to the influence of our formal training, we also noted that we may share a similar tendency to avoid personal narrative because it produces a general sense of discomfort. This "uncomfortable" feeling was rooted in the belief that sharing personal information or talking informally rendered us vulnerable to being perceived in potentially problematic ways, especially as women. Throughout our careers, we have focused on presenting ourselves in what could be labeled as stoic, unemotional, or engaging in behaviors we identified as traditionally more masculine—which we had associated with being "professional."

We also described to each other how we had generalized these ideas of adopting an impersonal, "professional" demeanor to the presentation of ourselves on our curriculum vitae, personal statements, and in the interview process, for fear of being perceived in a

Author's note: The authors' names are listed in alphabetical order and are regarded as having contributed equally to this chapter.

DOI: 10.4324/9781003216773-4

manner that potentially resulted in lost job prospects. In an ideal world, one in which we have ample opportunities for employment and systems are better designed to open doors to people from a range of backgrounds and lived experiences, we might feel better positioned to present ourselves more authentically. Nevertheless, we have each found ways to navigate securing employment in academic settings while embracing our unique learning histories and incorporating our personal values throughout our career. In the spirit of continuing to embrace the uncomfortable feeling of progressive change on a personal level, we incorporate those experiences here wherever possible. We hope that our own personal narratives combined with additional outside sources will be beneficial to readers and will provide insight into the challenges and considerations one may encounter when navigating the job market. Before diving deeper into different ways to navigate the job search, we would like to take a moment to describe our individual paths and current job functions.

Introduction to the Authors

Corina Jimenez-Gomez

I began my career in behavioral science in the Operant and Classical Conditioning Laboratory at the Universidad Central de Venezuela in the late 1990s. While there, I had the opportunity to get hands-on experience conducting behavioral research with nonhuman animals, learning to program on relay racks. I also conducted research evaluating basic behavioral processes, analyzed data, and read articles from the *Journal of the Experimental Analysis of Behavior* (*JEAB*). I fell in love with the field and decided to pursue it instead of the clinical psychology path for which I had been training. Upon graduating with a licensure in Psychology from the Universidad Católica Andrés Bello, I pursued a doctoral degree in the experimental analysis of behavior at Utah State University. While in graduate school, my research focused on evaluating behavioral and pharmacological interventions for the treatment of substance abuse in nonhuman animal models. Subsequently, I continued my training in the area of behavioral pharmacology as a postdoctoral fellow at the University of Michigan. Next, I moved to New Zealand, where I held a Research Fellow position at the University of Auckland. While in New Zealand, I participated in an early-childhood education program that sparked my interest in the application of behavior science to teach young children. During that same time, I became a mom, which further sparked my interest in the application of behavior science to teaching young children, particularly social communication and play skills, and adapting our science to address the needs of diverse populations. Both of these interests date back to my clinical work in La Vega, an underserved and under-resourced area of Caracas.

When I moved to Florida, my background and interests led me to work at The Scott Center for Autism Treatment, where I accrued the supervised hours necessary to become a Board Certified Behavior Analyst (BCBA). While at the Florida Institute of Technology, I worked both as a Research Assistant Professor in the School of Behavior Analysis and as Faculty Supervisor at The Scott Center for Autism Treatment. Having a background as a basic behavioral researcher and being a BCBA-D, I am always thinking about how to resolve questions and issues at both the level of the intervention as well as understanding the behavioral processes underlying application. When looking for an academic home, I was interested in finding a place that valued collaboration, that allowed me to pursue my interests, and one in which I could balance research and application of behavioral science.

I identify as a cisgender Latina, who immigrated to the US from a country to which I cannot easily return, whose homeland is spread all over the world wherever my family and friends reside. I am a first-generation advanced-degree graduate and academic, who experiences private events in Spanish. I am a primary caregiver of my children and aging parents. I have experienced firsthand systems of oppression in academia, and strive to use my privileged position to support others, as well as constantly aiming to keep my rich culture of food, music, and imagery embedded in all my endeavors.

Sarah M. Richling

I began my journey within the field of behavior analysis as a sophomore at University of Wisconsin, Eau Claire. Up until this point, I had been majoring in Biology and Chemistry in preparation for a career in the medical field. As an attempt to balance my difficult college course load, I decided to pursue classes in psychology and enrolled in a course called Introduction to Behavior Analysis taught by a prominent member of the field. Taking this class led me to serve as a teaching assistant, work in an animal laboratory, and introduced me to a university-based clinic providing onsite and in-home early intervention services for autistic individuals. In addition, my experiences helped me with my college job—working within a local juvenile detention facility. I was pleasantly surprised to find that the approach to psychology taken through behavior analysis aligned well with my worldview. Ultimately, my applied experiences led me to change my career plans entirely and I switched my major to psychology and began my career in behavior analysis at 20 years old.

In 2010, I received my BCBA and my master's degree in behavior analysis from St. Cloud State University in Minnesota. While enrolled, I took a course on the social bases of behavior and was introduced to different areas of application. This, combined with my previous history working in the juvenile detention center, solidified my interest in applying behavior analysis to social and cultural phenomena, with a particular focus on criminal recidivism. However, my actual practicum experience during this period involved providing consultation services within public elementary schools working with autistic students, students diagnosed with developmental disorders, and students struggling with behavioral and academic difficulties.

Thereafter, I completed my doctoral degree in behavior analysis at the University of Nevada, Reno. There, my interests in the molar application of behavior analysis to cultural phenomena were further developed as I was introduced to scientific system building from both a philosophical and an organizational and behavior management perspective. Although I was able to expand on that area of interest through my coursework and through teaching undergraduate classes in motivation, emotion, and gender, my practical training remained in the area of developmental disabilities. This included directing a day treatment clinic for adults with disabilities and providing BCBA supervision to fellow students in the clinic, teachers working in the Nevada school district, and students working in a clinic in Riyadh, Saudi Arabia.

As I was completing my doctoral degree, a former mentor alerted me to an employment opportunity at Auburn University which involved consulting with a juvenile-detention facility and my interest was immediately piqued. Although I will detail my experience with the job search later in this chapter, suffice it to say for now that at that stage I had only applied for and accepted one job offer, and I currently remain employed in that position as a clinical assistant professor. In this role, I am able to provide oversight of the clinical training of master's students in pursuit of their BCBA and teach graduate courses. In addition, I finally have the opportunity to expand my interests in applying behavior analysis to criminal behavior beyond an academic pursuit to an actual applied setting.

As for who I am aside from my career, I identify as a pansexual female, multiracial (Caucasian and Japanese), third-generation immigrant, and first-generation academic from a small-town, lower-middle-class background. I have chosen not to get married or have children and to live a sober lifestyle due to a family history of alcohol abuse and struggles with mental health. My paternal grandmother was a first-generation immigrant who had been orphaned and experienced homelessness in Japan prior to coming to the United States and raising five children on her own. She passed along her values for Japanese food, self-reliance and independence, and the Japanese notion of *honne* and *tatemae*. These words refer to an individual's true self and desires ("honne") and the self that aligns with societal expectations ("tatemae"). They highlight a culturally driven family expectation to avoid publicly divulging personal information (e.g., my personal identity and financial status), to avoid confrontation or disagreement in social contexts (e.g., negotiating salary), and to avoid public failure (e.g., struggles with mental health). As such, writing the current chapter was a challenging (and valuable) exercise in leaning into the uncomfortable development of new personal repertoires!

Shared Perspectives

Amid all that uncomfortableness, we also want to recognize our obvious positions of privilege. Among other things, we are two women with advanced degrees, who hold faculty positions and have the platform to write the present chapter. We recognize the many unique ways in which we have had advantages that others have not. We have shared a small portion of our history here but have also chosen to leave out some more significant and highly personal experiences. Our choice to publicly disclose personal information here does not imply we speak for any particular group. We speak for ourselves; the personal information shared was only intended for readers to gain a better understanding of our positionality.

The Path Toward an Academic Job

As mentioned earlier, each of the authors of this chapter took a very different route to reach the same job title, Assistant Clinical Professor, at the same institution. There is no single way to travel the path toward an academic job. In addition, we recognize that our current position as non-tenure track faculty may not be the ideal academic job target for many individuals. The specific detours, challenges, and opportunities encountered by each individual will differ. Nevertheless, we provide some general suggestions based on our experiences that we believe could be helpful when navigating the search for academic jobs.

The advice we provide can be useful to anyone starting their path towards an academic career, but it comes from the perspective of two women and is particularly aimed at women. The reasons for this include the historical underrepresentation of women, particularly women of color, in academia (American Association of University Women, 2021; Catalyst, 2020), and the unique barriers women face in academia (Howe-Walsh & Turnbull, 2016; Social Sciences Feminist Network Research Interest Group, 2017). Although the intersection of gender and other variables, such as race or gender identity, can pose further barriers to academic careers, we can only speak from the perspective of our own experiences and privilege. As a result, we acknowledge some of our recommendations may not apply equally to all readers but hope this chapter can serve as case studies for navigating the process of the academic job search. Given the limitations of our own learning histories and experiences, we encourage individuals who identify as members of minoritized groups to seek suggestions from people whose lived experiences might better inform challenges specific to those groups. With that being said, we will now discuss our subjective perspectives of the academic job-search process.

Before the Job Search

Networking

Before you start searching for jobs or preparing and submitting applications, there are various things you can do to help maximize your opportunities and build a strong foundation for your subsequent search activities. The first step begins during your time in graduate school, where you will interact with faculty and peers at your institution regularly and at other institutions during conferences and similar professional events. These interactions will help you begin to build your professional network, which can provide further opportunities for mentorship and professional growth later. The importance of professional networks cannot be overstated. For better or worse, professional networks play an important part in accessing career opportunities (Heffernan, 2021). Although it can be more difficult for people from minoritized or underrepresented groups to penetrate professional networks, it is important for attaining professional opportunities (Davis & Warfield, 2011). Seeking support from professional organizations or groups (e.g., Black Applied Behavior Analysts, Latino Association for Behavior Analysis, ABA Task Force) or connecting with mentors who share your background could be avenues to expanding your professional network (see Kelsky, 2020a for more advice for women of color).

Some ways to build networks include attending professional-development events (e.g., regional, national conferences), connecting with researchers conducting work similar to yours at other institutions, and mining your current network for connections and information that can be useful as you develop your career (e.g., upcoming grant announcements, job listings, etc.). Although some may suggest networking is for those who naturally engage in compatible social behaviors or behaviors labeled as extroverted (e.g., talking to strangers, speaking up during meetings), these are behaviors that can be shaped and learned. For me (Corina), building my professional network began while completing my training in Venezuela and seeking to pursue a graduate degree. I met with a professor who had earned his PhD in the US to ask for advice navigating the application process. This professor suggested contacting prospective mentors to introduce myself and approaching them at the first Association for Behavior Analysis conference I attended. As sound as these recommendations seemed, they required me to engage in behaviors that had not been encouraged or rewarded in my learning history: namely, approaching mostly older male authority figures, whose names I had seen on journal articles or covers of textbooks, to introduce myself and demonstrate my intellectual abilities. During graduate school, I continued to develop this behavioral repertoire, approaching people I did not know at conferences, sending "cold call" emails, and learning to navigate professional spaces dominated by people with backgrounds quite different from mine. None of these things were in my repertoire initially, and some clashed with my cultural background, but I identified the need to engage in these behaviors to access professional networks that would be closed off otherwise. As an international student, I did not have others to open doors or offer introductions for me, so I felt the need to acquire this behavioral repertoire to maximize my professional-development opportunities.

Whereas for me (Sarah), I have never quite mastered the art of initiating professional discourse in the manner just described and have adopted another potentially overlooked strategy for network building. My current professional network is almost entirely traceable to connections I had made with (and through) peers and mentees, as opposed to faculty or professional mentors. Even if some settings and institutions might foster competition with fellow students, my doctoral training required an especially heavy emphasis on socializing and collaborating with peers within and across psychological programs. Although a few opportunities have come about through approaching or being approached by people I did not know in professional settings, most introductions have been facilitated through already-established connections and friendships. Through this experience, I have found I am likely to be introduced to other individuals who share my values of creating networks of collaboration, the exchanging of ideas, and mutual support, both professionally and personally. As such, I often advise mentees to become aware of the resources that exist among them, both in the short and in the long term. Your peers can serve as a support system and as collaborative partners with unique and complementary ideas and skills. In addition, the field of behavior analysis is still relatively small; someone who is now your peer or mentee might later become a collaborator on a multisite grant application, a reviewer for a research paper, your boss as a clinical director, or a member of a faculty search committee. I, personally, have experienced each of these listed scenarios, among others. As I alluded to earlier, my master's advisor was the one to alert me to my current job opportunity, and now is my academic colleague. Therefore, I cannot stress enough how important it is to recognize that the way you conduct yourself as a student, a mentee, a peer, a supervisor, and a colleague will leave an impression which could later, in turn, foster (or hinder) opportunities for employment and professional advancement.

Another opportunity for networking involves utilizing online platforms. The advent of social media and professional networking sites such as LinkedIn have made building professional networks easier. Now it is possible to connect with people via shared connections and it is widely accepted that people you do not know personally can be your online "friend" or in your network. Learning to take advantage of these resources can be very useful for younger academics (Elson, 2020). Social media can be very useful for networking and career growth (Donelan, 2016). The use of online networks for professional purposes also highlights the importance of how young professionals portray themselves on these platforms. Anything that is publicly available online can be used to your advantage or detriment [Martis, n.d.]. Just like pictures from your participation in a regional conference can speak to your commitment to scholarly work, pictures from less flattering moments or controversial posts can limit your ability to access professional opportunities. In addition to directly connecting with others online, social media platforms allow users to connect to groups of individuals with shared interests (e.g., a students-of-behavior-analysis Facebook group). These groups can offer participants access to information, mentorship, and opportunities specific to the field of behavior analysis.

Taking on student leadership roles within university government, or state, national, and international professional organizations (e.g., state ABA student board positions, Association for Behavior Analysis International [ABAI] student representative, etc.) can also help give you the experience of academic service responsibilities and provide you with opportunities for networking. However, these positions are limited and difficult to access for many. As a graduate student, I (Corina) sought as many volunteer opportunities as possible, such as student representative in the ABAI executive council. Not only did I contact plenty of naturally occurring reinforcers while engaging in these activities (e.g., opportunity to have one-on-one interactions with leaders of the field), I also identified that it provided a valuable experience in my professional growth. It is important to recognize, however, these types of opportunities require one to allocate time and resources that may not always be available for all readers. As a graduate student who had an assistantship for financial support, I had the time available to devote to this service activity.

Exploring Available Resources

Yourself as a Resource

Another step you can take prior to searching for jobs and submitting applications is to view and utilize yourself as a primary resource. It can be useful to assess how your degree and professional experiences fit into your long-term career goals as well as how your personal values, goals, and reinforcers factor into the equation. Some individuals might have a very clear idea of the exact career position they would like to pursue, others might be weighing various options, and still others may not even be aware of what options are available outside of the expected tenure-track professor position (as was the case with Sarah). Later in this chapter, we discuss the various kinds of positions available to those interested in an academic career. Although nonacademic positions are outside the purview of this chapter, it is worth noting that those positions are equally valuable to academic ones and could better align with your values and professional goals.

For anyone still grappling with clarifying their overall career goals, there are several freely available career assessment tools which might be helpful (e.g., https://your.yale.edu/work-yale/learn-and-grow/career-development/career-assessment-tools). In addition, it may be beneficial to objectively identify areas of strength and weakness in reaching your overall career goals. Looking at your postgraduate career as another series of milestones may relieve some self-imposed pressure to find the perfect job and be the perfect candidate right away. This active and ongoing assessment of the alignment of your experiences and goals can help you to identify job opportunities where you can highlight your current strengths and allow for growth and/or mentorship in areas of weakness. For myself (Sarah), the funding mechanisms guiding my graduate experiences left me with a diverse and expansive list of clinical application, supervision, and teaching experiences. This made me an attractive candidate for applied positions where I would be responsible for the oversight and supervision of clinical services. However, the emphasis on these experiences during graduate school did not allow for the pursuit of more strictly research-oriented activities. As such, I wanted to identify a postdoc or a faculty position where I would be able to grow in that area, rather than take a position which might only further add to the clinical portion of my resume. Given my financial restraints and reliance on student loans throughout the entirety of my academic career, a postdoc position was not feasible. Ultimately, the role of a clinical assistant professor offered me the balance of utilizing my current skills while also being given the freedom and mentorship to expand on my research within a university setting. I originally viewed my current position as a milestone toward a tenure-track position later.

Just as each person's training and experience will differ greatly, so will each individual's unique values and reinforcers. For some, this might seem very straightforward, but for many women like the authors of this chapter, identifying what you really want and enjoy, rather than what you think you should do based on others' expectations and opinions, might not be strong in your repertoire. A simple but valuable piece of advice from a prominent and successful member of our field proved very helpful. This person suggested spending several weeks thinking about the reinforcers across all previous positions. The simple question of which tasks bring the most joy and to which tasks we gravitate easily during our downtime can lead to important insights. For me (Sarah), this contingency analysis made me realize I enjoy watching others learn the science and technology for the first time and appreciate the ability to explore new phenomena academically and in practice. I realized that although I had identified a tenure-track faculty position as my ultimate goal, mostly because I thought that is what I was supposed to aspire to, I was already in my ideal position as a clinical professor. So, dear reader, ask yourself: why academia? What are the contingencies maintaining your search for academic jobs? What professional behaviors or activities allow you to contact reinforcers? Thereafter, ask yourself if your strongest reinforcers are to be found in clinical application, research, teaching, mentorship, writing, or some combination of these. Then, identify positions where you are the most likely to encounter a dense schedule of reinforcement.

Organizational and Online Resources

For those still in graduate school, a variety of resources exist within institutions and online that can provide additional support while navigating the job market. As graduate students, we did not take advantage of all the resources we describe here, primarily because we were not aware they existed or did not actively seek them out. However, in our current roles we realize how beneficial these resources can be during the career-planning stage. For example, while at the University of Michigan as a postdoctoral fellow, I (Corina) took advantage of workshops offered on grant writing, preparing job applications, and delivering job talks. The opportunity to receive free training and advice from experts in these areas has been helpful throughout my career.

Many academic institutions have career centers that can provide access to services and resources including advising appointments, workshops, career events, career assessments, planning tools, mentorship programs, application-development support, doctoral-affairs support, and online resource repositories (e.g., https://careercenter.umich.edu; https://career.auburn.edu). Although some of the resources available are general and may not provide detailed recommendations specific to the field of behavior analysis, we recommend those who are able to take advantage of these services do so. Multiple sources of guidance and feedback, including institutional experts, may help uncover information you likely would not be exposed to through more field-specific avenues. Even if you encounter information that is not immediately relevant to your unique situation, it may be useful to relay to a colleague, peer, or mentee undergoing their own unique career-navigation challenges. This information also may be useful in the future as your professional goals and situation changes over time.

In addition to university-based resources, there is an overwhelming amount of information freely available online. This includes a plethora of assessments, career events, webinars, forums, industry trends, etc. Following are examples of promising resources:

- ImaginePhD (www.imaginephd.com) is a free online career exploration and planning tool for doctoral students and postdoctoral scholars in humanities and social sciences.
- The Professor Is In (https://theprofessorisin.com) is a website run by Karen Kelsky, who is a former faculty member turned academic-career coach. The website contains a wealth of useful information for those seeking employment within academia. I (Corina) have benefitted from the insight and advice from this website at many points in my career.

Interacting with mentors and peers (as will be discussed further) may also help in identifying the most helpful tools for successfully navigating specific careers within behavior analysis.

Mentors and Peers

Identifying one or more mentors can be invaluable to your ongoing career development. Obvious choices for mentors include current and former faculty advisors. However, some individuals may have found, through their graduate school experience and intimate collaboration with their faculty advisor, that they wish to go a different direction with their career path. While some students may establish a research line that is like that of their doctoral advisor, others may wish to expand their experiences into other areas. This was the case with me (Sarah). While I valued my experience working with individuals with developmental and intellectual disabilities, I had always hoped to gain additional experience in culturo-behavior science including criminal justice and other large-scale societal issues. As such, I became a volunteer and a board member for the ABAI special interest group, Behaviorists for Social Responsibility (BFSR), identified and collaborated with a faculty member in the criminal-justice department, and spoke with several individuals within the field who had successfully bridged the gap between ABA and other areas of scientific application at the societal level. As part of my first volunteer role with BFSR, I was tasked with interviewing prominent members of the field who had careers applying behavioral science to cultural phenomena. Through these interviews, I was able to reverse engineer a process map for my own career path—that is, find someone who does something similar to what you would like to do, and then take similar steps. This extends to any individual you have identified as successful in the area(s) you aspire to; look at what steps they have taken to get there and use it as a potential roadmap.

Mentorship, of course, is not limited to long-established academics. While the benefit of these mentors is a long history of experience in the field, the disadvantage is that they might not have an intimate connection to the job market as it currently exists. As such, it can be helpful to identify a group of peer mentors who are currently or have recently undergone the job-hunt process. Through this avenue, you may be alerted to new job opportunities, strategies, resources, and the exchange of templates for your professional portfolio materials (discussed in more detail later). In addition, creating peer networks can help to provide emotional support while you navigate through challenges, fears, and frustrations you will likely encounter in your job search and beyond.

Once you have identified valuable mentors and peers, reach out and foster the relationship. For instance, you may ask questions about their experiences and recommendations. As evidenced previously with the description of the differing career paths of the current chapter's authors, there is no single way to reach your destination. As such, take each person's perspective and advice in context. Their experience will likely be different from your own. Even if you follow the perfect advice for achieving an academic position to the letter, job market prospects at the exact time you graduate may not line up with your specific area of research or experience. There is only so much within your control. We suggest establishing ongoing mentorship relationships across your career in which you can ask questions, gain insight, and then reevaluate your personal goals, values, and plans accordingly.

The Search

The bulk of academic jobs tend to be posted in the fall with a start date the following fall semester. That means one must start looking for jobs at least a year before the intended start date. Often this means looking for jobs before having defended your dissertation or having completed data collection. Many job ads take this into account and will add a note that they will consider candidates who are ABD (all but dissertation). We mention this because being able to balance the job search with other stressful life events like preparing your dissertation requires advanced planning and leaning on your network as needed. If you determine that is not feasible for your situation or if you are not able to secure a position from the fall advertisements, that does not necessarily mean you have to wait until the next year. Some additional positions or unfilled positions may continue to be submitted throughout the entirety of the year. For instance, visiting professor lines tend to be advertised towards the end of the academic year. In addition, as was the case with Sarah, it might be possible to negotiate a spring semester start date to allow for adequate time to complete dissertation research activities (although it did require flying back to defend!).

You might be wondering where to look for jobs. There are sites dedicated to posting academic job ads (e.g., www.higheredjobs.com), where many academic departments submit job ads. You can also find job ads specific to psychology (e.g., APA) or behavior analysis on the websites of professional organizations (e.g., ABAI, APBA). You may be able to set up alerts on these sites to receive notifications of new postings that meet your requirements (e.g., specific location or area of expertise). Other sources of information about jobs include professional listservs, social media, and professional networks—again highlighting the importance of connecting with others in the professional community.

Different Types of Academic Positions

Because the authors live in the United States, we are writing this section describing academic jobs and ranks as they exist in this system. If readers are considering academic jobs outside the US, we encourage them to become familiar with the system of each country.

In the US, there are various types of academic positions: tenure track, research track, clinical track, instructional/lecturer track, visiting, or adjunct. Each of these comes with their own expectations and specific responsibilities. Briefly, tenure-track jobs are academic positions that have the option of promotion resulting in an indefinite appointment at the institution.[1] The job security, and the accompanying academic freedom, is what makes tenure-track jobs so attractive and sought after. Tenure-track faculty are expected to allocate their time to the areas of teaching, research, and service. The specific expectations regarding research productivity and teaching will depend on the institution. For instance, universities ranked as Very High Research Activity (i.e., R1 universities; Carnegie Classification of Institutions of Higher Education, 2021) are doctoral granting institutions where tenure-track faculty are typically expected to seek and obtain external funding for research and have a productive research program; whereas, universities with lower research activity (e.g., Doctoral/Professional or Master's universities, small liberal arts colleges, community colleges) may not require tenure-track faculty to seek external funding for research but may require faculty to teach more courses (i.e., higher teaching load). Thus, even within tenure-track jobs, there may be some variability regarding job duties depending on the institution (more on this later). Faculty hired for tenure-track jobs start at the Assistant Professor level, where they will remain until they are promoted to Associate Professor and receive tenure, usually within five to seven years. Subsequently, faculty may be promoted further to Professor, which is also referred to as Full Professor. Navigating your way through the tenure and promotion process can be a difficult and stressful experience as well. As such, this topic is addressed in more detail in Chapter 3.

When people think of academic jobs, what usually comes to mind is a tenure-track job. However, most academic jobs are now non-tenure track (AAUP, 2018; Flaherty, 2018). Non-tenure-track faculty do not have the option of promotion to an indefinite appointment and are expected to perform in specific areas depending on type of appointment (e.g., clinical, research, instructional). Some non-tenure-track faculty may also be promoted through the ranks of assistant, associate, and full. The funding sources and needs of the department determine the job duties. For instance, clinical-track faculty (such as the authors) have the main job duty of contributing to the clinical or practical training of students. Research-track faculty tend to have less of an emphasis on the instruction and devote most of their time to research endeavors that are supported by external funding. Instructional-track faculty tend to have the highest teaching load. Faculty who hold these positions are awarded the same institutional benefits as tenure-track faculty (e.g., retirement, health insurance) and participate in shared governance within universities and departments (e.g., members of university/college/departmental committees), but the degree to which they can participate and vote on all matters will be dependent on institutional culture. Because these positions do not lead to indefinite appointment, non-tenure-track faculty must regularly renew their contracts, sometimes as often as annually, and are offered less job security because their jobs may become redundant or unnecessary if institutional or departmental priorities change.

Finally, the least secure faculty positions include visiting and adjunct. Visiting faculty are hired for a limited time, usually one to two years, to fulfill a specific need for the department. For instance, if a tenured faculty member has to take a leave of absence or retires, departments may need to quickly fill teaching loads. Another way in which universities fulfill teaching loads is to hire adjunct faculty, who are hired to teach individual courses and are not eligible for any benefits, given the part-time nature of these positions.

The type of position that may be best suited for you will depend on a range of things, such as your career goals and professional interests, your ability to move to a different city or state, and other obligations. For instance, if you are interested in teaching master's students but want to continue working in your current job as regional clinical director of a residential facility, maybe an adjunct position would be a good fit. Therefore, it is important to not discard potential options based solely on the title and whatever preconceptions you may have. Consider, instead, what are the job expectations for each position and how these align with your professional goals and personal values.

Job Expectations

Before describing how to explore job expectations for positions you find, it is important to note that the title of the position itself may not convey specific details about the position. Take for instance the two authors of this chapter, who both have the same title, but have somewhat different responsibilities. Currently, we are both Assistant Clinical Professors in the ABA Program at Auburn University. In this role, we both teach courses in the Applied Behavior Analysis Master's program, conduct research, and supervise and mentor students, among other duties. Despite our identical job titles and the overlapping tasks, our jobs also include different responsibilities. A core part of Corina's position involves directing a university-based clinic providing early behavioral intervention services for children diagnosed with autism and related disorders. In this role, Corina oversees the administrative and organizational operation of the clinic, behavioral services delivered to all clients served at the clinic, outreach activities with members of the community, workshops and trainings for caregivers and practitioners, clinical supervision of students accruing practicum hours at the clinic, and research activities conducted with clinical populations. Corina also conducts translational and applied research, supervises student projects, and pursues external funding opportunities to support her research. A core part of Sarah's position, on the other hand, involves coordinating the various practicum sites and corresponding supervisors to ensure students are receiving a diverse array of quality clinical experiences, supervision, and training that complies with all professional and legal codes and guidelines. In addition, Sarah has a primary role at the practicum site for the juvenile-detention center. In this role, she provides oversight of the clinical research activities conducted by doctoral student supervisors and master's students as well as provides direct supervision of several master's students' clinical training.

As evidenced by the different job duties, the clinical job title does not fully capture the scope of the work we each conduct. Although the primary function of clinical-track faculty is to support the practical training of graduate students, in our roles we have the flexibility to engage in service and research activities that align with our personal and professional interests. This freedom allows us to pursue activities that benefit the university, program, and students as well as the achievement of our own professional goals and development. However, we acknowledge this may not be the case in all organizations. Job titles may have institution- or program-specific descriptions.

A term you will likely see when describing allocation of time among various job duties is FTE, or full-time equivalent. This refers to the percentage of your time dedicated to each activity. Assuming a 40-hour workweek (unrealistic perhaps, but just go with us for this example), a 0.5 FTE for research would assume you spend 50% of your time (or 20 hours per week) on research activities. Job listings will sometimes describe expectations regarding research, teaching, and mentorship of students in vague terms (e.g., applicant should have an active research program). How the FTE is divided among research, teaching, and service will depend on the institution (e.g., tenure-track at R1 universities will have higher research FTE) and departmental needs. Other times, job listings will include specifics regarding some aspects of the job, such as the teaching load. You will likely see this listed as a ratio (e.g., 2:2, 4:4, 3:3:1), with each number referring to a different semester (i.e., fall:spring:summer). Other important pieces of information you may find in job ads include whether the position is on a 9- or 12-month contract, whether there are clinical responsibilities, whether there is an expectation for obtaining external funding, and whether there are outreach or service requirements.

Because a job title and description may not give you a detailed and complete picture of what are the specific responsibilities and expectations of a particular job, we advise the reader to inquire beyond the job ad when searching for jobs.

Beyond the Job Ad

We encourage anyone interested in a position to contact the chair of the search committee to inquire about details of the job not listed on the ad. We also encourage readers to reach out to your professional network. You may directly or indirectly know someone who currently or formerly worked at, recently graduated from, or is currently attending the institution. These people can give you insights into the position, the institutional and departmental culture, and the location that you would not be able to access elsewhere. Just as the applicant will present themselves in the best light during the application process, the program/department/university will do the same. Tapping into informal sources of information may shed light into relevant and important features of the job. You might locate the curriculum vitae of faculty currently or previously employed at that institution and look for patterns of successful or non-successful track records of publications, funding, and retaining faculty, while also determining if your own research line or clinical skills will be complementary to the current faculty. In addition, online searches of current headlines in university or local newspapers also could provide information about the culture. The reason this is important is because, unless you are considering an online program, you will be relocating to a new place, where you will work *and* live. Knowing about the community and whether the culture aligns with your values, whether you will feel safe and welcome, and whether you will have access to certain amenities or services all might contribute to whether you are satisfied with your position and decide to remain there. For me (Corina), as a mom of school-aged children and a nature lover, educational and outdoor opportunities available are always at the forefront for me.

We each have a list of things to consider depending on our values and life situations. Some important and practical considerations include cost of living, job opportunities for partners, diversity on campus and in the community, family leave policies, access to research facilities, and organizational support for junior faculty (e.g., mentorship programs, internal funding mechanisms for research), among others. University websites often have a wealth of information about practical things such as benefits, research and clinical facilities, and internal funding mechanisms. You can also learn a lot about the town or city where the university is located by reading online resources (e.g., local newspapers, blogs). There are other things, however, that you can only gauge by directly asking. It is up to the reader how and whether to ask about things that are priorities for them. Although it is widely not advisable to discuss family and children during the application and interview process, before the move to my current position I (Corina) was very upfront about my need for partner accommodations, the importance of collegiality and collaboration, and the fact I have school-aged children who will sometimes pull me away from my work duties. It was important to me that prospective colleagues saw these parts of me before making any commitments. I understand this may not be advisable or possible for all readers. I had the privilege of having another faculty position before moving here, which allowed me to be more selective in my approach. Earlier in my career, I would not have disclosed these things so openly. I also had the benefit of asking for advice on this matter before taking the approach of disclosing personal aspects early in the application process, again highlighting the importance of building your network of colleagues and mentors.

You will often hear people talking about "fit," or whether there is alignment of your professional goals and personal values to the institution and position. I have interviewed for positions that seemed interesting and like a great fit professionally on paper, but once I learned more about the program/university/location I quickly realized the position would not allow opportunities for professional growth or did not align well with my values. At this point, one must decide whether the pros outweigh the cons (e.g., do you have other options? could you be successful/happy despite the cons?).

Although many of these contributing factors may not be fully clarified before the interview process, it is worthwhile to gather as much information prior, to both help prepare you for a successful interview and save you time, effort, and money applying for jobs that may not be a good fit for you. Assuming you have done your due diligence and have decided to apply for one or more positions, you can now start preparing your materials for the application and interview process.

Applying and Interviewing

Preparing Materials

Although some positions may only require you to submit your CV, personal statement/cover letter, and teaching evaluations, others may require you to develop a comprehensive teaching and research portfolio, each with their own philosophy statements, products, and evidence of success and evolution. Rather than reinventing the wheel, we suggest reaching out to mentors and peers who have successfully secured positions and asking them if they would be willing to share examples of their portfolios. You can then use examples to develop your own materials. We also encourage readers to utilize online and institutional examples. However, we must stress it is important to tailor your portfolio to you and the specific position and institution to which you are applying. It is very important to double-check your materials before submitting for accuracy regarding the institutional or position title for which you are applying. Recruit the help of peers/mentors, when possible, to avoid simple mistakes which could have major implications.

Navigating Interviews

The interview can be an informative step beyond the initial ad and application for both you and the institution to which you are applying. There is no "right way" to interview. As always, take advantage of peers, mentors, and the internet as potential resources (Kelsky, 2020b). However, every position and corresponding environment is as unique as every individual applying for those positions. As such, our main recommendation is to gain as much information as possible during the interview process and to present yourself authentically, professionally speaking. To the first point, remember that you are also interviewing the institution to determine if it is a good fit for *you*. The interview is a great opportunity to ask questions, learn about your potential future colleagues, and get insight into what life in this institution would be like. Take advantage of this opportunity. Asking different people the same questions (e.g., support for junior faculty, mentorship, life in the town/city, challenges, issues of diversity and inclusion) can be very informative. You can think of it as information gathering by assessing interobserver agreement. To the second point, you want to secure a position in which you are reasonably capable of being successful. Both you and the institution make a huge investment in the other party; it is important to ensure it is a wise investment on both ends.

It might feel strange to view yourself as an investment or a commodity, but it also may be beneficial to adopt this analogy as a means to consider fit with a particular job. Even if we may prefer to view academic institutions as human service settings, they are also financial organizations. As such, these organizations are going to look at candidates in terms of potential contributions you can make to the financial stability and success of the program, department, etc. This can include an evaluation of your ability to teach a wide variety of classes that will appeal to a large number of students (tuition-driven), your ability to secure extramural funding (research-grant-driven), and, in some fields such as behavior analysis and in some positions, your ability to secure service contracts with the community (service delivery/training-driven).

As such, it is once again important to do your research. Make sure you determine what the main funding mechanism is for the particular program and department, and your ability to contribute meaningfully to that initiative. The existent and expected funding mechanisms for your position will largely determine your day-to-day responsibilities and job function. If a given institution relies heavily on tuition, you can reasonably expect to have a large teaching load with large class sizes; whereas another institution designated as an R1 university will likely emphasize evidence of successfully securing federal grant money and require less teaching. If the job requires you to conduct research and/or secure student training opportunities and contracts, it is important to research the community in which you are expected to operate. Look for evidence of the demand for your particular skill sets and areas of research. Along this same vein, look for indicators of a saturated market. This also applies to the university and a department. It is best to identify a position in which your skill set will "diversify the portfolio," meaning, you will not be in direct competition with other professionals for the same funding. Rather, you want to be able to speak to how you can contribute and collaborate with other faculty members and highlight the demand for your particular skill set within that environment. As such, familiarize yourself with the other faculty, their research, and their role in the department. This will also prepare you for your interviews with them and will help you appear knowledgeable and invested in the department as a whole.

The aforementioned recommendations apply to interviews of all modalities (e.g., phone, live video, or in person). Institutions will often conduct an initial interview via phone or video conference with an initial pool of applicants before narrowing the pool to a smaller number of candidates to whom they will extend an invitation to interview in person. If you receive an invitation to interview in person, we highly recommend doing so, unless you have already determined there is a very small chance you would consider taking the position. In-person interviews can be costly for both you and the institution, but we do not recommend requesting a distance interview unless necessary for logistical or health reasons. This could be viewed as a lack of interest in the position. In addition, whether you have doubts about the position or think it is a perfect fit, experiencing the institution and community in person can be a game changer. For me (Sarah), I was initially lukewarm to the idea of moving to Alabama. My in-person experience was the main factor leading to my decision to accept the position. During my interview, I was able to see the beauty of the community and landscape. More importantly, I realized very quickly throughout my interview that I was actually an excellent fit for the position and that there was extreme potential for growth in my areas of interest. So even if you are unsure, take every opportunity to learn as much about the position as you can before making a final decision.

Negotiating Start-Up

Assuming you and the interviewing entity have determined a mutually beneficial relationship is likely, you will (hopefully) now move into the stage of receiving and negotiating a job offer. The offer you receive should be commensurate with the type of position to which you applied. That is, a position with a research load should include funds and resources to ensure you can be successful in your role. For instance, it is not uncommon for faculty with a research load to be offered a start-up package that includes funds to purchase research materials/equipment and relief from teaching duties during the first year. Talking about money and salary with people outside our family is typically frowned upon in our culture. However, mentors and peers can be extremely helpful resources for navigating the process of negotiating your offer. I (Corina) have been lucky to count on trusted friends and colleagues to have conversations about this throughout the years. Being able to get a sense of what is reasonable to expect (sometimes you will be given an offer) or to request (sometimes you will be asked to submit a proposal) can be extremely helpful when navigating the negotiations. It is important to note, however, that what is reasonable at one institution may not be so at a different institution. So, as with any piece of advice, take it in context and use it as a data point in your broader data collection of information.

The reason we are including a section on negotiating your job offer is because you may be so excited (or thankful) to have a job offer, it may not cross your mind to negotiate. Further, this is yet another behavioral repertoire that may not have been shaped in your learning history (it certainly was not for us). This is particularly true for women and people from minoritized backgrounds (Ro, 2021). This point of the hiring process is the only time when the applicant has any leverage to request funds, teaching-load reduction, partner accommodations, etc. We cannot afford to let this opportunity pass. Failing to negotiate at this point can have long-term negative impacts on income (all future raises will be a percentage of starting salary), productivity (time and resources available for research could determine your ability to complete studies), and overall satisfaction (a partner who cannot find employment will likely result in added stress).

There are some great existing resources for negotiating salary (e.g., Kelsky, 2021; UCSF, 2012; Wong, n.d.), but there are a few things specific to academic jobs worth noting.

Some Things you may be Able to Negotiate

It is important to note that each institution is different, but from our experience, salary, start-up funds, teaching relief, FTE allocations, partner accommodations, and moving costs may all be negotiable. Before you make your wish list, however, make sure you check with your resources. For instance, if the job is at a state university, you can check salaries in publicly available listings. You may also ask junior faculty in the department about their experiences negotiating their offer. Some people will offer this information candidly and unprompted, while others will be more reserved with this information. Use your judgment here and follow their lead. For instance, while interviewing for a faculty job, I (Corina) had a recently hired faculty member describe some of the areas they found were negotiable in the offer (e.g., start-up and course relief) and which were not (e.g., salary). I took this opportunity to ask follow-up questions regarding lessons learned and advice that I probably would not have asked if this person had not started this conversation. If you are talking to people in your network or mentors, however, you might be able to be more direct in your inquiry. You may also have a conversation with the search-committee chair or department head to clarify some of these issues. However, it may not necessarily be advisable to ask about these things early on in the interview process, unless they initiate the conversation.

Some Things may not be up for Negotiation

Some institutions have set limits on what they can offer based on budgetary or regulatory constraints. The only way to know what these are may be to directly inquire. Sometimes these things are clearly stated in the job ad or when you interact with administrators (e.g., department head, dean) during the interview process. It is important to note that being told something is not negotiable does not say anything about how valuable the department finds you to be, but it speaks to organizational constraints that extend far beyond your one position. Although it may feel very personal when your request for a higher salary (or other item you are negotiating) is denied, remember that the fact you are having this conversation means they want *you* in their department. Take a long view. For example, although a couple thousand dollars more per year would be ideal, there may be other positive aspects of your job offer (e.g., research funds, partner accommodation) that outweigh the lower salary. Although we said earlier it is important to negotiate because failing to do so could have long-term adverse consequences, not getting everything on your wish list should not be a reason to get discouraged. Evaluate the whole package and whether what is offered will allow you to be successful and happy in your position.

Conclusion

As we conclude the chapter, we want to note that although we wrote this chapter for women informed by our own lived experiences, the content is applicable to anyone navigating the search for academic jobs. We hope the advice and personal narrative provided in this chapter are useful to anyone navigating their own unique path toward (or away from!) an academic position. This process may lead you to unexpected and rewarding outcomes. Above all, we hope you are able to embrace the job search as a learning opportunity that can lead you toward encountering ample reinforcers, whatever that looks like for you.

Note

1. It is important to note university administrative practices continue to shift, making tenure-track jobs less stable than in the past. Financial challenges facing academic institutions impact salaries, number of jobs available, and renewal of contracts, even for tenure-track faculty (Woolston, 2021).

References

American Association of University Professors (AAUP). (2018). *Data snapshot: Contingent faculty in US higher ed.* www.aaup.org/sites/default/files/10112018%20Data%20Snapshot%20Tenure.pdf

American Association of University Women. (2021). *Fast facts: Women working in academia.* www.aauw.org/resources/article/fast-facts-academia/

Carnegie Classification of Institutions of Higher Education. (2021). https://carnegieclassifications.iu.edu/definitions.php

Catalyst. (2020). *Women in academia (quick take).* www.catalyst.org/research/women-in-academia/

Davis, D. J., & Warfield, M. (2011) The importance of networking in the academic and professional experiences of racial minority students in the USA. *Educational Research and Evaluation, 17*, 97–113. https://doi.org/10.1080/13803611.2011.597113

Donelan, H. (2016). Social media for professional development and networking opportunities in academia. *Journal of Further and Higher Education, 40*(5), 706–729. https://doi.org/10.1080/0309877X.2015.1014321

Elson, S. (2020). *LinkedIn for academics, professors, adjuncts, lecturers, instructors, school teachers, educators, tutors, researchers, deans and vice chancellors.* www.linkedin.com/pulse/linkedin-academics-professors-adjuncts-lecturers-school-sue-ellson/

Flaherty, C. (2018). *A non-tenure-track profession?* www.insidehighered.com/news/2018/10/12/about-three-quarters-all-faculty-positions-are-tenure-track-according-new-aaup

Heffernan, H. (2021) Academic networks and career trajectory: 'There's no career in academia without networks.' *Higher Education Research & Development, 40*, 981–994. https://doi.org/10.1080/07294360.2020.1799948

Howe-Walsh, L., & Turnbull, S. (2016) Barriers to women leaders in academia: Tales from science and technology. *Studies in Higher Education, 41*, 415–428. https://doi.org/10.1080/03075079.2014.929102

Kelsky, K. (2020a). *How to interview.* https://theprofessorisin.com/category/academic-job-search/how-to-interview/

Kelsky, K. (2020b). *Six ways to create sister circles in academe—WOC guest post.* https://theprofessorisin.com/2020/01/22/six-ways-to-create-sister-circles-in-academe-woc-guest-post/

Kelsky, K. (2021). *How to hop from one tenure track job to another.* https://theprofessorisin.com/category/academic-job-search/negotiating-offers/

Martis, L. (n.d.). *This social media mistake turns off recruiters even more than drunk pics.* www.monster.com/career-advice/article/social-media-mistakes-0517

Ro, C. (2021). Women and minorities ask for—and are offered—lower salaries than white men. It's a problem called the 'ask gap'—and fixing it can pay major dividends. *BBC.* www.bbc.com/worklife/article/20210615-how-the-salary-ask-gap-perpetuates- unequal-pay

Social Sciences Feminist Network Research Interest Group. (2017). The burden of invisible work in academia: Social inequalities and time use in five university departments. *Humboldt Journal of Social Relations, 39*, 228–245. www.jstor.org/stable/90007882

University of California San Francisco (UCSF), Office of Career and Professional Development. (2012). *Negotiating your start-Up package.* https://career.ucsf.edu/sites/g/files/tkssra2771/f/PDF/ResearcherNegotiatingStartupPackage.pdf

Wong, K. (n.d.). A woman's guide to salary negotiation. *New York Times.* www.nytimes.com/guides/working-womans-handbook/salary-negotiation-woman

Woolston, C. (2021, April 30). Job losses and falling salaries batter US academia. *Nature.* www.nature.com/articles/d41586-021-01183-9

3 The First Years of the Job

What My CV Doesn't Tell You

Shrinidhi Subramaniam

The First Years of the Job: What My CV Doesn't Tell You

If you were to read my curriculum vitae (CV), you would see someone who was on a clear path to academia. I earned master's and doctoral degrees in Psychology at West Virginia University, where I was trained in the experimental analysis of behavior by Dr. Elizabeth Kyonka and applied behavior analysis by Dr. Claire St. Peter. From there, I completed a postdoctoral fellowship in behavioral pharmacology with Dr. Ken Silverman at Johns Hopkins School of Medicine. As I am writing this chapter, I am going into my fourth year of a tenure-track position in the Department of Psychology at California State University, Stanislaus. All of my training was designed to prepare me for a position in academia. In many ways, I was absolutely prepared. In graduate school, I participated as a "junior colleague" in department and program committees. I took advantage of opportunities to engage in program and departmental service, even getting the rare opportunity to be a student member of a retention, promotion, and tenure committee. I learned how to present and publish my research under the guidance of some of the brightest people I have ever met. I learned to teach a few classes and even ran a few training workshops. I mentored undergraduate and junior graduate students in the lab and in the field. These experiences gave me discipline, responsibility, and ethical and professional skills. When I arrived at the academy, I knew what to expect.

The academy gave me what I expected . . . and much more. As an assistant professor at a teaching institution, I have been teaching three classes each semester, mentoring graduate students in their thesis research, participating in service committees, and conducting and disseminating some collaborative and independent research. I have been learning about the politics of my university and community, and have been developing relationships with faculty, colleagues, and service providers in the community. Engaging in all of these typical academic roles have made the first years of the job simultaneously fulfilling, surprising, and challenging. At moments, I pause with gratitude that I am being paid to be curious, but at other moments I think, "What the hell have I gotten myself into?"

What my CV does not say is that there are plenty of contextual variables that have influenced my behavior, some of which I am more eager to share than others: the former being my successes and my positive role models, and the latter being my failures and negative influences. In this chapter, I uphold the platitude that "the path of success never follows a straight line" and share with you my winding path. The unique roadblocks of the first years of an academic job—fitting in, establishing my worth, being subject to (sometimes irrelevant) evaluation and scrutiny—have been navigable because of lessons from my students and ancestors, an understanding of my values, and social support combined with the skills of self-management.

DOI: 10.4324/9781003216773-5

Where I Come From: Lessons From My Students and Ancestors

I have the pleasure of working with what are commonly referred to today as first-generation students: students who are the first in their family to go to college. I am inspired by their dedication and by the example they set for their families. During scholarship and application season, you may find me tearing up while reading their personal statements. The kind of openness and vulnerability that these students express is often discouraged by institutional powers. In fact, the American Psychological Association (APA) guide on writing personal statements for applications to graduate school references Norcross and Sayette's (2016) three Hs to avoid. These are humor, hyperbole, and hard luck. Another H, "humanity," might as well be added to the mix. While I agree that disclosure without purpose or premeditation of the consequences should be discouraged, I believe that by sharing our lives, having a sense of humor, and describing what experiences have been our cornerstones, we reduce stigma and connect with others. Some (e.g., Appleby & Appleby, 2006) may call this sharing a "kiss of death." To me, the Hs illustrate the diversity of experiences and values that students can bring to a graduate program. I welcome them. **Lesson #1: Be open about who you are.**

My students sometimes remind me of the women in my family who paved the way for me to follow my bliss. Nontraditional graduate students often remind me of my mother, who made the decision in mid-life to pursue her passion. After immigrating to the United States from India via Hong Kong, she left an unfulfilling career in real estate to become a high school English teacher. She continued her studies, eventually earning her doctorate in education. In doing so, she modeled how a person can be devoted to their interests, education, career, and family. Students who want to make their community a better place remind me of my sister, who is one of the most equity-minded people I know. Currently, she creates programs for high school students to connect with experts in the field so that they can prepare for college and a personally satisfying career. **Lesson #2: Do what you love to do.**

There have been examples of women in my recent ancestry who lived under British colonialism and had to navigate oppressive systems of patriarchy (e.g., early marriage; not being allowed to leave the house; expectations of having multiple children; poor social standing, especially if widowed). These women did so bravely and made sacrifices that I couldn't imagine. My great grandmother "Bada Pati" (or "Big Grandma") was exceptionally creative and curious. Where she grew up, many girls did not get an opportunity to graduate from high school because their responsibilities were located in the home. Bada Pati only attended elementary school. She had to teach herself, often through her voracious consumption of magazines, news, and documentaries, her many skills. She found inventive ways to stretch her limited resources. Ammami, Bada Pati's daughter and my grandmother, completed middle school and married at a young age. Although she lives her life without complaint of her circumstances, she made sure that my mother went to college before getting married. She also carries on Bada Pati's legacy of independent study. She spends much of her days reading books and magazines and teaching herself new recipes. **Lesson #3: Be curious and creative.**

My great grandmothers and grandmothers were either not permitted or actively discouraged from having a job or even stepping outside of the home. To the surprise and amusement of her community, my great grandmother, Janima, taught herself how to drive a car (in a sari that had nine yards of fabric, nonetheless). She was a big personality, speaking out on the radio in favor of helping those in need, and was responsible for starting a ladies' club in her community to encourage social advocacy. My grandmother, Muthamma, Janima's daughter, loved mathematics and wanted to be an accountant, but set that aside to have children and run her household. In one of my last conversations with her, she explained to me how incredibly proud she was that her daughters and granddaughters were all able to pursue their interests (and was especially excited that one of her granddaughters became an accountant). I have always had pride in my aunts, Muthamma's daughters, who became a doctor and an engineer. My aunt, who I call Janji Athai, Janima's namesake, was the first woman civil engineering student at the prestigious Indian Institute of Technology, Madras, paving the way for many future women engineers (Vijaysree, 2019). **Lesson #4: Be courageous.**

Although the older generations of women in my family did not go into academia, I have learned so much from them about how to navigate my first few years of the job. These have been some of the lessons that have been most important. They modeled important skills, formed the foundation of my value system, and helped me find balance in my life.

Where I've Been: Understanding My Values

Forgive my hyperbole and mentalism, but the first years of an academic job can feel soul-crushing. What was incredibly helpful in my adaptation to this career was to reflect on my values. I asked myself, "What is important to me?" "What drives me?" and "What brings meaning to my life?" (see Chapters 4 and 17 of this volume). This reflection can be an unstructured period of meditation, but it can also be structured, like the Values Card Sort Task used in Motivational Interviewing (Miller et al., 2011). In this task, a person is given a deck of cards with values and their descriptions. For example, "Acceptance: to be accepted as I am." They sort each card into one of several piles. The piles are usually labeled "Very important to me," "Important to me," and "Not important to me." After they sort all the cards, they go through their pile of values that are very important to them and select the top few. They then rank those values from most to least important and reflect on their ranking.

Values-affirmation tasks like the values card sort task have been shown to improve how students from underrepresented minority groups feel about themselves and can even reduce achievement gaps in STEM college courses (Jordt et al., 2017). In motivational interviewing, the clinician uses the client's values rankings as rationale for behavioral goals. They encourage the client to talk about the importance of engaging in desirable behaviors, which may be a motivating operation to engage in those behaviors. I teach several courses in which I ask students to complete a similar values-affirmation exercise. Students list their top ten core values, describe why those values are important to them, and list the concrete ways they can live up to their values. Figure 3.1 adapts this values-affirmation exercise to a personal practice I have found helpful in my first years of the job.

Now, I want you to forgive me for my hard-luck story. I have reflected quite a bit on the experiences that have been most valuable in my life. As I hinted earlier, some of these experiences have been things I am more hesitant to share about than my accomplishments and my inspiring ancestors. Although it puts me in a vulnerable position to share this story, I think that it may be worthwhile for those who have struggled or are struggling. In high school and the beginning of college, there were a few years that I will call my "lost years" when I was not able to engage in behaviors consistent with my values. As many people do, I found pleasure and avoidance in alcohol. I only did the bare minimum in school. My drinking took priority, I experimented with other drugs, and I began to face social and educational consequences. I made many unsuccessful efforts to quit or to drink in moderation; however, I failed repeatedly and began to lose hope. One day, I had what's called a moment of clarity. I knew that I had lost control, that I was living for myself in a way that made my life painfully small, and that I would not be able to accomplish anything in life if I kept on going the way that I was. I reached out to my family for help, and the right combination

1. Choose around ten values that resonate with you. You can choose your values from the image, which lists examples from the values card sort task developed by Miller et al. (2011). Do not overthink your selections, write down the words that you feel are core personal values.
2. Now place the list you selected in order of importance to you (most to least important). Explain why the values are important to you. Do they reflect how you live now or how you want to live?
3. Select one of your core values that you would like to focus on today. It would help to pick a value that you feel like you can currently live up to. What is one thing you can do (or are doing) today to live within this value?
4. Reflect on your values as they relate to work. Ask yourself: How can I live out my core values in my career? To what extent do my job expectations align with my values? To what extent does this institution align with my values?

Note: List taken from Miller et al. (2011) (Personal Values Card Sort, Public Domain)

Figure 3.1 Determining My Core Values in the First Years of the Job

Source: List taken from Miller et al. (2011) (Personal Values Card Sort, Public Domain)

of people entered my life at exactly the right time to change its trajectory. I found recovery and, without asking for it, got set on a very meaningful path.

When I found recovery, I found what I loved to do. Part of my own personal recovery involves trying to help people who have struggled with their own "lost years" get back on their feet. After my hiatus, I returned to school to pursue my Bachelors of Science in Psychology at Armstrong Atlantic State University (now Georgia Southern, Armstrong Campus). I began to ask myself how I can apply this value of service to the work that I do.

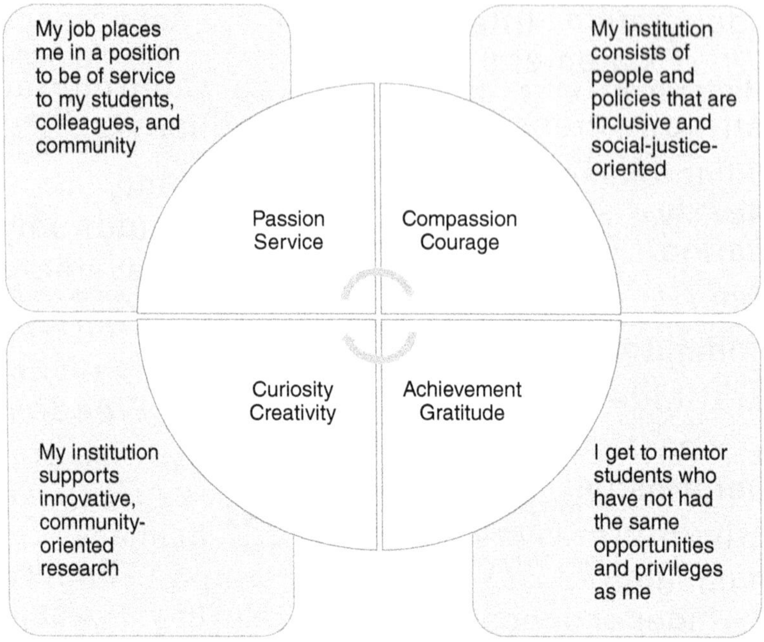

Figure 3.2 My Core Values at Work

I wanted to learn everything I could about scientific approaches to understanding and treating addiction. I approached my Psychology professor, Dr. Forrest Files, about my interest in addiction and asked if I could be a research assistant in his lab. Slightly surprised, he looked at me and said, "You know I do research with rats, right?" Thus began my journey in the experimental analysis of behavior. Since then, I learned about the spectrum of behavior analytic research in addiction: from laboratory-drug self-administration studies, to evidence-based behavioral interventions for addiction like contingency management, to ways we can engineer society to alleviate the conditions that drive health disparities.

My ancestors taught me the importance of passion, creativity, curiosity, courage, and achievement. My recovery gave me my passion and has taught me the importance of service, compassion, and gratitude. Collectively, these make up my core values. I am especially grateful for the mentorship I have received by experts in the field, which enabled me to carry out all of these values in my work. An example of how my values relate to work is illustrated in Figure 3.2, which places my core values at the center and their expression outside. For example, my values of passion and service lead me to a job that places me in a position to be of service to my students, colleagues, and community.

Returning to the values-affirmation exercise (Figure 3.1), as I was preparing my applications for academic jobs, I would ask myself, "What would bring meaning to my work?" "How can I live out my core values in my career?" and "To what extent does this job align with my values?" The wording in the call for applications and the mission statement of the organization are sometimes good indicators of alignment. However, the correspondence between an organization's stated mission and their practice can only be measured during extended observation during the first years of the job. As such, I have spent a good deal of time learning about the culture of my institution and either adapting to it or pushing for change. I continue to ask these questions, usually at the end of the spring semester when I reflect on how things have gone in each academic year.

Getting Pulled in Many Directions: Social Support and the Skills of Self-Management

It is easy to get pulled in many directions in an academic job. The three cardinal directions of academia are teaching, research, and service. Sometimes, hire letters or annual contracts spell out percentages of effort in each direction. For a tenure-track position, the standard is 40% teaching, 40% research, and 20% service. These percentages vary depending on whether the position is in a teaching- or research-focused institution. My department does not specify percentages, but presents elaborations for retention, promotion, and tenure that state,

> Teaching is central to the mission of the CSU and the Department of Psychology and Child Development. Because of this, the highest priority in evaluating candidates should be placed on teaching; accomplishments in scholarship and service, while important, cannot compensate for a lack of accomplishments in teaching.
>
> (California State University, Stanislaus, Department of Psychology and Child Development, 2021)

The elaborations go on to specify indicators of effective teaching, scholarship, and service, and expectations at each level of promotion (Assistant, Associate, and Full Professor). My unofficial estimate for percentage effort in each direction is 50% teaching, 30% research, 20% service. I will share with you some of my experiences in each area.

Cardinal Direction 1: Teaching

I was hired as a tenure-track faculty member in the behavior analysis core of my department in the fall of 2018. I was excited to teach courses in applied behavior analysis (ABA). I had expertise in the content, a well-crafted list of action-oriented learning objectives, and the goal of sharing my knowledge with students. Using the Association for Behavior Analysis, International (ABAI) Statement on Students' Right to Effective Education (Barrett et al., 1991) as a checklist, I believed I met many of the criteria for curriculum, assessment, method and evaluation. I walked in the classroom, threw down a copy of Baer et al. (1968), and informed my students about the dimensions of ABA and how ABA can be used to solve the world's problems. For those of you who have seen the Harry Potter movies or read the books, my approach was unintentionally Snape-like. Needless to say, that approach was not very successful. Since then, I have eased into presenting Baer et al. and focused on building relationships and interactions in the classroom first, much like I would working with clients in behavior analytic practice. Looking back at the ABAI statement, I must have missed the first set of principles, "The student's overall educational context should include schools that treat students with care and individual attention, comparable to that offered by a caring family." Anecdotally, building a therapeutic relationship and getting buy-in from the class has led to much more acceptance and critical interpretation of Baer et al. than leading with learning objectives.

A focus on the relational, caring component of teaching has been fulfilling, but has presented emotional labor and invisible work that I did not expect. According to Arlie Hochschild, who coined the term, emotional labor "involves trying to feel the right feeling for the job. This involves evoking and suppressing feelings" (Beck, 2018). The benefit of engaging in this labor has been that students feel relatively comfortable with me as a person. With that comfort has also come responsibility. It has opened the door to students sharing about trauma and negative experiences. When that happens, I remind myself that I am not the manager of other people's emotions. I must approach my students with empathy and compassion, recognizing the wholeness of their humanity and experiences. I try to make them feel seen, heard, and valued, by listening, being flexible, and referring them to places where they can find professional help, such as the student-counseling center on campus. Knowing what these resources are and how to link students with them has been incredibly important. Starting in my second year, I listed campus resources available to students in my course syllabus and described them to students on the first day of class and again at midterm. These included all of the basic-needs initiatives (food pantry, campus cares emergency funding, nutrition assistance program), health and wellness resources (disability resource services, student health center, psychological services), support centers (diversity center, undocumented student services), academic support (library, office of information technology, tech check-out, academic-success center, learning commons for tutoring), and professional support (career- and professional-development center).

Emotional labor can also involve the anxiety of being evaluated, real or imagined criticism of one's work, and fearing the probationary nature of the position. There is no doubt that I have experienced dread upon receipt of student evaluations of instruction (SEIs), especially because they are an important component of my retention and tenure reviews. In fact, early in my teaching, I would avoid reading SEIs until the following semester, even though students had some really nice things to say. It was hard for me to avoid focusing on the irrelevant evaluations. There have been comments about the way I look, dress, and talk that I am confident that male professors do not ever have to endure. The scholarship on bias in SEIs has shown that evaluations can be biased based on gender, race, ethnicity, age, and other nonverbal behaviors (for reviews, see Heffernan, 2021; Merritt, 2008). The first years of the job involved learning how to distinguish when a comment is irrelevant versus constructive. I also have learned how to advocate for myself by linking scholarship on the biased nature of SEIs in my promotion dossier and highlighting the multiple comments that speak to my skills and efforts in teaching and my attempts to address the useful feedback I have received.

My interactions in the classroom have been rich and fulfilling, especially since I have incorporated more culturally relevant teaching practices. However, I have experienced occasional discomfort. Recently, a student understood some of the suggestions that I gave them for resolving a conflict with a classmate as an attack on their character. My first instinct, which I fortunately only experienced covertly, was to get defensive ("Chill out, I'm trying to help you!"). Rather than acting on that event publicly, I immediately called my equity-minded sister who helped me to recognize the impact of what I said over the intention. In my response to the student, I acknowledged that my suggestions made them uncomfortable. I then clarified the options on how the student could resolve their conflict and then immediately documented the interaction in an e-mail to my department chair. Rather than triggering a power struggle, this general procedure showed compassion toward the student and looped in colleagues who can provide support for the student or advocate on my behalf: Pause, reach out to a trusted colleague or advisor, respond in a way that acknowledges the other person's experience, provide solutions, and document my actions. I will try to use this procedure in future uncomfortable interactions.

There were some pivotal moments in the first years of the job when I learned the value of just doing what I can and not trying to be perfect. In the fall of 2018, smoke from wildfires reduced air quality to unsafe levels in the California Central Valley. We lost two weeks of school and I had to refocus my course objectives to ensure that the most important content was retained. This experience taught me to be flexible and prioritize health over meeting all course objectives. In March 2020, the state of California was turned upside down by the COVID-19 pandemic. As I write this chapter, it has yet to turn around fully. My university abruptly transitioned to holding classes virtually and continued that mode of instruction for the next three semesters. Initially, I reacted to the pandemic like any academic sitting atop an ivory tower. I was reminded how Isaac Newton was inspired by the apple falling from a tree to develop his theory of gravity (Brockwell, 2020) and encouraged myself and others to "use the time wisely." Meanwhile, people were traumatized by the death toll of the pandemic, the continued structural racism in the United States, the social isolation, and the blurred boundaries between home and work. After a couple of months, I relearned the importance of being flexible. Rather than trying to use the time to be incredibly productive, I used it to seek out professional development on how I can be a more culturally responsive teacher. I incorporated a number of strengths-based assessments and reflection activities in my courses so that students had multiple outlets to express themselves. I feel like these practices will be beneficial long after the pandemic.

Cardinal Direction 2: Research

Because my position is at a teaching institution, the expectation that I start an independent program of research is not as heavily weighted as the expectation for effective teaching. That was a culture shock coming from research-intensive institutions. I conducted my postdoctoral fellowship at Johns Hopkins School of Medicine where I studied incentive programs to promote medication adherence and evaluated a model of the therapeutic workplace to promote drug abstinence and employment. These multiyear grant-funded evaluations were designed and carried out by talented scholars like Dr. Ken Silverman and Dr. August Holtyn and their teams of researchers and clinicians. In my transition to a teaching institution, I realized that I would not be able to replicate that work exactly, but my long-term goal to replicate the therapeutic workplace in my community remains.

In addition to maintaining collaborations with previous mentors, I tried to get to know the faculty at my institution. The first thing I did was get a sense of the work in which my colleagues were engaged when I attended my new-faculty orientation. I also tried to mingle about research while I was participating in teaching workshops at our Faculty Development Center. I chatted with faculty in my department about their research interests after attending students' thesis proposal and defense meetings. Some of these interactions have led to ongoing research collaborations. For example, I joined my university's faculty peer-mentor program, which allowed me to get to know Dr. Melanie Martin, a Professor in the Computer Science Department. I talked with her about the computer-skills training research I conducted while working on the therapeutic workplace and that led to a research collaboration where we evaluated computer skills in college students taking general education courses in Computer Science.

I also connected with practitioners in my community who were interested in piloting behavioral interventions. I built relationships with providers at a local addiction-treatment facility who were interested in evidence-based treatment. We met to discuss practices that might be helpful to them and I came up with a plan to start a pilot project on contingency management to support attendance at their outpatient treatment program. I applied for two small, institutional grants and received funding. That award resulted in a pilot project that I hope will establish the feasibility of an incentive program at the facility.

That was the CV version of my research plan and activities. The truth is that starting and running a research study at a teaching institution has been incredibly challenging. No one told me it would be easy, but, just like with teaching, there has been a lot of hidden and emotional labor involved. What I did not expect were the challenges I faced in dealing with the bureaucracy whenever I tried to start something new. For example, I needed to set up a way to pay participants remotely and repeatedly. I knew that some participants in my pilot project would lack stable housing and others were not able to maintain phone and internet services, so I ruled out mailing cards or using a web application to deliver incentives. I also knew that gift cards that are not linked to specific retailers carry a high fee, which would divert many of the funds that can otherwise be used for participant incentives. Therefore, a reloadable credit card seemed most appropriate. Unfortunately, no researcher in my university system had ever gotten a contract with a reloadable credit card company and the administrators at my institution had to build new systems for me. I didn't expect that I had to explain my procedures and rationale to administrators at every level of the university structure, be involved in a formal risk assessment, pay attention to the minor legal details in the contract from the credit card company, and wait for months while paperwork was being processed at the various levels of administration. I felt especially accomplished when the contract went through and now know to budget extra time for setting up new research systems. The moral of the story is, if you want to do something new, be patient with the people who have to build those systems, be prepared for well-meaning people to tell you that you should consider alternatives you have already considered, be persistent in your request, ask for what you need assertively, don't get discouraged, and just keep asking for what you need.

Cardinal Direction 3: Service

The general advice about service usually goes something like this: figure out what the expectations are and "*don't do too much service*" (Kelsky, 2017). When I started my position, the chair of my department suggested that I join the Graduate Committee and attend department faculty meetings once a month. That was reasonable. Since then, other opportunities have presented themselves. I have fallen into the pattern that many women and professors of color often find themselves, and it has been far too easy to overcommit to service. Because service usually comes with accountability to administrators and colleagues, deadlines for service activities and scheduled meetings can and have pulled me away from research and writing. I have gotten better at preventing myself from volunteering for positions and saying no to a few invitations to join committees. The script from Kelsky (2017) was helpful:

> Thank you for asking me; this is indeed a very important committee and one whose mission I support. Unfortunately, I'm already serving on XX committees and I feel I can't really add any more and still keep my research and writing on track for my tenure case. I'd love to revisit this next year, however.

That being said, I have found a few areas where service has been inherently rewarding or has helped me with my research and teaching. Participating in my department faculty and Graduate Committees allows me to voice student issues and have a say on graduate-program admissions. I also get to check in with my faculty colleagues and learn how their teaching and research are going at these meetings. Serving on a faculty-search committee gave me information and insight into unspoken hiring processes. I got involved in editorial service by saying "yes" to most ad hoc reviews that my mentors and advisers sent my way. That practice has led to editorial board memberships and the opportunity to serve as an associate editor for a journal, which helped expand my network of colleagues well outside of my institution.

All Other Directions: Applying the Skills of Self-Management to Work-Life Balance

In addition to balancing the three cardinal directions of the academic job, I find it most important to try to achieve a balance between work and my life outside of work. Most summers, I teach a class on self-management in which students come up with a self-change project and apply the principles of behavior analysis to their own behavior. Robert Epstein, a student of B.F. Skinner, recalled a lesson from his mentor about self-management:

> It is not enough to live your life, he told me; you also need to analyze it and make changes in it frequently and regularly.
>
> (Epstein, 1997, p. 559)

One of the most important points I make in the self-management course is that the people who are best at self-regulating observe and record their own behavior. They judge their self-management strategies by analyzing their behavior with and without the interventions that they implement. There are as many ways to analyze and change one's life as there are people, but I will share with you my strategy of analyzing my work-life balance. My approach, shown in Table 3.1, is based on principles of behavioral self-management and related fields.

Maintaining a work-life balance is easier said than done. This self-assessment is an example of how a person can foster self-awareness of how they spend time, resources, and energy. The resource can also be used to guide goal-setting and self-evaluation.

The work-life balance self-monitoring form in Table 3.1 lists major domains of lifestyle balance that are assessed in cognitive behavioral approaches to therapy (Daley & Marlatt, 2006). These are physical, emotional, creative/hobbies, relationships, spiritual, intellectual/work, and financial life. Below each domain are suggestions on how to self-assess behavior, set goals, and record progress. For example, getting adequate sleep is critical for overall health. I can monitor my sleep duration and/or rate the quality of my sleep. The targets that are measured and goals for each target are flexible. Since my sleep quality is fairly stable, I defined the target as sleep duration and set my sleep goal at 7–8 hours of sleep each night. In the third column, I can write whether my goal was met. There are also spaces for exercises that can help boost my mood and self-esteem like engaging in tasks I enjoy, participating in hobbies without guilt, and listing my strengths and talents. There are also places to envision how I set healthy boundaries with work and other people.

If I am in a maintenance period in which I am satisfied with my lifestyle balance, I can complete the assessment informally. In more tumultuous times (e.g., the onset of a global pandemic), I can complete the assessment formally and periodically. For example, I can reflect and fill out the datasheet at the end of each week to determine out-of-balance areas on which to craft a change plan. It is important to note that the goals should be achievable. After all, there are only 24 hours in a day. The task should also be approached with self-compassion. It is important to accept when an area is out of balance and to meet or fall short of goals without shame or guilt. For example, regarding my work quality, I can say to myself, "I didn't finish writing that manuscript today and that's okay." It also helps to arrange for others (e.g., companies, family, partners) to assist with or complete tasks. Hiring a cleaning service to clean my kitchen, bathrooms, and floors every other week was a game changer for me. I am also fortunate to have a partner who completes several household tasks and manages our finances, which leaves me free to engage in other activities.

Despite my best efforts to self-manage my work-life balance, the first years of the job can be emotionally taxing. With my newfound responsibilities and independence, I have experienced moments of confusion and self-doubt. I questioned whether I had imposter syndrome, a condition in which a person feels like they are a fraud who is in their position by chance and not merit (Clance, 1985). I recently retook the Imposter Phenomenon Scale (Chrisman et al., 1995). My score suggested that I have frequent imposter feelings. Before I label myself an imposter and suggest that others explore their own imposter feelings, it is important to acknowledge the influence of environmental contingencies. For example, if

Table 3.1 Self-Monitoring and Evaluation for the First Years . . . and Beyond

Self-Assessment	*Goal (with example)*	*Observed*
Physical Life		
<u>Sleep</u> How many hours of sleep per night did I get since the last observation?	*7-8 hours per night*	
<u>Illness</u> Yes/No: Do I get care and rest when I am sick?	*Yes*	
<u>Exercise</u> How regularly did I exercise?	*20 mins of yoga per day*	
<u>Nutrition</u> What is my nutrition goal and did I follow it?	*Nutrient-dense diet; Yes*	
<u>Hygiene</u> What basic self-hygiene practices should I follow and did I follow them?	*Brush/floss teeth, shower/bathe regularly; Yes*	
<u>Space</u> Yes/No: Is the environment around me clean, comfortable, and organized?	*Yes*	
Emotional Life		
<u>Stress</u> Rate my stress level on a scale of 1–10 (1 = no stress, 10 = extreme stress)	*Rating <7*	
<u>Mood: Anxiety & Depression</u> Rate anxiety and depression on a 1–10 scale (1 = no worry/fear/sadness, 10 = extreme worry/fear/sadness)	*Rating <5*	
<u>Strengths</u> What were my strengths/achievements from today?	*List 1–2 concrete examples*	
<u>Behavioral activation</u> What behavior(s) did I engage in that made me feel happy/joyful/comforted or at peace?	*List 1–2 concrete examples*	
Creative Life and Hobbies		
<u>Talents/Abilities</u> How have I used my creativity, talents and abilities?	*List 1–2 concrete examples*	
<u>Hobbies</u> Yes/No: Am I engaging in hobbies that involve me having fun without guilt?	*Yes*	
Family and Personal Relationships		
<u>Quality Time</u> How much quality time did I spend with my closest loved ones or in community each day?	*2+ hours per day with family, friends, significant others, pets*	
<u>Satisfaction: Family</u> How satisfied am I with my family relationships? Very Satisfied, Satisfied, Neutral, Unsatisfied, Very Unsatisfied	*Satisfied or Very Satisfied*	
<u>Satisfaction: Other Relationships</u> How satisfied am I with the quantity/quality of my personal relationships? Very Satisfied, Satisfied, Neutral, Unsatisfied, Very Unsatisfied	*Satisfied or Very Satisfied*	
<u>Perspective Taking</u> Yes/No: Did I exercise compassion with family, friends, coworkers, students, and strangers?	*Yes*	
<u>Boundaries</u> Yes/No: Did I set boundaries and hold family, friends, coworkers, and students accountable?	*Yes*	

Self-Assessment	*Goal (with example)*	*Observed*
Spiritual Life		
Values In what way am I living up to my values/ principles?	*List 1–2 concrete examples*	
Practices To what extent am I engaging in the following practices that fulfill me?	*1) Meditation (>5 min per day); 2) Gratitude List (3+ things per day); 3) Home altar*	
Intellectual and Work Life		
Work Time How many hours per day did I spend working since my last observation?	*M = 8 hours per work day*	
Curiosity In what way(s) am I following my bliss?	*List 1 example*	
Work Quality Am I satisfied with the time, effort, and quality of my work?	*Satisfied or Very Satisfied*	
Days off, Breaks Yes/No: Do I feel like I can take a day off if I am sick or need to engage in self-care? Do I take breaks during work?	*Yes; Yes*	
Boundaries What basic boundaries can I set and did I follow them?	*Block time, turn off notifications on nights & weekends*	
Financial Life		
Do I have sufficient income to meet my expenses?	*1/3 housing, 1/3 bills, 1/3 everything else, if possible*	
How secure do I feel with my financial situation? Very Secure, Secure, Neutral, Insecure, Very Insecure	*Neutral to Very Secure*	
Yes/No: Does money play a larger role in my life than I would like?	*No*	

Note: Domains are taken from Daley and Marlatt (2006). Domains can be added or removed to tailor the assessment to the individual. The italicized goals are examples and are meant to be placeholders rather than suggestions for personal goal.

self-doubt occurs in specific settings and not others, I should look for the function in the environment and see if I can address it. Are there social consequences like escape or attention that may be maintaining the self-doubt? Under what conditions do I feel like an imposter? Am I othered by those around me? Do I experience microaggressions or aggression from students or colleagues? Answering these questions can signal whether there are modifiable environmental conditions that I can address in specific settings. If self-doubt occurs globally across all settings, I should look for the function in the environment and may consider measuring and monitoring my own imposter feelings. There are several approaches that have been suggested to combat imposter feelings including talking to mentors, engaging in self-reinforcement, noticing that other people aren't perfect, reframing negative thoughts, and seeking therapy (Weir, 2013).

Where I Am Now

As I write this chapter, I am also preparing my dossier for promotion from assistant professor to associate professor. Reflecting on the first years of my job for the tenure process was much different than reflecting on the first years of my job for this chapter. In fact, conducting these two writing exercises simultaneously inspired me to subtitle this chapter, "What my CV Doesn't Tell You." While my tenure dossier contains a list of my accomplishments with supporting evidence, this chapter outlined a few of the contextual variables that made those accomplishments possible. Some of those variables are the lessons learned from my students and ancestors, the values I gained from learning from my own mistakes, and experiences with emotional labor and achieving a work-life balance. Although I sometimes deal with imposter feelings, I am confident that where I come from, where I've been, and a balanced approach to work and life have me exactly where I need to be right now.

References

Appleby, D. C., & Appleby, K. M. (2006). Kisses of death in the graduate school application process. *Teaching of Psychology, 33*(1), 19–24. https://doi.org/10.1207/s15328023top3301_5

Baer, D. M., Wolf, M. M., & Risley, T. R. (1968). Some current dimensions of applied behavior analysis. *Journal of Applied Behavior Analysis, 1*(1), 91–97. https://doi.org/10.1901/jaba.1968.1-91

Barrett, B. H., Beck, R., Binder, C., Cook, D. A., Engelmann, S., Greer, R. D., Kyrklund, S. J., Johnson, K. R., Maloney, M., McCorkley, N., Vargas, J. S., & Watkins, C. L. (1991). The right to effective education. *The Behavior Analyst, 14*(1), 79–82. https://doi.org/10.1007/BF03392556

Beck, J. (2018, November). The concept creep of "emotional labor." *The Atlantic*. www.theatlantic.com/family/archive/2018/11/arlie-hochschild-housework-isnt-emotional-labor/576637/

Brockwell, G. (2020, March 12). During a pandemic, Isaac Newton had to work from home, too. He used the time wisely. *The Washington Post*. www.washingtonpost.com/history/2020/03/12/during-pandemic-isaac-newton-had-work-home-too-he-used-time-wisely/

California State University, Stanislaus. (2021, August). *Department of psychology and child development: Retention, tenure, and promotion elaborations*. www.csustan.edu/sites/default/files/groups/Faculty%20Affairs/Positions3/f21_dept_of_psychology_and_child_development_rpt_elaborations.pdf

Chrisman, S. M., Pieper, W. A., Clance, P. R., Holland, C. L., & Glickauf-Hughes, C. (1995). Validation of the Clance imposter phenomenon scale. *Journal of Personality Assessment, 65*(3), 456–467. https://doi.org/10.1207/s15327752jpa6503_6

Clance, P. R. (1985). *The impostor phenomenon: When success makes you feel like a fake*. Bantam Books.

Daley, D. C., & Marlatt, A. (2006). *Lifestyle balance worksheet*. www.oxfordclinicalpsych.com/view/10.1093/med:psych/9780195307740.001.0001/med-9780195307740-interactive-pdf-026.pdf

Epstein, R. (1997). Skinner as self-manager. *Journal of Applied Behavior Analysis, 30*(3), 545–568. https://doi.org/10.1901/jaba.1997.30-545

Heffernan, T. (2021). Sexism, racism, prejudice, and bias: A literature review and synthesis of research surrounding student evaluations of courses and teaching. *Assessment & Evaluation in Higher Education*, 1–11. https://doi.org/10.1080/02602938.2021.1888075

Jordt, H., Eddy, S. L., Brazil, R., Lau, I., Mann, C., Brownell, S. E., King, K., & Freeman, S. (2017). Values affirmation intervention reduces achievement gap between underrepresented minority and white students in introductory biology classes. *CBE—Life Sciences Education, 16*(3), 1–10. https://doi.org/10.1187/cbe.16-12-0351

Kelsky, K. (2017, June). The professor is in: Service taking up too much time? How to do enough, but not too much, institutional service. *The Chronicle of Higher Education*. www.chronicle.com/article/the-professor-is-in-service-taking-up-too-much-time?

Merritt, D. J. (2008). Bias, the brain, and student evaluations of teaching. *John's Legal Review, 82*, 235–288.

Miller, W. R., Baca, J. C., Matthews, D. B., & Wilbourne, P. (2011). *Personal values card sort*. www.guilford.com/add/miller2/values.pdf?t

Norcross, J. C., & Sayette, M. A. (2016). *Insider's guide to graduate programs in clinical and counseling psychology: 2016/2017 edition*. Guilford Publications.

Vijaysree, V. (2019). In 1966, she was IIT Madras' first woman civil engineering student. *The Hindu*. www.thehindu.com/education/in-1966-she-was-iit-madras-first-woman-civil-engineering-student/article28759995.ece

Weir, K. (2013). *Feel like a fraud?* American Psychological Association. www.apa.org/gradpsych/2013/11/fraud

4 Building Values-Consistent Repertoires of Gender-Marginalized Academics

Emily K. Sandoz, Janani Vaidya, Brooke M. Smith, Jade Campbell, and Karen Kate Kellum

Building Values-Consistent Repertoires of Gender-Marginalized Academics[1]

There are a number of dimensions that can be used to characterize behavior as *effective*, or successful in producing an intended outcome. In the workplace, effectiveness is typically approached in terms of consistency of observed behavior both with task- or role-specific goals (i.e., task performance) and with a broader contextual vision (i.e., contextual performance; Borman & Motowidlo, 1993; Jex et al., 2006). In this way, the success of any one organization (e.g., a university) involves an individual's success with *both* performing specific tasks according to objective criteria *and* engaging in a variety of behaviors that contribute to a context that promotes organizational values. Prediction of contextual performance involves the employee's perception of organizational values as well as the fit between organizational values and their own (Goodman & Svyantek, 1999). In other words, it seems that people contribute most effectively to the workplace's culture when that culture converges with their personally held values. Values-consistent behavior also has benefits to the individual worker, as effective values-consistent behavior predicts less burnout (Veage et al., 2014; Vilardaga et al., 2011) and greater well-being (Veage et al., 2014).

Defining Values and Values-Promoting Contexts

Values have been explored conceptually and empirically from a variety of perspectives within the behavioral sciences (e.g., see Rohan, 2000). For example, Rokeach (1973) defined values as "an enduring belief that a specific mode of conduct or end-state of existence is personally or socially preferable to an opposite or converse mode of conduct or end-state of existence" (p. 5). This conceptualization of values as criteria for assessing personal success or integrity is foundational to the values (or self) affirmation literature (see Cohen & Sherman, 2014; Sherman, 2013). Here, values are conceptualized as an aspect of self, contact with which buffers the negative effects of threat (e.g., via values writing;

Authors' Note: The authors would like to note that we vary in the extent to which we identify as cisgender women—the assumed identity of the majority of the book's authors and the group on which this book is focused. We would like to take this opportunity to acknowledge our relative privilege in being invited, despite this variability, to speak to our gendered experiences of the academy. We hope, in part, to use this privilege to amplify the conversation around gender marginalization beyond contingencies for cisgender women. Even so, we are still speaking about gender from our particular perspectives, arising from our particular learning histories and the contexts in which we find ourselves today. For this reason, there are many whose experiences of gender marginalization within the academy will not be entirely captured by our efforts. We invite readers to reflect on your own perceptions of gender as an identity, as a behavior (i.e., gendering of the self or others), and as a context for others' behaviors toward you.

DOI: 10.4324/9781003216773-6

Sherman & Cohen, 2006). Common to many definitions of values in the psychological literature is the conceptualization of values as cognitive structures that produce meaning and guide behavior (Rohan, 2000). Behavioral conceptualizations of values diverge from the dominant perspective, abandoning cognitive constructs as causes of behavior (see da Silva Ferreira et al., 2020).

Behavior analysts have repeatedly considered values and values-consistent behavior as worthy of conceptual analysis. Skinner, in reflecting on control of human behavior, described values in terms of reinforcing contingencies: "any list of values is a list of reinforcers—conditioned or otherwise" (Rogers & Skinner, 1956, p. 1064). In this way, Skinner (1956) proposed that the values repertoire would potentially include any behavior maintained by reinforcement contingencies. Leigland (2005) further characterized these reinforcing contingencies as the effects of "motivational variables" (i.e., establishing operations and verbal augmentals; p. 138), of which values are a function. Bonow and Follette (2009) extended this analysis, distinguishing between valuing, functional values, and values statements. Here, *valuing* is emitted behavior, the pattern of which reveals values. Likewise, *functional values* are the consequences maintaining that behavior. Finally, *values statements* are augmentals that tact valuing, values, and the relationship between them, allowing for verbal transformation of the direct consequences of behavior to serve reinforcing functions (Bonow & Follette, 2009). Wilson and DuFrene (2009) integrate and extend these ideas, defining values as "freely chosen, verbally constructed consequences of ongoing, dynamic, evolving patterns of activity, which establish predominant reinforcers for that activity that are intrinsic in engagement in the valued behavioral pattern itself" (p. 66) and valued living as behaving in ways that allow for contact with these consequences. In this way, values are distinguished from rules that specify behavioral topographies or distinct outcomes (i.e., goals), specify aversive contingencies, or function as plys (i.e., specify socially mediated consequences; Plumb et al., 2009). Together, these behavioral conceptualizations of values converge to set aside a cognitive mechanism (e.g., an attitude or belief) as the cause of values-consistent behavior. Instead, values-consistent behavior is proposed to occur in contexts that allow for the detection, discrimination, and tacting of appetitive contingencies in such a way as to augment the direct consequences of the class of behaviors that participate in that contingency.

Influence of Values-Promoting Contexts

The primary body of research exploring the influence of values-promoting contexts is in social psychological research on values affirmation (see Cohen & Sherman, 2014; Howell, 2017). Typically, in values-affirmation work, participants rank or rate a list of values, then are randomly assigned to write about either a highly ranked or lowly ranked value (McQueen & Klein, 2006). Following the writing task, participant behavior is observed in terms of their response to threat (i.e., aversives), in terms of physiology (e.g., endothelial injury, Spicer et al., 2016), emotions (e.g., positive other-directed feelings, Crocker et al., 2008), attitudes (e.g., defensive, Van Tongeren et al., 2014), cognitions (e.g., accessibility of death-related thoughts, Schmeichel & Vohs, 2009), or actions (e.g., social behavior, Stinson et al., 2011; e.g., clinical performance, Salles et al., 2016).

For example, in one study, surgical residents were provided a list of 12 values, such as friends and family, sports, music, and religion. Then, they were instructed to either pick two or three that were most important to them and write about their rationale (affirmation condition), or to pick two or three that were least important to them and write about why someone else might find these important (control condition). Women in the values affirmation condition exhibited improved clinical performance at the six-month follow-up in terms of patient care, medical knowledge, practice-based learning and improvement, systems-based practice, professionalism, and interpersonal communication. The effect was not observed in men, or in the control condition, where there were no observed differences in clinical performance.

In general, contexts that facilitate contact with values seem to foster increased awareness of threat, openness toward threat, and committed, effective action in the presence of threat (see Sandoz & Anderson, 2015). In other words, contexts that allow for the detection, discrimination, and tacting of appetitive contingencies in such a way as to augment the direct consequences of the relevant appetitive response class can expand the function of co-occurring aversives, sometimes to the point of them no longer being aversive. Instead, aspects of context that have previously functioned to evoke and occasion behavior under aversive control are still detected in relevant contexts (e.g., Kessels et al., 2016), perhaps even with increased elicitation for those most sensitive to aversive learning conditions (e.g., Crowell et al., 2015; Finley et al., 2018), but without increased avoidance (e.g., Howell & Shepperd, 2012).

For example, a particular gender-marginalized person serving as a surgery resident might initially find surgical training aversive—thus their behavior to lack the sensitivity, responsivity, and flexibility required for effective clinical performance. Their training context, however, could provide accessible opportunities for the resident to detect, discriminate, and tact appetitive contingencies in such a way as to augment the direct consequences of the relevant appetitive response class. In addition to instructing values writing, their supervisor might inquire about their values or select clinical duties that allow for contact with appetitives. To the extent that the training context fosters values-consistent behavior, it will, as a whole, become less aversive, supporting improved performance and learning on the part of the resident.

Such shifts have been demonstrated with respect to a wide variety of repertoires. For example, most robust in the literature are impacts on health-related (see Epton et al., 2015) and academic (see Wu et al., 2021) repertoires. Early findings also support consistent effects with prosocial behavior (e.g., Creswell & Lindsay, 2014), problem-solving (e.g., Creswell et al., 2013), physiological stress responses (e.g., Sherman, 2013; Smith et al., 2019), self reported well-being (e.g., Nelson et al., 2014), and conflict resolution (e.g., Schumann, 2014).

Of course, contexts vary in the extent to which they promote values-consistent behavior (i.e., the detection, discrimination, and tacting of appetitive contingencies in such a way as to augment the direct consequences of the class of behaviors that participate in that contingency). And, from a behavioral perspective, the extent to which a context functions as values-promoting for a particular person is a product of an individual's history with functionally similar contexts. There are, however, typical characteristics of the academy likely to relate to values-consistent behavior in predictable ways.

The Academy and Barriers to Appetitive Control

The academy can be evaluated in terms of the extent to which it fosters values-consistent behavior—that is, the extent to which it fosters the detection, discrimination, and tacting of appetitive contingencies in such a way as to augment the direct consequences of the class of behaviors that participate in that contingency. Unfortunately, however, the most prominent overarching contingencies in the academy for many individuals tend to be aversive. In short, not every academic's learning history interacts with the context in such a way as to support effectiveness across teaching, research, mentorship, and service. In addition to the contingencies specific to each of these domains, the overall consequences for behaving in ways that do not meet requirements established via the institution and influenced by students often involve reducing the faculty member's impact, and offer very little by way of remediation (Bedenlier & Zawacki-Richter, 2015; Sheridan et al., 2015). For example, an academic struggling with teaching effectiveness may be pulled from upper-level and graduate courses, where they are likely to be able to teach their expertise to high-achieving students. Similarly, an academic struggling to supervise and mentor effectively may be prevented from developing substantive mentoring or supervision relationships, and be required to do more brief academic advising instead. The untenured academic who struggles to meet these expectations may soon find themselves without a position altogether.

Further, these contingencies are persistently shifting (e.g., new course assignments, course content being updated in conjunction with new literature and field norms, accreditation requirements, incoming and outgoing students, changes in administrators and leadership dynamics, and the impact of funding and legal changes on institutional capacity and resource allocation). The COVID-19 pandemic alone saw short- and long-term effects on academic contexts (e.g., transitioning to online education and the challenges to uphold both content and instructional quality, disparity among students' access to required technology, structural weakness in financial models, and limited resources to retain staff; see Salmi, 2021). In short, academic contexts may largely function to generate, shape, maintain, and generalize academic repertoires under aversive control (Skinner, 1965, 1968). This can be further observed in specific contingencies around research, teaching, service, and mentorship repertoires of academics.

Barriers to Appetitive Control Around Research

In tenure-track positions with a research requirement, publishing peer-reviewed research and generating grant funding are often seen as the most important activities in hiring, tenure, merit pay, and promotion decisions. The narrative of "publish or perish" (Coolidge, 1932)[2] is a relevant example of antecedent control, which multiple authors have suggested function aversively to many in academia (e.g., Salandra et al., 2021; Spurling, 2016). Frequency of publication is considered a metric of academic progress, serving as a significant criterion in measuring one's employability (Crawford et al., 2012; Rawat & Meena, 2014). And, once employed in academia, high-frequency publication allows access to potential generalized conditioned reinforcers like peer approval, release from other duties, and funding (Carson et al., 2013; Edwards & Roy, 2017; Moosa, 2018). That said, high-frequency publishing may not be sustainable for an academic when their responsibilities are multifold, and has been known to contribute to a rise in unethical research practice (Baykoucheva, 2015; Elliott, 2013), diminished quality of research (Bauerlein et al., 2010), fraudulent or predatory publishing practices (Freckelton, 2020; Retraction Watch, 2021; Rich, 2016), and other unwanted outcomes (see Moosa, 2018). For some, engaging in research has few built-in positive reinforcers and those that do exist are temporally distant. The behaviors of designing a study, obtaining appropriate institutional approval, collecting data, analyzing data, and writing a manuscript often comprise a years-long process (Maglaughlin & Sonnenwald, 2005). Often, manuscripts must be submitted to, and even reviewed by, multiple journals before finding an appropriate outlet (Roberts et al., 2003). Then, the editorial review process, at its fastest, takes many months, and at its slowest, may take years (Da Silva & Dobránszki, 2017). Depending on the academic's learning history, research involves a response class likely to be generated and shaped under aversive control.

Box 1—Personal Struggles with Research

JANANI: After obtaining my master's degree, I spent about five years attempting to acquire research experience in the field. I was repeatedly rejected from doctoral programs with the feedback to acquire research experience and publications, but with very little guidance on how to go about doing this. Being disabled, genderqueer, and not a US/European citizen made this particularly hard especially in my home country where the only option for work appeared to be as a traditional BCBA. This is not a values-consistent choice for me. All of my research and networking opportunities came via my specific network of peers I was fortunate to collaborate with. It required a lot of willingness on my part to pursue a fairly unorthodox route, and make choices such as traveling internationally to attend and present at conferences, freelancing, maintaining a day job completely unrelated to my expertise and field, and saying yes to a lot of unpaid labor. These are choices that I was only able to make because of my privilege and social location in my particular context, such as caste and finances. Virtual collaborative spaces and opportunities only became more available when the pandemic struck. It led to more opportunities, but during a particularly stressful and traumatic time. It is important to note that the needs for virtual collaborative spaces have always existed, but more people, especially those with leadership and access to resources, only selected working in that manner after the world shut down. However, we can already see how those from the global north/developed nations are returning to the status quo, with the resurgence of in-person work and collaborative efforts. I am aware that I am very lucky to have access to the several opportunities and working relationships in my career thus far. I am also aware that my unorthodox route has led me to work and commit to opportunities even when I do not have the capacity or resources because of the persistent fear that another one may not come by. So I can't say these haven't come without a price one way or the other.

Barriers to Appetitive Control Around Teaching

Teaching is probably the most common activity in which academics engage across various institutions, roles, and career stages. Most faculty in traditional academic departments teach courses, and graduate students may also serve as primary instructors or teaching assistants. Teaching repertoires include but are not limited to designing a course, creating syllabi, delivering lectures, creating course content and lecture materials, creating, conducting, and grading assignments, providing feedback to students, and keeping up with the literature (see Keeley et al., 2016). Mastery of such repertoires is typically considered in hiring, tenure, merit pay, and promotion decisions (Schimanski & Alperin, 2018). Although teaching is usually part of an academic's job description, the weight it carries with regard to advancing one's career varies depending on the institution, the department, and the individual's position. In some departments, teaching can be seen as an activity that impedes research, which may carry more weight in terms of career advancement (Green, 2008).

Teaching requirements can be less flexible than research. The level of control an instructor can exert on the content and style of their teaching tends to vary by course, institution, and employment type. Institutions may exert control over the content of courses in certain contexts (e.g., political climate, verified course sequences, accreditation standards). Ideally, an academic would teach courses in their areas of expertise. However, it may not always be the case that an academic is teaching courses they chose to teach, or that they even enjoy. For example, some instructors are required to "team teach" service courses such as Introduction to Psychology to maintain consistency across sections (e.g., see Minett-Smith & Davis, 2019). In some cases, they may be given course shells by their department and expected to teach the content as is, with little or no modification (Tippins, 2003). Alternatively, instructors may inherit courses that they have the ability to modify to some degree, or they may create courses from scratch and, in some instances, they may have the opportunity to change the curriculum and add courses that were not previously taught. Depending upon the instructor's level of control, they may be more or less able to align course content with topics that they consider values-consistent. Teaching also encompasses behavior management, public speaking, and oratorical fluency—skills that are generally not explicitly trained and, rather, are shaped over time by students' behavior. Depending on the academic's learning history and the amount of freedom they have at their institutions, teaching may involve a response class likely to be generated and shaped under aversive control.

Box 2—Personal Struggles with Teaching

KATE: I had the opportunity to take several courses about college teaching before leading a course of my own, which allowed me to build in activities that were appetitive for me and the students (e.g., lots of structured active responding, games). I love teaching, which is why I was somewhat surprised several semesters ago to find myself avoiding class-related tasks that were typically sources of appetitives (e.g., arriving early to visit, learning students' names, providing actionable feedback on student work). I watched myself, somewhat in horror, typing more numbers and fewer words on formative assessments, thereby reducing the effectiveness of such assessment. This likely directly impacted subsequent performance on summative assessments, making those assessments aversive to me (and likely the students as well). Except for the performance of brief lectures, I began to find teaching tiresome, repetitive, and directly competing with my administrative roles. In short, I started to dislike something I loved. A change in my behavior to create more appetitive contexts was necessary.

Barriers to Appetitive Control Around Service

Academics are also expected to provide ongoing service to the program, the department and college, the university, and the field. Service activities can include committee work, administrative duties, editorial work, establishing community partnerships, and more (Pfeifer, 2016). Ideally, service is factored into academic workload and compensated accordingly. However, there can be a tendency for service to become a catch-all category in which expectations placed upon academics do not reflect the compensation received (Boice, 2000) and in which duties become disproportionately distributed among faculty (Ward, 2003). Service typically carries the least weight in terms of tenure and promotion (Boice, 2000), and can take valuable time away from the research and scholarly activities. While service can be an opportunity for networking and potentially enhancing one's career, service efforts are less noticed and seldom rewarded (Toutkoushian & Bellas, 1999). Serving on committees often requires a demonstration of collegiality and influences how academics are perceived by their peers and superiors, which can influence promotion opportunities (Seldin et al., 2010). For example, if a committee is particularly contentious, serving as a member could actually harm faculty opportunities within the unit, thus closing avenues for advancement and potential positive reinforcement. Such situations may thus be ill-advised for more junior or untenured faculty. Depending on the academic's learning history, service may involve a response class likely to be generated and shaped under aversive control.

Barriers to Appetitive Control Around Mentorship

Participation in mentoring relationships contributes to students' satisfaction with and commitment to their academic programs (Phinney et al., 2011), and to their scholastic performance (Clark et al., 2000). For this reason, most academics are expected to maintain mentoring relationships which vary in their level of structure and formality. Mentorship goes beyond advising, which is restricted to sharing academic information and degree requirements. Mentors typically become the primary source of acceptance, support, advice, and guidance for the mentee (Angelique et al., 2002). Mentorship is considered a "soft" skill in the context of academia, which is reflected in the way it is undertrained, under-supervised, and undervalued (Johnson, 2015). Informal mentorship, in particular, with its lack of structure and requisite emotional labor, may disproportionately burden mentors (Baker & Griffin, 2010; Marina, 2015) and compete with other job requirements (Johnson & Zlotnik, 2005). Effective mentorship is also a time-intensive activity that competes with teaching, research, and service responsibilities of academics. Further, academics vary in the extent to which they enjoy, appreciate, or value the mentoring relationship (Coates, 2012). Depending on the academic's learning history, mentorship involves a response class likely to be generated and shaped under aversive control.

Box 3—Personal Struggles with Mentorship

BROOKE: As a junior faculty member, I have found supervision and mentorship the most challenging parts of my job. This was a surprise to me, because I began my job with the belief that proficiency in clinical work or professional activities would translate to proficiency in guiding others in these same activities, which turned out not to be the case. For me, many of my difficulties sprang from a lack of experience in these roles, self-doubts, and anxiety—"imposter syndrome." These activities also have less clear tangible outcomes than research or teaching. There are no publications to add to one's CV and there are no student evaluations (although in supervision there may be forms of this). The activities and the reinforcers that sustain them are ambiguous, and I found that navigating this complexity soon became aversive. These behaviors therefore came to be controlled by negative reinforcement contingencies—that is, I engaged in the behaviors in order to avoid the consequence of not doing so (losing my job) and engaging in supervision and mentorship was generally unpleasant. This was especially the case with mentorship, where the abrupt transition from student to mentor entailed navigating complex social and power relationships that had the potential to, and sometimes did, not go smoothly. I found myself plagued with uncertainty and frustration, and I was often angry and disappointed with myself for not responding to the situation in a more productive manner.

Marginalization as a Barrier to Appetitive Control

The academy—across research, teaching, service, and mentorship response classes—functions differently for individual academics, depending on their learning history and the way their repertoire interacts with others' behavior in the academic context. For example, an established hierarchy among faculty members may contribute to aversive academic contexts, where the most junior may be expected to take on unwanted departmental service roles, additional course loads, administrative responsibilities, and more (Kim et al., 2011). Such variability in how programmed academic contingencies function can also be observed in ways that are consistent with marginalization in other contexts.

Privilege in the Academy

Aversive control in academic contexts can be exacerbated for individuals who belong to marginalized groups, whose marginalization results in *underprivilege*, or a relative lack of privilege. Privilege allocation in the broader context with respect to race, ethnicity, nationality, gender, sexual orientation, class, and ability can be observed within the academic context (Antonio et al., 2000; Carson et al., 2019; Denker, 2009; Hirshfield & Joseph, 2012; Reybold & Corda, 2011; Toutkoushian & Bellas, 1999). This allocation is often attributed to standards of merit that claim neutrality and objectivity, but the availability of resources parallels contingencies selected by the context of privilege (Hirshfield & Joseph, 2012; Nocco et al., 2021). For example, service responsibilities (e.g., advising, mentoring, building community relations, hiring committees) are disproportionately borne by minority faculty members, including gender-marginalized individuals (Carson et al., 2019; Docka-Filipek & Stone, 2021). While the institution is lauded for diversity initiatives, minority faculty members are expected to demonstrate *good citizenship* by serving as ethnic representation or engaging in emotional labor to educate their peers about specific cultural groups (Padilla, 1994). Padilla (1994) described this phenomenon as "cultural taxation," which can impact minoritized faculty's psychological well-being. Minoritized faculty report excess service on committees in comparison to their privileged counterparts (Adams, 2002; Hanasono et al., 2019; Hirshfield & Joseph, 2012). Conflicts between appearing "collegial" on the one hand, while maintaining balance in one's service obligations on the other, may lead minoritized faculty to agree to service commitments that are not in their best interests, when requested to do so by faculty with more institutional power. This may be particularly problematic when the committee's work is sensitive or contentious. Because service carries less weight than research and publication during promotion considerations, excess service commitments contribute to the disproportionately lower tenure rates of marginalized faculty members in comparison to their privileged counterparts (Ginther & Hayes, 2003). These service appointments typically come with little or no compensation for tasks that require significant emotional labor and are controlled by unequal power dynamics (e.g. Denker, 2017; Eaton & Warner, 2021).

Another example of inequity is the systemic racism prevalent in academic contexts. Black, Indigenous, and People of Color (BIPOC) routinely experience macro- and microaggressions in academic contexts. These range from receiving disproportionate income in comparison to their White colleagues with comparable qualifications to being treated as inferior "diversity hires" by colleagues and students (Arnold et al., 2016; Subbaraman, 2020).

An analysis of privilege developed by the Louisiana Contextual Science Research Group (2022) can be applied to gender to understand how it can operate in an individual's academic context and repertoire. From a behavioral perspective, privilege can be considered an aspect of context, a contextually bound resource that enables certain lived experiences and learning opportunities of behaving organisms. As a *relative* ratio of appetitive to aversive control governing an organism's repertoire in a context, it allows us to consider access and equity from a functional rather than a topographical perspective. Privilege that allows the development of a broad, flexible repertoire enriched by appetitively-maintained behaviors is crucial, especially when individuals encounter aversive situations or contexts. As a corollary, the more underprivileged or marginalized an individual is, the more narrow, restrictive, and rigid their repertoire is likely to become. With repertoires largely operating under survival mechanisms (Kurantowicz & Nizinska, 2013), secondary reinforcers are elusive, aversives are more salient, and the appetitive learning repertoire becomes more impoverished. An analysis of values-consistent behavior in the academic context for gender-marginalized individuals thus requires an examination of the allocation and availability of resources as determined by privilege as a contextual variable.

Barriers to Appetitive Control Specific to Gender-Marginalized Academics

In addition to the aversive contingencies inherent in academic contexts, gender-marginalized academics experience explicit barriers to accessing the kinds of appetitives that would facilitate and maintain effective and meaningful engagement (Gregory, 2001; Park, 2011). At the structural level, gender discrepancies are apparent in income (Khan et al., 2019) and representation in faculty positions (Cardel et al., 2020). Roles disproportionately filled by gender-marginalized academics often result in few employee benefits (Caruth & Caruth, 2013), gross exploitation for labor (Rich, 2015), and instability as contracts are also governed by financial contingencies and meta-contingencies (Bolitzer, 2019; Rhoades, 2019). Gender discrepancies are also apparent at the interpersonal level. The academic context is more likely to be hostile for gender-marginalized academics, with interpersonal threats ranging from microaggressions to explicit harassment (see Blithe & Elliott, 2020). For example, gender-marginalized faculty in science, technology, engineering, and math (STEM) report experiencing discrimination and sexism (Riffle et al., 2013), ostracism and incivility (Miner et al., 2019), as well as sexual harassment (Vargas et al., 2020). Together, these contribute to an overall hostile and "chilly" work environment (Britton, 2017). The restricted access to appetitives in the presence of programmed aversives can result in ratio strain for the behaviors of gender-marginalized individuals in academic contexts. In short, barriers to appetitive control specific to gender-marginalized academics are apparent in perceptions of competence, gaps in training, lack of respect of personal and professional boundaries, disproportionate expectation of emotional labor, tokenization, and scarcity of appetitives in the academic context.

Perceptions of Low Competence and Punishment of Self-Advocacy

Gender-marginalized academics can be perceived as not having requisite skills and knowledge and, therefore, are less likely to be promoted to specific roles or perceived as capable of holding specific titles (Brissett, 2020; Harris & Nicolazzo, 2020; Robinson, 2018; Stout et al., 2007). Additionally, even when appointed to such roles, gender-marginalized academics are disproportionately denied key resources to support their adjustment and effectiveness (e.g., appropriate mentoring), but are penalized for not immediately meeting their new job requirements (Inzer & Crawford, 2005). As a result, failure to meet expectations and requirements is sometimes used as a demonstration of why gender-marginalized individuals may not be fit for their role (Bavishi et al., 2010; Griffin et al., 2013). In this way, it is common in academic contexts to allocate responsibility for learning on the organism and not on their environments, in direct contradiction to our scientific understanding of human behavior. This position is inconsistent, however, when it comes to perceptions of marginalized faculty that make efforts to make the academic context a better learning environment. Attempts to draw boundaries and prioritize one's health or well-being are often framed by gender-privileged academics as a values conflict rather than a result of competing contingencies and barriers to systemic support for gender-marginalized academics (Brissett, 2020; Docherty, 2013; Neumann & Finaly-Neumann, 1990). This serves to punish self-advocacy and boundary-setting behaviors.

Disparity in Training Opportunities

Academic contexts require individuals to engage in unspecified-but-required repertoires that typically characterize the learning histories of gender-privileged people (e.g., self-advocacy, institutional cultural competence, networking, leadership, teamwork, etc.; Verniers & Martinot, 2015). The same repertoires may be wholly untrained in learning histories that include gender marginalization. Even the availability of quality supervision and mentorship to shape and generate such repertoires for mentees and supervisees is often disparate across genders (Deanna et al., 2020; Llorens et al., 2021). Disparities in training opportunities continue on the consequential side. Heilman and Haynes (2005) suggested that when gender-privileged individuals engage in even the minimum service requirements that have been outlined as a job expectation, they are both lauded for effort and perceived as individuals with greater authority. Academic contexts also foster a disparate expectation of responsibility and ownership of emotional labor for those who are gender-marginalized, which can be seen even in the context of educating peers, superiors, and subordinates on the complexities and politics of gender dynamics and interactions in academic contexts (Anthym & Tuitt, 2019; Docka-Filipek & Stone, 2021; Hanasono et al., 2019; Turner et al., 2018).

Scarcity of Appetitives

The scarcity of appetitives available in some academic contexts itself may be a barrier to appetitive control. In addition to the abundance of aversives that gender-marginalized individuals are operating under in academic contexts, consequences that seem like positive reinforcers can also function aversively under conditions of scarcity. Gender-marginalized individuals in academic contexts with few appetitives available may still have narrow and rigid resultant repertoires even in the absence of clear aversives. The degrees of freedom (De Fernandes & Dittrich, 2018; Goldiamond, 1974) available in such cases may be too few for gender-marginalized individuals to build appetitive repertoires and thus, their behaviors are still operating under aversive control. For example, a lab led exclusively by gender-marginalized individuals may still not have access to appetitives if the overarching institution or governing body does not explicitly create contingencies of support for them. This is further amplified by the disparity in distribution of such labor expectations across gender marginalization under conditions of scarcity or competition (Saltmarsh et al., 2009; Singh et al., 1998). Additionally, active restorative measures taken to compensate for these pervasive, systemic barriers are rarely taken (McGill & Settle, 2012; Moore et al., 2015).

Intersection With Other Marginalized Identities

Gendered expectations of, and consequences for, gender-marginalized academics are further exacerbated when their gender intersects with other marginalized identities (e.g., race, ethnicity, nationality, sexual orientation, class, and ability). For example, gender-marginalized members of the LGBTQIAP+ community (transgender, nonbinary, intersex, etc.) also experience significant aversive control and barriers to appetitive control as a direct result of their identities. For LGBTQIAP+ academics, the academic context is likely to include harassment, unemployment, hiring discrimination, disclosure in a potentially unsafe context, misgendering, deadnaming (i.e., referring to a transgender person by the name assigned to them at birth without their consent), and more (Siegel, 2019). Research indicates that identity disclosure may occur at the cost of increased risk to personal safety (Pitcher, 2017) and lower course evaluations which influence promotion and tenure opportunities (Lewis, 2016). Additionally, coercive disclosure or outing may further perpetuate the myth of deception and potentially evoke anti-trans discrimination and violence (Bettcher, 2007). Trans academics are often *tokenized*—that is, treated merely as representatives of a group for the purpose of signaling inclusivity to observers (McKenzie, 2020). For example, they may be asked to perform emotional labor around "transgender issues" or serve as committee members in order for institutions to position themselves as "diverse" with little sensitivity to how those appointments serve, or do not serve, the trans person's well-being or career (Spade, 2010). The resultant *minority stress* (i.e., the stress experienced by marginalized individuals as a result of their social location; Meyer, 2003; Tan et al., 2019) of navigating transphobic environments can lead to limited resources available to trans academics to allocate to their career-related responsibilities (Catalano, 2014). Similar patterns are observed in intersections with other marginalized identities (e.g., Brown & Leigh, 2020; Harris & Nicolazzo, 2020).

Sourcing Appetitives to Promote Effective and Values-Consistent Academic Repertoires

Despite the relative imbalance of aversive to appetitive contingencies available in the academic context and barriers to accessibility for gender-marginalized academics, there are repertoires that can increase opportunities for academic work to come under appetitive control. Functionally speaking, success in developing a values-consistent academic repertoire involves several specific skills. In order to bring behavior under appetitive control, academics will need to first learn to detect potential appetitives. Next, academics will need to sample these appetitives—that is, will need to behave in ways that allow for contact with positive reinforcers and their discriminating and motivating antecedents. When under appetitive control, the academic repertoire will be sensitive enough to be maintained and shaped over time, and responsive to changing contingencies. This may be optimized to the extent that academics learn to tact those contingencies in ways that augment their appetitive functions. As this repertoire evolves, academics become more skilled at discriminating and sampling a broader range of potentially appetitive contexts. In this way, the academic becomes more effective at creating contexts that support an appetitive academic response class. As they expand their appetitive learning repertoires in the academic context, the context increasingly promotes research, teaching, service, and mentorship activities that are both effective and values-consistent.

Sourcing Appetitive Effectiveness in Research

Research effectiveness has been characterized by various behavioral patterns, including the development of confidence, engendering recognition, productivity, and sophistication as interactive and overlapping repertoires (Åkerlind, 2008). These repertoires can be further elaborated into specific activities. Academics with high research productivity, for example, tend to spend more time engaged in research activities, but are less likely to report perceived conflict between research and other academic activities (Ito & Brotheridge, 2007). Qualitative data from gender-marginalized researchers suggest that tracking and managing time effectively contribute to effectiveness (Dobele & Hafey, 2003). Research productivity is also more likely among academics who develop a program of research with a clear, strategic focus (Ito & Brotheridge, 2007). Here, qualitative data from gender-marginalized researchers suggest that this strategic focus may contribute most to research effectiveness when it is consistent with passion and interest (Dobele & Hafey, 2003).

Academics tend to have a lot of control over the content of their research as it is highly valued by the academy (Degn, 2018; Knights & Clarke, 2014). Therefore, locating institutional and departmental support for researchers can be a crucial source of appetitives, especially when the research is both contextually relevant and highly valued by individual researchers (Hardré, Beesley et al., 2011; Hardré, Miller et al., 2007). A 2003 study conducted by Ylijoki examined faculty values in the context of academic capitalism (i.e., universities and academics engaging in market-like behaviors related to the competition for academic resources such as grants, funding, partnership with industry, etc.; Slaughter & Rhoades, 2004). They found that despite barriers to financial appetitives, academics valued and desired producing work on their own research interests and intellectually challenging topics. Academics who are resourced to conduct high-quality research that influences their job performance and results in corresponding rewards may experience greater job satisfaction (Mamiseishvili, K., & Rosser, 2011). By aligning research interests with teaching and service responsibilities (e.g., by collecting and disseminating data on teaching, mentorship, and service activities), greater job satisfaction is likely to be fostered via the resulting values alignment (Mamiseishvili, K., & Rosser, 2011). Pushing for systemic change in the form of grassroots leadership (i.e., leadership by those who lack formal authority or delegated power to change the status quo; Lester & Kezar, 2012) in tandem with pursuing these individual valued behaviors can generate appetitives for the individual academic as well as their community at large.

Interpersonal behaviors also play a significant role in making appetitives available to academics. Researchers are more likely to maintain research success in terms of quality and quantity when they engage in international collaborations (Carli et al., 2019), with a moderate level of diversity in a collaborative team being ideal (Barjak & Robinson, 2008). Gender-marginalized researchers in particular may benefit from participating in a research group or other mentorship opportunities (Dobele & Hafey, 2003). These activities also seem to be cumulative, as a primary predictor of current research productivity is past productivity (Carli et al., 2019; Williamson & Cable, 2003).

Lechuga and Lechuga (2012) purported that shifting towards perceiving faculty as learners in the context of research, as opposed to knowledge producers and disseminators, can contribute to personal motivation with the potential for research productivity. When considering research as a learning activity, academics can engage in self-regulation to enhance and maintain motivation to conduct research. This perspective also relies less on appetitives that are controlled by departmental and institutional incentivizing structures. As learners, academics can exert greater agency over their research work and motivation by incorporating mechanisms that promote autonomy, community, contributing to society, and experiencing pleasure in the process rather than solely the outcome.

Box 4—Personal Success with Research

JANANI: I finally got an opportunity to join a research lab last year—Dr. Sandoz was willing to let me join and mentor me via their lab, and my personal growth and experience with a flexible and willing mentor has been phenomenal. The lab itself has moved to a completely virtual space since so many lab members are not in the same geographical location. Since joining the lab, I have been connecting with more people, learning more, and honing my skills as a researcher. I have access to a variety of appetitives in the research context, with opportunities to participate in ways that are values-consistent, such as working on research relevant to my interests. The opportunity to collaborate on this chapter is another instance. My experience in this lab has informed how I work with my own students now that I am a faculty member, by focusing on generating and finding appetitives for myself and my students in our student-teacher relationships, which would not have happened otherwise.

Sourcing Appetitive Effectiveness in Teaching

There are a number of activities that characterize teaching effectiveness. The function of teaching repertoires includes but is not limited to: demonstrating expertise, disseminating information, building and expanding student repertoires, contextualizing information in a manner relevant to students, shaping and generating high-quality professional repertoires for students, and more (Nicoll & Harrison, 2003). Given that the primary outcome of effective teaching practices is student learning, effective teaching is characterized by behaviors related to course content, content dissemination, as well as relationships with students (Kember & McNaught, 2007).

Some appetitives available for teachers with respect to course content include: designing and updating curriculum to currency, establishing the relevance of theoretical concepts using applied examples, and ensuring a thorough conceptual understanding for students. For content dissemination and instructional mechanism, appetitives can include designing teaching practices and curriculum that prioritize meeting student needs, ensuring that meaningful learning takes place by incorporating a variety of teaching modalities, and building a teaching repertoire that includes flexible and adaptive instructional design. These are skills that may converge with teaching experience, and whose effects can be found in student engagement and performance.

The effective student-teacher relationship involves enthusiasm to generate student motivation, genuine and empathetic rapport with students via meaningful individual interactions, and challenging student misconceptions in a respectful manner (Keeley et al., 2016). The combination of all these elements has the greatest impact on students' learning, therefore they can function as appetitives for academics as well. Effective teaching can generate consequences such as teaching awards, which can exert appetitive control on teaching behavior. For gender-marginalized individuals operating in the domain of teaching, peer relationships (i.e., sharing and mentorship) are valuable sources of appetitives (Macoun & Miller, 2014). These have a significantly positive impact on teachers' mental health and well-being, offer critical sociopolitical support, personal validation, information and material support, and a community within the institution that may be aversive in a gendered context. For academics with less control over the content or structure of their courses, focusing on higher-order appetitives (e.g., contributing to the training of competent professionals or shaping prosocial behavior) and positive interpersonal relationships with students can provide opportunities for positive reinforcement.

Box 5—Personal Success with Teaching

BROOKE: When I began my current academic appointment, I discovered that the psychology department lacked a course on diversity. I proposed including such a course in the curriculum, developed the course, and just finished teaching it for the first time as this chapter is being written. Developing this course, outside my area of research or clinical specialization, entailed a tremendous amount of work on a week-to-week basis. However, I approached the class as a learner; the discussion format of the class allowed me to build strong relationships with my students, and I often left class feeling rejuvenated and better able to sustain behavior in other domains (e.g., research, mentorship) due to the appetitives I was contacting in the domain of teaching. Because the institution in which I work and my position allowed me the flexibility and power to develop a new course that aligned with my values, the behavior of teaching became far more values-based than it previously had been. Having changed my own environment to be able to provide more values-based positive reinforcement, I was also able to influence the environment of students, who in many of their final assignments wrote about the positive impact this class had on their education and worldview.

Sourcing Appetitive Effectiveness in Service

There are a number of activities that characterize effectiveness in service. In this domain, effectiveness is most frequently conceptualized in one of two ways: retaining and progressing in one's academic position (e.g., Gentry & Stokes, 2015), and maintaining a sense of purpose and satisfaction with one's service roles (e.g., Ezell Sheets et al., 2018). In a review of the literature on engaging service toward tenure and promotion, Gentry and Stokes (2015) describe strategic service activities as those that advance one's career (e.g., collaborations, grant reviews), indirectly promote scholarly productivity, provide opportunities for professional leadership, and maintain the academic's sense of being needed. Some of these strategies are echoed in the recommendations of a group of multidisciplinary early- and mid-career faculty members from underrepresented groups to their peers on how to consider service invitations, including assessing the extent of alignment with research and career goals (Carson et al., 2019). Here, potential appetitives are indicated in the opportunities for advancement that service can afford.

Also of note are where recommendations for marginalized academics diverge. For example, marginalized academics are explicitly advised to seek more information about expectations, to assess the likelihood of a valued impact, to estimate the risks associated with declining, to resource themselves interpersonally (e.g., seek perspectives of others, pursue mentorship and support around service), and to engage in negotiation of duties to accommodate impactful service opportunities (Carson et al., 2019). It may be that appetitives of particular importance to gender-marginalized academics around service are clear discriminating and motivating antecedents, values-consistent consequences, and interpersonal resources.

Box 6—Personal Success with Service

EMILY: Last semester I took on a pretty terrible and highly sensitive service role at my university. What made it worse was that it was the kind of role that faculty tend to hang onto for quite a while. After compiling documents, meeting with administrators, repeatedly reviewing my charge, and leading a committee through some tough conversations, it was time to write a series of reports to our Graduate Council on our process and final decisions. Here, something became evident to me about the power I had in this role. I updated the language in my template to use all gender-inclusive language. It was a small thing that did not feel small at all. The more reports I wrote, the more meaningful this entire role felt. I was proud, and a little nervous, when it came time to send my reports to my committee. And I was touched, and a little nervous, when a number of faculty reached out to share how impactful they'd found this small shift. I'm not sure how the Council took my small act of rebellion, but I am eager to see what this pretty terrible, highly sensitive, and tremendously empowering role positions me to do next.

Sourcing Appetitive Effectiveness in Mentorship

There are a number of activities that characterize effectiveness in supervision and mentorship. For example, effective mentors train mentees in the ways of the institution, disseminating important and sometimes privileged information, offering visibility and exposure, and providing protection and advocacy via their institutional positioning (Angelique et al., 2002). Providing high-quality mentorship enhances mentee productivity, self-efficacy, career satisfaction, and reflects success for the mentor as well (Dolan & Johnson, 2009; Pfund et al., 2016). Additionally, the establishment of trust in the mentoring relationship cannot be understated (Johnson & Snider, 2016). Effective mentoring may also include shifting from traditional, one-on-one, top-down mentorship to the mentoring relationship as a collaborative effort. In this approach, both mentors and mentees are "learners" who engage in reciprocal activities with conscious, ongoing negotiation of expectations (McGee & Keller, 2007). Such a collaborative effort has the potential to generate appetitives for all parties in the mentoring relationship, including the mentor. Other modalities might include mentorship by multiple faculty members, which might increase potential appetitives for all participating members and facilitate socialization (Cawyer et al., 2002).

Mentors can access a number of appetitives via the mentor-mentee relationship (Johnson, 2007), such as: (a) personal satisfaction due to the mentee's growth and progress, (b) personal fulfillment derived from knowledge and skills transfer, (c) professional rejuvenation from working with students in a creative process, (d) networking, (e) personal and communal support as the mentorship relationship matures into a collegial one, (f) recognition as a result of successful mentee development, and (g) values-consistent behavior leading to their continued presence in the field. Rheingold (1994) also emphasized the rewarding nature of a student's decision to elect someone as their mentor, and the opportunity to create a personal legacy via mentorship.

Box 7—Personal Success with Mentorship

EMILY: An important lesson happened for me around 2015. I had a large, productive lab of brilliant, kind, hardworking students. The mission of our lab was explicitly values-focused, as were our research questions. And yet, it seemed there was a huge disparity between those who thrived in the lab and those who did not. We started taking data, formally and informally, on what behaviors look like in those who thrived. We noted that consistency in attending lab meetings, participating in multiple projects in both leadership and support roles, and spending time working in the lab on a regular schedule seemed to be associated with growth, vitality, and meaning in the research repertoire. Based on these data, I set formal expectations and attempted to intervene by setting rules and criteria for a formal commitment. And yet, still some expressed a desire to work in the lab, and clearly struggled—both to meet those expectations and to engage with the lab meaningfully. The problem with this became most clear to me when I found myself struggling. I was still engaging in ways that appeared consistent with the same level of commitment to the lab, but was beginning to feel constrained by the rules I'd made and the responsibility of enforcing them. The coronavirus pandemic brought, in March 2020, new perspective, as disparities in the relative privilege of the labbies became strikingly evident. We responded with four changes. First, we developed a behavior analytic conceptualization of privilege that could help us to move forward in ways that supported all of us more equitably. Second, we shifted away from emphasizing antecedent aversive control, which we came to understand as disproportionately harmful to the most vulnerable, least privileged of our members. Third, we began emphasizing consequential, appetitive control, which we came to understand as buffering impacts of the aversives that were increasingly all too common in our lives. Fourth, we created a number of channels to reduce response effort around communication regarding membership, needs, resources, and other contingencies. In other words, we supplemented our focus on data with attention to conceptual analysis, we replaced rules about when, where, and how to work with social norms about how to treat one another, we made lab way more fun in so many ways, and we empowered members to use their voices in ways most beneficial for them and for the group.

Making Use of (Even Limited) Power and Privilege

Several functional characteristics of the academy as a learning context challenge the development and maintenance of a values repertoire. In short, the academy systematically limits the detection, discrimination, and tacting of aversive, rather than appetitive, contingencies in such a way as to augment the direct consequences of the class of behaviors that participate in that contingency. This is especially true for those who lack the contextual privilege and power that tends to covary with cisgender male identity, which makes appetitives, and the repertoire functionally related to them, more readily accessible.

That said, privilege is an aspect of context, and power is contextually bound. Thus, even those in the academy that lack cisgender male privilege may develop values-consistent repertoires, if provided appropriate opportunities to build appetitive learning by maximizing the access and availability of appetitives not limited by gender (of course, these sources of power and privilege are not independent of gender, and may still be more elusive to those lacking cisgender male privilege).

Intersecting Identities

For one, gender is not the only aspect of identity that tends to covary with privileging contexts and the power that emerges from them. Race and ethnicity, education, ability, economic status, social class, sexuality, citizenship status, age, and religion all intersect with gender in ways that (1) characterize a person's individual identity and (2) predict interdependent and interacting patterns of contextual privilege and the lack thereof. For some, the challenges to accessing appetitives in the academy without cisgender male privilege are buffered by privilege associated with other aspects of identity. A gender-marginalized academic may still enjoy benefits to their values repertoire associated with their able-bodied status, their postdoctoral education, or their high level of income. In other words, these aspects of their identity may tend to covary with learning experiences that have sensitized them to particular appetitives and fostered the discrimination of patterns of behavior under appetitive control. Of course, the same person may find their repertoire lacking not only due to their gender, but also their mental health struggles, immigrant status, or minoritized religious affiliation. Thus, these aspects of their identity may covary with learning experiences that have sensitized them to particular aversives and fostered the discrimination of patterns of behavior under aversive control. The context needed to foster a values repertoire for any one academic is thus in part a product of the intersecting learning histories that covary with intersecting aspects of identity.

In addition, contexts within the academy vary in the extent to which they privilege particular identities. For example, some disciplines are currently dominated by women or non-binary academics (e.g., Forbes, 2020; Leslie et al., 2015), even in leadership positions (e.g., Porterfield & Kleiner, 2005; Winchester & Browning, 2015). This may provide (1) fewer systemic restrictions to appetitives at the departmental level that are typically gender-bound in other contexts and (2) more contextual support for the development of values repertoires.

Contextually-Bound Roles

Just as contexts vary in the extent to which they privilege particular identities, some sources of privilege and power are unique to particular contexts. For example, the academic whose context empowers them with control over the content and format of their courses likely has more ready access to appetitives supporting their teaching and instructional design. This includes both appetitives in the learning experiences they offer (e.g., lecturing on an enjoyable or meaningful topic, reading a beloved classic text, assigning an interesting exercise, or inviting an exciting guest speaker) and those in the (changing) repertoires of their students (e.g., identifying and building target student behaviors that are appetitive for the instructor). The academic whose learning history has fostered the detection, discrimination, and tacting of such contingencies in similar contexts is likely, then, to teach in a way that allows for contact with values. That is, they are likely to value teaching and to exhibit and enjoy all the benefits that come with valuing teaching.

Similarly, the academic whose context empowers them with control over their scientific focus and activities likely has more ready access to appetitives supporting their scientific work. This includes appetitives in the products of their scientific behavior (e.g., a riveting philosophical conundrum, an actionable behavioral conceptualization, an elegant research design, surprising empirical data, or an effective application) and in its focus (i.e., a fun or personally meaningful area of interest). The academic whose learning history has fostered the detection, discrimination, and tacting of such contingencies in similar contexts is likely, then, to do science in a way that allows for contact with values. That is, they are likely to value science and to exhibit and enjoy all the benefits that come with valuing science.

The same conceptual analysis could be applied to mentorship, supervision, and service to the university, community, or discipline. An academic is likely to value mentorship, to value supervision, and to value service to the extent that they are empowered to do so by being effectively afforded control over the focus and form of their activities. Of course, the effectiveness of this empowerment depends, in part, on the academic's history with detecting, discriminating, and tacting appetitive contingencies in such contexts.

Interpersonal Relationships

Privilege and power to access appetitives and build a values repertoire can also covary with interpersonal relationships across a power differential. This is possible when the more powerful person uses their sensitivity and access to appetitives to shape the detection, discrimination, and tacting of appetitive contingencies in such a way as to augment the direct consequences of the class of behaviors that participate in that contingency. This training of a values repertoire can be contrasted with using one's power to shape academic repertoires that are pliant, under aversive control, or both. For example, the academic whose history with teaching, service, research, and mentorship has been supervised such that the primary controlling contingencies were those mediated by their supervisor's approval or attention may find it difficult to detect, discriminate, and tact appetitive contingencies *not* mediated by their supervisor's behavior. To the extent that (1) disapproval and neglect have been more salient and/or (2) approval and attention have been particularly scarce, this difficulty will be even greater as a general insensitivity to appetitives might emerge. On the other hand, the academic whose supervisor has provided noncontingent acceptance *and* established or augmented appetitive contingencies in shaping teaching, service, research, and mentorship repertoires is likely to exhibit a more robust values repertoire. Such patterns are likely to be observed, not only in supervision relationships, but formal and informal mentorship, collaborative, and collegial roles where power differentials exist.

Rank and Responsibilities

Privilege and power to access appetitives and build a values repertoire can also covary with an academic's rank (e.g., assistant, associate, or full professor) and primary responsibilities (i.e., administration, clinical, teaching, or research). Traditionally the academy provides more privilege and power with increasing rank in terms of job security (e.g., tenured or non-tenured), access to system-level appetitives (e.g., prestigious awards, honorary roles, eligibility for sabbatical), and control over responsibilities. Thus, for many, promotion will allow for cumulative improvement to the values repertoire. Of course, the way appetitives covary with an academic's primary responsibilities may not be consistent with traditional conceptualizations of hierarchy in the academy. For some academics, their learning history is such that there are more appetitives available and accessible with their repertoire in the teaching context than in research. For others, their learning history provides that administration, and clinical contexts have the most appetitives available and accessible. Academics whose primary positions fit well with their appetitive learning history are likely to develop and maintain a values repertoire that includes ready detection, discrimination, and tacting of appetitive contingencies across contexts.

Contextualized Self-Assessment for Building Values-Consistent Repertoires

A thorough and ongoing self-assessment of one's own values-consistent repertoire as it relates to particular aspects of the academic context is recommended. First, this assessment should consider the values repertoire as it relates functionally to a particular context within the academy. Such an assessment might include an evaluation of both the availability and accessibility of appetitive antecedents and consequences. For example, we might ask ourselves:

1. What appetitives are potentially available to me in this context?
2. To what extent does the context allow me to predict when those appetitives are and are not available?
3. To what extent does the context allow me to predict when potentially appetitive contexts will function more or less appetitively?
4. To what extent are the behaviors I tend to engage in here accessing these appetitives effectively?
5. To what extent are the behaviors that might be necessary to access these appetitive behaviors I engage in (or have engaged in) in other contexts?
6. How easily can I tact appetitive contingencies at play in this context consistent with the previous questions?
7. How easily can I track the dynamic functional relationships between my behavior and the changing context in the moment?

Second, this assessment might consider how some contexts within the academy covary with identities, roles, relationships, ranks, and responsibilities in ways that are privileging and foster power. For example, we might ask:

8. What aspects of this context privilege me in this context? That is, what aspects of my identity, role, relationships, rank, or responsibilities increase my power here?
9. How am I currently using my power in this context to increase appetitives available to me and others?
10. How am I currently using my power in this context to increase the accessibility of appetitives for me and others?
11. What are the things my power and privilege here position me to change to make this context more appetitive for me and others?

Third, this assessment might consider the values repertoire as it relates functionally to contexts outside of the academy—that is, how our broader context is resourcing general needs that must be met in order for our values repertoire to come to bear. Specifically, we might ask ourselves what needs must be met in order for us to effectively detect, discriminate, and tact appetitive contingencies in such a way as to augment the direct consequences of the class of behaviors that participate in that contingency:

12. Is my broader context resourcing me with appetitives that foster health and safety?
13. Is my broader context resourcing me with appetitives that foster belonging and intimacy?
14. Is my broader context resourcing me with appetitives that foster self-awareness and intrapersonal growth?
15. Is my broader context resourcing me with appetitives that foster my values repertoire?
   Fourth, this assessment might include how our current behavior patterns relate functionally to the values repertoires of others in relationships where we have relatively more power. Often, when our behavior is under aversive control, we tend to use

antecedent interventions that rely heavily on rules specifying topographically defined behavior patterns and aversive consequences. For example, we might declare, "Students must have one written page a week, or our thesis meeting is canceled" as opposed to "Our thesis meeting will be most fun and productive for both of us if you have engaged in enough writing to have specific questions or a sample of your work." Specifically, we might ask ourselves:

16. Am I creating appetitive contexts for the students, junior colleagues, supervisees, staff, advisees, and mentees that I serve?
17. Am I creating a context that shapes the repertoires of those I serve to predict when those appetitives are and are not available?
18. Am I creating a context that shapes the repertoires of those I serve to predict when potentially appetitive contexts will function more or less appetitively?
19. Am I creating a context that shapes the repertoires needed for those I serve to access these appetitives effectively?
20. Am I creating a context that shapes the repertoires needed for those I serve to generalize behaviors they engage in (or have engaged in) in other contexts to the academic context?
21. Am I creating a context that shapes the tacting appetitive contingencies at play in this context consistent with the previous questions?
22. Am I creating a context that shapes tracking of the dynamic functional relationships between their behavior and the changing context in the moment?
23. Am I creating a context that shapes the engagement of those I serve in ongoing assessment of the power and privilege they may have, and how they are using it?
24. Am I creating a context that shapes the engagement of those I serve in ongoing assessment of how their broader context is resourcing general needs that must be met in order for their values repertoire to come to bear?

Conclusion

According to this conceptual analysis, the academy has mostly *not* evolved in a way that fosters the development and maintenance of values repertoires, despite the incredible advantage that this would have for those directly participating in the academy and for society at large. And, our assumption is that we (the authors), having had the opportunity to write this chapter and the learning history that afforded us something to say about the topic, are well positioned to evolve the behavior analytic corners of the academy further. And, our assumption is that you (the reader), having had the opportunity to read this chapter and the learning history to make sense of it, are well-positioned to support such an evolution. We recognize that the availability and necessity of engaging suggested behavior classes will depend upon your individual repertoire and the academic context in which you function. Thus, it is our hope that this chapter might complement our respective learning histories in such a way as to make such an evolution more likely.

Notes

1. A contemporary understanding of gender as a spectrum provides room for acknowledging commonalities and distinctions within academic contexts that are contextualized perceptions of one's gender. The authors examine the implications of gender within the academic context along the lines of privilege and marginalization that occur as a result of gendering repertoires of oneself and others. Instead of selecting specific gender identities, this chapter points to the experiences of those who are gender-marginalized and gender-privileged in the academic context.
2. There is some debate among scholars as to the origin of this term (see Moosa, 2018, pp. 4–5).

References

Adams, K. A. (2002). *What colleges and universities want in new faculty. Preparing future faculty occasional paper series*. Association of American Colleges & Universities, 1818 R Street, NW 20009.

Åkerlind, G. S. (2008). Growing and developing as a university researcher. *Higher Education, 55*(2), 241–254. https://doi.org/10.1007/s10734-007-9052-x

Angelique, H., Kyle, K., & Taylor, E. (2002). Mentors and muses: New strategies for academic success. *Innovative Higher Education, 26*(3), 195–209. https://doi.org/10.1023/A:1017968906264

Anthym, M., & Tuitt, F. (2019). When the levees break: The cost of vicarious trauma, microaggressions and emotional labor for black administrators and faculty engaging in race work at traditionally white institutions. *International Journal of Qualitative Studies in Education, 32*(9), 1072–1093. doi:10.1080/09518398.2019.1645907.

Antonio, A. L., Astin, H. S., & Cress, C. M. (2000). Community service in higher education: A look at the nation's faculty. *The Review of Higher Education, 23*(4), 373–397. doi:10.1353/rhe.2000.0015.

Arnold, N. W., Crawford, E. R., & Khalifa, M. (2016). Psychological heuristics and faculty of color: Racial battle fatigue and tenure/promotion. *The Journal of Higher Education, 87*(6), 890–919. https://doi.org/10.1080/00221546.2016.11780891

Baker, V. L., & Griffin, K. A. (2010). Beyond mentoring and advising: Toward understanding the role of faculty "developers" in student success. *About Campus, 14*(6), 2–8. doi:10.1002/abc.20002.

Barjak, F., & Robinson, S. (2008). International collaboration, mobility and team diversity in the life sciences: Impact on research performance. *Social Geography, 3*(1), 23–36. doi:10.5194/sg-3-23-2008

Bauerlein, M., Gad-el-Hak, M., Grody, W., McKelvey, B., & Trimble, S. (2010). We must stop the avalanche of low-quality research. *The Chronicle of Higher Education*. www.chronicle.com/article/We-Must-Stop-the-Avalanche-of/65890.

Bavishi, A., Madera, J. M., & Hebl, M. R. (2010). The effect of professor ethnicity and gender on student evaluations: Judged before met. *Journal of Diversity in Higher Education, 3*(4), 245–256. doi:10.1037/a0020763.

Baykoucheva, S. (2015). *Ethics in scientific publishing*. Elsevier.

Bedenlier, S., & Zawacki-Richter, O. (2015). Internationalization of higher education and the impacts on academic faculty members. *Research in Comparative and International Education, 10*(2), 185–201. https://doi.org/10.1177%2F1745499915571707

Bettcher, T. M. (2007). Evil deceivers and make-believers: On transphobic violence and the politics of illusion. *Hypatia, 22*(3), 43–65. doi:10.1111/j.1527-2001.2007.tb01090.x.

Blithe, S. J., & Elliott, M. (2020). Gender inequality in the academy: Microaggressions, work-life conflict, and academic rank. *Journal of Gender Studies, 29*(7), 751–764. doi:10.1080/09589236.2019.1657004

Boice, R. (2000). *Advice for new faculty members: Nihil Nimus*. Allyn & Bacon.

Bolitzer, L. A. (2019). What we know (and don't know) about adjunct faculty as teachers at four-year institutions. *The Review of Higher Education, 43*(1), 113–142. doi:10.1353/rhe.2019.0092

Bonow, J. T., & Follette, W. C. (2009). Beyond values clarification: Addressing client values in clinical behavior analysis. *The Behavior Analyst, 32*(1), 69–84. doi:10.1007/BF03392176

Borman, W. C., & Motowidlo, S. J. (1993). Expanding the criterion domain to include elements of contextual performance. In N. Schmitt & W. C. Borman (Eds.), *Personnel selection in organizations* (pp. 71–98). Jossey-Bass.

Brissett, N. (2020). Inequitable rewards: Experiences of faculty of color mentoring students of color. *Mentoring & Tutoring: Partnership in Learning, 28*(5), 556–577. doi:10.1080/13611267.2020.1859327

Britton, D. M. (2017). Beyond the chilly climate: The salience of gender in women's academic careers. *Gender & Society, 31*(1), 5–27. doi:10.1177/0891243216681494

Brown, N., & Leigh, J. (2020). *Ableism in academia: Theorising experiences of disabilities and chronic illnesses in higher education*. UCL Press.

Cardel, M. I., Dhurandhar, E., Yarar-Fisher, C., Foster, M., Hidalgo, B., McClure, L. A., Pagoto, S., Brown, N., Pekmezi, D., Sharafeldin, N., Willig, A. L., & Angelini, C. (2020). Turning chutes into ladders for women faculty: A review and roadmap for equity in academia. *Journal of Women's Health, 29*(5), 721–733. doi:10.1089/jwh.2019.8027

Carli, G., Tagliaventi, M. R., & Cutolo, D. (2019). One size does not fit all: The influence of individual and contextual factors on research excellence in academia. *Studies in Higher Education, 44*(11), 1912–1930. https://doi.org/10.1080/03075079.2018.1466873

Carson, T. L., Aguilera, A., Brown, S. D., Peña, J., Butler, A., Dulin, A., Jonassaint, C. R., Riley, I., Vanderbom, K., Molina, K. M., & Cené, C. W. (2019). A seat at the table: Strategic engagement in service activities for early career faculty from underrepresented groups in the academy. *Academic Medicine: Journal of the Association of American Medical Colleges, 94*(8), 1089–1093. doi:10.1097/ACM.0000000000002603
Carson, T. L., Bartneck, C., & Voges, K. (2013). Over-competitiveness in academia: A literature review. *Disruptive Science and Technology, 1*(4), 183–190. doi:10.1089/dst.2013.0013
Caruth, G. D., & Caruth, D. L. (2013). Adjunct faculty: Who are these unsung heroes of academe? *Current Issues in Education, 16*(3), 1–11. https://cie.asu.edu/ojs/index.php/cieatasu/article/view/1269
Catalano, D. C. J. (2014). *Welcome to guyland: Experiences of trans* men in college*. (Unpublished doctoral dissertation). University of Massachusetts—Amherst.
Cawyer, C. S., Simonds, C., & Davis, S. (2002). Mentoring to facilitate socialization: The case of the new faculty member. *International Journal of Qualitative Studies in Education, 15*(2), 225–242. https://doi.org/10.1080/09518390110111938
Clark, R. A., Harden, S. L., & Johnson, W. B. (2000). Mentor relationships in clinical psychology doctoral training: Results of a national survey. *Teaching of Psychology, 27*(4), 262–268. doi:10.1207/S15328023TOP2704_04
Coates, W. C. (2012). Being a mentor: What's in it for me? *Academic Emergency Medicine, 19*(1), 92–97. doi:10.1111/j.1553-2712.2011.01258.x
Cohen, G. L., & Sherman, D. K. (2014). The psychology of change: Self-affirmation and social psychological intervention. *Annual Review of Psychology, 65*, 333–371. doi:10.1146/annurev-psych-010213-115137
Coolidge, H. J. (1932). *Archibald Cary Coolidge*. Houghton Mifflin.
Crawford, C., Burns, R., & McNamara, R. H. (2012). Promotion to full professor: Moving beyond tenure and associate professorship. *Journal of Criminal Justice Education, 23*(1), 41–64. doi:10.1080/10511253.2011.645491
Creswell, J. D., Dutcher, J. M., Klein, W. M., Harris, P. R., & Levine, J. M. (2013). Self-affirmation improves problem-solving under stress. *PloS One, 8*(5), e62593. doi:10.1371/journal.pone.0062593
Creswell, J. D., & Lindsay, E. K. (2014). How does mindfulness training affect health? A mindfulness stress buffering account. *Current Directions in Psychological Science, 23*(6), 401–407. doi:10.1177/0963721414547415
Crocker, J., Niiya, Y., & Mischkowski, D. (2008). Why does writing about important values reduce defensiveness? Self-affirmation and the role of positive other-directed feelings. *Psychological Science, 19*(7), 740–747. doi:10.1111/j.1467-9280.2008.02150.x
Crowell, A., Page-Gould, E., & Schmeichel, B. J. (2015). Self-affirmation breaks the link between the behavioral inhibition system and the threat-potentiated startle response. *Emotion, 15*(2), 146–150. doi:10.1037/emo0000030
da Silva Ferreira, T. A., Simões, A. S., Ferreira, A. R., & Dos Santos, B. O. S. (2020). What are values in clinical behavior analysis? *Perspectives on Behavior Science, 43*(1), 177–188.
Da Silva, J. A. T., & Dobránszki, J. (2017). Excessively long editorial decisions and excessively long publication times by journals: Causes, risks, consequences, and proposed solutions. *Publishing Research Quarterly, 33*(1), 101–108.
de Fernandes, R. C., & Dittrich, A. (2018). Expanding the behavior-analytic meanings of "freedom": The contributions of Israel Goldiamond. *Behavior & Social Issues, 27*, 4–19. doi:10.5210/bsi.v.27i0.8248
Deanna, R., Baxter, I., Chun, K. P., Merkle, B. G., Zuo, R., Diele-Viegas, L. M., Geesink, P., Aschero, V., Navarro-Rosenblatt, D., Bortolus, A., Ribone, P. A., Welchen, E., de Leone, M. J., Oliferuk, S., Oleas, N. H., Grossi, M., Cosacov, A., Knapp, S., López-Mendez, A., & Auge, G. (2020). *It takes a village—overcoming gender-biased mentorship in academia*. doi:10.31219/osf.io/25h7p
Degn, L. (2018). Academic sensemaking and behavioural responses–exploring how academics perceive and respond to identity threats in times of turmoil. *Studies in Higher Education, 43*(2), 305–321. https://doi.org/10.1080/03075079.2016.1168796
Denker, K. J. (2009). Doing gender in the academy: The challenges for women in the academic organization. *Women and Language, 32*(1), 103–112.
Denker, K. J. (2017). Power, emotional labor, and intersectional identity at work: I would not kiss my boss but I did not speak. In *Organizational autoethnographies* (pp. 16–36). Routledge.
Dobele, A., & Hafey, N. (2003, January). Effective research tools for women in research at central Queensland university. *Proceedings of women in research conference*. Central Queensland University.

Docherty, J. S. (2013). What can we learn from a university that rewards faculty practice? *Negotiation Journal, 29*(2), 239–250. doi:10.1111/nejo.12021

Docka-Filipek, D., & Stone, L. B. (2021). Twice a "housewife": On academic precarity, "hysterical" women, faculty mental health, and service as gendered care work for the "university family" in pandemic times. *Gender, Work & Organization, 28*(6), 2158–2179. doi:10.1111/gwao.12723

Dolan, E., & Johnson, D. (2009). Toward a holistic view of undergraduate research experiences: An exploratory study of impact on graduate/postdoctoral mentors. *Journal of Science Education and Technology, 18*(6), 487–500. https://doi.org/10.1007/s10956-009-9165-3

Eaton, A., & Warner, L. R. (2021). Social justice burnout: Engaging in self-care while In M. E. Kite, K. A. Case, & W. R. Williams (Eds.), *Navigating difficult moments in teaching diversity and social justice* (pp. 31–43). American Psychological Association. doi:10.1037/0000216-003

Edwards, M. A., & Roy, S. (2017). Academic research in the 21st century: Maintaining scientific integrity in a climate of perverse incentives and hypercompetition. *Environmental Engineering Science, 34*(1), 51–61. https://doi.org/10.1089/ees.2016.0223

Elliott, D. B. (2013). Salami slicing and the SPU: Publish or perish? *Ophthalmic and Physiological Optics, 3*, 625–626. doi:10.1111/opo.12090

Epton, T., Harris, P. R., Kane, R., van Koningsbruggen, G. M., & Sheeran, P. (2015). The impact of self-affirmation on health-behavior change: A meta-analysis. *Health Psychology, 34*(3), 187–196. doi:10.1037/hea0000116

Ezell Sheets, J. K., Barnhardt, C. L., Phillips, C. W., & Valdés, P. H. (2018). The impact of faculty work-life factors on faculty service morale. *The Journal of Faculty Development, 32*(2), 53–66.

Finley, A. J., Crowell, A. L., & Schmeichel, B. J. (2018). Self-affirmation enhances processing of negative stimuli among threat-prone individuals. *Social Cognitive and Affective Neuroscience, 13*(6), 569–577. doi:10.1093/scan/nsy036

Forbes, T. D. (2020). Queer-free majors? LGBTQ+ college students' accounts of chilly and warm academic disciplines. *Journal of LGBT Youth*, 1–20. doi:10.1080/19361653.2020.1813673

Freckelton, I. (2020). Perils of precipitate publication: Fraudulent and substandard COVID-19 research. *Journal of Law and Medicine, 27*(4), 779–789.

Gentry, R., & Stokes, D. (2015). Strategies for professors who service the university to earn tenure and promotion. *Research in Higher Education Journal, 29*, 1–13.

Ginther, D. K., & Hayes, K. J. (2003). Gender differences in salary and promotion for faculty in the humanities, 1977–1995. *Journal of Human Resources, 38*(1), 34–73. doi:10.3368/jhr.XXXVIII.1.34

Goldiamond, I. (1974). Toward a constructional approach to social problems: Ethical and constitutional issues raised by applied behavior analysis. *Behaviorism, 2*(1), 1–84. www.jstor.org/stable/27758809

Goodman, S. A., & Svyantek, D. J. (1999). Person–organization fit and contextual performance: Do shared values matter. *Journal of Vocational Behavior, 55*(2), 254–275. doi:10.1006/jvbe.1998.1682

Green, R. G. (2008). Tenure and promotion decisions: The relative importance of teaching, scholarship, and service. *Journal of Social Work Education, 44*(2), 117–128. https://doi.org/10.5175/JSWE.2008.200700003

Gregory, S. T. (2001). Black faculty women in the academy: History, status, and future. *Journal of Negro Education, 70*(3), 124–138. doi:10.2307/3211205

Griffin, K. A., Bennett, J. C., & Harris, J. (2013). Marginalizing merit? Gender differences in Black faculty discourses on tenure, advancement, and professional success. *The Review of Higher Education, 36*(4), 489–512. doi:10.1353/rhe.2013.0040

Hanasono, L. K., Broido, E. M., Yacobucci, M. M., Root, K. V., Peña, S., & O'Neil, D. A. (2019). Secret service: Revealing gender biases in the visibility and value of faculty service. *Journal of Diversity in Higher Education, 12*(1), 85–98. doi:10.1037/dhe0000081

Hardré, P. L., Beesley, A. D., Miller, R. L., & Pace, T. M. (2011). Faculty motivation to do research: Across disciplines in research-extensive universities. *Journal of the Professoriate, 5*(1), 36–69.

Hardré, P. L., Miller, R. B., Beasley, A., Pace, T., Maxwell, M. S., & Xie, K. (2007). What motivates university faculty members to do research? Tenure-track faculty in research-extensive universities. *Journal of the Professoriate, 2*(1), 75–99.

Harris, J. C., & Nicolazzo, Z. (2020). Navigating the academic borderlands as multiracial and trans* faculty members. *Critical Studies in Education, 61*(2), 229–244. doi:10.1080/17508487.2017.1356340

Heilman, M. E., & Haynes, M. C. (2005). No credit where credit is due: Attributional rationalization of women's success in male-female teams. *Journal of Applied Psychology, 90*(5), 905–*916*. doi:10.1037/0021-9010.90.5.905

Hirshfield, L. E., & Joseph, T. D. (2012). "We need a woman, we need a black woman": Gender, race, and identity taxation in the academy. *Gender and Education, 24*(2), 213–227. doi:10.1080/09540253.2011.606208

Howell, A. J. (2017). Self-affirmation theory and the science of well-being. *Journal of Happiness Studies, 18*(1), 293–311. doi:10.1007/s10902-016-9713-5

Howell, J. L., & Shepperd, J. A. (2012). Reducing information avoidance through affirmation. *Psychological Science, 23*(2), 141–145. doi:10.1177/0956797611424164

Inzer, L. D., & Crawford, C. B. (2005). A review of formal and informal mentoring: Processes, problems, and design. *Journal of Leadership Education, 4*(1), 31–50.

Ito, J. K., & Brotheridge, C. M. (2007). Exploring the predictors and consequences of job insecurity's components. *Journal of Managerial Psychology, 22*(1), 40–64. doi:10.1108/02683940710721938

Jex, S. M., Cunningham, C. J. L., De la Rosa, G., & Broadfoot, A. (2006). Stress and employee effectiveness. In A. M. Rossi, P. L. Perrewé, & S. L. Sauter (Eds.). *Stress and quality of working life: Current directions in occupational health* (pp. 101–119). Information Age Publishing.

Johnson, J. M., & Snider, J. (2016). PhorwarD progress: Moving ahead through mentorship in the academy. In B. L. H. Marina (Ed.), *Mentoring away the glass ceiling in academia: A cultured critique*. Lexington Books.

Johnson, W. B. (2007). Student-faculty mentorship outcomes. In T. D. Allen & L. T. Eby (Eds.), *The Blackwell handbook of mentoring: A multiple perspectives approach* (pp. 189–210). Blackwell Publishing. https://doi.org/10.1111/b.9781405133739.2007.x

Johnson, W. B. (2015). *On being a mentor: A guide for higher education faculty* (2nd ed.). Routledge. doi:10.4324/9781315669120

Johnson, W. B., & Zlotnik, S. (2005). The frequency of advising and mentoring as salient work roles in academic job advertisements. *Mentoring & Tutoring: Partnership in Learning, 13*(1), 95–107. doi:10.1080/13611260500040443

Keeley, J. W., Ismail, E., & Buskist, W. (2016). Excellent teachers' perspectives on excellent teaching. *Teaching of Psychology, 43*(3), 175–179.

Kember, D., & McNaught, C. (2007). *Enhancing university teaching: Lessons from research into award winning teachers*. Routledge.

Kessels, L. T., Harris, P. R., Ruiter, R. A., & Klein, W. M. (2016). Attentional effects of self-affirmation in response to graphic antismoking images. *Health Psychology, 35*(8), 891. https://doi.org/10.1037/hea0000366

Khan, M. S., Lakha, F., Tan, M. M. J., Singh, S. R., Quek, R. Y. C., Han, E., Tan, S. M., Haldane, V., Gea-Sánchez, M., & Legido-Quigley, H. (2019). More talk than action: Gender and ethnic diversity in leading public health universities. *The Lancet, 393*(10171), 594–600. doi:10.1016/s0140-6736(18)32609-6

Kim, D., Wolf-Wendel, L., & Twombly, S. (2011). International faculty: Experiences of academic life and productivity in US universities. *The Journal of Higher Education, 82*(6), 720–747. https://doi.org/10.1080/00221546.2011.11777225

Knights, D., & Clarke, C. A. (2014). It's a bittersweet symphony, this life: Fragile academic selves and insecure identities at work. *Organization Studies, 35*(3), 335–357. https://doi.org/10.1177%2F0170840613508396

Kurantowicz, E., & Nizinska, A. (2013). How students "stay the course": Retention practices in higher education. *Studies in the Education of Adults, 45*(2), 135–147. doi:10.1080/02660830.2013.11661647

Lechuga, V. M., & Lechuga, D. C. (2012). Faculty motivation and scholarly work: Self-determination and self-regulation perspectives. *Journal of the Professoriate, 6*(2), 59–97. www.researchgate.net/publication/328889842

Leigland, S. (2005). Variables of which values are a function. *The Behavior Analyst, 28*(2), 133–142. doi:10.1007/BF03392109

Leslie, S. J., Cimpian, A., Meyer, M., & Freeland, E. (2015). Expectations of brilliance underlie gender distributions across academic disciplines. *Science, 347*(6219), 262–265. doi:10.1126/science.1261375

Lester, J., & Kezar, A. (2012). Faculty grassroots leadership: Making the invisible visible. *Journal of the Professoriate, 6*(2), 98–129.

Lewis, T. N. (2016). *Transgender student experience: Interactions with faculty and peers in the college classroom* (Unpublished doctoral dissertation). Texas A&M University.

Llorens, A., Tzovara, A., Bellier, L., Bhaya-Grossman, I., Bidet-Caulet, A., Chang, W. K., Cross, Z. R., Dominguez-Faus, R., Flinker, A., Fonken, Y., Gorenstein, M. A., Holdgraf, C., Hoy, C. W., Ivanova, M. V., Jimenez, R. T., Jun, S., Kam, J. W. Y., Kidd, C., Marcelle, E., & Marciano, D. (2021). Gender bias in academia: A lifetime problem that needs solutions. *Neuron, 109*(13), 2047–2074. doi:10.1016/j.neuron.2021.06.002

Louisiana Contextual Science Research Group (2022). Beyond checking: A behavior-analytic conceptualization of privilege as a manipulable aspect of context. *Behavior and Social Issues, 31*, 343–365. https://doi.org/10.1007/s42822-022-00091-5

Macoun, A., & Miller, D. (2014). Surviving (thriving) in academia: Feminist support networks and women ECRs. *Journal of Gender Studies, 23*(3), 287–301. https://doi.org/10.1080/09589236.2014.909718

Maglaughlin, K. L., & Sonnenwald, D. H. (2005). *Factors that impact interdisciplinary scientific research collaboration: Focus on the natural sciences in academia.* Proceedings of the 10th International Conference of the International Society for Scientometrics and Informetrics.

Mamiseishvili, K., & Rosser, V. J. (2011). Examining the relationship between faculty productivity and job satisfaction. *Journal of the Professoriate, 5*(2), 100–132.

Marina, B. L. H. (2015). *Mentoring away the glass ceiling in academia: A cultured critique*. Lexington Books.

McGee, R., & Keller, J. L. (2007). Identifying future scientists: Predicting persistence into research training. *Cell Biology Education, 6*(4), 316–331. doi:10.1187/cbe.07-04-0020

McGill, M. M., & Settle, A. (2012). Identifying effects of institutional resources and support on computing faculty research productivity, tenure, and promotion. *International Journal of Doctoral Studies, 7*, 167–198.

McKenzie, B. J. (2020). *Workplace experiences of transgender faculty at institutions of higher education* (Doctoral dissertation). Northcentral University.

McQueen, A., & Klein, W. M. (2006). Experimental manipulations of self-affirmation: A systematic review. *Self and Identity, 5*(4), 289–354. doi:10.1080/15298860600805325.

Meyer, I. H. (2003). Prejudice, social stress, and mental health in lesbian, gay, and bisexual populations: Conceptual issues and research evidence. *Psychological Bulletin, 129*, 674–697. doi:10.1037/0033-2909.129.5.674

Miner, K. N., January, S. C., Dray, K. K., & Carter-Sowell, A. R. (2019). Is it always this cold? Chilly interpersonal climates as a barrier to the well-being of early-career women faculty in STEM. *Equality, Diversity and Inclusion: An International Journal, 38*(2), 226–245. doi:10.1108/EDI-07-2018-0127

Minett-Smith, C., & Davis, C. L. (2019). Widening the discourse on team-teaching in higher education. *Teaching in Higher Education, 25*(5), 579–594. https://doi.org/10.1080/13562517.2019.1577814

Moore, C. L., Wang, N., Davis, D., Aref, F., Manyibe, E. O., Washington, A. L., Johnson, J., Eugene-Cross, K., Muhammad, K., & Quinn, J. (2015). Disability, health, independent living, and rehabilitation research leaders from traditionally underrepresented racial and ethnic populations: Career development and success factors. *Journal of Rehabilitation, 81*(1), 19.

Moosa, I. A. (2018). *Publish or perish: Perceived benefits versus unintended consequences*. Edward Elgar Publishing. doi:10.4337/9781786434937.00007

Nelson, S. K., Fuller, J. A., Choi, I., & Lyubomirsky, S. (2014). Beyond self-protection: Self-affirmation benefits hedonic and eudaimonic well-being. *Personality and Social Psychology Bulletin, 40*(8), 998–1011. doi:10.1177/0146167214533389

Neumann, Y., & Finaly-Neumann, E. (1990). The reward-support framework and faculty commitment to their university. *Research in Higher Education, 31*(1), 75–97. doi:10.1007/BF00992558

Nicoll, K., & Harrison, R. (2003). Constructing the good teacher in higher education: The discursive work of standards. *Studies in Continuing Education, 25*(1), 23–35. doi:10.1080/01580370309289

Nocco, M. A., Mcgill, B. M., Mackenzie, C. M., Tonietto, R. K., Dudney, J., Bletz, M. C., Young, T., & Kuebbing, S. E. (2021). Mentorship, equity, and research productivity: Lessons from a pandemic. *Biological Conservation, 255*, 108966. doi:10.1016/j.biocon.2021.108966

Padilla, A. M. (1994). Ethnic minority scholars, research, and mentoring: Current and future issues. *Educational Researcher, 23*(4), 24–27. doi:10.2307/1176259

Park, T. (2011). Do faculty members get what they deserve? A review of the literature surrounding the determinants of salary, promotion and tenure. *The Journal of the Professoriate, 6*(1), 28–47.

Pfeifer, H. L. (2016). How to be a good academic citizen: The role and importance of service in academia. *Journal of Criminal Justice Education, 27*(2), 238–254.

Pfund, C., Byars-Winston, A., Branchaw, J., Hurtado, S., & Eagan, K. (2016). Defining attributes and metrics of effective research mentoring relationships. *AIDS and Behavior, 20*(2), 238–248. doi:10.1007/s10461-016-1384-z

Phinney, J. S., Campos, C. M. T., Kallemeyn, D. M. P., & Kim, C. (2011). Processes and outcomes of a mentoring program for Latino college freshmen. *Journal of Social Issues, 67*(3), 599–621. doi:10.1111/j.1540-4560.2011.01716.x

Pitcher, E. (2017). *Being and becoming professionally other: Identities, voices, and experiences of U.S. trans* academics*. Peter Lang Inc.

Plumb, J. C., Stewart, I., Dahl, J., & Lundgren, T. (2009). In search of meaning: Values in modern clinical behavior analysis. *The Behavior Analyst, 32*(1), 85–103. doi:10.1007/BF03392177

Porterfield, J., & Kleiner, B. H. (2005). A new era: Women and leadership. *Equal Opportunities International, 24*(5/6), 49–56. https://doi.org/10.1108/02610150510788150

Rawat, S., & Meena, S. (2014). Publish or perish: Where are we heading? *Journal of Research in Medical Sciences: The Official Journal of Isfahan University of Medical Sciences, 19*(2), 87–89.

Retraction Watch. (2021). *Retraction watch: Tracking retractions as a window into the scientific process*. Retraction Watch. http://retractionwatch.com

Reybold, L. E., & Corda, K. W. (2011). Faculty identity and the "lesser role": Service to the academy. *Journal of the Professoriate, 5*(1), 121–148.

Rheingold, H. L. (1994). *The psychologist's guide to an academic career*. American Psychological Association.

Rhoades, G. (2019). Taking college teachers' working conditions seriously: Adjunct faculty and negotiating a labor-based conception of quality. *The Journal of Higher Education, 91*(3), 1–26. doi:10.1080/00221546.2019.1664196

Rich, T. (2015). A worthy asset: The adjunct faculty and the influences on their job satisfaction. *To Improve the Academy, 34*(1–2), 156–170. doi:10.1002/tia2.20010

Rich, T. (2016). Predatory publishing, open access, and the costs to academia. *PS: Political Science & Politics, 49*(2), 265–267. doi:10.1017/S1049096516000172

Riffle, R., Schneider, T., Hillard, A., Polander, E., Jackson, S., DesAutels, P., & Wheatly, M. (2013). A mixed methods study of gender, STEM department climate, and workplace outcomes. *Journal of Women and Minorities in Science and Engineering, 19*(3), 227–243. doi:10.1615/JWomenMinorScienEng.2013005743

Roberts, M. C., Brown, K. J., & Smith-Boydston, J. M. (2003). The scientific process and publishing research. In M. C. Roberts & S. I. Stephen (Eds.), *Handbook of research methods in clinical psychology* (pp. 31–51). Blackwell Publishing.

Robinson, C. S. (2018). Hiding in plain sight: Early career experiences of a non-binary, queer faculty member. *Women & Language, 41*(1), 110–127.

Rogers, C. R., & Skinner, B. F. (1956). Some issues concerning the control of human behavior. *Science, 124*(3231), 1057–1066. doi:10.1126/science.124.3231.1057

Rohan, M. J. (2000). A rose by any name? The values construct. *Personality and Social Psychology Review, 4*(3), 255–277. doi:10.1207/S15327957PSPR0403_4

Rokeach, M. (1973). *The nature of human values*. Free press.

Salandra, R., Salter, A., & Walker, J. T. (2021). Are academics willing to forgo citations to publish in high-status journals? Examining preferences for 4 and 4-rated journal publication among UK business and management academics. *British Journal of Management*. doi:10.1111/1467-8551.12510

Salles, A., Mueller, C. M., & Cohen, G. L. (2016). A values affirmation intervention to improve female residents' surgical performance. *Journal of Graduate Medical Education, 8*(3), 378.

Salmi, J. (2021). Impact of COVID-19 on higher education from an equity perspective. *International Higher Education, 105*, 5–6.

Saltmarsh, J., Giles Jr., D. E., O'Meara, K., Sandmann, L., Ward, E., & Buglione, S. M. (2009). Community engagement and institutional culture in higher education: An investigation of faculty reward policies at engaged campuses. In B. E. Moely, S. H. Billig, & B. A. Holland (Eds.), *Creating our identities in service-learning and community engagement* (pp. 3–29). IAP Information Age Publishing.

Sandoz, E. K., & Anderson, R. S. (2015). Building awareness, openness, and action: Values work in behavior therapy. *The Behavior Therapist, 38*(3), 60–69.

Schimanski, L. A., & Alperin, J. P. (2018). The evaluation of scholarship in academic promotion and tenure processes: Past, present, and future. *F1000Research*, 7(1605), 1–20. http://doi.org/10.12688/f1000research.16493.1

Schmeichel, B. J., & Vohs, K. (2009). Self-affirmation and self-control: Affirming core values counteracts ego depletion. *Journal of Personality and Social Psychology, 96*(4), 770. doi:10.1037/a0014635

Schumann, K. (2014). An affirmed self and a better apology: The effect of self-affirmation on transgressors' responses to victims. *Journal of Experimental Social Psychology, 54*, 89–96. doi:10.1016/j.jesp.2014.04.013

Seldin, P., Miller, J. E., & Seldin, C. A. (2010). *The teaching portfolio: A practical guide to improved performance and promotion/tenure decisions*. John Wiley & Sons.

Sheridan, L., Murdoch, N. H., & Harder, E. (2015). Assessing mentoring culture: Faculty and staff perceptions, gaps, and strengths. *Canadian Journal of Higher Education, 45*(4), 423–439.

Sherman, D. K. (2013). Self-affirmation: Understanding the effects. *Social and Personality Psychology Compass*, 7(11), 834–845. doi:10.1111/spc3.12072.

Sherman, D. K., & Cohen, G. L. (2006). The psychology of self-defense: Self-affirmation theory. *Advances in Experimental Social Psychology, 38*, 183–242. https://doi.org/10.1016/S0065-2601(06)38004-5

Siegel, D. P. (2019). Transgender experiences and transphobia in higher education. *Sociology Compass*. doi:10.1111/soc4.12734

Singh, S. N., Mishra, S., & Kim, D. (1998). related burnout among faculty in higher education. *Psychological Reports, 83*(2), 463–473. doi:10.2466/pr0.1998.83.2.463

Skinner, B. F. (1956). A case history in scientific method. *American Psychologist, 11*(5), 221–233. doi:10.1037/h0047662

Skinner, B. F. (1965). *Science and human behavior*. Simon and Schuster.

Skinner, B. F. (1968). *The technology of teaching*. Appleton-Century-Crofts.

Slaughter, S., & Rhoades, G. (2004). *Academic capitalism and the new economy: Markets, state, and higher education*. The Johns Hopkins University Press.

Smith, B. M., Villatte, J. L., Ong, C. W., Butcher, G., Twohig, M. P., Levin, M. E., & Hayes, S. C. (2019). The influence of a personal values intervention on cold pressor-induced distress tolerance. *Behavior Modification, 43*(5), 688–710. doi:10.1177/0145445518782402

Spade, D. (2010). Be professional. *Harvard Journal of Law & Gender, 33*, 71–84.

Spicer, J., Shimbo, D., Johnston, N., Harlapur, M., Purdie-Vaughns, V., Cook, J., Fu, J., Burg, M. M., & Wager, T. D. (2016). Prevention of stress-provoked endothelial injury by values affirmation: A proof of principle study. *Annals of Behavioral Medicine, 50*(3), 471–479. doi:10.1007/s12160-015-9756-6

Spurling, L. (2016). On different forms of 'publication anxiety.' *Psychodynamic Practice: Individuals, Groups and Organisations, 22*(4), 366–372. doi:10.1080/14753634.2016.1181919ndra

Stinson, D. A., Logel, C., Shepherd, S., & Zanna, M. P. (2011). Rewriting the self-fulfilling prophecy of social rejection: Self-affirmation improves relational security and social behavior up to 2 months later. *Psychological Science, 22*(9), 1145–1149. doi:10.1177/0956797611417725

Stout, P. A., Staiger, J., & Jennings, N. A. (2007). Affective stories: Understanding the lack of progress of women faculty. *NWSA Journal, 19*(3), 124–144. doi:10.1353/nwsa.2007.0050

Subbaraman, N. (2020). How #BlackInTheIvory put a spotlight on racism in academia. *Nature, 582*(7812), 327–328.

Tan, K. K. H., Treharne, G. J., Ellis, S. J., Schmidt, J. M., & Veale, J. F. (2019). Gender minority stress: A critical review. *Journal of Homosexuality*, 1–19. https://doi.org/10.1080/00918369.2019.1591789

Tippins, M. J. (2003). Implementing knowledge management in academia: Teaching the teachers. *International Journal of Educational Management, 17*(7). 339–345. https://doi.org/10.1108/09513540310501021

Toutkoushian, R. K., & Bellas, M. L. (1999). Faculty time allocations and research productivity: Gender, race and family effects. *The Review of Higher Education, 22*(4), 367–390. doi:10.1353/rhe.1999.0014

Turner, G. W., Pelts, M., & Thompson, M. (2018). Between the academy and queerness: Microaggressions in social work education. *Affilia, 33*(1), 98–111. doi:10.1177/0886109917729664

Van Tongeren, D. R., Green, J. D., Hulsey, T. L., Legare, C. H., Bromley, D. G., & Houtman, A. M. (2014). A meaning-based approach to humility: Relationship affirmation reduces worldview defense. *Journal of Psychology and Theology, 42*(1), 62–69. doi:10.1177/009164711404200107

Vargas, E. A., Brassel, S. T., Cortina, L. M., Settles, I. H., Johnson, T. R., & Jagsi, R. (2020). MedToo: A large-scale examination of the incidence and impact of sexual harassment of physicians and other faculty at an academic medical center. *Journal of Women's Health, 29*(1), 13–20. doi:10.1089/jwh.2019.7766

Veage, S., Ciarrochi, J., Deane, F. P., Andresen, R., Oades, L. G., & Crowe, T. P. (2014). Value congruence, importance and success and in the workplace: Links with well-being and burnout amongst mental health practitioners. *Journal of Contextual Behavioral Science, 3*(4), 258–264. doi:10.1016/j.jcbs.2014.06.004

Verniers, C., & Martinot, D. (2015). Characteristics expected in fields of higher education and gender stereotypical traits related to academic success: A mirror effect. *Social Psychology of Education, 18*(4), 719–733.

Vilardaga, R., Luoma, J. B., Hayes, S. C., Pistorello, J., Levin, M. E., Hildebrandt, M. J., Kohlenberg, B., Roget, N. A., & Bond, F. (2011). Burnout among the addiction counseling workforce: The differential roles of mindfulness and values-based processes and work-site factors. *Journal of Substance Abuse Treatment, 40*(4), 323–335. doi:10.1016/j.jsat.2010.11.015

Ward, K. (2003). Faculty service roles and the scholarship of engagement. *Higher Education Report, 29*(5), 1–188. http://files.eric.ed.gov/full text/ED476222.pdf.

Williamson, I. O., & Cable, D. M. (2003). Predicting early career research productivity: The case of management faculty. *Journal of Organizational Behavior: The International Journal of Industrial, Occupational and Organizational Psychology and Behavior, 24*(1), 25–44.

Wilson, K. G., & DuFrene, T. (2009). *Mindfulness for two: An acceptance and commitment therapy approach to mindfulness in psychotherapy*. New Harbinger Publications.

Winchester, H. P. M., & Browning, L. (2015). Gender equality in academia: A critical reflection. *Journal of Higher Education Policy and Management, 37*(3), 269–281. doi:10.1080/1360080X.2015.1034427

Wu, Z., Spreckelsen, T. F., & Cohen, G. L. (2021). A meta-analysis of the effect of values affirmation on academic achievement. *Journal of Social Issues*, 77(3), 702–750. doi:10.1111/josi.12415

Ylijoki, O. (2003). Entangled in academic capitalism? A case-study of changing ideals and practices of university research. *Higher Education, 45*, 307–335.

5 Mentoring Relationships

Finding a Mentor, Being Mentored, and Mentoring Others

Erin B. Rasmussen, Sierra Baca-Zeff, and Morgan Musquez

Introduction

One of the richest, most rewarding aspects of academic life is the opportunity and process of mentoring students in their research endeavors and professional development. There are fewer things more gratifying in one's career than watching graduate students develop and deepen the skills of independently conceptualizing and executing research, thinking critically, masterfully presenting information, and writing scientifically. Mentoring undergraduate research is also an enriching experience, as mentors get to see firsthand their students begin putting into practice what they learn in the classroom and the sparks of excitement that ignite as students assist in the conduct of scientific studies.

This chapter on mentoring was written by a senior research mentor in the latter part of her career and her two graduate students who, at the time of writing, are at the beginning of their third year in an experimental psychology doctoral program. We hope that sharing the perspective of a seasoned faculty member and two graduate students midway through their doctoral training provides a developmental perspective to mentoring. While this chapter was written mostly in the context of graduate research training, there are certainly bits of advice and information that also apply to mentoring undergraduate research. While we recognize there are many ways to mentor students in research, we provide our views of what has worked well in our research laboratory.

Some faculty members may envision their role with graduate training as *supervisory* only—that is, more focused on training, monitoring performance, and evaluating the trainee's work and providing feedback (Leblanc et al., 2020). These aspects of the job are foundational and critical for developing strong scientists. Others also envision themselves as *mentors*, in which they perform these functions of the job, but also view their role as an *opportunity to establish and cultivate meaningful and sustaining relationships* between mentor and mentee. It has been the experience of these authors and others (see Allen et al., 2004) that mentoring leads to better job satisfaction and a more gratifying experience for the mentor. Likewise, this experience is also more fulfilling for the mentee. In this chapter, we share the experiences in the development and cultivation of the mentoring relationship.

Selecting a Mentor and Selecting Mentees

While Esquierdo-Leal (see Chapter 1) describes the many considerations in selecting a graduate program, one factor that will be explicated here is finding a mentor. Indeed, the mentoring relationship begins with identifying a strong fit between mentor and mentee as the potential student searches for an appropriate graduate program. From the perspective of a student searching for a mentor for graduate training, there are a number of considerations,

DOI: 10.4324/9781003216773-7

from the larger and more broad concerns of academic interests to more personal concerns of personality and how mentors interact with their students. From an academic viewpoint, graduate students should select potential mentors who have similar research interests to their own with an established record of publishing and grant awards in that area. Mentors do not necessarily need to have *identical* interests to one's own, but if a potential mentor has interests in a vastly different area, it is unlikely that a student will have opportunities to explore their interests outside of the mentor's area. If there is a question of whether a potential mentor would be willing to explore a topic tangential to their area of study, it may be worth contacting them and having a conversation beforehand. We recommend an email, phone, or online video chat with potential mentors in general to discuss the extent to which research areas overlap and what required experiences the mentor expects before applying to a program.

The interview is another opportunity for information gathering. If a student's record looks satisfactory on paper, they may be invited for an interview to visit the university campus and meet the mentor in person (online interviews are also possible, though we have found they do not characterize a program or campus as well as an in-person interview). While mentors indeed are interviewing potential students, consider that students are also interviewing potential mentors. Students should look for a mentor to whom they believe they have a good interpersonal fit, which of course means different things to different students. Even though all students will value expertise and professionalism, some students may also value friendliness, patience, or a greater amount of communication than others. They may look for these signs as compatibility when having conversations with potential mentors. When talking to a potential mentor, it will likely be for a short period of time, whether in an in-person interview (e.g., a couple of hours across a couple of days), a video chat, or a short follow-up email. Given this limited amount of interaction, holding these hopes and expectations when interacting with the potential mentor may help with drawing attention to elements of the interview that are most important to the student.

While interviewing, it is also important to identify traits or "red flags" that would make the relationship difficult. For example, if a student values kindness and personability from a mentor and during the interview the mentor comes across as cold and keeps the topic purely on academics (e.g., testing their statistics knowledge) or redirects the conversation every time the student has a question about mentoring style, that may be a sign of a poor fit. That is not to say that the mentor is bad at mentoring, of course, but they may be more focused on supervising, as opposed to mentoring. As mentioned before, the interview process tends to be brief; so to better understand a person's mentoring style, it may also be beneficial to ask other graduate students their opinions of the mentor. Graduate students tend to be more honest in private spaces of what a mentor is like, which might allow potential students to make a more informed decision.

From the mentor's perspective, selecting students is an exciting endeavor. It goes without saying that academic and laboratory experiences and potential for success are factors that most mentors look for when selecting a student to join their lab. Often objective indicators such as GRE scores have traditionally been used to predict success in graduate programs, though research shows that GRE scores at best predict only a small amount of the variability in graduate-student success (e.g., Boles, 2018; Kuncel et al., 2001; Morrison & Morrison, 1995; Moneta-Koehler et al., 2017; Sealy et al., 2019). Moreover, underrepresented groups are less likely to be selected for graduate programs when only GRE and GPA are used for selection, as opposed to more holistic approaches (ETS, 2014; Kuncel et al., 2001; Miller & Stassun, 2014; Sampson & Boyer, 2001). It is not surprising that fewer schools are using GRE scores to evaluate admissions (Benderly, 2017). Grade point averages, another more objective measure, are also indicative of student success in college (i.e., high GPAs as undergraduates often predict high GPAs in graduate school), but sometimes do not necessarily reflect characteristics such as work ethic, perseverance, problem-solving ability, and subsequent success as a scientist (Benderly, 2017).

Student experience and expert opinion, by way of letters of recommendation, may better characterize the experience and potential a student may have (Benderly, 2017). Students who have laboratory experience that matches or complements the mentor's research program will allow for an easier transition into graduate school and earlier success in developing research projects than those without this experience. Moreover, a record of presentations at conferences and publications (though less likely for students coming from undergraduate programs) shows that a student has strong interests and some incoming skills in conducting and disseminating research. Using these indicators in addition to GPA and GRE scores represents a more holistic approach to selection and increases the odds that qualified members of underrepresented groups get selected.

As mentioned from the student perspective, interpersonal fit with the mentor and research team is also important. For example, if a mentor tries to create a collaborative tenor to their research team, a person whose personality characteristics are consistent is likely to keep the collaborative dynamic going. Even though it is not always possible to characterize someone's personality in a single interview, sometimes it is possible to detect who creates competition, or even tension, in the team dynamic. Having this information up front may prevent a potential problem in the future.

The Vertical Team Structure

Once a mentor has selected students, they may want to consider developing the structure of the research team. The organization of a research team varies from mentor to mentor. One strategy that we have employed with success is the "vertical team" approach, which ensures that each team member gains experience as both mentee and as mentor. Here, the team dynamic follows a ladder-like hierarchy with the mentor directing the overall direction of research (i.e., their program of research) from the top and each successive team member actively participating in both the mentee and mentor roles. The participation level for each role is determined by relative experience. For example, new team members may seek training in laboratory techniques from team members who most recently occupied the same role as a new team member (i.e., first-year graduate students seeking help from second- or third-year students). Second- and third-year students can also help provide guidance and advice from the student perspective on other aspects of research, such as first drafts of papers or posters for a conference before the drafts go to the mentor. Moreover, the more seasoned student's advice on "how to survive graduate school" is often a more relevant perspective than the mentor's view, though it is important for the mentor to provide their experienced views on this as well. A preprofessional student (i.e., a fourth- or fifth-year student) can provide guidance to second- or third-year students, such as how to prepare for a thesis defense, an oral presentation, or submit a grant proposal. They also serve more as a mentor as they near the end of their program training and become more independent. This approach also allows one to mentor the mentoring repertoire of a seasoned graduate student.

The vertical team approach has some benefits. First, this approach frees the faculty member to spend more time on higher-order tasks that keep their research program moving forward, such as mentoring the submission of scientific papers by their students, grant writing (which can be used for student graduate research assistantships and tuition), and preparing their students for public presentation of research at conferences or job or postdoctoral interviews. Being able to count on seasoned students to teach the specifics of data collection via an experimental protocol, for example, means more time devoted to the overarching aspects of keeping a program of research running. Faculty members have a great deal of pressure to publish research, seek funding, teach courses, and serve on committees within the university and professional community. Therefore, providing opportunities for experienced students to take on some of this workload may be beneficial. Two, this approach is not only helpful for the mentor but allows the mentees an opportunity to practice mentoring and teaching those in the lower "rungs" through sharing the knowledge and skills imparted to them from the more sophisticated team members. Though they likely are not aware at the time, these beginnings of mentoring will become a foundation on which they will build. A fourth- or fifth-year student, for example, will likely mentor undergraduate students on how to follow an experimental protocol for data collection for their dissertation, which will nicely translate to leading independent studies at a postdoctoral fellowship or their first academic position.

Another benefit of the vertical team approach is that team members learn to work with one another, which may decrease the possibility of competition, enhance interpersonal connections, enhance the skills of interacting with others in an academic environment (i.e., collaboration), and can be building blocks for lifelong friendships. When students rely on each other, a small community and lab culture can be built, not only reinforcing efficiency of work, but allowing others to rely on one another and creating a welcoming and collaborative space for team members.

There are also potential costs of the vertical team approach. First, a mentor must be willing to relinquish a portion of control over the mentee's learning process and place it in the hands of other team members. However, if a mentor has done an effective job of training those in the higher rungs, then that trust can be easy to place. Second, the vertical team approach may mean that newer students may have less contact with the mentor in the initial year(s), given much of their training (e.g., assisting with data collection on someone else's project) is mentored by more senior team members. It should be stated, however, that a mentor's involvement at *all* levels of a student's time in graduate school is still crucial. A mentor's contact with their more junior students can occur in a number of contexts besides the laboratory. One context is regular (e.g., weekly) research team meetings in which projects can be discussed, research troubleshooting can occur, data can be presented, and presentations can be practiced in a supportive environment. Importantly, this is also a place in which interpersonal connections among the team can be established, as it is likely one of the few times during which everyone will meet at one time.

Mentors should also meet individually with more junior mentees on a basis that is individualized to their needs. Some students may need more support than others, especially during the first year and it is important to recognize the differences so that time is not wasted or opportunities are not missed to provide assistance. More on the importance of these meetings will be discussed later in this chapter. And finally, less formal research team activities or parties with members of the entire group are also important in developing the interconnections of all members of the vertical team, including the mentor. Our research team has two to three lab parties per year hosted by Rasmussen and we also join for other activities, such as mud runs, hikes, river floats, and trips to the local amusement park.

When more seasoned team members mentor less seasoned members, oversight of this mentoring should still occur to some extent. The mentor should emphasize to the more senior student mentor the importance of giving clear instructions, reminding the seasoned mentee that new students do not yet have the experience that they now have, so taking their perspective is critical. Further, when more senior students teach more junior students, there tends to be information given on *what* to do, but not *why* it is done. The *why* can be just as important as the *what*, so senior students should consider inclusion of the rationale. Finally, large amounts of training can be overwhelming to a new mentee. Therefore, it is advisable for training, especially for large tasks like writing a thesis, to be given in smaller steps. This makes tasks easier for newer lab members to learn.

Characteristics of Effective Mentoring

In this section we describe our views of what we envision as the most important aspects of mentoring.

Professionalism: Respect, Equality, and Equity

Mentors should treat their mentees with respect and professionalism when giving opportunities, resources, and offering guidance and feedback. A starting point for this assumes that all mentees are treated equally; that is, regardless of gender identity, ethnicity, sexual orientation, able-bodiedness, and the like, students will receive equal treatment in terms of research opportunities and expectations. This, of course, helps mentees feel valued and treated fairly. However, even if mentors may feel like they are treating their students equally, it is important to verify this by more objectively examining potential personal biases (implicit or otherwise). One may do this by humbly asking students or colleagues if there are ways in which more respectful and equitable practices can be improved. Mentors can also create a "brave" environment in which students feel comfortable talking to their mentors about difficult topics, such as feeling devalued. This will be discussed later in the chapter.

A mentor's time and resources should be allocated equitably and fairly among their students. For example, consider two graduate students who are similar in ability, experience, and year in the program. If one person receives lab resources (e.g., a competitive graduate research assistantship salary and tuition package) one year, the other student should be prioritized to receive the resources the next time they are offered, if possible. There should also be a conversation with the student who did not receive the resources about how this decision was made ("the decision-making body saw the two of you as equal in merit and experience and we couldn't decide, so we flipped a coin") and what will happen later to adjust for this ("you will be prioritized for this type of funding next year"). Often the easy approach for an uncomfortable conversation such as this is for a mentor to say nothing when a student is given more than an equally deserving student. Students, in the absence of information, may try to fill in the blanks of situations in which they feel overlooked. It is best to not assume they understand. We encourage mentors in most instances to have those uncomfortable conversations. The fair allocation of resources is indeed a delicate balance, where fairness and clear communication is key.

Equal treatment does not necessarily mean equitable treatment. The reality is that graduate students vary in their abilities and relative experience. Some mentors select students to mentor who have extensive experience and therefore require less mentoring, for example, students who already have master's degrees or extensive undergraduate or graduate research experience. This is advantageous to freeing the mentor up to work on the products they need to keep their research program continuing (i.e., publications and grant applications). On the other hand, some mentors may be in situations in which they are more likely to attract students with less research experience (e.g., they're at institutions with less established graduate programs, or they're an early-career faculty member) and these types of students require relatively more mentoring. Most mentors likely have a mix of abilities in their beginning students, so it is important to assess what students need based on their previous experience and current abilities. For example, a student with a master's degree and published research will need less guidance on writing and running experiments, but perhaps more attention on collaboratively writing a research grant or preparations for postgraduation interviews. A less seasoned student may need more scaffolding with foundational skills, such as how to follow an established experimental protocol or execute the steps of a research technique. Some students do well with accepting an assignment and independently completing it. Others need regularly scheduled meetings in person such that they can review progress with their mentor on projects. As they gain experience, this scaffolding should become less frequent. Discussing the type and frequency of individualized instruction with the mentee can help clarify the expectations for each person. In addition, these conversations can also clarify long-term goals and expectations—not only for the mentor with respect to the mentee, but also the mentee's career and personal goals.

Individualized Constructive and Compassionate Feedback

Related to differences in student needs, the frequency and method of communication will be as diverse as any other need. Feedback is a necessary and consistent part of working within academia; indeed, there is nothing more useful than criticism to improve scholarship. As mentioned, frequency of feedback is one consideration, however, the *method* of relaying the feedback is also important.

Whenever possible, *compassionate feedback* is ideal. Compassionate feedback starts first with reminding oneself how it feels to receive hostile v. constructive feedback; most people are open and receptive to feedback that is constructive and corrective, as opposed to feedback that is hostile. Answering the question of "how would I respond best to this kind of feedback?" may help direct a mentor's approach. In addition, creating a context can also help with being compassionate in feedback. Consider an instance in which a mentee submits a manuscript draft for edits by their mentor. If this is a mentee's first draft, it is likely to require substantial revision and organizational change. Reminding them of the context of where they are in their writing career (i.e., at the beginning) and that they are going to experience a large learning curve with these early drafts is helpful for them in terms of what to expect for extensiveness of editorial feedback. One can also remind them on a moderately edited second or third draft, that the draft was a large improvement from the first draft, and acknowledge their use of the previous draft's feedback in getting them to this one. This not only helps the student's receptivity and understanding (e.g., the *why*) of another round of feedback, but also reminds the mentor that the student *is learning* from what they offer.

It is also important to remind students that scientific writing and speaking are lifelong skills to develop, and that expecting, accepting, and using feedback is part of learning and a part of the scientific process. In the Rasmussen lab, we always say "ink is love," meaning the more ink you see on your draft, the more your evaluator loves you and wants to see you improve as a writer (though now we might say "track changes is love"). Indeed, taking time to thoroughly review and edit a draft of a paper takes a substantial amount of time and cognitive energy, and can be viewed as an act of love. Part of this conversation can include the expectation that science is a corrective process and as such, we practice and cultivate the skills of humility, openness, and responsiveness to criticism.

Another component of compassionate feedback is to highlight the successes of the work that a mentee performs. Most of the feedback that graduate students receive is corrective, so recognition of what is done correctly is appreciated. This could be something as simple as praising a good point made in a lab meeting, a well-worded paragraph in a manuscript, or admitting a mistake (especially a big one) in the execution of an experimental protocol. It goes without saying that reaching milestones (defending a thesis, presenting at a conference, publishing a paper, getting a grant funded, winning a research award) should be shared and celebrated with the entire research team as well as the program, department, or other academic unit. These types of recognition allow the mentor to reward a small or large effort (i.e., perseverance) on the part of the student, showing that their hard work has payoffs. These recognitions may also reinforce behavioral aspects of good science, and strengthen bonds between mentor and mentee.

Mentors can also effectively communicate and strengthen a mentee's scientific writing by focusing on the content of the work rather than making assumptions or implications about the mentee's abilities (e.g., the *writing* could be improved by adding more examples of <content term> v. the *writer* is incompetent for leaving examples out). Overall, feedback should be specific and proactive in terms of how to improve rather than simply pointing out failures and expecting the necessary changes to be obvious. By incorporating the former, mentees will be given the opportunity and motivation to learn from mistakes and make proper changes to grow in their field.

Finally, because effective mentoring of students takes time, thought, and consideration, it is also important for a mentor to know limits in terms of their ideal graduate-student load. Mentoring too many students at once will spread the mentor too thin among their students, making a less satisfying experience for the students and an overworked faculty member. Too few students can allow for more high-quality mentoring, but the research program of the faculty member will not be as productive. For example, for Rasmussen, the ideal load is four graduate students. However, that load will also depend on the relative experience of each student. If she has four graduate students who have come in with less laboratory and writing experience, they will likely need more scaffolding, so taking a fifth student may stretch her beyond her capacity to give high-quality instruction. If, however, three mentees have extensive laboratory and writing experience and one is less experienced, taking a more experienced fifth student might be reasonable. In this example, the nature of the vertical team is not lost. It only works when there is an array of abilities and levels.

Appropriate Power Differentials

Regardless of mentoring style, there is no circumventing the fact that there are power differentials between mentors and mentees; that is, the relationship between the mentor and the mentee has a clear hierarchy. One individual has the degree and years of experience while the other was specifically selected to learn from them. While not inherently negative, power differentials are something to be aware of within the mentoring relationship. Having this power dynamic allows a clear chain of response when help is needed. It creates an essence of professionalism and allows the vertical team to be maintained. The mentor provides training and the oversight of a high-functioning team and, when needed, can pinpoint when the team or a task is not running efficiently and can suggest alternatives of how to move forward. Therefore, power differentials have a clear function.

There are different types of power differentials that exist on teams. On one extreme, unhealthy power differentials exist, for example, those that lead to exploitation of the mentee, such as severe overwork or sexual harassment. These types of problems can have negative outcomes for mentees and require alleviation and may require the assistance of a department chair, dean, or human resources director to solve. On the other hand, there are situations in which very little to no power differential exists and mentees are treated as friends, as opposed to trainees. This makes it difficult for a mentor to train and give the necessary feedback to a mentee, and may also be challenging in terms of running a research team.

Most power differentials are somewhere in the middle of these two extremes—that is, there is a clear hierarchy, but it functions to create an effective team. One such example is the "junior-colleague" model, in which the mentee is viewed as a colleague in training. It begins with eschewing titles and using first names in interactions. The foundation is the promotion of open communication and respect between mentor and mentee and among all members of the team. Input and ideas from mentees are actively sought and encouraged through respectful interactions that shape the appropriate behaviors of a scientist, but do not discourage inquiry. Team members are also escorted into professional networks by ensuring dissemination of their work and being introduced to professionals and included in professional conversations, e.g., networking conversations at conferences. The junior-colleague model not only allows the mentee to feel valued as a contributing member to the discipline, but it will ease their transition into the professional world.

The junior-colleague model also helps with the more subtle problems surrounding power differentials that include the fear of speaking up when something goes wrong, or having difficult conversations, such as those surrounding a research error, communication misunderstandings, or life struggles that may influence a mentee's work. When a junior colleague feels more comfortable speaking to their mentor about these types of issues, it can reduce tension and conflict in relationships between mentor and mentee (in addition to establishing lower power differentials, a mentor can help create these conditions by practicing effective communication and compassionate feedback, all discussed in this chapter). From the mentee's side, practicing *brave behavior*, that is verbal behavior, in which one feels uncomfortable to approach the mentor about a topic, but does so in spite of the discomfort, should be part of the repertoire. Mentors should reinforce brave behavior, even if the outcome of the conversation is not in line with mentee's expectations (e.g., "I know it took a lot of courage to ask me if you could remove one of the conditions from your study. I'm glad you feel comfortable talking to me about this. But given that we want a publishable study, it would not be in your best long-term interests to do that. Let's brainstorm if there are other ways we can reduce the time it takes to complete your study."). Indeed, if the relationship is functioning as it should, the mentee should feel comfortable approaching the mentor with all questions relating to research, professional development, and seeking support when needed.

Opportunities, Growth Mindset, and the Building of Frustration Tolerance

Like many apprenticeships, mentees enter the academic environment with a goal in mind: often graduation and/or specific career aspirations. However, there are many milestones to reach before achieving this goal, each testing students' abilities along the way. Some will be more challenging than others, e.g., thesis defenses or comprehensive exams. Students may sometimes feel ill prepared or overwhelmed for these milestones, especially because they are novel to them and have high stakes. From the mentor's standpoint, however, the mentee is often viewed as ready for these challenges, as they have the prerequisite skills in place. Therefore, the mentee must work through the discomfort of their own expectations and trust those of the mentee. They must "learn to be comfortable with being uncomfortable," as this is a necessary step for every new scientist. Instead of avoiding situations that cause this discomfort, mentees can learn to accept and tolerate their own discomfort (i.e., frustration tolerance) as they work through the development of new skills and milestones.

Growth mindset (see Dweck, 2007) and frustration tolerance go hand in hand. Growth mindset, taken from the field of psychology and applied to education, refers to essentially training students to thrive on challenge. Errors and failure are viewed not as evidence of ineptness, but as an opportunity for correction, growth, and for expanding our existing abilities. Fixed mindset, conversely, assumes that abilities are perceived as overall unchanging. Because a standard is already set, people either seek to succeed at what they already do and if they stretch beyond that and fail, they stop trying to change and grow. In other words, with a fixed mindset, opportunities for growth are avoided and it is this avoidance that keeps people from taking risks and expanding their repertoire. Growth mindset can be incredibly valuable in that a challenging situation can be reframed as one that is an opportunity to learn. Almost any challenge can be broken down into smaller steps and specific behaviors. Consider the example of students who may enter academic programs without a strong background in statistics. When it comes to running analyses, they may encounter frustrating barriers. Through changing a verbalization to oneself such as, "I don't know how to do this" to "I don't know how to do this *yet*, but I do know where to go for help and I will utilize these resources," and then following through, allows growth to take place, as compared to the behavior of giving up or avoidance. Others have identified the effectiveness of this method. The Think Aloud Pair Problem Solving (Whimbley et al., 2013) and Talk Aloud Problem Solving (Robbins, 2011) identify this as "keeping a positive attitude" and suggest such statements are a part of that important characteristic of a good problem solver and thus good scientist.

Frustration tolerance, also relevant to challenges, refers to an acceptance of the emotion toward what seems a challenging or insurmountable condition, as opposed to an escape or avoidance response, and is a necessary skill in the academic world (Meindl et al., 2019; Shi et al., 2021). For example, consider a common situation in experimental programs in which mentees are asked to program code for an upcoming project. Although students may have minimal coding experience, a mentor can give them the tools (e.g., a manual or access to a class) to learn this rather large and at times frustrating challenge. Being taught to expect and label such emotions when they occur, and to take short breaks when needed, but to return to the task later, helps build an insensitivity or tolerance to frustration, such that the individual feels less affected by setbacks, failures, feedback, or the instances in which part of a project must be redone. Given that mistakes are a part of learning and students are learning constantly, mistakes will be expected and emotions to those can be accepted as part of the process. When the process is complete, the student feels a tremendous sense of accomplishment and ownership in what they have done.

Mentors may also shape frustration tolerance by providing more support, especially when the student is more junior. This may occur through offering resources, conducting check-ins and one-on-one chats, and then eventually allowing the student to complete tasks more independently as they progress through the program. However, as students become more independent, they may make more mistakes. As part of this, patience and support is needed. When mistakes happen, students are likely to feel bad about them, whether it be due to questioning their own abilities or feeling as though they have let the team down. It helps to provide a realistic view of how impactful the mistake is (often it is small in the grand scheme of things). Reminding the student how far they have come in the program and letting them know if they are on the right track helps reinforce their efforts.

Finally, it is important to also mention that sometimes the weight of learning some of these more challenging tasks can be compounded by other difficulties a student may be suffering, such as a personal loss. Some of these life events may require additional support than what the mentor may provide. In instances like this, normalizing the seeking of psychological support should be practiced and having some referrals of trusted counselors or psychologists on hand, especially those for students, may assist a student.

Communication

Communication about expectations and execution of tasks is an essential practice for effectively running a research team and for mentoring students. Without clear communication, confusion ensues and mistakes are made, creating conflict and disappointment. Rasmussen begins every academic year with a list of general expectations she has of her graduate and undergraduate students (see Appendix); note that the list also contains what students can expect of her (she also often gives this to potential students when they interview for graduate school, as well, so they get an idea of the type of mentoring she does). Note that the list contains not only academically related expectations, but also those related to professional and interpersonal conduct. Beginning the academic year in this manner gets everyone on the same page in terms of what is expected and sets the tone for the year. It also allows Rasmussen to explain why these expectations are in place, rather than just stating them.

It is also important to remember that when an assignment or task is communicated, the mentee may not understand exactly what has been stated. As mentors, recall that the less experienced student may not yet have learned certain scientific terms or jargon. For example, if a mentor directs a newer student with a comment like "You should look into <some topic>," it may not be clear to the student that what the mentor means is to ask a more seasoned student about the issue or perhaps to conduct a literature search. Clearer instruction might be to "ask Luis to provide you with the protocol for how to obtain participant consent," or, "if you conduct a literature search on <content>, that might be a good first step. What databases are you familiar with and which keywords do you think would be useful to your search?" Asking a probing question like this helps the mentor get a feel for where the student is skill-wise for literature searches, for example, and then additional guidance can be given if necessary. Being clear about the steps needed to do something is important to a less experienced student.

On the student's end, particularly if they are more junior, asking clarifying questions is important. Mentors do not expect you to know everything. They may forget what you do and do not know, especially when they see a pattern of competence and success. Stating, "I am unsure which resources you would like me to consult when you ask me to look into that. Can you please give me a little more direction?" will likely lead to a mentor apologizing for forgetting that the mentee is only a first-year student, for example, and happily filling in the details. It is also important for the student to record in some way (i.e., writing it down or typing on a laptop) what the mentor says for a detailed task. It can be time consuming and therefore frustrating for mentors to repeat themselves with the same information, especially when a mentee makes no attempt to record it the first time.

Styles of communication, and preferences for those styles, vary among mentors and among mentees. For instance, when talking with a mentor, some students may have a tendency to overshare their life experiences, while others prefer to stay more private. Even though it may seem unnecessary to some mentors, the student who overshares may do so as a way of informing their mentor of life events that may impact their work and mental health, which may influence their productivity. When the individual listening does not understand this and punishes this behavior (e.g., stating, "I don't need to hear the details of your personal life"), the student may be left confused and stop sharing, which may decrease their overall communication with the mentor. Instead, when instances like this happen, it is important to try to understand the function of the behavior and shape accordingly, e.g., reinforce the overall reporting of an important life event by stating something like, "it sounds like you have a heavy emotional load right now. What can I do to support you while you work through this? Do you need an extension on a project, for example?" Of course, as a mentor, it is possible to shape this behavior and reinforce what may be the essential pieces of these conversations, such as project check-ins and overall emotional well-being of students, as opposed to details that may be more appropriate for a therapist or counselor, for example. As mentioned previously, it can be helpful to have a list of referrals on hand for students (e.g., physicians, student counseling services, etc.), so they can get the appropriate support they may need.

E-Communications

Electronic communications (email, instant messaging, texting, etc.) have transformed the amount of communication that can be had effectively and in a brief amount of time and effort without requiring an in-person meeting. Mentors and mentees can check in with one another daily (if necessary) on small matters or details of a task or project, and very little time is taken. It is important to note, however, that there are nuances when communicating electronically. Without in-person interaction, it is more difficult to pick up on tone, facial expressions, and other nonverbal communication aspects that affect overall communication. Therefore, communication difficulties may arise, particularly for newer students who are not yet familiar with their mentor's communication style. For these students, electronic-based feedback may not provide a clear blueprint for the student to move forward on a project, for example. It is also possible for the student to misinterpret the feedback or not realize if a mistake was made, and therefore move forward in a way that does not address the issue. When these discrepancies happen repeatedly, or over an extended period of time, it may lead to escalation of strong emotions, creating tension in the relationship. In these instances, it may be best to opt for meeting in person to clarify the problems and work through the conflict. Regular in-person meetings can also prevent the problems that online communication may bring with students who require more structure and feedback. One other potential side effect of e-communications is that their use may blur the line between work-life balance by setting up expectations of when responses to emails should happen. Often individuals expect an immediate e-mail response, so if an email is sent after 5:00 p.m. or on the weekends, and a clear boundary for a mentor is that those are hours meant for their family, that barrier needs to be explained and consistently practiced by the mentor. More on this topic can be found in Donlin-Washington & Helvey (see Chapter 15).

Research Meetings

Mentors should communicate with team members one-on-one, and they must communicate to the group. No matter the team dynamic, there will always be a need for the mentor to step in and provide instruction and feedback both on an individual basis and to the entire research team. An easy and effective way to promote this cohesion is through regular, in-person meetings. This may be a time to discuss progress, roadblocks, and next steps in a way that is transparent to all team members. These group meetings allow for communication to be done all at once, as opposed to many individual meetings that may not only be time consuming, but may actually cause more communication errors as information is passed secondhand from one team member to another. The lab meeting allows everyone to be on the same page, to ask questions, and clarify information. Lab meetings also allow for professional behavior, such as the practice of presentations for a conference, discussion of data, and discussion and critique of research articles, to be shaped and modeled.

Admitting Mistakes

Despite experience, the best of communication efforts, or one's place within the team, mistakes happen and are inevitable. How one handles mistakes is important for any relationship, including that between mentor and mentee. A mentor who can admit they made a mistake models honesty and vulnerability (see Chapter 20 of this volume) for mentees and cultivates trust in the relationship. Practicing honesty and humility as a mentor also makes it easier for mentees to imitate these skills. Additionally, mentors who are "life-long learners"—a form of admitting errors—better prepare mentees in the field as they are able to embrace new knowledge that advances or contradicts old knowledge. In the Rasmussen lab, we refer to admitting mistakes as a willingness to "fall on one's sword." To do this, there is ownership for the mistake, a sincere apology, and the individual amends the situation to the best of their ability. When a mistake is ignored, defensiveness occurs, or when dishonesty is used to cover up a mistake, tension in the team may be heightened, and trust and confidence may erode.

Some conflicts and mistakes take place within the working environment. Perhaps a team member misunderstands a task and completes it in a way that is incorrect or not useful to the rest of the team, resulting in someone needing to redo the task. Although discouraging, these mistakes tend to have a clear path for amends. The individual might apologize, recomplete the task after learning what is expected instead, and ask more specific questions in the future to avoid repeating the same mistake. However, interpersonal mistakes with other team members may have a less clear path for making amends. For example, if a team member is a member of another group (e.g., a person of color or sexual minority) and something insensitive or hurtful is said to them, an apology may not completely alleviate the problem. After a sincere apology is issued, it is the role of the person who made the comment to not only learn why that comment is inappropriate and what might be said instead, but to address biases that may influence similar statements in the future. When faced with these situations, some individuals may become defensive, as it often feels like an attack on one's character. However, it is important to note that the person who informs someone of hurtful statements often does so out of respect for the individual and as an effort to continue the relationship. Mistakes and their subsequent apologies, whether academic or personal, are essential for team functioning. Not only does it provide a foundation for learning and productivity in working environments, but it allows individuals to be more aware of others' experiences and to build stronger relationships. Working through a mistake can strengthen team dynamics by promoting trust that there is room for mistakes and forgiveness.

Balancing Professional and Interpersonal Roles

The role of a mentor in communicating can be a delicate balance between professionalism and interpersonal connection. Not only do mentors provide structure and information for their mentees, but often it is important for them to know more about the mentee to build a relationship with them. In other words, a mentorship completely founded in professionalism may be interpreted as cold, while one completely founded in interpersonal connection may inhibit the mentee's growth as a professional. While a fuller characterization of the many roles mentors may provide is explored in Chapter 6, we provide a few thoughts here.

In a perfect world, keeping the relationship strictly professional is ideal as to not blur potential boundaries within the relationship. Unfortunately, life events beyond one's control happen for which strict professionalism is ill equipped to address the needs of the mentee. These events may include, but are not limited to: a family tragedy, personal insecurities related to one's field (e.g., imposter syndrome), socioeconomic stress (e.g., paying for rent, health costs/concerns, etc.), or simply being overwhelmed. Academia is challenging. These are all instances in which allowing for interpersonal connection through compassion is needed for the emotional, physical, and educational well-being of the mentee. However, boundaries must be clean enough to avoid problems like oversharing inappropriate information or building a relationship that blurs the dynamic of mentor and mentee, which can complicate the mentor's ability to perform their professional role.

When comments are made that may blur these boundaries, it is a mentor's job to "reel in" the conversation in individual or group settings to focus more on work-related activities, allowing mentees to share information but only responding to what is appropriate in that instance (e.g., it is often not relevant to know about someone's sex life or recreational drug use, especially if it makes others uncomfortable). If the oversharing continues, having a one-on-one talk with the individual to more directly address content would be appropriate. Mentors may be friendly, but they are not their mentees' friend during the graduate school context (though, this relationship may change after graduation). It is important to remember that the goal of the program is not to build friendships, but to instead build the knowledge and skills needed to not only earn a degree and gain employment, but also to learn about the other aspects of science not tied to these goals (such as critical thinking). There are exceptions to this general role, however. We encourage readers to consult Peterson et al. (see Chapter 6) for more information and further discussion of this topic.

On some occasions, a mentor may be the one who overshares or influences a relationship beyond what is professional and appropriate, to a point that makes the mentee uncomfortable. One strategy for dealing with this as a mentee is to diplomatically, but abruptly, leave the conversation when it happens. Hopefully, this may send the message to the mentor that the topic caused discomfort. But what happens if oversharing persists? Given the difference in the power dynamic, it may be difficult for the mentee to "reel in" the conversation or confront the mentor about the inappropriate dynamics of the relationship. However, it is important that the mentee realize the responsibility rests also on them to address the expectations (e.g., professionalism, guidance, etc.) they have for the mentor. From the mentee's side, practicing this brave behavior should be part of the repertoire. This may be an in-person conversation. For others, it may be an email (we suggest the former, as email communications, especially those with more difficult topics, may contain a tone that is unintended). Starting the conversation by stating, "I have something to talk to you about, but it is a difficult topic for me because . . ." is a good lead-in.

Talking one-on-one with the mentor may be intimidating, but we recommend it as a good strategy to reduce triangulation. Just as it would be unfair for the mentor to talk about the mentee's shortcomings with others before addressing those concerns with the mentee, the same logic applies for the mentor. We are all human and should be given the opportunity to correct our errors. However, if the issue continues after the conversation, the mentee may need to contact an outside resource such as the department chair, dean, or the human resources department.

Creating a Collaborative Environment

Research teams differ in their interpersonal dynamics for collaboration and competition. One type of environment may not necessarily be better overall than another, yet it is important for a student to know in which type of environment they will thrive. Some laboratories will be more competitive, while others are more collaborative. On one end of the continuum, competitive settings tend to be those in which opportunities are awarded to the most meritorious or those in which resources in a lab, such as paid positions, or other forms of funding are scarcer. While competitive labs may breed productivity because students may vie for these resources with one another, they may also promote a higher-stress environment and feelings of unfairness among the team.

In a collaborative environment, all team members are recognized as unique with diverse experiences, knowledge, and skill sets that are appreciated and valued. Moreover, their continued development and sharing of their skills is acknowledged and rewarded by the mentor. Because of this, competition for superiority is lessened. Some team members will have better fits for specific projects based on their own experiences and skill sets over others, but there are opportunities for everyone. A collaborative environment encourages the symbiotic sharing of these skills on projects. For example, if one student is highly statistically skilled, while another person is excellent at experimental design, placing these two individuals together on a project in which they can teach the other their area of excellence not only fosters collaboration and provides an opportunity to learn from someone else, it also teaches the values of humility and openness, which are important to the scientific process (Neuringer, 1991).

In a collaborative environment, the mentor can establish the expectation that each team member should be valued and encouraged to help others. It is not uncommon in these environments that team members are welcome to contribute to a manuscript or poster presentation or that resources are shared such that if one person receives a low-probability (i.e., competitive) opportunity for financial resources (a higher salary graduate research assistantship) one time, another team member will receive a similar opportunity the next time.

Even though the collaborative environment is ideal for some, it is not always easy to achieve. Resources are often limited and are not always guaranteed in graduate programs, as state, federal, and local funding circumstances can change without notice. If grants or paid positions are not plentiful and decisions are not made by the mentor (i.e., made by the program, department, or college) and team members do not know when opportunities will be offered again, a more competitive environment may form. In these situations, other forms of collaboration should be reinforced as much as possible and honest conversations about the amount of control the mentor has over these decisions should happen. At the interview stage, it can be beneficial to query faculty and students in graduate programs about funding and other opportunities, but also the type of environment of the program (i.e., level of collaboration v. competitiveness) and particularly the climate of the lab to make sure the environment is one that is compatible with the student. More on creating cooperative and collaborative environments can be found by Dillenburger (see Chapter 21).

Balancing Graduate School With Nonacademic Alternative Reinforcers

Graduate school is challenging in that mentees are expected to balance their program requirements, conduct and disseminate research, complete assistantships and internships, and even participate in leadership and service. This hefty load does not leave much time for developing other parts of life, such as hobbies and cultivation of relationships outside of the graduate school context. Nonetheless, these are important parts of life for which mentees should make time (see Chapters 10 and 14 for more on these issues). Importantly, mentors should not only remind their students of the balance of academic with nonacademic life, but also model it personally.

First, foundational aspects of good mental and physical health should be prioritized. Sleep, healthy eating, and exercise have long been recognized as essential (Breslow & Enstrom, 1980; Rippe, 2018). Stress-relieving activities, such as meditation, team sport participation, outdoor activities, or nonacademic group activities (e.g., painting, book groups, etc.) should be prioritized. Scheduling time for these activities can be done and should be practiced (see Chapter 14). From an alternative reinforcement perspective, nonacademic hobbies in graduate school will also help on days that are particularly challenging or difficult. Having other sources of reinforcement will ease the blows of challenges that all students face. Mentors should also normalize (as opposed to stigmatize) the process of help-seeking (e.g., when a student may be in crisis or suffer a life event) by talking about this behavior as just one more way to take care of foundational needs.

Establishing and prioritizing the development of meaningful relationships is also important. Developing an intimate relationship in graduate school or as an academic can also be exciting and add balance to life, while also being a large source of reinforcement outside of the duties of the department (see Chapter 10). Sometimes students enter a graduate program with a partner or spouse. This relationship can serve as a source of support; however, graduate students often feel spread thin with the expectations of the program and finding time to give their loved one. It is not surprising that rates of divorce and break-ups in graduate school are high (Wedemeyer-Strombel, 2018) (see Chapter 22). Having honest conversations about the challenges of graduate school and work with one's partner may assist in the balance. Making sure to allocate time for them may help with keeping these important relationships a priority.

Some graduate students are parents. Historically, academia has been a male-dominated field, and female representation has been low (Parker, 2015). Little attention was paid to the dual role of academic and parent, particularly because male academics who were parents had wives and partners at home to raise children. More recently, the dynamic is much different. Women now earn over half of the PhDs that are awarded (and 60% of the master's degrees), and therefore are more likely to enter into academia (Council of Graduate Schools, 2020). Many of them choose to have children. Moreover, all genders now play a role in parenting; it is not only for women. Therefore, changing the landscape to be more supportive of parenthood in the academic environment is important.

This change can start at the level of graduate interview. Many women with children have been instructed to not disclose this status on interviews for programs, as it may impact the way in which a mentor will see your dedication. Some mentors have historically discounted the contributions of graduate students with children because they are wrongly perceived to be not fully committed to a graduate program (Verniers & Vala, 2018). This kind of rhetoric is harmful and places women in a situation in which they feel they need to hide the fact that they are mothers. Parenthood does not need to be part of the discussion of a graduate school interview necessarily; however, if a potential student feels safe enough to disclose this information during the interview and is devalued for this (e.g., acceptance is withheld, which is also illegal), an honest examination of this issue at the individual, program, and departmental level is required.

The process of change continues with what types of comments are made to students, in particular women, about having children. Rasmussen remembers a moment at a conference when she was pregnant with her first child; she was an assistant professor at the time. A female colleague stated to her "well, you can kiss your career goodbye." It was hurtful and it was untrue. When Rasmussen considered the female former presidents of this same organization, a number of them came to mind who had children (for example, Dr. Linda Hayes, Dr. Beth Sulzer-Azaroff—see also Chapters 10 and 23). These types of caustic comments can be stated by mentors to students also. The notion that one cannot be successful both as an academic and as a mother—that you have to choose between the two—is untrue and harms the choices for a student. Instead, create spaces to have discussions about the balance of career and the choice to have children with the underlying assumption being there is no one path for all individuals.

Mentors, especially those with children, can also model the "having it all" with their students. It is okay and even beneficial for a mentor to talk about their children, and the manner by which they balance the duties of an academic with those of a parent. Part of this conversation should be that one should not sacrifice their own mental health in the process of this balance; learning to establish healthy boundaries and prioritizing some opportunities over others (i.e., saying no) should be an ongoing conversation. It is important also to model these boundaries to students so that they feel they can and should prioritize their children. Rasmussen's students know, for example, that on the weekends and after 5:00 on weekdays, this is sacred time with her family and academic issues must wait.

From the mentee's perspective, setting boundaries with oneself as a parent is also important. Sometimes the desire to "have it all" translates into "I must do it all" and an overwhelming amount of work is taken on. It is important to remember that when a mentor offers new opportunities (e.g., a new project) it is possible to say no. Like any student, it is important to recognize one's limits in order to avoid burnout. It is not a sign of weakness to decline an opportunity, rather it is a sign of maturity to identify one's capabilities. Hence, there may be a need for increased communication between mentor and mentee when the mentee is a parent. Regardless of position, children are a priority and when working within a system that did not historically account for this, mothers are deserving of a voice to therefore balance both school and children. Being able to have open, honest conversations about expectations, challenges, and problem solving about the balance of academic work and children is important.

Providing mentees who have children with flexibility and opportunities is crucial to their feeling like a valued team member. However, another observation that should not be overlooked is ensuring that mentees *without* children are also fairly treated. With equity being the overarching goal, it would not make sense to promote balanced workload expectations from team members with children, but not for those team members without children. For example, imagine a scenario in which one team member has a child and another does not and both need individual access to the lab. Just as it would be unreasonable to schedule the team member with children to only have access to the lab during the evenings or weekends, it would be equally unfair to have this expectation for the team member without children. In these instances, an open dialogue between both students and a *quid pro quo* arrangement ("if I do this for you, can you help me with something else . . . ?") may assuage both parties and make the parenting graduate student feel less like they are burdening another student.

Summary and Conclusions

In this chapter, we discussed how to select a mentor (for students) and mentee (for faculty members) and provided a description of an organizational strategy that has been beneficial to our research team—the vertical team approach. In addition, we discussed our views of the most critical elements of mentoring, which include professionalism, compassionate feedback, appropriate power differentials, and effective communication. Additionally, we talked about the importance of development of a growth mindset and of frustration tolerance, effective communication, the elements of collaborative environments, and balancing graduate school with nonacademic alternative reinforcers. Even though this may not be an exhaustive list of topics within the mentor-mentee relationship, we believe these topics hold great value and provide a foundation for healthy mentoring relationships to be built within the academic environment. As discussed throughout the chapter, each of these topics are complex. Mentors and mentees are likely to have come from different academic and sociocultural backgrounds and may have different communication styles. While there are many paths and facets of effective mentoring, and this is certainly not an exhaustive list, we feel that the key features of a successful mentor-mentee relationship are respect for individual differences and the promotion of effective communication.

References

Allen, T. D., Eby, L. T., Poteet, M. L., Lentz, E., & Lima, L. (2004). Career benefits associated with mentoring for proteges: A meta-analysis. *Journal of Applied Psychology*, *89*(1), 127–136. https://doi.org/10.1037/0021-9010.89.1.127

Benderly, B. L. (2017). GREs don't predict grad school success. What does? *Science*, *373*. www.sciencemag.org/careers/2017/06/gres-dont-predict-grad-school-success-what-does

Boles, L. (2018). Predicting graduate school success in a speech-language pathology program. *Teaching and Learning in Communication Sciences & Disorders*, *2*(2). https://doi:10.30707/tlcsd2.2boles

Breslow, L., & Enstrom, J. E. (1980). Persistence of health habits and their relationship to mortality. *Preventive Medicine*, *9*, 469–483. https://doi.org/10.1016/0091-7435(80)90042-0

Council of Graduate Schools. (2020). *Graduate enrollment and degrees 2009 to 2019*. https://cgsnet.org/ckfinder/userfiles/files/CGS_GED19_Report_final2.pdf

Dweck, C. S. (2007). *Mindset: The new psychology of success*. Ballentine.

Educational Testing System. (2014). *A snapshot of the individuals who took the GRE revised general test*. Retrieved June 25, 2018, from www.ets.org/s/gre/pdf/snapshot_test_taker_data_2014.pdf

Kuncel, N. R., Ones, D. S., & Hezlett, S. A. (2001). A comprehensive meta-analysis of the predictive validity of the graduate record examinations: Implications for graduate student selection and performance. *Psychological Bulletin, 127*, 162–181. https://doi.org/10.1037/0033-2909.127.1.162

Leblanc, L. A., Sellars, T. P., & Ala'i, S. (2020). *Building and sustaining meaningful and effective relationships as a supervisor and mentor.* Sloan.

Meindl, P., Yu, A., Galla, B. M., Quirk, A., Haeck, C., Goyer, J. P., Lejuez, C. W., D'Mello, S. K., & Duckworth, A. L. (2019). A brief behavioral measure of frustration tolerance predicts academic achievement immediately and two years later. *Emotion, 19*(6), 1081–1092. https://doi.org/10.1037/emo0000492

Miller, C., & Stassun, K. (2014). A test that fails. *Nature, 510*, 303–304. https://doi.org/10.1038/nj7504-303a

Moneta-Koehler, L., Brown, A. M., Petrie, K. A., Evans, B. J., & Chalkley, R. (2017). The limitations of the GRE in predicting success in biomedical graduate school. *PLoS One, 12*, e0166742. https://doi.org/10.1371/journal.pone.0166742

Morrison, T., & Morrison, M. (1995). A meta-analytic assessment of the predictive validity of the quantitative and verbal components of the Graduate Record Examination with graduate grade point average representing the criterion of graduate success. *Educational and Psychological Measurement, 55*, 309–316. https://doi.org/10.1177/0013164495055002015

Neuringer, A. (1991). Humble behaviorism. *The Behavior Analyst, 14*, 1–13. https://doi:10.1007/BF03392543

Parker, P. (2015). The historic role of women in higher education. *Administrative Issues: Connecting Education, Practice, and Research, 5*(1), 3–14. https://doi:10.5929/2015.5.1.1

Rippe, J. M. (2018). Lifestyle medicine: The health promoting power of daily habits and practices. *American Journal of Lifestyle Medicine, 12*(6), 499–512. https://doi.org/10.1177/1559827618785554

Robbins, J. K. (2011). Problem solving, reasoning, and analytical thinking in a classroom environment. *The Behavior Analyst Today, 12*(1), 41–48. http://dx.doi.org/10.1037/h0100710

Sampson, C., & Boyer, P. G. (2001). GRE scores as predictors of minority students' success in graduate study: An argument for change. *College Student Journal, 35*, 271.

Sealy, L., Saunders, C., Blume, J., & Chalkley, R. (2019) The GRE over the entire range of scores lacks predictive ability for PhD outcomes in the biomedical sciences. *PLoS One, 14*, e0201634. https://doi.org/10.1371/journal.pone.020163

Shi, S., Zhang, Z., Wang, Y., Yue, H., Wang, Z., & Qian, S. (2021). The relationship between college teacher's frustration tolerance and academic performance. *Frontiers in Psychology, 12.* https://doi.org/10.3389/fpsyg.2021.564484

Verniers, C., & Vala, J. (2018). Justifying gender discrimination in the workplace: The mediating role of motherhood myths. *PLoS One, 13*(1), e0190657. https://doi.org/10.1371/journal.pone.0201150

Wedemeyer-Strombel, K. R. (2018). Why does graduate school kill so many marriages? *Chronicle of Higher Education.* www.chronicle.com/article/why-does-graduate-school-kill-so-many-marriages/?bc_nonce=0jp20abpn9rt08uzn2jodhav&cid=reg_wall_signup

Whimbley, A., Lochhead, J., & Narode, R. (2013). *Problem solving and comprehension* (7th ed.). Routledge.

Appendix 5.1

Expectations of graduate and undergraduate students in the Rasmussen lab.

What My Students Can Expect of Me

1. I will provide high-quality, individualized research and professional mentorship. The type and structure of mentoring and the relationship with the mentor depends on each student's unique abilities and level of independence.
2. I will return drafts of written documents (e.g., thesis, dissertation, manuscripts) in a timely fashion (usually within 1–2 weeks). If I cannot do this because of workload, I will tell the student when to expect his/her draft. In other words, I won't leave you hanging.
3. I will provide opportunities and help prepare students for research presentations at conferences.
4. I will mentor students in submitting manuscripts for publication.
5. I will promote my students by nominating their meritorious work for awards and honors. I also will promote them for primary funding opportunities.
6. I will support my students when they are struggling with life events and difficulties. This can mean behaviors like providing flexibility on deadlines to referring them to professionals who can help. I will also help them solve time-management problems.
7. If a student is not making progress on a project or in the program, I will provide scaffolding to help them. This can mean many things, as each student's needs are individual. Examples may include regular verbal check-ins, meetings, or grading contracts.
8. I will conduct myself with honesty and integrity in all dealings with my students. Confidentiality can be assumed. There may be an occasion when I have to break a confidence, but this is only in the event of a major problem (e.g., academic dishonesty, health or welfare risk).
9. If I have not met one of the expectations listed here, I invite you to talk with me about it. I'm human and can make mistakes, too. But you can expect me to take responsibility for it and make it right.

My Expectations of You

1. I expect students to attend weekly lab meetings regularly. This includes summer. If you need to miss lab meeting, please contact me ahead of time to let me know. Be on time. Attendance also means being prepared and looking prepared. This means reading the articles or book chapters that are assigned, thinking about them, and being prepared to contribute. Showing up without the materials is a sure way to look unprepared.

2. I expect timely completion of theses, dissertations, and independent projects. Specifics of this can be found in #3 and #4. I also expect my students to submit internal and external grants to help fund their research.
3. The departmental expectations for work and credit is as follow: students work 4 hours for every credit of research for which they register (4483, 5583, 6650, 8850). If a student is working under a research assistantship, CPI, or other contract, they should be working whatever hours the contract specifies.
4. When verbal agreements have been made about progress on a research project, I expect students to fulfill these agreements. For example, if an agreement is reached about when a student proposes his/her thesis, then that agreement needs to be met. If I, or the student, foresees a legitimate problem that will interfere with the agreement, then the agreement can be renegotiated. If the agreement is not met by the student, then we will create a written contract. Failure to meet multiple agreements might lead to a question of mentor-mentee fit and the mentoring relation may need to be reconsidered.
5. I expect students to work on other independent research projects in the lab besides his or her own research. How much time they devote to this depends on other responsibilities they have. Each student should lead at least one project beyond their requirements for the doctorate.
6. I expect my students to regularly attend conferences and present their research at these conferences. Poster presentations are expected of greener students. Oral presentations are expected of more seasoned students. Students should also represent the lab by participating in departmental and university research colloquia (e.g., Research Forum, Brown Bags, Data Blitz, university conferences) by presenting research.
7. I expect my students to submit their completed research (i.e., theses, dissertations) for publication if their results are publishable. Of course, we will co-author these manuscripts together and I will provide appropriate mentorship of the writing of the document. Authorship is decided before the manuscript is written and we adhere to the APA ethical guidelines for decision making. In general, authorship is determined by how much relative work each author completes. If a full draft or revision is not completed by a pre-determined agreed-upon date, I have the right to reassign authorship, such that the paper can be submitted in a timely manner.
8. I expect my students to work interpersonally well and help each other. We function as a team. Conflicts happen sometimes but should try to be resolved internally by directly discussing the issues with the person with whom you are having conflict. Discussion of conflicts with people who are not directly implicated in the conflict (i.e., triangulation) can exacerbate the conflict. Therefore, it is highly discouraged. Also, respect the vertical team approach (i.e., consult with the person above you before going above them). If conflicts cannot be handled individually, it is important to the team to bring them to my attention for assistance or mediation.
9. Integrity and trust are critical to the function of a lab team. I expect my students to have integrity and honesty in coursework, in the laboratory, and professionally. Mistakes happen and forgiveness is our practice. Failing to take responsibility by covering up a mistake or being dishonest is not acceptable. Remember that your behavior is a reflection of me and mine is a reflection on you.

6 Mentoring, Mothering, Sistering, and Friending

Building a Caring Mentoring Community

Stephanie M. Peterson, Cynthia M. Anderson, and Jennifer R. Wolgemuth

Mentoring, Mothering, Sistering, and Friending: Building a Caring Mentoring Community

We were honored to be asked to contribute a chapter on the topic of mentoring women for this book. We were also a bit intimidated, to be frank. Sure, all three of us have served as mentors to a number of individuals over the years, but it's fair to say that we felt like we were muddling through it most of the time. Good mentoring is a difficult task. The working title *Mentoring, Mothering, Sistering, and Friending* struck a resonant chord, because it suggested that being a mentor involves many different types of relationships between mentor and mentee. Sometimes—ok, a lot of the time—mentoring feels messy. It can be difficult to know which role to play and whether any of these roles are appropriate at any given point in time and context. It can be such a challenge! At the same time, engaging in these different mentoring relationships is incredibly rewarding and joyful. In writing this chapter, we explore these different relationships, both as a mentor and as a mentee, and sometimes both simultaneously (we did say mentoring was messy!). After all, we have been and continue to be mentored ourselves over the years and not always by those we would quickly label "mentors." Though each of us are in mentoring roles presently, we each still have mentors we turn to for guidance and support, and our mentees surely mentor us as well. Thus, our reflections on mentoring are omnidirectional. We obtain mentoring and guidance from colleagues and from those more senior to us (and hopefully provide the same to them, at least on occasion). We provide guidance to more junior professionals, and likewise they offer us guidance, often with their own generational perspective (Clapp, 2010). In this approach, wisdom and insight are all around us. In this sense, mentorship is a cultural practice, one that requires all participants to work collectively as a unit, seek out colleagues working at a variety of levels, and have genuine curiosity for each other. Participants in a mentoring culture engage in these behaviors for the purpose of meaningful learning and teaching exchanges (Clapp, 2010).

After agreeing to write the chapter, our next task was to decide how we would do it. Peterson and Anderson, as behavior analytic researchers, felt a little out of their elements, because the topic didn't lend itself to direct observation of measurable behavior using experimental research designs—something with which both have expertise. Instead, the task at hand seemed to demand the sharing of our experiences with mentoring and, thus, a more qualitative approach. Peterson and Anderson, recognizing that this was not their strength, sought out collaboration with another researcher and mentor—one who had strength in qualitative research. Enter third author Wolgemuth, a qualitative methodologist with an education background and lens. We engaged in discussion and ultimately settled on an approach that drew inspiration from collaborative reflection and storytelling design traditions like trio-ethnography (Sawyer & Norris, 2013) and collaborative auto-ethnography (Chang et al., 2013). What these design traditions have in common is they 1) value personal

DOI: 10.4324/9781003216773-8

storytelling, 2) involve a process of collective sharing, reflection, and analysis informed by theoretical and empirical literature, and 3) place an emphasis on interpreting individual and collective experience in the context of a cultural milieu. We shared our mentoring experiences with each other; we discussed together what those experiences might mean; and, we reflected on the academic and disciplinary cultures that exerted influences on how we thought about and enacted mentoring across our careers and now.

Our process involved multiple Zoom meetings, during which we discussed our experiences in mentoring from the perspectives of both mentor and mentee. We shared anecdotes and stories. We made observations about successful experiences, mistakes we made, things we enjoyed about our own mentors, and experiences we wished we had had as mentees. We brought in academic readings to inform our dialogues and drew on them to structure and interpret our experiences. We posed questions to each other. We responded to those questions both during our discussions and in writing, as reflections following our discussions. We learned a lot from each other. We identified stories that very much resonated with each of us. We found areas in which we completely disagreed with one another. We laughed at our former selves (and at our current selves!). We sometimes found ourselves envious of each other's experiences. We realized how difficult mentoring really is—as if we didn't already know that. From these discussions and writings, we identified themes or perhaps ideas and insights that seemed to us important to write about—things we think are helpful to share, things that may provoke others to think (with us) about mentoring a bit differently. We discuss these later. But first, we introduce ourselves and provide some background so readers can understand the contexts from which each of us come.

Before we introduce ourselves, we offer a note about our writing style for this chapter. As you may have already noticed, we've chosen a writing style that is both casual and conversational. It seemed appropriate to adopt this style of writing for the chapter, given the conversational approach we took for our research strategy. We infused an academic perspective as well, but we wanted the content of this chapter to be, above all, approachable and readable, a relatable mentoring text in and of itself. We use first-person narrative whenever we can and identify the author who shared an example when possible. However, when an example involves one of our former students, we do not identify which of us shared the example in order to maintain privacy for our students. Further, at times, gender-neutral pronouns are used in some cases to maintain privacy. Finally, at least one of us is no longer working in an academic role. Whether we are working in academic, clinical, or other professional roles, we all continue to mentor and be mentored. We use the word "student" to indicate the person being mentored. We chose this word because we were all "raised" in an academic environment; therefore, it feels most comfortable to us. However, it should be noted that our intention is to use the word in a way that is inclusive of many different types of learners and we do not restrict the word to mean only those studying in academic environments.

About Us

Stephanie M. Peterson

I began my career as a special education teacher. One of my earliest mentors was Susan Lagos, the Director of Monroe Developmental Center, a school for children with severe disabilities in Cedar Rapids, Iowa. It was here that I had my first experience with children with disabilities, and Ms. Lagos inspired my passion for ensuring equity, inclusion, and therapeutic environments for all individuals with disabilities. Interestingly, Ms. Lagos reappeared in my professional life a few other times, once in my master's program and again after I earned my Ph.D. By then, she was Dr. Lagos and had become an Associate Dean at The University of Iowa. Upon reflection, she was a very important early female role model for me. Dr. Lagos showed me early on that women could be powerful, strong leaders and mentors.

Although I was exposed to behavior analysis during my undergraduate education, it was never labeled as such. I took courses from several behavioral faculty at the undergraduate and master's levels: Drs. Alan Frank, Gary Sasso, and Jo Hendrickson. However, it was not until I took a behavioral assessment class from Dr. David Wacker at the end of my master's program that I was formally introduced to behavior analysis. Dr. Wacker became my graduate mentor and, subsequently, a career mentor and friend. He was an outstanding mentor, and I frequently feel intimidated by trying to live up to that standard of mentorship for my own students. After earning my Ph.D. in Special Education at The University of Iowa, I accepted a faculty position at Gonzaga University, where I taught for four years. During that time, I was fortunate to have a number of mentors, who shaped and reinforced my teaching skills: Drs. Betty Williams, Randy Williams, Vikki Howard, and Tim McLaughlin. I also taught at Utah State University, Idaho State University, The Ohio State University, and Western Michigan University. At each of these institutions, I was fortunate to work with esteemed colleagues who took me under their wings and served as mentors and wonderfully collaborative colleagues: Drs. Ben Lignugaris/Kraft, Tim Slocum, Charles Salzberg, Nancy Neef, Tim Heron, Bill Heward, John Cooper, Wayne Fuqua, Dick Malott, and Alyce Dickinson, just to name a few. I was very fortunate to have opportunities to connect with a number of other individuals in the field of behavior analysis over the years who graciously shared their time and talent with me and provided expert mentorship when I needed it. Rather than name them all, suffice it to say that there are many, and they consist of men and women across a variety of areas within behavior analysis, from a variety of locales, and from both academic and clinical settings. I am so grateful to all of them for what they have taught me and continue to teach me. Over the years, I have mentored a number of undergraduate and graduate students, many of whom have become friends, colleagues, and mentors, themselves. In 2015, I received an Outstanding Mentor Award from the Association of Behavior Analysis, International Student Committee (as runner up to Nancy Neef, mind you). Like my own graduate-student mentor, Dave Wacker, I often use the Socratic method as a strategy for mentoring. I believe that mentoring is one of the most important tasks with which I am charged in my academic role. After all, teaching and mentoring shape not only the lives of those I mentor, but also the future of the field and the lives of all the individuals my mentees interact with in the future.

Cynthia M. Anderson

My first experience with mentoring occurred during my undergraduate years, at a liberal arts women's college. I was assigned an advisor in the psychology department (by luck of the draw), and she quickly became a touchstone for me as I explored different majors (psychology, biology, philosophy, English), and even different personas (punk rocker, Deadhead, scholar). My undergraduate advisor was a phenomenal teacher and managed to make all students in her classes feel valued, accepted, and as if they mattered. She inspired me to consider a career in academia, largely focused on teaching. She also showed me the importance and value of listening and learning from others, skills I've tried (and often failed) to emulate over the years. After earning my undergraduate degree, I began my career working on the Neurobehavioral Unit at Kennedy Krieger Institute (this position was due entirely to my advisor, who had completed her predoctoral training here). I was fortunate to be mentored by another woman, this one a behavior analyst who introduced me to the science and practice of behavior analysis; using a shaping process, she helped me develop skills in the practice of behavior analysis, as well as a passion for our science. During graduate school and in ensuing years, I also have been fortunate to be mentored by esteemed colleagues, some of whom were in the institutions I was studying or working in, but many others who I met via professional associations or via colleagues. Although I am no longer in an academic position, I am lucky to have opportunities to continue providing mentorship to postdoctoral fellows and more junior colleagues. I view mentoring as an honor and as one of the most important tasks I have. As Stephanie said, through mentoring I shape not only the lives of those I mentor; they also shape the future of the field and the lives of all the individuals my mentees interact with in the future.

Jennifer R. Wolgemuth

As a qualitative methodologist, I'm a bit of an oddball in this group (side note: this is considered a feature of collaborative ethnographic work where an outsider serves as a critical friend, offering a different perspective on shared assumptions). I might trace the origins of becoming a methodologist to my Ph.D. program in Educational Research. My advisor, and very much a "quant guy," Dr. R. Brian Cobb, was and remains a treasured mentor—he guided me through experimental designs, meta-analyses, advanced me into leadership roles in his research center, and then . . . stepped back and watched with what I expect was a mixture of appreciation, skepticism, and confusion as I became passionate about narrative inquiry and poststructural feminism. He didn't particularly (want to) understand Foucault, but it was okay that I did. He bragged that he actually read every word of my 400+-page dissertation. He taught me, both directly and indirectly, that good mentorship does not mean replicating yourself or your agenda. Recently I published a pretty heavy-handed theoretical critique of a WWC(ish) systematic review I'd worked on with Brian as Principal Investigator (PI). Even though he is quite happily retired, I reached out to share the publication. I was surprised at my nervousness and apparently still strong desire for his approval. His response was, as ever, affirmative: "In reading the abstract, this sounds like precisely the article I would have expected you to have authored and wouldn't have it any other way." He taught me that good mentorship also means affirming and caring.

Recently I've coedited a book with Kelly Guyotte (Guyotte & Wolgemuth, 2022), who is also a qualitative methodologist, on philosophy and mentoring in qualitative research. We argue in the introduction that mentoring is a philosophical practice, whether parties to the mentoring relationship reflect on it as such or not (and of course we argue they should). What we think about mentoring, what we think about how we should mentor, what we think about the mentoring relationship all matter—they say a lot about our personal ethics and the values of our discipline, both current and aspirational. Qualitative research often values caring, creativity, advocacy, and risk-taking—and as such, so often does our mentorship. It turns out, though, that mentoring in qualitative research may not be so different from mentoring in behavior analysis, at least from the mentoring into the field I've received from my admired coauthors, Stephanie and Cynthia. While I may never self-define as a "woman in behavior analysis," I appreciate the opportunity to learn about the field from them and to challenge my perhaps unfair assumptions that (mentoring in) behavior analysis is overly structured, clinical, and maintains an untenable separation between subject and object. Mentoring is messy, after all.

A Word About "Women"

As we collaborated on writing this chapter, we all wrestled with restricting our discussion to "women" mentoring "women." After all, each of us witnessed and experienced people who identified as men and women as exceptional and caring mentors. In addition, we recognize that "woman" and "man" are socially defined constructs and that many of us do not fit so neatly into a single construct or category. Further, mentoring in and of itself is hard work, and the issues mentors face are not often easily assigned or attributed to their gender identifications. Mentors, regardless of their gender identifications, may want to be home with their families and likely struggle with the amount of time being a good mentor, academic, researcher, and/or clinician can take away from other life priorities and obligations. Surely these issues are not unique to women. For example, one of us recalls a time when one of her male students was interviewing for a job. Her student stated he wanted to have a job where his hours were flexible, so he could attend his children's ball games and otherwise be present for his family. Much later, when he was not offered the job he had interviewed for, he learned that his statements about family were largely the reason he did not receive a job offer. Flexibility in working hours so that an individual can assume family responsibilities may be more often attributed to a woman's needs than a man's, given that women spend more than twice the number of minutes each day caring for children than men (U.S. Bureau of Labor Statistics, 2021). However, Halpern (2005) found that flexible work policies may increase both men's and women's commitment to their employer and result in fewer symptoms of stress, suggesting there are no gender differences in the desire for flexibility in the workplace.

At the same time, being or being perceived as a woman *is* a unique experience. Women report being sexually assaulted or harassed at a rate of 81% compared to 43% of men (Kearl, 2018). Feminized professions such as teaching, childcare, and home health are arguably underpaid (Scheider & Gould, 2016)—on average women earn 84 cents for every dollar paid to a man (Barroso & Brown, 2021). While the pay gap between women and men at the assistant professor level seems to have narrowed in recent years, women who are full professors earn 83 cents to every dollar their white male counterparts make (Bichsel et al., 2021). Women in higher education bear the brunt of what is described as "emotional labor" and are more likely to be judged negatively on course evaluations for not being "friendly" or "caring" (e.g., Shreffler et al., 2019). For example, during her first year in an academic profession, one of us received teaching evaluations in a graduate course in which several students noted, "She is not as warm as we thought she'd be." Women also remain underrepresented in many disciplines, such as STEM (Science, Technology, Engineering, Math) fields (National Science Board, 2016). While women comprise 50% of all academic deans, they are concentrated at the assistant and associate dean levels and make up less than 33% of the highest-paid deans (Pritchard et al., 2019). The proportion of women in leadership positions decreases as the level of academic leadership increases. As of 2016, only 30% of university presidents were women and a mere 5% were women of color (American Council on Education, 2017). Identifying as a woman comes with its own particular struggles, pressures, stereotypes, disparities, and violence, and it is under and with these assumptions that we speak about our individual and collective experiences with mentorship in academic, research, and clinical spaces.

In general, we ultimately conclude it's messy trying to discuss mentoring from a woman's perspective. The issues faced by those who identify as women are real and probably need to be part of the conversation in a mentoring relationship (we recognize and acknowledge that issues faced by those who identify as men also are quite real and should be part of the conversation in mentoring relationships, but that is a topic for another chapter). We believe that women in leadership roles can serve as effective role models for other women (and men). The perspectives and insights a woman can offer another woman are important and likely unique. At the same time, men can and do face similar challenges in their own right. Further, the insights, perspectives, and modeling men can offer women are also important and unique. This "messiness" maps on to the omnidirectional nature of mentorship neatly, in the sense that insights from multiple perspectives can inform the views and practices of all members in the mentoring relationship and contribute to the teaching and learning of the group.

Rules for Success

During our discussions, Peterson noted that her graduate school mentor often referred to the "Eleven Rules for Success" he had gleaned from Steve Hayes at an Association for Behavior Analysis (now Association for Behavior Analysis, International) conference in 1985. Peterson has used these rules for success as guideposts throughout her career and referred to them often during the group's discussions. The rules resonated with all of us, so we decided to use them as a way to organize our thoughts about mentoring and as a lens through which our experiences as "women" scientists could be viewed. Hayes (1998) later published these rules. At that time, the number of rules had expanded to 13, and they were framed specifically for graduate students. Though slightly different from the rules Peterson "grew up with," we based what follows on these later rules for our purposes here because readers can locate and refer to the rules more easily in the literature. Next, we reflect on these rules as they relate to mentoring, friending, sistering, and mothering, simultaneously updating his rules to reflect today's sociocultural context.

1. Care About the Process, not Just the Outcome

Here, Hayes (1998) encourages graduate students to value the process of learning rather than to remain solely focused on the goal of obtaining the degree (i.e., letters behind your name, piece of paper, diploma). He advises graduate students to care about the mental exercise of considering problems, studying the research literature, proposing solutions or methods of determining functional relations, analyzing data, and drawing conclusions. In our discussions, one theme that emerged was that it is important to care—*really care*—about your mentees, the mentor/mentee relationship, and working together as a team. We focus heavily on interpersonal care, caring for mentees as people with unique experiences, histories, cultures, communities, and values. Further, it is important that both mentor and mentee have a shared vision and mission regarding at least some specific issues. That is, both mentor and mentee need to care deeply about some similar issues. Often, in behavior analysis, this shared vision and mission can equate to advocating for positive social change. For example, a mentor and mentee might have differing political perspectives but both care deeply about addressing health disparities in rural areas—this shared mission could help to align their work together. While we all had different ideas about "care," and how we might enact it, our general sense was that caring should reflect an appreciation of mutuality and interdependence (see, for example, Chatzidakis et al., 2020). Our conversations for this chapter occurred during a worldwide COVID-19 pandemic that amplified the importance of caring—caring for ourselves, our families, our communities, public health and policy, and even our planet—and made exceedingly real to us the ways in which we are interconnected over space and time. Rather than retreat into isolation, we embraced interdependence as a touchstone for caring mentorship. Care was not something we did to and for mentees. Rather, care is something to be cultivated in our interdependent mentoring networks that extends beyond caring for/about academic growth to caring for the person in the context of their families, communities, and histories (including histories of trauma and oppression).

One example that emerged in our discussion was when we asked the question, "What do you look for in a mentee?" We observed that the expected answers might be things like knowledge of behavior analysis, experience with research, high Graduate Record

Examination scores, and the like. However, we agreed that the most relevant characteristics we look for in mentees are (1) a shared vision for making life better for the population of interest (e.g., animals, children, teachers, people with intellectual disabilities), and (2) a commitment to a strong work ethic. One of us noted that teaching the behavior analytic skills needed to be successful is relatively easy. We are fairly skilled at teaching these repertoires. However, teaching people to care deeply about the work they are doing is a much more difficult task. We look for mentees who can "show up" with passion and a willingness to work hard to learn the behavior analytic skills to produce social change. After all, this deep caring creates motivation for the challenging, time-consuming work that is involved in learning the behavior analytic repertoires, completing the research projects, and implementing the clinical strategies necessary for our clients (i.e., work ethic).

Conceptualizing "care" as an ethic in an interdependent world also helped us wrestle with/against gendered and sexist notions of care as "women's" work. As an ethic, care is appropriately a responsibility of all gendered bodies. Yet, in academia, those who identify as women in STEM fields often shoulder more heavy teaching, service, and mentoring responsibilities (Armstrong & Jovanovic, 2015; Hermanowicz, 2012; Kulis et al., 2002; Madge & Bee, 1999; Urry, 2015). In other words, women are often expected to take on the caring labor of the department and be the academic, mentor, friend, and mother. Further, women in STEM fields are highly represented in helping professions and much less in non-helping professions, such as those related to physics and chemistry. This is exemplified in behavior analysis by the overrepresentation of women who are Board Certified Behavior Analysts (BCBAs). As of January 28, 2022, over 85% of BCBAs are women (BACB, n.d.), and the professional practice of behavior analysis is largely a "helping" profession (i.e., providing behavior analytic treatment for individuals with autism and/or developmental disabilities). Caring mentoring, we believe, should work to change these gendered inequities and the gendering of "care" work in behavior analysis.

2. *Talk—and Write—a Lot*

Here, Hayes (1998) notes that successful scientists speak, write, debate, and persuade a lot. To learn these skills, one must engage in these behaviors. However, women may engage in fewer of these behaviors in the workplace. For example, Eakins and Eakins (1976) and Edelsky (1993) found that men spoke more often and longer than women during faculty meetings. These trends continue today and seem to be present outside the academy. For example, in a meta-analytic review of studies comparing men's and women's conversation styles, Anderson and Leaper (1998) showed that men are significantly more likely than women to interrupt others when speaking (interestingly, these effects were smaller when men were first authors on publications). Even on the Supreme Court, this occurs with male justices interrupting female justices about three times as often as they do males (or females interrupt others; Jacobi & Schweers, 2017). Further, women often receive negative feedback (and other aversive consequences) if they talk more than men in meetings (Brescoll, 2011). Aries (1976) found similar patterns among undergraduate students participating in group discussions, and Lee and Mccabe (2021) found that little has changed in ensuing years. Men tend to speak out more frequently and for longer durations. Further, they found that men are more likely to interrupt others and to speak without raising their hands and waiting to be recognized. Lee and Mccabe reported that style and tone differed as well, with men using assertive language whereas women's statements came across as more hesitant and apologetic. These findings are troubling and suggest that societal change remains needed. Often, the implication is that women should be less apologetic (and humble) and more outspoken (and assertive). This may be true, but women should not bear the brunt of being required to change. Societal change means some men, including men in the academy, may need to be *more* apologetic (and humble) and *less* outspoken (and assertive). As mentors, we believe it is important to provide space for *all people* to develop (a) skills in speaking, debating, and persuading, *and* (b) skills in listening and encouraging others to share. After all, as scientists we should be both humble and confident simultaneously. We need to have intellectual humility, as this is how science proceeds. The virtue of open curiosity and the commitment to the fact that what we think we know could be wrong (i.e., the principle of falsifiability) are what allow science to proceed. At the same time, it takes confidence to ask questions that are difficult to answer and to challenge prevailing ideas and schools of thought.

When mentoring, it is important to provide mentees with forums in which they have opportunities to speak, write, debate, persuade, and listen to others. In the earlier version of the rules that Peterson had learned, this rule was framed as "create a forum for your ideas." In other words, if forums for discussing ideas don't currently exist, mentors can help create and monitor them to teach and coach speaking, debating, and persuading skills, as well as skills in truly listening to others and encouraging others to share. An example of creating forums for speaking, debating, persuading, and listening that emerged from our discussion was creating book and/or journal clubs. In one of our research labs, we regularly choose books to read together as a group, and we host discussions on these books. We sometimes choose books that are behavior analytic, and sometimes the books are non-behavior analytic but related to autism or disability themes. Recent examples include *Coercion and Its Fallout* (Sidman, 1989), *Mad in America* (Whitaker, 2002) and *Supervisor and Mentor* (LeBlanc et al., 2020). Sometimes we choose books we are confident will spark debate and disagreement so mentees can practice debate, persuasion, and listening.

Another strategy for creating discussion opportunities is to provide mentees opportunities to practice public presentations in front of their peers. Peer mentees are asked to critique each other's presentations, both in style and content. This provides opportunities for mentees to practice writing and talking about behavior analytic ideas, and peer mentees get practice analyzing speaking performances, identifying strengths and limitations of the performance, and delivering verbal feedback on the performance. In turn this provides additional speaking, and potential writing, opportunities for peer mentees. Mentors can create opportunities for mentees to engage in public presentations and write together.

Mentors can also talk with mentees about their own comfort level with skills in these areas. Sometimes these discussions are best one-on-one and can follow observations made by a mentor. For example, one of us mentored a student who spoke up only rarely in class and during research team meetings, yet shared and argued convincingly in writing. This student (who identified as male) came from a cultural tradition that valued listening over speaking and viewed others as "over sharing." Together, the mentor and the student discussed the student's learning history and perspective, as well as the student's career goals and aspirations (an academic position in a university). They identified specific activities and times when the student felt it would be appropriate and acceptable to speak, and even to debate and persuade, and the student began to engage in these behaviors during those times, and to look for other opportunities. Together they discovered that, if the student had identified situations as appropriate ahead of time (e.g., during planned class discussions, participating in a symposium, presenting a poster, during lab meetings when the person discussing a project asked for input), he was comfortable speaking up, sharing ideas, and such.

3. Say "Yes" Easily—and Mean It

Hayes (1998) notes that graduate students need to broaden their repertoires and the way to do so is to say "yes" to projects when invited to participate in them. After saying "yes," the student needs to show they "mean" it by following through and actually doing *more* than what is asked of them. He suggests that the student complete the task elegantly. As one of Peterson's mentors, Bill Heward, always used to say, "You gotta be there." In this, he meant you have to show up. You have to be dependable. You have to be present. You have to participate. We discussed this at some length and agree with this sentiment. Yet we also recognize that it can be easy to say yes to opportunities, sometimes at the expense of other commitments or important areas of life. One important role of a mentor is to help mentees learn to evaluate opportunities and to consider whether they will be able to fully engage in the opportunity without either shirking other responsibilities or neglecting one or more aspects of their life. For example, one of us recently mentored a doctoral student who, in addition to working a full-time job while in graduate school, was also attempting to be a coauthor on two papers and had agreed to coauthor a book chapter. The student repeatedly insisted that they could handle all these obligations and that they'd been told by another faculty member to "never say no, or you won't be asked again." Over a period of weeks, this student started to become physically ill and began struggling to sleep at night. In a discussion of costs and benefits, the student decided to regretfully decline additional writing opportunities and to focus on their dissertation and only one of the papers, letting the additional manuscript and book chapter go. In sum, we believe that mentoring in saying no can be just as important as saying yes (see Rule #12).

4. *Work With Others and Share Easily*

Hayes (1998) encourages students to form teams, collaborate, and share ideas. He encourages students to worry little about authorship and who gets credit for ideas. We agree with the underlying message here, which is to work together and collaborate out of motivation to learn and engage in the process of sharing ideas. Peterson noted that in her lab as a graduate student, the sentiment was that the group accomplished much more working together than individuals could accomplish working alone. Collaboration should be encouraged and valued. Collaboration has the added benefits of expanding professional networks and learning from one another by exploring divergent ideas (see Rule #2). An important role of a mentor can be to model sharing of ideas and collaboration. In graduate school, mentors frequently model this by helping students develop ideas for theses, dissertations, and other projects. We can also model sharing ideas via research teams, and by describing our interactions with colleagues in these areas. We model this by inviting researchers from other universities to attend lab meetings for discussions around shared interests. Often, ideas for collaborative research emerge from these discussions. Further, such discussions help create professional networks for our students. For example, Peterson assigns students to seek out individuals who were guests at her lab meetings at professional conferences, sending them armed with thank-you cards and small tokens of appreciation for attending the lab meeting, which provides the student with a purpose for approaching an esteemed member of the field. The hope is that doing so reduces the potential anxiety that can surround approaching an admired individual and not knowing what to say. Having a task, such as saying "thank you" on behalf of the lab gives the student "entry" into a conversation with valued colleagues, as well as a small step toward a relationship with the individual.

Although we agree with Hayes (1998) that individuals should worry little about who gets credit for what, we also encourage students (and colleagues) to have open, frank, and early conversations about authorship when engaging in collective work together. It is important that roles, expectations, and authorship are explicitly defined early in the collaborative activities. This can help avoid professional disagreements and confrontations later in the activity. Indeed, in unfortunate situations, professional relationships have been ruined or forever tarnished because of such disputes, which may not have been the case had those conversations occurred during the project's early stages. Further, if an individual is to say "yes easily and mean it" (see Rule #3), one needs to understand what one is signing up for, in terms of expected work output, as well as credit for that work. If the two seem mismatched, it may be important to consider saying "no easily and mean it" (see Rule #12); or to disagree appropriately and negotiate with the team (see Rule #2).

5. Keep Your Commitments

According to Hayes (1998), this is the most important of all the rules (if so, then why isn't it Rule #1, we wondered?). This rule is simple and straightforward. If you say yes—that you're going to do it—then do it. We agree with this rule completely, and yet . . . see Rule #3. In an ideal world, we say yes only to what is possible, and we mentor others to do so. If, however, a mentor has taken on more than they can manage, an important role of mentoring becomes how to "back out" of a commitment gracefully. As described under Rule #3, one of us had exactly this experience with a mentor. When one of our students realized that keeping her writing commitments would come at the expense of her health, she and the mentor role-played conversations that the student could have with the collaborating senior authors, explaining both her initial enthusiasm for the project and her decision to extract herself from the collaboration. The mentor also helped the student identify other people who might be willing to collaborate on the projects, should the lead author desire other contributors.

Ideally of course, all commitments are kept. We, therefore, view the role of the mentor in this area as largely happening before a commitment is made (again see our caveat to Rule #3). Rather than encouraging our mentees to "blindly" say yes to every opportunity, we encourage them to carefully consider the opportunity, not just the joy involvement will bring or its outcome (e.g., another publication), but also the cost of engaging, in terms of time and other resources. We ask students to consider what they will need to stop doing or do less of if the presented opportunity is accepted. Taking time to engage in this exercise can lead to less deleterious outcomes including reneging on commitments. It is important to understand that it can be worse (e.g., detrimental to academic reputations, professional relationships, and personal lives) to say "yes" to something but not be able to deliver, than it might be to say "no" and miss an opportunity to participate in a potentially reinforcing activity. Professionals often appreciate it when another professional can recognize their own limits and say "no" when necessary (see Rule #12). In fact, those other professionals may actually be jealous of your ability to engage in this skill! Peterson notes that she often presents students with opportunities, even if she believes they are too busy to accept. She does this with purpose, to provide them with opportunities to analyze their personal situation/context and to say "no easily and mean it" (see Rule #12) if necessary. It can be difficult for a student to say no to their mentor, just as it can be difficult to say no to a future supervisor, such as a department chair or PI. Thus, these practice opportunities are instructive, and it is important that a mentor reinforces rather than punishes good decision making on the student's part. Leadership is demanding. Learning to cope with the high demands is an important part of the student's development. A resource that may be helpful is *Your Oxygen Mask First* (Lawrence, 2017), which may make for a good book club discussion (see Rule #2).

6. Even Dogs Never Urinate in Their Own Beds

Hayes (1998) notes he has observed many a student begin to complain when things aren't going well. However, he notes that complaining to other students, who are powerless to remedy the situation, is not productive. At the same time, this can be highly reinforcing, because complaining can result in others commiserating and otherwise attending to this unproductive behavior. Complaining can contribute to a negative culture, and because complaining is so highly reinforced it can contribute to a verbal community that is not conducive to constructive problem-solving. Hayes suggests that students should avoid complaining and if they observe others complaining, they should walk away (i.e., put the complaining behavior on extinction). We agree with Hayes that complaining and commiserating can be reinforcing. At the same time, we offer some alternative perspectives here. First, if we wish to establish a caring culture, simply walking away from someone who is complaining demonstrates neither compassion nor caring. At least acknowledging the issue and providing the complainer with some constructive problem-solving strategies may be more helpful. Second, we are not sure complaining is always a bad thing. It is important for students and mentors to discriminate between a student voicing an objection to inequitable treatment and "gossiping" or "stirring the pot." We admit that this discrimination is not always easy. Allowing for discussions of complaints and openly talking about whether the complaint appears to be gossip or potential inequitable treatment and strategies for dealing with each is important. Third, we are not convinced that graduate students should be viewed as "powerless to remedy the situation" and worry that putting complaining on extinction can actually perpetuate many conditions that are neither healthy nor productive. For far too long women in the academy experienced harassment, and this continues today (e.g., National Academies of Science, Engineering, and Medicine, 2018; Tenbrunsel et al., 2019). For an in-depth example, please see Nebbe, 2022. As Fernando and Prasad (2019) note, women who experience harassment often are persuaded by others (e.g., colleagues, staff in human resources) to simply keep quiet. This kind of "complaining" should never be viewed as problematic. In fact, it is important for mentors to make students (and others) aware of formal complaint processes available to them (e.g., Title IX offices, offices of institutional equity) and to support students in making a complaint if necessary. For example, one of the authors remembers a time when one of her students was experiencing sexual harassment. The mentor advised the student how to file a formal complaint. The student wanted to file a complaint but was afraid to do so. The mentor asked the student if she wanted the mentor to go with her as she made the complaint. Relieved, the student readily agreed and asked the mentor to please come with her. Agreeing to come with the student allowed the student to feel supported and the complaint to be made in an appropriate forum.

Other situations can be more difficult to navigate. For example, one of us worked for some years in a setting where it was expected that all faculty and students would go to a happy hour (which often became happy evening) every Friday afternoon. Although often fun and a great opportunity for connecting (and developing research ideas), this commitment was difficult for faculty and students who had families or other commitments outside of the program and department, religious practices/obligations, and/or family values that precluded alcohol consumption, for example. Those who tried to bow out often experienced both direct and indirect social pressure and consequences. In these situations, a mentor can help their students by first being approachable when a concern arises. The mentor can teach students how to have difficult conversations, such as raising concerns appropriately. Further, ensuring students know to whom they can express a concern and what resources are available to them when a concern arises is important. At the same time, mentors can be good models for planning and organizing events that are considerate of family, social, and religious obligations and values, for example also planning potlucks in the park and opportunities to play together (e.g., bowling, outdoor games). Peterson frequently plans events for her students, and her students also frequently plan social events together. These events are varied and include potlucks, painting ceramics, hiking, shopping, and games, just to name a few. At many events, the students bring their "plus ones" and children.

One of us recalls a situation in which students had a concern about a professor and their approach to teaching the course, as well as the grading of assignments in the course. The students thought the professor's expectations were too high and unattainable. Rather than addressing the concern directly with the faculty member, the students complained to each other, banded together, expressed their concerns as a group to another faculty member, who then approached the professor. The professor felt blindsided and, quite frankly, bullied. The professor asked the other faculty member why they didn't direct the students to her directly. The other faculty member said it was not realistic to expect students to express a concern to a professor, despite the fact that the department handbook stated that when a concern arises, the first step is to speak directly with the individual with whom the concern has arisen. As described in examples provided in Rule #5, a mentor can guide students here by discussing the concern with the student, role-playing how the student might approach the problem and what they might say when reaching out to the professor, and then following up with the student to discuss how the interaction went to determine next steps. Providing students with resources, such as books like *Crucial Conversations* (Patterson et al., 2012) and *How to Win Friends and Influence People* (Carnegie, 1936; required reading for Peterson's lab), can be very helpful. These are examples of books that can be helpful to read as part of a book club (see Rule #2).

7. *Acknowledge Your Own Power and Behave Accordingly*

Hayes (1998) encourages students to recognize that they can make a difference in the world. In this, he asks students to behave in a way that creates the change they want to see in the world. In Rule #6, we discussed how to teach students to express a concern when one arises. Teaching students these skills empowers them, especially if their mentors are standing beside them, assisting them through the difficult situation. It is important that mentors reinforce and not punish behaviors associated with creating change. Rather, they encourage students to question . . . well, everyone and everything. For example, Peterson explicitly tells her students that if they have a concern with any of the clinical cases reviewed on a weekly basis in the lab that they should ask a question, whether that is directed to a more senior student in the lab, their supervisor, or herself. Questioning others is praised, because it is viewed as protecting each other, not "calling someone out." LeBlanc and colleagues (2020) note that good supervisors ask their supervisees to "bring them smoke." This metaphor relates to "where there is smoke, there is fire," and supervisees who bring you smoke allow you to solve problems while they are small, before they are big, raging fires. Thus, when students ask questions of each other or of their supervisors when they sense something could be wrong, they are helping everyone around them avoid a fire and potentially more severe consequences down the road. Framed in this manner, a culture of helping one another resolve potentially damaging situations develops. For example, one of us recalls a situation in which a White student made a comment about police brutality that a Black student found offensive. Rather than initiating a confrontational argument about the situation, the Black student exerted their power and initiated a discussion about how they felt about the comment in a supervised group meeting. An excellent discussion ensued, apologies were made, and every member of the team learned and grew because of the interaction. In fact, further conversations happened after the event, so continued learning occurred and a forum for discussing racial issues was created (see Rule #2). In this example, the Black student created the change that they wanted to see in the world.

How do students come to realize their power? Perhaps, as mentors, we need to give it to our students. That is, we need to put them in the position of power over us. Perhaps our students need to see us, their mentors, as vulnerable and themselves as powerful. Peterson recalled a recent example of how this was accomplished. She had decided to apply for a leadership position at her institution. As part of her interview, she was asked to prepare a talk she would give to the entire campus community. The job was for an associate dean position and, as such, the focus of the talk was how the academic college should tackle the challenges and opportunities that lay ahead. Peterson prepared her talk, but she was very, very anxious about giving the talk, having always had much more anxiety about public speaking with local audiences (with whom she must work day in and day out) than with national and international audiences (at least you don't have to look the people from your international audience in the face every day at work if you really flub your talk!). So, she asked the students in her lab if they would be willing to give up one of their lab meetings to allow her to practice her talk in front of them, just as they routinely practice their talks in front of her and their labmates. The students graciously agreed to do so. On the day of the rehearsal, Peterson told the students she wanted them to critique her talk, just as they would one another's talks. She reminded them that their criticism would help save her from later embarrassment (see smoke/fire discussion in Rule #7). Peterson was extremely nervous to practice her talk in front of her students, just as they were when they practiced in front of her. Following her rehearsal, the students critiqued the ideas she presented, as well as her slides. They encouraged her to re-sequence some of her ideas, gave her feedback on how she could make her slides more engaging, and were very warm, gentle, and supportive (just as Peterson tries to be with them). The talk was far better the following week when it was performed publicly, because of their feedback and input. While this activity was self-serving, in the sense that Peterson wanted and needed the practice opportunity and feedback, it also served the students. It was good for the students to see Peterson nervous and humble. It put them in the "power" seat, while Peterson was in the vulnerable position. It also gave the students the opportunity to exercise their power with grace, compassion, and dignity. They saw the effects of their power the following week, when the changes they suggested were implemented, which served as reinforcement for their exercise of power. These are important opportunities for students, and the mentor has it in their power to provide them. Fries-Britt and Snider (2015) note that students must be willing and able to be professionally vulnerable with their supervisors. They do this by being open about what they know and do not know, and they ask for help when they need it. Mentors can do the same thing with their students. Doing so allows students opportunities to acknowledge their power and behave accordingly.

8. Acknowledge Your Own Finitude and Behave Accordingly

Here, Hayes (1998) encourages students to recognize that life is short and, thus, we should all use our time wisely. He asks students to consider how they want to spend their time and to ensure they are spending their time in ways that matter. See Rules #3, #5, #11, and #12. We are all getting older. As we said earlier, the COVID-19 pandemic has caused all of us to consider more carefully how we spend our time. Rule #1 asks that we care about caring. It is important that we spend our time working on issues for which we have passion and that we establish our priorities, both personally and professionally. Most professionals we know confess that they have never found that elusive "work-life balance." Perhaps that is part of the journey—striving for that balance is just what it is all about.

9. Network With Your Betters

Hayes (1998) encourages students to take initiative to meet more senior members of the field by going to their talks, asking them about their work, sharing ideas, and so forth. This is good advice. It is good for students to take the initiative to meet others in the field and talk with them about their work. This takes confidence. Sellers et al. (2016) note that supervisors should strive to develop behavior analysts who are competent, *confident*, and effective. A mentor can play a large role in helping their students develop confidence. See Rule #4 and suggestions for inviting recognized researchers into the students' space (i.e., their lab meetings) first, which can be a more comfortable space than at a professional conference for an initial interaction. Further, assigning the students to go thank those individuals for attending a lab meeting gives the students entry into a conversation with a recognized researcher at a professional meeting.

Cirincione-Ulezi (2020) notes that mentorship may grow into sponsorship over time. Sponsorship helps advance the career of those they sponsor, grooming individuals for leadership positions. She notes that sponsorship relationships often develop outside of the traditional work hours, suggesting that for such relationships to develop, the lines and boundaries may be complex and blurry (sistering, mothering, friending). One of the things a sponsor does is introduce the individual being sponsored into their professional network, allowing them to make the contacts they need to participate in collaborative efforts (see Rule #4). For these introductions to be authentic and have impact for the student, the mentor needs to know and care about the student, their interests, their goals, and their aspirations (see Rule #1). At the same time, the student must be competent and have developed a successful body of work the sponsor can support and talk about with others. While some of this is on the student, it is also incumbent on the mentor/sponsor to have helped shape these skills over time. A mentor serves their student well by helping them become competent and effective, which can lead to confidence and make the student easy to sponsor. Lacking sponsorship, students may not have access to leadership positions (Cirincione-Ulezi, 2020).

When we were discussing sponsorship during our Zoom meetings, one of us bristled at the idea of sponsorship, suggesting that sponsorship might lead to an insular network. The limitation of an insular network is lack of diversity, especially of ideas and thought. This is ironic, given that one point Cirincione-Ulezi (2020) makes is that "Black women continue to be grossly underrepresented in positions of leadership within the field of ABA" (p. 722) and that without sponsorship, many Black women may not have the support they need to move into leadership positions. In Cirincione-Ulezi's view, sponsorship may be necessary for increased diversity in the field. However, the point is well taken that sponsorship may lead to restricted groups of individuals (and creating replicas of ourselves). A mentor could guard against this by ensuring their own network is broad and diverse and seeking out opportunities to establish connections with individuals who conduct research in areas that differ from their own so that they can introduce their mentees to a broad network of potential collaborators.

10. Guard Your Integrity

Losing your integrity is a slippery slope. Hayes (1998) notes it is easy to violate our integrity just a little bit to achieve a desired outcome. However, Hayes notes that the consequences for doing so are quite dire. Violating your integrity can result in more and more future violations, and it can result in the loss of reinforcement for doing good science. As behavior analysts, of course, we have professional codes of ethics (American Psychological Association, 2017; Behavior Analyst Certification Board, 2020). One of us remembers our mentor saying that the ethics codes are great, but they kind of state the obvious (e.g., "Don't sleep with your clients.").

Although ethics codes provide some guidance on the more difficult dilemmas, they really aren't nuanced enough to provide clear guidance on the multiple gray areas we all deal with on a day-to-day basis. This is necessarily so, as no set of ethical guidelines can spell out what to do in every situation one might encounter, nor could a single set of ethical guidelines take into account all the contextual variables that could be at play in any given situation. Fortunately, the nature of a behavior analyst's work provides many opportunities for discussion regarding ethical dilemmas—client-related work, research, supervision, academic integrity, and social integrity. We all agreed that creating a context where students can have open discussions with each other about the multitude of dilemmas that will undoubtedly face them during their academic career and beyond is critical to the development of the problem-solving repertoire that will be necessary during and long after graduate school. In fact, we try to cultivate relationships with our mentees and among our mentees that stand the test of time, creating a trusted professional community that our students can reach out to and depend upon throughout their careers. As Peterson heard one of her colleagues Jim Carr put it, our mentoring comes with an "extended warranty." The mentoring relationship typically does not end when the student earns their diploma. In fact, often the relationship further develops after graduation, and as described repeatedly here continues to be omnidirectional. We all recalled times when we had called upon former students to seek guidance on a difficult issue and that we had all had former students call upon us for guidance long after they had graduated.

11. Follow Your Bliss

Hayes (1998) encourages students to be true to themselves—to know what they are interested in and to follow those interests. He also notes here that students should proceed with confidence, even if they don't *feel* confident. We have already discussed confidence in Rule #9. Further, it may be important for our students to understand that we, as mentors, don't always feel confident, either (see Rule #7). Many women experience "imposter syndrome" (Clance & Imes, 1978), meaning they feel as though they are imposters in their careers. Langford and Clance (1993) defined imposter syndrome as believing that one's accomplishments are a result of chance rather than ability, having been lucky, or having somehow manipulated others' impressions of one's skills. While not a behavior analytic concept, perhaps imposter syndrome could be conceptualized behaviorally as attributing others' views about one's competence as based on something other than one's own behavior—to variables out of our own control.

In a recent longitudinal study of imposter syndrome in STEM fields (astronomy and astrophysics), Ivie and colleagues (2016) found that women were more likely to feel as imposters than men. Individuals who changed advisors during graduate school or rated their graduate advisor poorly were more likely to leave the field. Also, women tended to be less satisfied with their advisors, which made it more likely they would change advisors, and thus might result in them leaving the field. The authors concluded that advisors who were more encouraging might be more highly rated and that students who receive more encouragement may be more likely to stay in the field. From a behavior analytic perspective, the results of this and other, similar studies suggest that positive reinforcement, such as behavior-specific praise, is important in the mentoring relationship. This type of "encouragement" links the positive feedback specifically to the student's behavior. In addition, being clear about *why* you are providing the encouragement may indicate sincerity and genuine care (see Rule #1) on the part of the mentor.

Another way to increase student confidence is for mentors to give a name to the work that their students are doing, especially if their work does not fit directly within the mainstream. Wolgemuth shared Elizabeth St. Pierre's (e.g., 2011, 2019, 2021) development of "post-qualitative" inquiry as an example. St. Pierre (2016) had been teaching poststructural theories and/as approaches to qualitative inquiry for many years, but lamented that her students' scholarly products were often met with incredulity and dismissiveness from other academics, reviewers, and editors. Her development of and advocacy for post-qualitative research as a named—viable and established—methodological approach carved out a space of legitimacy and recognition for qualitative scholars and methodologists whose bliss was poststructural theorizing.

12. Say "No" Easily—and Mean It

Hayes (1998) notes that to follow Rule #5 (Keep Your Commitments), one must learn Rule #12. It is easy to become overcommitted. When you are overcommitted it is difficult to "mean it" when you say "yes" (see Rule #3). As we reflected on this, we all identified this as an important skill but one that each of us is working on. And some of us noted we really stink at this skill and are not always good role models for those we supervise when it comes to this rule. Both Anderson and Peterson agreed that being a scholar and behavior analyst is like "being a kid in a candy store," where every opportunity simply looks great and is hard not to take on. There are many competing reinforcers and opportunities. As one of our mentors used to say, "Those choices between two approach responses are really hard!" As stated previously, creating practice opportunities for students to say no can be useful.

We have found success in strategies for saying no. For example, one reason saying no is difficult for Peterson (and likely others) is that she doesn't want to let others down. Saying no feels like letting people down. If providing help is a reinforcer for someone, saying no and not providing help withholds a reinforcer (automatic extinction). Teaching a strategy that results in saying no but also helps is one solution. For example, one script for saying no but that still helps might be saying no when asked to complete an editorial review of a manuscript when one's time is limited, and one knows the task cannot be completed on time. If the naysayer responds to the associate editor with a no but also provides suggestions for other reviewers who are also competent and might be highly likely to say yes, the naysayer has provided assistance to the associate editor. The naysayer may still experience positive reinforcement for helping if the associate editor expresses gratitude for the assistance. At the same time, the naysayer experiences negative reinforcement through the avoidance of a stimulus that will take unavailable time and by the avoidance of an aversive stimulus (i.e., being tardy on a review). It can be helpful for mentors to model variations of such scripts for students when saying no themselves and to help students develop their own scripts for situations they may encounter.

Of course, in order to say no, one must first discriminate that a no response is necessary. One of us recalled seeing a meme that displayed a car's side-view mirror. Instead of saying "Warning: Objects in mirror are closer than they appear," the mirror said, "Warning: Dates on calendar are closer than they appear." One of us covertly makes this statement when committing to a talk or other event later on the calendar. We have heard others use statements, such as "Present me really wants to say yes to this talk. How will future me feel about it as the date approaches?" Both of these strategies involve considering delayed consequences and examining other commitments on the calendar that both precede and conflict with the date of the targeted activity. Teaching students to make such evaluations can help in this area. Having conversations with students about these issues can be an important part of the mentoring process. These conversations can be facilitated through discussions of books such as *Deep Work* (Newport, 2016) and *Essentialism* (McKeown, 2014) as part of a book club (see Rule #2).

13. Open Your Mail, Return Your Phone Calls, and Keep Your Desk Clean

Hayes (1998) admits complete defeat on this rule and doesn't even bother to discuss it. These are very practical skills and are still important to model and practice with students. In fact, we mused that this is one area in which those we mentor often mentor us. Our students are often more adept than we are with apps to help manage practical systems. Some of us often ask our students about their strategies here, and we benefit greatly from that mentoring. Further, although we agree that opening emails, returning calls, and the like is important, we also recognize the importance of boundaries and both modeling and supporting boundaries between "work time" and "personal time." We reflected upon many times in which we initiated and/or returned emails in the wee hours of the morning, simply because we happened to be awake, and also how receiving emails sent at these odd hours could inadvertently send a message that we expect others to be working at those times. Each of us noted that we had been making efforts to not send messages outside of common work hours to avoid this implicit message, either by simply refraining from emailing when awake at odd hours or using email tools such as "delay send."

Summary

In summary, though intimidated when asked to write this chapter (imposter syndrome, anyone?), we really had fun talking about our experiences with mentoring and being mentored. We enjoyed struggling through multiple issues, starting with the construct of "woman" and whether our experiences mentoring differ from those of men. We also enjoyed digging into the literature on several topics related to mentoring, gender issues in higher education, and issues of diversity. We (Peterson and Anderson) enjoyed having the opportunity to learn a little more about qualitative research, and work with someone outside the field (Wolgemuth; diversify your network!). We found this to be a highly introspective activity, causing us to more closely examine how we mentor and why we do the things we do. In some cases, we do things the way we do because our own mentors did it that way. In some cases, we do things the way we do because we want to avoid an experience we had when we were being mentored. In yet other cases, we really aren't sure why we do things the way we do. Engaging in the activity of writing this chapter caused us to be more purposeful about our actions in mentoring. And that is a good thing. We hope that reading this chapter helps you to be more purposeful as both a mentor and mentee. We also found it difficult to write—or maybe better put, to stop writing—this chapter, because the nature of mentoring is so dynamic. Each day, when mentoring our students, we would observe yet another example that could be worked into the chapter. Further, we continued to change and grow as mentors as we studied and wrote about mentoring. In short, writing this chapter changed us. Every time we interact with our students, we continue to change and grow. In truth, this chapter will never really be "done." Each of us will continue writing this chapter covertly as we continue to interact with our students and learn to be better mentors. Furthermore, our mentoring processes will continue to grow and evolve across generations of students.

Mentorship is a cultural practice. We work to establish a culture where all members of our research teams have genuine care and curiosity for each other so that we can have meaningful teaching and learning exchanges. Creating nurturing environments is essential for producing the caring and productive individuals our society values (Biglan, 2015). Developing such caring and nurturing environments is important to help the people with whom we work grow into behavior analysts with the skills, interests, and daily habits needed to live healthy, happy, and productive lives (cf. Biglan). What behaviors are involved in developing a culture of caring and nurturing? Though written for graduate students, we found Hayes' (1998)

Thirteen Rules of Success a helpful framework for identifying and organizing strategies mentors can use to guide their students and create a culture of caring and nurturing. We have described examples of what each of the 13 rules mean to us, strategies we have used in the mentoring process that are guided by these rules, and examples of how we have implemented these strategies. You may infer different meanings and strategies from these rules. Indeed, our own understanding of these rules changes and matures over time. We hope you will consider these rules in the context of your own mentoring and will reflect on them often, as their meanings may change over time for you as well. Indeed, Hayes' (1998) rules, while published over 20 years ago, still resonate today. The rules are flexible and easily incorporate different interpretations, particularly our perspectives as women in today's sociocultural context. We suspect they will still be relevant 20 years from now as they continue to evolve in response to changes in mentoring, our field, and the broader sociopolitical dynamics of academic life.

Racial and ethnic diversity in the STEM workforce remains low, especially at the doctoral level and beyond (Bernard & Cooperdock, 2018; HESA, 2018; National Center for Science Engineering Statistics, 2019). Women are also underrepresented in STEM fields (National Science Board, 2016). Some (e.g., Chaudhary & Berhe, 2020) argue that these problems of underrepresentation persist for a number of reasons, including continued marginalization and power imbalances. Implementing some of the strategies described here may help to disperse power in research groups. Creating a caring and nurturing context as we have described means that all members of the group are in the role of mentor and mentee at different points in time. Multi-mentor models, which can be conceptualized as having multiple mentors both within and outside the research group, are becoming favored over a single-mentor, top-down approach (Montgomery & Page, 2018). Such mentoring models may be more responsive to the individual needs and goals of individuals in the research group and may, therefore, create a more nurturing, caring context.

All three of us have had the good fortune of having some wonderful mentors in our careers. We have also experienced some not-so-wonderful mentoring relationships. We have had open conversations with our students about mentoring relationships, which has occasionally prompted discussion among our current and past students about the group cultures in our mentoring communities. Related to the community culture of one group, while we were writing this chapter, a woman who is one of our former students sent the following unsolicited email (shared here with permission from the former student):

> Academia can be so toxic, especially for students of color. Every university has its issues, but I think our [group] protected me from a lot. Of course I still saw things and experienced things, but you and the community you created kept me shielded and protected.
>
> In my current research I have now learned that building community, taking care of each other, looking out for each other . . . all those things are . . . evidence-based practices for ensuring success of students of color in higher ed. All the things you foster and promote in your [group] contribute heavily to the success of all students, and especially students from marginalized communities.
>
> . . . I now see how my other colleagues of color experienced grad school and it is scary and sad to say the least. I was really lucky to land where I did.
>
> I hope this sense of community and family continues to thrive in your [group] now. I now make it a priority to ensure my students feel like a community.

This anecdote was timely and informative regarding the importance of building a caring community between the mentor and mentees. Mentoring in an omnidirectional fashion as described here means the mentor can find herself in the role of mentor, mother, sister, and/or friend at any given point in time—perhaps all in the same day. There is no doubt this makes mentoring complex and challenging. Considering the importance of the task at hand—shaping behavior analysts, setting the occasion for a successful and happy career for budding behavior analysts, and more broadly shaping the future of the field—it is a task that should not be taken lightly. These challenges come with the turf because the task is paramount. With any luck, the payoff is that the cultures we establish with our students will generalize to their own research groups such that similar cultures are established in their own mentoring communities, wherever they go next. For example, these rules for success have already been passed from Hayes (1998) to one of our mentors, to one of us, to our own students, and now to their students. This is how the future of the field is shaped and where the mentor's impact may be felt for many generations.

References

American Council on Education. (2017). *Women presidents*. www.aceacps.org/women-presidents/#:~:text=In%202016%2C%20three%20out%20of,progression%20to%20care%20for%20others

American Psychological Association. (2017). *Ethical principles of psychologists and code of conduct* (2002, amended effective June 1, 2010, and January 1, 2017). www.apa.org/ethics/code/

Anderson, K. J., & Leaper, C. (1998). Meta-analyses of gender effects on conversational interruption: Who, what, when, where, and how. *Sex Roles, 39*(3), 225–252.

Aries, E. (1976). Interaction patterns and themes of male, female, and mixed groups. *Small Group Research*, 7(1), 7–18. https://doi:10.1177/104649647600700102

Armstrong, M. A., & Jovanovic, J. (2015). Starting at the crossroads: Intersectional approaches to institutionally supporting underrepresented minority women STEM faculty. *Journal of Women and Minorities in Science and Engineering, 21*(2), 141–157.

Barroso, A., & Brown, A. (2021, May 25). *Gender pay gap in U.S. held steady in 2020*. Pew Research Center. www.pewresearch.org/fact-tank/2021/05/25/gender-pay-gap-facts/

Behavior Analyst Certification Board. (2020). *Ethics code for behavior analysts*. https://bacb.com/wp-content/ethics-code-for-behavior-analysts/

Behavior Analyst Certification Board. (n.d.). *BACB certificant data*. Retrieved April 12, 2022, from www.bacb.com/bacb-certificant-data/

Bernard, R. E., & Cooperdock, E. H. (2018). No progress on diversity in 40 years. *Nature Geoscience, 11*(5), 292–295.

Bichsel, J., Fuesting, M., Nadel-Hawthorne, S., & Schmidt, A. (2021, March). *Faculty in higher education annual report: Key findings, trends, and comprehensive tables for tenure track, non-tenure teaching, and non-tenure research faculty and summary data for adjunct faculty for the 2020–21 academic year (research report)*. CUPA-HR. www.cupahr.org/surveys/results/

Biglan, A. (2015). *The nurture effect: How the science of human behavior can improve our lives and our world*. New Harbinger Publications.

Brescoll, V. L. (2011). Who takes the floor and why: Gender, power, and volubility in organizations. *Administrative Science Quarterly, 56*(4), 622–641. https://doi.org/10.1177/0001839212439994

Carnegie, D. (1936). *How to win friends and influence people*. Simon & Schuster.

Chang, H., Ngunjiri, F. W., & Hernandez, K. C. (2013). *Collaborative autoethnography*. Left Coast Press.

Chatzidakis, A., Hakim, J., Litter, J., & Rottenberg, C. (2020). *The care manifesto: The politics of interdependence*. Verso Books.

Chaudhary, V. B., & Berhe, A. A. (2020). Ten simple rules for building an antiracist lab. *PLoS Computational Biology, 16*(10), e1008210. https://doi.org/10.1371/journal.pcbi.1008210

Cirincione-Ulezi, N. (2020). Black women and barriers to leadership in ABA. *Behavior Analysis in Practice, 13*(4), 719–724. https://doi.org/10.1007/s40617-020-00444-9

Clance, P. R., & Imes, S. A. (1978). The imposter phenomenon in high achieving women: Dynamics and therapeutic intervention. *Psychotherapy: Theory, Research & Practice, 15*(3), 241.

Clapp, E. P. (2010). Omni-directional mentorship: Exploring a new approach to inter-generational knowledge-sharing in arts practice and administration. In *A closer look 2010: Leading creatively* (pp. 66–79). National Alliance for Media Arts and Culture.

Eakins, B. W., & Eakins, R. G. (1976). Verbal turn taking and exchanges in faculty dialogue. In B. L. Dubois & I. Crouch (Eds.), *The sociology of the languages of American women* (pp. 53–62). Trinity University.

Edelsky, C. (1993). Who's got the floor? In D. Tannen (Ed.), *Gender and conversational interaction* (pp. 189–227). Oxford University Press.

Fernando, D., & Prasad, A. (2019). Sex-based harassment and organizational silencing: How women are led to reluctant acquiescence in academia. *Human Relations*, *72*(10), 1565–1594.

Fries-Britt, S., & Snider, J. (2015) Mentoring outside the line: The importance of authenticity, transparency, and vulnerability in effective mentoring relationships. *New Directions for Higher Education*, *171*, 3–11. https://doi:10.1002/he.20137.

Guyotte, K., & Wolgemuth, J. R. (Eds.). (2022). *Philosophical mentoring in qualitative research: Collaborating and inquiring together*. Routledge.

Halpern, D. F. (2005). How time-flexible work policies can reduce stress, improve health, and save money. *Stress and Health*, *21*(3), 157–168.

Hayes, S. C. (1998). Thirteen rules for success: A message for students. *The Behavior Therapist*, *21*, 47–49.

Hermanowicz, J. C. (2012). The sociology of academic careers: Problems and prospects. In *Higher education: Handbook of theory and research* (pp. 207–248). Springer.

HESA. (2018). *Widening participation: UK performance indicators 2016/17*. HESA.

Ivie, R., White, S., & Chu, R. Y. (2016). Women's and men's career choices in astronomy and astrophysics. *Physical Review Physics Education Research*, *12*(2), 020109.

Jacobi, T., & Schweers, D. (2017). Female supreme court justices are interrupted more by male justices and advocates. *Harvard Business Review*, *11*.

Kearl, H. (2018). *The facts behind the #metoo movement: A national study on sexual harassment and assault*. Stop Street Harassment.

Kulis, S., Sicotte, D., & Collins, S. (2002). More than a pipeline problem: Labor supply constraints and gender stratification across academic science disciplines. *Research in Higher Education*, *43*(6), 657–691.

Langford, J., & Clance, P. R. (1993). The imposter phenomenon: Recent research findings regarding dynamics, personality and family patterns and their implications for treatment. *Psychotherapy: Theory, research, practice, training*, *30*(3), 495.

Lawrence, K. (2017). *Your oxygen mask first: 17 habits to help high-achievers survive and thrive in leadership and life*. Lioncrest Publishing.

LeBlanc, L. A., Sellers, T. P., & Ala'i, S. (2020). *Building and sustaining meaningful relationships as a supervisor and mentor*. Sloan Educational Publishing.

Lee, J. J., & Mccabe, J. M. (2021). Who speaks and who listens: Revisiting the chilly climate in college classrooms. *Gender & Society*, *35*(1), 32–60.

Madge, C., & Bee, A. (1999). Women, science and identity: Interviews with female physical geographers. *Area*, *31*(4), 335–348.

McKeown, G. (2014). *Essentialism*. Crown Publishing Company.

Montgomery, B. L., & Page, S. C. (2018). *Mentoring beyond hierarchies: Multi-mentor systems and models*. National Academies of Sciences, Engineering, and Medicine Committee on Effective Mentoring in STEMM.

National Academies of Science, Engineering, and Medicine. (2018). *Sexual harassment of women: Climate, culture, and consequences in academic sciences, engineering, and medicine*. The National Academies Press. https://doi.org/10.17226/24994

National Center for Science and Engineering Statistics. (2019). *Women, minorities, and persons with disabilities in science and engineering: Special Report NSF* 19-340. National Science Foundation.

National Science Board. (2016). *Science and engineering indicators 2016*. National Science Foundation (NSB-2016–1).

Nebbe, C. (2022, April 26). *The decade-long discrimination a Chinese American doctor at the UI faced and the legal battle that brought it to light* [audio podcast]. Iowa Public Radio, Talk of Iowa. www.iowapublicradio.org/podcast/talk-of-iowa/2022-04-26/the-decades-long-discrimination-a-chinese-american-doctor-at-the-ui-faced-and-the-legal-battle-that-brought-it-to-light

Newport, C. (2016). *Deep work: Rules for focused success in a distracted world*. Hachette UK.

Patterson, K., Grenny, J., McMillan, R., & Switzler, A. (2012). *Crucial conversations tools for talking when stakes are high*. McGraw-Hill Education.

Pritchard, A., Li, J., McChesney, J., & Bichsel, J. (2019, April). *Administrators in higher education annual report: Key findings, trends, and comprehensive tables for the 2018–19 academic year (research report)*. CUPA-HR. www.cupahr.org/surveys/results/

Sawyer, R. D., & Norris, J. (2013). *Duoethnography: Understanding qualitative research*. Oxford University Press.

Scheider, J., & Gould, E. (2016, July 20). *"Women's work" and the gender pay gap: How discrimination, societal norms, and other forces affect women's occupational choices—and their pay*. Economic Policy Institute. www.epi.org/publication/womens-work-and-the-gender-pay-gap-how-discrimination-societal-norms-and-other-forces-affect-womens-occupational-choices-and-their-pay/

Sellers, T. P., Valentino, A. L., & LeBlanc, L. A. (2016). Recommended practices for individual supervision of aspiring behavior analysts. *Behavior Analysis in Practice*, *9*(4), 274–286. https://doi:10.1007/s40617-016-0110-7

Shreffler, M. B., Shreffler, J. R., & Murfree, J. R. (2019). Barriers to the advancement of female faculty in higher education: Evaluations of teaching, work-family conflict and perceived organizational support. *Journal of Higher Education Theory and Practice*, *19*(8), 72–85.

Sidman, M. (1989). *Coercion and its fallout*. Authors Cooperative.

St. Pierre, E. A. (2011). Post qualitative research: The critique and the coming after. In N. K. Denzin & Y. S. Lincoln (Eds.), *Sage handbook of qualitative inquiry* (4th ed., pp. 611–635). Sage.

St. Pierre, E. A. (2016). A brief and personal history of post qualitative research: Toward 'post inquiry.' *Journal of Curriculum Theorizing*, *30*(2), 2–19.

St. Pierre, E. A. (2019). Post qualitative inquiry in an ontology of immanence. *Qualitative Inquiry*, *25*(1), 3–16.

St. Pierre, E. A. (2021). Why post qualitative inquiry? *Qualitative Inquiry*, *27*(2), 163–166.

Tenbrunsel, A. E., Rees, M. R., & Diekmann, K. A. (2019). Sexual harassment in academia: Ethical climates and bounded ethicality. *Annual Review of Psychology*, *70*, 245–270. https://doi.org/10.1146/annurev-psych-010418-102945

U.S. Bureau of Labor Statistics. (2021, September 10). *American time use survey summary*. Economic News Release. www.bls.gov/news.release/atus.nr0.htm

Urry, M. (2015). Science and gender: Scientists must work harder on equality. *Nature*, *528*, 471–473.

Whitaker, R. (2002). *Mad in America: Bad science, bad medicine, and the enduring mistreatment of the mentally ill*. Perseus Publishing.

Part II

Striving and Surviving

7 Scholarship Expectations and Practices Across the Academic Landscape

Kelly M. Banna, Amy L. Odum, and Erin B. Rasmussen

Scholarship Expectations and Practices Across the Academic Landscape

Within the American academy, faculty in tenure-track positions are universally—or nearly universally—assessed across three domains of professional behavior: teaching, scholarship, and service. Although each university or university system defines these categories in its own way, the category regarding scholarship is perhaps the most variable. Most definitions, however, are variations on themes articulated by Boyer (1990) and include activities that discover, integrate, and/or apply knowledge within the academic discipline or to the areas of teaching and learning. Universities—and in many cases, the academic departments contained therein—may also set expectations for the quantity of scholarly activity, the scope at which it is disseminated, the weight allocated to refereed (v. non-refereed) products, and the reputation of the outlet, just to name a few.

Specific scholarly expectations for tenure and promotion—the "golden rings" of the academy—can vary widely both as a function of academic discipline and the nature of the institution. In this chapter, we provide an overview of our academic training, scholarship expectations in our departments, strategies for including students in and obtaining funding for our research, and advice for establishing and maintaining productive lines of research. We are all behavior analysts housed in psychology departments but hold appointments at universities that carry different Carnegie classifications (Carnegie Foundation for the Advancement of Teaching, 2022).

Millersville University of Pennsylvania (MU): Master's Granting, Larger Programs (M1)—Millersville University is one of 14 comprehensive, four-year,[1] public universities in the Pennsylvania State System of Higher Education (PASSHE) that are accredited by the Middle States Commission on Higher Education. It is located in Millersville Borough, which has a population of just over 8,000 people, though the surrounding Lancaster area is much larger (~ 85,000). As of Fall 2021, MU's enrollment stood at 7,213 students, approximately 85% of which were undergraduates.[2] Pennsylvania residents make up 92% of the undergraduate body. PASSHE has been charged by the state legislature to provide exceptional education to Pennsylvania residents at the lowest possible cost to our students.

Kelly M. Banna, Ph.D, Associate Professor: I earned my B.S. in psychology from James Madison University in 1999. I became interested in the experimental analysis of behavior (EAB) while working on my undergraduate thesis with Sherry Serdikoff. My project evaluated the discriminative stimulus effects of gamma hydroxybutyric acid using rats as subjects. By the time I completed that project, I knew two things: first, that I wanted to pursue a career in academia and second, that I wanted to study behavioral pharmacology. While my primary area of interest was drug self-administration, Sherry convinced me to apply to

DOI: 10.4324/9781003216773-10

graduate programs in the experimental analysis of behavior where I could get a solid foundation in the science of behavior; afterwards, I could specialize in self-administration.

I decided to take Sherry's advice. Following graduation, I headed to Auburn University, where I completed my M.S. and Ph.D. in experimental psychology under the mentorship of Chris Newland. Most of my graduate research focused on behavioral pharmacology and mathematical modeling of choice behavior maintained under concurrent schedules of reinforcement, the latter of which I studied in both aquatic (bluegill sunfish) and rodent (rat) species. I also completed formal minors in statistics at both the undergraduate and graduate level (pro tip: if you want job security, find something no one else likes doing and get really, really good at it).

Following graduate school, I accepted a postdoctoral position in the Department of Neuroscience at the Medical University of South Carolina (MUSC) working in the lab of Ronald See. Here, I gained experience studying animal models of substance abuse and relapse using the drug self-administration and reinstatement paradigm. In this model, rats are trained to respond for (i.e., self-administer) small amounts of a drug. Responding is subsequently extinguished, and several challenges are presented to the subjects to determine whether those challenges occasion drug seeking. The challenges most often employed—exposure to stressors; a small, passively-administered amount of the drug; and drug-paired cues—have been selected because they are associated with relapse to drug seeking in humans (see Venniro et al. [2016] and Shaham et al. [2003] for reviews). During my time at MUSC, I also taught Introductory Psychology as an adjunct at the College of Charleston.

For a variety of reasons, I decided to take a hiatus from academia at the end of my postdoctoral scholarship. I ended up in Wichita, KS for four years because my husband was stationed at McConnell Air Force Base. After two years of working as a veterinary assistant at a friend's clinic, I had the opportunity to teach as a visiting assistant professor at Wichita State University. Two years later, I accepted a tenure-track position at Millersville University of Pennsylvania, where I continue to work as an associate professor in the Psychology Department. My primary research interests are behavioral economics and animal models of substance abuse, which often overlap. All of my formal training and most of my current scholarship involves nonhuman animals, but I occasionally dabble in human research.

My professional service to the field includes holding several elected positions in the Southeastern Association for Behavior Analysis (program chair, president-elect, president, past president, and board of directors [twice]). I have also served on the Editorial Board for *Perspectives on Behavior Science* and as an ad hoc reviewer for a number of other publications. I am very involved in service activities at MU, including a current position as the chapter president for our faculty union (the Association of Pennsylvania State College and University Faculties [APSCUF]). I am an active member of the Institutional Animal Care and Use Committee (IACUC) and have chaired MU's Mentored Undergraduate Summer Experience committee, which awards summer grants to undergraduates for research and creative activities.

Department Overview: Our Psychology Department has approximately 14 full-time, tenure-track faculty members at any given time, and contains four programs: a Bachelor of Arts program in Psychology and graduate programs in Clinical Psychology (M.S.), School Psychology (M.S./Ed.S), and School Counseling (M.Ed). The bachelor's program serves just under 400 majors,[3] approximately 20% of whom are transfer students. The psychology major is heavy in coursework for research, statistics, and laboratory work, including a capstone course with a research option. Students also select 12 and 6 credit hours from a menu of core and general electives, respectively.

Two-thirds of the required credits in the Psychology core are in research-focused, laboratory courses, which illustrates the premium our department places on psychology as a research enterprise. Further, our honors program spans three semesters, during which time undergraduates propose, carry out, and defend senior theses, working under the mentorship of faculty advisors. I teach both methods-based courses and the Advanced Laboratory in Learning and Behavior Analysis on a regular basis, and I typically have one or two honors students working in my lab at any given time. I also teach our introductory courses in Learning and Behavior Analysis and Physiological Psychology one to two times per academic year.

Expectations for Scholarship: The guidelines for faculty evaluation and decisions regarding tenure and promotion (T&P) are provided in the statewide collective bargaining agreement (CBA) and associated policies, which are negotiated by PASSHE and State APSCUF. Each chapter of the faculty union (one per campus) also negotiates local policies related to T&P with local administration.

Like most institutions of higher education, the CBA specifies teaching, scholarship, and service as the bases for faculty evaluation. Because PASSHE universities are teaching-centered, the expectations for T&P are weighted in favor of teaching effectiveness. In fact, statewide policy requires that each university explicitly weight teaching as the most impactful of the three when assessing applications for promotion. Our local policy, for example, requires that each promotion application be scored using one of three weighting algorithms:[4] (a) .60-.20-.20, (b) .50-.30-.20, and .50-.20-.30. These numbers represent the weighting factors for teaching, scholarship, and service, respectively. These weighting algorithms indicate that scholarly activity only accounts for 20–30% of faculty members' overall promotion score (v. 50–60% for demonstrating effective teaching). This is reasonable considering that a full teaching load is 24 c.h. per academic year (i.e., a 4:4 load).

While categories for evaluation among PASSHE universities mirror those at other institutions of higher education, we are somewhat unique in that the evaluation and granting of tenure is independent from that of promotion to associate professor. Faculty are required to apply for tenure in their fifth year of employment. Applications are reviewed by the University Promotion and Tenure Committee (UPTC), which then recommends to the provost whether or not to tenure each applicant; it is an "up or down" decision. In contrast, the decision to go up for associate is entirely up to individual faculty members. They may apply for associate along with tenure or wait to do so at a later date. In theory, faculty in PASSHE institutions could retire at the rank of assistant professor.

In general, the expectations for scholarship in my department are broad; the CBA provides a list of activities that count as scholarship across campuses and disciplines, and our local agreements on T&P specify that more weight is given to those activities that have been subjected to external review processes (e.g., peer-reviewed articles, juried exhibitions) than to those that have not. There are currently no minimal requirements for any type of scholarly product specified in the CBA, related statewide policies, or local agreements. Generally speaking, faculty must demonstrate some minimal amount of scholarship to earn tenure (e.g., one to two publications, two to three conference presentations). Expectations for promotion to associate are a bit higher, but not specified; the same goes for promotion to full professor. In many ways, MU takes the Justice Potter Stewart (*Jacobellis v. Ohio*, 1964) approach to identifying quality scholarship: we'll know it when we see it.

Student Involvement: Completing my graduate work and postdoctoral fellowship at large, research-intensive institutions confirmed what I had always known: that I did not want a career in that environment. These experiences were critical in preparing me to establish my own lab at Millersville, so I wouldn't trade them for anything—that sort of work just wasn't (and still isn't) what I want to spend my time doing. While I like research, I *love* teaching, and I especially love recruiting undergraduate students and training them in the behavior analytic tradition. Therefore, when I applied for tenure-track positions, I only applied to small-to-medium liberal arts universities emphasizing undergraduate education that would allow me to build a meaningful research program dedicated to training undergrads. Luckily, I found an opportunity to do just that at MU.

Given the teaching-intensive nature of my position, I have had to creatively design my research program such that it overlaps significantly with my teaching responsibilities. First and foremost, I am an active mentor in the Psychology Honors Program. I typically mentor one to two thesis students every year and employ two to three additional undergraduate laboratory assistants who are paid with MU student wage funds. Students complete projects that are (in theory) publishable and align with my research goals. Many of these projects are variations on those that I completed as a graduate student or a postdoc, or replicate studies involving animal models of substance abuse and/or behavioral economics. Typical animal projects include two experimental sessions a day, six days a week, *all of which are run by undergraduate students*. Students are also paid to do husbandry work (e.g., weigh, feed, clean cages) and lab cleaning on one day every weekend.

I employ a junior-colleague model of mentorship common in graduate programs (see Amy's more extensive description shortly). I work closely with students in the beginning of a project and gradually give them more independence as the project evolves. New students and lab assistants are trained by more experienced students, and eventually graduate to working independently. We have regular lab meetings, during which time we address any experimental/animal-care issues that arise and discuss journal articles (when there is time). This is also the forum in which my thesis students practice their proposals and defenses. Essentially, my lab is modeled after the experience I had as a graduate student.

Unfortunately, supervising honors theses does not count towards my course load. In order to use my time more efficiently, I've begun using honors projects as the basis for classroom projects in my advanced laboratory course. Students in this class gain experience handling rats, shaping behavior, and carrying out husbandry duties. Course readings are drawn from the primary literature related to the project, and we spend the semester reviewing readings and building a research paper around the lab project. By doing this, I am combining prep work for honors theses with that for one of my (labor-intensive) courses, which also allows me to prepare and write my own manuscripts.

I've used a similar strategy in my statistics class—class projects replicate (or replicate and extend) projects described in the primary literature that align with my research interests. The results can be written up for publication and/or presented at conferences, either by students or by me. Such a strategy also provides opportunities for publishing and/or presenting in journals or at conferences related to either the research topic or to teaching and learning.

Sources of Funding: At many institutions, faculty are expected to negotiate "start-up packages" before accepting academic positions. This involves securing the resources (e.g., financial, physical space) necessary for a new faculty member to begin and complete enough research to apply for additional, external funding over the following years. The size of these packages can range from a few thousand to over a million dollars depending on discipline, scholarship expectations, and the availability of laboratory/office space, and can often be *the* selling point or *the* deal breaker of a job offer.

Luckily for me, I didn't have to deal with any of that for the following reasons. First, I was hired, in part, to teach a course that includes a rat-lab component. This meant that the laboratory space I would need to teach *and* conduct my own research was already available. Second, the academic building that houses the Psychology department was undergoing significant renovations at the time I was hired. Because of the timing, I was able to work with the university architect to design the laboratory space according to my needs and industry standards before I even started my first day of work. Finally, one of the expectations was that I would modernize both the methodological and technological aspects associated with maintaining an operational rat lab and teaching a related course. When I arrived, all the equipment was antiquated (think analog operant chambers and hanging wire cages), which meant that everything needed to be replaced. Because the laboratory space was used as a teaching facility (i.e., was tied to our curriculum), the entire cost of upgrading the housing and experimental equipment was covered by the college in which my department is housed. This amounted to over $50,000 of equipment, which I was also expected to use for my own research and research involving students—jackpot!

Start-up costs are only the beginning of the financial resources required to maintain an animal laboratory. Additional and recurring costs include purchasing animals, *per diems* (i.e., husbandry costs associated with animal care, such as food, bedding, and animal facility staff), maintenance costs, and the cost of any additional equipment needed for new research projects. Because all of my research involves students, and (to date) all of their projects have been associated with required or elective courses, I have been able to maintain my lab using nothing more than funding from my department/college and internal grants to me and (mostly) my students. This has the added benefit of providing students with experience writing grant applications, which is an excellent addition to their CVs, especially if they intend to apply to graduate school. The lab also offers opportunities for employing students on campus in a way that gives them research experience and skills they would find useful if they wanted a career in research. Undergraduate-focused universities are often happy to support these activities because they provide the foundation for student research (a high-impact practice), give students unique experiences that increase their competitiveness in graduate school applications, and contribute to the educational mission of the school.

I am not unique in my department. Among those of us who regularly mentor student research, none of us currently has significant sources of external funding (e.g., more than $5,000). In fact, aside from the animal research I conduct, most or all of the research being done by faculty in my department can be done at little to no cost. Student funding is available through internal grants, some of which are paid for through a significant endowment to the department made by my predecessor. This money is specifically set aside to support student research and travel, and is available to faculty who engage those students.

Words of Wisdom: The following suggestions are anecdotal and are based on my experience at an undergraduate-focused, public university with high teaching demands. I suspect that these strategies would prove fruitful at most similarly situated institutions and at smaller private colleges where undergraduate research is considered a highly valued, high-impact practice.

Kill two (or more!) birds with one stone. Because teaching loads tend to be heavier at baccalaureate and master's institutions, look for opportunities in which your scholarship and teaching can overlap. Applying a graduate school model to student theses and/or independent projects provides one such opportunity. Rather than separating your research from student collaborations, align student projects with your scholarly interests and goals. Projects should be selected based on intellectual merit and the potential to produce publications or presentations at state, regional, or national conferences. This approach requires that you identify and recruit academically strong students who demonstrate high levels of responsibility and the ability to work independently. Depending on how long data collection lasts, it may also require you to identify students who can commit to a multi-semester project (more on this shortly).

A second mechanism for combining teaching and scholarly activities is to bring your research interests into the classroom. While many of us do research on complex topics that, as a whole, are more advanced than what is typically covered in undergraduate courses, they can often be broken down into smaller, simpler writing and laboratory assignments. By doing this, much of the preparation you do for your classes will provide at least a foundation for manuscripts and conference presentations.

Replicate (and extend). Replication is the gold standard for demonstrating the reliability of scientific findings; it is the key to discovering "truths" about the natural world. Unfortunately, it is undervalued in both grant funding and publication, which makes it a low-value activity for faculty employed at research-intensive universities. However, undergraduate research projects provide an excellent opportunity for such studies for the following reasons. First, undergraduates, by their very nature, are not prepared to conduct extensive literature searches to identify "holes" in the literature or to design studies on how to fill them. Second, their time with us is limited. While graduate school can go on for a seemingly indefinite period of time, most undergraduates expect to complete their degree in four years. Further, many do not take research-based courses or begin doing mentored research until their junior or senior year. Replication studies provide the opportunity to conduct research using well-defined methods, eliminating the time it would take to design a novel study. Further, replicating a published study specifies and limits the scope of the literature review students need to do; it is a much more tractable endeavor. Given that the scientific community—including the field of behavior analysis—has begun to acknowledge the value and necessity of replication in advancing science, opportunities for publishing such studies are likely to increase in the coming years (see, for example, the special issue of *Perspectives on Behavior Science* addressing replication and reproducibility).

Because the scholarship and funding expectations for faculty at teaching-intensive universities are often less stringent than those at larger institutions, there is less pressure to chase after shiny new projects or to obtain large grants. This means we are free to do things like replicate existing studies and present the results at conferences or in publications. We also get bonus points for including students. Also, once you've successfully designed and implemented a replication for use in a class or as a student research project, it is relatively easy to (re-)replicate and extend. This is particularly efficient for those of us who teach multiple sections of lab-based courses on an annual basis.

Identify good students and recruit/train them early. In order to maintain a successful research program at an undergraduate institution, you will need to identify and recruit strong students early in their career (e.g., late sophomore/early junior year). My strategy has been to reach out to students who do well in my (or colleagues') classes, especially the research methods and statistics sequence and the introductory behavior analysis course. I look for students who are actively engaged in class activities and discussion, demonstrate advanced critical-thinking skills, attend class regularly and on time, work well with their classmates, interact well with me, submit all of their assignments on time, and who (ideally) are decent writers. I know that sounds like a lot, but in ten years at a small, public university in relatively rural Pennsylvania that has an admissions rate of over 90%, I have never had trouble identifying one to three students a year who meet these criteria and who want to work in a rat lab. Given the heavy teaching load I carry and the fact that I spend a substantial amount of time engaged in university service, I cannot commit enough time or resources to training students who are not already well prepared for working in a live animal lab. Inviting underprepared students into my lab would set us both up for failure, so I don't do that.

It is also my belief that this relationship should be symbiotic: if these talented students are willing to dedicate a significant amount of time and effort to my lab, I owe it to them to be an attentive and active mentor. In their time with me, I try to teach them about the ins and outs of running a lab (tl;dr—85% of it is trouble-shooting, 10% is sciencing, 5% is screaming into the void); the ethical responsibilities associated with caring for live animals; and designing, executing, analyzing, and presenting research. Successfully navigating this process is rewarded with detailed and glowing letters of recommendation. In short, my goal is to create a research environment in which students will flourish, provide them with the experiences they need to successfully apply to graduate school, and make it so that—when they get there—they are *under*whelmed by the workload.

Idaho State University (ISU): Doctoral-Granting, High Research Activity (R2)—Idaho State University is a university located in rural mountainous Pocatello, ID—a city of over 55,000 residents. ISU has over 240 undergraduate degree programs and 140 graduate programs, 20 of which are doctoral-level. ISU also has the health mission for the state of Idaho and leads the state in training for health professions. We have satellite campuses in three other cities—in Idaho Falls, Meridian, and Twin Falls—as well as one in Anchorage, AK. ISU typically enrolls over 12,000 undergraduate students and over 2,000 graduate students. Most undergraduate students are from Idaho and 40% are first-generation college students. About 57% of the student body identifies as female. Because our undergraduates are from Idaho, they generally reflect the demographics of the area—73% are White and at least half identity as members of the Church of Jesus Christ of Latter-Day Saints. We have seen a rise in Hispanic students attending ISU in the last decade, which currently make up about 12% of our student body. About 52% of our undergraduates receive some form of financial aid.

Erin B. Rasmussen, Ph.D, Professor: I completed my B.S. in Psychology at Utah State University; my undergraduate advisor, Carl Cheney, heavily influenced my direction into the experimental analysis of behavior. From there, I earned my Ph.D. from Auburn University in the Experimental Analysis of Behavior (emphasis in Behavioral Pharmacology and Toxicology) under the supervision of Chris Newland. Much of my training is in animal research, though I also learned a great deal from Tom Critchfield on how to do human operant research. I also learned the philosophy of behaviorism and tools of science from Peter Harzem, Jim Johnston, Bill Buskist, Mona El-Sheikh, Bill Hopkins, Rick Fleming, and Dudley McGlynn. After graduating from Auburn, I accepted an assistant professorship at the Department of Psychology at the College of Charleston, which has three to four behavior analytic core faculty, for three years. Then in 2004, I accepted an assistant professor position in ISU's Department of Psychology, which is where I have resided since. I am now a full professor and am also the chair of ISU's IACUC.

During my graduate and postgraduate training, I developed a wealth of research skills in both animal and human research, and I benefitted greatly from training in general processes that underlie the behavior of many species. Because of this, my research program has involved the study of behavioral processes that can be examined from the highly controlled and reductionist rigor of the animal lab to real-world settings that have broad social significance. My research team typically includes four to five doctoral students from both of ISU's PhD programs (Experimental Psychology and Clinical Psychology) and some talented undergraduates; all of them contribute substantially and meaningfully to my research program.

My current research interests tie together health, behavioral economics, and behavioral pharmacology. I have two laboratories (human and animal) that investigate choice and decision-making involved in obesity and health. My human work focuses on behavioral economic and socioeconomic factors related to food-based delay discounting. My animal work investigates the effects of diet on neurotransmitter systems that play a role in the valuation of food reinforcement (including delay discounting) in diet-induced and genetic models of obesity. More recently, we have been examining the establishment of food cues as triggers for binge eating and delay discounting.

I have over 60 peer-reviewed publications and was awarded a three-year research grant from the National Institutes of Health (NIH) to investigate the relations among food insecurity, obesity, and food impulsivity. I have served as Associate Editor for *Perspectives on Behavior Science* (2015–2019) and have completed two terms on the editorial board of the *Journal of the Experimental Analysis of Behavior*. I also served as the president of the Association for Behavior Analysis International for a three-year term (2019–2022) and recently received authorship of the seventh edition of the textbook *Behavior Analysis and Learning: A Biobehavioral*

Approach with Drs. Casey Clay, Carl Cheney, and the late David Pierce. I teach undergraduate and graduate courses on Learning & Behavior, Food & Behavior, Senior Seminar, and Psychopharmacology.

Department Overview: The number of faculty in the Department of Psychology is smaller than most universities with doctoral programs, with 13 tenure-track faculty members, one visiting line, one full-time lecturer, and a varying number of adjuncts. We have over 400 students in our undergraduate major.

We have two doctoral programs—an APA-accredited Clinical Psychology program that is over 30 years old and an Experimental Psychology program that is over ten years old. Our faculty are collaborative across programs—research and mentoring students across the two graduate programs is standard practice. We have 40–50 graduate students in the department; most are from out of state. Most come here to work with particular faculty members. Our faculty are productive publication-wise; many have acquired federal funding, and many are well known in their fields, which also adds to the exciting climate of the department.

The standard teaching load at ISU is 3:3, which means everyone must teach three courses in the fall and three in the spring. This teaching load is set by the Idaho State Board of Education. Each faculty member is accountable for 15 units of work output and nine of those must be teaching. Therefore 60% of the load is required to be teaching. However, each department can determine what qualifies as teaching. For example, in our department, the clinical faculty count practica (training clinical doctoral students in therapy) as a class; other universities often include this requirement on top of regular teaching loads. Our department also gives faculty one course credit per year if they are supervising at least three graduate students in terms of theses and dissertations. Therefore, most faculty in our department have a 2:3 or 3:2 teaching load. Course releases are also offered for administrative roles in the department, such as for chair or graduate-program directors or for university administrative roles, such as chairing the IACUC. You can also "buy out" of courses with research grants.

Based on this teaching load, the research requirements for each department at ISU vary a great deal. In our department, since the number of classes we teach includes graduate mentoring, we meet the state law's requirements for nine units of teaching. But if you consider the distribution of work to the three areas (teaching, research, and service) by counting courses only as teaching, the distribution looks more like 40–50% teaching, 45–55% research, 5–15% service. Because we have two doctoral programs, it is easier to get studies published because the work of conducting the studies is done primarily by graduate students. Faculty conduct research mainly by supervising the design, analysis, and dissemination of the studies, as well as applying for grant money, but the data collection and foundational work is done by the graduate students.

Expectations for Scholarship: Our departmental guidelines for T&P state that a faculty member must have published at least three to four peer-reviewed publications during the five-year review period (with data collected from ISU) to earn a satisfactory rating for T&P to associate professor; more publications are required for a superior rating. At least six to seven peer-reviewed publications (high-impact are more heavily weighted) during the review period are required for a satisfactory rating for promotion to full professor; again, more are required for a superior rating. You must have at least one superior rating in the areas of research or teaching for promotion to associate and two superiors in the three areas of teaching, research, and service for promotion to full professor.

The mean productivity in the department, though, is much greater than these minimal requirements. Once their labs are established, faculty members publish an average of two to three peer-reviewed papers per year, which results in ten or more papers on average for promotion to associate professor and 15 or more for promotion to full professor. The contingencies for publishing seem to be less about department requirements and more about the social or personal contingencies. Many of us enjoy the process of publishing papers and helping our graduate students reach the next level (e.g., postdoctoral fellowship, academic position). This greatly maximizes productivity because publishing research is controlled by appetitive, as opposed to aversive, contingencies. In other words, a published paper is a positive reinforcer, as opposed to a negative reinforcer. For me, I have been a full professor for ten years now, and I am hitting my peak level of research productivity. I am not required by my university to publish much at this point; my employment is safe. But producing research under these conditions is enjoyable and an act of intellectual stimulation. It is an ideal arrangement for me.

Everyone in my department is expected to submit grants for tenure and promotion to the rank of associate and full professor. Internal grants are minimal requirements—everyone needs them to fund their research and they are relatively easy to get. As such, they don't count for much in terms of progress toward T&P. Submitting external grants to federal agencies like the NIH and the National Science Foundation, which require a great deal of preparation and are highly competitive, is weighted much more heavily. Everyone is expected to *submit* grants to appropriate federal agencies for T&P, but because of the highly competitive nature of federal funding, the grant's *funding* is not required. If the grant is funded or if a high score is achieved, however, the chances of T&P are very high. This is also true for promotion from associate to full professor. About half of our faculty has received external funding from federal agencies—some were funded pre-T&P, some post-T&P, and some were funded after reaching the rank of full professor. But the reality is that most who receive federal funding do so later in their career. For example, the average age of a scientist getting their first grant (R01) funded by the NIH in 1995 was 40 years old. Since then, that age has increased to 44 years old. There are no gender-related differences in age of first grant, incidentally (Lauer, 2021), though women make up less than 30% of grant awardees at NIH (Lauer & Roychowdhury, 2021). Given that most faculty begin their careers (i.e., obtain an assistant professorship) in their late 20s or early to mid-30s, one can see that these grants are not really intended to help launch careers; they are awarded after a principal investigator (PI) has demonstrated an ability to establish a program of research (this is true even of New Investigator initiatives).

Student Involvement: At ISU, my graduate students conduct the empirical studies that my research team generates, and I offer developmentally appropriate levels of supervision and support from the first step of conceptualizing and designing the study to the last steps of dissemination, such as publishing the study or presenting it at a conference. My students submit the protocols for research ethics review (Institutional Review Board if a human study or IACUC if an animal study), help design the studies, collect the data, and conduct the analyses. I help them hone their skills of writing, presenting, and critical thinking. I also help them prepare for their thesis and dissertation proposals and defenses. With more experience, they become more self-sufficient with these skills and earn the ability to design their own studies more independently. We use the vertical team approach (see Rasmussen et al.'s Chapter 5 on mentoring in this volume), in which each student, based on their experience, serves as a mentee and mentor to someone more junior, in terms of research. Undergraduates on the team often serve as research assistants to my graduate students' studies. Once in a while I will have an especially gifted undergraduate who I will mentor in designing a study. I have had several undergraduates publish their honors thesis, for example.

My graduate students also get opportunities to publish non-empirical papers, too, such as reviews or book chapters. These projects are usually led by me, and their duties are more circumscribed (e.g., a specific section of a paper is assigned to a student). All of my graduate students are expected to submit research grants (usually internal grants or smaller-value external grants) to help fund their studies and to get experience with grant writing. They are also expected to present research (e.g., posters, symposia) at professional conferences annually, consistent with program and laboratory requirements. Advanced undergraduates also get these opportunities, though usually as posters.

Sources of Funding: For my first three years, my start-up package funded the building of my operant research (rat) laboratory and seed money for the first projects. I also negotiated an office space for a potential human lab, should the need arise to do human research. After those three years were up, I took advantage of internal grants, the Idaho IDeA Network of Biomedical Research Excellence program, and a university-wide National Science Foundation grant that offered seed money for research to female PIs. I also applied for NIH grants, though none of my applications were funded in the early years. Much of my time was spent looking for money to fund research. It was enough, though, to earn T&P to the ranks of associate and full professor. I also ended up designing a human operant lab, which was a good move. It allowed my research team to conduct studies in a shorter time with less money than was required for animal research (and a side note: my human research gets cited much more frequently than my animal research. Serendipity.).

Shortly after reaching full professor, I finally landed the NIH grant, and it was fantastic not to have to worry about funding for a short time. True to the data, I was 44 when I received the news from the NIH. Now, I am at a point in my career where I am not required to submit grants, but to continue my research program, money is required. I also feel that because ISU invested in me and my research early on, I need to continue the return on their investment (ROI—a buzzword we hear a lot in universities these days). So, my plan is to continue submitting grants to fund more extensive projects.

Words of Wisdom: The following suggestions are intended to help young (and not-so-young) faculty navigate the world of grant applications and publication.

Publish in a variety of journals. As behavior analysts, it is both an honor and duty to publish in and support our journals. However, there are some limits to this. If your department or institution values peer-reviewed research in high-impact journals, they may undervalue research published in behavior analytic journals—even the flagship journals of the field—simply because the scope of impact (i.e., impact factors) is lower. At the time of this writing, we are seeing a rise in the impact factors of some of our flagship journals (e.g., *Journal of the Experimental Analysis of Behavior, Journal of Applied Behavior Analysis*, and *Perspectives on Behavior Science*, formerly *The Behavior Analyst*) due to efforts to broaden the range of authors, content, and citations outside of the field; however, the impact factors are still on the lower end (impact factor range = 2.11 to 2.83) when comparing them to multidisciplinary journals in psychology and other fields. Nonetheless, depending on departmental and university practices, publishing in journals with lower impact factors (even those flagship journals in the field) may harm one's chances of T&P. In addition, when submitting grants for external fundings, grant reviewers want to see that the PIs have published research in high-impact journals. Therefore, doing so increases the odds that a grant application will be taken seriously.

My approach is to publish both in behavior analytic journals and in higher impact, multidisciplinary journals. Some examples of the latter include *Experimental and Clinical Psychopharmacology, Health Psychology, Appetite, Physiology and Behavior, Journal of Experimental Psychology*, and *Behavioral Research and Therapy* (impact factor range = 3.2 to 5.87). Publishing more broadly also has several other benefits. One, a wider range of scientists are exposed to behavior analytic research, which keeps our science visible. Two, greater exposure means more citations of your research, which increases your *h*-index—a measure of impact that is often used for T&P and funding decisions (though, the interested reader should also see Koltun & Hafner, 2021 for why an *h*-index may not be the best indicator of impact). Third, publishing in journals with greater impact increases your competitiveness for faculty positions across a wider range of institutions. For example, I can credibly market myself as a psychopharmacologist, health psychologist, behavioral economist, and even behavioral neuroscientist because my research has been published in journals representing these fields. Therefore, my profile may fit a wider range of available positions both within and outside of the academy. I also train my students to market themselves more broadly in this way.

Reach out to scientists from other fields if you want federal grants and higher-impact publications. The contingencies of getting grants and publishing in higher-impact journals are collaborative and multidisciplinary. Therefore, staying insular in behavior analysis is unlikely to pay off. It is perfectly appropriate to reach out to others outside of your field and talk about a potential grant idea or research project. Being flexible with the technical language of behavior analysis and how others talk about our field will be important in ensuring that conversations are productive. I personally feel like my research has been more meaningful to me because of my collaborations outside the field. The perspectives I have gained are invaluable.

Scholarship is a life-long process. When I look back at myself after graduating with my Ph.D., I see someone who was still very green in terms of research. I did not know this at that time. I had eight peer-reviewed publications, so I figured I knew a little something. But I still had a great deal to learn about scientific writing and grant writing in particular. Graduate school gives you the foundational skills you need to begin the academic journey, but practice and peer-reviewed feedback (surprise!) hone these skills. The peer review process will teach you repeatedly how to sharpen your writing skills, how to anticipate how reviewers will respond to what you write (and prevent those responses), and to develop openness and humility to critical comments (i.e., a thicker skin). I am not the same writer I was 20 years ago as a fresh Ph.D.; I am not the same writer I was ten years ago. And I hopefully will not be the same writer ten years from now. Be kind to yourself as you remember that research is a lifelong skill. Don't give up when you receive harsh criticism. Instead, make some time and space for the emotional responses and self-doubt, then come back to the critical comments as feedback that will strengthen your skills as a writer and scientist, rather than as a threat to your identity. Every revised draft I have made has been improved by the critical feedback of reviewers—every single one.

Specialize your research program. As a fresh Ph.D., I had big ideas about chasing multiple topics for research. My graduate advisor warned me against this, reminding me that the contingencies for a research program are in specialization—picking one area and sticking with it. It took me some time to realize that what he said was true. External grant reviewers want to see that you have a program of research; dedication to one area reassures them that you are an expert, and that the money will be spent wisely. Spreading yourself too thin across multiple topics might occasion others to characterize your record as "jack of all trades, master of none." This is perfectly fine if that is your goal, but if your goal is to get an external grant or to be recognized as an expert in a specific research area, then specializing is the way to go.

External funding: if at first you don't succeed. . . . The nature of NIH (and other institutional) funding awarded to mid- or late-career scientists has implications for the new faculty member. First, be wary of institutions in which the funding of external grants is *required* for T&P; this places a faculty member in a precarious position, especially given that even some of the most meritorious applications do not receive funding (see NIH, 2021; Rocky, 2015). It is in your best interest to ask about T&P requirements before accepting a tenure-track position. It is also important to realize that requirements may change over time, so contingencies at the time of hire may not be the same ones later. Having ongoing conversations with your chair can ensure you are current in expectations along the way. Second, to build one's research credibility, one tactic that can pay off is to submit grants that are funded by nongovernment agencies (e.g., foundations or private companies) and take advantage of other organizations for seed money, such at the Center for Translational Research, state programs that fund seed money for research (e.g., the Idaho IDeA Network for Excellence in Biomedical Research), and internal grants to supplement research and provide preliminary data for the larger grants. Your Office of Research, Office of Sponsored Programs, or others in your department can be a valuable resource for learning of such opportunities.

And finally, do not give up! It can be demoralizing when a grant application gets triaged (i.e., not discussed because it is not in the top 50%). It can also be confusing when a revision that initially received a high score gets a lower score or even triaged on the second round. It can also be frustrating when an application receives a high "fundable" score, but then receives no funding. It is helpful to understand the peer review process of the institution of interest. For example, at the NIH, funding decisions are made by the institute (there are 27) and this is a separate process from scientific evaluation, which is conducted first by the Center for Scientific Review (CSR). A high score from the scientific-review process is necessary for the next decision of funding by the institution (see NIH, 2019, 2022). To complicate matters further, the lore around NIH funding is that decisions are based 75% on merit and 25% on luck. For example, three scientific reviewers from the Scientific Review Group (SRG; also called study sections) are assigned to review an application. The application must be meritorious and enthusiastically regarded and promoted to the SRG by all three reviewers (but especially by the primary and secondary reviewers) to receive a high score, which is contributed by the SRG. PIs do not have any say or prediction in who will be the three specific reviewers of their application, though they do have access to a roster of those on the SRG (40–50 names usually). This is where luck comes in: if one reviewer is just a little lukewarm about the topic (even though the science is strong), this will affect your score. Further, even if the application receives a high score and is recommended for funding, the institute may not list your topic as a funding priority (contacting a representative from the institute to determine funding priorities is always a good idea before starting an application). Either one of these events can lead to an outstanding application not being funded. Despite these unknowns, doing some detective work in terms of knowing your SRG roster and institutional funding priorities can still increase your likelihood of funding. The advice of "just keep submitting applications" is sound—a worthy application can indeed eventually align with the planets and pay off.

Utah State University (USU): Doctoral-Granting, Very High Research Activity (R1)—the main campus of Utah State University is located in Logan (population 53,000), in the mountains in high-elevation northern UT, and is situated in the greater Cache Valley area, which has an estimated population of 150,000. Utah State has over 24,000 undergraduate students and 3,000 graduate students across the main and branch campuses, and over 900 professors on the main campus, which encompasses 400 acres. The mission of Utah State is to be "one of the nation's premier student-centered land-grant and space-grant universities by fostering the principle that academics come first, by cultivating diversity of thought and culture and by serving the public through learning, discovery and engagement." Of undergraduate students, 53% identify as women, 83% White, and 7% Hispanic. Over 50% of undergraduates receive federal grants, 20% are first-generation college students, and 77% are from Utah. Utah State has one of the oldest and most prestigious undergraduate research programs in the U.S.

Amy L. Odum, Ph.D, Professor: I have been a professor for over 20 years. I began my higher education at the University of Florida in Gainesville (UF), having grown up mostly in rural north Florida. At UF I was strongly influenced by a host of prominent behavior analysts, most notably Ed Malagodi, Tim Hackenberg, Marc Branch, Brian Iwata, and Hank Pennypacker, who were my professors. I helped to conduct research in the Malagodi/Hackenberg laboratory, where my first job was to clean pigeon operant chambers. It was a very dirty job. Eric Jacobs, who was a graduate student at the time, was a kind and wise mentor to me. After graduating with my B.S., I worked for a couple years as a program director at a residential facility for people with developmental disabilities, a position I obtained because I had briefly served, frankly rather poorly, as an undergraduate research volunteer in Brian Iwata's laboratory with Jennifer Zarcone, Tim Vollmer, and others (graduate students at the time), studying self-injury in people with developmental disabilities.

These experiences made me realize that I was not, in fact, well suited for applied work, and I began looking for graduate programs in basic behavior analysis. I enjoyed basic research in which I could more fully control the relevant variables and experimental conditions, although over time I have come to realize that even in the laboratory, there is only so much we can control and understand. I earned my master's and Ph.D. at West Virginia University (WVU), where my mentor was Dave Schaal. I also was highly influenced by other faculty there at the time, including Andy Lattal, Mike Perone, Kent Parker, and Phil Chase. My research at WVU was in Behavioral Pharmacology and basic EAB with pigeons. I was interested in the effects of delayed reinforcement on behavior as well as how environmental factors influence the effects of drugs on behavior.

After I completed my Ph.D, I began a postdoctoral fellowship at the University of Vermont's Human Behavioral Pharmacology Laboratory, mentored by Warren Bickel, studying delay discounting in people with drug addiction. Steve Higgins and John Hughes were influential to me as well. For example, Steve Higgins gave me my first review to conduct for the *Journal of the Experimental Analysis of Behavior*, which he read and gave me feedback on. In particular I recall his suggestion to be more helpful and kind, advice which has stuck with me to this day. Academia and the peer review process are difficult enough, so I do my best to be a caring and positive force within it.

After a year as a postdoctoral fellow, I became an assistant professor. I started at the University of New Hampshire (UNH), where Billy Baum had recently retired. Things went well overall at UNH, but in 2003 I accepted a position as assistant professor at Utah State University in Logan, where I remain today. Unlike UNH, where I mentored graduate students in a general Ph.D in psychology, USU offered the opportunity to revitalize a specialized graduate program in behavior analysis. While I was at UNH, I learned about their Preparing Future Faculty program, which emphasizes training in research, teaching, and service; this has continued to influence my approach to graduate training to this day as the majority of my students ultimately become professors.

My current research focuses broadly on delay discounting (the decline in the value of temporally proximal reinforcers) and animal models of licit drug use. My laboratory conducts research with both people and nonhumans (mostly rats but in the past, pigeons as well). We have conducted research on topics that range from basic determinants of delay discounting (e.g., delay distribution and the order in which it is presented, the impact of history variables [e.g., cigarette smoking status]) to more applied and clinical research on strategies for decreasing the extent to which delayed outcomes are discounted. Some of these projects have been conducted in collaboration with clinical behavioral analysts in my department, and other projects in collaboration with faculty from other specializations, such as the brain and cognition. As my career has advanced and I have been tenured longer, I have been focusing more on projects that are interesting to me but at higher risk for not producing publishable data in a timely manner. For example, as a full professor, I have been spending a lot of time and effort on developing a rat model of e-cigarette use (vaping), which has come with a host of technical challenges. My hope ultimately is to link these two lines of research to examine history factors like vaping that influence delay discounting in preclinical models, and how we may remediate the heightened delay discounting that may result.

I have been fortunate to hold a number of roles in the field of behavior analysis. I served as Associate Editor for the *Journal of the Experimental Analysis of Behavior* (*JEAB*), and then was chosen as Editor in Chief. This position held some mixed feelings for me, because although I was surely not the first woman to be qualified for the position, I was the first woman to hold it since the inception of the journal in 1958. I am also serving the second of two eight-year terms on the board of directors of the Society for the Experimental Analysis of Behavior, which publishes JEAB as well as the *Journal of Applied Behavior Analysis* (*JABA*), and have held the roles of vice president and president each, twice (I am currently president). I also served as president of Division 25 (Behavior Analysis) of the American Psychological Association. I am a fellow in the Association for Behavior Analysis International (ABAI) and was a founding member of the science board. For the ABAI program, I served as area coordinator for behavioral pharmacology as well as program committee chair. I am excited to have joined Jim Mazur as a coauthor on the ninth edition of the textbook *Learning and Behavior*.

Department Overview: The psychology department has grown tremendously during my time at USU, and we have currently over 30 tenure-track professors as well as five clinical/research track professors and a full-time lecturer. There are nearly 800 undergraduate psychology majors and approximately 225 graduate students in the department. The Ph.D. program comprises seven graduate specializations. Behavior analytic faculty work both in Combined Clinical/Counseling, which has been continuously accredited by the APA for nearly 50 years, and in the Behavior Analysis specialization, which has been active for over 50 years and currently features basic as well as applied and translational emphases. In conjunction with the department of Special Education and Rehabilitation Services, students in the Behavior Analysis specialization can meet the requirements to become Board Certified Behavior Analysts. Faculty frequently collaborate across programs, and the department prides itself on undergraduate education and involvement in addition to a thriving graduate program and highly productive faculty, many with large federal grants.

The typical teaching load for tenure-track faculty in the psychology department is 2:2, indicating that faculty are expected to teach two courses in the fall and two in the spring. Pre-tenure faculty have a reduced teaching load for their first few years, and course reductions are also available for intensive external service roles, such as journal editor or president of a society. We have role statements that describe the percentage of "evaluative weight" that teaching, research, and service hold for us, and the majority of professors have 45%, 50%, and 5% respectively, meaning that teaching makes up 45% of our evaluation, research 50%, and service 5%. Notably, these weights do not describe how much time faculty spend in these activities, but how these activities are weighted in our evaluations. This fact provides an important caution as well as tension for those who would take on major service roles. Course buy outs are also available, in which faculty can contribute a set amount of money from an external grant to help cover the cost of hiring someone else (graduate student or adjunct) to teach their assigned course. Faculty can buy out of all but one course a year, and in practice even this is negotiable.

Expectations for Scholarship: Criteria for annual evaluation are spelled out in the role statement, and for research incorporate multiple elements. One of these is a steady and consistent record of research endeavors supporting scholarly activity, which includes peer-reviewed materials like journal articles as well as books and book chapters, invited review articles, symposia presentations, and success in extramural funding. The output is expected to be sustainable over time, with the professor acquiring the resources needed to maintain their program of research. Professors are also expected to keep a positive professional reputation based on their scholarly activity. Furthermore, professors must articulate and sustain a focused and coherent theme in their research program. The role of the professor on any collaborative work with colleagues from other disciplines must be clearly described and documented. It is expected that over time, professors will be major contributors and/or leaders in their research and scholarship, including in funding which supports their work.

Evaluations take place annually with the department head and, as of recently, incorporate the previous five years of work. To "meet expectations" for research, faculty must average at least three peer-reviewed products per year and submission of at least one external grant proposal per year. These publishing expectations have increased from two per year when I was first hired, and in practice, a number of faculty publish far more (e.g., 10–15 per year). Exemplary research performance in terms of number of articles and/or a large external grant received are required for "exceeding expectations" in annual reviews.

Promotion and tenure reviews are a separate process from annual evaluations and are conducted with a committee of faculty rather than the department head. To receive promotion and tenure, assistant professors need to meet the standard published in the USU faculty code, which states that promotion requires "an established reputation based upon a balance of teaching, research and service; broad recognition of professional success in the field of appointment; evidence of effectiveness in all of the professional domains in which the faculty member performs; and evidence of excellence in the major emphasis of his or her role statement." Excellence is defined by the standards for associate professors within the person's national professional peer group. Thus, in order to receive tenure and be promoted from assistant professor to associate professor, faculty must demonstrate excellence in the main area of their role statement, which is in most cases research.

Note that in the role statement, as well as in the criteria for promotion and tenure, there is no explicitly stated number of peer-reviewed products required, grants submitted or funded, etc. Furthermore, the function of the promotion and tenure committee is meant to be strictly evaluative, rather than advising or mentoring. Although advice may be given by the committee (and in practice often is), it is explicitly stated that promotion and tenure strategies as well as materials included in the portfolio are solely the candidate's responsibility. These facets of the promotion and tenure process can be anxiety-provoking, but the annual reviews provided by the committee provide an assessment of the likelihood of the candidate's record meeting the criterion of excellence for the main emphasis (typically research) and effectiveness for the other emphases (typically teaching and service) each year prior to the tenure and promotion decision. Thus, the ultimate judgement when it is made in the critical year should ideally come as a surprise to no one. Promotion to full professor requires the same criteria as promotion to associate professor, but with the additional requirement that promotion to the rank of professor "shall require an outstanding reputation in at least the major emphasis as defined in the role statement." When you compare the annual evaluation process with the promotion and tenure process, it becomes clear that being "excellent" in the promotion and tenure process is "meeting expectations" in annual evaluations. Thus, the expectation and the norm are excellence. It can be difficult to feel like "enough" in this type of context, so it is important to work out what your values are and let your goals and efforts be guided by these. Then you can evaluate yourself with respect to how you've met your value-driven goals in addition to how you have met the department's expectations of excellence.

Student Involvement: Undergraduate and graduate students are an integral part of my research. The involvement of students in my research program is very similar to that of Erin's described earlier, so I won't repeat the valuable information that she presented. Rather I will simply say that involving students in a meaningful way and inviting them to make contributions to the work at every stage is extremely fulfilling and substantially increases the creativity and relevance of the research conducted in my lab. In conjunction with my students, who have different life histories and knowledge than I have, we can think of ideas that wouldn't occur to us individually. Their fresh takes on long-time topics keep the work interesting and timely. I give them a great deal of autonomy in their research so that they can learn many of the things that come only from experience. Rules go only so far, and may not be remembered as well as contingency-shaped procedures when they have their own laboratories.

I follow a junior-colleague model, in what we have termed the "lab family" approach, which is a form of vertical mentoring in which all laboratory members (myself included) mentor and guide members who have less experience and knowledge. This means that my graduate students get a lot of mentoring experience while still in graduate school. My goal is that when students leave my laboratory, I am confident that they will be able to establish their own laboratory, with everything that goes into that large and complex task. Therefore, I give them increasing levels of independence so that by the time they earn their Ph.Ds, they can function virtually autonomously, although I still oversee their work and give advice and guidance. It can be a bit scary and challenging to let students make decisions about the course of a project after discussing the pros and cons of different directions rather than to *tell* them what to do, and it can also be the same for students to bear that responsibility. For that reason, I let students know that I can make decisions if they don't feel ready and provide additional direction at their request. Over the years, I have tried to identify the optimal level of support and scaffolding my students need to develop into their own, and to be open to and welcoming of feedback from my students regarding my mentoring and supervision. I highly recommend LeBlanc et al.'s (2020) "Building and Sustaining Meaningful and Effective Relationships as a Supervisor and Mentor," which I am working to incorporate into my relationships with my students.

Sources of Funding: Research at USU is funded in a variety of ways. First, there are a number of mechanisms through which my undergraduate and graduate students can apply for direct funding. These include guaranteed internal funds from the department and college for undergraduate honors theses, master's theses, and dissertation research. Additionally, students may compete for internal grants. These are increasingly competitive, and recently have been funded at rates not unlike that of external grants. Finally, my students often write and receive external grants from associations, societies, and foundations.

USU also provides a number of funding opportunities for research that is not student-led. As is common, I received a start-up funding package that provided initial financial support to cover the cost of equipment and other necessities, such as animal purchases and per diems and payments for human participants. Importantly, after the start-up funding, most resources available to USU professors in psychology are highly competitive. For example, internal grants come from the Office of Research, which receives applications from all disciplines across the university. The competitive nature of this process often requires second-round submissions with award rates similar to that of external sources. In recognition of the lack of ready internal funding, our department recently transformed our individual travel fund to an individual research and professional-development fund. This small amount of guaranteed funding for each faculty member will be helpful, but for animal research, which is quite costly, external funding is required. This requirement is one of the more stressful aspects of research at USU to me. My salary is completely covered by my institution, but at some major research universities, even portions of tenure-track professors' salaries must come from external funding.

Over the years, I have collaborated on a number of successful external grants as well as received some as principal investigator from the NIH. These include grants from the National Institute of Mental Health, the National Institute on Alcohol Abuse and Alcoholism, and the National Institute on Drug Abuse. All of Erin's advice about grants is excellent, and I won't duplicate it here. One thing that is helpful about USU is the way that indirect costs on an external grant are handled. Indirect costs are the general costs charged by the institution to support the research in addition to the direct costs of actually conducting the research. USU returns a portion of indirect costs to the college of the investigator, which in my case is the College of Education, which then returns a portion of the indirect costs to the department (in my case Psychology), which then in turn returns a portion of the indirect costs to the principal investigator on the grant project. These dollars form a general research fund that investigators can use to support research projects other than the grant. Research in my animal laboratory has been funded extensively by indirect costs generated by grants for other animal projects or even those that fund human research. The amount of indirect cost returns varies widely across universities, with some offering none, but at some institutions, this source of money can be a real boon to creativity and productivity as not all research must be funded with specific external sources.

Words of Wisdom: I have a few bits of advice to add to Erin and Kelly's very helpful and detailed recommendations. They include strategies for establishing and maintaining healthy writing habits, which many faculty find challenging.

Distinguish between the writing and editing processes. I remember sharing a lovely dinner with one of my favorite mentors and research collaborators Tony Nevin, by then emeritus faculty at UNH and well into his 70s. After dinner—glass of wine in hand—he said he was going to go write for a while. To my surprise, no sooner had he sat down at his laptop than the clickety clack of his keyboard started up at a vigorous pace. As a new assistant professor, it still took me quite a while to get started when I sat down to write, and so I thought a great deal about how it was that Tony could sit down and begin writing immediately. Obviously, he had a great deal more experience, but in talking to him, I found he also wrote without concern for the exact word choice or turn of phrase. On reflection, I realized that sometimes I took a long time to write because I conflated the writing and editing phases. By giving myself permission to write imperfectly, with a commitment to edit my writing *later*, I was able to get going much faster and to maintain a higher speed once I was writing. At times, I even resorted to a bit of absurdity. If I didn't know what to write for a topic sentence, for example, I would write something to hold the space, like "this is a topic sentence," and move on to the details of the paragraph if I could. If I was really struggling, I would even say aloud and concurrently type things like "I'm typing! I'm at my computer and I'm typing! I'm at my computer and I'M TY-PING!" (thanks to Will Ferrell in the movie *Elf* for this idea). Somehow typing, even if the content wasn't *right*, set the occasion for more typing, and eventually I would be on my way. I find I no longer need this strategy to get going, but it was a lighthearted way for me to deal with what can be a serious issue.

Better living through (applied) behavior analysis. In the past, I found myself struggling to get started on large writing projects; I still do, on occasion. My solution is inspired by basic EAB research in which pigeons respond for reinforcers on fixed-ratio schedules. Under such schedules, a certain number of responses are needed to produce a reinforcer. The larger the upcoming ratio, the longer the pigeon will pause before getting started. If you break it up and give the pigeon a conditioned reinforcer, like a flash of the key light, for smaller units within the ratio (called a second-order schedule), the pauses are much shorter and the pigeon works more steadily (Ferster & Skinner, 1957). Thus, for myself, I break up larger writing tasks into smaller units until I reach a unit I can easily complete. For example, it may be difficult to get started if you tell yourself you are writing an NIH grant, but much easier to begin if you tell yourself you are writing the first paragraph of the specific aims. This tactic of breaking up projects into small-enough units so that you can easily complete the task, combined with the other tactic of separating writing from editing, has been enormously helpful for me over the years and others I have shared it with. If you share these struggles in your writing, then I hope it will be helpful to you too.

Strive consistently to improve your writing. I recommend a writing diary. Writing *well* is a long-term learning process, as Erin noted, and at this point, I enjoy honing my craft. In the beginning of my graduate school career, however, back in the days of red pen on hard copy, it was daunting. For my graduate students, I have them note each piece of feedback they receive on their writing in a document, and how they addressed the feedback. For example, they may receive the suggestion to strengthen a topic sentence so that it covers the contents of the paragraph. They can then note how they did so. Sometimes students receive comments on grammar, such as use of a semicolon v. comma. In this case, they would write the rule for when to use which. Over time and with consistent review, the writing diary is refined and condensed as patterns become clear. The student eventually has a guide that they generated with solutions to their unique writing challenges and growth points. They can then review this guide as they are editing their work, and thus become more and more independent. If you are already past the stage where you regularly receive detailed feedback from a mentor on your writing, consider requesting some from a trusted colleague or mentor. Additionally, you could start a writing diary with feedback from the peer review process, like manuscript reviews and grant reviews. The goal is to notice your common challenges as well as build a ready-to-deploy arsenal of solutions to those challenges. As you are writing that manuscript or grant, you can review your specific issues and improve them *before* you hit submit.

Some Final Thoughts

The previous narratives highlight some similarities in the scholarship practices and expectations across the academic landscape. These include the integral role that students play in research and our approaches to mentoring, expectations to produce scholarly products, and the necessity of research funding. However, there are some explicit and important differences, especially between undergraduate-focused institutions, such as MU, and the more research-intensive universities. The most notable include the amount of scholarly productivity required for tenure and promotion and the amount of external funding faculty members are expected—and even required—to secure.

These differences should be taken into account when going on the job market, especially when applying for your first academic position. None of these models is better than the other—rather they emphasize different aspects of scholarship, broadly defined, and each provides opportunities for growing the field. For example, faculty at R1 and R2 schools are producing the lion's share of peer-reviewed publications and producing doctoral-level behavior analysts. Faculty at smaller schools, however, have the freedom to focus on recruiting talented undergraduates and preparing them for graduate study; in a way, they serve as feeder schools to the larger institutions. Together, they form a sort of "training ecosystem" for the field. The type of institution that is right for *you* is the one that most closely aligns with your personal professional goals and plays to your strengths. Ideally, it will also provide a supportive environment for you to work on your weaknesses, whatever they may be. Whichever career path you choose, remember that you are more likely to succeed at an institution at which you can spend the majority of your time engaged in activities that are personally fulfilling. Don't let others coerce you into taking one path or the other based on *their* personal and professional values.

Finally, remember that to be a scholar is to be a lifelong learner. This does not simply mean the accumulation of more factual knowledge; it primarily refers to the consistent and intentional cultivation of new skills and growth within your professional field over the course of your academic lifetime. The ability to demonstrate such a pattern is indispensable in successfully navigating the scholarship expectations at any academic institution.

Notes

1. As of July 1, 2022, PASSHE will comprise ten universities after three schools in the west and three schools in the northeast are integrated to form two universities.
2. Full time = 4,916; Female = 59%; White = 75%, Hispanic = 10%, Black = 8%; Pell Grant Recipient = 25%; First-Generation ~ 17%
3. PA resident = 95%; Female = 84%; White = 72%, Hispanic = 14%, Black = 8%; Pell Grant Recipient = 34%
4. The weighting algorithm that produces the highest score for each applicant is the one that is used.

References

Boyer, E. L. (1990). *Scholarship reconsidered: Priorities of the professoriate*. The Carnegie Foundation for the Advancement of Teaching. https://files.eric.ed.gov/fulltext/ED326149.pdf

Carnegie Foundation for the Advancement of Teaching. (2022, April 24). *The Carnegie classification of institutions of higher education* (2021 ed.). https://carnegieclassifications.acenet.edu/definitions.php.

Ferster, C. B., & Skinner, B. F. (1957). *Schedules of reinforcement*. Appleton-Century-Crofts. https://doi.org/10.1037/10627-000

Jacobellis v. Ohio, 378 U.S. 184 (1964). www.oyez.org/cases/1963/11

Koltun, V., & Hafner, D. (2021). The h-index is no longer an effective correlate of scientific reputation. *PLoS One*, *16*(6), e0253397. https://doi.org/10.1371/journal.pone.0253397

Lauer, M. (2021). *Long-term trends in the age of Principal Investigators supported for the first time on NIH R01-equivalent awards*. https://nexus.od.nih.gov/all/2021/11/18/long-term-trends-in-the- age-of-principal-investigators-supported-for-the-first-time-on-nih-r01-awards/

Lauer, M., & Roychowdhury, D. (2021). Inequalities in the distribution of national institutes of health research project grant funding. *eLife*, *10*, e71712. https://doi:10.7554/eLife.71712

LeBlanc, L. A., Sellers, T. P., & Ala'i, S. (2020). *Building and sustaining meaningful and effective relationships as a supervisor and mentor*. Sloan Publishing.

National Institutes of Health. (2019). *NIH peer review: Grants and cooperative agreements*. National Institutes of Health Office of Extramural Research. https://grants.nih.gov/grants/peerreview22713webv2.pdf

National Institutes of Health. (2021). *NIH success and funding rates*. NIH Data Book. https://report.nih.gov/nihdatabook/category/10

National Institutes of Health. (2022). *Peer review*. NIH Central Resource for Grants and Funding Information. https://grants.nih.gov/grants/peer-review.htm

Rocky, S. (2015). *What are the chances of getting funded?* National Institutes of Health. https://nexus.od.nih.gov/all/2015/06/29/what-are-the-chances-of-getting-funded/

Shaham, Y., Shalev, U., Lu, L., de Wit, H., & Stewart, J. (2003). The reinstatement model of drug relapse: History, methodology, and major findings. *Psychopharmacology*, *168*, 3–20. https://doi.org/10.1007/s00213-002-1224-x

Venniro, M., Caprioli, D., & Shaham, Y. (2016). Animal models of drug relapse and craving: From drug priming-induced reinstatement to incubation of craving after voluntary abstinence. *Progress in Brain Research*, *224*, 25–52. https://doi.org/10.1016/bs.pbr.2015.08.004

8 Promotions

Rocío Rosales

Preface

I am the proud daughter of immigrant parents from Mexico who dedicated their life to the pursuit of opportunity and education for their children. I am a first-generation Mexican American and first-generation college student. My experience in academia may share similarities with but is also likely vastly different from that of esteemed colleagues who hold a position of privilege as a White woman and/or who come from a higher socioeconomic background. In turn, my own privilege as a cisgender, able-bodied woman, grants me a unique experience and perspective. This context is important to share because my lived experience inevitably contributes to my writing on this topic and may speak to some more than others. I hope the content will be helpful for all who read it, and that my voice will reach and inspire those who share similarities with my own background—one that is not well represented in academia, and even less so in behavior analysis. I am grateful to the editors of this book for the opportunity to share my perspective, and especially to Ruth Anne Rehfeldt, for her unwavering mentorship and sponsorship throughout my career.

Promotions

There are many exciting opportunities that come with your first academic position. You meet new colleagues who may become potential research collaborators, others who may become lifelong friends. You are in a new space, with new courses to prep, new students to mentor, and new partnerships to forge. The more immediate tasks that require your attention could take up all your time: prepping that new course, department and committee meetings, trainings and orientations for new faculty, and students who need your help and advice. When is there time to think about and plan for tenure? What about your research and writing? These activities are not scheduled for you. You must make the time. The tenure process requires that you focus on protecting your time and promoting your work.

Balancing the many and varied responsibilities that come with being a faculty member is crucial to your ultimate success. There are three areas that will make up the formal evaluation: teaching, research, and service. There are also *informal* areas of evaluation (i.e., collegiality tends to be a major factor; more on this later). During the provisional period at the rank of assistant professor, which typically lasts six to seven years, there are opportunities for structured feedback on your performance in teaching, research, and service. When a tenure dossier is sent for review, it is evaluated by various committees starting with colleagues in your home department and culminating with the University President or a Board of Trustees. A successful evaluation results in tenure and promotion to associate professor. In case of an unfavorable outcome, a new search for employment must begin. Annual reviews are designed to avoid this potentially devastating situation.

DOI: 10.4324/9781003216773-11

Promotion to full professor follows a similar process, but there is a wide timeframe ranging anywhere from another six to ten years (or more) following tenure, and the qualifications or requirements are broader in scope. For example, a national and/or international reputation in your field, showing academic leadership, and securing a certain amount of external funding may all be required for promotion from associate to full. An important distinction between these two levels of promotion is that the second is not a requirement to keep your job. Earning tenure equates to a lifetime appointment with the institution. The position is secure unless a crime is committed, or some other severe offense occurs, or in the unfortunate event that a department is cut due to funding considerations or low program enrollment. The second promotion results in an added increase to your base salary, and it is the highest faculty rank until retirement and status as Regent Emeritus is granted, which are often given even higher status than full professor. Both factors have a lasting impact on a career in academia. For both promotions it is critical to have a solid understanding of the department and institution's expectations and requirements.

Written and Unwritten Rules of Tenure and Promotion

Each institution has a set of written rules and guidelines for new faculty to reference in preparation for promotion and tenure. Even after a careful read of this chapter, it is likely that you will have questions. As questions come up it is critically important that you seek clarity from colleagues and mentors within the institution. Criteria for promotion and tenure, although guided by a set of written rules, are often not explicit or clear. To complicate matters, there are *unwritten* rules that are not applied in the same manner within or across departments. Regrettably, these unwritten rules are part of the culture of academic institutions. As a new faculty member your task is to read, and then interpret the rules—but you cannot do this on your own (nor should you try). The decisions surrounding faculty roles and responsibilities have both intellectual and political components that will be unique to each department. As a graduate student, you were likely not privy to all the department politics. As a faculty member, you must understand the political aspects of decision making in your department to ensure your own success. Mentors within the institution can be a valuable resource for learning about the university and department's culture to successfully navigate these unwritten rules.

Most institutions will provide new faculty with formal orientation and annual workshops in preparation for promotion and tenure. If these meetings are available to you, do not skip them. This is especially important if there are frequent changes in the university's upper administration (i.e., chancellor, president, provost). The information shared at these annual workshops will vary from year to year, and the requirements for preparing your dossier may change slightly. If the institution is implementing large-scale changes, the requirements for promotion and tenure may seem like a moving target. For example, if a research university is making strides to achieve an R1 status, the requirements for promotion and tenure may increase from year to year. In some cases, promotion to associate may be considered under the "old" promotion and tenure guidelines (or those that the individual faculty person was hired under); however, requirements for promotion to full typically will fall under the new or most recent guidelines. If there are changes to the guidelines or requirements for promotion and tenure, it may be advantageous to follow the new guidelines in promotion to associate. Doing so puts faculty in a better position to transition from associate to full. Another advantage of attending workshops related to promotion and tenure on a regular basis is that recently promoted faculty can supply insights into the process, and this is an ideal time to meet and network with colleagues outside of your department.

Preparing a tenure dossier may not be the only requirement at your institution. Some universities require external letters of support, which are different from letters of recommendation. External reviewers are not typically selected by the faculty person who is being considered for tenure and promotion. This means that colleagues in the field will be invited by your department chair to comment on your promotion materials, although in some cases you may be invited to make *suggestions* both for potential reviewers and those to exclude. Ask early if this is a requirement of the tenure process at your institution. External reviewers generally cannot be colleagues with whom you have an existing relationship (personal or professional). For example, your primary mentor from a doctoral program cannot serve in this role, nor can colleagues you have partnered with on grants (internal or external) or publications. If external reviewers will be called on to comment on the tenure dossier, it will be important to think strategically of how to grow your professional network and increase your visibility in the field. Some of this may be accomplished via professional service so long as there is a balance with research activities. Later sections of this chapter will be dedicated to recommendations for balancing teaching, research, and service activities.

Although the tenure and promotion process and its written guidelines should be transparent, the reality is that you will need to do some work to interpret unwritten rules and navigate department politics. This has been described as navigating a "foggy climate" (Banerjee & Pawley, 2013). Tenured faculty members can help clear up the fog by presenting clear and explicit information to untenured colleagues. Doing so helps to create equity in the tenure and promotion process (O'Meara et al., 2019).

Mentorship and Sponsorship

Finding mentors to help guide you through the process of promotion and tenure may be the single most important thing you do to increase your likelihood of success and protect your well-being. Mentors provide information, encouragement, support, and advocate on your behalf (although this last role may be best described as a *sponsor*, as will be defined shortly). If you have a mentor assigned to you within your department, also look for one outside of your department and outside of your institution. If you have both, look for more. It is unlikely that one or two people will be able to fulfill all your needs as a new faculty member. These needs are compounded if you are a member of a historically marginalized group.

Think of having multiple mentors in the same way you might think of having friends who support you in unique ways. The relationship is different, but the idea is the same. Who can you ask specific questions to about department politics? Do you have a trusted source to help you understand the campus environment? Who will you call on if you need advice on a student issue? Who is your go-to person for bouncing around research ideas? Who can you share teaching ideas with? Is there someone who will read and comment on your work before it is sent in for peer review? Who will you turn to for emotional support? Do you have a role model within the department? Do you have a role model within the profession? Do you have someone that shares your cultural identity that you can look up to in the field? For faculty from historically marginalized groups, a role model or mentor of the same or similar background is especially influential (Boyd et al., 2017), yet one may not be available. The National Center for Faculty Development and Diversity (NCFDD) provides a wide range of tools and supports that I recommend exploring. This includes a "mentor map" (National Center for Faculty Development and Diversity, n.d.) that will get you thinking of the various roles mentors can play in your success in academia.

Some institutions have formal mentorship programs that assign new faculty to at least two different mentors (one within and one outside the department). But what if the mentors aren't a good match? What if you need someone to help hold you accountable in a safe space? You may find that the best mentor relationships are those that happen organically, and that peer mentorship can be just as important as non-peer mentors. The best part of peer mentorship is that it need not be formalized. A group of peers you can talk openly to without fear of repercussion can provide a sense of empowerment and in turn, improve career satisfaction (Faloye et al., 2021). If you formalize some aspects of the group by holding writing sessions or professional-development workshops, this can also affect your productivity and career growth.

By creating a *network* of mentors, you alleviate the pressure of relying on one or two people to meet all your needs or to have all the answers. As a mentor myself, I often send my mentees to seek input from others. My perspective on certain topics will be unique and therefore not shared by all. Moreover, it is important for new faculty to connect with multiple colleagues in and outside of their department. Mentors within the profession also play a critical role. If you have a good relationship with your graduate school mentor, continue to foster that relationship after you secure an academic position. Stay connected. Share personal developments and professional accomplishments. Staying connected creates a lifelong opportunity for senior colleagues to open doors for your career advancement. This is an example of *sponsorship*, which differs from mentorship in several ways (Ayyala et al., 2019).

What is sponsorship? Briefly it is when a mentor uses their own social capital (the network of relationships they have built over the course of their career) to help advance or influence their protégé's career (Chow, 2021). It is the difference between providing one-on-one advice and individual feedback to speaking well of the mentee to a larger audience when the mentee is not present. The sponsor uses their status and visibility in the field to give visibility to their mentee. But this is not as simple as putting someone's name forward or inviting them into professional circles. The mentee will have questions and may need help navigating the new space. They may experience imposter syndrome (Clance & Imes, 1978) and feel pressured to work harder than everyone else to prove their worth and status. Imposter syndrome has been described as a feeling that individuals may experience when they perceive their status and/or position was granted due only to some blunder, mishap, or stroke of luck. This inevitably leads to feelings of not belonging in certain groups (e.g., academia, leadership positions in professional organizations, invited speakers at conferences, etc.). Recent discussion has called for a reframing of "imposter syndrome" as "imposter *phenomenon*" in order to highlight the role of context both in its development and maintenance (Feenstra et al., 2020). By acknowledging the complexity and multidimensional origins of this construct, individuals may be better able to address imposter feelings if they are contextualized as a response to a dysfunctional context rather than some intrinsic characteristic. This may be especially true for faculty from marginalized groups who have fewer role models in elite spaces (Ayyala et al., 2019; Boyd et al., 2017), and thus, may be more susceptible to the imposter phenomenon.

There are actionable steps that sponsorship entails. Rosalind Chow (2021) describes these as the "ABCDs of sponsorship": Amplifying, Boosting, Connecting, and Defending. Amplifying is the equivalent of self-promotion (here, the sponsor promotes the work of the mentee). As someone in a position of power and privilege, the sponsor shares the accomplishments of the mentee to create or increase positive impressions by an external audience. Women hesitate to self-promote (Exley & Judd, 2019). When a sponsor amplifies on behalf of the mentee it validates their work and can elevate its status. Boosting is the equivalent to serving as a reference. When a sponsor vouches for a mentee, they put their own name and reputation on the line. Connecting is when the sponsor elevates the status and recognition of the mentee by facilitating new relationships. Defending is the equivalent of offering protection against unfair critiques or biased opinions. This is a key role of a sponsor. Defending is particularly important for women faculty of color who have an increased likelihood of being viewed negatively by colleagues (Ong et al., 2017). For example, women's interactions may be more likely to be viewed as "confrontational" or they may be viewed as being "too outspoken." On the other hand, some women may be viewed as indifferent if their cultural background encourages or teaches them to be silent.

Many of us have benefited from sponsorship at some point in our professional lives. Once we recognize and acknowledge its power, we may be tempted to seek it out and to serve as sponsors to new colleagues in the field. Mentorship and sponsorship are a constant state of learning and growth. It is never too late to seek out or to become a sponsor.

The Big Three: Teaching, Research, and Service

One consistency across academic institutions in the promotion and tenure guidelines is the focus on three different components of the dossier: teaching, research, and service. How much value or emphasis is placed on each will vary. As mentioned previously, seeking clarity on how written guidelines are interpreted by the department, college, and university is critically important. I will review each of these components for general considerations and important aspects that should be considered for women faculty and members of historically marginalized groups.

Teaching

All tenure-track positions require faculty to teach. The number and types of courses faculty are assigned to teach vary depending on the needs of the department and of the institution. While most tenure-track appointments are nine-month positions, some offer added teaching opportunities in the summer, generally for more compensation. Teaching in the summer is not required and some institutions may frown upon those who opt for summer teaching because it inevitably takes time away from research activities. Teaching loads may be negotiable. For example, an appointment at a state college or university with a strong emphasis on teaching may carry a 4:4 load (4 courses in the fall, 4 courses in the spring), but this can be reduced to 3:3 with course buyouts for faculty who are actively conducting research and show research productivity (i.e., via publications in peer-reviewed journals). At research institutions, the teaching load may start at 3:3 or 2:2 but can be further reduced when faculty show research productivity (e.g., via a certain number of peer-reviewed publications and/or success securing external funding). Course reductions may also be negotiated if faculty are involved in service activities at the institution (e.g., director of a graduate program) or in their profession (e.g., editor of an academic journal).

An important aspect related to teaching is the number of new course preps you are assigned during the first few years of your appointment. While it may be exciting to develop courses from the ground up, this can take considerable time away from your research activities. Academic departments may have systems in place to protect new faculty and avoid overburdening them with teaching and service activities. If you do not feel support in this regard, seek advice from a mentor about best ways to address this issue. Perhaps the culture of the department or institution does not match your needs and that could be a good reason to start seeking employment elsewhere. When you are developing new courses or making updates to courses you previously developed, it is easy to lose yourself in course prep. If you tend to be a perfectionist and/or if you have a large teaching load, this is a particularly difficult trap to escape. Set accountability checks for the maximum time you will dedicate to any given course. You can (and should, in my opinion) integrate teaching with research, as this is an excellent way to show your commitment to high-quality teaching. If you are unsure about topics or research questions you can address in the classroom, there are several resources that may serve as inspiration (see Bernstein & Chase, 2013; Brodsky & Fienup, 2018; Querol et al., 2015).

A key area of teaching is how you are evaluated as an instructor. Unfortunately, student evaluations have consistently shown low correlations with teaching effectiveness, and are known to be biased to favor White, older, male instructors (Bavishi et al., 2010; Kreitzer & Sweet-Cushman, 2021). Hence, women faculty and members of other historically marginalized groups start the semester at a disadvantage. Knowledge of these biases may lead to self-imposed internal pressures to perform at higher-than-expected levels to avoid negative evaluations. To alleviate this concern, it may be helpful to seek out regular feedback from students during the semester. For example, instead of waiting until the end of the term, create and distribute a simple two- to three-question anonymous survey to seek input at the midterm. Include a section for narrative feedback as this may provide valuable information that will not be captured by numbers. Encourage students to complete the narrative part of the survey by sharing that you plan to make changes based on their input. Then do it. This shows students that you take their input seriously and can set the stage for improved scores at the end of the term. Feedback loops tend to improve performance and overall satisfaction and can serve to build rapport with students. If you can show how you use student feedback to make continuous improvements to your courses, this will be viewed as a strength in your teaching.

Importantly, teaching evaluations are not limited to student input. Your department chair and/or department colleagues may also conduct regular observations of your teaching. These observations are typically scheduled with advance notice and followed by a written summary of the observation. In this case, unlike with end-of-semester student evaluations, there is an opportunity for the faculty member to respond to the chair's comments in a formalized manner, especially if these comments become part of a permanent record. If your department or institution does not have a formal peer teaching-evaluation process, you can still ask colleagues to observe your teaching and comment in a formal manner to include as part of your teaching dossier. Opening your classroom to outside observation can be intimidating but getting input from multiple perspectives may lead to positive outcomes.

Finally, evaluation of teaching also includes performance as an advisor and mentor. Keep good records of the number of students who work with you each term and what they do or where they go after they graduate or leave your research lab. If you supervise undergraduate or graduate-student research projects, offer research or service-learning opportunities, and provide professional-development opportunities to students in your research lab. When students are part of a conference presentation and/or peer reviewed manuscripts, make note of it. Peer-reviewed publications that include students as first authors (on theses and dissertations) may still "count" as first-authored publications by colleagues in your department and help to demonstrate a commitment to high-quality mentorship. These are all forms of teaching and mentorship outside of a classroom setting. Gather formal feedback from students who take part in these activities at the end of each term. These experiences can have a significant impact on student success, but they are not often formally evaluated as teaching activities by institutions.

Research

All tenure-track positions require faculty to engage in research. The expectations and requirements for research productivity can vary widely by institution. Considerations in the evaluation of a faculty's research may include not only the number of peer-reviewed publications on a curriculum vitae, but when the research is published (e.g., if there is a record of consistent productivity from the time of the appointment), where the research is published (e.g., journal impact factors), how often the research is cited (e.g., a presence on platforms that track citations of your work), and how the research is evaluated by peers (e.g., what external reviewers say about the work and its impact on the field).

Publishing steadily is likely to be a key factor in the evaluation of research. This means that, ideally, there are no large gaps in the record of publications. Start by publishing your dissertation. The timeline from submission to publication can be a year or longer. Set a writing schedule and stick to it. Form or join a writing group to help with accountability for writing (20–30 minutes a day can help you develop a habit of writing). The format and schedule of the writing group can be adapted to meet your needs. Personally, I have found that people I work with best are reliable with checking in on my progress and provide intermittent encouragement. If you can't meet in person, meet virtually. One of the benefits of meeting virtually is that you can expand your writing group to colleagues in different time zones. Set up a Zoom or Google meeting, check in at the beginning for no more than five minutes, and set a timer for your next check-in. If you do meet in person, follow the same schedule to keep everyone on track and hold each other accountable.

Deciding where to send your work for peer review and eventual publication is also an important part of this process. A brief description of each journal where you have published should be on the version of your curriculum vitae that is sent with your tenure application (this is customary practice in some departments). For example, it may be relevant to include information about each journal's acceptance and/or rejection rates, the number of subscribers, and the relevance of the journal within your area of research (e.g., *The Analysis of Verbal Behavior* focuses on research in a niche area v. *Behavior Analysis in Practice* if the work you are doing is practice-oriented). It is important to weigh the pros and cons of publishing your work in a variety of journals. If you only send manuscripts for peer review to the top journals in the field, and you are successful with publications in these journals, your visibility within the field will likely grow. Citations may also be higher for journals that are more commonly referenced within your scientific community. There are advantages to publishing in journals that are considered second-tier or outside of behavior analysis, namely dissemination of your work to a broader audience, and possibly an increased likelihood of success with the peer review process. If you are collaborating on an interdisciplinary project, your collaborators may need to publish the work in journals in their own field. In some departments, you may have to present a strong case for publishing outside of discipline-specific journals even when those journals have higher impact factors.

Conference proceedings may carry varying weight in the evaluation of research. While some institutions place a high value on conference presentations, others may not consider this work as "counting" toward your research productivity. If you have a good sense of what your department and institution expect and value for research activity, it can guide your decision-making process to distribute your time. For example, if you are providing supervision to graduate students for required theses or dissertations, these projects can easily convert to conference proposals. But if conference proceedings are not held in high regard at your institution, it may be wise to be selective in the number of student presentations you supervise. On the other hand, collaborating with colleagues outside of your institution on conference symposia can also contribute to visibility in the field and may lead to future research collaborations.

Success with external funding may also be considered a factor for promotion and tenure. This does not mean that you will always have to secure grant monies to qualify for tenure, but it is important to inquire how external funding is evaluated at your institution. If it is part of the evaluation process it will be critical for you to at least show a commitment to securing external funding by submitting applications for external grants and securing internal funding. Getting a grant from a national funding agency is difficult, and most proposals are not funded on the first attempt. Funding agencies will typically provide feedback on proposals. Use this feedback to make improvements and resubmit the application during the next grant cycle. The skills and experience you gain applying for external funding during your graduate training can vary widely. Some programs place a stronger emphasis on teaching and publishing, with little if any time dedicated to grant writing. If there is an opportunity to take a grant-writing course as part of a graduate program, take the class. If your institution offers grant-writing workshops, sign up. If there are other services offered through an office of research, take time to learn about these resources and use them to your advantage. Finally, grant-issuing agencies offer resources online that may also be useful as a starting point (e.g., U.S. Department of Education, 2007; U.S. Department of Health and Human Services, 2020).

Overall, it is best to stick close to the guidelines for promotion and tenure at your institution during the first years on the job. Find out what your institution values, and aim to do that first. Pursuing external funding is time consuming and the probability of success is lower than pursuing peer-reviewed publications. First-time applicants may require several attempts before they are successful, and once the grant is awarded there is an added delay to receive the award. Carefully consider (and seek mentorship) on how best to distribute your time. Mentors can be colleagues within your own department who have been successful with obtaining external funding, or colleagues that you meet while attending conferences and/or grant-writing workshops within or outside of your institution. Remember that standards vary widely across institutions, however, so it is best to seek mentorship from within your own university and department.

Service

All tenure-track positions will have service requirements. As with teaching and research, it is critical to find out how service is weighed in your evaluation for promotion and tenure. What kind of service is considered important? How much is "enough" or "too much"? A strong record of service could be indicative that you will be a good colleague, but too much of a focus on service will distract from teaching and research. Most research institutions will evaluate teaching and research more heavily than service. In fact, even with a stellar service record, if teaching or research are not up to the standards of the institution, a favorable tenure and promotion outcome is less likely. Teaching institutions may put more emphasis on teaching than research but will still place service at a lower priority than both teaching and research. Some institutions weigh all three requirements equally but service to the department or institution is most valuable for promotion and tenure, with more emphasis on service in the promotion from associate to full professor.

There are several levels of service that will be considered as part of your evaluation. Departmental service can include advising and mentoring students and serving on committees. Distribution of service activities at the department level can take various forms. For example, faculty may be asked to volunteer to serve, faculty may be invited to serve, or less commonly, faculty may be appointed to serve on a committee for the department. Untenured faculty members may feel pressured to volunteer if they are unfamiliar with the expectations of the department. Senior colleagues can help avoid this uncomfortable situation by creating different structures of service assignment for committee activities.

Service at the college and university level also typically means serving on or perhaps leading a committee. Seek advice from someone more senior in your department about the types and amount of service that is expected. It may not be in your best interest to decline an invitation by your department chair, dean, or provost to serve on a committee, but there may be ways to prioritize the types and amount of service you are involved in pre-tenure. As an untenured faculty member in my first academic appointment, I recall volunteering to serve as department senator because this service was presented as an opportunity to connect with colleagues outside of my department. I now feel strongly that untenured faculty members should not be encouraged to serve in this role. Although attending college- and university-wide meetings may, in fact, result in connecting with faculty who may not meet otherwise, being new to the institution means you are not familiar with its history or culture. Voicing opinions on a topic that may be contentious puts untenured faculty in an uncomfortable and vulnerable position, especially when voting is not anonymous. Aim to identify service opportunities that complement your areas of focus or that are in line with your strengths so that you can embed research with teaching and service.

Service to the profession is also important, although there may be less of an emphasis on this type of service for promotion from assistant to associate professor. There are many opportunities to get involved with professional organizations like the Association for Behavior Analysis International (ABAI) as well as state and regional associations. As a freshly minted Ph.D., you may not think you have enough experience to serve in a leadership position for a professional organization, but you may be just what the organization needs. Start with the various Special Interest Groups (SIGs) of ABAI. I am grateful that a friend and colleague reached out to invite me to serve on the Verbal Behavior SIG during my first few years in academia. Although I was already familiar with the VB SIG, I had not thought of "throwing my name in the hat" to serve on the executive board. Perhaps it was because I didn't feel that I fit in, nor that I had sufficient experience to serve in one of these positions. My experience serving on the executive board of the VB SIG boosted my confidence, afforded me opportunities to connect with leaders in the field, and helped me gain visibility.

Service to the profession can also include volunteering to serve as a reviewer for academic journals. This is typically a prerequisite to serving on the editorial board. Now that I have served as associate editor for two journals, the best advice I can give is to accept the invitation to review manuscripts and spend time reading and commenting on the *content* of the manuscript (skip over copyediting other people's work). Overall, serving as a reviewer and on committees for professional organizations is an excellent way to make connections and get exposure within the field. As with other types of service, it is important to evaluate how much time serving as a peer reviewer will take away from your own research.

Faculty from marginalized groups may be more likely to be called on or be inclined to provide professional service within their community (Jimenez et al., 2019). If you are the only member of a marginalized group in your department, students may seek you out as an advisor or mentor (June, 2015) or you may be called on to help with relevant student organizations. You may also be more often asked to serve on university committees relating to diversity (Aguirre, 2000), or you may be inclined to do this work on your own and not wait for an invitation. If you are called to provide this type of service because of your personal background, it is critical to ensure the service will be recognized more than minimally by your institution. It may be possible to request release time for professional service, especially if there are concurrent invitations or opportunities to serve in these capacities.

If you have a good understanding of how service is viewed and evaluated, you will be better able to make decisions about how to distribute your time. Finding this balance is not easy, especially because women faculty get asked to do more service (Guarino & Borden, 2017) and tend to do more as a result. If you find that you are having a tough time saying "no" or you are getting multiple requests, there may be ways to spread out your participation by declining an invitation but offering to take part the following semester or academic year. Alternatively, if you are asked to give your time for service to a new committee, seek input from your department chair and/or dean to gain their perspective on your service commitments. Tenured colleagues can also help in this regard by having clear guidelines about the amount and type of service that are expected from untenured faculty in their department.

The Coveted "Work-Life" Balance

Balancing teaching, research, and service activities is a job in and of itself. Faculty face various sources of stress and may often struggle to make time for themselves and their loved ones. The coveted work-life balance may be by far the hardest task we face as academics, and there is no right or wrong way of meeting this need. In the section that follows I highlight various sources of stress that all academics face, with particular attention to how stress impacts women and other members of historically marginalized groups in the academe.

The first type of stress can be described as work-life stress, related to the time you have or the time you make for interests outside of work compared to the number of hours you are working each week. A factor (at least for me) that makes this balance a constant struggle is the flexible, but never-ending, work schedule. There is no "clocking out" at 5 p.m., but you *can* and *should* clock out, figuratively speaking, every day. Be available for yourself and for your family—whether that be a partner, children, extended family, or pets. Do what makes you happy that is unrelated to work every day—go for a run, walk, or hike, grab a meal or a drink with a friend, meditate, watch that favorite TV show, talk to your partner, spend uninterrupted screen-free time with your kids, or cuddle with those fur babies.

Sadly, academics tend to glorify the 60+ hour workweek. This is the culture of praising someone privately or publicly for responding to emails late into the evening or early morning hours, or constantly talking about the amount of work they have or how busy they are. This is the culture that creates perceived and real disparities for women who may have young children at home. The "mommy shift" is well recognized by those who constantly balance the demands of being a parent and the responsibilities of academia. If you are a parent or aspire to be a parent in the future, the amount and types of support offered for parental leave, childcare facilities, and the culture of your department and institution when it comes to balancing parenthood with academia have the potential of contributing to elevated levels of stress and your decision of the "right time" to have children. There is no right answer. If there are other women in your department who have children, seek their mentorship. Not only is the decision of having children a deeply personal one, but if your institution is not family-friendly this will bring added stressors that you may need to consider. Policies that make a university family-friendly include parental leave for both men and women following the birth or adoption of a child (e.g., partial or full relief of teaching and service duties for an academic semester); options for stopping the tenure clock (e.g., the time on parental leave is not counted toward the provisionary period that is granted before a tenure application must be submitted); and paid leave (e.g., granting base pay for six weeks or more) during or after a pregnancy (Mason & Goulden, 2004). Several women in behavior analysis have shared their perspectives and personal journey on balancing motherhood in academia that may serve as a valuable resource (e.g., Favell, 2015; Pétursdóttir, 2015; Sulzer-Azaroff, 2015). Your health and your family's health and well-being will contribute to the balance you have at home with your partner, children, and extended family members. With the right mentorship and support, this balancing act comes a bit easier.

The second type of stress can be described as climate stress, or the stress associated with the social climate of the department, the institution, and the field. This source of stress can contribute to overall well-being and feelings of work and career satisfaction. The constant competitive nature of academia can contribute to feelings of not belonging. Letters of rejection and critique of one's work require a "tough skin." As mentioned in an earlier section, women are more likely to experience bias in student evaluations. Members of historically marginalized groups face incidents of subtle and overt discrimination on a regular basis. I was not familiar with the term microaggression until 2013. As soon as it was defined and described, however, I could easily identify several incidents of microaggressions I had experienced in my career, and I felt validated. Microaggressions are defined as "brief and commonplace daily verbal, behavioral, or environmental indignities, whether intentional or unintentional, that communicate hostile, derogatory, or negative racial slights and insults toward persons of color" (Sue et al., p. 271). Maybe I wasn't being too sensitive after all. First-generation college students who are now college faculty tend to keep their status quiet, further contributing to feelings of isolation in academia. It was only in recent years that the "I'm First" campaign (Council for Opportunity in Education, n.d.) allowed for faculty and students to self-identify and more easily connect. First-generation faculty may continue to experience the disparity in knowledge and, by default, access to resources, navigating a career where the rules are not all written in a handbook (or playbook); yet the fact that there *is* an unwritten handbook makes everything more confusing. First-generation faculty and members of historically marginalized groups may experience internal self-imposed pressure to perform at higher levels than their colleagues. The metaphor "the squeaky wheel gets the grease" is all too accurate. This places faculty who are not comfortable speaking up, voicing their opinions, never mind asking for or negotiating resources, at a clear disadvantage. There is a powerful unwritten rule to "keep your head down" until you have tenure for fear of retaliation. I was once told by a White peer (also untenured at the time) that it would be disingenuous to stay silent if I did not agree with a departmental decision. This colleague had the public enthusiastic support of a few senior White faculty members in the department, something I did not share. Faculty retention is critical yet there are fewer programs in place to support faculty of color in academic environments (Griffin, 2019; Zambrana et al., 2015). The importance of mentoring and sponsorship outlined previously needs to be stressed because the climate in academia requires it.

A third type of stress can be described as financial stress. Assistant professor salaries nationwide vary widely with an average of $82,508 and a range of $62,243 to $108,195 (American Academy of University Professors, 2020). The stress associated with finances may not always be related to the base salary. There is stress in knowing that there are well-documented disparities in salary for women and for faculty of color (Li & Koedel, 2017; Li et al., 2019). There is stress related to student loan repayment which reportedly takes 20 years, on average, for those who complete a doctoral degree at a public university (Hanson, 2021), meaning that a substantial part of your monthly salary will be set aside for this payment, which affects planning for future life events (e.g., buying a home, starting a family). Financial literacy may help to improve the long-term outcomes of planning for a graduate education, especially for first-generation college students who face more uncertainty in financing their education (Lee & Mueller, 2014). Student loan forgiveness programs and repayment plans can help reduce the total monthly payment. For many people in this position, the reprieve on student loan payments at the start of the COVID-19 pandemic was a breath of fresh air, however, plans for people to restart the payments post-pandemic is a source of growing anxiety. There are options for student loan forgiveness. Research loan-repayment programs at the state, regional, and national level. Depending on your area of expertise, there may be programs for working with underserved populations (see U.S. Department of Education, n.d.; U.S. Department of Health and Human Services, 2021).

A Few Takeaways

In closing, I offer some advice from my personal journey in academia to date. First, keep good records of your work. At my first new-faculty orientation, the advice someone gave was to keep three boxes in the office: one labeled research, one labeled teaching, and one labeled service. No one keeps boxes in their offices (at least not anymore), but you can create three folders that live on your desktop to start saving relevant documents as they come up (e.g., student evaluations, research publications, an updated copy of your CV, etc.). During my first year in academia, I also started a work log. I wrote down everything I had done each day. It was a simple Word document that took no more than five minutes to complete before I left the office. I have since switched to an electronic calendar where I track my tasks and how long I spend on each one. The narrative from the work log was helpful. I went back to it many times over when asked to write self-evaluations, academic plans, a pre-tenure application, and eventually to prepare my tenure dossier. The work log kept me accountable and reminded me of everything I had done each day. This was especially important for days when I felt I had not done much. Those tended to be days when I was teaching all afternoon, meeting with students, writing letters of recommendation, or when a colleague sat down to chat over lunch but stayed longer than planned. These activities are all important aspects of a life in academia.

Second, make efforts to create meaningful connections with your colleagues. Collegiality is often used as a criterion for promotion and tenure, but it is never part of the written rules or guidelines. Your department will be a second home. These are the colleagues you will interact with for the rest of your academic career (until they retire or leave, or until you retire or leave). These are the people who should be your strongest supporters when you go up for tenure. Get up and out of your office to roam the halls intermittently throughout the semester; stop by to check in with the department administrator(s); say hello if colleagues have their office door open; arrive to department meetings early; pair yourself with positive interactions as much as possible. Ask questions. Maybe it's a question about a teaching award you are hoping to receive; or you are looking to make connections in the community and need some guidance; or you want to hear various perspectives on how the tenure requirements are interpreted; or maybe you want recommendations for dining out in the area or a local dentist or hair stylist. I believe that making these personal connections may lead to more involved conversations (at times) that can provide insight into the department's culture and history. These conversations can also naturally lead to development of friendships and identification of mentors within the department. Moreover, I believe that connecting with colleagues on a personal level is vital to the overall health of an academic department and to your own well-being.

Third, do not shy away from negotiations. Women are more likely to avoid negotiating (Leibbrandt & List, 2015). Think of negotiating as an important self-advocacy skill to practice in academia. Remember that negotiations do not happen only before you sign a contract or start a new position. Negotiations are also not always related to monetary compensation (e.g., you can negotiate office and research space, teaching schedules, etc.). When I moved into my second academic position, there was one major aspect of negotiations that I initially overlooked. There was discussion about the years of service I had accumulated at my earlier institution, and my understanding was that these would be counted toward the required six years of service I had to complete before becoming eligible for promotion and tenure at my new institution. However, I neglected to ensure those specific terms were written into my formal contract. It was not until I attended the first tenure workshop at my new institution that this information dawned on me—and here I was a full year into my new position. Thankfully, I had email communication related to these specifics before I accepted the offer. The lesson here is to put everything in writing.

Finally, the importance of finding mentors along the way can't be stressed enough. I have been fortunate to have both mentors and sponsors in my academic career, but I find that there is always room for more. As an associate professor with tenure, I continue to look for mentors who I can lean on to help me navigate the next promotion. I have found that peer mentorship has become even more important for me at this stage in my career, and I continue to look for mentors who share multiple parts of my personal identity. To date, I have only been able to find these mentors outside of my professional circle, but I look forward to serving in this role for those who come after me as they blaze their own trails.

References

Aguirre, A. J. (2000). *Women and minority faculty in the academic workplace: Recruitment, retention, and academic culture* (Vol. 27). Jossey-Bass.

American Academy of University Professors. (2020). *The annual report on the economic status of the profession, 2019–20.* www.aaup.org/report/annual-report-economic-status-profession-2019–20

Ayyala, M. S., Skarupski, K., Bodurtha, J. N., González-Fernández, M., Ishii, L. E., Fivush, B., & Levine, R. B. (2019). Mentorship is not enough: Exploring sponsorship and its role in career advancement in academic medicine. *American Medicine: Journal of the Association of American Medical Colleges, 94*(1), 94–100. https://doi.org/10.1097/ACM.0000000000002398

Banerjee, D., & Pawley, A. L. (2013). Gender and promotion: How do science, technology engineering, and mathematics (STEM) faculty members survive a foggy climate? *Journal of Women and Minorities in Science and Engineering, 19*(4), 329–347.

Bavishi, A., J. Madera, M., & Hebl, M. R. (2010). The effect of professor ethnicity and gender on student evaluations: Judged before met. *Journal of Diversity in Higher Education, 3*(4), 245–256. https://doi.org/10.1037/a0020763

Bernstein, D., & Chase, P. N. (2013). Contributions of behavior analysis to higher education. In G. J. Madden, W. V. Dube, T. D. Hackenberg, G. P. Hanley, & K. A. Lattal (Eds.), *APA Handbook of behavior analysis, vol. 2. Translating principles into practice* (pp. 523–543). American Psychological Association. https://doi.org/10.1037/13938-021

Boyd, B., Caraway, J., & Flores-Neimann, Y. (2017). Surviving and thriving in academia: A guide for members of marginalized groups. *American Psychological Association.* www.apa.org/pi/oema/resources/brochures/surviving

Brodsky, J., & Fienup, D. M. (2018). Sidman goes to college: A meta-analysis of equivalence- based instruction in higher education. *Perspectives on Behavior Science, 41*(1), 95–119. https://doi.org/10.1007/s40614-018-0150-0

Chow, R. (2021). Don't just mentor women and people of color. Sponsor them. *Harvard Business Review.* https://hbr-org.cdn.ampproject.org/c/s/hbr.org/amp/2021/06/dont-just-mentor-women-and-people-of-color-sponsor-them

Clance, P. R., & Imes, S. A. (1978). The imposter phenomenon in high achieving women: Dynamics and therapeutic intervention. *Psychotherapy: Theory Research and Practic, 15*, 241. doi:10.1037/h0086006

Council for Opportunity in Education. (n.d.). *First-generation celebration day.* https://coenet.org/first-generation.shtml

Exley, C. L., & Judd, B. K. (2019). *The gender gap in self-promotion.* National Bureau of Economic Research Working Paper Series, No. 26345. https://www.nber.org/papers/w26345

Faloye, A. O., Bechtel, A. J., & Methangkool, E. (2021). Peer mentorship: An often overlooked tool in under resourced academic departments. *Academic Medicine, 96*(1), 16. https://doi.org/10.1097/ACM.0000000000003776

Favell, J. E. (2015). A career in behavior analysis: Notes from the journey. *The Behavior Analyst, 38(2)*, 229–236. https://doi.org/10.1007/s40614-015-0037-2

Feenstra, S., Begeny, C. T., Ryan, M. K., Rink, F. A., Stoker, J. I., & Jordan, J. (2020). Contextualizing the impostor "syndrome." *Frontiers in Psychology, 11*, 575024. https://doi.org/10.3389/fpsyg.2020.575024

Griffin, K. A. (2019). *Redoubling our efforts: How institutions can affect faculty diversity. Race and ethnicity in higher education: A status report.* American Council on Education. www.equityinhighered.org/resources/ideas-and-insights/redoubling-our-efforts-how-institutions-can-affect-faculty-diversity/

Guarino, C. M., & Borden, M. H. (2017). Faculty service loads and gender: Are women taking care of the academic family? *Research in Higher Education, 58*(6), 672–694. https://doi.org/10.1007/s11162-017-9454-2

Hanson, M. (2021). *Average time to pay off student loans.* Educationdat.org. https://educationdata.org/average-time-to-repay-student-loans

Jimenez, M. F., Laverty, T. M., Bombaci, S. P., Wilkins, K., Bennett, D. E., & Pejchar, L. (2019). Underrepresented faculty play a disproportionate role in advancing diversity and inclusion. *Nature Ecology & Evolution, 3*(7), 1030–1033. https://doi.org/10.1038/s41559-019-0911-5

June, A. W. (2015, November 8). The invisible labor of minority professors. *The Chronicle of Higher Education*. www.chronicle.com/article/the-invisible-labor-of-minority-professors/

Kreitzer, R. J., & Sweet-Cushman, J. (2021). Evaluating student evaluations of teaching: A review of measurement and equity bias in SETs and recommendations for ethical reform. *Journal of Academic Ethics*, 1–12. https://doi.org/10.1007/s10805-021-09400-w

Lee, J., & Mueller, J. A. (2014). Student loan debt literacy: A comparison of first-generation and continuing-generation college students. *Journal of College Student Development*, *55*(7), 714–719.

Leibbrandt, A., & List, J. A. (2015). Do women avoid salary negotiations? Evidence from a large-scale natural field experiment. *Management Science*, *61*(9), 2016–2024. https://doi.org/10.1287/mnsc.2014.1994

Li, A., Gravina, N., Pritchard, J. K., & Poling, A. (2019). The gender pay gap for behavior analysis faculty. *Behavior Analysis in Practice*, *12*(4), 743–746. https://doi.org/10.1007/s40617-019-00347-4

Li, D., & Koedel, C. (2017). Representation and salary gaps by race-ethnicity and gender at selective public universities. *Educational Researcher*, *46*(7), 343–354.

Mason, M. A., & Goulden, M. (2004). Do babies matter (Part II)? Closing the baby gap. *Academe*, *90*(6), 11–15.

National Center for Faculty Development and Diversity. (n.d.). *NFCDD Mentor Map*. https://www.facultydiversity.org/home

O'Meara, K. A., Lennartz, C. J., Kuvaeva, A. A., & Misra, J. (2019). Department conditions and practices associated with faculty workload satisfaction and perceptions of equity. *The Journal of Higher Education*, *90*(5), 744–772. https://doi.org/10.1080/00221546.2019.1584025

Ong, M., Smith, J. M., & Ko, L. T. (2017). Counterspaces for women of color in STEM higher education: Marginal and central spaces for persistence and success. *Journal of Research in Science Teaching*, *55*(2), 145–206. https://doi.org/10.1002/tea.21417

Pétursdóttir, A. I. (2015). Influences on my early academic career. *The Behavior Analyst*, *38*(2), 255–262. https://doi.org/10.1007/s40614-015-0039-0

Querol, B. I. D., Rosales, R., & Soldner, J. L. (2015). A comprehensive review of interteaching and its impact on student learning and satisfaction. *Scholarship of Teaching and Learning in Psychology*, *1*(4), 390–411. https://doi.org/10.1037/stl0000048

Sue, D. W., Capodilupo, C. M., Torino, G. C., Bucceri, J. M., Holder, A., Nadal, K. L., & Esquilin, M. (2007). Racial microaggressions in everyday life: Implications for clinical practice. *American Psychologist*, *62*(4), 271. https://doi.org/10.1037/0003-066X.62.4.271

Sulzer-Azaroff, B. (2015). Joy and fulfillment as a female behavior analyst. *The Behavior Analyst*, *38*(2), 275–282. https://doi.org/10.1007/s40614-015-0038-1

U.S. Department of Education. (2007). *Grant application technical assistance resources*. https://www2.ed.gov/admins/grants/apply/techassist/index.html

U.S. Department of Education. (n.d.). *Public service loan forgiveness*. https://studentaid.gov/manage-loans/forgiveness-cancellation/public-service

U.S. Department of Health and Human Services. (2020). *NIH central resource for grants and funding information*. https://grants.nih.gov/grants/how-to-apply- application-guide/format-and-write/write-your-application.htm

U.S. Department of Health and Human Services. (2021). *Loan repayment program*. www.nimhd.nih.gov/programs/extramural/loan-repayment.html

Zambrana, R. E., Ray, R., Espino, M. M., Castro, C. Cohen, B. D., & Eliason, J. (2015). Don't leave us behind: The importance of mentoring for underrepresented minority faculty. *American Educational Research Journal*, *52*, 40–72. https://doi.org/10.3102/0002831214563063

9 Understanding the Importance of Intersectionality in Advancing Community-Engaged Scholarship and Increasing Diversity

Jomella Watson-Thompson and Eric C. Thompson

"The Road Not Taken" by Robert Frost (1916)

Two roads diverged in a yellow wood,
And sorry I could not travel both
And be one traveler, long I stood
And looked down one as far as I could
To where it bent in the undergrowth;
Then took the other, as just as fair,
And having perhaps the better claim,
Because it was grassy and wanted wear;
Though as for that the passing there
Had worn them really about the same,
And both that morning equally lay
In leaves no step had trodden black.
Oh, I kept the first for another day!
Yet knowing how way leads on to way,
I doubted if I should ever come back.
I shall be telling this with a sigh
Somewhere ages and ages hence:
Two roads diverged in a wood, and I—
I took the one less traveled by,
And that has made all the difference.

Community Engagement: The Road Less Traveled

I once characterized my journey as a community-engaged scholar as the road less traveled when considering the traditional standards for matriculation as a tenure-track faculty member (Watson-Thompson, 2018). In mainstream academia, there are often few conditions that may serve as reinforcers for supporting community-engaged scholarship due to the often-competing requirements and contingencies on behavior, including traditional guidelines and expectations related to attaining tenure and promotion. Now, after working in academia for over a decade and having acquired tenure as a community-engaged scholar, I will reflect on my journey and consider both the opportunities and challenges experienced in supporting this path.

Community Engagement: Road Traveled by Scholars of Color

More recently, I realized that for me and many faculty of color, community engagement is often the more common road traveled in supporting research, learning, and service on

DOI: 10.4324/9781003216773-12

a grassy, but less weathered path. Now that I consider my journey, I have noted a winding but similar path with other colleagues and peers, particularly women of color, who have a sustained commitment to community engagement. Yet, the motivation and rewards for supporting community-engaged scholarship are often external and provided by the communities served rather than the academic institutions.

According to Corbin et al. (2021),

> There is considerable evidence faculty of color and/or women are more likely than their white and male counterparts to pursue community engaged forms of scholarship and to view the academic profession as an opportunity to influence social change for the common/public good. . . . For example, data from the 2016–17 faculty survey administered by the Higher Education Research Institute at the University of California, Los Angeles provides valuable insights into faculty practice. One of the questions asks whether, in the previous three years, the faculty member 'collaborated with local community on research/teaching to address their needs.' Across the entire sample, 47% of faculty answered yes. For faculty of color, 92%, 56%, and 52% of Indigenous, Latinx, and Black faculty, respectively, answered yes (as compared with 46% of white faculty).
>
> (Faculty Diversity and Community Engaged Scholarship section)

Faculty of color with a commitment to engaging and serving communities may often represent and broker participation of communities in which they are a member (e.g., geographical place) or identify themselves (e.g., persons of color). Corbin et al. (2021) further suggest,

> research also indicates that minoritized faculty are less likely to pursue academic careers or to remain in faculty positions on campuses where emerging forms of scholarship, including community engaged scholarship, are not valued, and rewarded. If community engaged scholarship is clearly defined, fairly evaluated, and fully rewarded, the evidence suggests that faculty positions will become more appealing to minoritized faculty. Supporting community engaged scholarship is thus an important strategy for diversifying the professoriate.
>
> (Faculty Diversity and Community Engaged Scholarship section)

Yet, there is often little recognition or rewards for persons of color in academia that acknowledge the importance of the contributions made in diversifying learning and research, including who is served and engaged both from the campus and in the community. It has been well documented that community engagement is a critical factor that enhances academic persistence and retention in higher education for not only faculty and researchers, but also for students of color (Holsapple, 2012; Ling Yeh, 2010).

Corbin et al. (2021) summarized,

> Diversifying the faculty can help advance research that has a broad social impact, assist communities in addressing social issues, and improve student learning outcomes. Unfortunately, faculty evaluation and reward systems remain antagonistic to academic work that would fulfil these goals. Understanding the importance of community engaged scholarship as a strategy for diversifying the faculty should motivate educational leaders to shape and support community engaged scholarship.
>
> (How Higher Education Can Fulfill Its Democratic Aspirations section)

Examining Opportunities for Advancing Community-Engagement Through Academia

Historical Purpose and Present Challenges of Institutions of Higher Education

Although the academe was intended to be bastions of knowledge to advance the public good, including through discourse, the institution was intentionally designed for White males as both students and in the professorate. Thus, some challenges experienced by women in academia, which are even more exacerbated for women of color, are due to operating in a system not designed for them. Some of the standard processes for matriculation, including promotion and tenure requirements, were gatekeeper systems.

Matias et al. (2021) explained,

> Tenured scholars who, as we've noted, are mostly white and male, largely make the rules that determine who else can join the tenured ranks. This involves what sociologists call 'boundary work,' or the practice of a group setting rules to determine who is good enough to join. And as such, many of the rules established around tenure over the years work really well for white scholars, but don't adequately capture the contributions of scholars of color. For instance, getting tenure often requires some combination of demonstrating excellence in research (measured by publication metrics and funding) and teaching (measured by teaching evaluations). It turns out though, that the topics that scholars of color often research are less likely to receive research funding and, at least in some fields, are less likely to be included in the very journals that are valued for promotion. Scholars of color are also less likely than white scholars to be cited when their work is published. And on the teaching front, women and people of color are often evaluated more poorly than white men, even when they are teaching identical content. What this all adds up to is that when colleges and universities invite scholars of color to join their ranks and increase the diversity of their faculty, they are inviting them to play a game that's set up for them to lose.
>
> (Universities Faculties Haven't Become Much More Diverse section)

Institutions of higher education were designed to advance the public good through research, teaching, and service. Throughout the history of higher education in the United States, academic institutions have been generators of knowledge and producers of the public good, including during periods of war and restoration (Boyer, 1996). However, toward the end of the 20th century, the role of the scholar through the professorate was under critical consideration, which have continued as challenges in the 21st century.

Ernest Boyer (1990) summarized the tension,

> The time has come, we believe, to step back and reflect on the variety of functions academics are expected to perform. It's time to ask how priorities of the professoriate relate to the faculty reward system, as well as to the missions of America's higher learning institutions. Such an inquiry into the work of faculty is essential if students are to be well served, if the creativity of all faculty is to be fully tapped, and if the goals of every college and university are to be appropriately defined. While we speak with pride about the great diversity of American higher education, the reality is that on many campuses standards of scholarship have become increasingly restrictive, and campus priorities frequently are more imitative than distinctive. . . . According to the dominant view, to be a scholar is to be a researcher—and publication is the primary yardstick by which scholarly productivity is measured. . . . Beyond the campus, America's social and economic crises are growing—troubled schools, budget deficits, pollution, urban decay, and neglected children, to highlight problems that are most apparent. . . . Given these

realities, the conviction is growing that the vision of service that once so energized the nation's campuses must be given a new legitimacy. The challenge then is this: Can America's colleges and universities, with all the richness of their resources, be of greater service to the nation and the world? Can we define scholarship in ways that respond more adequately to the urgent new realities both within the academy and beyond?

(p. 2–3)

Continuum of Community-Engaged Scholarship

In Scholarship Reconsidered, Ernest Boyer (1996) presented integrated functions of scholarship including discovery, knowledge/teaching, integration, application, and engagement. The scholarship of the discovery of knowledge advances research as a critical component, which then supports the integration of scholarship across disciplines through multidisciplinary collaboration. The scholarship of knowledge focuses on ensuring that knowledge, including through teaching and reciprocal learning, has utility. Engagement as a distinct form of scholarship was refined more precisely by Boyer over time. Initially, Boyer (1990) proposed the scholarship of application, which focused on applying knowledge based on discovery and integration to improve human condition as a form of scholarly service. However, several years later, Boyer (1996) extended the scholarship of application and refocused the functions to include the scholarship of engagement more explicitly.

Often, in applied behavior analysis, we interchangeably equate application or addressing applied problems of social significance to engagement. Application is one of multiple components of the scholarship of engagement. Applied work is not necessarily community engagement. The scholarship of application is a component of engagement. The scholarship of engagement includes the application of knowledge to address issues of societal importance. However, engagement focuses on the process by which academic and community partners reciprocally facilitate the co-creation of knowledge, integration, and discovery.

Community-engaged scholarship supports the integration of research/discovery, knowledge/learning, and application through a collaborative process with community partners who set the issue agenda for action. Community-engaged scholarship is "the collaboration between academics and individuals outside the academy—knowledge professionals and the lay public (local, regional/state, national, global)—for the mutually beneficial exchange of knowledge and resources in a context of partnership and reciprocity" (Post et al., 2016, p. 113). Therefore, in the strongest form of community-engaged scholarship, research, teaching, and service are interrelated and an integrated process of scholarship. Boyer (1996) proposes,

> The scholarship of engagement means connecting the rich resources of the university to our most pressing social, civic, and ethical problems, to our schools, to our teachers, and to our cities. . . . Campuses would be viewed by both students and professors not as isolated islands, but as staging grounds for action . . . what's also needed is not just more programs, but a larger purpose, a larger sense of mission, a larger clarity of direction in the nation's life . . . the scholarship of engagement also means creating a special climate in which the academic and civic cultures communicate more continuously and more creatively with each other.
>
> (p. 19–20)

My Road Traveled as a Community-Engaged Scholar

In 2009, when I began my career as an early-career faculty on the tenure track, the traditional mechanisms and pathways in academia did not fully support the conditions for advancing as a community-engaged scholar. In mainstream academia, community-engaged scholarship is often the exception rather than the norm due to competing conditions and requirements for success as a scholar. Early in my career, in a conversation with Dr. Betty Hart, she challenged me to consider both the benefits and tensions of timely progress in achieving tenure as a community-engaged scholar. Based on our discussion, I placed a sign in my office that remains and serves as a reminder of the challenges faced by faculty who often must choose between what Dr. Hart stated as either community service or academic achievement.

During my early career, multiple colleagues and mentors highly encouraged me to delay my focus on community-engaged scholarship, particularly in the areas of research and service, until post tenure. In academia, it is well known and understood that the standard of success for matriculation through the professorate is based on the traditional system of obtaining tenure and promotion. The traditional system of success in academia is often dichotomized as "publish or perish" for tenure-track faculty in academia. Pre-tenured faculty members are often encouraged to support a traditional approach to obtaining tenure by focusing on standard forms of teaching, research, and scholarship, particularly during early career. Often, early-career faculty are advised against participating in community-engaged scholarship prior to tenure. It is intended to be protective of the time and effort of faculty to support traditionally recognized forms of scholarship that are considered necessary based on quantitative measures of publications in scholarly journals, student ratings on course evaluations, and commonly accepted forms of service to the institution and discipline Then, after attaining tenure it is more commonly accepted for faculty to support community-engaged activities.

Exploring Community-Engaged Scholarship

Like many academicians, I had a limited understanding of community-engaged scholarship when I began my journey as an assistant professor. At most institutions of higher education, there is often not formal training for graduate students or early-career faculty in community-engaged approaches. Although some may engage in the practice of community engagement through research or curricular experiences, there is often less structured and intentional supports. All too often, formal training or technical support in understanding community-engaged scholarship as not only a pedagogy but guided practice is not a standard component of graduate training or early-career support. There is a continuum of participatory and community-engaged approaches that all too often academicians stumble upon as they support the work, with limited prior context for intentionally understanding and identifying how their work may fit within a range of community approaches. Additionally, based on the disciplinary affiliation, often similar terms are used interchangeably or as variants across fields, which may further contribute to lack of clarity related to community-engaged approaches.

Advancing Behavioral Community Approaches Through Participatory Research

The Center for Community Health and Development (KU CCHD) is a research center affiliated with the Department of Applied Behavioral Science and the Schiefelbusch Institute for Life Span Studies. The vision of the KU CCHD is "people working together to transform environments and conditions to assure health and well-being for all" (University of Kansas, 2022). The CCHD focuses on community-engaged partnerships that advance community and public health, child and youth health and development, and community capacity-building efforts. The CCHD is grounded in applied behavioral science but integrates principles, values, and approaches also from community psychology, prevention science, and public health. As a core value, the CCHD advances social justice and health-equity work.

The KU CCHD facilitates a behavioral community approach to community problem-solving. Behavioral community psychology is a sub-discipline that integrates applied behavior analysis and community psychology. "It attempts to understand and change community problems through the application of behavioral theory and technology" (Bogat & Jason, 2000, p. 101). Fawcett (1980) noted, "in the sub-field of behavioral community psychology, the methods of applied behavior analysis are used to analyze community problems and to develop and evaluate replicable methods for solving such problems and improving the capacities of communities to achieve their own goals" (p. 7).

Now, in my administrative role at the University of Kansas as the Director of the Center for Service Learning, I advocate for changes in systems and conditions that advance community engagement, including in considering how to address the limited reward mechanisms, training, and technical supports. However, my commitment to serving as a proponent and champion of community-engaged scholarship at not only my local institution but more broadly within and across fields was guided by my own experience.

My Journey as a Community-Engaged Scholar

When I was an assistant professor, I was nominated by the Center for Service Learning at the University of Kansas for a national award in community engagement. In 2014, I was blessed to be the recipient of the Ernest A. Lynton Award for the Scholarship of Engagement of Early Career Faculty, which is now administered by Campus Compact. However, it was during the award-nomination process that I was introduced to community-engaged scholarship as an approach, which was transformational to my career trajectory as a scholar. Although community-engaged scholarship was the work I had been supporting, I did not have a framework to guide my efforts. Through community-engaged scholarship, I found an approach supporting the integration of my community-engaged efforts across my academic responsibilities of research, teaching, and service. I also identified a community of multi-disciplinary scholars, as well as a sub-discipline that studies and examines the scholarship of engagement.

Community-Engaged Research

As a graduate research assistant with the Center for Community Health and Development (CCHD) at the University of Kansas (KU), I became familiar with participatory approaches, including participatory action research and community-based participatory research (CBPR). Community-engaged scholarship is a broader orientation for supporting the integration of research, teaching, and service. Thus, CBPR may be considered a form of community-engaged scholarship (Blanchard & Furco, 2021).

As a graduate student, I supported the work of a community-engaged scholar through the facilitation of community-based participatory research as a graduate research assistant, service-learning as a graduate teaching assistant, and participation in related service and outreach activities with community partners as both a student and community member. I was fortunate to be trained as a community-engaged scholar as a graduate student although I was unaware of the existing pedagogy. Since my work was community-engaged, I already had established community-based research projects and partnerships, which fueled my commitment to remain affiliated with the University of Kansas after graduation. However, when

I was hired as an assistant professor on the tenure track, the broader conditions by which I needed to ensure I could satisfy requirements for tenure and promotion while also advancing community-engaged scholarship became more conflicting. I was effectively facilitating community-based participatory research and evaluation efforts with partners, maintaining dozens of service-learning partnerships through teaching, and serving with community partners to advance outreach. Yet, there were few established mechanisms within my discipline or the institution to evaluate and promote such integrated work.

As a faculty member, I developed a research program that integrates interdisciplinary methods from behavioral science, community psychology, prevention science, and public health to help understand and improve outcomes related to youth and community development. Overall, my research studies have focused on the: (a) experimental analysis of community-based interventions to address youth violence and substance abuse; (b) study of community implementation of evidence-based prevention approaches, particularly related to violence prevention; and the (c) implementation of community-based assessments and interventions to understand and promote health behaviors among groups experiencing disparities.

My professional mission is to cultivate healthy, safe, and prosperous communities through the integration of research, teaching, and service through community-engaged scholarship. My research approach uses methods of engaged scholarship and community-based participatory research. Through community-engaged scholarship, our research supports a mutual process of knowledge discovery and application between researchers, community partners, and students. Community partners are involved throughout the research process, from intervention development to data review and interpretation, to help assure culturally appropriate interventions and outcomes of social significance. Community-based scholarship requires a longer-term investment over time, in place, and with people and partners to ensure a commitment to engagement that is both meaningful and sufficient to observe sustained changes in both the environments and behaviors within the community. I have now partnered with some community-based partners organizations for nearly two decades.

As a researcher affiliated with the KU CCHD, I lead the Community Youth Development and Prevention Team. We have developed a program of research in the areas of community development and positive youth development, particularly related to adolescent substance abuse prevention, community- and youth-violence prevention, and youth justice. Ultimately, we are contributing to improvements in community-level outcomes related to behaviors of interest at the level of the population or group of people.

As a team, we have contributed to advancing research and evaluation of youth- and community-violence prevention efforts, particularly in our Kansas City region. For instance, in our youth- and community-violence prevention efforts, we partner to support community-based interventions that will prevent and reduce shootings (i.e., aggravated assaults), killings (i.e., homicides, fatalities), and intentional injury-related hospitalizations of youth ages 10 to 24. Also, for 15 years, our research team has served as the participatory evaluation partner for Aim4Peace, a local community-violence prevention program implemented through the Kansas City, Missouri Health Department (Watson-Thompson et al., 2013; Stewart et al., 2021).

Since 2021, I have led the Youth Violence Prevention Center-Kansas City (YVPC-KC), which is one of five National Centers of Excellence in Youth Violence Prevention designated by the Centers for Disease Control and Prevention. The YVPC-KC supports implementation of the ThrYve (Together Helping to Reduce Youth Violence for Equity) model of youth-violence prevention, which integrates a behavioral-community approach (Watson-Thompson et al., 2020). Through ThrYve, we facilitate a coalition of more than 40 partners across 14 sectors of the community (e.g., schools, justice system, health) to advance environmental changes across systems to prevent and reduce youth violence. ThrYve serves communities, including youth and families, who are primarily Black and Hispanic and disproportionately experience youth violence.

Additionally, we have supported behavioral-community studies examining the effects of community processes such as planning (e.g., Watson-Thompson et al., 2008) and participatory evaluation (e.g., Watson-Thompson et al., 2018) on community capacity to facilitate prevention efforts (Watson-Thompson et al., 2014). For nearly two decades, we supported participatory evaluative research in partnership with the Learning Tree Institute and with other partners of the Kansas Prevention Collaborative (KPC) through the Kansas Department on Aging and Disability Services. Through the efforts of the KPC, our team has worked with more than 50 adolescent substance abuse prevention coalitions across the state of Kansas through longitudinal studies documenting the environmental change process to advance adolescent substance abuse prevention efforts (e.g., Anderson-Carpenter et al., 2016).

Our team has established lines of community research to advance a behavioral analytic approach to assessing and reinforcing pro-social behaviors for youth. For instance, we have developed the Assessment of Preferred Leisure Alternatives for Youth (A-PLAY), a web-based preference assessment to examine whether youth participation in preferred alternative activities (e.g., physical activity) during out-of-school time increases participation in healthy pro-social behaviors (Kadavasal & Watson-Thompson, 2022). Additionally, we worked with Dr. Dave Jarmolowicz as a joint team to develop an emergent line of research assessing decision-making processes of youth with risk for violence (e.g., Moore, 2021).

Service Learning and Community Outreach

My teaching mission is to prepare students to address important societal problems through course instruction, group-based cooperative learning, and service learning that fosters sustained civic and community engagement. I teach multiple courses that train students in community health and development competencies (e.g., community assessment, strategic planning, evaluation) using a behavioral-community approach. I instruct courses on Community Leadership, Building Healthy Communities (i.e., community health and development competencies), Behavioral Community Psychology, and the Practicum in Community Health and Development. Additionally, I mentor students who are in the joint Master of Public Health and behavioral psychology doctoral program.

Through the coursework, I connect students with our research partnerships and initiatives to collaboratively address community issues through integrated research and teaching endeavors. I arrange opportunities for student learning through service learning and community engagement with community partners to meet community-identified needs. Service learning enables students to immediately apply and generalize knowledge and skills to novel community problems with diverse populations and settings. In my courses, all partners—students, community partners, and the instructor—are collaborators in the reciprocal process of engagement, feedback, and learning. Taken together, these objectives support an integrated model of action-oriented cooperative learning that is grounded in behavioral science in a manner that prepares students to develop, implement, and lead community-based interventions and efforts.

Additionally, the service and outreach component of my academic role is often integrated through the community-engaged research and teaching commitments. For instance, my research team in partnership with community partners and students in my courses across years have developed the LEAD UP (Leadership, Education, Adolescent Development with Unlimited Potential) Youth Achievement Program, which provides leadership and college-readiness supports for racial and ethnic youth. Now, after supporting LEAD UP for nearly a decade, the initial outreach effort is evolving into a line of community-engaged research. Ultimately, across research, teaching, and service endeavors, I work with a group of student and staff scholars who are committed to improving outcomes and conditions for youth and families in the communities we serve. Through community-engaged scholarship, I have a guiding framework and approach to integrate across research, teaching, and service activities to contribute to meaningful and sustained improvements in community-level outcomes over time and in dedicated places.

Challenge With Community-Engaged Scholarship

The opportunity to advance community-engaged scholarship in ways that meaningfully contribute to addressing community-identified needs with communities is important work. Prior to learning more about community-engaged scholarship, I focused on my work as isolated components across research, teaching, and service. However, now through a community-engaged scholarship orientation, I think of research, teaching, and service as interdependent activities that are reciprocal in supporting the community-identified needs of partners. Therefore, it was difficult when I went through the promotion and tenure process to respond to the format required for my personal statement and dossier which did not permit the fluidity across components of the academic responsibilities and my approach as a community-engaged scholar. Additionally, since many in academia are not formally trained on community-engaged scholarship, it is also challenging for peers in academia to evaluate the work as is done through more traditional approaches in which teaching, research, and service are isolated into different and distinct activities. Lastly, the reward mechanisms, related to performance evaluation and merit, including in the tenure and promotion processes, do not always consider the additional contributions of a community-engaged scholar. For instance, the maintenance of community partnerships requires a substantial investment of time to establish and maintain trust, rapport, and a common agenda. However, once established, there are lasting benefits to both the academic and community collaborators that accelerate research, teaching, and service endeavors.

In traditional systems of academic institutions, community-engaged scholarship is punished. The time and commitment required to advance community-engaged scholarship is not often recognized or acknowledged. Additionally, often the products that are of value to the community partner (e.g., program evaluation report, community assessment) may be different than what is valued in academia (e.g., peer-reviewed publication). Those in academia who chose to persist in advancing community-engaged approaches are then often supporting parallel and dual activities, meaning we are producing multiple and varied products of meaning and utility to community partners (e.g., evaluation report), but then for academic processes often must reproduce it for traditional peer review (e.g., scholarly journal publications). Therefore, community-engaged scholars must respond to two different audiences, sets of contingencies, and systems of reinforcement, which results in duplicative work and effort for the scholar.

A preferred and more modern approach is to recognize and reward community-engaged products through the academic systems, including in performance evaluations, promotion and tenure, and as a collective part of the university impact (Blanchard & Furco, 2021). For instance, allowing community experts to serve on student committees, be recognized as community peers in peer review processes, and to review and validate community products (e.g., evaluation reports, community assessments) would support functional mechanisms for social validation of goals, procedures, and effects. If ultimately in academia we are producing interventions that have potential for impact, but are not serving the intended audiences, the interventions are not being adopted and sustained, or generalized across settings and behaviors, then we are doing a disservice to the application of our science. A strength of community-engaged approaches is that generalization is programmed for as part of the process; thereby, social validity of the goals, procedures, and effects are embedded activities.

Advancing Community Engagement as a Black Behavioral Community Psychologist

In 2009, I began my journey as an academician as a newly minted doctoral graduate in behavioral psychology. I entered with a clear vision to contribute to meaningful change and improvement by advancing systems change. However, early in my career, there were uncertainties about how I could most effectively contribute to the field of applied behavior analysis. As an early-career faculty member both trained and hired into an applied behavior science program, I experienced initial uncertainties in my professional identity in the field of applied behavior analysis due to my race, gender, religion, and area of concentration or subspecialty, which is focused in behavioral-community application. Now as an associate professor, I unequivocally identify as a Black woman and protestant Christian who is a community-engaged scholar and behavioral community psychologist. However, it took me over a decade to really understand and be confident in the cross sections of my personal and professional identities, particularly within the context of our discipline. Only after being both granted tenure and having developed positive rapport with established colleagues in the field am I now comfortable sharing my journey as a Black woman scholar in academia who advances community-engaged scholarship through behavioral community approaches.

Based on the evolutionary process, I have become well versed in navigating being the only or one of the few Black people in a professional setting. Yet, my experience and journey may not be comparable to that of many of my peers in my department, at my institution, or in the field who are majority White. As a Black woman of color, a general consideration for me is always will I be the only, the first, or who came before me from my community. For those who are from dominant majority backgrounds and never have to ask or wonder, it is a place of privilege.

Overall, I have been blessed to work in supportive environments with colleagues at my institution and in the field more broadly who are committed and care deeply for their applied work and those they serve. Yet, my experience as a Black woman even in a supportive setting is still quite different and one that cannot be understood by many of my professional peers. Thus, my experience is one that I do not share often, even with those who are empathetic and supportive, as I recognize it may be difficult to fully understand. As such, I acknowledge my vulnerability in writing this chapter.

Intersectionality as a Black Woman Scholar in Applied Behavior Analysis

This book chapter culminates my experience and perspectives as an academician and scholar. As I contemplated the development of this chapter, I determined I was unable to describe my journey without acknowledging the intersectionality of my personal and professional identities as a Black woman. In 1989, Dr. Kimberle' Crenshaw coined the term intersectionality based on her work, in which she noted,

> With Black women as the starting point, it becomes more apparent how dominant conceptions of discrimination condition us to think about subordination as disadvantage occurring along a single categorical axis. I want to suggest further that this single-axis framework erases Black women in the conceptualization, identification and remediation of race and sex discrimination by limiting inquiry to the experiences of

> otherwise-privileged members of the group. . . . This focus on the most privileged group members marginalizes those who are multiply-burdened and obscures claims that cannot be understood as resulting from discrete sources of discrimination. I suggest further that this focus on otherwise-privileged group members creates a distorted analysis of racism and sexism because the operative conceptions of race and sex become grounded in experiences that actually represent only a subset of a much more complex phenomenon. . . . These problems of exclusion cannot be solved simply by including Black women within an already established analytical structure. Because the intersectional experience is greater than the sum of racism and sexism, any analysis that does not take intersectionality into account cannot sufficiently address the particular manner in which Black women are subordinated.
>
> (p. 140)

In 1989, Dr. Crenshaw introduced the work of intersectionality and multidimensionality to better understand the experiences of Black women that challenged the single-axis analysis of experiences often dominated by the perspective of the Black male and White woman. Thus, the framework of intersectionality emerged to better understand and address the experience of the Black woman across multiple interrelated areas of identity. Since this time, the concept of intersectionality has broadened to understand a range of experiences related to identity.

Intersectionality was included in the seventh edition of the Publication Manual of the American Psychological Association to provide guidance for how to address intersectionality in writing. APA (2020) suggests,

> When authors write about personal characteristics they should be sensitive to intersectionality- that is, to the way in which individuals are shaped by and identify with a vast array of cultural, structural, sociobiological, economic, and social contexts (Howards & Renfrow, 2014). Intersectionality is a paradigm that addresses the multiple dimensions of identity and social systems as they intersect with one another and relate to inequality. . . . Thus, individuals are located within a range of social groups whose structural inequalities can result in marginalized identities. . . . To address intersectionality in a paper, identify individuals' relevant characteristics and group memberships (e.g., ability and/or disability status, age, gender, gender identity, generation, historical as well as ongoing experiences of marginalization, immigrant status, language, national origin, race and/or ethnic status, among other variables), and describe how their characteristics and group membership intersect in ways that are relevant to the study.
>
> (American Psychological Association, 2020, pp. 148–149)

Within the context of my own experience, I am writing this chapter and recognize the importance of understanding how intersectionality and my personal characteristics have shaped my professional identity and work, including in my commitment to advancing community-engaged scholarship as a behavioral-community psychologist. My work and commitment as a community-engaged scholar is very much informed by my identity as a Black woman who is a protestant Christian and is committed to positively impacting communities of color, including in the communities in which I work, reside, and identify.

Assuring Social-Emotional Supports as Scholars and Academicians in Higher Education

When writing this chapter, I had to ensure that I wrote it during a time that my emotional stamina would permit probing and reflection on my journey over the past decade. All too often, as scholars, we neither have the time nor opportunity to allow for the cognitive and emotional space required to probe deeply into our own lived experiences, which is particularly critical when writing from the position and perspective of a minoritized group. To this end, my husband, Eric Thompson, a higher education professional, is a co-author of this chapter. He has observed, endured, supported, and shared in my journey as a Black academician and community-engaged scholar. The path has been one that I neither crossed nor am able to share on my own, but in partnership and through the support of my spouse Eric, our family, and collegial mentors who along the way have provided a safety net as my community of compassion and care.

Exemplars of Macro Aggressions Experienced by Faculty of Color

During the early and formative stages of my career, I was told by a White male of influence that they did not know of anyone Black in the field of behavior analysis who was appropriate for a position I was desiring to attain. The person further opinionated that they were unable to identify hardly any persons of color in our discipline, and of the few there was only one White Hispanic male who may be appropriate for the position. Then, the person further went on to provide me with the named examples of prior Black women who had tried to pursue this path and were unsuccessful. Additionally, the person was critical of my application of behavioral science through a behavioral community approach as it deviates from standard behavioral approaches. In my private thoughts, when this opinion was verbalized, I decided to support the mantra "I can show you better than I can tell you." Thus, my nonverbal response to refute the criticism was to behave in the context experienced all too often by women, which is then to over-perform. Unfortunately, for Black women, the default response and expectation to over-perform may be a modern-day form of mammification (Beauboeuf-Lafontant, 2009).

As a person of color, prejudice and discrimination are common and understood as a way of life. Since I was a child, I have been continuously prepared for the reality that at times I will first be judged by the color of my skin despite my credentials, degrees, and expertise. Yet, it was not until a decade later when offering my support and advocacy to a friend who is Hispanic and had experienced discrimination in the workplace that I understood the gravitas and weight of my own experience in shaping my professional career and presence in the field. I have an enduring commitment to supporting community-engaged efforts with often minoritized and marginalized groups in both the academic and community settings.

Although the experience occurred over a decade ago, it is still a moment for me that is etched in history. Since this time, there has not been a week that in some manner I have not reflected on those comments of disparagement. At times it has been motivating and other times disheartening that people of color, particularly those who are Black, still must combat the ignorance of others in multiple environments, including in the field and workplace. I understand that as a professional I must continue to demonstrate the worth of not only myself as an individual, but then I also have the weighted responsibility to serve as a symbol and demonstrate the merit of our [Black] people in the discipline and profession. The result of continuous taxation of proving one's worth as a Black scholar is layered on top of the already exhausting demands of the professorate, which is even more complex as a community-engaged scholar. Collectively, over time such conditions may further contribute to untenable conditions experienced by some persons of color in both the field and in institutions of higher education.

Only after I had become established in the field did I confront the person and candidly raise this macroaggression that I experienced early in my career. For this person, the experience that I had reflected on at least weekly for over a decade was but an insignificant moment in time that they had not remembered. Much later, after a decade, I shared with another White colleague in the field about the experience. In that moment of discomfort and unrehearsed responding in dealing with matters of race and prejudice, the default response was to inquire if I was sure that is what the person meant or intended. At that moment, I realized that unless you have walked a mile in one's shoes or have been on the road with a person of color in time proximal to an experience, it may be incomprehensible to understand the daily micro and macroaggressions encountered.

When afforded the opportunity and privilege to support the conditions that may enable the success of scholars of color, particularly those who are women, it is imperative that we facilitate and advocate for changes in systems that are necessary to truly disrupt and diversify our institutions within and across our disciplines and field. Additionally, when we have overtly or covertly contributed to systems of inequities and oppression for people of color in academia or in our field, it is important to both acknowledge the ill, as well as communicate and engage in the active demonstration of behaviors with those involved to meaningfully support reparative efforts to foster healing. Lastly, when working with or serving minoritized groups, it is of upmost importance for people from the dominant group to not self-identify as an ally or advocate, as that determination must be bestowed by those within the community you are supporting or serving based on one's active behaviors with the group.

Although there is a long way to go, I have been involved in more recent efforts in the field of behavior analysis to better support diversification. In 2020, I was invited to serve on the inaugural Diversity, Equity, and Inclusion Board for the Association of Behavior Analysis International. In 2021, I had the immense opportunity to contribute as a guest associate editor, along with Kaston Anderson-Carpenter for the special issue on police brutality and systematic racism in Behavior Analysis in Practice in which Denisha Gingles served as the guest editor and Jonathan Tarbox as the editor. Additionally, in 2022, I was elected to serve on the Executive Council for the Association for Behavior Analysis International as the first Black person to have served in this capacity since its development in 1974. Although there is modest progress, there are great strides yet to make as a discipline and field, including through our professional associations and academic programs, to further enhance and maintain the diversity of our field, including with those we serve in the community. As I reflect on my journey as a Black academician and community-engaged scholar, I choose to share this experience within the context of my intersectionality as a demonstration of the conditions in which I have operated. Additionally, I hope to exemplify the challenges presented in academia as a person of color, as well as in my practice as a community-engaged scholar.

Impact of Disparities of Blacks in Psychology and Applied Behavior Analysis

Racial Diversity in the Discipline

As a Black woman, I am a member of an underrepresented group in our discipline. Based on the 2021 membership data, only 4% (229) of the members of the Association for Behavior Analysis International (ABAI) (2021) were Black or of African descent. Similarly, the American Psychological Association (2018) also found that only 4% (4,200) of active psychologists in 2016 were Black or African American, although nearly 14% of the United States population is Black or African American (U.S. Census Bureau, 2022).

According to Dr. Nasiah Cirincione-Ulezi (2020), one common denominator for many Black women within the field of ABA is that at some point in their careers, they are likely to be in the unique position of being the only Black woman ABA professional at the school, clinic, agency, or program where they are employed. Being the "only one" of any group in the workplace may serve as an incredible disadvantage, specifically as it relates to pursuing and attaining positions of leadership. . . . As the only Black woman, or one of two or three other Black women in a work environment, Black women often report feelings of isolation and invisibility at work (Robinson-Wood et al., 2015).

Institutional Diversity

At my institutional campus, in 2021, only 3.4% of faculty and faculty administrators were Black, and even fewer were Black women (University of Kansas, 2021). Presently, as the only Black woman faculty in my academic home department, approximately 5% of the tenure-track faculty (i.e., me) identify as a Black woman. During my time as faculty, I have been one of two faculty who were Black in our department across the duration of my employment, which resulted in approximately 10% of the faculty in our unit identifying as Black.

When hired, my academic institution was engaging in a set of practices to recruit and retain racial and ethnic students and faculty. In 2009, at the time that I began my tenure-track faculty career, the institution had just hired an associate vice provost for diversity and equity for the first time, which at that time was the most senior diversity officer at the institution. Now that I am a tenured faculty member, I am comfortable sharing that I was a minority direct hire or a target of opportunity hire. Based on the human resources guidelines at the University of Kansas, targets of opportunity hire "fall into two categories: a) The hire of a prominent, nationally sought-after scholar or researcher; or b) The hire of an underrepresented group member in an area where there is evidence of underutilization" (University of Kansas, 2015). At the time, a minority direct or opportunity hiring strategy was supported by the institution to specifically recruit and retain qualified racial and ethnic faculty candidates. As an opportunity hire, the process was the same as is standard for any faculty hire and involved a series of interviews, a job talk, and completion of other requirements that then culminated in a vote by the faculty for the position, which then was approved at various levels of the university.

Anecdotally, in recent conversations with faculty on our campus, multiple other Black women tenured or tenure-track faculty with whom I have come into contact have often been successfully recruited through this mechanism. However, rather than public recognition and celebration of a strategy that may be effective for at least the hiring of Black women into academia, it is not often openly discussed. Now that I am a tenured associate professor who has demonstrated the merit of my contributions and commitment to my department, institution, and in the broader field, it is important to acknowledge hiring mechanisms that intentionally support increased representation of minoritized groups at some institutions of higher education.

Community Matters in Advancing Representation for Minoritized Groups

I am a native Kansan, so for me, being at a predominantly white institution (PWI) in Kansas was not of as much concern since it was the geographic and cultural setting in which I was reared. Excluding the period in which I pursued my undergraduate studies at Jackson State University, a historically Black college and university (HBCU), I have been a proud Kansan. However, my decision to complete my undergraduate work at an HBCU was very intentional and afforded me the opportunity to be part of a majority group through a community of academic peers and mentors. It was a transformational period in my academic and professional development in which I was trained by Black faculty, including Black women, who both understood and prepared me for the journey ahead, including as an engaged scholar. After completing my undergraduate studies, I returned to Kansas to be closer to my family, but also largely because of an informal pipeline that had been established in collaboration with Dr. Eric Strauss, who at the time was the director of the Master of Urban Planning

Program at the University of Kansas, and Dr. Jacqueline Franklin, a Black woman faculty in the Urban Affairs undergraduate program at Jackson State University. Through the mentorship of Dr. Franklin, I was supported in navigating the process of applying for and attending graduate school, including in understanding the graduate-admissions timeline, exploring opportunities for graduate assistantships, and having an established network of faculty and Black alumni from the University of Kansas. Once more, the intentionality and support provided by my mentor team in navigating higher education from my undergraduate, to graduate, and now professional career has been critical.

While in the Master of Urban Planning program, I was introduced to applied behavior analysis as a graduate research assistant (GRA). During my last year in the urban planning program, I served as a GRA with the Center for Community Health and Development at the University of Kansas (KU). Upon graduation from the Master of Urban Planning program, I was admitted to the doctoral program in behavioral psychology and Dr. Stephen Fawcett served as my faculty mentor. I was introduced to the behavioral community approach for addressing community problems and goals through the KU Center for Community Health and Development (CCHD), then under the leadership of Dr. Fawcett. The KU CCHD became a safe place in which I was able to grow in advancing the work of behavioral-community applications through community-engaged scholarship.

Importance of Community-Engaged Scholarship to Faculty Hiring and Retention

I am a tenured associate professor in the Department of Applied Behavioral Science at the University of Kansas. I have contributed to furthering the community health and development specialty area, within the applied behavior science department at KU, as well as hold an administrative appointment as the Director of the Center for Service Learning. Since I completed my graduate training at the University of Kansas, I entered my faculty position with strong community partnerships, which otherwise takes multiple years to develop and maintain. My commitment to advancing community-engaged efforts began with and in communities as a graduate student and has been paramount to my commitment to remaining at the University of Kansas for over a decade. For me, as a Black woman in a predominantly white institution, my commitment to serving the broader community and advancing community-engaged scholarship has been a key factor that has influenced my professional goals and decisions. As a graduate trained in the practice of community-engaged scholarship, my dedication to serving my community was critical to my career decisions. It is important both for the community, but also as an institution to contribute to sustaining community-engaged scholarship activities through established partnerships, including in teaching and learning, research, and through service and outreach.

According to Corbin et al. (2021),

> Making the connection between faculty diversity and community engaged scholarship is essential for creating institutional environments where a new and more diverse generation of faculty members can thrive. . . . Research also indicates that minoritized faculty are less likely to pursue academic careers or to remain in faculty positions on campuses where emerging forms of scholarship, including community engaged scholarship, are not valued and rewarded. If community engaged scholarship is clearly defined, fairly evaluated, and fully rewarded, the evidence suggests that faculty positions will become more appealing to minoritized faculty. Supporting community engaged scholarship is thus an important strategy for diversifying the professoriate. Diversifying the faculty can help advance research that has a broad social impact, assist communities in addressing social issues, and improve student learning outcomes. Unfortunately, faculty

> evaluation and reward systems remain antagonistic to academic work that would fulfil these goals. Understanding the importance of community engaged scholarship as a strategy for diversifying the faculty should motivate educational leaders to shape and support community engaged scholarship.
>
> (Section Attaining and Retaining a Diverse Faculty)

Community-engaged scholarship (CES) not only positively impacts the community but also provides meaningful experiences for community and academic partners, including students, staff, and faculty. CES may also be a recruitment and retention strategy, particularly for faculty of color. For a community-engaged scholar, the commitment to the community partnerships and interventions may be a critical consideration in the recruitment and retention of racial and ethnic scholars. Additionally, for scholars who must relocate to communities in which they may not have support systems, it can be very daunting and isolating to be one of the few Black scholars in a community. Therefore, the partnerships with the community served may also provide a sense of community for the scholar. Often, the value of community-engaged scholars investing in lasting and meaningful change in the community is discounted by the institution and the discipline, including in the application of behavior science.

Road Taken: Advancing Diversity Through Community-Engaged Scholarship

To further advance the application of behavior science, it is important to enhance the diversity of the field including in expanding areas of application through the engagement of those involved in training, practice, and service delivery. The scholarship of engagement supports a participatory process for collaborating with community and academic partners to identify and address problems of social significance through the application, integration, and discovery of knowledge. Additionally, community engagement fosters social validation of the goals, procedures, and effects as part of the integrative process.

Community-engaged scholarship may serve as a conduit for faculty, researchers, and students of color to meaningfully contribute to diverse communities and populations through research, teaching and learning, and service. Often, community engagement is of value particularly to faculty and researchers of color who may want to serve communities of interest or identity through the application and science of behavior. Thus, community-engaged scholarship may be an overlooked strategy for the recruitment and retention of diverse scholars of color in the academic or practice settings, including in applied behavioral science and analysis.

A benefit of community-engaged scholarship is the diversification of who may have improved access to our services and behavioral interventions. The field can occasion opportunities for those who are from minoritized, underrepresented, and underserved groups to expand the communities and populations served by recognizing community-engagement as a merited form of scholarship in our academic training programs and practice. However, the traditional structures for evaluating the merit of scholarly contributions in academia or the field are not adept in examining community-engagement as a form of scholarship.

It is important that we consider how to support the conditions that can advance community-engaged scholarship through our academic training programs and as a profession. Opportunities to support community-engaged scholarship may serve as a recruitment and retention strategy for scholars of color. In the field of behavior analysis and applied behavior science, there are opportunities to partner in advancing the efforts of community-engaged scholarship. When afforded the opportunity and privilege to support the conditions that may enable the success of scholars of color, particularly those who are women, it is imperative that we facilitate and advocate for changes in systems that are necessary to disrupt and diversify our institutions and discipline. In this chapter, I have shared the journey of a Black academician who supports a behavioral community psychology approach through community-engaged scholarship. I am cognizant that my road traveled through community-engaged scholarship as a Black academician and behavioral community psychologist is making the path a little more weathered so that there may be better traction for others who choose to journey along.

References

American Psychological Association. (2018). *Demographics of the U.S. psychology workforce: Findings from the 2007–16 American community survey*. Author.

American Psychological Association. (2020). *Publication manual of the American psychological association* (7th ed.). American Psychological Association. https://doi.org/10.1037/0000165-000

Anderson-Carpenter, K., Watson-Thompson, J., Chaney, L., & Jones, M. (2016). Reducing binge drinking in adolescents through implementation of the strategic prevention framework. *American Journal of Community Psychology*, *57*, 36–46. https://doi.org/10.1002/ajcp.12029

Association for Behavior Analysis International. (2021). *ABAI diversity data membership*. Retrieved February 27, 2022, from https://media.abainternational.org/dei/DEI%20Data%202020-2021%20Membership.pdf.

Beauboeuf-Lafontant, T. (2009). *Behind the mask of the strong black woman: Voice and the embodiment of a costly performance*. Temple University Press.

Blanchard, L., & Furco, A. (2021). *Faculty engaged scholarship: Setting standards and building conceptual clarity*. Academy of Community Engagement Scholarship. https://doi.org/10.17615/0xj1-c49

Bogat, G. A., & Jason, L. A. (2000). Toward an integration of behaviorism and community psychology. In J. Rappaport & E. Seidman (Eds.), *Handbook of community psychology* (pp. 101–114). Springer.

Boyer, E. (1990). *Scholarship reconsidered: The priorities of the professoriate*. Carnegie Foundation for the Advancement of Teaching.

Boyer, E. (1996). The scholarship of engagement. *Journal of Public Service and Outreach*, *1*(1), 11–20.

Cirincione-Ulezi, N. (2020). Black women and barriers to leadership in APA. *Behavior Analysis in Practice*, *13*, 719–724. https://doi.org/10.1007/s40617-020-00444-9

Corbin, G., Kehal, S., & Saltmarsh, J. (2021). Why community engaged scholarship is important to diversity, inclusion, and equity in higher education. *Scholars Strategy Network*. Retrieved July 1, 2022, from https://scholars.org/print/pdf/node/22301

Crenshaw, K. (1989). Demarginalizing the intersection of race and sex: A black feminist critique of antidiscrimination doctrine, feminist theory and antiracist politics. *University of Chicago Legal Forum*, *1*(8), 139–167. doi:10.4324/9781315582924-10

Fawcett, S. B. (1980). Behavioral community psychology. *American Psychological Association Division of Community Psychology Newsletter*, *13*(3), 7–8.

Holsapple, M. A. (2012, Spring). Service-learning and student diversity outcomes: Existing evidence and directions for future research. *Michigan Journal of Community Service Learning*, 5–18. https://files.eric.ed.gov/fulltext/EJ988316.pdf

Howard, J., & Renfrow, D. (2014). Intersectionality. In J. McLeod, E. Lawler, & M. Schwalbe (Eds.), *Handbook of the social psychology of inequality* (pp. 95–124). Handbooks of Sociology and Social Research. Springer. https://doi.org/10.1007/978-94-017-9002-4_5

Kadavasal, P., & Watson-Thompson, J. (2022). Examining PLAY to increase levels of physical activity among youth during leisure time. *Behavior and Social Issues*, *31*(1), 215–233. https://doi.org/10.1007/s42822-022-00090-6

Ling Yeh, T. (2010, Spring). Service-learning and persistence of low-income, first-generation college students: An exploratory study. *Michigan Journal of Community Service Learning*, 55–65. https://files.eric.ed.gov/fulltext/EJ904634.pdf

Matias, J. N., Lewis, N., & Hope, E. (2021). Universities say they want more diverse faculties. So why is academia still so white? *FiveThirtyEight*. https://fivethirtyeight.com/features/universities-say-they-want-more-diverse-faculties-so-why-is-academia-still-so-white/

Moore, C. (2021). *A behavioral economic approach to preventing adolescent violence* (Doctoral dissertation). University of Kansas, Behavioral Psychology.

Post, M. A., Ward, E., Longo, N. V., & Saltmarsh, J. (Eds.). (2016). *Publicly engaged scholars: Next generation engagement and the future of higher education*. Stylus.

Robinson-Wood, T., Balogun-Mwangi, O., Boadi, N., Fernandes, C., Matsumoto, A., Popat-Jain, A., & Zhang, X. (2015). Worse than blatant racism: A phenomenological investigation of microaggressions among Black women. *Journal of Ethnographic & Qualitative Research, 9*(3), 21–236.

Stewart, D. E., Jessop, N., & Watson-Thompson, J. (2021). Examining conflict mediations to prevent violence through multisector partnerships. *Peace and Conflict: Journal of Peace Psychology, 27*(2), 170–181. https://doi.org/10.1037/pac0000536

U.S. Census Bureau. (2022). *Quick facts: United States*. Retrieved July 1, 2022, from www.census.gov/quickfacts/fact/table/US/PST045221

University of Kansas. (2015). *Guidelines for successful recruiting*. Retrieved February 27, 2022, from http://humanresources.ku.edu/sites/humanresources.drupal.ku.edu/files/docs/2015%20Guidelines%20for%20Successful%20Recruiting_0.pdf

University of Kansas. (2021). *KU fact book*. Retrieved March 20, 2022, from https://aire.ku.edu/faculty-and-staff

University of Kansas. (2022). *About the center*. Retrieved March 20, 2022, from https://communityhealth.ku.edu/about-center

Watson-Thompson, J. (2018). The road taken: Contributions to advancing community-engaged scholarship. *Metropolitan Universities, 29*(4), 107–121. https://journals.iupui.edu/index.php/muj/article/download/22837/22260/doi:10.18060/22837

Watson-Thompson, J., Fawcett, S. B., & Schultz, J. A. (2008). A framework for community mobilization to promote healthy youth development. *American Journal of Preventive Medicine, 34*(3), S72–S81. https://doi.org/10.1016/j.amepre.2007.12.016

Watson-Thompson, J., Woods, N. K., Schober, D. J., & Schultz, J. A. (2014). Implementing the capacity for change model with substance abuse prevention coalitions. *Journal of Community Psychology, 42*(6), 748–763. doi:10.1002/JCOP.21650

Watson-Thompson, J., Jessop, N., Hassaballa, I., Vanchy, P., Henderson, J., & Moore, C. (2020). Together helping reduce youth violence for equity (ThrYve): Examining the development of a comprehensive multisectoral approach to youth violence prevention. *American Journal of Community Psychology*. https://doi.org/10.1002/ajcp.12449

Watson-Thompson, J., Jones, M. D., Colvin, J. D., Schober, D. J., McClendon-Cole, T., & Johnson, A. M. (2013). Supporting a community-based participatory evaluation approach to violence prevention. *Journal of Prevention and Intervention in the Community, 41(3)*, 155–166. www.tandfonline.com/doi/full/10.1080/10852352.2013.788342

Watson-Thompson, J., May, M. J., Jefferson, J., Young, Y., Young, A., & Schultz, J. (2018). Examining the contributions of a community coalition in addressing urban health determinants. *Journal of Prevention & Intervention in the Community, 46*(1), 7–27. https://doi.org/10.1080/10852352.2018.1385936

10 Family-Career Balance

Professional and Personal Repertoires Shaped with Love, Enthusiasm, and Strong Models

Martha Hübner and Luiza Hübner

Family and School Until 18 Years Old: The Shaping of a Scientist and a Teenage Leader

The importance of family has been significant to me during all phases of my life, in addition to the concept of working hard, the relevance of a career, and the mission of doing my best in everything.

Over the past 22 years, every year, the whole Hübner family got together for an official meeting, called the "Annual Convention of the Hübner Family," where grandmothers, uncles, aunts, cousins, sisters, brothers, mother, and father, about 30 people, were in the same place (usually a hotel) for three days. We would have fun sharing inside jokes, unforgettable plays, scavenger hunts, speeches, and minutes (reports)! Some Hübners were medical doctors, psychiatrists, professors, businesspeople, and housewives. They were famous for writing and speaking well, generally loving to read, and loving language, including poetry. They were also famous for their eccentric sense of humor (jokes and stories). There was a joke that we shared among ourselves: *Hübners are famous for being intelligent, beautiful, and modest.* After saying this, we added: *But we disagree about being modest.*

On those convention days, we made presentations, which were generally musical or performative shows and poems read aloud or recited by heart. Since the time we were young children, we learned that art, language, and music were also important and that we had to cultivate these talents. Of course, some anxiety and competition grew as well.

In behavior analytic language, I had learned at a very early stage that a big family was there to socially reinforce my talents, as I was close to them. With these contingencies, I developed love and a caring attitude toward them, but I also developed a general repertoire of doing my best, be it when performing or learning skills at school or in other areas of life.

In our core family (mother [Martha], father [Celson], two sisters [Maria Regina and Maria Helena], and one brother [Celson]), I grew up with a model of a strong and affectionate father, who was an airline captain at a commercial company (Varig Airlines), and a very present mother, a homemaker, who gave me the same name as hers: Maria Martha Costa Hübner.

I was born in São Paulo, the capital of São Paulo state, Brazil, South America, on March 18, 1955. São Paulo is the largest city in South America. I am the youngest of four siblings (with two sisters and one brother). I am 11 years younger than my brother, the third sibling, and 13 years younger than my oldest sister. When I was ten years old, we moved to Rio de Janeiro due to my father's career at the Varig airline company. I spent the happiest days of my childhood and adolescence in Rio. When I was 16 years old, we moved back to

Authors' note: We would like to thank Editage (www.editage.com) for English-language editing.

DOI: 10.4324/9781003216773-13

São Paulo state—this time, to a countryside city called Sorocaba. We moved there because of my uncle, Hudson Hübner França, a cardiologist who lived in the city. He was my father's youngest brother. By that time, my father, a retired airline captain, had a heart attack and needed his brother close to him.

In Sorocaba City, from 11 to 18 years old, I started to experience different kinds of leadership among my friends and at school. Having studied at well-renowned schools in Rio, high school in a small city was somehow easy for me. The lowest mark I used to receive was nine out of ten. I scored full marks on the majority of my tests. When I received a nine, my father would ask me, "What happened here, darling?" This high performance shaped my repertoire. Of course, anxiety, a sense of competition, and high academic performance had to coexist.

In the arts field, I also continued to shape my repertoires early during the annual meetings of the Hübner family, mentioned earlier. I had created a musical band with three other friends. We used to play at our school parties and events. My role was to sing, play the guitar, coordinate the logistics of the events, and plan and decide on costumes. We explored the possibility of participating in a music festival, and on one Thursday evening, we presented at the festival. On Friday morning, I went to school to write a math test, and I got a nine out of ten on a very difficult test. On Friday evening, we received an award: we won the music festival, with a song presented by us, which was composed by a friend and myself. Fortunately, due to a double victory, my father did not negatively react to my score of nine on the math test. Our victory at the festival was also well received by him. To sum up, good results in the arts were also reinforced by my family (father and mother), but academic performance had to be high as well.

My sisters and brother were also very important in shaping a good balance between career and family in my behavior patterns. My oldest sister, Maria Regina, was a leader in her area (social science), and when she was a teenager, she used to play the guitar; she also spoke English fluently. I learned to imitate her in both abilities. My other sister, Maria Helena, taught me how to study when I was about nine years old, helping me with homework and school tasks. She used to work all day and study at night, but if I needed some help with school tasks, the only thing I had to do was to ask her for help, through a small written message. In the next morning, my homework was completely finished.

My brother helped me a lot when I had a terrible eye accident. When we were in Rio, I was shot with a bird-killing weapon and the bullet hit my right eye. My brother read me part of a storybook (*The Adventures of Tom Sawyer*) every day for a month (at that time, I was unable to go to school). With love and enthusiasm, he taught me that even in difficult times, we had to move on and accomplish our responsibilities.

University and Graduation: The Importance of Family Support

I had to make a decision about which course to take at the university (in Brazil we are required to choose a course—either a four-year course or a five-year course—in the same discipline. There is no "minor" or "major" for a postsecondary course in Brazilian universities). I attended vocational counseling, which helped me choose the psychology course.

In the early days of my undergraduate classes, while answering a question about my conception of psychology, I realized, years later after rereading my answer, that I conceived psychology not only as a science but as a behavioral science. It was an answer that already outlined the notion of contingencies and the relationship between human beings and their environment.

My ontogeny could help explain the positive experience that I had with Behavior Analysis, right in the first semester of my Psychology course. As a daughter of a commercial aviation pilot, I grew up listening to exciting stories about "the passengers, the plane and the pilot," which always emphasized the important relationship between behaviors, the constant attention to the countless stimuli on a plane's control panel, the detail of each analysis, and the skillful handling of complex contingencies. My mother, in turn, was never tired of saying, with a smile, that I was "born for science." I did not know what that meant, but now I understand that she implied that I study hard and build a career for myself. Besides, because she always said this with a smiling face and tender gestures, the word "science" must have acquired reinforcing properties early on. However, this message might have also started a kind of conflict between love, family, and academia. I used to be a very good student in high school. When I started dating, my mother kept saying, "You are a woman of science. Keep studying hard." The message became even clearer to me: "Pursue the life of academia rather than that of being a wife and building a family." The conflict has probably been established by conflicting sources of verbal governance.

I will describe how I solved this conflict by playing different roles: as a scientist, a therapist, a wife, and a mother, without losing the joy of being a woman, a mother, and a hard worker, as a scientist, and as an applied behavior analyst. Challenges, suffering, hard work, happiness, leadership, and awards are part of this complex journey.

Right at the beginning of the psychology course, I was invited to monitor the behavioral disciplines and, at one of them, I started research with an echolalic young girl, applying Skinner's (1957) verbal operant concepts. This research, which I started during my undergraduate course, turned out to be part of my master's thesis, at the suggestion of my advisors, Maria Lucia Dantas Ferrara and Larry Williams. This master's thesis was considered the first one in Brazil about verbal behavior. At the same time, during my undergraduate studies, I met my first boyfriend, and the relationship lasted five years. In 1979, I met my first husband and the father of my daughter, Luiza Hübner, who was born in 1986.

During my undergraduate years at the Catholic University of São Paulo and my graduate courses at the University of São Paulo, my academic performance maintained a high standard. The management of personal and professional contingencies taught me that the conflict between personal life and academia existed only in verbal governance, not in direct contingencies. I was able to manage both living a romantic life and being a researcher at the same time. My father gave me some help: when I was getting married, he whispered in my future husband's ear, "Please, do not disturb her career. She will go far." Indeed, my first marriage was very balanced in terms of female-related and male-related housework and the tasks of raising a daughter. During my 14 years of marriage, I received a master's degree, got my PhD, and became a university professor and a child psychologist counselor (behavior therapy) at the same time. My husband admired me (and vice versa). He gave me all the support to conduct my professional life and shared with me all domestic tasks, including cooking. This is an important point for achieving a balance between career and family: we have to manage contingencies day by day, with mutual positive reinforcement with our partner, as well as sharing values that become verbal governance in your daily life regarding what you consider important in your life. For me, my career was as important as my family. I could not live without both.

Some Highs and Lows During Graduation Programs and University Teaching

With the conclusion of my master's thesis, I was excited about the fact that I was perhaps inaugurating a line of research in the experimental analysis of verbal behavior in my country. However, I did not have many interlocutors. Few Brazilian colleagues were interested in and/or researching verbal behavior. Therefore, I decided to write to Skinner himself. In the letter, I revealed my difficulty in distinguishing between echoic, tacts, and mands during the acquisition process, recognizing a clear distinction only in the final acquired operants. In other words, I "complained" about the existence of multiple controls in verbal behavior. Later, I found from Skinner himself that this was not a problem, as long as we identified, as much as possible, the controlling variables in a functional analysis of language (Hübner, 2021, in press). In his response to my letter, Skinner alerted me to the fact that distinguishing the referred operants during acquisition was a minor issue. He said that the terms were only there to make the rest of the analysis possible, that is, the entire functional analysis of verbal behavior. Some colleagues, who were specialists in analyzing Skinner's books, told me that this concept was not found in his books.

I continued with my attempt to further discuss issues relating to verbal behavior and behavior analysis with the author of the book *Verbal Behavior.* On a visit to the United States of America in 1983, I called Harvard and scheduled an interview with Buhrrus Frederic Skinner. He attended to me kindly and surprised me with his answers. I left the interview with an unforgettable feeling of having met a sage, not because I agreed with his ideas and considered them fantastic and unique, like the young fan I was, but above all, because he considered them incomplete. When I asked during the interview (a question that I would certainly not have the courage to ask today) about Chomsky's criticism that he did not have a complete science in the study of language, he told me that he was tired of misreading his proposals and concluded that he, in fact, did not present a complete science. He said to me at the time, "And who would have it?" (Hübner, 2022).

When my daughter was four years old, I finished my doctoral dissertation. When she was drawing or pretending she was writing and someone asked what she was doing, she quickly answered that she was writing her dissertation. This small detail probably reveals an imbalance between family and career. It shows that I was spending a huge amount of time writing and this behavior of mine was the most frequent my daughter was seeing. True or not, I spent most of the following years without going to the Association for Behavior Analysis International (conferences that I loved) because my daughter was now going to school (the Association of Behavior Analysis International [ABAI] generally occurs in May, which is in the middle of the school semester). This is another example of how family and career controlled my decisions in terms of time spent with both. If I felt an imbalance, I tried to redirect my journey. However, I have to admit that my maternal duties were a priority until Luiza was 15 years old. After that, I returned to my international trips, and it was possible to leave her in Brazil for some days, while I was attending international events.

Another indicator that it was not easy to balance career and family, in terms of raising a child, is a behavior that I saw Luiza displaying at a bookstore: looking for books to read, she chose a book entitled *When I am alone: A guide to children at home.* This broke my heart. I felt miserable and that I had failed as a mother. At the same time, I concluded that she was somehow coping.

To give an idea of my worries and exaggerations about maternal duties, I used to tell my friends that I could not stay away from my daughter for more than four hours. My friends, laughing, used to reply, "In my case, I cannot stand four hours with them."

My professional career was developing well, while Luiza was growing up: teaching at universities (Catholic University of São Paulo and Mackenzie University, both considered two of the three main universities of São Paulo city), conducting research, and finishing my PhD with Maria Amelia Matos in 1990 at the University of São Paulo. When I look back at my professional journey, I see that everything was an effort that was the confluence of many different people, behaviors, and strong models, most of them women behaving in a magnanimous way to improve our field.

My behavior analytic repertoire was shaped by great professors (Helio Guilhardi, Amalia Pie Andery, Maria Luisa Guedes, Celia Gonçalves, and Sonia Meyer at the Catholic University of São Paulo and Maria Amelia Matos, Rachel Kerbauy, Lígia Marcondes Machado, Maria Lucia Dantas Ferrara, at the University of São Paulo [USP]). Two professors (Carolina Bori and João Claudio Todorov) taught me how to manage, as president with two mandates, the largest scientific psychology association in Brazil (SBP), from 2002 to 2005. It is not a coincidence that both were previous Brazilian recipients of the same ABAI award that I would receive years later. I will describe this soon.

My marriage was not going well, though. The problem was not the theme of the present chapter; it was not due to an imbalance between career and family. Well, maybe partly so. In some sense, I tried hard to have both, and I would have liked to see and reinforce it in my husband's repertoire. In this aspect, I did not manage it very well, and the marriage ended. The problems were more complex, and like many other couples, we divorced in 1993. However, we have remained friends. It was a good marriage of 14 years.

The Second Marriage and the Explosion in the Leadership of Scientific Associations

After two years of being divorced, while I was teaching at Mackenzie University, one of my students and advisees in the Mackenzie Master Degree program in Education, Juliane Pozzetti de Campos, introduced me to Domingos Pozzetti Neto, her uncle, who became my husband, for 26 years.

Domingos is a university professor in language (Portuguese) and a man admired as a hero by his family and students. Family is one of the highest priorities for him, as well as the responsibility of daily work and the sustenance of his life and obligations. His niece introduced us to each other as a personal happiness plan for both of us, and she was successful. Domingos admired a woman who could speak English, play the guitar, and sing. He also admired a successful and independent woman. He told me that I had all these attributes. I admired a man with a great sense of responsibility, who was handsome and had political and social values congruent with mine. We matched. At 40 years of age, I gained a loving and large family of two nephews, seven nieces, and one stepson, with their wives, husbands, daughters and sons—the Pozzetti family!

I found love again in perfect harmony with a soaring career in different and new dimensions. In summary, during this phase of my career, I continued to write books and papers and to teach at universities. In 2003, I taught at the largest university in South America and one of the most famous in Brazil, the University of São Paulo (USP). In the first phase, the president of the Brazilian Association of Psychology (SBP), the first scientific association in the area, was founded by behavior analysts. I was reelected for the second mandate.

During my years at SBP, we conducted four national conferences for scientists and practitioners to present their work during the same panel discussion or symposium. We also led the development of the guidelines of undergraduate psychology programs for the whole country. As Professor João Claudio Todorov, one of the founders of behavior analysis in Brazil, liked to highlight, at SBP, we invited everyone to participate in the discussions on psychology at the national scientific association, but the political control was behavior-oriented.

Immediately afterward, I was elected president of the Brazilian Association for Behavioral Psychology and Medicine (ABPMC), with two mandates. This was a flourishing time for agapic love (Skinner, 1989), and working hard for the development of behavior analysis in Brazil.

During my presidency at the Brazilian Association of Behavior Psychology and Medicine, we kept the dream of continuing the reunion of scientists and practitioners, now strictly in the field of behavior analysis, believing that we needed to teach Behavior Analysis to the audience to navigate all the domains of our field: Experimental Analysis of Behavior,

Applied Behavior Analysis, Services, and our Philosophy—Behaviorism. These domains, I used to say, are like rooms in our home—Behaviorism—and without knowing each other well, it is hard to know our science and philosophy in a complete way. Without knowing them well, it is easy to get into a technical way of doing Behavior Analysis. Doing so is an easy way to disappear. Why? Science and technology help in the comprehension of processes in order to conduct them at several levels and occasions in a better way. Techniques refer to knowing how to conduct them only in specific situations. We need both to survive as a science and epistemology and to solve problems in new situations.

Working with scientific policy in Brazil did not separate me from my students at USP. Having students was the most effective way to disseminate behavior analysis and to keep our hope for the future alive. The students were lovely. In some way, they became a part of our family.

The students were at USP, and pursuing a career at USP was not easy. To stay there, professors had to submit to many contests: the first contest was to enter; the second one was to make it stable (they call it effectuation); the third one was called "Livre Docência," and the fourth one was called "professor titular" (full professor).

The competition to obtain the title of "Full Professor" was, with no doubt, a special, important, and unforgettable moment. When the contest was over, I had the added privilege of receiving a letter from one of my mentees (Felipe Gomes), which included a detailed personal report on the three days of the contest, in his view. With some reluctance, I decided to reproduce an excerpt from that letter, which moved me a lot, especially because I realized that such a moment had an impact on this dear student:

> If the first day was marked by the recognition of your wisdom and competence in planning experiments, analyzing results and discussing them with equally competent colleagues, on the second day, during the examination of your memorial, we walked along the beautiful trajectory that justifies all this recognition. It was wonderful to see colleagues and friends chatting about your already long career in Psychology and Behavior Analysis and to hear fun and exciting stories that marked your trajectory, both for you and for those who have followed you throughout these years. Each member of the board remembered different aspects and achievements of your career, always emphasizing your plurality, your willingness to embrace everything—almost always successfully. For me, it was very exciting to hear about several things that day: your courage in debating with Skinner, your engagement in coordinating the Program, in the direction of ABPMC, in our representation at ABA, the award won this year, your insertion and growing relationship with the University Hospital, your work in teaching, research and application, your passion for what you do and for always trying to do better. I was especially moved when you talked about your father and the values you learned from him, when you told the episode with Luiza (which in itself is exciting, but also because you know how to use everyday examples so well to demonstrate the application and practical implications of our work as behavior analysts), when Professor. Maria Teresa Araújo Silva said that she would have liked to have been you as student, when Professor Gerson Tomanari confessed that he was relieved when you joined USP, among many other beautiful and sincere speeches, from people who admire you as a person and as a professional. Anyway, I would like to remember them all, but it's not possible; at least the sensations and emotions I felt these days were all saved, and that's what counts.
>
> The third day was the icing on the cake, of course. After all the achievements, professional achievements, dedication, studies (and I'm not just talking about 40 days) and considerations from the board, we didn't expect to hear less than ten for each grade given by each teacher. You deserved them all, no doubt about it.

> In view of all this, I feel very grateful and privileged to be part of your group of advisees and to be able to count on all this experience, dedication, willingness and, above all, on your affection, welcoming and always in a reinforcing way you have to deal with me and the group. I confess that going through this experience of following your competition generates anxiety—good, I admit—, as I have the obligation to do my best in my Master's dissertation, in return, and try hard if I want to be, one day, a little of the professional and teacher you are for all of us.
>
> (Felipe Gomes, August 2015)

Felipe Gomes had finished his master's and doctoral degrees with outstanding performance and his letter had a deep impact on my confidence to move forward as a professional and as a person, in a similar direction I had been taken before.

International Journey: The Essential Role of ABAI

Since 1979, I have been interested in the Association of Behavior Analysis International (ABAI, then known as ABA). The 1979 meeting was my first meeting in Dearborn, Michigan, USA. With three other colleagues (Celso Goyos, Lúcia Williams, and Luiz Carlos de Freitas), we prepared a slideshow on behavior analysis in Brazil. With four slide projectors, Brazilian songs in the background, and time coordination among the four of us, we presented the major university programs, initiatives, and centers for Behavior Analysis in Brazil, from the north to the south of the country. I remember exactly the moment when Buhrrus Fredric Skinner, Fred Keller, and Murray Sidman were walking down the hotel corridor to see our presentation. What an honor and pleasure!

From 1982, I became the contact person for ABA (ABAI) in Brazil, and I had the privilege of taking the post of Professor João Claudio Todorov (one of the founders of Behavior Analysis in Brazil) to be presented at the 1990 convention because he could not attend.

After the 1990 convention, it took a while to return to the annual meetings, as I mentioned earlier. Maybe this gap of going to international meetings was a reflection of an imbalance between family and career, showing that maternal duties were a priority for me. This also reveals the challenges faced by a woman in coordinating the duties of taking care of a child, going to work, and being married, even when you have a good partner who helps with the domestic tasks. We should also remember that in Brazil, middle-class people can hire a helper who works at home. Such individuals are of great help in terms of cleaning the house and cooking. Even so, from 1990 to 2002, I stopped attending international meetings in my area of study, but I continued to work every day as a psychology teacher at Mackenzie University and as a behavior therapist, as well as being the president of Brazilian scientific associations from 2002 to 2010.

It is interesting that as I continue to write about the theme of the present chapter, some new facts from the past come to mind, and I reinterpret them. At the time of writing these words, I realized that the exaggeration of the maternal duties could be seen as contradictory to my mother's verbal rule of not getting married and not being a mother (she did not say that explicitly, but she meant it, I think). It taught me, because of my childhood and adolescent contingencies, to conceive academia and maternal duties as a challenge, but totally possible. My mother was a very present mother and, at the same time, had multiple talents. For example, she was an excellent sewer, although she was not professionally trained. I used to wear formal, stylish dresses almost every weekend. In other words, my mom implied the opposite. Knowing that coherence between verbal and nonverbal behavior does not always occur and that we can find different controls between them (verbal and nonverbal), nonverbal contingencies played a major control over my behavior and reinforced the coexistence of high standards of behaviors in professional and personal lives. Phylogenic variables also explain the priority I gave to maternal duties.

In 2003, I received a phone call from Dr. Maria Malott, consulting about the idea of an international ABAI conference in Brazil. I accepted the idea immediately and, with Dr. Helio Guilhardi from the Brazilian Association of Behavioral Psychology and Medicine (ABPMC), we organized the 2004 International Meeting of ABAI, with around 2,000 participants. It was the largest meeting on Behavior Analysis in Brazil and the largest international meeting of ABAI.

In 2007, ABAI invited me to be part of a group of professors to teach Behavior Analysis in Jordan, in the Middle East. It was one of the most unique experiences I had in my life, with the unconditional support of my husband and daughter, Domingos and Luiza, who encouraged and convinced me to go. In Jordan, it was clear to me how I had a life of freedom in terms of the role of a woman in a family and in a professional context. The limits of women there were evident, and the master's program that I was teaching at Jordan University of Science and Technology, as part of the ABAI delegation, had a huge impact on the lives of some students in the class.

Years later, in 2014, when I was reading the journal *The Analysis of Verbal Behavior*, I saw a paper that was a systematic replication of a paper that I gave the Jordanian students to read and present as a seminar during our classes in 2007. The original paper was titled "Effects of praising qualifying autoclitics on the frequency of reading" (Hübner et al., 2008), and the paper published in 2014 was "An extension of the effects of praising positive qualifying autoclitics on the frequency of reading" (Sheyab et al., 2014). It was very pleasing to see this.

The highlight of my international journey was about to happen. In 2009, I was nominated to be an international representative at the Executive Council of ABAI and I was elected for a second mandate until 2014. In 2015, I was elected president, which I never expected.

During my speech as president-elect, in San Antonio, Texas, I showed a tendency to find balance. The title of my speech was "Behavior Analysis Without Borders." The objective of the text was to propose an approach of greater interaction among dimensions within behavior analysis, starting with a description of ABAI initiatives to break geographical and technical borders.

Under the leadership of its Executive Council, ABAI has crossed geographical borders for the past decades, disseminating behavior analysis around the world through: a) annual conferences and conventions all over the world, receiving more than 40 countries at every convention; b) its international conferences, which allowed ABAI to go to different countries, such as Italy, Canada, Brazil, China, Norway, Spain, Mexico, Japan, France, and Sweden; and c) supporting affiliate chapters in five continents, reaching around 40 affiliate chapters outside the borders of the USA and 46 within the USA.

After being on the council since 2009, ABAI made huge progress in considering all the chapters—non-USA and USA chapters—as being ABAI chapters. Because of this, we could say that there are more than 20,000 ABAI people worldwide. Awarding international development grants and awards is another way ABAI is breaking geographical borders.

Finally, I mentioned that another initiative that ABAI took to break international borders through Behavior Analysis was the delegations, whereby ABAI leaders go to countries where Behavior Analysis is incipient and ask for help to develop it. I mentioned that continuing this kind of initiative would be one of my main directions as president, and it was. During my presidency, we went to India as a delegation, and the results were quite fruitful, as I will describe later. In my view, ABAI showed that it was possible to break geographical borders through the consistent and unique epistemology of behavior analysis. Thus, we can say that geographical borders are not barriers to the advancement of our field.

Paradoxically, however, the domains within behavior analysis have presented borders that are not easy to cross or navigate, although many authors have pointed out that such navigation is critical. Therefore, in my presidential speech, I analyzed how imbalanced our field was. For example, Moore and Cooper (2003), citing Hawkins and Anderson (2002), argued that at

> any point in time, any particular behavior analyst might function as a basic behavior analyst, an applied behavior analyst, and a behavior-analytic practitioner. A behavior analyst might fill one or more of those roles at any given time and perhaps all three roles over the course of a career.
>
> (Moore & Cooper, p. 71)

One of the reasons for this is that there are nodes among the internal domains. The ABAI has been developing strategies to ensure healthy navigation through borders.

In the direction of breaking internal Behavior Analysis borders among the domains, the ABAI Program Committee has provided important suggestions, such as the "Task Force Report" of 2014 Convention (Jennifer Austin, Jesse Dallery, Jonathan Friedel, Ramona Houmanfar, Dick Malott, Mark Mattaini):

> If you are inviting someone who does primarily basic research, you might ask him/her to mention the applied implications of his/her work. . . . If you are inviting someone who does primarily applied work, you might ask him/her to mention the theoretical implications of his/her work. Consider developing a mechanism for invited symposia or other invited events that involve multiple Program Areas. For example, two Program Areas. . . . This could provide a means for developing "translational" symposia. Consider including someone who can represent a purely practitioner point of view (i.e., someone who is not an educator or a researcher, but works full time delivering ABA services).
>
> (ABAI handbook of program, 2014)

This last suggestion by the Program Committee is clear evidence that the ABAI program task force, under the leadership of its executive council, is enhancing the participation of practitioners in our home, because their presence at ABAI not only means that we are, indeed, *The home of science and practice* but because by having them within ABAI, with the strategies of integrating the domains, we can truly welcome and shape a very important category of constituency: the scientist-practitioners.

Therefore, ABAI has been making great efforts to keep the constituency of practitioners inside, because we know that theory and basic research without practice are lame, with the risk of being hermetic or being only a pleasant intellectual game, and practicing without theory and basic research inspiration is blind and poses the risk of the extinction of behavior analysis as a whole.

Establishing a parallel between that presidential address I had presented in San Antonio, Texas in 2015, and my text here and the theme of the present chapter, I think a previous paragraph reflects what I think about family and career balance: career without a family and vice versa are incomplete paths, because we can neither live being fed by love only nor live with science only, without a love to feel. Besides, I think it is part of my repertoire to develop and propose a balance between domains.

If we search carefully, we can find strong models of behavior analysts who have tried hard to find this balance, for example, Fred Keller, Fred Skinner, Charles Ferster, Don Baer, Azrin, Murray Sidman, Rachlin, Bill Heward, Jack Michael, Fergus Lowe, Doug Greer,

Sigrid Glenn, Linda Hayes, Carol Pilgrim, Gladys Williams, Susan Schneider, Jim Carr, Maria Mallot, Janet Twyman, and Mike Perone. This group of appealing people come from different domains and they are still active at ABAI conferences, through their presence, references, or warm memories, appealing to a broad audience with their generosity, knowledge, and extensive expertise in the field.

I totally agree with Jay Moore (2003) when he said,

> We can then identify at least four roles that a behavior analyst might fill: conceptual behavior analyst, basic behavior analyst, applied behavior analyst, and behavior-analytic practitioner. . . . Each of these four roles is an extremely valuable part of behavior analysis, and each deserves full and equal respect.
>
> (Moore, 2003, p. 119)

If an author of the stature of Jay Moore published this, it is because something was wrong or deficient in terms of equality of respect among the areas. Probably, he meant that the basic researchers were receiving more attention and prestige in our area than the practitioners. Is that fair? Why?

Well, basic researchers are the discoverers of principles and processes; they are the ones who understand the process in order to derive procedures/techniques for the applied researchers and practitioners. However, it is also possible that the equivalence paradigm boom started with applied research in which Murray Sidman (1971) taught, for the first time, a 17-year-old boy (named Cosmo) to read.

The success of this applied work led to the proposal of an equivalence paradigm ten years later. This is an example of how a necessity in a service delivery (applied problem) inspires a basic procedure to be tested and theorized.

In 2007, Murray Sidman wrote a paper titled "What's in Behavior Analysis for us," in which he said that the term

> Experimental Analysis of Behavior not only summarizes a set of behavioral facts and theories, but it is also a name of a set of behavioral repertoires, and, as we know, if we want to understand what somebody does, we have to find out the reinforcers of his behavior, in our case, the behavior of behavior Analysts.
>
> (p. 309)

In that paper he presented his own reinforcer for what he was doing:

> The moments of exultation became even more frequent when I began doing experimental investigations with people as subjects. . . . The day Cosmo went through that program successfully, I went home and listened to Sousa marches, imagining Cosmo and me leading the band down the street. Why are we so unwilling to let people know that laboratory work can generate such reactions? As many practitioners know very well, one of the joys that comes from working with the same person for a long period of time is the affection—the mutual affection—that often develops. That happens in the laboratory, too. One of the features that I prize the most about the photograph is the sight of Cosmo's fingers, indicating that he had placed his arm about my waist.
>
> (Sidman, 2007, p. 314)

I am also fortunate, as was Sidman, to have my own "Cosmo" in my own life, not as a participant in a research study but as a member of my family.

From this moment, I am also authorized to talk about the fifth domain of Behavior Analysis: the domain of the consumer. Obviously, I had inserted my family in my 2015 presidential speech, talking about a nephew's history with Applied Behavior Analysis.

Louis was born in October 2006. After six months, we started to notice some signs of autism; after a year and some months, we started to look for neurologists, psychiatrists, and behavior therapists in Brazil. He had greatly improved during the first year of behavior therapy, but he still showed palilalia and stereotypical behavior. At three years of age, even presenting this problem, the therapist group at that time decided to reduce the number of therapy hours (making an error that I call a "decision not based on scientific evidence and showing an error that is known as applying 'Light ABA,'" which does not exist in literature).

After that, I decided to call an international Behavior Analyst and my students at the University of São Paulo (USP) and started intensive ABA therapy.

When Dr. Gladys Williams started the treatment, Louis did not look into others' eyes; he had a high frequency of palilalia, some stereotypic behavior, and few interactions with other people.

After five years of solid treatment, totally evidence-based, and with a controlled practice, he was dismissed from his ABA therapy.

For me, this is an example of behavior analysis without borders: a multicultural team, interacting and navigating inside all the borders of our field.

As president of ABAI, I incorporated my view of the balance between career and family into my speech and I also took some art to the annual convention. During the 2016 annual convention in Chicago, USA, we had a classical-music presentation of the pianist Fabio Luz, considered one of the major interpreters of Debussy. It was a new kind of event at the annual convention and, for me and some of my colleagues, it was a magical moment. I also sang the most famous Brazilian song titled "The Girl from Ipanema"—which had family and career influences on one person: myself.

When I thought I had experienced the maximum joy that could happen at ABAI, I was surprised with an award for the International Development of Behavior Analysis, which I received in 2018, in San Diego, California from the Society for the Advancement of Behavior Analysis (SABA). Of course, many members of my big Hübner family (brother, oldest sister, sister-in-law, niece, and cousins) attended this prestigious event to support me. At the International ABAI meeting in Japan, 2015, under my presidency, there were so many Hübner family members at the hotel convention that Dr. Maria Malott had difficulty finding my room. If you have a big family and they go to Japan with you to attend a conference that has no connection with what they do, you realize that you are the connection. It is an ecstatic feeling. Unforgettable. Family and career in the same place!

During my ten-minute speech at the award ceremony, I created images of an airplane journey in motion, where I was the pilot, and I informed the audience about the different places and trips I took to disseminate behavior analysis in the world. Any clue about who inspired me to present this slideshow? My father and his profession (airline pilot), of course!

During my time as president of ABAI, we also had an opportunity to go to Italy at the kind request of Fabio Tosolin to participate at a national conference. We set the first steps to create another chapter, besides the affiliate chapter that already existed. Fabio Tosolin, with Aristide Saggino, proposed an Associate Chapter of ABAI, which reflects the increasing number of people interested in behavior analysis in Italy, introducing more areas in our field, such as organizational behavior management (OBM).

I presented a picture of myself at the top of the Italian mountains. Two details were important in the picture: the T-shirt I was wearing had the ABAI logo and the woman in the picture was the president of ABAI at the time when the picture was taken.

The last journey I described in my ten-minute award speech was my visit to India as part of another ABAI delegation. Maria Malott organized the main activities of this delegation with Dr. Smita Awasthi. We went with two other special colleagues: Drs. Linda Hayes and Ingunn Sandaker. We spent a week talking to high-level scientists and government decision makers, as well as with the press. With the authorities and scientists, we showed the importance of Behavior Analysis, the importance of creating graduate and undergraduate programs on Behavior Analysis, and the huge necessity of mutual interactions between science and practice for the survival of our field.

One of the persons from India, a behavior analyst, commenting on the role of our delegation, telling us that in one week, they had learned more about Behavior Analysis than in many years. The person mentioned the focus change from techniques only to the beautiful process of scientific analysis and discoveries through research. I had the feeling that we took to India the important notion that Behavior Analysis is not only practice and not only behavior therapy. Considering the improvements that India showed in 2021 (the recognition of Behavior Analysis as a profession, communicated by Smita Awasthi), the delegation, somehow, had a significant impact. Thus, the journeys were valid and worthy, mainly because they were journeys with many extraordinary people. I dedicated that award to all of them and to my family, my safe port (among them, my brother and my older sister were there again)!

We could stop this chapter right here. The balance between career and family has been well described. However, the COVID-19 pandemic has hit the world at large and Brazil in particular. In March 2020, the federal Brazilian government showed terrible management of the crisis, minimizing the serious effects of COVID-19. Their verbal behavior showed denial and anti-science attitudes. Therefore, I desperately started to present videos on the Internet. Six videos and three interviews with important Brazilian media were produced. One interview was given to the *Nexo* newspaper and two others to GloboNews. Each video and interview addressed the principles of experimental analysis of behavior that explained the actual contingencies from the beginning of the pandemic until November 2020, with instructions on behaviors that should be presented and those to be avoided, as well as the possible determinants of each. Principles, such as positive and negative reinforcement, verbal control, aversive control, anxiety paradigm, three-term contingency, and the model of selection by consequence were addressed in the videos and interviews. The contents also included data about the reality of COVID-19 in Brazil at the time, such as the number of deaths, social distancing rates, and behavior of the population in the city of São Paulo, which controlled my behavior in spreading science on a larger scale. The emphasis of the videos and interviews was that, in the absence of a vaccine and pharmacological treatments, the treatment should be behavioral. In this context, the importance of scientific dissemination and constant communication with the lay population, facing the challenge of maintaining a simple language, without losing precision, clarity, and empirical base, besides exercising the social responsibility of the scientist, was emphasized.

I spent the whole of 2020, until now, at my home office, but also accepting invitations to "Instagram live presentations" and "webinars," spreading out the notion of contingency and how to cope with the crisis, teaching new behaviors for the moment. With a large number of interviews, lives, and a personal history of doing this with the press since 1976, two results emerged from disseminating Behavior Analysis around Brazil: 1) I wrote a scientific paper about Behavior Analysis and scientific diffusion about the communication of a behavior analyst with the public (Hübner, 2021, accepted); 2) with the amazing support of Dr. Dick Malott and João Lucas Bernardy (a doctoral student), I was nominated to the Society for the Advancement of Behavior Analysis (SABA) for an award and the board of directors accepted it. With this initiative, I received the honor to be the 2022 recipient of the SABA award for "Effective presentation of Behavior Analysis in the mass media." This was unexpected, of course. What an honor!

At the same time, my large Hübner family was divided: some of them agreed with the Brazilian federal government and the management of the pandemic, and some of them were shocked about their denial attitudes. We are still divided, even with more than half a million deaths due to COVID-19 in Brazil. The divisions in the large Hübner family because of politics were not new. However, the antagonism between life and death, the value of the vaccine, and the resulting contempt were all difficult to cope with. The pain I experienced in seeing that my attitudes and communications in the mass media during the pandemic were receiving the support of my colleagues, scientists, and the public, yet part of my own larger family was against the major part of my orientation, broke my heart for some months and brought a huge imbalance in my concept of family. Many Brazilian families are experiencing divisions, like ours. Fortunately, my husband, my daughter, and one of my sisters are on the same side: the side of life, vaccines, and science! This balance is still solid and full of love and comprehension. Following this section is a text written by Luiza Hübner, my daughter. Some "reliability" of previous contents is presented, somehow.

Luiza Hübner's Perspective

How do I put into words such a unique life story? Sometimes, adjectives escape me to describe it in all its complexity. At this moment, with my 35th year of life just starting, I will risk telling some chapters of my story that made me who I am today: a story full of love, affection, mutual learning between a mother and her daughter, with their intertwined paths in Psychology and Behavior Analysis.

When I started thinking about my professional life and chose psychology as a career, I already knew that my psychologist mother had an immense influence on this choice. I confess that thinking about psychology has always been unquestionable for me, even though I was not sure why. Today, reflecting more carefully, I know that this choice was a consequence of the important female, maternal, and professional reference I had in my life: my mother, Martha Hübner. Her image and her way of being always had a strong impact on me, as well as her presence since the beginning of my life.

Although she had a remarkably intense and busy work routine, her presence was always marked by her effort to establish a pleasant, creative, and welcoming family environment. I remember her as a smiling mother who was excited about motherhood during my childhood, her reading to me before bed, my trips to her room in the middle of the night, and the ceiling with luminous stickers and a toy star that always glowed in the dark, thus alleviating any fear that might occur during the night. In my eyes, my mother was always a very busy professional. When people asked me as a child what my mother did for a living, I used to say, "My mother reads theses." However, she did much more than that. She lovingly organized birthday parties, took me to school and picked me up every day (one day she "forgot" to pick me and arrived very late, but that was not on purpose). If the day at school had been good, we sometimes went out to celebrate, stopping by the bakery to pick a sweet of my choice, or going to a newsstand to buy something I liked.

Our moments together were never rare; they were pleasant and quality moments, which makes me believe that my mother was successful in balancing motherhood with her professional life. After all, she always prioritized being present at the important moments of her children's routines and did not hesitate to ask when she needed a little extra help (from my father or someone else).

While I was at school, my mother saw patients in her office (as a behavioral therapist), prepared classes, studied, and organized things at home. All this was always done in a very generous and participative atmosphere, including the school environment. I have friends who even today comment on how my mother was always one of the coolest mothers in the class; many of them are still close to her and keep in touch to this day through social networks. Of course, the principles of behavior analysis have also always been part of my upbringing, with a good dose of positive reinforcement, which certainly contributed to making our bond stronger and to making her choices as a mother and educator, so to speak, more successful and aligned with her goals for her daughter's education.

During my late teens, when I was about to take the entrance exam to university, I did not think much about the possibilities available for a professional life as a psychologist, but I knew that psychology involved much reading (including Skinner, Fred Keller, the Wistar lineage rats, dissertations, theses), highlighter pens, Post-it notes, trips to the ABAI Congress, foreign colleagues (mostly North Americans), and clients who relied on our listening and competence in the therapeutic setting.

Today, going back in time, I realize that psychology was always a choice influenced by the very choices my mother made in my education. The choice of the school (based on the principles of behavior analysis) and its community, the relationship between friends and their families, the first celebrated homework, and the readings before bed were all always experienced with great affection and a great emotional investment. Even in challenging periods, such as adolescence, I have memories of a mother who was always willing to educate only with affection.

Although journalism and medicine haunted my thoughts, when the time for the entrance exam came, there was no doubt that Psychology had chosen me since childhood.

My five years at the Faculty of Psychology at PUC-SP, the same university where she graduated and taught, were memorable and were lived fully. I am proud to have built a trajectory similar to hers in this respect. When I started to specialize in Behavior Therapy at USP, I had the opportunity to be her student and learn from her in an academic environment. As if what I had learned throughout my life was not enough, I received this additional gift.

Over the past few years, we have built a stronger relationship as professionals and have formed a duo, so to speak. She usually says that I am her counterpart and that she likes it. In her contest to become a full professor at the University of São Paulo, our dear Prof. Dr. Maria Amália Andery described Martha's professional trajectory as a spiral. Perhaps this description also makes sense for our mother-daughter as well as professional relationship: firm, circular, constant, and always in motion.

In relation to all of her prestigious and honorable achievements, I know that they are the absolute result of all her strength, competence, excellence, and passion for what she does. My mother is a passionate psychology scientist and is also sincerely dedicated to motherhood. As I once wrote, if today I am a psychologist and a better human being than I was yesterday, rest assured that this is a result of the professional values that my mother taught me and still teaches to this day.

References

ABAI. (2014, May 23–27). *ABAI Convention program handbook*. Annual Association for Behavior Analysis International Conference, USA. Association for Behavior Analysis International. Handbook program.

Hawkins, R. P., & Anderson, C. M. (2002). On the distinction between science and practice: A reply to Thyer and Adkins. *The Behavior Analyst*, 25, 115–119.

Hübner, M. M. C. (accepted). Scientific dissemination and COVID-19: A behavior analyst in communication with the public. *Sociedade Brasileira de Psicologia: Cadernos de Psicologia*, 1, 1–18. doi: 10.9788/CP2021.1-03

Hübner, M. M. C., Austin, J., & Miguel. C. (2008). Effects of praising qualifying autoclitics on the frequency of reading. *The Analysis of Verbal Behavior, 24*, 55–62. https://doi.org/10.1007/bf03393056

Hübner, M. Strapasson, B. & Dittrich, A. (2022). *História da Análise do Comportamento em autobiografias.* Curitiba: Juruá.

Moore, J., & Cooper, J. O. (2003). Some proposed relations among the domains of behavior analysis. *The Behavior Analyst, 26*(1), 69–84. https://doi:10.1007/BF03392068

Sheyab, M., Pritchard, J., & Malady, M. (2014). An extension of the effects of praising positive qualifying autoclitics on the frequency of reading. *The Analysis of Verbal Behavior, 30*, 141–147. https://doi.org/10.1007/s40616-014-0017-8

Sidman, M. (1971). Reading and auditory-visual equivalences. *Journal of Speech and Hearing Research, 14*, 5–13. http://doi:10.1044/jshr.1401.05

Sidman, M. (2007). The analysis of behavior: What's in it for us? *Journal of the Experimental Analysis of Behavior, 87*, 309–316. https://doi.org/10.1901/jeab.2007.82-06

Skinner, B. F. (1957). *Verbal Behavior.* New York: Appleton-Century-Crofts.

Skinner, B. F. (1989). Recent issues in the analysis of behavior. Columbus, OH: Merrill.

11 Spiritual Activism

Paula Danquah-Brobby

Spiritual Activism

It has always been my belief that people belonging to historically minoritized and marginalized groups or who have intersectional identities cannot afford to navigate a life that is *not* rooted in some form of spirituality or connection to what some may refer to as the divine, universal energy, Gaia, or God. If you belong to a marginalized group or possess intersectional identities that are multiply oppressed, you cannot escape or avoid the constant deluge of nefarious social narratives, psychological contingencies, social/cultural metacontingencies, and macrocontingencies that have been maintained and perpetuated in order to *other* you. powell and Menendian (2016) explained "othering" as "a term that not only encompasses the many expressions of prejudice on the basis of group identities, but we argue that it provides a clarifying frame that reveals a set of common processes and conditions that propagate group-based inequality and marginality" (p. 17).

For those of us who are subjected to othering behavior, systems of oppression and inequity that maintain and reinforce othering practices are incompatible with optimal physical and mental health and quality-of-life outcomes (Centers for Disease Control and Prevention, 2021, 2022; powell & Menendian, 2016; Yearby, 2020). Othering behavior creates recurring punishment contingencies that decrease the likelihood that someone who belongs to multiple marginalized identities/groups will behave in ways that express and reflect their authentic self. Furthermore, the aversive stimuli associated with othering practices have powerful control over the behavior of the othered (Saini & Vance, 2020; also see Chapter 4). For example, during the Jim Crow era, Black men and women were not allowed to look White people in the eyes and had to avert their gaze upon seeing a White person on the street. In fact, Black people had to move off the sidewalk to allow White people to pass. To maintain "obedient" behaviors such as these, controlling agencies, such as religious institutions, educational systems, government, family, media, etc. (Al-Nasser et al., 2019; Saini & Vance, 2020; Skinner, 1953; Todorov & Freitas Lemos, 2020), established laws and rules that were meant to reinforce compliance and submissive behaviors, and punish what were considered to be oppositional behaviors amongst the outgroup/those who have been othered (i.e., minoritized and marginalized groups such as lesbian, gay, bisexual, transgender, queer and/or questioning, intersexed, asexual, and two-spirit [LGBTQIA2S+] individuals and Black, Indigenous, People of Color [BIPoC individuals]). Saini and Vance (2020) explained,

> These contingencies represent a new cultural norm, which assures a cultural practice is followed. In these cases, controlling agencies (i.e., agencies and systems) enforced cultural practices and provided aversive consequences when the individual behavior was

DOI: 10.4324/9781003216773-14

> incongruent with the cultural practice (e.g., an individual behaved inconsistently with the law and must be punished). In this sense, racist laws consist of operant contingencies interlocked into metacontingencies.
>
> (pp. 55–56)

Still, the Jim Crow era has come and gone, yet our society still suffers from the plague of othering and oppression. How can this be? It is because although cultural practices and controlling agencies evolve and change over time, and the controlling agencies, socio-interlocked behaviors (socio-IBs), interlocking behavioral contingencies (IBCs), aggregate products (APs), and macrobehaviors may not have the same topography or structure across time and space; the consequences still benefit the ingroup (e.g., White people, cisgender individuals, heterosexuals, men). Thus, the advantages to the ingroup are preserved and upheld from one generation to the next:

> The concept of the metacontingency highlights the functional relation between racist IBCs (e.g., the coordinated efforts of two or more majority individuals that exclude minorities), their aggregate product (e.g., the greater availability of resources for members and less availability for nonmembers), and the cultural consequences (e.g., access to greater wealth or opportunities for the majority group) created by and for a society of majority individuals. Moreover, conditional relations are supported by members of the majority over successive generations, even after the original reasons for discrimination have been eliminated. That is, metacontingencies support cultural practices designed by initial controlling agencies, even when those agencies have been removed or changed.
>
> (Saini & Vance, 2020, p. 56)

Certain socio-IBs, metacontingencies (Glenn, 2004; Houmanfar et al., 2010; Saini & Vance, 2020; Todorov & Freitas Lemos, 2020), and even macrocontingencies (Al-Nasser et al., 2019; Glenn, 2004) can be brutal, oppressive, dehumanizing, and deadly for people who look like me, and their recurrence can have life-altering consequences and cumulative effects (Al-Nasser et al., 2019; Glenn, 2004). In the instance of othering metacontingencies at play in our current culture and society, the cultural-organizational milieu (antecedents that allow for the occurrence of specific socio-IBs and APs; Houmanfar et al., 2010; Saini & Vance, 2020; Todorov & Freitas Lemos, 2020) is comprised of government, judicial, and educational systems, the media, economic institutions, and what powell and Menendian (2016) refer to as *classification schemas*. Classification schemas are humans' natural and innate tendency to categorize stimuli in order to make sense of their environment for the purpose of survival (of the species). As it relates to othering, these schemas can lead to ethnocentrism and extreme relativism. Socio-IBs, in this case, are the concerted effort by multiple members of the ingroup to other/exclude members belonging to the outgroup. The AP of these socio-IBs is increased access to and availability of resources (e.g., financial, housing, educational, health/medical, food, employment) for the ingroup and decreased/limited access to and availability of resources for the outgroup. These socio-IBs and APs influence consumer practices such as racism, homophobia, transphobia, sexism, xenophobia, religious/spiritual persecution, etc. (i.e., othering practices, beliefs, and attitudes) that are reinforced by controlling agencies and milieu leaders (e.g., teachers, news-media executives, pastors/spiritual leaders, job supervisors, family members, bankers, elected officials). These individuals then generate group rules (i.e., social narratives) that perpetuate othering behavior toward minoritized and marginalized groups (i.e., outgroup). Examples of said rules may be that outgroup members are aggressive, unsafe, unworthy, less than and, simply put, the "other." Moreover, the non-interlocked macrobehaviors of individuals can lead to the cumulative effect of othering and exclusion that establishes a dangerous macrocontingency for the outgroup that benefits the ingroup. Saini and Vance (2020) highlighted how ethical self-control and social discounting (loss of reinforcement on the individual level to strengthen social contingencies that benefit the ingroup) can result in the cumulative effect of othering (see also Tourrinho, 2013). Figure 11.1, adapted from Al-Nasser et al. (2019), shows the interplay between othering metacontingencies and macrocontingencies. It illustrates how socio-IBs and APs influence consumers' othering practices, and how said practices generate group rules that further shape, reinforce, and maintain socio-IBs and APs.

For me, one major remedy for combatting the destructive impact of othering on an operant level (i.e., ontogenetic) has always been my engagement in spiritual practices that serve to deepen my connection to the divine, universal energy (i.e., God). Because I am Black (race), Ghanaian (ethnicity), American (nationality), queer (sexual orientation), female/nonbinary (gender identity; she/they pronouns), and someone who clearly possesses an intersectional identity, my spirituality has literally saved my life, time and time again. It has been my security blanket, my confidante, my life partner, and the love of my spiritual life. Somé (1998) wrote about the healing wisdom of indigenous West African spiritual beliefs and practices: "from an indigenous perspective, the individual psyche can be healed only by addressing one's relationship with the visible worlds of nature and community and one's relationships with the invisible forces of the ancestors and Spirit allies" (p. 17). Accordingly, this chapter will center on the multidimensional intersection of my lived experiences and identity (Crenshaw, 1989) with a rich and deeply personal spiritual life. Thus, I begin this chapter by sharing that there is an immense degree of vulnerability and safety that I have to presume (whether real or imagined) in order to *allow* you, the reader, into my spiritually intersectional queer world. As such, I invite you to engage this content with an open heart and mind (metaphorically speaking).

I

> "If I knew nothing else, I knew I was dark-skinned before I knew anything else about myself. . . . It was always a measure of . . . my value. And in so knowing that I was dark-skinned, I also knew that I wasn't beautiful. The potential didn't even exist for me to be beautiful."
>
> —Dr. Yaba Blay (2022; podcast: We Can Do Hard Things with Glennon Doyle)

My mother, father, and older sister emigrated from Ghana in the 1970's. Upon settling into their new life in the United States (US), they had to engage in acculturation strategies (Berry, 2010). Acculturation refers to the psychological and cultural changes that occur when a non-dominant ethnocultural group/outgroup (e.g., Ghanaian immigrants/ex-patriots or "expats") comes in contact with a dominant cultural group/ingroup (e.g., the larger society, members of the host country). Acculturation strategies are the behaviors involved in the process of acculturating (i.e., integration, assimilation, separation, and marginalization). Berry (2010) stated,

> Four acculturation strategies have been derived from two basic issues facing all acculturating peoples. These issues are based on the distinction between orientations towards one's own group, and those towards other groups. This distinction is rendered as (i) a relative preference for maintaining one's heritage culture and identity . . . and (ii) a relative preference for having contact with and participating in the larger society along with the other ethno-cultural groups.
>
> (p. 198)

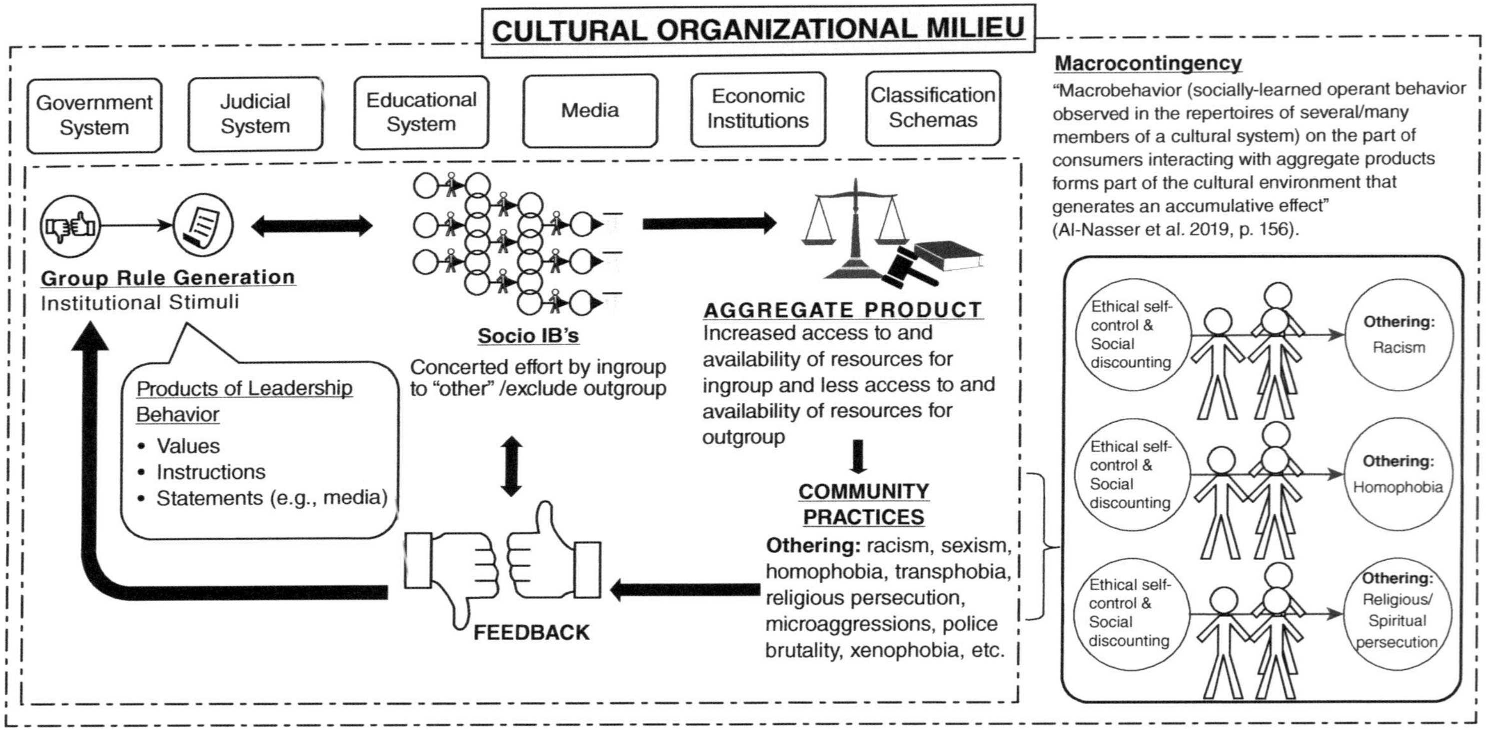

Figure 11.1 Othering Metacontingency and Macrocontingency

My parents held on to their cultural values, beliefs, and behaviors but also actively participated in the social organization of their new country. Berry called this acculturation strategy *integration.*

A few years into their time in the US, my mother became pregnant with me. However, shortly after my birth, my parents separated and later divorced; my mother gained primary custody of my older sister and me. It was not in her plan to become a single mother of two children in a new environment that presented a very different set of socio-IBs and metacontingencies. For the majority of my elementary school years, my mother worked two to three jobs, leaving my sister to care for me as a secondary mother/caregiver; she is ten years older than me. Imagine being 12 or 13 years old and having to care for a young child because your mother is forced to work multiple jobs to provide a better life and opportunities for you. It was a raw deal for all of us, but we made it work.[1]

My mother raised us as if she was still living in Ghana. She only spoke Ga in the house, we bathed inside the bathtub but used a bucket,[2] and we only ate Ghanaian food. Despite working five to six days a week, my mother cooked entire Ghanaian meals almost every day, and if you have ever eaten West African food, you know that meals take an abundance of loving care and time—there were no instant meals being cooked at my house (fun fact, I did not eat macaroni and cheese until my senior year of high school). In Ghana, everyone in the family is expected to contribute to the needs of the group and pull their own weight, even the children. Ghanaian culture and society can be described as collectivist in nature. From a very young age,[3] I was responsible for cleaning the bathrooms, sweeping the kitchen, hand-washing the dishes (we used the dishwasher for storing dishes—why waste money on dishwasher soap when your two hands, a sponge, and Palmolive are exponentially cheaper?), and doing the family laundry (the laundry was about a block or two away from our apartment).

When I was nine years old, my sister moved out and the household responsibilities grew. I also spent a significant amount of time by myself. They called us "latchkey kids" because we would wear house keys around our necks so that we would not lose them and we needed those keys to get into empty homes where no parent would arrive from work until dark. Consequently, the neighborhood kids, mostly children of immigrants like myself, cared for and looked after each other until dusk. It was during these twilight hours that you could hear a cacophony of children's names being called by exhausted working mothers throughout the neighborhood, directing children to return to home for dinner.

Between my Ghanaian upbringing and time spent with my first-generation American friends, I could not tell that I was growing up in America—except when I was at school or watching American TV. All of my early childhood experiences were rooted in my family's Ghanaian identity and culture. The result was a lived Black experience that has been extraordinarily different than my Black American brothers and sisters who are descendants of enslaved Africans. The intersection of xenophobia, racism, and sexism offered multiple opportunities for me to come in contact with othering behavior that was difficult for my young spirit to process. I often felt unseen and alone with little guidance to help me navigate the profound weight of being multiply oppressed. The concept of intersectionality was first proposed by Dr. Kimberle Crenshaw (1989). Crenshaw centered her analysis on the multidimensional nature of Black women's lived experiences. Crenshaw (2017) illuminated,

> Intersectionality is a lens through which you can see where power comes and collides, where it interlocks and intersects. It's not simply that there's a race problem here, a gender problem here, and a class or LGBTQ problem there. Many times that framework erases what happens to people who are subject to all of these things.
>
> (para. 4)

DeFelice and Diller (2019) defined intersectional feminism from a behavior analytic perspective—as "an array of variables (e.g., race, gender, sexual orientation) [that] interact to create the experience and perspective of individuals, modifying the salience of particular environmental events influencing behavior" (p. 831). My mother's intersectional identity brought her in regular contact with an exceptional set of aversive systemic, cultural, and social circumstances for the first time in her life: racism, xenophobia, and othering, to name a few. Born and raised in a country where people who looked like her were the standard—standard of beauty, intelligence, aptitude, innovation, etc.—I can only imagine what she must have been going through and how this, coupled with acculturative stress, must have been compounded by a divorce that left her raising children alone in a foreign land. Moreover, the age difference between my older sister and me made it a challenge to understand, let alone discuss, the complexities of our overlapping yet distinct intersectionality.[4]

Still, I found solace and peace within my Ghanaian family and our chosen extended family of aunties, uncles, and cousins (i.e., a community of African immigrants with whom my mother formed lifelong bonds).[5] Within the safety of this community, I was never "too dark-skinned" or made to feel ugly, or less than. But, when I stepped outside of this protective bubble, especially into predominately White spaces, which included school, the onslaught of ruthless tacts was damaging. I was called names like *African booty scratcher, burnt toast, ugly, darkie*. I was teased about being African and asked, ad nauseam, if my family used to live alongside giraffes and lions (and tigers and bears, oh my!). What I always found ironic was that the attacks came from White *and* Black American children alike.

Despite coming in frequent contact with reinforcement from my West African, immigrant community, these negative experiences conditioned me to view myself as ugly, and they challenged my sense of worthiness. In order to survive the brutality of heteronormative White supremacy, colorism, and xenophobia, I clung to my spirituality like one clings to a life preserver. At that young age, my spiritual life manifested in the form of spending hours at a time in the woods or by the creek, curious about and marveling at the vibrational energy of nature. If I was not exploring the wonders of the woods, I could always find God in the night sky as I wished and prayed to be among the moon and stars. With the universal divine (i.e., God) in tow, my imagination was limitless, and I was free to be anyone and anything I wanted. Miracles and magic abounded.

To this day, I dream of relatives long gone who bring words of wisdom (and warning). I can hear the whispers of my ancestors among the rustling trees or the stillness of the night sky. As a child, I carried this spiritual gift like a compass, guiding my path forward toward the discovery of my own divine light, or what Maparyan (2012) called *Innate Divinity*:

> Innate Divinity means that the fundamental essence of human existence, of the human condition, is a spiritual one, is energetic rather than material, and is constituted by a 'seed of light' connecting all embodied beings to the Great Light, otherwise known as Divine Intelligence, God, or the All.
>
> (p. 9)

Unfortunately, it would require many more life-altering experiences before I could fully comprehend and access the magnitude and power of my Innate Divinity. This would include the discovery of my queer sexuality, gender identity, and forgiving myself for ever being tricked into thinking that I was anything other than spectacular—inside and out.

II

When I was in my early twenties, I ended a long-term romantic relationship and moved across the country from Maryland to California. Although I had lived abroad in France, had visited my family's homeland of Ghana numerous times throughout my life, and had been living on my own for several years at that point, it was the first time that I would be on my own as a single, childless, and well-paid (for a 25-year-old) young adult. The possibilities of foolishness and reckless abandon were endless; I was looking forward to the mayhem. Accordingly, I packed up what little belongings I had (two cats and a new car) and headed westward to a new reality.

My new environment afforded me the opportunity to craft novel identities and expand my behavioral repertoires—a restart or sorts. This was an opportunity to explore new behaviors, come in contact with new social contingencies, and have certain behaviors come under the control of novel stimuli. It was an exciting time, but I was truly lost. It would take me coming across a months-old video recording of my bikini-clad Black body at a Hollywood pool party for me to wake up. It would also serve as the catalyst for my continued self-actualization. Self-actualization, self-expansion, and inner transformation are the cornerstone of what author and Women's Studies professor, Dr. Layli Maparyan (2012) refers to as the *Womanist Idea*. She wrote, "self-actualization is the foundation of positive social change because free, creative, expressive, self-loving individuals make the most altruistic political actors and the responsible and accountable servants of humanity" (p. 43).

Life in California brought a new cast of characters, interests, and opportunities for growth. I worked my nine-to-five, dated, and partied. The latter two activities were relatively new to me being that I had just ended a seven-year relationship. I was proudly out and dated boys, girls, and everyone in between.[6] I did not consider myself to be bisexual or pansexual,[7] but rather saw myself as queer.[8] Over 20 years later, married to my beloved wife, I still use the term queer to describe my sexuality—not because I have romantic attractions to men (notice I said romantic—meaning I have no desire to be in a romantic relationship with a man), but because I have never been one to put myself or allow anyone else to put me in a metaphorical box. I am just "Paula" and I always strive to expand, grow, and transcend. It is important to me to have the freedom to be every bit of who I am. However, it was my time in California that shaped and strengthened these beliefs.

While living in Los Angeles, I went to lavish parties and met various celebrities. I made new "friends" who were fabulous, superficial, drank heavily, and who were mostly White. One new friend was a woman who was known for throwing exclusive pool parties at famous Hollywood and Beverly Hills hotels. At the time, I felt honored to be counted amongst her inner circle of friends. Gone were the days of feeling othered, less than, ugly, too queer, too dark, not close enough in proximity to Whiteness, unwanted, invisible . . . or so I thought. I was too naïve and too desperate to fit in that I failed to see that I was being fetishized and tokenized.[9] I was too engrossed in my own self-hatred to notice . . . or care. I had rejected many aspects of my former self and, in its place, accepted and engaged in various forms of detrimental behaviors. My spiritual life took a backseat to my desire for acceptance.

Autumn in southern California was quite different than autumn on the East Coast. Palm trees do not have leaves that change, offering breathtaking hues of orange, red, and yellow as they end their life cycle in preparation for winter. I found myself feeling homesick and missing everything from my family and friends to my childhood autumn weather, to the interlocking behavioral contingencies that enriched the life that I knew and loved back in Maryland. As the pool parties wrapped up and the summer fever died down, we slowed our pace and spent more time together in smaller social groups. It was on one of these random fall afternoons that a bored, self-absorbed group of friends decided to watch video recordings of ourselves at the various pool parties we had attended over the summer months. We watched videos for hours—drinking, laughing, and slowly drifting off to other parts of the house to have nonsensical and at times comical, boozy conversations. Nonetheless, I remained in front of the TV, fascinated by what had been captured of our summer shenanigans and utterly heartbroken over my lack of inclusion in the hours of footage. I saw one familiar White face after another, frolicking in the pool, walking here and there, drinking, smoking, and making asinine comments to the camera. I was invisible again: unseen and undervalued. Right before switching off the TV, there I was.

My image on the screen was powerful in contrast to the White bodies moving all around me. The image was unapologetically Black, magical, and divine, but I did not see any of those attributes at the time. I watched as my dark-skinned, long-limbed body swayed to the beat of house music.[10] I watched as my hips moved in perfect harmony with the beat and pounding bass pouring out of the large speakers. I threw my head back in ecstasy, stretched my long arms and fingers towards the hot summer sky, and became one with the vibrational energy of the music.[11] Watching the video, I was utterly mesmerized—not because I thought I was beautiful, but because I could tell I was performing. All I could see was desperation. I was desperate to be pretty, seen, worthy, and part of the in-crowd. The wounded child inside of me was seemingly dancing for her life, engaging in a fruitless attempt to keep White supremacy,[12] colorism,[13] oppression,[14] institutional racism,[15] homophobia,[16] xenophobia,[17] and all other violence towards my intersectional identity at bay. Suddenly, the music seemed to trail off to a whisper as two voices abruptly cut through the video. I immediately recognized the voices; it was two of my "friends," who, I should note, were White. The conversation went something like this:[18]

Person 1: Oh my God! Look at Paula's skin and how dark it is; it looks like velvet.
Person 2: She's so exotic, so dark.
Person 1: I bet she'll never know how beautiful she is.

Exotic? My dark skin? I'll never know how beautiful I am? What in the name of microaggression was this? No comments about how great of a friend I was? No mention of gratitude for my contributions to our friend circle? Nothing about how they valued me or saw ME, my spirit, or my essence? You see, microaggressions do not always come in the form of overt, nefarious verbal or physical behavior; they can present as "compliments" and sweet nothings from others. This notion of invisibility is pervasive in the lives of Black, Indigenous, People of Color (BIPoC) individuals and communities. Ralph Ellison (1980) wrote about this sentiment in his book *Invisible Man*:

> I am an invisible man. No, I am not a spook like those who haunted Edgar Allan Poe; nor am I one of your Hollywood-movie ectoplasms. I am a man of substance, of flesh and bone, fiber and liquids—and I might even be said to possess a mind. I am invisible, understand, simply because people refuse to see me. . . . When they approach me they see only my surroundings, themselves, or figments of their imagination—indeed, everything and anything except me.
>
> (p. 3)

When I hear non-BIPoC individuals speak of their ability to be colorblind to race, it does nothing more than affirm that we truly are not seen—which is a form of racism.

The realization that I was nothing more than the token Black person in the friend group brought back memories of being excluded and othered. There was the time in the seventh grade when my Black elementary school friends said that I could no longer sit with them at lunch, nor would they continue to be my friend because they perceived me to be an Oreo.[19] In junior high school, I had been accepted into a humanities magnet program where I was one of about five Black students. And although this dynamic came with its own set of challenges, it was something that I was used to since I had been in gifted programs throughout my academic career. My Black elementary school friends watched me socializing with the plethora of new White peers in my new program and felt the need to share their judgement and disgust. Then there was the time when I was called the n-word during undergrad, while in the process of defending myself from the racist verbal behavior of another White male student. The tokenism also made me think of the time when I was at a party with a dear friend and a White woman walked up behind me, ran her fingers through my short dreadlocks, and exclaimed that my hair reminded her of her grandmother's carpet that she loved to nap on as a child. Comparing my hair to carpet was awful enough but, if you do not already know this, *never ever* touch a Black person's hair unless you have been given permission to do so. Despite the false societal narrative that continues to claim that Black bodies (especially Black transgender female bodies) belong to everyone but us (recall the White American history of trafficking and enslaving Africans in this country; the continued sexualization and exploitation of Black bodies such as Sarah Baartman; and the state-sanctioned killings of Black bodies like George Floyd, Breonna Taylor, Botham Jean, Philandro Castile, Sandra Bland, Freddy Gray, Eric Garner, Michael Brown, Travon Martin, Tamir Rice, and Elijah McClain by corrupt police officers). *Absolutely no one has ownership of our bodies.*

Ultimately, that 30-second video clip of me dancing was my salvation. I eventually withdrew from that social group and focused heavily on my work. However, as is the case with both individual and systemic disenfranchisement, it is pervasive. Not only was I experiencing othering in my social circle, I was also experiencing it at my job. Needless to say, I left that employment situation and accepted a new opportunity that deepened my understanding and love for applied behavior analysis (ABA). It also presented me with several positively reinforcing behavioral contingencies that changed the trajectory of my career and life.

I began working for a new company, providing ABA services to low-income Latinx families living further inland. Although my ABA training could have been better, I naturally and quickly grasped behavior principles. I could see the impact of the four-term contingency at work as my young clients acquired new skills and challenging behaviors were reduced. It was not until I worked with a five-year-old boy named Orlando that my future as a behavior analyst/scientist would be cemented.[20] My ABA training with this new company did not include any education on verbal behavior; however, looking back, I can see that I was implementing my own version of a mand training program that took place in the natural environment. After our discrete trial training (DTT) work, I always ended our sessions with outside play.[21] Orlando had a huge front yard that had a chicken coop and playground equipment. Left to his own devices, Orlando would perseverate on wiggling any long pliable object (e.g., a belt, hose, or sock). Consequently, I tried my best to keep him engaged during our outside time, but also made sure he had some downtime to do what he wanted (i.e., I followed his lead, which often meant watching him wiggle an object that he had brought outside with him or found in the yard). Because he preferred to play on the slide, non-vocal mands to push him were reinforced, contingent on his approximated sign for "go." As time went on, his signs were successively shaped until they matched the correct topography for signing and manding go. Witnessing Orlando's progress reinforced my abilities as a behavior technician.[22] In addition, working with my amazing Latinx and Hispanic families was one of the only times in my career that my ABA knowledge and skills were not called into question.

One day, as I was leaving Orlando's house, I opened and closed the front chain-link fence and watched him as he squatted in the yard and wiggled a black belt in the grass. Whenever I left his home I would watch him play in his yard for several seconds and then yell "bye-bye" while waving to him; Orlando never looked up at me or responded when I did this. But, on this particular day when I said bye and waved, Orlando stopped wiggling the belt, looked up, made eye contact with me, smiled, flopped his hand forward one time (i.e., approximated a wave), and said, "buh-buh." In total and utter shock, I stood there and cried for several minutes as he went back to his belt play. Despite my understanding of behavior analytic principles and technology to explain what had just happened, I also knew that there was something bigger, something divine that was occurring. Once again, I was bearing witness to the phenomenon of God in action. Why had he responded in that moment and not any of the ones prior? What had occurred in his private world that elicited vocal verbal behavior in that moment? How was he able to coordinate such a complex response class and chain of behaviors (listening to me saying bye, raising his head, looking me in the eye, smiling, raising his hand, and vocally emitting the sound buh-buh) without me teaching him each behavior in the chain? Our science has an explanation for this, predicated on behavior principles. Conversely, others who hold tight to spirituality would call this act divine. I know that the convergence of matter and spirit flies in the face of determinism; I am not attempting to challenge scientific assumptions. However, as a spiritual being, I have never been able to separate my faith from my science. It was in that moment that I decided to become a behavior analyst/scientist and knew that the universal energy was conspiring in my favor. But first, a spiritual liberation was on the horizon.

III

> "[T]he fundamental essence of human existence, of the human condition, is a spiritual one, is energetic rather than material, and is constituted by a 'seed of light' connecting all embodied beings to the Great Light, otherwise known as Divine Intelligence, God, or the All."
>
> —Maparyan (2012), p. 8, The Womanist Idea

When I experienced shaktipat,[23] I was visiting an ashram and had just completed an intense, two-hour meditation and chanting session. Chanting sacred mantras in a space full of light workers and like-minded, spiritual beings brings about a divine ecstasy that I wish everyone could experience. The magnetic energy of a group chanting in unison, as one sacred spirit, produces a tangible vibrational frequency that courses through your body and soul. It is akin to being internally *and* externally enveloped by a warm, loving bath. It is similar to a massage, except it is happening internally. This is what I had just experienced as I was sitting on a bench outside of the meditation hall. I was waiting for my friend to return from the lavatory. As I attempted to gain my bearings and re-center myself, I noticed that I had been sitting in front of a large, floor-to-ceiling painting of the previous guru, Baba Muktananda. Now, I had a very special bond with Baba. I listened to audio cassette tapes of his chants (yes, cassette tapes—this was well over 20 years ago), read his books, watched videos of his interviews, anything I could find that would give me a glimpse into who this magnificent being was. I did not fully understand my connection to Baba and how hearing his voice could only be described with one word: *nectar*. The significance of Baba Muktananda in my life was pure nectar. Furthermore, the translation of his name, Muktananda, literally meant the *bliss of liberation*. It was a spiritual liberation, expansion, and transformation that took place in front of Baba's imposing picture as I waited for my friend to return. What occurred next was a spiritual and energetic shift that, prior to this event, was both inconceivable and unfathomable.

As I studied Baba's image, allowing my eyes to trace and retrace the outline of his eyes, nose, mouth, arms, cinnamon-brown skin and orange robe, my eyes became locked in with his image and my immediate environment simply slipped away. All noises, voices, and people moving about ceased to exist. The only thing I could see was Baba's image. I stopped tracing his form and seemed to dissolve into the picture. All of a sudden, I lost my breath and began gasping for air, but all I could manage were short, rapid breaths (much like when someone is hyperventilating—but faster). At the same time, I had no fear. I had zero concern about my breathing or what was happening to me. I was at complete peace. What swelled through my spirit next was an overwhelming, overpowering, and absolutely godly feeling of unconditional love. Love that was not of this world; love that I had never in my life before or since. It was absolute nectar. In that moment, I knew I was experiencing God's divine love. I wish there was another word in the English language for the feeling of love that I had experienced that day because "love" does not begin to truly capture what this felt like. It was as if I was being cradled in God's arms as she plugged into my soul and let her omnipotent energy flow through every inch of my body, my existence. In that moment, as I openly wept, I surrendered utterly and completely to this spiritual awakening. My life was forever changed.

When my friend emerged, she was startled by what she saw. Octavia immediately ran over and knelt down, asking if I was okay; asking what had taken place; asking who had made me upset. I kept my eye trained on Baba's life-size image, barely blinking, and slowly recounted what happened. She remained silent. When I finally drew my gaze to her face, she was smiling and crying. "You just experienced shaktipat! It's when the guru transfers their divine energy to you!" Octavia had introduced me to Siddha Yoga Meditation (SYM) no more than a year before, and this was my first time at the ashram. She had been faithfully practicing SYM since childhood yet had never experienced shaktipat. Octavia was ecstatic for me but was also in complete shock. One does not typically experience shaktipat from an image of a guru, much less one who is no longer living. I should also note, I had never seen or met Baba in real life; he transitioned (passed away) in 1982 when I was a young child. I did not become aware of Baba or SYM until adulthood.

After experiencing shaktipat, everything in my life changed. The first change that I noticed was my sense of smell. I have horrible allergies and always hated the smell of cut grass. I am not sure if my strong aversion stemmed from pairing my allergic reactions to fresh cut grass and pollen, but I found the smell abhorrent. That all changed once I returned from the ashram. To this day, I absolutely love the smell of cut grass (it smells like nectar). I can also smell trees—all of them, something I was not able to do before. What do trees smell like, you ask? The only way that I can describe it is the smell of God. I would drive through Rock Creek Park in DC, on the way home from work each day, and weep as I hung my head out of the car window and took deep, deep breaths of air. In these moments I felt another iteration of shaktipat that was less intense but profound, nonetheless. The change in my olfactory senses reinforced the behavior of spending more time in the woods, as I had done during my childhood. As a result, my relationship and appreciation for nature was reestablished and persists. Another change was an increase in unexplainable phenomena related to clairvoyance, visions, and strengthened connections with my ancestors. These events continue to this day and are beyond the scope of this chapter. They are also deeply personal and private. However, I will say that my recognition of my ancestors' work in my life, along with my teenage son coming out as transgender male,[24] helped me discover and tact my own gender identity: gender non-binary. Shaktipat allowed my meditation practice to flourish. My deepening practice brought with it a sense of inner peace, knowing, and self-love that grew exponentially with each opportunity to become still and quiet my internal verbal behavior. The bliss of liberation untethered me from the harmful false narratives maintained by racism, homophobia, sexism, misogynoir, and other aversive interlocking behavioral contingencies rooted in my subjugation. Although unable to escape the existence, function, and reinforcement of systemic oppression and White supremacy, I no longer allowed it to define any aspect of who I was or how I showed up in the world. My liberation was indeed quite blissful, and I owe so much of who I am today to that moment on the bench in the ashram. Thus, it is my sincerest hope that our science can begin to focus on and offer stronger analyses of spiritual occurrences that our field usually relegates to the world of mentalism and immaterialism (Hayes, 1984). In his writings about the impact of White, Western colonization on West African indigenous spirituality, Somé (1998) explained,

> Healers in the village taught that Westerners tried to control magic by insisting on knowing a visible cause for anything that might happen. This expectation had the sad and inevitable effect of mystifying rather than clarifying reality, since as the village people know, different laws operate in different dimensions of reality.
>
> (p. 11)

To this day, I thank God for working through me and starting me on the path of spiritual awakening, spiritual activism (Maparyan, 2012) and radical, unapologetic self-love.[25] The fact that self-love can be a revolutionary act for people with intersectional identities, people who look like me, and people whose lived experiences are similar to mine, affirms the need for *justice-oriented spiritual activism, rooted in a behavior analytic, culturo-behavioral science.*

IV

> "We are beginning to envision a new kind of politics fundamentally grounded in spirituality and not simply strengthened by it," that is, "a more spiritually informed vision of what is necessary to achieve revolution."
>
> —Maparyan (2012), p. 103, The Womanist Idea

Working with neurodiverse children and their families for over 20 years, coupled with my own personal battles for justice, fueled my passion to protect and advocate for the "underdog" throughout my career. I worked with families from all racial/ethnic backgrounds and socioeconomic levels but focused the last ten years of my clinical work on serving families who lived in low- and middle-income countries (LAMICs). I have worked with families and organizations all over the Middle East and North Africa (MENA), and in my family's homeland of Ghana. As a behavior analyst/scientist working with families with different cultural and world views than my own (including international families), it was imperative that I study cultural responsiveness and humility, tailoring my assessments and treatment plans to meet the specific individual and cultural needs of the family or organization.

My ability to practice cultural humility was further shaped and reinforced by my doctoral education in the emerging field of International Psychology (IP).[26] IP was created in reaction to and is a critique of the historical exclusivity and Whitewashing of mainstream psychology and its dogged focus on Western, White notions of human functioning and development (Stevens, 2007). It comprises cultural, cross-cultural, indigenous, and mainstream psychologies with the goal of moving closer to becoming a global psychology (global in the sense that psychologists adopt a global perspective when examining and addressing the historical, political, economic, and social conflicts impacting the mental, psychological, physical, and behavioral health/well-being of our international community). IP is an inclusive psychology that views human development and functioning through a less ethnocentric perspective and a more global, ecological,[27] and moderate universalism-relativism lens.[28] It was through my IP education that I was able to better understand and communicate the need for a behavior science that is diverse, equitable, culturally responsive, and inclusive—but also activist and action-oriented. Our field is changing, but it has a long way to go to achieve this goal. Likewise, higher education has much work to do to address its perpetuation of White supremacy and the continued marginalization of students and faculty belonging to disenfranchised populations.

Since my start in the academy, both as a graduate student and, later, as faculty/administrative faculty, I have been quite candid in my human right to be my authentic self in any space—especially in White, heteronormative ingroup spaces. When I became the department chair of an ABA program at a minority-serving institution (MSI), I brought along all of my ABA, IP, multidimensional/intersectional identity (which includes my sexuality), and spiritual activism with me. You would think that showing up as who you truly are would be a simple act but in fact, it is a privilege. For Black women, Black queer women (trans or cisgender), and Black queer non-binary individuals, being unapologetic about who you are is considered to be revolutionary, radical, and in defiance of systemic oppression (e.g., White supremacy, sexism, misogynoir, homophobia, transphobia, cisgender heteronormativity). My dear colleague and friend Dr. Nasiah Cirincione-Ulezi published a powerful article in *Behavior Analysis and Practice* (Cirincione-Ulezi, 2020) about the barriers that Black women face in higher education—especially when it comes to accessing leadership opportunities within the field and academy. Cirincione-Ulezi highlighted that Black women typically feel unheard, invisible, isolated, and/or like the *only one* (the only Black woman or person of color at their place of employment or school). Moreover, Black women are often made to prove their qualifications and ABA aptitude, fight against stereotypes (e.g., angry Black woman) and implicit/explicit biases, or work in toxic conditions that do not support our well-being or our professional development and success. This can result in stalled career growth and hesitation to capitalize on leadership opportunities:

> After more than three decades of interventions, people of color are still progressing to leadership at a disproportionately lower rate than their White counterparts in the professional labor force . . . Black women have the least statistical parity in leadership positions across the labor force, meaning their representation at the leadership level is not equal to that of the wider population.
>
> (p. 719)

I have experienced every single barrier that Dr. Cirincione-Ulezi outlined in her paper.[29] The feelings of invisibility, verification of credentials that reinforce imposter syndrome, knowing that you are the only one or one of a few who look like you at school, in the workplace, or on leadership teams—it all amounts to othering. This is why it was especially imperative in my role as department chair to create a safe place—a place of belonging and inclusivity—for my faculty and students.

The first student that I met in the department was an African master's student who was in the hallway studying their SAFMEDS for an upcoming quiz. This particular student was going through their flash cards as I was approaching and looked away from the cards to meet my gaze. As their beautiful smile stretched across their face, they exclaimed, "Dr. Danquah-Brobby! Hi! We NEED you!" I will never forget this student's comment. No explanation was needed; I knew exactly what they meant by the statement, *we need you*. The previous chair was not BIPoC but the majority of my students were. What they were saying was, *it is about time we had someone that looked like us in this position, to properly guide and mentor us. We need someone who looks like us to show us the way and tell us the truth about this field and the academy. We need you here to keep us safe and have our best interests at heart. We need to see ourselves reflected in you so that we know what is possible.* It was a responsibility that I did not take lightly, especially being the first Black ABA chair in that department, at that specific campus' location.

During my tenure as department chair, my spiritual activism took the form of establishing numerous partnerships with external stakeholders (ABA companies, K-12 schools, etc.). I also worked with a popular ABA test-preparation company to provide a 40% discount on courses for my students. One general disadvantage for students belonging to historically minoritized and marginalized groups is that said marginalization also contributes to and perpetuates economic disenfranchisement. Thus, it is quite common for students belonging to marginalized groups and identities to lack the financial means to afford test-preparation courses that can cost hundreds of dollars. A 40% discount was monumental and provided access to an opportunity that is not typically available to them. I also developed an articulation agreement with a local historically Black college/university (HBCU) that allowed their undergraduate psychology seniors to use half of their allotted elective credits towards graduate courses in one of my ABA programs. This was an opportunity that afforded minoritized students access to graduate school education at an overall reduced cost. At the end of the day, I knew every single one of my students by name and prioritized mentorship, advising, and advocacy in order to help them gain the skills needed to navigate this field. Our field has yet to offer any truth and reconciliation for decades of exclusionary practices and perpetuating systemic racism (Saini & Vance, 2020), homophobia and transphobia—to name a few (Barlow & Agras, 1973; Callahan & Leitenberg, 1973; McGuire & Vallance, 1964; Rekers & Lovaas, 1974, as cited in DeFelice & Diller, 2019). We still hold various annual conferences that are not inclusive or accessible for students and professionals—especially those who belong to marginalized groups: tickets are astronomically priced, hotel accommodations, flights, and food are expensive, conferences lack diversity and/or diverse supply chain vendors, BIPoC attendees tend to feel ignored/excluded, there are limited presentation topics related to social matters of importance to minoritized individuals, etc.

Early into my behavior analytic career, I stopped attending ABA conferences after a horrible experience at a local event. Everything felt elitist and exclusive, and I was the only Black person there. Despite attending with someone who I looked to as a mentor, I felt extremely isolated and lonely. To make matters worse, a very well-known BCBA struck up a conversation with my colleague as I stood right next to her. During that five-minute conversation, I was not introduced and neither one of them acknowledged my presence. I literally stood right next to this person with a painful smile on my face, wishing I could elope from the area and flee to safety—yes, safety. For people who look like me, being othered and feeling unsafe is common and, as such, it is important for us to have safe spaces where we do not have to worry or be hypervigilant about microaggressions and dehumanization. This is why organizations such as Black Applied Behavior Analysts, Inc. (BABA) and the Latino Association for Behavior Analysis (LABA) were established, and why their presence in the field is vital for BIPoC behavior analysts/scientists—we see ourselves, our humanity, and all that is possible for us, reflected in the values, initiatives, and actions of these organizations. Yes, we NEED you!

I eventually resigned from the MSI and transitioned into a new role as the Chief Diversity Officer (CDO) for a college within a university system. The role is challenging but extremely rewarding. I am grateful for my ABA, culturo-behavior science (CBS), and IP knowledge and education, as they have aided me tremendously in my efforts to effect macro-level changes across our academic community. However, CDOs, BABA, LABA, and access, justice, equity, diversity, and inclusion (AJEDI) efforts within our field and the academy are not enough. Allyship is not enough. We need more spiritual activists, and we need accomplices.

V

> [I]f you don't trust yourself to be involved in transforming that which needs to be changed, then you end up waiting for someone else to come along and do the work for you.
>
> —Somé (1998), p. 36, The Healing Wisdom of Africa

Author and activist Glennon Doyle has a weekly podcast called *We Can Do Hard Things*. She addresses and unpacks tough subject matters in an honest and loving manner. On episode 79, she and her wife, soccer Olympian Abby Wambach, spoke with Dr. Yaba Blay, a Ghanaian American scholar-activist, public speaker, and cultural consultant (Doyle, 2022). Dr. Blay shared many profound reflections on the podcast, but one topic that resonated with me was the need for accomplices, as opposed to allies (Doyle, 2022). The gestalt of Dr. Blay's opinion was that allies tend not to have "skin" in the game and have the privilege of supporting justice-oriented causes from afar, when it is convenient to them. Dr. Blay went on to state that allies tend to stop short when sacrifices need to be made. On the other hand, accomplices show that they have skin in the game by their willingness to sacrifice or lose something of importance to them because they are deeply committed to the right of all humans to live a life that is free of othering, oppression, disenfranchisement, marginalization, and White supremacy. Think back to videos and images of Dr. Martin Luther King marching against racism during Jim Crow and recall the images of young White women and men being beaten, hosed, and bitten by police dogs—right alongside their Black sisters and brothers*; they were accomplices*. There were also the Freedom Riders, some of whom were White, who were beaten and almost killed by a White mob in 1961; *they were accomplices*. Fast forward to the Black Lives Matter marches in the summer of 2020, that took place all over the US (and world) to protest police killings of Black and Brown (i.e., Latinx and Hispanic) individuals. I saw many images of White, Latinx, Asian, and Arab individuals being punched, kicked, tear gassed, and arrested—they were accomplices who were willing to lose or sacrifice something, including their freedom and lives, to fight for human rights. We no longer need allies, we need accomplices. Anti-racism, homophobia, transphobia, ableism, xenophobia, classism, and so forth, is a fight we all must actively work to dismantle. Oppression never sleeps, never tires, never stops and neither can we.

Having intersectional, marginalized identities necessitates spiritual activism, and spiritual activism requires cultivating a community of people (including accomplices) who support, nurture, and nourish your soul. The communities we build are safe and sacred and something I never had within this field. I have been a behavior analyst/scientist for over 20 years, and, over the course of my career, I have been on an island of one . . . until recently. The pandemic has been a brutal reality check for most of us yet, despite the challenges, it has afforded me the opportunity to develop or strengthen relationships with amazing people in our field. My community, my circle, is still being shaped and continues to grow, but I am ever so grateful for their presence in and impact on my life. I do not regret that it has taken over 20 years to find "my people" since I wholeheartedly believe that we connected at exactly the right, divine time. My people are not only spiritual activists, accomplices, and much more, but they continue to help me to feel less alone, less othered. Their behaviors affirm and reinforce my own spiritual activism, deepen my love for my own intersectional identity, and hold me accountable for showing up as my authentic self in all that I do and work to achieve.

As our field continues to evolve and engage in more inclusive and culturally responsive practices, spiritual activism, community, and accomplices will be critical to the success, longevity, and relevancy of our science. We can no longer continue to perpetuate or be complicit in othering and oppressive practices. Likewise, we need more research on and exploration of issues that are of importance to marginalized and minoritized groups, specifically as it relates to people belonging to LGBTQIA2S+ and BIPoC communities. There is a dearth of research and literature focusing on the needs, challenges, and lived experiences of these specific groups, and there is limited research and commentary on how we as a field begin to dismantle systems of oppression and othering utilizing our amazing science (Matsuda et al., 2020; Morris et al., 2021). We cannot claim to be an inclusive science if we remain largely silent on key social issues. We will never be the change we wish to see in the world if we fail to hold ourselves accountable and atone for past transgressions. Maparyan (2012) offered sage advice that should resonate with all behavior analysts/scientists and behavior change agents: "Changed beings require a changed environment, and a changed environment is unsustainable without changed beings" (p. 125). Let this be a clarion call for our field and science. Àse and Amen.

Notes

1. In Ghanaian culture, older siblings are expected to care for and look after younger ones, often establishing a secondary caregiver role for the older child.
2. Because only cold water runs out of the faucet in most Ghanaian households, Ghanaians have to fill up a bucket with cold water, boil water, and then add it to the bucket of cold water. Although hot and cold water run from the faucets in America, my mother maintained this behavior in our household until I reached middle school.
3. This is very common in Ghanaian culture. Everyone must contribute to the upkeep of the household.
4. Because my mother and sister were immigrants, their intersectional identity and othering experiences overlapped with mine, but were also quite different than my own.
5. In Ghanaian culture, your parents' close friends are considered your aunts and uncles. For Ghanaian immigrants who are attempting to establish a community in a foreign land, other Africans who are befriended and become a part of said community are now seen as family.
6. When LGBTQIA2S+ individuals are open to all about their sexual and/or gender identity, this is known as being "out."
7. Bisexual means that you are attracted to both men and women. Pansexual means you are attracted to men, women, and trans/gender nonconforming individuals.
8. When I say queer, I mean that I am a part of the LGBTQIA2S+ community but do not adopt any specific label but see myself as the totality of the labels, hence my preference for the term queer.
9. Tokenism: the policy or practice of making only a symbolic effort (Merriam-Webster, n.d.)
10. House music: a type of electronic dance music
11. Vibrational energy: "Vibrational energy experts claim that certain emotions and thought patterns, such as joy, peace, and acceptance, create high frequency vibrations, while other feelings and mindsets (such as anger, despair, and fear) vibrate at a lower rate" (Stanborough, 2020, para. 20).
12. White supremacy: "the social, economic, and political systems that collectively enable White people to maintain power over people of other races" (Merriam-Webster, n.d.)
13. Colorism: "prejudice or discrimination especially within a racial or ethnic group favoring people with lighter skin over those with darker skin" (Merriam-Webster, n.d.)
14. Oppression: "unjust or cruel exercise of authority or power" (Merriam-Webster, n.d.).
15. Institutional racism: "the systemic oppression of a racial group to the social, economic, and political advantage of another" (Merriam-Webster, n.d.)
16. Homophobia: "irrational fear of, aversion to, or discrimination against homosexuality or gay people" (Merriam-Webster, n.d.)
17. Xenophobia: "fear and hatred of strangers or foreigners or of anything that is strange or foreign" (Merriam-Webster, n.d.)
18. I still recall what was said but, clearly, I no longer have access to the video to capture what was said verbatim. This is the gestalt of the conversation.

19. An Oreo is a Black person who is deemed to "act White."
20. Orlando's name has been changed to protect his identity.
21. I am no longer in the practice of creating treatment plans that have children sitting at tables and doing DTT for long periods of time.
22. There was no such thing as a behavior technician or registered behavior technician at this time in my career.
23. Shaktipat: "On the Siddha Yoga path, the initiation (*diksha*) by which a Siddha Guru transmits the divine grace that awakens Kundalini, the inner spiritual energy in an aspirant" (SYDA Foundation, n.d., para 1).
24. Although my son is already out, he has given me permission to share in this chapter that he identifies as a transgender male/boy.
25. Dr. Maparyan defined spiritual activism as "putting spirituality to work for positive social and ecological change" (p. 114).
26. As a professional with an eclectic professional background, education, and training, I have known about these terms and practice for several years and did not learn about them via behavior analytic education, literature, or training. Many disciplines and fields *outside* of behavior analysis have been discussing the importance of (and how to practice) cultural responsiveness, competency, awareness, and humility (e.g., international, cross-cultural, and community psychologies).
27. Ecological: "of or relating to the environments of living things or to the relationships between living things and their environments" (Merriam-Webster, n.d.)
28. Universalism-relativism: "To what extent are psychological functions and processes common to humankind and to what extent are they unique to specific cultural groups" (Berry et al., 2011, p. 6)?
29. If you would like to learn more about this topic, I invite you to read Dr. Cirincione-Ulezi's work.

References

Al-Nasser, T., Burleigh, K. J., Ardila Sánchez, J. G., & Houmanfar, R. (2019). Metacontingency and macrocontingency analysis related to honor crimes in the Hashemite Kingdom of Jordan. *Behavior and Social Issues*, *28*, 140–159. https://doi.org/10.1007/s42822-019-00021-y

Berry, J. W. (2010). Mobility and acculturation. In S. C. Carr (Ed.), *The psychology of global mobility* (pp. 193–210). Springer.

Berry, J. W., Poortinga, Y. H., Breugelmans, S. G., Chasiotis, A., & Sam, D. L. (2011). *Cross- cultural psychology: Research and applications* (3rd ed.). Cambridge University.

Centers for Disease Control and Prevention. (2021, November 24). *Racism and health*. www.cdc.gov/healthequity/racism-disparities/index.html

Centers for Disease Control and Prevention. (2022, March 29). *Social determinants of health*. www.cdc.gov/chronicdisease/programs-impact/sdoh.htm

Cirincione-Ulezi, N. (2020). Black women and barriers to leadership in ABA. *Behavior Analysis in Practice*, *12*, 719–724. https://doi.org/10.1007/s40617-020-00444-9

Columbia Law School. (2017, June 8). *Kimberlé Crenshaw on intersectionality, more than two decades later*. www.law.columbia.edu/news/archive/kimberle-crenshaw-intersectionality-more-two-decades-later

Crenshaw, K. (1989). Demarginalizing the intersection of race and sex: A Black feminist critique of antidiscrimination doctrine, feminist theory and antiracist politics. *University of Chicago Legal Forum 1*(8), 139–167.

DeFelice, K. A., & Diller, J. W. (2019). Intersectional feminism and behavior analysis. *Behavior Analysis in Practice*, *12*, 831–838. https://doi.org/10.1007/s40617-019-00341-w

Doyle, G. (Host.). (2022, March 17). The power of rethinking everything with Dr. Yaba Blay (No. 79) [Audio podcast episode]. We can do hard things with Glennon Doyle. *Apple Podcasts*. https://podcasts.apple.com/us/podcast/the-power-of-rethinking-everything-with-dr-yaba-blay/id1564530722?i=1000554326811

Ellison, R. (1980). *Invisible man*. Vintage Books.

Glenn, S. S. (2004). Individual behavior, culture, and social change. *The Behavior Analyst*, *27*(2), 133–151. https://doi.org/10.1007/BF03393175

Hayes, S. C. (1984). Making sense of spirituality. *Behaviorism*, *12*, 99–110.

Houmanfar, R., Rodrigues, N. J., & Ward, T. A. (2010). Emergence and metacontingency: Points of contact and departure. *Behavior and Social Issues*, *19*, 53–78. https://doi.org/10.5210/bsi.v19i0.3065

Maparyan, L. (2012). *The womanist idea*. Routledge. https://doi.org/10.4324/9780203135938

Matsuda, K., Garcia, Y., Catagnus, R., & Ackerlund Brandt, J. (2020). Can behavior analysis help us understand and reduce racism? A review of the current literature. *Behavior Analysis in Practice, 13*, 336–347. https://doi.org/10.1007//s40617-020-00411-4

Merriam-Webster. (n.d.). *Tokenism*. www.merriam-webster.com/dictionary/tokenism

Morris, C., Goetz, D. B., & Gabriele-Black, K. (2021). The treatment of LGBTQ+ individuals in behavior-analytic publications: A historical review. *Behavior Analysis in Practice, 14*, 1179–1190. https://doi.org/10.1007/s40617-020-00546-4

powell, J. A., & Menendian, S. (2016). The problem of othering: Towards inclusiveness and belonging. *Othering & Belonging, 1*, 14–40.

Saini, V., & Vance, H. (2020). Systemic racism and cultural selection: A preliminary analysis of metacontingencies. *Behavior and Social Issues, 29*, 52–63. https://doi.org/10.1007/s42822-020-00040-0

Skinner, B. F. (1953). *Science and human behavior*. Free Press.

Somé, M. P. (1998). *The healing wisdom of Africa*. Tarcher/Putnam.

Stanborough, J. (2020, November 13). *What is vibrational energy?* www.healthline.com/health/vibrational-energy

Stevens, M. J. (2007). Orientation to a global psychology. In. M. J. Stevens & U. P. Gielen (Eds.), *Toward a global psychology: Theory, research, intervention, and pedagogy* (pp. 3–33). Lawrence Erlbaum Associates.

SYDA Foundation. (n.d.). *Shaktipat initiation*. www.siddhayoga.org/shaktipat-spiritual-initiation

Todorov, J. C., & Freitas Lemos, R. (2020). Applying behavioral science to large-scale social changes. In T. M. Cihon & M. A. Mattaini (Eds.), *Behavior science perspectives on culture and community. Behavior analysis: Theory, research, and practice* (pp. 171–193). Springer. https://doi.org/10.1007/978-3-030-45421-0_8

Tourrinho, E. Z. (2013). Cultural consequences and interlocking behavioral contingencies: Selection at the cultural level. *Behavior and Philosophy, 41*, 60–90. www.jstor.org/stable/behaphil.41.60

Yearby, R. (2020). Structural racism and health disparities: Reconfiguring the social determinants of health framework to include the root cause. *The Journal of Law, Medicine & Ethics, 48*(3), 518–526. https://doi.org/10.1177/1073110520958876

12 The Experiences of Female Scientists in the Global Network

Louise McHugh and Lynn Farrell

The Experiences of Female Scientists in the Global Network

Where Are We Now?

It's becoming increasingly harder to remember a time when we didn't have endless (though not always accurate) information at our fingertips and an ever-expanding connection to others through the global network. However, I (Lynn) was served a gentle reminder of the relative recency of our digital lives while going through my beloved late Nanny's belongings. I found a school "newspaper" she had kept that I had produced as a primary school student in which I had earnestly written an article to help people learn how to search the internet and access websites. So, while it may seem like we have been living in the Information Age forever, here in Ireland we were still getting to grips with the internet back in the 90s after it first arrived in 1991. It was two universities (namely Trinity College Dublin and University College Dublin) that first connected to the internet in Ireland (RTE, 2016), and its rollout has spread (albeit imperfectly) since then to varying degrees across the country and beyond. The idea of networking on a global scale and disseminating research using the internet is arguably an even more recent development with the rise of social media sites such as Facebook and Twitter since the early 2000s.

Sometimes it feels like academia still isn't quite sure what to do with the possibilities of global connection and research dissemination outside of paywalled journals and associations. However, we have seen the power of the global network for community building and social change through initiatives such as the "me too" movement or #MeToo (addressing sexual assault and harassment; https://metoomvmt.org) and #BlackLivesMatter (tackling white supremacy and violence against Black communities; https://blacklivesmatter.com) —both of these movements were initiated by Black women activists and went viral across the world, facilitated by social media and its power for connection.

These movements and the rise of the internet have been defining moments for our generations but what do these new dynamics mean for a woman navigating her career in science? Certainly, our academic fields must seem much larger now given the increasingly global and social nature of the network of science—just think for instance of the potential audience of #AcademicTwitter with tweets able to reach around 300 million active users on any given day (see Kaseda, 2020). This chapter will highlight some of the main themes we have seen emerging in terms of the possibilities that a global network provides, acknowledging both the benefits and potential drawbacks of engaging with science, networking, and conducting research in this digital age. Of course, we cannot speak for all women (we are not such a homogenous bunch despite what popular gender stereotypes would like you to believe) and so we wish to acknowledge that we will speak about this topic from our perspectives as

DOI: 10.4324/9781003216773-15

early-career (Lynn) and mid-career (Louise) White Irish psychology academics both with a background in Contextual Behavioral Science but with differing social-class backgrounds and identities. We will address the relative privilege of our positions and identities later in the chapter.

Send a Message to the World

Gatekeepers of science prior to the digital age were journal editors, conference programme chairs and reviewers. Traditionally these gatekeepers of science dissemination were mainly White males, who continue to make up the majority of academic, tenured and senior leadership positions compared to women and people of color (National Science Foundation, National Center for Science and Engineering Statistics [NSF/NCSES], 2019; She Figures, 2019; Woolston, 2020), though numbers vary across subfields with psychology typically faring better for female representation. There have been known historical blocks to female scientists' work which has led to anonymous peer review processes and affirmative action initiatives as forms of redress. Even though these initiatives are making a difference, progress is slow and even increased female representation on editorial boards may not necessarily eradicate unconscious biases that contribute to women being less likely to be invited to write commissioned pieces (see Nature, 2012).

Social media has allowed a platform for global knowledge transfer that evens the playing field for diverse scientists. Content on social media is user-generated; therefore, communicating and disseminating research is less limited by the usual gatekeepers, as is the audience of research on social media. A defining characteristic of social media platforms is that the diffusion of content largely occurs through social network processes that are enhanced by technology. Each active user is a participant in the diffusion process, because their engagement with knowledge being transferred (i.e., liking, commenting, and sharing) makes the content visible to their social network. Different platforms can be used to get the research out there to both the academic community and also stakeholders and potential users of the research findings. This broadens the reach of academic content that would traditionally have been locked behind paywalled journals and rather expensive conferences.

Personally, this has allowed us to connect more quickly and easily with colleagues who may not have reached out formally via academic emails or perhaps even have been aware of our work if we hadn't been able to promote it ourselves via personal and professional social media accounts. This helps us step into an international and interdisciplinary arena—we are not just talking to our colleagues at conferences anymore; we are sharing our work for all to see, including those outside of academia who may have similar interests and/or valuable insights or experiences that can better inform our perspectives as researchers. We have certainly witnessed valuable teaching moments around gender identity and expression, for example, through social media engagement and blogs that have and continue to influence our work around gender. With access to many more perspectives on a global scale, there is incredible potential to develop more nuanced understandings both through academic discourse and exposure to people's lived experiences.

Choices, Choices, Choices

In addition to its wider reach, the internet allows for a broader range of methods of knowledge transfer and exchange. Many of these outlets are typically free to use and relatively user-friendly, though certainly one can engage with them at varying levels of complexity (and we do not claim to be experts!). Since joining University College Dublin in 2012, I (Louise) have been able to create an entity and virtual presence for my lab. Once I settled on a title for the group (UCD CBS lab) all I had to do was create a logo (with the help of an online graphic designer) and the lab was born. From this I was able to set up a lab webpage, Twitter account, and YouTube channel where all the lab members could share resources and materials. The freedom to create a virtual entity allowed interested students and researchers to approach me about conducting research in my lab. Indeed, Lynn Farrell came to work with me as a doctoral student in 2013 having seen that I was establishing this lab focused on both Relational Frame Theory (RFT) and Acceptance and Commitment Therapy (ACT). She was part of the collaborative process of establishing the lab online, which has continued to grow as new students and postdoctoral researchers have come, flourished, and moved on, bringing their own style and interests to add layers to the lab's identity. This process has also allowed these researchers to establish their own online presence through and in collaboration with the lab's evolving identity that acts as both a launching point and as a safety net. They can flex their creative muscles while getting experience with new styles of science communication and research engagement, which has been really useful networking. An online lab presence allows people from around the world to see the work that the lab is doing with just a Google search. There is also a sense of community established through this collaborative research and dissemination—as Lynn will attest, once a UCD CBS labbie, always a UCD CBS labbie!

It also allows for the sharing of resources and materials as they are being produced. Materials and protocols developed can be accessed by others in real time. The UCD CBS lab has been able to develop materials funded by the University College Dublin SPARC funding scheme that has allowed us to host online sessions to use our academic knowledge on mental health to promote well-being for UCD staff and students. We also produced an animated series of mental health videos that aimed to equip young people with evidence-based skills to take charge of their well-being and live meaningful lives, allowing the general public to capitalize on the applications of research in free and accessible ways.

With greater accessibility than paywalled journals, social media is, therefore, a powerful tool for discovery and sharing research. Indeed, recent surveys have shown that a large proportion of scientists (at least in the US) use social media for exactly these purposes with ResearchGate, LinkedIn, Facebook and Twitter ranking among the most visited sites by scientists (see Nature Cell Biology, 2018). This variety and novelty of platforms can also bring its own form of pressure, however. There can be an expectation now that academics are adept at navigating these new outlets, that they are also graphic designers, programmers, and web designers able to present their research quickly, easily and in an engaging manner in a variety of formats online. And while there are certainly an increasing number of websites, tutorials, etc., that can help you hone these skills, this can take time—time that you must fit into your already-busy work schedule.

Additionally, some of the beauty of science communication online is that it offers choice—the choice of platform to engage with, but also whether and when to engage. There is, however, a possibility that rather than social media engagement and online science communication being a personal choice, it becomes (perhaps implicitly) part of the job. The rise of "altmetrics" that measure an article's online exposure on social media platforms, as well as in traditional reference managers, shows that even academic publishers are starting to track these nontraditional routes of impact. This may not suit everyone with academic acumen and adds additional demands to an already demanding (though rewarding) profession. It can also blur the lines between the personal and the professional depending on how you use your social media accounts. This added expectation may involve tricky navigation for women in particular who have on average been found within the organizational literature to be less likely to self-promote (e.g., Exley & Kessler, 2019), and may avoid such visibility to avoid backlash for violating typical feminine gender norms (e.g., Ballakrishnen et al., 2019).

This won't apply to all women of course (and may indeed be relevant for some men and non-binary individuals) but requires consideration as the nature of research dissemination changes and grows. Certainly, more formal requirements for social media engagement may drain some of the magic and freedom from this nontraditional outlet.

Role Models and Stereotypes

Role models influence our actions and motivate us to strive to uncover our potential and overcome our perceived weaknesses. "If you can see it, you can be it" is a quote often heard in discussions about propelling minority groups forward. Finding female role models has become much more possible in the digital age. This is largely due to earlier issues raised around gatekeepers of knowledge. Women's voices were not as central in science even up until recent times. In the area of psychology, when you look at lists of famous psychologists, many female contributors are overlooked. In the field of behavior analysis, for example, Mary Cover Jones is not given as much prominence as that of John Watson. The key figures remembered from our past are predominantly men. Men such as Skinner and Pavlov made great contributions to the field which should be recognized; however, it can make you question where the women were. More insidiously, as a woman in Psychology, this can make you think are women as successful in this field as men—do they belong, do *I* belong? Now, wherever there are people living, breathing, thinking, etc., *of course* women belong and there have been and continue to be many successful women in science and Psychology—take, for example, Mary Cover Jones, Marsha Linehan, Elizabeth Loftus, Jennifer Eberhardt. However, before the advent of the global network, our exposure to these kinds of role models depended on who was included in textbooks and college courses, which typically underrepresented women and people of color (Simpson & Bouhafa, 2020). When I (Louise) came into science, the female role models I would like to have had, in terms of academics getting promoted and due recognition for their work, were hard to come across. The situation had improved when I (Lynn) entered the field but there is still much progress to be made.

Publication trends in science continue to reflect a lack of representation of women to this day although there are signs of improvement. A recent analysis of sex trends in publication in behavior analysis examined seven behavior-analytic journals and found that female contribution to the field, as authors and editors, increased between 2014 and 2017, with percentages varying across the journals (Li et al., 2018). However, with data demonstrating that females represent the majority of certified behavior analysts (Behavior Analyst Certification Board; Nosik & Grow, 2015), Li et al. (2018) noted that they remain proportionally underrepresented as both editors and authors.

Nosik et al. (2018) provided a more comprehensive analysis of females' participation in behavior analysis among categories such as professional awards, invited speakers, editors and authorship, and so forth. They found that the percentage of females among the majority of the categories was generally below 50%. Farrell et al. (2019) conducted an analysis of publication trends related to author sex on all articles published in the *Journal of Contextual Behavioral Science (JCBS)* between 2012 and 2017. Results indicated that there was near parity in the overall numbers of male and female authors, with approximately equal numbers of male and female first authors. However, a significant difference was observed among corresponding authors, with males more likely to fulfil this role. Male authors also produced more single-author articles. Interestingly, male-authored articles received significantly more citations than female-authored articles.

The "WikiProject Women" sheds light on this further in the online space. A group of editors came together to discuss the coverage of women's content across Wikipedia in response to the fact that only 17% of Wikipedia biographies are about women. A subgroup of the WikiProject Women is the "WikiProject Woman Scientists" who are bringing attention and responding to the systemic bias in the lack of the representation of women scientists on Wikipedia. A positive action we can all take today is to set up a Wiki page for a woman scientist in our field who does not currently have one.

Wider access to information and information dissemination through the likes of blogs, social media, personal websites, etc., have reduced the level of gatekeeping involved in finding and promoting role models. We can more actively seek out role models effectively. This doesn't just mean finding female role models (though same-sex role models can be really important, e.g., Stout et al., 2011). Rather, having access to academics from all over the world and all sorts of diverse backgrounds allows us to more effectively find role models we can relate to across multiple levels.

An issue related to role models is how stereotypes can block females in the scientific community. Stereotypes about women's gender roles and intellectual ability (e.g., Carli et al., 2016; Leslie et al., 2015) can make a career in science more of an uphill battle for women, and the grip these stereotypes have on women's choices vary in strength across the globe; it is important to keep those perspectives in mind when we engage with the global network as they can keep some women from being able to engage with this network full stop.

One stereotype that can block woman scientists is that men are more likely to be associated with science than women (e.g., Farrell et al., 2020). There are studies to suggest, however, that certain behavioral interventions can reduce the gender bias against women in science. For example, Farrell et al. (2020) assessed the impact of three brief interventions aimed at influencing implicit gender bias in Science, Technology, Engineering and Math (STEM) fields by strengthening a positive relation between women and STEM (i.e., psychoeducation, exposure to positive counter-stereotypical exemplars and perspective-taking). Gender-STEM bias was assessed at the implicit level (via the Implicit Relational Assessment Procedure; IRAP) and the explicit level (via rating scales). The findings indicated that implicit gender-STEM bias is malleable, at least in the short term with psychoeducation as the most effective, followed by exposure to positive counter-stereotypical exemplars. Therefore, moving forward, exemplars and education can increase a positive relationship between people's perception of women and science. An online campaign that is a great example of this is the #ILookLikeAScientist and #EuPareçoCientista Twitter initiatives that aimed to break the stereotype of old white males as the only scientists, showing diversity among researchers. People from different backgrounds posted pictures of themselves on Twitter with the hashtags in order to give visibility to the diversity of scientists globally.

Via the global network, a more communal, collaborative vision of science is developing. This is one that will appeal to those who perhaps were put off by the stereotype of science as a lonely, competitive endeavor that doesn't really help people. The stereotype that STEM fields do not afford communal goals to work or help with others has been shown to be a deterrent to recruiting students to STEM pathways. Clark et al. (2016) conducted experiments that involved the impact of cueing communal goals to work or help with others in science and demonstrated that the stereotype of non-communal goals in STEM could be shifted. Moving forward, we as scientists can combat the stereotype that science does not involve communal goals by highlighting communal aspects of our work in our writing, our classes, and on online platforms. Indeed, recent research by Hofstra and colleagues (2020) has supported the idea that more collaborative and diverse science will bring more innovation.

Diversifying Science

Diversifying science is connected to the issue of role models and stereotypes. As we saw there are initiatives on changing what the typical scientist looks like (see the #ILookLikeAScientist trend on Twitter) and how they operate. Our lives have been transformed with the emergence of global digital platforms, allowing us to break through geographical and cultural borders. Now we have the capacity to communicate with almost anybody in the world irrespective of culture, social context, or language (to an extent). The exponential increase in access to people across diverse contexts has allowed people to connect across diverse perspectives and with shared values and ideas, and also to share perspectives and ideas that have allowed for some disruption in the status quo. The "invisible women data bias" has highlighted this point. The scientific field being dominated by white males leads to research that does not consider diversity. Examples from the invisible women data bias include seat belts not being designed for women, women's health conditions being under-researched, personal protective equipment (PPE) not designed to fit women, etc. (Criado Perez, 2019). More women in science from different backgrounds, race, and ethnicities, and more visibility of these women in science will help diversify the topics researched.

There's Always a But . . .

Of course there are negatives to the global network. Trolls and digital silencing are serious issues and ones that can disproportionally impact women. Trolling is a form of harassment that involves sustained or repeated attempts of emotional and psychological harm and physical threats over time and across contexts (Essed, 1991; Tynes et al., 2008; Williams et al., 1997). A study by Ortiz (2020) surveying online users found that respondents suggested that trolls target women, feminists, people of color, and disabled persons by activating group position and exercising power. They surveyed 120 online users and found that these users perceived trolling as aligned to the group positions of male, White, and conservative. Todd and Melancon (2019) in a qualitative study on gender differences in perceptions of trolling found that females were more sensitive to trolling cues and likely to be silenced by them than males, and also more likely to be the targets of sexual harassment.

Fichman and Sanfilippo (2015) found that gender also impacts responses to trolling. Although this is nuanced and culturally dependent, it can, in some cases, result in silencing certain voices. This has been referred to as a digital spiral of silence. A prime example of this in the academic context is the case of Dr. Melissa Zimdars. She created a Google Doc of false news sources post the 2016 general election in the USA. Dr. Zimdars was an assistant professor of communication and media at Merrimack College in Massachusetts. Her Google Doc went viral, but she received such a volume of threats and harassment that she removed the document and had to get protection measures put in place by her academic institution. Unfortunately, Dr. Zimdars is only one example of women in academia that fear the ramifications of participating in or starting certain conversations because of the harassment they may face. This is particularly evident in the case of gender-based research and feminist issues.

Both authors of the current chapter have been involved in research looking at gender biases towards women in science. It is clear that sharing this topic on social media platforms is met with hostility that other research topics are not. We have all seen tweets celebrating women on International Women's Day being met with "When is men's day?" responses. I (Lynn) have dealt with disparaging comments through professional social media accounts dismissing my research or similar research I've shared because of its focus on women and gender bias. I received a comment from a stranger on a presentation I uploaded about gender biases and implicit responding saying that I wasn't a real psychologist and telling people to watch a real psychologist debunk gender bias and implicit bias with a link to a video presentation from a well-known, controversial male psychologist (the commenter was not that psychologist of course). I was a student at the time, and you can imagine how deflating that experience was, especially during a time where you are hypercritical of your work yourself with thoughts of the viva (i.e., final exam to defend your doctoral work in the Irish context) looming. I put a check on video comments going forward so that they wouldn't be added unless approved as I feared worse comments might follow. This perception, that women may face harassment online for expressing certain views, which is based on our own experience and the stories of other women, can have a (likely intended) silencing effect.

And this is not just a perception, research supports this assessment as true and there are certainly far worse incidences than what we have experienced. In 2014, a study of online harassment (Duggan, 2014) found that of women between 18 to 24 years of age, a staggering 25% had experienced online stalking. We say staggering but actually from our experience this is sadly not surprising. It is all too common that Twitter direct messages come into our inboxes unsolicited that refer to our appearance for example. And we only use our Twitter accounts for professional reasons—well, I (Louise) do post the odd tweet about Gaelic Football!

A report by Amnesty International (2018) labelled Twitter as an often toxic space for women due to abusive and threatening incidents of harassment including death threats. Across eight countries, almost a quarter of women surveyed said they had experienced abuse or harassment online at least once, mainly from strangers. Women of multiple marginalised identities often face this kind of abuse more intensely, such as women of color, transgender women, bisexual and lesbian women and women with disabilities (Amnesty International, 2018). Female politicians, journalists and women's rights activists are also prime targets due to their visibility and use of social media as part of their profession. This can have a silencing and censoring impact on women even when they want to be able to freely engage on this platform. This is not to say that men do not experience online harassment; of course they do and just because we do not focus on it here does not mean that we don't think that all forms of online abuse need to be addressed (a common charge levelled at initiatives and research with a focus on women). But this is not about comparisons, this is about the experience of women in the global network and there are uniquely gendered components to the harassment that women face online that need individual consideration in context.

Despite this, it is so important to emphasise that to combat the gendered digital silencing of women engaging on social media, we must advance women's voices in online spaces. Women have fewer followers, and their tweets receive fewer likes and retweets in certain research areas (Zhu et al., 2019). We can change this. In order to create a safe space for women's voices, we as women must engage on social media on key issues and all issues of scientific interest to us and we must support other women and allies to do the same. One example of this within ACBS has been the formation of a Women's Special Interest Group (SIG) to promote women's voices and research. The development of this SIG has not been without its challenges—the experience of gender differs across individuals and cultures, and dialogue can be difficult when the subject matter is as contentious and socially sensitive. However, that doesn't mean there hasn't been (and continues to be) value in the process. It remains important to create and develop these spaces where difficult conversations can be had. We may not be there yet, and we may not always get it right—in fact we certainly won't as we're still only human! But our success is in our continued efforts. We need to avoid self-censoring into silence. From a professional perspective, a dangerous by-product of self-censoring can be the loss of opportunities to network and promote our work. From a personal perspective, it keeps our world and our lives small in a way that they no longer have to be.

Privilege

We are conscious of the fact that our experiences do not speak for the experiences of all women. Our unique contexts have shaped our interactions with and access to the global network. As such, we wish to be as transparent as we can about our backgrounds and relative privileges as White women living in Europe.

I (Lynn) come from a working-class background. Someone from my area getting into university (or even wanting to) was a relatively rare occurrence, though this is slowly changing. Although I was a good student and my teachers were very supportive, I was still warned not to aim too high—if I got into any of the top universities I was told I'd be a little fish in a big pond. This was my guidance counselling. Occasionally I was met with shocked faces at university when I said where I was from—they only knew the bad news stories, not the ones of good, hard-working people living in these communities. My parents worked hard to send me to university. I worked part-time to help support my studies and fund the first two years of my PhD before I was successful in achieving (much needed) funding. My first laptop was the result of an academic award, my second I got through Irish Research Council scholarship funding. A laptop and internet access were and are necessary tools for study and research. Academia remains prohibitively expensive particularly as you move into postgraduate study—I was lucky to have a supportive partner and parents; I couldn't have afforded to live and study at the same time otherwise. Though I've come quite far from my "little fish" days, those kinds of things stay with you. I didn't have family or older friends who could tell me how to navigate university or academia. I doubted myself and my ability often, and still do. This is where social media can have a positive influence, however (despite its equal capacity for ill). When I joined Twitter, there were first-generation university students like me posting about their experiences online, normalizing the obstacles (both physical and mental) that I was coming up against. I was too shy and nervous myself to come out and speak about these things publicly on these platforms but here were these everyday role models saying to anyone that could see their post, "You are not alone! Keep going! Academia needs your perspective!"

Being exposed to and being able to connect with these networks if you choose is part of the magic of the global network but it is also a privilege. Not everyone has equal access to the internet or the resources to develop their digital skills both globally (OECD, 2018) and even within our very own Ireland (Accenture, 2020). In addition to being a social class and regional issue, this is a gender issue. Globally, women are less likely than men to have a smartphone and access to the internet by a margin of hundreds of millions (OECD, 2018). Access to resources and education along with safety and harassment concerns and gender stereotypes about women's roles and technology as a male domain presents barriers to closing this gendered digital divide (UNESCO, 2019). Additionally, domestic gender imbalances in terms of housework and caregiving impinge on women's ability to participate in digital labor, connection, and training (OECD, 2018; UNESCO, 2019).

COVID-19 has further exacerbated some of these disparities as increasingly our lives were made to turn online. This shift also served to further highlight the domestic gender imbalances that limit women's ability to engage digitally. Women have traditionally been more involved in housework and caregiving (e.g., McMunn et al., 2020). These responsibilities have increased during the pandemic for women, caregivers, and mothers in particular, especially during periods of homeschooling when women have had to balance their personal and professional lives in the same space (e.g., Adams-Prassl et al., 2020; Andrew et al., 2020; Petts et al., 2021). In relation to academia, early indications are that the publication productivity of women and parents has been negatively impacted by lockdown conditions (e.g., Breuning et al., 2020; Myers et al., 2020), particularly Black women and women with young children (Staniscuaski et al., 2021). Globally there is a need for more gender-aware policies and initiatives that target the structural and gendered bases of these divides, as digital access and skills can empower people in many areas of modern life (OECD, 2018, UNESCO, 2019).

From the standpoint of academia, the advent of online conferences in response to COVID-19 is a positive step that can utilize the power of our digital capabilities to become more accessible for attendees from a diverse range of countries and personal situations (e.g., caregivers who previously would have been unable to attend physical conferences in far-flung places). Online conferences better facilitate asynchronous attendance through recordings, and this may facilitate later translations of presentations into a wider range of languages. However, in some cases, online conferences remain as expensive as the physical events, limiting their potential to reach wider, less privileged or disadvantaged academic audiences. This is something that requires further serious consideration from organizers, and, hopefully, more accessible online conferences will be retained as a valid form of dissemination post-pandemic.

Additionally, as we have noted in the previous section, women of various identities can face harassment online that ranges in severity. In their report on Twitter in particular, Amnesty International (2018) flagged that violent and abusive harassment is most often directed at women and particularly women with intersecting marginalized identities. We cannot speak for these women experiencing this terrible abuse, but we can use this privileged opportunity in writing this chapter to highlight this issue and acknowledge how serious and damaging it can be for women's digital engagement, and join calls for social media providers to improve their reporting mechanisms and processes and their responses to these interactions (e.g., Amnesty International, 2018). We can commit ourselves to reporting instances of abuse when we see them and encourage others to do the same. There are also more positive steps we can take around amplification of marginalized voices that we wish to highlight in our closing section.

Take-Home Message

Amplifying the voices of traditionally marginalized groups such as women, particularly women of color and women with other intersecting identities, is something we can see the global network offer a space for. There are many ways that we can support this amplification:

(1) Retweet women's tweets on their scientific work.
(2) Reach out to junior colleagues and amplify their work online.
(3) Use the global network to collaborate outside our usual bubbles.
(4) Model the collaborative, supportive scientific endeavors and relationships that we want to see online.
(5) Try not to feed the trolls and report abusive comments or profiles that we see.
(6) Continue to grow and develop in a digital space as the possibilities of what it can offer continue to grow and develop with us.

We hope this chapter on the experience of female scientists in the global network can be a call to arms to our readers. Women scientists—when possible—do not step back from getting your science out there and voices heard! And if we have relative privileges, we can and should use them to amplify marginalized voices and flag research from other communities so that we can use the global network to create more innovative and inclusive science for all.

References

Accenture. (2020, July 22). *Bridging the gap—Ireland's digital divide*. Accenture. www.accenture.com/ie-en/insights/local/digital-divide

Adams-Prassl, A., Boneva, T., Golin, M., & Rauh, C. (2020a). *Inequality in the impact of the coronavirus shock: Evidence from real time surveys*. IZA Discussion Papers, No. 13183, Institute of Labor Economics (IZA), Bonn. www.econstor.eu/bitstream/10419/216495/1/dp13183.pdf

Amnesty International. (2018). *Toxic Twitter—A toxic place for women*. Amnesty International. www.amnesty.org/en/latest/research/2018/03/online-violence-against-women-chapter-1/

Andrew, A., Cattan, S., Dias, M. C., Farquharson, C., Kraftman, L., Krutikova, S., Phimister, A., & Sevilla, A. (2020). How are mothers and fathers balancing work and family under lockdown? *Institute for Fiscal Studies*. https://doi:10.1920/bn.ifs.2020.bn0290

Ballakrishnen, S., Fielding-Singh, P., & Magliozzi, D. (2019). Intentional invisibility: Professional women and the navigation of workplace constraints. *Sociological Perspectives*, *62*(1), 23–41. https://doi.org/10.1177/0731121418782185

Breuning, M., Fattore, C., Ramos, J., & Scalera, J. (2020). *Gender, parenting, and scholarly productivity during the global pandemic*. APSA Preprints. https://doi:10.33774/apsa-2020-ffg5r. This content is a preprint and has not been peer-reviewed

Carli, L. L., Alawa, L., Lee, Y., Zhao, B., & Kim, E. (2016). Stereotypes about gender and science: Women ≠ scientists. *Psychology of Women Quarterly*, *40*(2), 244–260. https://doi.org/10.1177/0361684315622645

Clark, E., Fuesting, M., &. Diekman, A. (2016). Enhancing interest in science: Exemplars as cues to communal affordances of science. *Journal of Applied Social Psychology*, *46*(11), 641–654. https://doi:10.1111/jasp.12392

Criado Perez, C. (2019). *Invisible women: Data bias in a world designed for men*. Harry N. Abrams.

Duggan, M. (2014). *Online harassment*. Pew Research Center.

Essed, P. (1991). *Understanding everyday racism: An interdisciplinary theory*. Sage.

Exley, C. L., & Kessler, J. B. (2019). *The gender gap in self-promotion* (No. w26345). National Bureau of Economic Research.

Farrell, L., Cocoran, F., Sandoz, E., & McHugh, L. (2019). Examination of sex-specific publication trends within the *Journal of contextual behavioral science* between 2012 and 2017. *Journal of Contextual Behavioral Science*, *11*, 27–33. https://doi.org/10.1016/j.jcbs.2018.11.006

Farrell, L., Nearchou, F., & McHugh, L. (2020). Examining the effectiveness of brief interventions to strengthen a positive implicit relation between women and stem across two timepoints. *Social Psychology of Education: An International Journal*. Advance online publication. https://doi.org/10.1007/s11218-020-09576-w

Fichman, P., & Sanfilippo, R. (2015). The bad boys and girls of cyberspace: How gender and context impact perception of and reaction to trolling. *Social Science Computer Review*, *33*(2), 163–180. doi:10.1177/0894439314533169

Hofstra, B., Kularni, V., Munoz-Najar Galvez, S., & He, B. (2020). The diversity-innovation paradox in science. *Proceedings of the National Academy of Sciences*, *117*(17). https://doi:10.1073/pnas.1915378117

Kaseda, E. (2020, May). *Academic Twitter. American psychological association: Psychological science agenda*. www.apa.org/science/about/psa/2020/05/academic-twitter

Leslie, S. J., Cimpian, A., Meyer, M., & Freeland, E. (2015). Expectations of brilliance underlie gender distributions across academic disciplines. *Science*, *347*(6219), 262–265.

Li, A., Curiel, H., Pritchard, J., & Poling, A. (2018). Participation of women in behavior analysis research: Some recent and relevant data. *Behavior Analysis in Practice*, *11*(2), 160–164 https://doi:10.1007/s40617-018-0211-6

McMunn, A., Bird, L., Webb, E., & Sacker, A. (2020). Gender divisions of paid and unpaid work in contemporary UK couples. *Work, Employment and Society*, *34*(2), 155–173. https://doi.org/10.1177/0950017019862153

Myers, K. R., Tham, W. Y., Yin, Y., Cohodes, N., Thursby, J. G., Thursby, M. C., Schiffer, P., Walsh, J. T., Lakhani, K. R., & Wang, D. (2020). Unequal effects of the COVID-19 pandemic on scientists. *Nature Human Behaviour*, *4*(9), 880–883. https://doi.org/10.1038/s41562-020-0921-y

National Science Foundation, National Center for Science and Engineering Statistics [NSF/NCSES]. (2019). *Women, minorities, and persons with disabilities in science and engineering: 2019*. National Science Foundation. https://ncses.nsf.gov/pubs/nsf21321/report/academic-careers#representation

Nature. (2012). *Nature's sexism*. *Nature*, *491*, 495. https://doi.org/10.1038/491495a

Nature Cell Biology. (2018). Social media for scientists. *Nature Cell Biology*, *20*, 1329. https://doi.org/10.1038/s41556-018-0253-6

Nosik, M., & Grow, L. (2015). Prominent women in behavior analysis: An introduction. *The Behaviour Analyst*, *38*(2), 225–227.

Nosik, M., Luke, M., & Carr, J. (2018). Representation of women in behavior analysis: An empirical analysis. *Behavior Analysis: Research and Practice*, *19*(2), 213–221. http://dx.doi.org/10.1037/bar0000118

OECD. (2018). *Bridging the digital gender divide: Include, upskill, innovate*. www.oecd.org/digital/bridging-the-digital-gender-divide.pdf

Ortiz, S. (2020). Trolling as a collective form of harassment: An inductive study of how online users understand trolling. *Social Media and Society*, *6*(2), 205630512092851. https://doi.org/10.1177/2056305120928512

Petts, R., Carlson, D., & Pepin, J. (2021). A gendered pandemic: Childcare, homeschooling, and parents' employment during COVID-19. *Gender, Work & Organization*, *28*(S2), 515–534. https://doi.org/10.1111/gwao.12614

RTE. (2016, June 17). *25 years of internet in Ireland marked*. RTE. www.rte.ie/news/technology/2016/0617/796241-25-years-of-internet-in-ireland-marked/

She Figures. (2019). *She figures 2018*. European Commission. https://op.europa.eu/en/publication-detail/-/publication/9540ffa1-4478-11e9-a8ed-01aa75ed71a1

Simpson, A., & Bouhafa, Y. (2020). Youths' and adults' identity in STEM: A systematic literature review. *Journal for STEM Education Research*, *3*(2), 167–194. https://doi.org/10.1007/s41979-020-00034-y

Staniscuaski, F., Kmetzsch, L., Soletti, R. C., Reichert, F., Zandonà, E., Ludwig, Z., Lima, E. F., Neumann, A., Schwartz, I., Mello-Carpes, P. B., Tamajusuku, A., Werneck, F. P., Ricachenevsky, F. K., Infanger, C., Seixas, A., Staats, C. C., & de Oliveira, L. (2021). Gender, race and parenthood impact academic productivity during the COVID-19 pandemic: From survey to action. *Frontiers in Psychology*, *12*, 663252. https://doi.org/10.3389/fpsyg.2021.663252

Stout, J. G., Dasgupta, N., Hunsinger, M., & McManus, M. A. (2011). STEMing the tide: Using ingroup experts to inoculate women's self-concept in science, technology, engineering, and mathematics (STEM). *Journal of Personality and. Social Psychology*, *100*(2), 255–270. https://doi.org/10.1037/a0021385

Todd, P., & Melancon, J. (2019). Gender differences in perceptions of trolling in livestream video broadcasting. *Cyberpsychology, Behavior, and Social Networking*, *22*(7), 472–477. https://doi.org/10.1089/cyber.2018.0560

Tynes, B. M., Giang, M. T., Williams, D. R., & Thompson, G. N. (2008). Online racial discrimination and psychological adjustment among adolescents. *Journal of Adolescent Health*, *43*(6), 565–569. https://doi.org/10.1016/j.jadohealth.2008.08.021

UNESCO. (2019). *I'd blush if I could: Closing gender divides in digital skills through education. UNESCO*. https://en.unesco.org/Id-blush-it-I-could

Williams, D. R., Yu, Y., Jackson, J. S., & Anderson, N. B. (1997). Racial differences in physical and mental health: Socioeconomic status, stress and discrimination. *Journal of Health Psychology*, *2*(3), 335–351. http://journals.sagepub. com/doi/pdf/10.1177/135910539700200305

Woolston, C. (2020, March 12). White men still dominate in UK academic science. *Nature*. www.nature.com/articles/d41586-020-00759-1

Zhu, J. M., Pelullo, A. P., Hassan, S., Siderowf, L., Merchant, R. M., & Werner, R. M. (2019). Gender differences in Twitter use and influence among health policy and health services researchers. *JAMA Internal Medicine*, *179*(12), 1726–1729. https://doi.org/10.1001/jamainternmed.2019.4027

13 Transitions

Ariana D'Arms, Amoy Kito Hugh-Pennie, and Denise Ross-Page

Transitions

Introduction

This chapter is titled *Transitions*, and it is about why and how women in the behavior sciences may transition within higher education and even between professional fields. Generally, women transition in higher education for a multitude of reasons. The extremely fortunate among us may find one or two universities and settle into a tenure-track position. However, as we will discuss in this chapter, this is rarely, if ever, the case. Tenure-track positions are not doled out like candy and the path to tenure can sometimes be long and arduous (also see Chapters 2, 3, and 8). Further, the expectations for success in higher education can be demanding; and establishing a body of research, demonstrating both expertise and relatability when teaching students, and committing to unpaid and volunteer service to the university and your profession can be strenuous work (also see Chapters 7 and 17). Consequently, as our lives change over the course of our academic careers, we may find ourselves packing our bags, uprooting our families, and sacrificing essential support such as friends, families, and community ties to give it a "good old college try" in a new institution, career, or city. These sometimes-necessary transitions can be both exciting and scary at the same time.

We are honored to share pieces of our stories about transitioning as part of this book about Women in Behavior Analysis. This chapter assumes that most women will transition in their careers at some point, so its focus is not on the choice to transition but the reasons why we may transition and how to make a transition "successful." By writing this chapter, we hope to accomplish four objectives:

1) Describe insights into the work lives of women and especially women of color.
2) Discuss some considerations we have used when deciding how to transition.
3) Share our personal stories of transitioning in higher education.
4) Give practical recommendations for those who are transitioning.

The editors of this book asked us to be transparent, vulnerable, and authentic as we considered how to write this chapter, and we will attempt to honor their request. We, the authors of this chapter, are a group of women from diverse backgrounds and we represent a range of experiences in higher education. Ariana D'Arms recently completed her doctorate in behavior analysis and is in her first year of an academic position. Denise Ross-Page and Amoy Kito Hugh-Pennie are both doctoral graduates of the behavior analysis program at Teachers College and each have 20+ years in the field of behavior analysis working in higher

DOI: 10.4324/9781003216773-16

education and PK-12 schools and agencies. Together, we hope that we accomplish our goals for this chapter as we share our stories with you and that, in doing so, the experiences we share will serve as a source of encouragement and support for your career choices.

Why Women Transition: Facts About Women in the Workplace (Ariana D'Arms)

My mother and I have always been very close. So close that we were able to non-vocally communicate with one another until I started speaking one-word sentences when I was around three years old. Even then, Spanish was my first language due to the time I spent with my Mexican grandfather and babysitters. It was not until I was about five years old that I started to speak English. This English-language delay, I believe, affected my ability to read on par with same-age peers. Luckily, my reading challenges were caught in early elementary school, and I received in-school reading tutoring. While my current reading abilities have at least helped me to successfully obtain a PhD, my early reading struggles stuck with me and fueled my desire to work with other struggling readers.

Learning about behavior analysis and its application to all students in education made me hopeful about providing effective education to students who the school-aged version of me would have considered my friends—students who were otherwise considered "bad" and "beyond help." Seeing how behavior analysis could be used to change learning environments for these students and help them become successful readers was what inspired me to further pursue education in this field. My desire to study and practice applied behavior analysis kept me going in pursuit of my PhD.

Despite my interest in behavior analysis, I would not have obtained this degree or transitioned very well between the stages of graduate school and my career without my family helping me let go of defining myself by my productivity and self-imposed perfectionism. During my recent transition between my PhD program to my career, I was provided with ample opportunity to reflect on what I wanted my life to look like. This opportunity came from being isolated from loved ones and work relationships during the COVID-19 pandemic. During my time of reflection, I realized that throughout graduate school, I had prioritized study, research, and practice while leaving very little room for development outside of this work.

As I approached my dissertation defense and graduation, I grieved the loss of my student self. I questioned who I was without school and felt lost. Additionally, I was overwhelmed by the number of ways my career could turn based on the types of positions I might receive. Should I stay in academia? Should I pursue applied work? Should I remain in administration? But shortly before my dissertation defense, I was met with an opportunity to develop my personal life and family. Taking this opportunity limited the choices I needed to make professionally but greatly enriched my personal life; and having fewer options made the transition less overwhelming.

Although I only recently transitioned from graduate school to a teaching position in higher education, I have observed the importance of being aware of the dynamics of my professional field as I navigate my transitions. In what follows I provide some insights into the work lives of women with a specific focus on women of color.

1. **Promotional opportunities are few.** Within the general workplace, women are underrepresented in senior ranks (Ely & Padavic, 2020) and are less likely than men to be promoted early on in their careers (LeanIn.Org, 2019). Even fewer women of color are promoted (LeanIn.Org). More specifically, women with intersecting identities,

especially women of color and women with disabilities, receive less support, advocacy, and opportunities from managers; fewer opportunities to illuminate work; and lower access to senior workers (LeanIn.Org).

When Ely and Padavic (2020) surveyed employees about why women are underrepresented in senior ranks, men and women both contended that senior rank roles require long working hours and, as such, women's familial obligations prevent them from completing those hours. However, when women were actually observed in the workplace, researchers found that both men and women had difficulties with the types of work-life balance that would make them successful in higher-ranking positions. Men, though, were not encouraged to take accommodations that would impact their ability to achieve a senior rank (e.g., maternity leave) while women were encouraged to take such accommodations (Ely & Padavic, 2020). In some cases, these accommodations were stigmatizing for those who took them (Ely & Padavic).

2. **Bias and discrimination:** A majority of women, especially women with intersecting identities, report daily discrimination at work (LeanIn.Org, 2019). Within academia, women make up 60% of university administrators and faculty members (Flaherty, 2021). However, only 24% of all women are considered top earners and women of color represent only 2% of research universities' highest-paid administrators and faculty members (Flaherty). These disparities are especially disheartening because women earn the majority of doctorate, master's, and bachelor's degrees (Flaherty). Women of color may have an even more marginalizing experience in higher education. For instance, Woldai (2021) argued that the persistent Eurocentric foundation of academia can leave Black women with feelings of isolation in the academy. Microaggressions against women of color as either students or faculty in academia can make higher education settings aversive for them and prompt their transitions to new institutions or careers. Notable microaggressions experienced by female Black students include being asked in meetings and courses to give an account or perspective based on their identity and having their actions being interpreted as intimidating (Morales, 2014). A reported microaggression against faculty of color includes having their competencies questioned by students and other faculty members (DeCuir-Gunby et al., 2020; Johnson & Joseph-Salisbury, 2018). For more about the experience of faculty members of color, readers are encouraged to read *Written/Unwritten: Diversity and the Hidden Truths of Tenure* (Matthew, 2016; also see Chapters 4 and 11).

   In our field, the Behavior Analysis Certification Board (BACB) reported that while 85% of Board Certified Behavior Analyst (BCBA) certificants were women, only 22% were Hispanic, 8% Black, 6% Asian, 0.6% Pacific Islander, and 0.35% American Indian. Although there is limited research available regarding the work life of women in our field—including the experiences of women of color—it is important to consider how reports about microaggressions both in academia (Woldai, 2021) and the general workplace (LeanIn.Org, 2019) may reflect the experiences of women in behavior analysis. Experiences with bias and discrimination, combined with witnessing male colleagues receive more promotions and earnings, may motivate professional behavior analysts to transition out of their current positions in hopes of better overall treatment.

3. **Quality of work:** Although this book is about higher education, we also want to address transitions within schools and agencies since many behavior analysts will work in these settings at some point. Most certified behavior analysts work in agencies with

individuals with autism (BACB, n.d.) and are compensated through insurance billing. However, schools and agencies may not have oversight that holds them accountable for issues that are of concern to professional behavior analysts such as adhering to the BACB Ethics Code or having a balanced caseload (Britton et al., 2021; Brodhead & Higbee, 2012; Brodhead et al., 2018; Silbaugh & Fattal, 2021).

> Further, autism clinics are businesses and may push BCBAs to accrue billable hours, which can result in large caseloads and insufficient supervision. Thus, significant responsibility is placed on the individual BCBA to make sure that they adhere to the ethical professional standards of the field in the midst of financial pressures on their job. When these issues are present, a BCBA may transition from direct service in agencies and schools to another company or field in order to practice within the confines of the ethical standards and to maintain their mental health.

In conclusion, among many possible reasons, some women in higher education may transition to other institutions or fields when they experience limited opportunities for promotion, bias and discrimination, or imbalanced workloads (Ely & Padavic, 2020; LeanIn.Org, 2019; Woldai, 2021; Yellen, 2020). Regardless of the reason for our transitions, our goal is usually to have the lives that we desire.

Choosing to Transition: Considering Your Values and Goals (Denise Ross)

I have made five transitions in the nearly 25 years since I completed graduate school. I have multiple identities that have affected my choice to transition from one institution, position, or city to another. First, I am an African-American woman who is a wife, daughter, sister, and musician as well as an aunt to three beautiful nieces—one of whom I helped raise. I am also a researcher and a writer—two activities that have held my interest since I was a young child. Finally, I am a third-generation college graduate (my great aunts graduated from college in the 1940s and 50s when it was very uncommon for Black women to be permitted to attend college). My parents both held graduate degrees and my father worked in corporate America while my mother was a nurse administrator. When I was a young child, they moved my brother and me to a predominantly white, middle-class suburb because of the school system, and that decision afforded me educational opportunities that most of my large extended family did not have. It is through this lens of economic and educational privilege, identity as a Black student who attended school in a predominantly white district, and my proud racial identity as an African-American woman that I view my career choices.

I was blessed to finish graduate school at Columbia University at age 26 and entered my first faculty position right away (looking back, though, I was way too young to know exactly what I wanted to do for an entire career). Yet, I appreciated my first position since it was the first and only time in my career that I had a Black female department chair as a mentor, and she was fundamental to my career because she made tenure and academia transparent for me. After four years at that institution, however, I realized that I wanted to focus more on research and I became a visiting and then term (non-tenured, temporary) faculty member for three years at an Ivy League institution in the Northeast. In my fourth year there, my position was converted to a tenure-track position. At the same time, my father was in a serious accident, and he needed my care, so I found a position in the Midwest to be near him. While in the Midwest, I led program development in behavior analysis for about five years at a non-tenure-granting institution and four years at a tenure-granting institution. I eventually went up for tenure for the first time in my career and then moved into an administrative role at the University of Wisconsin-Milwaukee, which is where I currently work.

During my career, as is true for other women, life happened. I bought a house, overcame an illness (also see Chapter 14), said goodbye to my dear father who passed away from COVID complications (see Chapter 22), parented my goddaughter, and got married (also see Chapters 6, 10, and 19). Despite the shifts in my career and life, however, I will never forget the first time I transitioned in higher education right after graduate school. During my last semester in graduate school, I found myself feeling conflicted about going to a teaching institution versus a research institution (also see Chapter 2). I had accepted a university position at a teaching institution in a city where I thought I would enjoy working, but a couple of weeks after I accepted the position, I was offered a different position at a research institution in our field. I questioned my decision to work at the teaching institution, and advice from the department chair at the research institution only added to my confusion. "You won't be able to do your research there," he said, giving voice to my own fears.

I wasn't sure what to do but I remembered a Biblical proverb that I had read: "A good name is more to be desired than silver or gold" (Proverbs 22:1). As I reflected on this proverb, I realized that if I took the position that looked better on paper but did not keep my commitment to the teaching institution, I would be making a career choice based on how lucrative the position was instead of basing my decision on my own values and goals. So, at age 26, I turned down the position at the research institution and packed up my things to work at Florida Atlantic University. What I did not realize at the time was that there would be many opportunities for me to transition throughout my career and that this lesson—the idea that I should make decisions based on my personal values and goals and not because of the lure of an opportunity—would be essential for my future choices.

In reflecting on my experiences transitioning since graduate school, I have realized that my decisions to change institutions or jobs were based on at least four values (also see Chapters 4, 18, and 20) or considerations that I will share here. I hope that by sharing them, others will find them useful as they consider transitioning. The four considerations are: 1) **Knowing my "why":** what motivates me to do the work I do? 2) **Knowing my "who":** what are the priorities of the most important people in my life? 3) **Knowing my "win":** what does "success" mean to me personally? and 4) **Knowing my "worth":** what makes me feel valued? What are my strengths and weaknesses? I describe these in further detail here.

1. **Knowing my "why."** Knowing my "why" refers to my motivation for the work that I do. Since high school, I have been interested in addressing social justice issues related to economically disadvantaged families. This interest developed from observing differences in educational opportunities within my own extended family. As I mentioned earlier, I grew up in a middle-class family with parents who moved me to the suburbs so that I could have a good education. That was not the case for most of my 22 first cousins, many of whom struggled to finish high school because the quality of the schools they attended in lower-income school districts was poor. One poignant example is when my favorite childhood cousin had to move to my school district to finish high school because there were too many barriers for her to finish school in her community. She finished high school at age 19 while I was a junior in college at age 19.

   I realized that the situation I was observing in my family was not unique to them but described the experiences of many children who were disenfranchised in their schooling opportunities due to their family's income status. I have had the opportunity to observe the effects of poverty up close and to experience the marked difference that access to better schooling and other resources made. Thus, helping to improve the lives of economically disadvantaged children became my "why."

Knowing this "why" helps me make decisions that align with the reason I became a behavior analyst. It has also helped with the cities I have chosen to live in because I will usually choose a job in a city where I can continue my work with economically disadvantaged children. Thus, to me, knowing my why means that I have a purpose for my choices and that I pursue those purposes no matter where I am.

2. **Knowing my "who."** Knowing my "who" refers to considering the priorities and needs of the most important people in my life in my decisions to transition. My family was and is my "who." As a woman, I have learned that it is fine to make a transition that lets me better support my family. If possible, I try to find a position that allows me to pursue my career goals, but I do not apologize for making a transition that lets me take care of my family first.

    When I was a faculty member at an institution in the Northeast, my father was in a very bad accident. My brother was in law school and my parents were divorced so there was no one else to help care for my dad. I searched for a position in the Midwest that was only a six-hour drive and an easy one-hour plane ride from my father's home. I took the position that would let me continue my work in behavior analysis while being close to my father. My dad recovered from that accident, but I stayed in the Midwest and did not leave again because I was able to better support my family. In another example, I negotiated for a spring-semester start date to let my five-year-old niece (whom I was raising) finish her first semester in kindergarten. In these scenarios, I told my jobs that my family was important to me and that their needs would have to be considered in my decision making.

3. **Knowing my "win."** Knowing my win means that I define *success* for myself—not based on the expectations of others. In one chapter of my life, success may mean pursuing tenure at a research institution in a large city while in another chapter it may mean working at a non-tenure-granting institution so that I can be closer to my parents—even if colleagues disagree with my choices. This is a principle that I have had to embrace repeatedly—whether I was choosing a lower salary in a place that would let me do my research or chose not to apply for a position in a small city because I would feel isolated as a single African-American woman.

    Throughout my career, I have usually been the only African-American woman or one of just a couple of African-American faculty members in my department. Thus, my colleagues, who have largely been white, married, and/or had children, usually did not experience the institution or city in the way that I did. Generally, I have found that working at an institution in a small town with little diversity is not a good fit for me even if it provides unique opportunities to advance my career or do my research. Instead, living in a diverse city where there is an education department that values my work as a behavior analyst has been a better fit for me because I can pursue my career interests in PK-12 education and find community there. Thus, it is always important for me to differentiate a professional win in the eyes of others from a win for me personally.

4. **Knowing my "worth."** I was ecstatic to be asked to work as a visiting assistant professor at an Ivy League institution. It was a dream come true. But three years later, when the administration had not converted my position to a tenure-track position (nor had they converted the positions of several other Black female faculty members who were also on temporary lines), I knew it was time to make a move. I applied for a faculty position at a different institution and received a great opportunity: a tenure-track position,

promotion to a higher rank, and the freedom to go up for tenure whenever I wanted. At that point, I was willing to leave everything on the table at the Ivy League institution. The decision I ultimately made was to remain in the visiting position so that I could do my research (this goes back to knowing my win). *However, I was willing to walk away from it all because I had learned that the institution—while an amazing place to work—did not define my worth.* Defining my own worth is another principle that I have had to repeatedly rely on, especially when I thought that I was facing racial bias in a position. I have tried to minimize the number of times that I use this consideration in my decision making because not feeling valued is not always enough of a reason to leave an institution. However, I do think that as women we can sometimes be loyal to institutions that are not loyal to us, as evidenced by heavy workloads or marginalizing experiences that negatively impact our health and mental well-being. In the rare circumstance when this has happened to me, I have decided to walk away and be somewhere that, as a mentor said, "celebrates my gifts and does not tolerate them."

> I also think that knowing my worth means knowing myself and being able to grow when needed. For example, I was once given some feedback in a pre-tenure review that I did not like, and that I thought was biased. The feedback was hard for me to hear, and I wanted to run from it and the racial bias that I eventually had to confront. I decided, though, to also grow through it instead of only confronting it. I asked myself if I had heard the feedback at any other point in my career (and I had). I then asked myself what would happen if I changed in this area. Could I take on positions and projects that I had previously avoided? With the help of some supportive colleagues, I chose to listen to the criticism and intentionally work on those areas that were critiqued. Later, when a position opened that would require that I use skills in the areas that were criticized, I felt like I could at least apply for it. It turned out that receiving the criticism as feedback worked in my favor and I learned what I needed to strengthen. So, to me, part of knowing my worth is also taking the time to find out more about myself. What are my strengths and weaknesses? How can knowing them help me decide which opportunities to turn down, pursue, or even put in a "maybe" pile until I'm ready for them?

Intersectionality and Transitions (Amoy Kito Hugh-Pennie)

My name is Amoy Kito. The name "Amoy" is an English transliteration of the Zhangzhou pronunciation of the words 厦门 and has different pronunciations and spellings in different Chinese dialects such as Hokkien, Taiwanese, Mandarin, and so on. It may be seen as Xiamen, Amoi, Amoy, or pronounced in several ways in different dialects. It has at times been shortened to May May or Moy Moy to refer to the youngest female child in a family as a pet name. "Kito" is Swahili for masterpiece or precious jewel. My father gave me this Chinese and African name to honor his Chinese father and African mother and so that I may know my roots and forge my own identity in relation to it.

My mother used to say to me very plainly, "In life anything can be taken from you. Your home. Your job. Your life. The one thing no one can take from you is your education." She was the daughter of a college professor and ambassador of an HBCU who recruited students from the West Indies to attend one of the first colleges for free black slaves in the United States. She started her family early and went to college later in life; she also worked two, sometimes three, jobs to ensure that her children's schooling began with a private-school education. In this way my mother taught me the power of advocacy, parental involvement and overcoming obstacles. My father instilled in us discipline through the regular practice of meditation and martial arts at his small martial arts studio in Miami after school. He provided a healthy respect for alternate self-learning through music, eastern philosophy, reading, and questioning the status quo. Thus, overcoming obstacles and resilience was ingrained early and with regularity so that when I became ill, I viewed it as another obstacle to overcome. However, being other-abled is not something to overcome, it is a part of one's identity that requires attention, planning, and management through navigating transitions in similar fashion to any of my other identities.

I say this by way of introduction because often Black people are much more than the color or shade of their skin. Racial, ethnic, cultural and gender identities are often easy to pinpoint as ways in which barriers exist societally and professionally. However, although many of my transitions have been driven by a need to explore and gain more insights into my own identity (and some to accommodate or push past some of these barriers), living with invisible disabilities has been as much, if not more, of a driving force.

My most significant transitions were those that took me outside my comfort zone and outside of the United States. My transition to Canada professionally allowed me to expand my skills and knowledge of government-funded programs, establish criteria for excellence, develop blind-review processes for group ABA curriculum, learn and engage in the accreditation process for medical programs, and gain a deeper understanding of human rights, legal and ethical issues in a position of quality assurance, program evaluation, and ethics review. At the same time, I was expanding my academic skills by teaching ethics and other graduate-level courses in ABA. All the while I learned the subtle and not-so-subtle differences of a new culture. It was also when my mother died.

Further, it was significant because it allowed for greater connection to my Hakka Chinese roots. In the United States, identity is so wrapped up in black and white that a very prominent part of my ethnic culture was often overlooked both in society and my surroundings. This connection through the Hakka Preservation Society of Toronto allowed me to gain a better sense of self and fill in some of the missing pieces of information in my own family. This connection led me to other connections that deepened my journey when transitioning to Hong Kong.

Living in Hong Kong opened many opportunities both personally and professionally. It allowed for an opportunity to work with alumni from graduate school who collectively expanded services and educational opportunities through inclusive education and the further dissemination of ABA abroad. My skills in education, tied with my knowledge of ABA, allowed for translation across professionals to effectively assist transitions from a 1:1 ABA model fading to lesser systems of support to independence.

These are not solo accomplishments. Collaboration is a major key to success. Having colleagues who shared the same academic background and essentially spoke the same language was extremely beneficial because it assisted in understanding and communicating goals and outcomes. The challenge that assisted in my development was the international setting. There were so many different cultures, languages, and priorities that learning to navigate and communicate with parents and families who had different backgrounds and often spoke different primary languages was key.

Personally, these transitions in higher education as adjunct faculty abroad, while also engaging in full- or part-time roles in education, nonprofit or private sector employment have allowed for growth while also presenting some challenges. It allowed more personal relationships with colleagues, more freedom of travel, more balance between work and life priorities. Being in a bit of an "expat bubble" in Hong Kong specifically after my mother's death and during a time of increasing tension and violence in the United States allowed breathing room, further exploration and a deeper connection to my Chinese identity.

Knowing I could not live a life of avoidance and having to make choices that affect my family as well, a return was imminent and so I have transitioned once more. I try to use these experiences in my teaching and the application of my work wherever and whatever it happens to be.

Navigating Transitions (Amoy Kito Hugh-Pennie and Denise Ross-Page)

It takes discipline and resilience to consistently transition from post to post and then readjust to your new surroundings. Trailing spouses and children can be impacted by each of these transitions for better or worse. Depending on years of service, position offered, and tenure status, we can have several or few options available for desirable positions, locations, and institutions. Our choices often depend on several factors we have discussed in this chapter to navigate successfully. What is most important when transitioning to new institutions, cities, or jobs, though, is to not make assumptions or have your own agenda but to ask questions and find out what is significant to the people you will serve. This is an ongoing learning process and competence requires regular self-reflection and asking ourselves why we do what we do. In what way may we be biased for or against certain procedures, interventions, or practices? We must begin to question how we interpret information about ourselves or others that may come from sources that are steeped in intentional and unintentional racism and sexism (American Psychological Association [APA], 2021). In this section, we will describe some specific considerations when transitioning:

1. *The Art of Negotiation:* A mentor once said that you get what you negotiate for, so ask for what you want up front. This is important when negotiating salary, benefits, time off, and relocation. When transitioning, there will be a window of opportunity to ask for what you need to be successful in your new position. This window typically comes after the offer for a position, so be prepared to ask for what you want (also see Chapter 2). Do you need research resources such as time off for research, lab space, or graduate assistant support? Were you offered an acceptable salary and is it equitable when compared to other salaries at the institution or your field? Do your research by talking to your colleagues in similar positions, carefully reflect on what you need for your specific work, and then negotiate by telling the department what you need, why you need it, and how it will help you be successful at the institution. In all of your negotiations, remember that women—and especially women of color—are asked to do a lot of service in institutions. Pre-tenure, we advise that women only perform university service that has a benefit for their career or advances them toward tenure. This becomes even more important if you are other-abled or have an invisible disability. You may not even know what you need to be "successful." You may need to consult with a career counselor or professional organizations that offer services or recommendations for accommodations to support you in your role. Having the most information up front can make all the difference.
2. *Build Bridges, Don't Burn Them:* When you leave a position or turn one down, try to maintain your working relationships. Behavior analysis, education, psychology, social work, and related social science fields are small; it is likely that you'll collaborate with or at least cross the paths of these colleagues again at conferences or in other professional settings. Try to find common ground or areas of similarity that will build trust and lay the groundwork for future collaborations. If a working relationship does not work out, part ways in the most professional way possible. We find that it is also helpful to remember that at any given time, we are all at different personal and professional stages.

It is helpful to remember to try to both show and receive grace and understanding for another person's stage in life.

3. *Jill of All Trades:* Each of us has had to transition between fields within behavior analysis. For instance, both Amoy and Denise attended the same behavior analysis graduate program at Teachers College where we finished with a special education teaching certification and completed a K-12 administrator's license. While Denise began in higher education after graduate school, Amoy started in school administration and part-time higher education. We each have had to transition between K-12 administration and higher education to pursue our *why*. We have also transitioned between departments of psychology and education to find positions. Understanding your profession and any professions that intersect with yours is important for transitioning (also see Chapter 17).
4. *Your Career Is Your Career:* Whether you are at an Ivy League institution or a community college, your publication record, service, and teaching belong to you. While it is true that your teaching and service loads will affect your ability to publish, you can find a way to remain relevant and scholarly even under difficult circumstances (also see Chapter 7). The payoff is that continuing to engage in some type of scholarly activity no matter where you are, such as presenting at conferences or engaging in leadership within the greater professional organization, will keep your CV relevant so that you have choices in the types of opportunities you can take. As we said earlier, your life may have different demands at different stages that allow you to move between types of institutions or related fields based on your needs. Your academic record is yours. It is not wholly dependent on the institution where you are; it follows you. So, no matter where you are, try to find a way to do your work and tell your story.
5. *Time, Time, Time:* When choosing to transition, give ample time to your position out of respect if you can. Given how slowly academic searches move forward sometimes, you may not always have the option to do this but at least try to give your institution enough time to replace your position. At times you may find yourself working in multiple roles such as in a full-time private sector or nonprofit role as well as an adjunct faculty member. There may seem to be a default way of behaving in your environment by others in your same position. However, ensure a separation of responsibilities and clear communication about what is expected and acceptable. What is acceptable for some or even most may be held against you if not communicated clearly.
6. *Evaluate Your Skills, Add to Your Toolbox!:* The field of behavior analysis is constantly evolving. When I, Amoy, entered the field of applied behavior analysis, I literally stumbled across a sign on campus in the psychology department at my undergraduate institution that read, "Free training to work with children with Autism." It was an independent study to learn the Lovaas Method. My first thought was, "When will I ever get a chance to work with children with autism (insert laughter here)?" The field has experienced many transitions since that time in the early 90s and I have needed to keep up through continuing education and my own professional preparation. Transitions, especially if you can anticipate them early enough, are an excellent way to begin the process of self-evaluation, continued learning, and improvement.

Conclusion

We have learned and experienced much when serving in our various roles. Working in higher education can be a rewarding career with the institutional support and external communities that you need to be successful. However, although achieving tenure is the aim of many professionals in higher education, it does not have to be the driving force for everyone. Perhaps you are not interested in or well suited to participate in committee work, advising, grant writing, or other aspects of full-time or tenure-track positions. If not, you can pursue research independently or with colleagues as we all have done, while engaging in part-time roles in academia. Regardless of the choices you may face in your career, we hope this chapter of our collective experiences in higher education will provide some guidance or validation along your journey.

References

American Psychological Association. (2021). *Apology to people of color for APA's role in promoting, perpetuating, and failing to challenge racism, racial discrimination, and human hierarchy in U.S.* Resolution adopted by the APA.

Behavior Analyst Certification Board. (n.d). *BACB certificant data.* www.bacb.com/BACB-certificant-data

Britton, L. N., Crye, A. A., & Hayes, L. K. (2021). Cultivating the ethical repertoires of behavior analysts: Prevention of common violations. *Behavior Analysis in Practice, 14*(2), 534–548. https://doi:10.1007/s40617-020-00540-w

Brodhead, M. T., & Higbee, T. S. (2012). Teaching and maintaining ethical behavior in a professional organization. *Behavior Analysis in Practice, 5*(2), 82–88. https://doi.org/10.1007/BF03391827

Brodhead, M. T., Quigley, S. P., & Cox, D. J. (2018). How to identify ethical practices in organizations prior to employment. *Behavior Analysis in Practice, 11*(2), 165–173. https://doi.org/10.1007/s40617-018-0235-y

DeCuir-Gunby, J. T, Johnson, O. T., Edwards, C. W., McCoy, W. N., & White, A. M. (2020). African American professionals in higher education: Experiencing and coping with racial microaggressions. *Race Ethnicity and Education, 23*(4), 492–508. https://doi.org/10.1080/13613324.2019.1579706

Ely, R. J., & Padavic, I. (2020). What's really holding women back? *Harvard Business Review.* https://hbr.org/2020/03/whats-really-holding-women-back

Flaherty, C. (2020). Academe's sticky pay-parity problem. *Inside Higher Ed.* www.insidehighered.com/news/2021/02/24/women-make-just-24-percent-research-universities-top-earners

Johnson, A., & Joseph-Salisbury, R. (2018). 'Are you supposed to be in here?' Racial microaggressions and knowledge production in higher education. In J. Arday & H. S. Mirza (Eds.), *Dismantling race in higher education: Racism, whiteness and decolonising the academy* (pp. 143–160). Palgrave Macmillan Ltd. https://doi.org/10.1007/978-3-319-60261-5_8

LeanIn.Org. (2019). *Women in the workplace.* https://leanin.org/women-in-the-workplace-report-2019/progress-at-the-top

Matthew, P. A. (Ed.). (2016). *Written/unwritten: Diversity and the hidden truths of tenure.* University of North Carolina Press. https://www.jstor.org/stable/10.5149/9781469627724_matthew

Morales, E. M. (2014). Intersectional impact: Black students and race, gender and class microaggressions in higher education. *Race, Gender & Class, 21*(3–4), 48–66.

Silbaugh, B. C., & Fattal, R. E. (2021). Exploring quality in the applied behavior analysis service delivery industry. *Behavior Analysis in Practice.* https://doi.org/10.1007/s40617-021-00627-y

Woldai, L. (2021, February 11). Black women in higher education: A reflection on inequity and injustice. *The Emory Wheel.* https://emorywheel.com/black-women-in-higher-education-a-reflection-on-inequity-and-injustice/

Yellen, J. L. (2020). *The history of women's work and wages and how it has created success for us all.* The Brookings Institution. www.brookings.edu/essay/the-history-of-womens-work-and-wages-and-how-it-has-created-success-for-us-all/

14 Sickness, Health, and Love

Managing Life and Work Demands

Julie M. Slowiak

Sickness, Health, and Love: Managing Life and Work Demands

The night before my invited presentation at the 2018 Association for Behavior Analysis International (ABAI) convention set the stage for what would be the beginning of my journey with a chronic and debilitating vestibular condition. Instead of attending the Expo Poster Session to represent the Behavior Analysis in Health, Sport, and Fitness Special Interest Group, I found myself nauseous with a pounding headache and lying in the dark on the bathroom floor of my hotel room. I was experiencing my first full-blown migraine.

The next morning, I experienced lingering effects of light sensitivity (photophobia) and sound sensitivity (phonophobia), along with a general sense of unsteadiness and brain fog. Feelings of anxiety and nervousness consumed me as I worried about whether I would be able to give the presentation I had worked on for several months later that afternoon. I contacted my friend and colleague who was chairing the event to let him know what I was experiencing. After some back and forth about how I was feeling, I ultimately decided to move forward with my talk under the condition that he would watch me in case I lost my balance onstage and that we request that the lights in the ballroom be dimmed as much as possible.

I don't recall much of my presentation. I do remember that the ballroom was packed; without enough chairs to accommodate them, conference attendees were standing and sitting along the outside walls of the room! My undergraduate mentor was in the audience, along with several other familiar faces. As I stood looking out into the sea of people, I shared a very personal story of early-career professional burnout as a precursor for the focus of my talk on broadening the reach of our science to support individual health and well-being within the work environment. I remember feeling enormously grateful that my then boyfriend, now husband, had carefully reviewed my presentation slides and that I had made the effort to write out my speaker notes in advance. I also recall a great sense of relief when I heard the loud applause. The presentation was over, and I was still standing, still breathing, still smiling.

How Did I Get Here?

I started my journey as a faculty member in academia in 2008, after completing my doctoral studies at Western Michigan University. As I write this chapter, I am in my 14th year at the University of Minnesota Duluth, where I am a tenured, associate professor in the Psychology Department. During my first ten years in academia, I experienced mostly some nagging, intermittent chronic back and hip pain that relate to a car accident I was in when I was in high school. I also experienced a handful of acute and treatable physical health-related issues. I had my share of stress fractures while trying to be a long-distance runner, as well

DOI: 10.4324/9781003216773-17

as a broken wrist while cross-country skiing (an attempt to embrace northern Minnesota winters that didn't bode well!). I was diagnosed with amenorrhea and osteopenia in 2013 as a result of trusting a personal trainer who didn't have my health in his best interest (and likely lacked sufficient expertise) when I simply wanted to shed some post-injury weight. In response to his rigid rules, I became overly obsessed with getting leaner and had severe body dysmorphia. About 12 months later, I found out that, likely due to the nutritional methods this personal trainer recommended, my hormones became horribly imbalanced. Fortunately, my experience treating and overcoming amenorrhea and the associated osteopenia opened my eyes to the importance of maintaining my physical and mental health.

That experience also prompted me to take the initiative to learn about and study nutritional science, female hormones, proper training, and how these three factors interact with one another. Had I not had that experience, I may not have discovered that I enjoy lifting weights and strength training. I also probably would not have decided to complete a certification course in exercise nutrition, become an advocate for living a healthy, more holistic lifestyle, or refocus some of my scholarly interests toward issues related to worker well-being. Overall, I have done my best to live and model a healthy lifestyle. I exercise daily, eat a diet of minimally processed foods, aim for seven hours of sleep per night, refrain from alcohol except on very rare occasions, and quit smoking (for the last time) over 14 years ago.

Effectively managing stress and figuring out how to have a life outside of work are what I considered my biggest challenges . . . up until 2018. Though I was diagnosed with one chronic health condition (endometriosis) when I was in college, I was misinformed about the chronic and progressive nature of endometriosis and did not think much of it until around 18 years later in 2018 when symptoms resurfaced. Strangely, 2018 was also the year during which my husband, who had been struggling with chronic health issues long before we met due to post-traumatic brain injury syndrome, received a life-changing diagnosis. Three months later, after episodic experiences of visual vertigo, migraines, unsteadiness, and difficulty with anxiety and panic while driving, I received my own life-changing diagnosis (persistent postural perceptual dizziness [PPPD] and vestibular migraine).

An Uncanny Invitation

When I was invited to write this chapter, my initial urge was to turn it down. I even considered it once after initially accepting. Why? The week before I received the invitation, I had told my husband that I was not going to take on any new commitments; my academic plate was full, and my husband's and my life was fuller than usual. On top of managing our own health and supporting one another, my father-in-law was diagnosed with terminal cancer in February 2020 and started in-home hospice in late summer 2020. I spent most of the 2020–2021 academic year living out of state with my in-laws and working remotely during the pandemic so that we could help care for my father-in-law and spend as much time with him as possible. In the midst of it, in March 2021, my father was involved in a severe, "freak" accident while driving his semi-truck. His injuries, while non-life threatening, were serious. We had to make the hard decision to leave my in-laws for a couple of months to help support my parents through my father's surgeries and the beginning of his recovery. In May 2021, we traveled back to be with my in-laws, and we were able to spend the final month of my father-in-law's life by his side. At the time of this writing, my father has recovered well enough to return to work, and my husband and I have been playing catch-up from being away from our home and medical care in Minnesota.

I realize that everyone who is reading this knows what happened during spring 2020. The pandemic impacted each and every one of us and made managing life and work demands more challenging. For many who were living with chronic health conditions before the pandemic, managing their condition effectively and safely was hindered by limited, reduced, or virtual access to routine care (Chudasama et al., 2020). Concerns about contracting COVID-19 among those with chronic conditions led to a greater avoidance of urgent or emergency care (Czeisler et al., 2020). Even so, my husband and I are grateful for the timing. We kept as many medical appointments as possible. While I did have to fly back for a couple of appointments, virtual communication with our health care team became a norm, and in many ways, more convenient. Importantly, I was able to continue working through our travels back and forth across the Midwest and Eastern United States, and I even taught a graduate class and held work meetings from hotel lobbies on a couple of occasions. Was it ideal? No, but it was possible for us to care for and provide support to both of our families when they needed it, and this was both important and aligned with our values.

The Inevitable Reality of Health as We Age

In the United States, 60% of adults have one chronic health condition, and 40% have two or more (Centers for Disease Control and Prevention [CDC], 2021). In their *Caregiving in the U.S. 2020* report, AARP and the National Alliance for Caregiving (2020) revealed that 19.2% of 1,392 surveyed American caregivers aged 18 and older provided care for an adult in the 12 months prior to their participation in the survey; this percentage represents an estimated 47.9 million US adult caregivers. Among adult caregivers, 63% provide care for adults with a long-term physical condition, while about half as many provide care for adults with memory problems (32%), short-term physical conditions (30%), and emotional or mental health issues (27%). In the same report, adult caregivers reported spending 23.7 hours per week providing care, 61% reported working while caregiving, 61% reported work-related impacts (e.g., going into work early or staying late), and 45% have experienced at least one financial impact (e.g., reduced savings, more debt). Taken together, these statistics highlight the inevitable reality that each of us, a loved one, or both will experience a health crisis or be diagnosed with a chronic health condition at some point during our lives.

As you might imagine, maintaining professional productivity while living with chronic health conditions and/or serving in a caretaker role for a significant other or a loved one comes with several challenges. The situation becomes more complex when both partners in a relationship are diagnosed with chronic health issues. Throughout the remainder of this chapter, I will provide an overview of chronic health conditions while sharing personal narratives to offer insight into managing the daily challenges of living and working with my chronic health conditions and simultaneously offering support to, and caring for, my husband. I will share reflections on the decision to informally and formally disclose my conditions as a way to seek support and resources. I will discuss how health issues have affected my perspective on my life and career, requiring that I reassess how current actions align with my values. Finally, I will offer strategies that have been helpful to me as I continue to navigate working in academia and learn to respond effectively to never-ending changes and uncertainties.

Chronic "What"?

You have likely heard the words health, illness, and disease preceded by the word *chronic*. My impression is that the terms chronic health, chronic illness, and chronic disease are often used interchangeably, and some have discussed the confusion and implications that stem from varied use of these terms in medical information disseminated worldwide (e.g., Bernell & Howard, 2016). To keep things simple, I am going to use the term chronic health conditions to encompass all physical and mental human health conditions, illnesses, and diseases that require long-term management and impact daily living. In doing so, I believe the term encompasses the array of definitions used by professional communities (e.g., CDC, World Health Organization [WHO], Pan American Health Organization [PAHO]).

According to the CDC, chronic diseases are defined as "conditions that last one year or more and require ongoing medical attention or limit activities of daily living or both" (CDCP, 2021). Chronic diseases are sometimes referred to as non-communicable diseases (NCDs), and they account for 71% of all deaths worldwide (WHO, 2021a). While cardiovascular diseases, cancers, chronic respiratory diseases, and diabetes are the most common types of chronic disease, others include, but are not limited to, some types of autoimmune disease, pain disorders, gastrointestinal diseases, vestibular disorders, sleep disorders, etc. Mental health conditions and some injuries are also considered chronic diseases (PAHO, n.d.). While genetic, physiological, and environmental factors contribute to the prevalence of chronic disease, modifiable lifestyle behaviors associated with physical inactivity, poor nutrition, tobacco use, and excessive alcohol use lead to an increased risk of chronic disease (CDCP, 2021; WHO, 2021a). The majority of chronic diseases can be prevented, or their onset and progression delayed, through interventions that target behavioral risk factors.

That said, not all chronic health conditions are *preventable*. Many individuals, including myself and my husband, live with conditions that do not fall into the "preventable" category. To make the situation more complicated, the causes of many non-preventable chronic health conditions—including ours—are unknown or difficult to identify and, sometimes, difficult to diagnose, treat, and manage. For example, the time lapse from the onset of symptoms to clinical diagnosis for those with endometriosis is 4–11 years (Agarwal et al., 2019). Managing our health often feels like a full-time or second job for my husband and me, respectively.

Furthermore, not all chronic health conditions are *visible*, though many are classified as disabilities. An individual with a disability is defined by the Americans with Disabilities Act (ADA) as a person who "has a physical or mental impairment that substantially limits one or more major life activities, has a history or record of such an impairment, or a person who is perceived by others as having such an impairment" (ADA.gov—U.S. Department of Justice Civil Rights Division, n.d.). According to the Centers for Disease Control and Prevention (2020), 61 million (26%) of adults in the United States live with a disability. While work-related and other accidents (e.g., vehicle accidents) can result in long-term disabilities, the majority of disabilities are linked to chronic health conditions (Council for Disability Awareness, 2021). Of those with severe disabilities, 74% do not use assistive devices or technologies (e.g., wheelchair, walker); their disability is considered invisible or hidden (Invisible Disabilities Association [IDA], 2020). Therefore, the vast majority of disabilities are hidden.

Some disabilities are *episodic*, adding yet another layer of complexity to living with a disabling chronic health condition. Episodic disabilities are those "where there are times of comparative wellness punctuated by intermittent periods of more severe symptoms that can contribute to activity limitations" (Gignac, Bowring et al., 2021, p. 154). Even when they are well managed, episodic disabilities can be unpredictable and sudden, many are invisible or hidden, and associated symptoms can create work-related challenges for the employee and their employer (Gignac, Bowring et al., 2021). I can relate to this because of the semi-unpredictable nature of symptoms associated with my conditions. I recall, early into my persistent postural perceptual dizziness (PPPD) diagnosis, walking through one of the primary corridors that connects several campus buildings. The floor of the corridor near the Geography Department is covered in maps, and display cases in the wall are illuminated by bright fluorescent lights. As I walked through the area, I suddenly felt unsteady and fell into the wall! Thankfully, I did not sustain an injury from this episode. I had been hugging the wall while walking because I have learned that doing so gives me a sense of security while walking solo through campus. On other occasions, it is not unusual for me to have to stop walking abruptly, either because of a sense of instability or because my legs feel like they are suddenly stuck in mud. While I typically regain my sense of stability and motor control quickly, things I used to take for granted, such as crossing the street and going grocery shopping, are much more anxiety-provoking now that I know there is a chance my body might "freeze up" or I might lose my balance. As such, my PPPD does bring with it safety-related risks that I need to consider on a day-to-day basis.

Over the last few years, I have increased my level of self-awareness regarding triggers (e.g., visually complex environments, lack of quality sleep, food ingredients such as gluten and dairy, fluorescent lights) and have learned how to respond effectively to reduce the severity of symptoms. However, there are times when my symptoms still seem to appear out of nowhere. I have also witnessed first-hand how life with multiple chronic health conditions can feel like a never-ending life experiment to find what works and what doesn't, sometimes only to find what works in the present moment or a very short period of time.

My Chronic Health Conditions

Until recently, I didn't consider the frequent headaches, gastrointestinal issues, and the long-term nagging issues associated with my car accident as part of my identity as someone having chronic health conditions. I simply accepted them as part of my "normal." When I talk about my experience with chronic illness/disability, I mostly focus on the conditions that impact daily functioning: endometriosis, PPPD, and migraines. Most readers are likely familiar with headaches and migraines and less familiar with endometriosis and PPPD. I will share a brief definition with associated symptoms, as I believe they provide necessary context for my experience living and working with chronic health conditions that are considered invisible disabilities.

According to the WHO (2021b), endometriosis affects approximately 10% of women of reproductive age worldwide and is a chronic disease "characterized by the presence of tissue resembling endometrium (the lining of the uterus) outside the uterus." Symptoms associated with endometriosis include but are not limited to severe and chronic pain during menstrual cycles, sexual intercourse, bowel movements and/or urination; chronic pelvic pain, abdominal bloating, and nausea, as well as fatigue/lack of energy, mental health issues (e.g., anxiety, depression), infertility, and difficulty fulfilling work and social commitments. PPPD is a "a chronic vestibular disorder that manifests with waxing and waning symptoms of dizziness, unsteadiness, or nonspinning vertigo that last for three months or more and are exacerbated by upright posture, active or passive motion of self, and exposure to environments with complex or moving visual stimuli" (Staab, 2020, p. 130).

As mentioned earlier, I was diagnosed with endometriosis in 2000, and my PPPD and migraine diagnoses came in 2018. For reasons I now understand better after a great deal of reading and research, debilitating symptoms associated with my endometriosis were largely dormant until mid-to-late 2018. The flare-ups I experience today are fairly predictable, allowing me to plan in advance and structure my day and schedule accordingly. Living with PPPD and migraines has been a different kind of challenge from endometriosis. I encounter potential triggers in my natural environment daily, and symptoms are a constant reminder that things can suddenly get worse at any time. Lifestyle changes, in addition to vestibular rehabilitation therapy, strength and balance training, and regular practice of habitation exercises, allow me to function fairly well even *while* experiencing mild symptoms. That said, I often feel like I can never let my guard down because a threat is almost always present. Even on a day where my symptoms seem mild, things can change suddenly at any moment, and I can find myself in a debilitating situation.

The Decision to Disclose

For those with disabling conditions, especially disabilities that are invisible and progressive, the decision to disclose is personal and comes with its own set of challenges. Do I want to self-identify as a person with a disability? Do I disclose my disability at work? If yes, to whom and how much do I share? In recent years, I made a purposeful and very personal decision to be open about my experiences, especially with regard to how my chronic health conditions can impact my work and ability to engage in a variety of work and non-work activities. You might say I decided to get comfortable with, and take ownership of, my conditions versus hide them, similar to how I refuse to hide the colorful tattoos on my arms. Who knows, perhaps the stigma surrounding chronic illnesses and disabilities will diminish one day, similar to how tattoos were once "taboo."

People often ask why I made the decision to disclose to my colleagues and, more recently, the university, particularly given the episodic and invisible nature of my conditions. It is a valid question, as most people I come into contact with at work would never suspect I have a disabling and chronic health condition because I don't "look" sick or disabled, I have managed to maintain an acceptable level of work productivity, and working mostly from home over the past two years has provided a shield for the visible side effects of the increased frequency of my symptoms.

Above all else, I strive to live my life in accordance with my values. When I entered academia fresh out of graduate school, I recall feeling as though I had to put on what I refer to as my "professor face" and keep the personal side of myself out of my classroom and hidden from my colleagues. I was a tenure-track assistant professor with a goal to attain tenure and promotion to associate professor, and I felt the need to show up in a way that met everyone else's expectations. This seemed to work for me until I realized that my passion and excitement for teaching was dwindling. I decided to start sharing more stories and letting my students and colleagues "see" that I was more than a professor, that I was a human who has experienced many of the same or similar ups and downs as they have. I also began to reach out more frequently for general support and advice from my colleagues. In 2016, I attended a Courage to Teach retreat with other faculty colleagues on my campus; we reflected on, and renewed, our identity as educators. Through these experiences, I learned that my students and colleagues appreciated my authenticity, and I felt a renewed sense of self and purpose in my work.

Those earlier, positive experiences of showing up as my authentic self while teaching, advising, mentoring, and engaging with coworkers and colleagues made the decision to disclose my chronic health conditions much easier. I talked to my department chair almost immediately at the start of the Fall 2018 semester, as I made preparations to travel to Mayo Clinic in Rochester, MN, for a two-day evaluation of symptoms associated with my vestibular disorder.

A short side note about that trip because it highlights a unique struggle of living alone and being unable to drive on the highway: at the time, my husband was not living in Minnesota. We were dating and not yet married. Because I was unable to drive myself to the Mayo Clinic and needed to be out of town for several days, I had to find a way to get myself to Rochester (located 3.5 hours south of Duluth). I ended up using the shuttle van service from Duluth to the Minneapolis-St. Paul (MSP) Airport; I was still a little over an hour away from my destination. My younger sister (who lives in the Rochester area) drove up to get me and then drove the rest of the way. Thankfully, I was able to schedule my medical evaluation on the two days immediately preceding my invited presentation at the Minnesota Northland Association for Behavior Analysis conference in Minneapolis. My sister drove me back to Minneapolis, I gave my presentation, and with the help of a former student and friend who lives in the area I made it back to the MSP Airport the next day to take the shuttle back to Duluth. I share this experience as an example of a challenge that does not cross the minds of most people.

———

From the time since I received my PPPD and migraine diagnoses, I have kept my department head informed, particularly as it has related to the need to schedule regular appointments to manage and treat my conditions and to discuss how to navigate work expectations. I also have not shied away from sharing with other colleagues when it has felt right to do so or as a way to advocate for support or resources. For example, I noticed that the lights in one of my assigned classrooms flickered when I tried to use the dimmer during lecture on the first day of class. As I left my classroom, I encountered a facilities management staff person and explained the issue with the light, how it impacted my vestibular condition, *and* asked whether they thought anything could be done before the next time I would teach in that room. When I returned to the same classroom two days later, the light issue was fixed! I wouldn't find out until after class that day that my request to fix the lights also provided relief to a student in my class who also suffered from a migraine condition.

While feelings of embarrassment, anxiety, and worry often accompany me during conversations about my symptoms and experiences, both the seemingly positive and supportive reactions of others and the immediate feeling of relief that followed reinforced my decision to disclose within a variety of contexts. It has been heartening to observe how my own disclosure has led to an increase in others' sense of security to disclose their own experiences with me. My hope is that through modeling for others, I can help reduce the stigma and stereotypes related to invisible disabilities, and more generally, mental health and disability.

Another very practical reason I chose and continue to disclose is for safety purposes. If I am walking with someone, it is possible I may need to reach out and hold their arm for stability, especially if we are walking outside in the bright sun, inside under bright, fluorescent lights, or in a visually complex environment with a lot of movement (e.g., grocery stores and large department stores). Alternatively, if I am standing or walking alone and begin to experience visual vertigo and a sensation as if I am swaying forward and backward, I may need to stop momentarily, sit down, or ask for help. Before my PPPD diagnosis—when I wasn't sure what was happening or why I would experience these sensations, I did have to yell out for help from strangers while crossing the street a couple of times. Thankfully, these strangers were receptive and kind enough to assist me. Living with a disabling chronic condition for which symptoms can appear suddenly can be downright scary. The more I learn about my condition, it's not surprising to me that several individuals from an online forum in which I participate report struggling with high levels of anxiety and are unable to continue to work.

Most recently, I had to go through a more formal process of disclosure when I made the decision to request work accommodations for the 2021–2022 academic year. While campus operations were returning as much as possible to the way they were pre-pandemic, all of my classes were scheduled to be offered completely online. I want to note that this is not unusual. The Psychology Department at UMD offers an Online Psychology major program; as a result, our department regularly offers completely online, asynchronous courses to serve our online students and simultaneously offer flexibility to students in our on-campus program. I have taught a mix of in-person and online classes for most of the time I've been in my position.

What *is* unusual about the current academic year is that UMD administration provided new guidelines for faculty. Our Chancellor stated that "faculty must be available for in-person advising/meetings/office hours," and college-level administration expects that faculty be available on site for a minimum of four hours per week. While this wouldn't have been an issue of concern for me last year, I quickly realized that the regression of progress, or perhaps the progression of my vestibular condition, was going to make working on campus this year very difficult (regardless of the continued concerns surrounding COVID-19). Therefore, I requested accommodations to support both my physical and mental well-being, as well as to allow me to sustain employment and continue to be a productive and effective professional.

Employees with disabling chronic conditions are protected by the ADA. After discussions with and encouragement from both my former Department Head and our Interim Department Head, I submitted a formal request for work accommodations through the UReturn, a division of the university's Disability Resource Center, which exists to serve faculty and staff with any disability or medical condition requiring accommodations. While apprehensive at first, I found the experience of working with the access coordinator and my physician very supportive and validating. The process was quicker than anticipated, and I felt good knowing that I had the formal and legal support for my request to work remotely from home. I was relieved when my request was approved, and while it did result in a change to my teaching assignment in the Spring semester, I am grateful to be able to continue to work effectively from home while beginning a new round of vestibular rehabilitation paired with biofeedback and occupational therapy. My hope is that I will be able to effectively return to work on campus in Fall 2022.

Outside of work, disclosure to friends, family, and neighbors has been mostly supportive, though I have picked up on some looks of disbelief and minimizing comments while discussing both my and my husband's chronic and disabling health conditions. In addition to hearing, "But you don't look sick," I have also heard "I just don't get it" in response to my difficulty with driving. Others' reactions have sometimes left me feeling as though our conditions are inconvenient, especially when making plans that include getting together in person. While an overnight or weekend trip might seem simple and easy for most, it requires advanced planning and preparation for us. If we visit my parents for a weekend, we arrive with so much stuff (e.g., food that meets both of our dietary needs, medications/supplements, medical equipment) that you would think we were staying for a month!

Additional stigma and medical or healthcare gaslighting (Fetters, 2018) is not unusual for those with invisible disabilities and chronic conditions for which causes are not easily explained. Those with invisible disabilities may not be taken seriously or be given the same level of understanding and compassion and may have to exert more effort to *prove* their condition (Aimone, 2019; Dobson, 2021). My husband has experienced a higher number of negative health care experiences than me, including dismissive, insulting, and invalidating comments (e.g., "That's not even possible," "you sound like a hypochondriac"), unnecessary and often invasive and painful testing, as well as incorrect diagnoses, medications, and prognoses. While going through the process of applying for social security disability benefits, a medical examiner questioned whether one of my husband's diagnoses was "a real thing!" Only once a medical professional reviews his blood work, MRIs, and past medical history do they change their tone and behavior; a common statement he has heard is, "Oh! I'm not sure what is wrong, but something is VERY wrong." Unfortunately, I do believe the saying is true that, sometimes, you need to live or see it to believe it. While navigating the medical disability process for my husband, I have commented numerous times that anyone who spends 24 hours with us would understand just how bad things are and "get it."

Those interested in learning more about the topic of disability disclosure, working with a disability, or supporting employees with a disabling chronic condition might find it helpful to read some recent literature on chronic illness stigma in the workplace (e.g., Beatty, 2018; Santuzzi & Keating, 2020); disclosure and work accommodation of episodic disabilities (e.g., Gignac, Bowring et al., 2021); goals and strategies associated with disclosure (e.g., Ganesh & Lazar, 2021; Gignac, Jetha et al., 2021); identifying and addressing barriers to provide support to employees with chronic conditions (e.g., Bosma et al., 2021; Ganesh & Lazar, 2021), and the impact of chronic illnesses and perceived severity job-related burnout (Cook & Zill, 2021). The Job Accommodation Network ([JAN]; https://askjan.org/) is a free resource for employees looking for advice, guidance, and resources related to disclosing and requesting work accommodations, as well as for employers seeking advice and guidance related to providing job accommodations.

Before moving on, I want to share my final thought about the decision to disclose. Disclosure has been the right decision for me; however, I do not want to suggest that disclosure will be the best or right decision for everyone. While the decision to disclose may not be an option for everyone, I advocate for doing what's best for you and your situation. For me, the primary benefit of disclosing was gaining the formal and legal support needed to obtain work accommodations that have allowed me to continue to work effectively with my condition. In addition, disclosing my conditions with colleagues and students has resulted in meaningful conversations, opened lines of communication should I need added support or assistance, and given me a sense of relief because I do not feel as though I am hiding this part of myself.

How Health Issues Have Affected My Perspective on My Life and Career

The diagnosis of a chronic health condition is a major life event for both the individual and those around them. Daily challenges can have a negative impact on one's life and career goals, and life choices are often impacted and can become or feel limiting. For example, chronic health conditions may impact decisions related to starting a family; forming and sustaining or ending relationships; making job and career changes; participating in social and leisure activities; celebrating holidays; pursuing/completing education; and modifying lifestyle habits (Bhatti, 2011). On numerous occasions, I have taken time to reflect on—and remind myself of—my purpose, clarifying my values, and reassessing my priorities.

Grief and Loss

An unexpected side effect of living with navigating my and my partner's chronic health conditions has been learning how to respond effectively to the feelings of grief and loss. While grief and loss can result from a number of things, being diagnosed with and learning how to live with a chronic health condition—many of which are progressive in nature—is a loss of your former, healthy self and requires a grieving *process*. My husband is unable to do the work he did before his health conditions became disabling; when I met him, he was noticeably fused with his former identity and has since found it helpful to reflect on the question, "who am I if I am not who I used to be?" My husband and I were already living with chronic health issues when we first met; while we do not grieve over the loss of how our relationship used to be, there are times when we grieve over how we envisioned our future.

Both my husband and I have found the application of Acceptance and Commitment Therapy/Training ([ACT]; Hayes et al., 2012) to chronic health to be extremely helpful. Practicing and applying ACT has helped us clarify our values, make space for whatever "junk" shows up, and see ourselves as more than our diagnoses. Russ Harris' (2021) latest book, *When Life Hits Hard: How to Transcend Grief, Crisis, and Loss with Acceptance and*

Commitment Therapy, turned out to be a very timely and useful resource for identifying additional strategies for responding effectively and healing as we continue to navigate our chronic health conditions, as well as supporting our families through significant life events. In his book, Harris (2021) encourages readers to be curious and to view losses and major life events as opportunities to learn and grow (see also Chapters 4 and 12). Within a span of six months, my father was hospitalized with COVID-19, my mother had COVID-19, my father was in a serious accident, and my husband's father passed away. Over the course of one year, we bounced around between our home in Minnesota, my in-laws' home in Pennsylvania, and my parents' home in Wisconsin. I used these experiences as an opportunity to reflect on the values I hold regarding family relationships and how I want to act and engage as a daughter, sister, and wife.

Thoughts of Worry

I often notice thoughts of worry related to the uncertainty of how my endometriosis and PPPD conditions might progress, as well as how each might continue to affect my life and my ability to do the things I want to do. Symptoms associated with my vestibular condition, in particular, are noticeable on a daily basis. Learning to respond effectively to most of my symptoms has allowed me to continue to work. Within the last year, however, my ability to drive has rapidly worsened to the point where I cannot drive outside of my neighborhood.

As a result, I often notice thoughts of worry that my condition will continue to worsen. A common thought is whether I might need to change careers or become unable to work altogether. That thought elicits strong feelings of anxiety and worry because I am the sole income provider, and financial burden is common among those with multimorbidity, the presence of two or more chronic health conditions (e.g., Larkin et al., 2021). In addition to costs related to health insurance premiums and copays for medical appointments and prescription medications, we also have to consider costs for dietary supplements and groceries (we both have dietary restrictions) and other health-related self-care (massage, physical therapy, etc.). While grateful for health insurance, the costs associated with copays add up quickly when you have frequent appointments, and the overall cost of health care continues to increase. Because of this, I take advantage of my flexible spending account benefit, more carefully consider the necessity of non-essential purchases than I have in the past, and look for other ways to save money on a regular basis (e.g., watching for sales and special promotions).

I also notice feelings of embarrassment associated with sharing my worries with friends, family, and colleagues. I regularly notice feelings of frustration, anger, and grief related to a perceived loss of independence and feeling as though I am trapped. What will I do if there comes a time where I cannot drive and need to travel, and no one is available to help me? While a concern for one's health and some amount of anxiety and worry is normal, evidence that those with chronic health conditions are susceptible to develop pathological levels of fear representative of DSM-5 illness anxiety disorder or somatic symptom disorder exists (Lebel et al., 2020).

One of the hardest things for me with regard to living with these conditions has been to stay focused on what I can do versus what I can't do, especially when I'm having a bad day. It's easy for me to get "stuck" by feelings of embarrassment and shame when I can't do something that I used to do with ease and when I have to ask for help, even when the person I have to ask is my husband (who is always ready, willing, and wanting to help). When these feelings and thoughts overwhelm and hook me, I find it helpful to first notice and then name the thoughts and feelings (Harris, 2021). Naming them helps me acknowledge what I am noticing. Harris (2021) offers five naming techniques: (1) I'm having the thought that . . .; (2) I'm noticing the thought that . . .; (3) Here's my mind telling me that . . .; (4) I notice my mind telling me that . . .; and (5) I notice I'm having the thought that . . . . He states: "We can't stop our minds from telling us stories, but we can learn to catch them in the act. And we can learn to choose the way we respond: to let the helpful stories guide us and let the unhelpful ones go" (p. 70). The first step in unhooking from the unhelpful stories, thoughts, feelings, and sensations we experience is to notice them. Noticing them gives us a moment to pause and reflect on the next small action that we can take to move toward what is important to us.

My Career

My career in academia has always been important to me. I feel grateful to have my position at UMD and to be part of a department that is filled with a group of supportive colleagues. Teaching, providing mentorship, conducting research that interests me, and sharing my passion and excitement about the field of behavior analysis with students continues to be both personally and professionally fulfilling. One thing that has changed over the years and especially in response to my chronic health conditions is the way in which I prioritize things related to my health and well-being, my family, and my career. The process looks different now in comparison to my early, tenure-track career years. My intention is to remain in academia as long as I am able to effectively do my job, with or without reasonable work accommodations. To do so, I know I will need to continue to set boundaries, make intentional decisions related to service commitments, and advocate for and request flexible work arrangements when necessary. The pandemic was a blessing in many ways, allowing me to continue to work from home effectively while also caring for myself, my husband, and our families. Having worked from home since May 2019—except for the first eight weeks of the Spring 2020 semester—I realize I will encounter a new challenge when and if I return to campus and teach classes in person. Symptoms associated with my conditions have increased in frequency and severity, and I will need to think ahead when prepping my classes so that I have a back-up plan for days when I feel flattened by brain fog, fatigue, intense pain, and the inability to stand or sit upright without feeling like I'm swaying back and forth.

Another change is that I no longer worry about the fact that I haven't yet been promoted from the rank of associate professor to full professor. This revelation came after a conversation with a female faculty member in another department who seemed surprised that I wasn't yet a full professor. The simple truth is that the response effort not only feels higher but *is* higher now that I am managing significantly more non-work "stuff." I'm not saying I won't continue to work to attain the rank of full professor. I am, however, saying that I am okay with knowing that it might take longer than I anticipated because I am hampered by chronic health conditions. I understand and have accepted that my level of work productivity and capacity for work may be compromised for both shorter and longer periods of time. At this stage, I would rather slow down and make adjustments versus risk my health or my relationships for a promotion.

My health has also encouraged me to focus more of my attention on engaging in meaningful work. As much as possible, I align the focus of my research with personal interests (e.g., self-care, burnout). I also consider more carefully my available time and energy before taking on a new project or service commitment. Finally, I do my best to commit only to those things that will allow me to move closer to my goals and are aligned with my values.

A seemingly unsurprising consequence of living with a disabling health condition and caring for my husband is my heighted curiosity about the experiences of others who live with and/or support others with chronic health conditions. While I have always been supportive of students who need class-related accommodations, I have a newfound appreciation for work accommodations. I have plans to conduct research to better understand organizational factors (structure, policies, and procedures) that support sustained employment. Within the disability literature, there appears more on issues concerning those who have visible, physical disabilities, and less on those with chronic, invisible illnesses, let alone on couples who each live with chronic illness. I am also intrigued to learn more about other faculty members' experiences as they maintain their roles in higher education.

Strategies for Managing Daily Work and Non-Work Challenges

I believe that many academics with chronic health conditions can maintain high levels of work productivity and navigate professional expectations within the areas of teaching, research, and service, though some barriers will inevitably arise. Under the umbrella of teaching, we consider face-to-face courses, online courses, office hours, advising, grading, and curricular development, among others. Within the area of research and scholarship, we consider time and effort spent reading to stay current on research in our field, looking for opportunities to expand knowledge and expertise, writing and publishing, applying for grants, overseeing lab work, and attending conferences. Service commitments may include involvement to support departmental and programmatic operations, participation on college/campus/system-wide committees and professional committees, as well as editorial responsibilities, peer review, and mentoring/supervision. One should keep in mind that expectations can differ widely from one institution to the next and that equitable and supportive institutional policies and practices at the organizational level are critical to sustain employment as long as possible. In this final section, I share seven strategies that I (and my husband) have found helpful to manage daily life and work demands and respond effectively when challenges arise.

1. ***Advocate for Your Health.*** UPMC HealthBeat (2019) provides sound advice for being your own health advocate, including bringing someone with you to your appointment, documenting your symptoms, learning as much as possible about your condition (doing your own research), asking questions, and remembering that you have options. My husband and I also take notes on triggers for our symptoms, take data on our symptoms after we start or stop medications and treatments, and share all of this information with our health care team. We have also learned the importance of speaking up when we need additional information or clarification and when we do not feel comfortable with or agree with medical advice or recommendations.

   Actively participating in the treatment and management of our conditions and remembering that we are the expert when it comes to our body and the covert sensations we experience has been critical to our progress. Finally, we have found that getting involved with and supporting one another's treatment plan has increased awareness and understanding of what the other experiences. It's not unusual for us to read research about one another's conditions and to share information that we feel might be useful.

2. ***Become an Expert Self-Manager.*** The topic of chronic health self-management is well known in the medical and public health literature (e.g., Anekwe & Rahkovsky, 2018), and the self-management of behavior is certainly not a stranger to those in the field of behavior analysis. According to Epstein (1997a), "we manage our own behavior when we deliberately alter the variables of which that behavior is a function; that is, when we act in some way *in order to* change our subsequent behavior. Epstein described how B. F. Skinner's management of Skinner's own behavior was a *lifestyle* and something that

he did continuously and with ease. In his book, *Self-Help Without the Hype*, Epstein (1997b) reveals three "secrets" of self-management: modify your environment, monitor your behavior, and make commitments. I have shared with others my gratitude for having graduate training in the field of behavior analysis, as I believe it equipped me with the knowledge and skills to apply the principles of behavior to more effectively live with and manage my chronic health conditions. In fact, my physical therapist was excited when I showed up to an appointment with a notebook full of data and a graph to visually analyze progress from one appointment to the next!

3. ***Learn to Prioritize (When Everything is Important).*** Before managing multiple disabling chronic conditions, I would have described myself as a creature of habit and someone who thrived on structure and routines. Living with and caring for someone with chronic health conditions that impact daily living has encouraged me to practice what I call "intentional flexibility" in nearly every part of my life. It is a rare day when I am able to complete everything on my to-do list in the way I had intended, especially on days when I am highly symptomatic and energy is low. How do I/we manage? I gave up my pen-and-paper planner for work a few years ago in favor of using my Google Calendar and the "Tasks" feature. I often tell others that I feel like I am playing Tetris with my calendar, frequently rearranging events and tasks in order to try to make everything fit in an orderly fashion! My husband and I also use a whiteboard on the front of our refrigerator for non-work, household-related tasks.

Learning to prioritize is essential; for each task, I take into consideration its level of importance and urgency, how and whether completing it aligns with my values and goals, as well as the consequences of task completion. I identify a single, top-priority work task that I complete as early in the day as possible so that I feel like I have accomplished *something* even if the rest of the day goes awry. Work activities associated with the classes I am teaching or student advising/mentoring are those that typically rise to the top of my priority list. Not only am I evaluated more heavily on those activities, but those activities align with my value to engage in meaningful work that is mutually beneficial to myself and my students. Non-work activities associated with scheduling/attending medical appointments, grocery shopping, exercising, taking care of our dog, and spending time with my husband come before things such as non-urgent house cleaning tasks and never-ending home projects.

When you throw chronic health conditions in the mix, navigating day-to-day activities can be tricky, especially depending on the limitations you have. As my husband says, a chronic condition completely changes the way you live your life; it's a process of adaptation through learning how to live a new, meaningful life rather than simply modifying your old life. One strategy that has been particularly helpful is to experiment with organizing my days into blocks and identifying days and times of day that are best for writing/research, teaching, holding meetings, and running errands. I also find it helpful to put everything on my calendar, including what I call "me time." It's also not unusual to schedule walking "phone dates" with friends and family while taking our dog on his longer morning walk. Finally, my husband and I have anchor activities—non-negotiable non-work activities—such as our evening walk together with our dog and quiet time together before I go to bed. Anchor activities give us some sense of "normalcy" amidst whatever else happens on a given day.

4. ***Embrace the Chaos.*** My husband and I often refer to our life with multiple chronic health conditions as an adventure; to his credit, my husband warned me that he would

bring chaos into my life the first time we ever spoke to one another! Learning to be flexible, adaptable, patient, and compassionate can improve your ability to effectively respond to never-ending changes, the unknown, and the inevitable challenges. While having a long-term plan sounds like a nice idea, I find that weekly, daily, and sometimes hourly plans work best in this stage of my life and career. While plans give us a sense of control, it is essential to build in flexibility for unpredictability. In doing so, I am able to more effectively tune into what my body needs and make adjustments in the moment. For example, I've had days where I've had to make changes to a planned workout or cancel a social activity because I was experiencing brain fog and low energy as after-effects of a vestibular migraine, or intense pain related to an endometriosis flare-up. Rather than being discouraged or defeated by these changes, I embrace the chaos and accept these events as opportunities to practice flexibility, patience, and self-compassion. A simple reframing can be so relieving. Rather than "I have to change my plans," I think of it as "I get another opportunity to challenge myself to embrace the chaos and practice flexibility."

My husband has post-traumatic brain injury syndrome; as a result, he has several medical appointments and procedures, regular testing, and a high frequency of bad days. His sleep phase disorder is disruptive to having a "normal" daily schedule because it is not unusual for him to go to bed around the time I get up and sleep until sometime in the mid-to-late afternoon. Because I am currently unable to drive, we do our best to schedule all medical and other appointments as late in the day as possible. While I used to run errands on my way to/from work, I now have to wait for my husband to wake up (and sometimes ask him to wake up earlier than he would if I didn't need him to get up to take me somewhere). While I know and appreciate that he doesn't mind getting up, I struggle with making the requests because of my desire for him to get as much sleep as possible.

Learning to live more mindfully in the present moment is a skill that has been essential to our ability to lean into the chaos. I have found that using grounding techniques to contact the present moment gives me a moment of pause to reflect and fosters more patience and self-compassion, especially when everything feels difficult and overwhelming. My husband and I have learned over the last several years that we are more effective in navigating and responding to the unanticipated changes when we intentionally practice flexibility. It is also one of the many ways we can show love for one another through our actions.

5. ***Form a Support System.*** Not being able to drive like I used to has been the most significant and frustrating obstacle associated with my PPPD condition. I stopped driving on the highway, as well as on roads and in areas that are visually complex (bridges, tunnels, hills, winding roads), in summer 2018. I was still able to drive locally, which allowed me to drive myself to work and run errands, so I wasn't terribly concerned and only felt annoyed and frustrated when I did want to leave the city to visit family and friends. Before the pandemic, I was taking steps to manage my driving-related anxiety, which became a very strong conditioned response after repeated pairings with PPPD symptoms and scary driving situations (e.g., tunnel vision, loss of feeling in my limbs, panic attacks). My hope was that I would eventually regain my ability to drive with continued effort to do vestibular rehabilitation exercises, many of which are habituation exercises. With PPPD in particular, I have found that it is important to continue doing the things that you normally do, including driving.

Having made the decision to leave the state and live with my in-laws to care for my father-in-law for nearly a year, I was unable to drive in my normal surroundings. Tackling my ability to drive took a back seat to more pressing issues over the past several months, and that's okay. Why? I have learned that it is okay to ask for help from friends, family, and neighbors. I also have an amazing husband who has never complained about having to be in the driver's seat, no matter how short or long the trip. My husband frequently tells me that he is grateful that driving is something that he *can* do to help me live with my condition, and he reminds me that we are a team. That's what partners and teammates do—they help one another and take turns being strong for one another when one partner is struggling. While it is possible that PPPD—like many chronic health conditions—is progressive, I am hopeful that I will regain the ability to drive again, even if only locally.

6. ***Communicate!*** When asked by others who live with or care for someone with chronic health issues, the number one piece of advice my husband and I give is to communicate. I believe communication is the most important thing for people in a relationship where one or both partners have a chronic illness. While I sometimes wish it were possible, your partner cannot read your mind. They are not always able to tell when you're feeling well or when you're feeling sad, hurt, angry, in pain, etc. And, when you react inappropriately (because it will happen), communicate and apologize. There are a lot of ups and downs. Sometimes, my husband and I are both struggling to keep it together, and sometimes one of us will refrain from letting the other know how bad things are on a particular day because we know the other is already having a bad day. Usually, by the end of the day, we have a talk about it because we know something is up. We are in tune with one another's emotional state and how this influences one another's behavior.

If you're going to make your relationship work, you need to take those feelings of shame, pride, and embarrassment along for the ride and communicate how you are feeling. We joke that we are a pair of brutally honest a-holes, and it works for us! There's something special about being able to be completely open, raw, and unfiltered with someone who "gets it" when it comes to managing, experiencing, and supporting one another through the challenges of living with our chronic health conditions. We say it how it is, and it's not always PG! For better or worse, we committed to a lifetime of love and open, brutally honest communication.

We make time for the hard conversations, even when we don't want to, when it's uncomfortable, and when it means taking time from other things on our to-do lists. If talking out loud and face-to-face is too hard or not an option at the moment, find another way to communicate. Because of the limited number of hours we see each other each day, my husband and I will send each other text messages or leave notes on the whiteboard on the refrigerator. In the end, the difficult conversations bring us closer and reflect our love for one another.

7. ***Practice Personal and Professional Self-Care.*** This last strategy is one that applies to anyone, with or without a chronic health condition. Dorociak et al. (2017) defined self-care as "a multidimensional, multifaceted process of purposeful engagement in strategies that promote healthy functioning and enhance well-being" (p. 326). In their work, they identified five dimensions of self-care that encompass behaviors across personal and work domains: professional support, professional development, life balance, cognitive awareness, and daily balance. Some of my own research has focused on job-related

burnout, which results from prolonged exposure to work-related stressors. Burnout has been linked to numerous physiological, psychological, and occupational consequences, including chronic health conditions (e.g., Salvagioni et al., 2017), and research suggests that chronic stress is a common risk factor of 75–90% of chronic health conditions (Liu et al., 2017). In a recent study on practitioners in the field of behavior analysis, we found that increased frequency of engaging in self-care strategies predicted lower levels of emotional exhaustion and disengagement, two dimensions of job-related burnout (Slowiak & DeLongchamp, 2021). Therefore, it seems reasonable to suggest that practicing self-care may play a role in preventing or delaying the progression of chronic health conditions through reducing job-related burnout.

Conclusion

If you've read this far, thank you. Thank you for letting me share my stories, experiences, and viewpoints. My hope is that what I've shared with you will help you if you or someone you love and care for lives with one or more chronic health conditions. I also hope this chapter serves its purpose to help lessen stigma surrounding chronic health conditions and equip you with strategies that will help you continue to work in academia *and* live a meaningful and fulfilling life while managing whatever challenging health-related issues come your way.

Acknowledgments

I would like to thank Chad Cilli (my husband) for all of his support and love as we have learned, together, to navigate a life full of chaos, and for his feedback and encouragement while writing this chapter and sharing pieces of our story. I would also like to thank Traci M. Cihon, Ruth Anne Rehfeldt, and Erin B. Rasmussen (editors of this book) for extending this invitation at exactly the right, albeit challenging, time.

References

AARP and National Alliance for Caregiving. (2020). *Caregiving in the United States 2020*. AARP. https://doi.org/10.26419/ppi.00103.001

ADA.gov—U.S. Department of Justice Civil Rights Division. (n.d.). *Introduction to the Americans with disabilities act*. https://beta.ada.gov/topics/intro-to-ada/

Agarwal, S. K., Chapron, C., Giudice, L. C., Laufer, M. R., Leyland, N., Missmer, S. A., Singh, S. S., & Taylor, H. S. (2019). Clinical diagnosis of endometriosis: A call to action. *American Journal of Obstetrics and Gynecology, 220*(4), 354.e1–354.e12. https://doi.org/10.1016/j.ajog.2018.12.039

Aimone, L. (2019). *Living under the stigma of an invisible illness*. www.distortedperceptions.org/articles-main/2019/11/17/living-under-the-stigma-of-an-invisible-illness

Anekwe, T. D., & Rahkovsky, I. (2018). Self-management: A comprehensive approach to management of chronic conditions. *American Journal of Public Health, 108*(Suppl 6), S430–S436. https://doi.org/10.2105/AJPH.2014.302041r

Beatty, J. (2018). Chronic illness stigma and its relevance in the workplace. In S. Thomson & G. Grandy (Eds.), *Stigmas, work and organizations*. Palgrave Macmillan. https://doi.org/10.1057/978-1-137-56476-4_3

Bernell, S., & Howard, S. W. (2016). Use your words carefully: What is a chronic disease? *Frontiers in Public Health, 4*, Article 159. https://doi.org/10.3389/fpubh.2016.00159

Bhatti, Z., Salek, M., & Finlay, A. (2011). Chronic diseases influence major life changing decisions: A new domain in quality of life research. *Journal of the Royal Society of Medicine, 104*(6), 241–250. https://doi.org/10.1258/jrsm.2011.110010

Bosma, A. R., Boot, C. R. L., Snippen, N. C., Schaafsma, F. G., & Anema, J. R. (2021). Supporting employees with chronic conditions to stay at work: Perspectives of occupational health professionals and organizational representatives. *BMC Public Health, 21,* Article 592. https://doi.org/10.1186/s12889-021-10633-y

Centers for Disease Control and Prevention. (2020). *Disability impacts all of us* [Infographic]. www.cdc.gov/ncbddd/disabilityandhealth/infographic-disability-impacts-all.html

Centers for Disease Control and Prevention. (2021). *About chronic diseases.* www.cdc.gov/chronicdisease/about/index.htm

Chudasama, Y. V., Gillies, C. L., Zaccardi, F., Coles, B., Davies, M. J., Seidu, S., & Khunti, K. (2020). Impact of COVID-19 on routine care for chronic diseases: A global survey of views from healthcare professionals. *Diabetes & Metabolic Syndrome, 14*(5), 965–967. https://doi.org/10.1016/j.dsx.2020.06.042

Cook, A., & Zill, A. (2021). Working with chronic illness: Investigating individual health status and burnout. *Academy of Management Proceedings, 1,* 11557. https://doi.org/10.5465/AMBPP.2021.11557abstract

Council for Disability Awareness. (2021). *Disability statistics.* https://disabilitycanhappen.org/disability-statistic/

Czeisler, M. É., Marynak, K., Clarke, K. E. Salah, Z., Shakya, I., Thierry, J. M., Ali, N., McMillan, H., Wiley, J. F., Weaver, M. D., Czeisler, C. A., Rajaratnam, S. M. W., & Howard, M. E. (2020). Delay or avoidance of medical care because of COVID-19–related concerns—United States, June 2020. *Morbidity and Mortality Weekly Report (MMWR), 69,* 1250–1257. http://dx.doi.org/10.15585/mmwr.mm6936a4

Dobson, J. (2021). Invisible illness and measurability. *AMA Journal of Ethics, 23*(7), E512–E513. http://dx.doi.org/10.1001/amajethics.2021.512

Dorociak, K. E., Rupert, P. A., Bryant, F. B., & Zahniser, E. (2017). Development of a self-care assessment for psychologists. *Journal of Counseling Psychology, 64*(3), 325–334. https://doi.org/10.1037/cou0000206

Epstein, R. (1997a). Skinner as self-manager. *Journal of Applied Behavior Analysis, 30*(3), 545–568. https://doi.org/10.1901/jaba.1997.30-545

Epstein, R. (1997b). *Self-help without the hype.* Performance Management Publishers.

Fetters, A. (2018). The doctor doesn't listen to her. But the media is starting to. *The Atlantic.* www.theatlantic.com/family/archive/2018/08/womens-health-care-gaslighting/567149/

Ganesh, K., & Lazar, A. (2021). The work of workplace disclosure: Invisible chronic conditions and opportunities for design. *Proceedings of the ACM on Human-Computer Interaction, 5.* https://doi.org/10.1145/3449147

Gignac, M. A. M., Bowring, J., Jetha, A., Beaton, D. E., Breslin, F. C., Franche, R. L., Irvin, E., Macdermid, J. C., Shaw, W. S., Smith, P. M., Thompson, A., Tompa, E., Van Eerd, D., & Saunders, R. (2021). Disclosure, privacy and workplace accommodation of episodic disabilities: Organizational perspectives on disability communication-support processes to sustain employment. *Journal of Occupational Rehabilitation, 31*(1), 153–165. https://doi.org/10.1007/s10926-020-09901-2

Gignac, M. A. M., Jetha, A., Ginis, K. A. M., & Ibrahim, S. (2021). Does it matter what your reasons are when deciding to disclose (or not disclose) a disability at work? The association of workers' approach and avoidance goals with perceived positive and negative workplace outcomes. *Journal of Occupational Rehabilitation, 31,* 638–651. https://doi.org/10.1007/s10926-020-09956-1

Harris, R. (2021). *When life hits hard: How to transcend grief, crisis, and loss with acceptance and commitment therapy.* New Harbinger.

Hayes, S. C., Strosahl, K., & Wilson, K. G. (2012). *Acceptance and commitment therapy: The process and practice of mindful change* (2nd ed.). Guilford Press.

Invisible Disabilities Association. (2020). *Annual report—2020.* https://invisibledisabilities.org/pubs/2020_ida_annual_report

Larkin, J., Foley, L., Smith, S. M., Harrington, P., & Clyne, B. (2021). The experience of financial burden for people with multimorbidity: A systematic review of qualitative research. *Health Expectations, 24*(2), 282–295. https://doi.org/10.1111/hex.13166

Lebel, S., Mutsaers, B., Tomei, C., Leclair, C. S., Jones, G., Petricone-Westwood, D., Rutkowski, N., Ta, V., Trudel, G., Laflamme, S. Z., Lavigne, A-A., & Dinkel, A. (2020). Health anxiety and illness-related fears across diverse chronic illnesses: A systematic review on conceptualization, measurement, prevalence, course, and correlates. *PLOS One, 15*(7), e0234124. https://doi.org/10.1371/journal.pone.0234124

Liu, Y. Z., Wang, Y. X., & Jiang, C. L. (2017). Inflammation: The common pathway of stress-related diseases. *Frontiers in Human Neuroscience, 11*, Article 316. https://doi.org/10.3389/fnhum.2017.00316
Pan American Health Organization. (n.d.). *Noncommunicable diseases.* www.paho.org/en/topics/noncommunicable-diseases
Salvagioni, D., Melanda, F. N., Mesas, A. E., González, A. D., Gabani, F. L., & Andrade, S. M. (2017). Physical, psychological and occupational consequences of job burnout: A systematic review of prospective studies. *PLoS One, 12*(10), e0185781. https://doi.org/10.1371/journal.pone.0185781
Santuzzi, A. M., & Keating, R. T. (2020). Managing invisible disabilities in the workplace: Identification and disclosure dilemmas for workers with hidden impairments. In S. L. Fielden, M. E. Moore, & G. L. Bend (Eds.), *The Palgrave handbook of disability at work* (pp. 331–349). Palgrave Macmillan. https://doi.org/10.1007/978-3-030-42966-9_19
Slowiak, J. M., & DeLongchamp, A. C. (2021). Self-care strategies and job-crafting practices among behavior analysts: Do they predict perceptions of work–life balance, work engagement, and burnout? *Behavior Analysis in Practice.* Advance online publication. https://doi.org/10.1007/s40617-021-00570-y
Staab, J. P. (2020). Persistent postural-perceptual dizziness. *Seminars in Neurology, 40*(1), 130–137. https://doi.org/10.1055/s-0039-3402736
UPMC HealthBeat. (2019). *How to be your own health advocate.* https://share.upmc.com/2019/07/being-your-own-health-advocate/
World Health Organization. (2021a). *Noncommunicable diseases* [Fact Sheet]. www.who.int/news-room/fact-sheets/detail/noncommunicable-diseases
World Health Organization. (2021b). *Endometriosis* [Fact Sheet]. www.who.int/news-room/fact-sheets/detail/endometriosis

15 Leisure

Wendy Donlin Washington and Casey Irwin Helvey

Leisure

The goal of this chapter is to assure you that leisure can be meaningful: it contributes to the state of mental health, facilitates meaningful social connections, and enriches our lives. However, the story is not as simple as "leisure is good." Different types of leisure are associated with differential outcomes. Prioritizing leisure can be difficult, so suggestions for self-intervention are provided.

What Is Leisure?

Leisure has many meanings across populations, age groups, cultures, genders, and socioeconomic status. Finding an operational definition for leisure has proven difficult, but most definitions stress that leisure is "time that is not spent working." Petty and Trussell (2019) describe that some researchers define leisure in terms of "free or discretionary time" while others define it in terms of a *state of mind* that emphasizes enjoyment, freedom, and fulfillment. Though studies from the field of leisure studies conceptualize leisure and recreation as separate concepts, this chapter combines variations of the definition to include free time, recreational activities, sports, and travel. Leisure will refer to non-work activities with which individuals freely choose to engage.

Leisure is an essential part of life, leading to its inclusion in the *Universal Declaration of Human Rights* (1948) in article 24: Everyone has the right to rest and leisure, including reasonable limitation of working hours and periodic holidays with pay. This inclusion stemmed from various worldwide movements to limit the duration of the workday. Across the globe, there are varying limitations on workday durations, inclusions of breaks, and vacation time. As a result, leisure industries have boomed, contributing significantly to the gross domestic product (GDP) in many nations (World Travel & Tourism Council, 2021). Therefore, leisure is important from a human rights perspective, and economically. Given the significance of leisure, scientific scrutiny is warranted.

In behavior analytic journals, many articles describe the provision of access to leisure as a reinforcer. In the *Journal of Applied Behavior Analysis*, the word "leisure" occurs in 501 articles, many identifying a leisure type that will serve as a reinforcer for an individual. Other articles identify leisure behaviors as targets for intervention. The *Journal of the Experimental Analysis of Behavior* reveals 47 articles including "leisure," spanning analysis of leisure as a reinforcer in matching research and delay discounting. The topic has broader coverage in

DOI: 10.4324/9781003216773-18

leisure studies, recreation therapy, and traditional psychology. For example, the journal *Leisure Studies (2021)* indicates that the scope of their journal includes:

> [Q]ualitative and quantitative research which critically analyzes both the creation and consumption of leisure, including sport, travel and tourism, hospitality, media (including digital media), events, heritage, and the arts. Articles which examine the inter-relationships between leisure and work, civic engagement, health and well-being, major resources of social inequality and forms of social (in)justice.

Access to leisure and engaging in non-work activities are reinforcing across many contexts, species, and throughout the lifespan. Research by Premack (1959) and Timberlake and Allison (1974) provide a useful way to conceive of engaging in leisure as reinforcing through manipulations of response deprivation. By measuring the duration of behaviors throughout the day, access to specific behaviors could be identified as possibly reinforcing. Premack described restricting access to behaviors that occur at a high frequency or for a long duration, to use as reinforcers for less probable behavior. Timberlake and Allison refined this idea by pointing out that engaging in low-probability behaviors may still be reinforcing if access is sufficiently restricted. Response deprivation can be framed as an establishing operation. Restricting access to behavior increases its reinforcing efficacy and increases the probability of engaging in behaviors that reinstate access (Klatt & Morris, 2001). Many behavior analysts (and even non-behavior analysts) likely employ these restrictions on their own behavior: they restrict access to leisure activities contingent on engaging in some other activity (e.g., work tasks, cleaning, writing book chapters, etc.). Both authors have tried restricting access to leisure with varying degrees of success. Reasons that these tactics may not be ideal for maintaining well-being, health, or even work productivity are described in following sections.

Given that behavior analysis has not extensively examined the competing effects of engaging in leisure time activities on other behaviors, this chapter also includes behavioral interpretations of research from traditional psychology, leisure studies, and business. Many of the suggestions in this chapter warrant additional empirical exploration with behavioral methods.

Types of Leisure Activities

Leisure (including recreation and travel) includes many classes of behavior, which may consist of *active* or *passive* features. Active leisure emphasizes the involvement of physical activity and movement (e.g., sports, walking, exercising), while passive leisure is more sedentary (e.g., television viewing, reading, video games, smartphone use, social media, and computer use). Active leisure has stronger and more positive correlations with well-being than passive leisure. These relations have been found across the lifespan, from children (e.g., Holder et al., 2009) to older adults (e.g., Yamashita et al., 2019). Passive leisure, however, can include activities that are intellectually and emotionally stimulating. Reading books, socializing with friends and family, listening to a concert, going to religious services, and visiting art exhibitions have been correlated with higher subjective well-being (Brajša-Žganec et al., 2011). Leisure is also categorized based on features of social interaction, purposefulness, cognitive stimulation, or artistic expression.

Leisure and Work

Leisure and work have a dynamic relationship. Kuykendall et al. (2020) reviewed how work might constrain leisure. Individuals may have commitments, deadlines, specific hours to work, and may suffer fatigue from those work activities. "Ideal worker norms" may pressure workers to forgo leisure time in favor of spending extra hours on work tasks (Kuykendall et al., 2020, p. 3). Supervisors may directly reinforce conforming to the idea of worker norms, requiring that workers be available (e.g., via email) during non-work hours, and may discourage taking breaks or having access to leisure in the workplace.

In the digital age, work often "follows" us to other contexts when we use smartphones to check work-related email or texts or when we receive work-related calls. Son and Chen (2018) examined how smartphone use interacts with leisure and life satisfaction in Taiwanese workers who used a smartphone for work tasks. Workers self-reported on their smartphone use, stress, workload, life satisfaction, and the "segmentation culture" at their workplace. Segmentation culture refers to practices that guarantee minimum periods of disconnection time from work. Younger individuals reported more work overload, and older individuals benefited more from segmentation cultures. Higher education levels and daily smartphone use were directly associated with more work stress. Higher smartphone use was also negatively correlated with motivation to engage in leisure and boredom during leisure. Unexpectedly, smartphone use was also directly associated with higher life satisfaction.

These results reveal an interesting and complicated relationship between work, leisure, and life satisfaction. The nuanced relations between smartphone use and life satisfaction could be due to the ability to transition between work and leisure contexts quickly. Workers might be more likely to feel comfortable engaging in leisure if they can easily check on work tasks via a smartphone. Having a smartphone present during work hours, one might have more freedom to engage in short bouts of leisure (e.g., browsing social media, shopping, playing video games, watching videos, listening to music).

Others who have difficulty with the transition from work to leisure may need more infrastructural support to protect their leisure time, especially with the digital age. Some European countries have been adapting "right to disconnect" (a good example of segmentation culture) laws to protect workers from being penalized for failure to respond to work requests outside of work hours. Von Bergen and Bressler (2019) describe the cultural shift in which work would occur during set blocks of time (e.g., nine to five) at a specific location, such as an office or worksite to the more recent arrangements in which employees are often able to complete some or all work activities while away from the work location during more flexible hours (indeed, the COVID-19 pandemic has helped move this shift in work culture). They describe this shift as a "double-edged sword," as it allows for more flexibility for workers to complete tasks but has been accompanied by employers expecting to be able to contact employees during non-work hours. These expectations can be associated with higher work-related stress levels, lower productivity, health issues, workplace safety issues, and personal life conflict, especially problematic for employees who have children or must care for aging relatives.

Workplace Burnout

Workplace *burnout* can occur when chronic job stressors affect the motivation and ability to engage in work. Leiter and Maslach (2003) describe that burnout is characterized by "exhaustion, cynicism and inefficacy" (p. 93). Sabagh et al. (2018) identify the most defining feature of burnout as emotional exhaustion, most often an outcome of chronic stress and work demands. Few studies examine burnout in behavior analytic faculty and practitioners, and none examine how leisure may be a tool to mitigate burnout. Bottini et al. (2020), however, investigated workplace features that influence burnout in service providers working with individuals on the autism spectrum and found that workload is directly correlated with emotional exhaustion and burnout. Workplaces that were perceived as fair and equitable, rewarded performance, and had values that aligned with the worker's own values were inversely correlated with burnout. It would be important and interesting to investigate whether access to breaks, and engagement with leisure could weaken the effects of workplace stressors in behavior analytic settings.

Self-care and job-crafting strategies might mitigate burnout in some contexts. Slowiak and DeLongchamp (2021) evaluated these strategies in behavior-analytic students and practitioners who self-reported high levels of burnout, including disengagement and exhaustion. Importantly, cognitive awareness (e.g., self-monitoring, self-exploration, and self-reflection) and life balance (e.g., engaging in enjoyable activities, sources of social support and connection outside of work) were the most reported self-care strategies. Life balance was negatively correlated with exhaustion. In addition, job-crafting strategies such as increasing structural job resources (e.g., professional development), "challenging" job demands (e.g., allowing access to meaningful and stimulating tasks), and social job resources (e.g., asking coworkers for feedback) were reported as commonly used. Challenging job demands were negatively correlated with exhaustion. Self-care strategies in general and overall job-crafting were positively associated with work-life balance and work engagement.

In fields that could be considered similar to those in behavior analysis, especially applied behavior analysis, leisure has been shown to be protective for work stress, burnout and well-being. Wolff et al. (2021) asked US healthcare workers to self-report physical activity (on the job and during leisure), well-being, job stress, exhaustion, and disengagement. Physical activity on the job was associated with more exhaustion, whereas leisure time physical activity was associated with a reduction in exhaustion and stress. They note that the degree of control that one has over their own job demands likely interacts with the relationship between leisure time physical activity, exhaustion, and stress.

Workplace stress is also found in academia and is therefore relevant to behavior analysts in the academic workplace. Sabagh et al. (2018) reviewed 36 empirical studies on burnout in college faculty in 13 countries. Workload (general job demands) most consistently predicted burnout. In most of those studies, older faculty members, and faculty members with higher rank reported lower levels of exhaustion. However, in a few studies, lecturers with teaching duties only reported lower exhaustion and depersonalization compared to tenure-track faculty. Social support, whether at work or outside of work, was associated with lower levels of burnout. No gender differences were found.

Petty and Trussell (2019) propose that leisure should be considered "self-care" and should be considered as vital as other types of self-care, like universal basics (e.g., food, air, water), developmental, and health needs. They also propose that self-care, including leisure, may interact with gender roles, as society often expects women to "put others' needs before our own" (p7). Guarino and Borden (2017) support this idea, noting that women are less likely to turn down requests for performing service in academia, especially internal service (to the department or college). Women indeed spent more time per week on service activities (~36 minutes) and engaged in 1.4 more service activities per year (e.g., committees, administrative roles) when compared to male counterparts. The authors note that women may also be reluctant to turn down a request for service, as it may shift the burden to other female faculty members, especially those who are working toward tenure. The tendency to care for others at their own expense, then, is a phenomenon with women.

The leisure-work dynamic may be influenced by cultural disparities in higher education. Fong et al. (2017) reviewed specific barriers related to achieving diversity in the field of applied behavior analysis that may have implications for leisure. For example, minority students and junior faculty without mentorship opportunities may lack the guidance and modeling for adjusting to work demands and establishing an appropriate work-life balance. Additionally, select members of a minority group may be especially recognized and included in the majority social group (i.e., tokenism) that can be associated with undue responsibility for mentorship and supervision of minority students (Fong et al., 2017). This increased workload may prevent minority students and faculty from arranging proper leisure time. Finally, microaggressions can evoke feelings of rejection or isolation (Fong et al., 2017), leading to overcompensation by increasing work effort, greatly reducing leisure time.

These studies begin to paint a picture of workplace stress and burnout. Stress and burnout among practitioners and faculty is common, can be exacerbated by implicit and explicit workplace policies, and differentially affect members of varying demographic groups. Stress and burnout can be mitigated by disconnecting from work, reducing workload, and having social support both at work and away from work. Leisure may address some of these problems.

Leisure and Health

Work stress can impact physical health, morbidity, and mortality. In a pair of seminal studies of British civil servants (known as The Whitehall I and II studies), a strong inverse correlation was found between employment grade and cardiovascular disease in men (Marmot et al., 1978) and in a follow-up replication in men and women (Marmot et al., 1991). Workers with higher job stress and lower job status were also most likely to engage in health-risk behavioral patterns (smoking, lower exercise levels, poor diet, etc.) which can further increase cardiovascular risks. Therefore, in addition to the quality-of-life benefits that were mentioned in the previous section, some types of leisure can directly impact physical health. Leisure that involves physical activity can be especially impactful. The U.S. Department of Health and Human Services (2018) provides guidelines for levels of physical activity across the lifespan. For healthy adults, they suggest engaging in at least 150 minutes of moderate-intensity physical activity per week, which they describe as equivalent to a rank of 5 or 6 on a 10-point scale of an individual's personal physical activity capacity. These levels of physical activity are associated with dozens of health benefits, including improved bone health, lower risk for all-cause mortality, lower risk of cardiovascular disease, lower risk of type-2 diabetes, lower risk of many cancers, lower risk of dimension, reduced anxiety, reduced risk of depression, improved sleep, improved physical functioning, lower risk of fall and fall-related injuries, improved quality of life, and improved cognition.

Pushing one's physical activity to a higher level can have even greater benefits. Increasing physical activity from 150 to 300 minutes a week can lead to more profound impacts in the areas listed in the previous paragraph. It is important to note also that physical activity intensity categories may change with experience. For example, performance initially categorized as moderate physical activity may become easier with practice, and therefore drop to the light physical activity category. Sensor-based technologies can help ensure physical activity results in target heart rates that would count as moderate (64–76% of our maximum heart rate) or vigorous activity (77–93% of our maximum heart rate; CDC, 2020).

A note about physical activity and its health benefits is warranted. Only about one in four adults in the US meet the minimum physical activity guidelines. The Centers for Disease Control (CDC, 2020) list sedentary behavior (inactivity) as one of the four main risk factors for preventable chronic diseases (along with tobacco use, poor nutrition, and excessive alcohol use). It has also been shown that long durations of sedentary behavior (greater than 6.8 hours per day) are associated with increased risk for cardiovascular disease, even in those who engage in recommended levels of physical activity (Pandey et al., 2016). In addition to affirming that physical activity doesn't attenuate the risk associated with sedentary behavior, Ekelund et al. (2016) report that watching television for more than three hours per day was associated with increased risk of mortality in most people (the lowest 75% in ranks of physical activity levels.)

Incorporating physical activity into leisure time can be accomplished by engaging in many types of activities, ranging from taking brisk walks to joining a sports team. Short bouts of physical activity can be incorporated into breaks at work (e.g., Batchelder & Washington, 2021; Green & Dallery, 2019) to mitigate the effects of long-duration sedentary behavior. Some individuals may prefer to engage in physical activity by themselves, while others may prefer group activities. Costs vary for active leisure (e.g., gym memberships, equipment, and travel). Multiple options exist for active leisure, and websites like Meetup.com offer opportunities to find local groups with shared interest in leisure.

Leisure may also impact mental health. Some interventions for behavioral health incorporate leisure as tools for therapy. Behavioral Activation Therapy, an empirically validated technique used in cognitive behavioral therapy (CBT), stresses the incorporation of enjoyable activities into the daily lives of those suffering from mental illness, especially depression (Kanter et al., 2010). Conceptually, mood can be improved by engaging in activities associated with pleasant emotions (e.g., engaging in hobbies, reading, cooking, spending time with friends), which carries over to other activities as well. Benefits of behavioral activation can also be seen when one masters new skills. Behavioral activation stems from early work by Ferster (1973) but has grown extensively in scope within CBT. Relevant features of behavioral activation include "activity monitoring, activity scheduling, contingency management . . . and a focus on values assessment (Kanter et al., 2010, p. 611)." Some of the features of Behavioral Activation Therapy can be used to protect leisure time.

Strategies for Protecting Leisure Time

Leisure time is an important contributor to well-being. However, time is a limited resource, and many other obligations compete for that time. Some leisure requires substantial financial resources (e.g., travel, gym memberships, photography equipment, etc.). How, then, can we make sure to protect time and resources for leisure activity?

Identify Short-Duration and Long-Duration Activities That You'd Enjoy

The first step to protecting leisure time is to list all preferred or potential leisure activities, including at least a few activities that require physical activity. Then, categorize the frequency, duration, or rate at which you would be able to engage in the behaviors (e.g., daily, weekly, monthly, during vacation, etc.). Identify the financial costs associated with the activities. Keep the list handy and amend it when necessary, to inspire you when you have time for leisure.

Planning to Engage in Leisure: Scheduling (Some of) Your Leisure Can Be Useful

When leisure requires significant time or money, plan ahead. Anticipating those big activities also may have a positive emotional impact. Recently, the concept of Episodic Future Thinking (EFT) has been explored as a tool for changing choice behavior in clinical and non-clinical populations (Rung & Epstein, 2020). EFT involves imagining or "pre-experiencing" a future event. Interventions involving EFT have noted increases in positive affect and a reduction in delay discounting (e.g., Rung & Epstein, 2020). Though no studies directly investigated EFT interactions with work and leisure, there may be similar positive impacts. Vacation planning is a good example; the act itself may be fun. The positive effects of planning are further illustrated by research on "savoring," which refers to the ability to predict, discriminate, or remember the pleasure or enjoyment occurring in association with a specific event. Savoring has been shown to enhance subjective enjoyment in the moment and can evoke enjoyment both prior to a future experience and when remembering a prior experience (see Chun et al., 2017 for a review).

However, overplanning your everyday leisure may be contraindicated. Tonietto and Malkoc (2016) studied the effects of impromptu, specifically scheduled, and roughly scheduled leisure. They found that overscheduling leisure led to leisure taking on obligation/work-type characteristics. More rigidity reduced enjoyment, suggesting that scheduling leisure might devalue it.

These opposing findings, combined with the demands of work, create a dilemma. How does one prioritize leisure? One solution might be to reserve time for leisure on your calendar but refrain from preselecting activities. Free-flowing, impromptu leisure could have bigger impacts on your enjoyment. When leisure activities are social, members of the group might need to know when a get-together is occurring but wait to pick an activity or location until the day of the meetup.

Budgeting Leisure

Most people have a limited financial budget for leisure, which competes with other expenses. Experiential consumption is more strongly tied to well-being than material consumption (Gilovich et al., 2015; Kumar et al., 2020), and predicts before-, during-, and after-leisure savoring (Chun et al., 2017). To illustrate this point, recall a non-essential object you have purchased that costs a substantial amount of money. Also, recall an enjoyable vacation or recreation in which a comparable amount of money was spent. Does thinking about the object or the event occasion more pleasant memories? Evidence predicts that experiences have a bigger impact.

Pre-commitment Responses May Increase the Likelihood of Leisure Activity

Emitting a behavior that "commits" someone to engaging in a future behavior has been shown to increase the frequency or likelihood of that future behavior. Pre-commitment responses can vary in topography (e.g., a self-promise, a verbal agreement, a formal contract, or even a down payment). One may even consider buying a gym membership a pre-commitment response that increases the future probability of engaging in physical activity. Buying a dog should help ensure that you take walks and engage in other fun pet-related activities. These pre-commitment responses are not 100% effective (e.g., it is not uncommon to join a gym and rarely attend), but it may shift the odds of contacting the leisure activity to a higher probability. In operant research, engaging in a pre-commitment response can lead to the removal of a competing reinforcement arrangement, which often leads to an increase in target behavior (e.g., Rachlin & Green, 1972). Though these pre-commitments should be balanced given the previously described overplanning effects, agreeing to engage in leisure with others, or pre-purchasing access to leisure may help us appropriately prioritize leisure.

Avoid Workplace Communication During Non-Work Hours

Enhancing stimulus control of work and leisure may increase engagement and enjoyment of leisure time. Communicate your boundaries to others when it is appropriate. For example, "away" messages on email can inform others of your availability. For professors, including a description of when you are available for meetings, and when you will typically answer email or phone messages can prevent unreasonable expectations from students. Also respect others' leisure time by avoiding after-hours emails and requests.

Addressing Engagement and Efficiency in the Workplace

Efficiency and engagement in the workplace can impact the freedom you have to engage in leisure. Humans, including students (Perrin et al., 2011), faculty (Ackerman & Gross, 2007), and practitioners procrastinate. There are obligations that we cannot avoid or escape. Procrastination on work tasks may reduce the time spent on sleep, leisure, and self-care. Procrastination can be characterized by a delay or failure to initiate a task, and also failure to persist on a task. Frequent disengagement from tasks (i.e., transitioning to other behaviors) can lead to inefficiency. Addressing work inefficiency can help protect time away from work.

The behavioral work on rich-to-lean transitions may be useful in understanding and addressing problems associated with procrastination. "Rich" reinforcement refers to conditions where reinforcers are more frequent, have higher magnitude, require less effort, or are more immediate. "Lean" reinforcement conditions are characterized as those that have less reinforcement, relative to the rich conditions. Work behaviors may vary in intrinsic reinforcement as well (e.g., making graphs of data might be preferred to answering emails). Determining which tasks would be more highly probable (high-p) or less probable (low-p) under unrestrained conditions could help facilitate engagement in low-p tasks. Transitioning between reinforcement conditions occasions predictable patterns of responding in the basic literature (e.g., Perone & Courtney, 1992; Williams et al., 2011). Often, longer pauses occur when upcoming reinforcement is discriminable as leaner, especially after just experiencing a rich reinforcement condition. Stimuli associated with rich-to-lean transitions can function aversively and escape-maintained behavior may occur during these transition periods (e.g., Langford et al., 2019; Retzlaff et al., 2017).

Applied research has evaluated relatively extended periods of pausing between behaviors, called dawdling, during rich-to-lean transitions in children with autism spectrum disorder (Jessel et al., 2016). Dawdling was not specific to any given topographies of behavior, but rather referred to instances in which the relative duration of pausing during one transition type was greater than during other transitions. In academia, such dawdling may take the form of surfing the web or checking social media, chatting with colleagues, or taking naps relatively more frequently or for relatively longer durations during rich-to-lean transitions. Even when work tasks are reinforced, we may delay engagement because the payoff is less than what we just experienced. Examining how these conditions affect behavior in workplaces for behavior analysts and academics would be an interesting endeavor.

During work, we may engage in other responses, such as cell phone use and/or checking social media, during rich-to-lean transitions or when going from high-p to low-p tasks. It may be beneficial to arrange for a terminal richer or high-p task every so often to help maintain responding. For example, Jessel et al. (2016) arranged 50% of rich-to-lean transitions to include unsignaled access to preferred activities. In other words, on 50% of occasions, participants would have unsignaled access to high-p activities when transitioning to the lean context. A decrease in dawdling was observed when unsignaled access to high-p activities were arranged following a rich-to-lean transition. It would be important to experimentally evaluate these strategies for self-management and academic tasks, as it may not be feasible to schedule such a high probability of unsignaled access to high-p activities or tasks for behavior analysts and academics. It may also be difficult to keep such access to high-p activities or tasks unsignaled during rich-to-lean transitions when self-managing and it may therefore be necessary to solicit support from others when arranging these contingencies.

When we cannot fit leisure into our schedule, working on preferred academic tasks may be a compromise. Preferred academic tasks can be arranged in a high-p sequence to promote compliance with low or non-preferred academic tasks (Lee et al., 2004). The high-p sequence involves delivering a series of high-probability requests that have a history of compliance prior to the delivery of the targeted low-probability request. Contingent reinforcement, such as praise or some other stimulus that can be quickly delivered and consumed, for compliance with these high-p requests is thought to increase the likelihood of compliance with the final low-p request (Lipschultz & Wilder, 2017).

Though research is needed to evaluate the high-p sequence as a self-management strategy, especially in workplace contexts, it may be beneficial to identify a preference hierarchy of academic or work-related tasks and other obligations and arrange them according to the high-p sequence. One important consideration may be whether an upcoming low-p task is signaled. In a review of the high-p sequence, Lipschultz and Wilder (2017) indicated that responding to high-p requests may decline over time and that removing stimuli associated with low-p requests may improve responding. This suggests that we may need to remove stimuli associated with upcoming low-p tasks when arranging our schedules, such as calendar reminders, to-do lists, or task materials to maintain productivity over time.

Though these behavioral strategies may help manage work engagement, there are a few more important things to remember about academic work. First, you will never be "caught up." Never. Making access to leisure contingent on getting caught up at work could lead to a situation in which you never earn access to leisure. In academia, business, and in practice, the amount of workload will vary. Some deadlines will be less flexible than others. Submitting grades, evaluating data to make immediate treatment decisions, and finishing slides before a presentation are examples of behaviors that will likely have immediate and inflexible deadlines. In these situations, leisure can be influenced by meeting these types of work deadlines. Plan for smaller bouts of leisure time activity during predictable heavier workloads. It is precisely during those busy times that we are likely most stressed and need a break.

Additionally, be deliberate in which roles you accept, committees you join, and tasks you agree to complete. The freedom to choose work tasks varies greatly both across and within fields. As you progress through your career, the more freedom you likely will have to select tasks. Service requests in academia and science can disproportionately burden newer faculty and women (e.g., Petty & Trussell, 2019). Presumably, these burdens at least partially exist because of the lower likelihood of these individuals refusing requests. Supervisors may make many requests to take on new roles, join committees, teach new classes, or add to your caseload. Requests for your time may not be restricted to only your direct workplace. Journal editors may call on you to review manuscripts or join the board of editors. Local and national organizations may request that you serve on or chair committees. Colleagues may ask you to contribute manuscripts for special issues of journals or chapters for books. Overcommitting to work will likely lead to higher stress and less free time to engage in non-work activities.

Of course, you should say yes to *some* of these requests. The advice of the authors is that you should never say yes immediately. Delaying your answer by a few days will allow you to more fully consider the impact to your workload and career. Early in your career, it's important to consider which tasks will have the biggest impact on career goals, like promotions (e.g., peer-reviewed publications, grant applications, meeting service requirements), and increasing your standing in the field (e.g., serving on the board of editors of a journal, holding leadership roles in professional organizations). Also consider whether you are "effort discounting," where one discounts the effort required if that effort requirement is delayed (Białaszek et al., 2019). For example, are you more likely to consider saying yes to writing a manuscript if you do not have to start it for several months? Always be aware of what saying yes will cost you; effort and time must be diverted to take on new responsibilities. If you're unsure whether you have enough time and effort to dedicate to something new, ask if you can reduce some other aspect of your workload. When the first author (WDW) was new in an academic position, she was unaware that she could ask for reductions in teaching load or service in exchange for accepting new roles. Sometimes you will have to delay committing to a new task, and other times you will have to decline. You do not have to say yes to all requests.

Promote Leisure-Facilitating Workplace Culture

Support and help develop a workplace culture where the need for leisure is recognized, and even codified. Creating a culture of intentional disconnection with work can improve our ability to engage in leisure activity and is associated with higher subjective well-being. Acknowledge the need for free time in others. Avoid expecting your peers, supervisors, students, supervisees, or employees to be immediately accessible when away from work. Ask others at the workplace if they have time to engage in leisure-time activities. Encourage employers to facilitate physical activity-based leisure breaks and access (e.g., walking areas, access to showers, access to gym equipment). Appeal to the workplace to facilitate the ability for workers or students to be able to plan for leisure. Workplaces that use just-in-time scheduling, or reactive scheduling of work hours based on customer demands, disrupt the ability to engage in leisure (Kuykendall et al., 2020). Unpredictability in one's schedule, estimated to be as high as 41% in US early-career workers, can also lead to increased work stress, family stress related to obtaining childcare, and transportation difficulties (Kuykendall et al., 2020).

Normalize the need for leisure. In academia, and in many business settings, the *cult of overwork* (Surowiecki, 2014) is often present. Faculty and graduate students often state that work is overwhelming and spend more than 40 hours a week working. This verbal behavior sometimes has a competitive tone, in which we point out the most aversive aspects of our workload to others to show just how dedicated we are. We might even make these statements with deliberate exaggeration. Though the function of these behaviors has not been established, we can guess that on some occasions these statements are socially reinforced. On other occasions, these statements may allow us to avoid new demands or requests for our time and effort. Hearing these types of statements repeatedly among our peers may influence us to work longer hours, forgo leisure, and change our verbal behavior to conform to this culture. The first author (WDW) notes that on occasion she hides evidence of leisure from colleagues because she feels guilty for engaging in leisure when there are unfinished work tasks. Upon writing this chapter, she has made a self-commitment to cease engaging in this kind of behavior (though the effects of this pre-commitment have yet to be measured).

Layer Leisure Over Other Activities

Combining necessity with leisure could allow for more opportunities for leisure experiences. For example, try listening to podcasts or books during a commute. Invite a colleague to have coffee outside while discussing work. Read a journal article while walking on a treadmill. Though these layered leisure activities may not be the ideal, they can still allow us to benefit from activities we would not otherwise have time to do.

Two Case Studies: Leisure at Different Career Stages

Though two cases hardly make for scientific rigor, the authors thought it would be useful to examine our different experiences and perspectives on leisure integration, given that we are in different stages of our careers. At the time of this writing, Wendy Donlin Washington (WDW) is a tenured faculty member, an administrator in a graduate school, membership coordinator of Association for Behavior Analysis International (ABAI), and has been in the field of behavior analysis since 1994. She has conducted animal and human research on health-related behaviors and best practices in higher education. Casey Irwin Helvey (CIH) is a BCBA and a fourth year Ph.D. student at the University of North Carolina Wilmington. She has completed research in the areas of the assessment and treatment of severe behavior, assessing and increasing physical activity in both children and adults, and evaluating issues of diversity in behavior analysis graduate programs. Additionally, the authors have different economic situations, different histories of reinforcement, and different ages.

Here we post several leisure-related questions and answers from both authors. It also might be useful for the reader to answer the questions for themselves before reading the author's answers:

How Do You Make Time for Leisure in Your Current Situation?

WDW: This varies with academic year schedules. During semesters, it is difficult to engage in leisure without deliberately scheduling free time. Tenure-track faculty are typically expected to dedicate time to teaching, research, and service. I engage in research activities (grant writing, manuscript writing, graduate student meetings, Institutional Review Board protocols, data analysis, etc.), and service (university committees, administrative duties, reviewing manuscripts, serving ABAI, etc.). Until accepting an administrative appointment a few months ago, I was also teaching three classes each semester, but now only teach one per semester. There are also unclassified activities that steal my time, like the 50 emails a day I get during busy periods. I spend between 50–70 hours a week on these activities. During the workday, I take walks around my campus, play Pokémon Go, or take a fiction book to lunch to work in small bits of leisure. These breaks typically make it easier to stay focused when I am on task. I sometimes unintentionally scroll through social media on my computer or my phone, distracting me from being on task and leading to inefficiency.

To "turn off" work while away from my office, I avoid opening email, which I found greatly interfered with leisure. Without this self-imposed rule, I would find myself checking email right before I planned on engaging in leisure, and then my efforts would divert to whatever request or task was required by the email. Not checking email after 7 p.m. and rarely on weekends is one of the best ways I've found to protect my time. I state when I'll read emails in my syllabus and will put away messages on my mail to let senders know I will not respond immediately. I've also decided to refrain from sending emails on late Friday afternoons that require behavior on the part of the reader, in an effort to respect others' free time as well (send those emails Monday morning instead.)

I need to schedule active leisure, or I end up spending my time in passive leisure. My spouse and I will plan specific times for kayaking, fishing, visiting parks, etc. On weekends, I make elaborate meals (which I consider a fun activity). During COVID restrictions, I have become a better bread baker because I can work small increments of bread time in between work-related tasks. I also make it a practice to carry my camera in my car to allow for impromptu landscape and wildlife photography (see Figure 15.1), one of my favorite leisure time activities.

During winter break and summer, it is easier to have unplanned leisure. Instead, I schedule specific times to engage in work (~4 hours a day, usually in the mornings). These breaks are typically the only times that I can travel, as faculty really cannot take vacations during the academic year.

At different points in my career, my leisure and the amount of time dedicated to those activities has greatly changed. When I was a student, I had a much bigger social circle, and that led to more organized leisure being available (like parties, going dancing, exercising together, etc.). Though I had a lot less money, I engaged in a lot more leisure. I would sleep

Figure 15.1 Photo Taken by Wendy Donlin Washington of Savannah the Leopard During a Visit to a Wildlife Sanctuary

less to fit in work and leisure activities (which I cannot do now that I'm older). My leisure is no longer limited by finances, allowing me better vacations and better toys (like kayaks), but I spend less time in leisure now than at any other point in life.

CIH: As I have progressed through graduate school, it has gotten easier to make time for leisure. During my first and second years of graduate school, days were consumed by academic tasks, or at least engaging in covert verbal behavior about the tasks that needed to be done. Then, I would make time for leisure only after working myself to the point that I was no longer productive or able to focus. I sometimes forced myself to take a night off from work or spend a day on the weekend doing something other than academic tasks. Leisure would often come in the form of "bedtime procrastination" (Kamphorst et al., 2018), in which I would delay bedtime (to 2 a.m.) by spending an hour or so scrolling through social media or watching television late in the evening. Perhaps lack of leisure contributed to ineffective self-management. Unclear contingencies of reinforcement for contributing to class discussions, getting good grades, presenting at conferences, and publications competed with non-academic reinforcers. To more effectively arrange for leisure time, graduate students might benefit from learning to solicit praise and feedback and ask for clarification for standards of academic work.

Because of reduced academic demands and working from home during the COVID-19 pandemic, I find that I can arrange time strictly for leisure. The natural breaks in my schedule have made it easier to arrange leisure. Based on the Premack principle, I program leisure to be available contingent on completing a given academic task or a specified period of time spent working on one or more academic tasks. I've subsequently had higher productivity in academics and leisure, better mental health, and healthier relationships. Nonetheless, I am cautious of occasions on which I self-deliver reinforcement outside of the programmed contingency when using self-management. There are days of only leisure, or maybe even several days in a row are spent this way (outside of scheduled courses and meeting times). It is difficult to get back on track in these cases, and there are times when I risk falling behind. Additionally, COVID-related delays and postponement of deadlines exacerbate this problem. There are also days when I skip leisure breaks and spend more time engaged in academic tasks.

Another self-management tool I use is a mobile application called Forest, which allows users to set timers and if you exit the application to send text messages, use social media accounts, etc., while the timer is going, then you lose points. If you do not exit out of the application to do anything else while the timer is going, then you earn points to plant trees in a forest. I set timers to stay focused during academic tasks and leisure time. Overall, using self-management strategies helps establish a more meaningful balance between academics and leisure in my current schedule. My advice to current graduate students would be to employ self-management strategies early on and to have a discussion with their research mentors or supervisors about what is expected of them.

How Do You Disperse Your Leisure Activity?

WDW: During the academic year, I tend to engage in my active leisure on weekends, and most passive leisure in evenings after work. I give myself short breaks between classes, or at lunchtime, to walk or browse social media. Given that I do research on physical activity, it is embarrassing to admit that I do not typically follow CDC (2020) guidelines to disperse my physical activity throughout the week. During winter break and summer, I am more likely to engage in active leisure that is more dispersed throughout the week.

CIH: My leisure time tends to occur both in big "chunks" and dispersed throughout the week. I take small leisure breaks throughout the day between classes, meetings, and individual work. If I am spending the day working on my dissertation or writing a manuscript, then I schedule breaks (e.g., 30 minutes per 2 hours of work). Having leisure dispersed throughout the day helps me to enjoy my time working and I am more productive. I also have longer leisure breaks dispersed throughout the week for activities such as yoga, dinner with friends, or simply to sit by myself and watch a movie on the couch. I am strict on keeping my physical activity leisure breaks no matter what and I tend to schedule those about three to four times per week.

Are there Big Fluctuations in Your Ability to Engage in Leisure?

WDW: Academic cycles contribute to big fluctuations in leisure. The last three weeks of a semester are very busy, and I often have little leisure time, because graduate students are more likely to defend theses, end-of-semester papers and tests must be graded, and students are more likely to require office-hour visits. This takes a toll on my productivity and mental state. I become tired and cranky, less efficient in my work tasks, and I eat poorly. This cycle has become harder on me the older I get, yet I have been unable to break that cycle. When I am "off-contract" (not technically being paid to work), during the summer, I allow myself a lot more time to engage in leisure while still completing discretionary work activities.

CIH: There may be minor fluctuations in my ability to engage in leisure from day to day or from week to week, but I generally have a predictable schedule. Any major fluctuations tend to be a result of my own procrastination or inability to effectively self-manage. My ability to engage in leisure has fluctuated with changing responsibilities. For example, my most recent summer has been the least demanding academically. The increase in leisure time has been enjoyable, though I have found it difficult to create and stick to a schedule for academic tasks that are necessary, such as writing my dissertation. I also find that the more time spent engaged in leisure at the expense of my academic work tends to evoke a high level of guilt, which seems to serve as an establishing operation for academic-related behaviors. I then only complete as much academic work as necessary to terminate the feelings of guilt, which is not enough to be sufficiently productive. I get stuck in this cycle of leisure and procrastination, followed by guilt and short, inefficient periods of work.

How Does Leisure Time Correlate with Your Mental Health?

WDW: Leisure seems to improve my mental health and reduce stress. After physical activity, I tend to sleep better. Social leisure activities strengthen my relationships with friends and family. However, there is also a side effect of engaging in leisure: guilt. As mentioned earlier, academics are never "caught up" with work. Engaging in leisure activity sometimes feels like cheating on work. I have had conversations with many other academics, and this guilt seems to be common. This guilt sometimes leads to a failure to engage in leisure or work, resulting in even more guilt because I have neither been productive nor had fun. This guilt spiral is not healthy and does not improve productivity. I have also noticed myself conceiving of leisure to align with response deprivation arrangements. That is, I "deserve" access to leisure only upon completion of some work task. If I engage in leisure activity without meeting whatever arbitrary goal I have set, I feel like I am cheating, and getting access to the reinforcer without deserving it. Even recognizing this is a problematic conception does not always eliminate this guilt cycle. I am convinced this is a common phenomenon given memes I've seen on academic social media sites (e.g., www.facebook.com/academicssay).

CIH: When I have not engaged in leisure and I have many academic tasks to complete, I notice stress and depression-like behaviors. These include drinking more coffee throughout the day, grinding my teeth, shaking my feet and/or legs while sitting or lying, and complaining or other negative statements. I also tend to start eating and sleeping less. I feel less productive because I am distracted and "scatterbrained." All of these events together lead to taking a much-needed leisure break, though I always feel guilty during leisure in these instances because I have been less productive and still have a long list of things to do. I try to notice precursors before I get to this state and plan to improve my environment.

When I make time for leisure, my emotional state is more positive, and I am more productive in my work. Under these circumstances, I do not feel guilty when engaging in leisure, which makes it more enjoyable. One strategy to allay guilt is to write down the task (e.g., grade papers by end of day tomorrow, send email in the morning). Then, I can work on getting it completed or resolving the issue soon, but it also does not take away from a positive experience during leisure activities.

Do you Find that You are Able to Engage in Many Leisure Activities in Contexts Outside Academia (e.g., Non-academic Friends/Colleagues and Settings)?

WDW: While in college and my postdoc, most of my leisure time was spent with academic peers. However, since becoming a professor, and getting married, much less of my time is spent with colleagues. With a few exceptions, engaging in social leisure with colleagues tends to turn into complaining about work (even when we declare that there will be no work discussion). Over time, I have sought more of a delineation between work and leisure, which I believe has been beneficial.

CIH: It is difficult for me to maintain relationships outside of my academic program. It seems easier to spend time with graduate students than older friends (another source of guilt). I am able to commiserate with other graduate students during leisure: it gives me a sense of comfort to know that I am not the only one feeling this way. It does get exhausting to always talk about school during leisure time. When spending time with non-academics, I hear comments like "aren't you on vacation?" or "why are you responding to that email now?" I attempt to make time for my family and long-time friends because these relationships are important to me. Having these other relationships is also a good way to structure strict leisure time that has nothing to do with school and helps keep feelings of guilt or otherwise about school at bay.

Conclusions

Correlational evidence supports a positive relationship between leisure activity with subjective well-being, mental health, and work productivity. Therefore, we feel leisure time is important and should be prioritized. It should be considered a universal need rather than a luxury. Leisure time has the most impact when it is active, not interrupted by work, and dispersed regularly. Both authors report feeling guilt (and noticing it in peers) when engaging in "undeserved" leisure, perhaps stemming from treating access to leisure as a reinforcer for work-related behavior. The strategies suggested by the authors may help individuals protect and benefit from leisure.

Some academic, business and practice workplaces support a culture of overwork, where leisure is not facilitated. Further study of leisure engagement and policies that support the "right to disconnect" from work are warranted in our field. Behavior analysis certainly has tools to study the impacts of workplace interventions, self-management strategies, and leisure engagement on outcomes indicating higher well-being, quality of life, and work satisfaction in members of our field.

References

Ackerman, D. S., & Gross, B. L. (2007). I can start that JME manuscript next week, can't I? The task characteristics behind why faculty procrastinate. *Journal of Marketing education*, *29*(2), 97–110. https://doi.org/10.1177/0273475307302012

Batchelder, S. R., & Washington, W. D. (2021). Effects of incentives and prompts on sedentary and walking behaviors in university employees. *Behavior Analysis: Research and Practice*. Advance online publication. https://doi.org/10.1037/bar0000214

Białaszek, W., Ostaszewski, P., Green, L., & Myerson, J. (2019). On four types of devaluation of outcomes due to their costs: Delay, probability, effort, and social discounting. *The Psychological Record*, *69*(3), 415–424. https://doi.org/10.1007/s40732-019-00340-x

Bottini, S., Wiseman, K., & Gillis, J. (2020). Burnout in providers serving individuals with ASD: The impact of the workplace. *Research in Developmental Disabilities*, *100*, 103616. https://doi.org/10.1016/j.ridd.2020.103616

Brajša-Žganec, A., Merkaš, M., & Šverko, I. (2011). Quality of life and leisure activities: How do leisure activities contribute to subjective well-being? *Social Indicators Research*, *102*(1), 81–91. doi:10.1007/s11205-010-9724-2

Centers for Disease Control. (2020). *Target heart rate and estimated maximum heart rate*. www.cdc.gov/physicalactivity/basics/measuring/heartrate.htm

Chun, H. H., Diehl, K., & MacInnis, D. J. (2017). Savoring an upcoming experience affects ongoing and remembered consumption enjoyment. *Journal of Marketing*, *81*(3), 96–110. https://doi.org/10.1509/jm.15.0267

Ekelund, U., Steene-Johannessen, J., Brown, W. J., Fagerland, M. W., Owen, N., Powell, K. E., Bauman, A., & Lee, I. (2016). Does physical activity attenuate, or even eliminate, the detrimental association of sitting time with mortality? A harmonized meta-analysis of data from more than 1 million men and women. *Lancet*, *388*(1), 1302–1310. https://doi.org/10.1016/S0140-6736(16)30370-1

Ferster, C. B. (1973). A functional analysis of depression. *American Psychologist, 28*(10), 857. https://doi.org/10.1037/h0035605

Fong, E. H., Ficklin, S., & Lee, H. Y. (2017). Increasing cultural understanding and diversity in applied behavior analysis. *Behavior Analysis: Research and Practice, 17*(2), 103–113. http://dx.doi.org/10.1037/bar0000076

Gilovich, T., Kumar, A., & Jampol, L. (2015). A wonderful life: Experiential consumption and the pursuit of happiness. *Journal of Consumer Psychology, 25*(1), 152–165. https://doi.org/10.1016/j.jcps.2014.08.004

Green, N., & Dallery, J. (2019). Evaluating the effectiveness of education, feedback, & task clarification to increase workplace physical activity. *Journal of Organizational Behavior Management, 39*(3–4), 237–246. https://doi.org/10.1080/01608061.2019.1632239

Guarino, C. M., & Borden, V. M. (2017). Faculty service loads and gender: Are women taking care of the academic family? *Research in Higher Education, 58*(6), 672–694. https://doi.org/10.1007/s11162-017-9454-2

Holder, M. D., Coleman, B., & Sehn, Z. L. (2009). The contribution of active and passive leisure to children's well-being. *Journal of Health Psychology, 14*(3), 378–386. https://DOI:10.1177/1359105308101676

Jessel, J., Hanley, G. P., & Ghaemmghami, M. (2016). A translational evaluation of transitions. *Journal of Applied Behavior Analysis, 49*, 359–376. https://doi.org/10.1002/jaba.283

Kamphorst, B. A., Nauts, S., De Ridder, D. T., & Anderson, J. H. (2018). Too depleted to turn in: The relevance of end-of-the-day resource depletion for reducing bedtime procrastination. *Frontiers in Psychology, 9*, 252. https://doi.org/10.3389/fpsyg.2018.00252

Kanter, J. W., Manos, R. C., Bowe, W. M., Baruch, D. E., Busch, A. M., & Rusch, L. C. (2010). What is behavioral activation? A review of the empirical literature. *Clinical Psychology Review, 30*(6), 608–620. https://doi.org/10.1016/j.cpr.2010.04.001

Klatt, K. P., & Morris, E. K. (2001). The Premack principle, response deprivation, and establishing operations. *The Behavior Analyst, 24*(2), 173–180. https://doi.org/10.1007/BF03392028

Kumar, A., Killingsworth, M. A., & Gilovich, T. (2020). Spending on doing promotes more moment-to-moment happiness than spending on having. *Journal of Experimental Social Psychology, 88*, 103971. https://doi.org/10.1016/j.jesp.2020.103971

Kuykendall, L., Zhu, Z., & Craig, L. (2020). How work constrains leisure: New ideas and directions for interdisciplinary research. *Journal of Leisure Research, 51*(5), 635–642. https://DOI:10.1080/00222216.2020.1807841.

Langford, J. S., Pitts, R. C., & Hughes, C. E. (2019). Assessing functions of stimuli associated with rich-to-lean transitions using a choice procedure. *Journal of the Experimental Analysis of Behavior, 112*(1), 97–110. https://doi.org/10.1002/jeab.540

Lee, D. L., Belfiore, P. J., Scheeler, M. C., Hua, Y., & Smith, R. (2004). Behavioral momentum in academics: Using embedded high-p sequences to increase academic productivity. *Psychology in the Schools, 41*(7), 789–801. https://doi.org/10.1002/pits.20014

Leisure Studies. (2021). *Aims and scope*. www.tandfonline.com/action/journalInformation?show=aimsScope&journalCode=rlst20

Leiter, M. P., & Maslach, C. (2003). Areas of worklife: A structured approach to organizational predictors of job burnout. In *Emotional and physiological processes and positive intervention strategies*. Emerald Group Publishing Limited. doi:10.1080/11745398.2019.1652661

Lipschultz, J., & Wilder, D. A. (2017). Recent research on the high-probability instructional sequence: A brief review. *Journal of Applied Behavior Analysis, 50*(2), 424–428. https://doi.org/10.1002/jaba.378

Marmot, M. G., Rose, G., Shipley, M., & Hamilton, P. J. (1978). Employment grade and coronary heart disease in British civil servants. *Journal of Epidemiology & Community Health, 32*(4), 244–249. doi:10.1136/jech.32.4.244

Marmot, M. G., Stansfeld, S., Patel, C., North, F., Head, J., White, I., Brunner, E., Feeney, A., & Smith, G. D. (1991). Health inequalities among British civil servants: the Whitehall II study. *The Lancet, 337*(8754), 1387–1393. https://doi.org/10.1016/0140-6736(91)93068-K

Pandey, A., Salahuddin, U., Garg, A., Ayers, C., Kulinski, J., Anand, V., Mayo, H., Kumbhani, D. J., de Lemos, J., & Berry, J. D. (2016). Continuous dose-response association between sedentary time and risk for cardiovascular disease: A meta-analysis. *JAMA Cardiology, 1*(5), 575–583. doi:10.1001/jamacardio.2016.1567

Perone, M., & Courtney, K. (1992). Fixed-ratio pausing: Joint effects of past reinforcer magnitude and stimuli correlated with upcoming magnitude. *Journal of the Experimental Analysis of Behavior, 57*(1), 33–46. https://doi.org/10.1901/jeab.1992.57-33

Perrin, C. J., Miller, N., Haberlin, A. T., Ivy, J. W., Meindl, J. N., & Neef, N. A. (2011). Measuring and reducing college students' procrastination. *Journal of Applied Behavior Analysis, 44*(3), 463–474. https://doi.org/10.1901/jaba.2011.44-463

Petty, L., & Trussell, D. E. (2019). Leisure self-care, health and well-being in women's lives. *Annals of Leisure Research*, 1–12. https://doi.org/10.1080/11745398.2019.1652661

Premack, D. (1959). Toward empirical behavior laws: I. Positive reinforcement. *Psychological Review, 66*(4), 219–233. https://doi.org/10.1037/h0040891

Rachlin, H., & Green, L. (1972). Commitment, choice and self-control 1. *Journal of the Experimental Analysis of Behavior, 17*(1), 15–22. https://doi.org/10.1901/jeab.1972.17-15

Retzlaff, B. J., Parthum, E. T., Pitts, R. C., & Hughes, C. E. (2017). Escape from rich-to-lean transitions: Stimulus change and timeout. *Journal of the Experimental Analysis of Behavior, 107*(1), 65–84. https://doi.org/10.1002/jeab.236

Rung, J. M., & Epstein, L. H. (2020). Translating episodic future thinking manipulations for clinical use: Development of a clinical control. *PLoS One, 15*(8). https://doi.org/10.1371/journal.pone.0237435

Sabagh, Z., Hall, N. C., & Saroyan, A. (2018). Antecedents, correlates and consequences of faculty burnout. *Educational Research, 60*(2), 131–156. https://DOI:10.1080/00131881.2018.1461573

Slowiak, J. M., & DeLongchamp, A. C. (2021). Self-care strategies and job-crafting practices among behavior analysts: Do they predict perceptions of work-life balance, work engagement, and burnout? *Behavior Analysis in Practice.* https://doi.org/10.1007/s40617-021-00570-y

Son, J. S., & Chen, C. C. (2018). Does using a smartphone for work purposes "ruin" your leisure? Examining the role of smartphone use in work–leisure conflict and life satisfaction. *Journal of Leisure Research, 49*(3–5), 236–257. doi:10.1080/00222216.2018.1534074

Surowiecki, J. (2014). "The Cult Of Overwork." *The New Yorker, 89*(46), 23. Gale Literature Resource Center, link.gale.com/apps/doc/A357473899/LitRC?u=nclivewilm&sid=googleScholar&xid=a2dec638. Accessed 6 Feb. 2023.

Timberlake, W., & Allison, J. (1974). Response deprivation: An empirical approach to instrumental performance. *Psychological Review, 81*(2), 146–164. https://doi.org/10.1037/h0036101

Tonietto, G. N., & Malkoc, S. A. (2016). The calendar mindset: Scheduling takes the fun out and puts the work in. *Journal of Marketing Research, 53*(6), 922–936. https://doi.org/10.1509/jmr.14.0591

U.S. Department of Health and Human Services. (2018). *Physical activity guidelines for Americans* (2nd ed.). U.S. Department of Health and Human Services. https://health.gov/sites/default/files/2019-09/Physical_Activity_Guidelines_2nd_edition.pdf

UN General Assembly. (1948). *"Universal declaration of human rights" (217 [III] A).* www.un.org/en/about-us/universal-declaration-of-human-rights

Von Bergen, C. W., & Bressler, M. S. (2019). Work, non-work boundaries and the right to disconnect. *The Journal of Applied Business and Economics, 21*(2), 51–69. https://doi.org/10.33423/jabe.v21i1.1454

Williams, D. C., Saunders, K. J., & Perone, M. (2011). Extended pausing by humans on multiple fixed-ratio schedules with varied reinforcer magnitude and response requirements. *Journal of the Experimental Analysis of Behavior, 95*(2), 203–220. https://doi.org/10.1901/jeab.2011.95-203

Wolff, M. B., O'Connor, P. J., Wilson, M. G., & Gay, J. L. (2021). Associations between occupational and leisure-time physical activity with employee stress, burnout and well-being among healthcare industry workers. *American Journal of Health Promotion, 35*(7), 957–965. https://doi.org/10.1177/08901171211011372

World Travel & Tourism Council. (2021, June). *Travel & tourism economic impact 2021: Global economic impact & trends 2021.* https://wttc.org/Portals/0/Documents/Reports/2021/Global%20Economic%20Impact%20and%20Trends%202021.pdf?ver=2021-07-01-114957-177

Yamashita, T., Bardo, A. R., & Liu, D. (2019). Experienced subjective well-being during physically active and passive leisure time activities among adults aged 65 years and older. *The Gerontologist, 59*(4), 718–726. https://doi.org/10.1093/geront/gny106

Part III

Thriving

16 Making Something out of Nothing or Very Little

A Tale of How to Plant Seeds of Behavior Analysis, How to Cultivate Them, and Enjoy Watching Them Grow and Multiply

Zuilma Gabriela Sigurðardóttir

Making Something out of Nothing or Very Little: A Tale of How to Plant Seeds of Behavior Analysis, How to Cultivate Them, and Enjoy Watching Them Grow and Multiply

I have been in academia for 22 years. A colleague at the psychology department encouraged me to apply for an assistant professor position to teach behavior analysis in the first graduate program in psychology in Iceland. I was the only Ph.D.-level behavior analyst available at that time who had clinical experience. The antecedent to my academic job was seven years of practice as a behavior analyst in human services in Iceland (disguised as a psychologist) and two years abroad while receiving supervision and training, five years of part-time teaching miscellaneous courses at the University of Iceland in three different departments, and nine years of studies in two countries, Iceland and the United States. In 2004 I was promoted to associate professor and in 2018 to full professor.

My years in academia have given me countless opportunities to reach my goals, in particular to establish and disseminate behavior analysis. They have also given me the flexibility I needed to rear and educate my two children and function in my many life roles (e.g., mother, daughter, friend, spouse) despite the enormous workload (also see Chapters 6, 10, and 19). Academic demands have shaped me professionally and personally as no other occupation did. However, the personal contacts, the reputation of my work in the field, and the socio-cultural insights I acquired during my years of practice outside of academia facilitated and opened the door to so many of my academic projects. It is my conviction that this interplay between academic work and practice has also been key for the dissemination of the science of behavior analysis in this country. Iceland's population only counts approximately 365,000 inhabitants. One thing that happens in such a small society is that for better or for worse, words travel fast, with or without social media. I will therefore tell the tale of the events in both arenas, i.e., in academia and clinical practice, that have impacted my career in behavior analysis in this very small but very modern and fast-paced society.

Before I began a career in academia I was able to plant seeds of behavior analysis in various contexts, in one way or another. However, there were practical and societal limitations to the impact I could have during my years of clinical practice. I did not see that until later. I was able to influence colleagues and administrators, sometimes the public, but always locally, temporarily, depending on my status and the status of my colleagues within an organization, and even on the political climate in the country. Entering academia opened the possibility for long-term, more stable, and general dissemination of behavior analysis. The seeds I planted during clinical practice flourished more after I entered academia and I was able to continue cultivating them resulting in their diffusion and multiplication beyond my horizon.

DOI: 10.4324/9781003216773-20

I will start my tale in the beginning, in academia, when I was a student and how I became first a radical behaviorist and later a behavior analyst who practiced and ended up in academia, where the mission of establishing behavior analysis in Iceland really took off.

The Importance of Behaviorism and a Strong Scientific Base

During my undergraduate years at the University of Iceland in the 1980s, I had to read extensively. Books and articles were my sources and inspiration long before the times of the internet, PowerPoint slides, social media, YouTube videos, podcasts, and other resources that summarize main points neatly. Texts were in English and they were often heavy; it sometimes felt like I was trying to find my way out of a large forest with foggy areas. I first became aware of applied behavior analysis in an elective course on rehabilitation during my second year. The "Behavior Principles" (Ferster et al., 1975) that I had learned in my first year and found so unattractive acquired significance. The feeling that I wanted to head in that direction began to grow. However, what really convinced me of that was reading *About Behaviorism* (Skinner, 1976) one term later, in a required course on personality psychology. In addition, I read various criticisms and replies to criticisms of radical behaviorism, and other "-isms" in psychology with emphasis on logical analysis. I read Skinner's book three times over the course of a few weeks. That was the point of no return for me; I became a radical behaviorist. During my third year I became a fan of Murray Sidman, when I read his *Tactics of Scientific Research* (1960) in an elective course. I found that this book gave me such a valuable perspective not offered in any of my methodology and (mainly) statistics and advanced statistics courses. Reading Sidman's book was an eye-opening experience that shifted my perspective on what kind of research methods were most valuable in the study of human behavior and why. His book taught me what a behavior analyst should do.

When I completed my first academic degree, I knew that nothing in psychology made as much sense as radical behaviorism and single-subject experimental methodology. I wanted to learn how to apply behavior principles to clinical problems, evaluate my interventions with each future client, and, when unsuccessful, try to find the reason until I would find a way to solve the client's problem and that way learn more about the functions of the behavior at hand. I was immensely excited when I discovered behavior analysis master's programs in the United States (also see Chapter 1). I am thankful to the Icelandic Government Student Loan Fund and to the Behavior Analysis & Therapy Program of Southern Illinois University-Carbondale (SIUC) for allowing me to earn a master's degree in behavior analysis before the decade ended.

Having a good understanding of science, radical behaviorism, single-subject experimental methodology, critical thinking about issues in psychology, -isms, and debates did help me enormously during my master's studies. The strong pro-science orientation and basis I was given in my undergraduate studies made everything fit smoothly. This taught me the importance of a strong undergraduate degree with a scientific emphasis that teaches how to discriminate science from pseudoscience and non-science, to think critically and know the arguments for and against an issue or idea, especially logical analysis, to be a skeptic until logic or sufficient data convinces me, and to have the basis for evaluating data. Books, articles, hands-on projects, and occasional feedback from teachers and fellow students during ardent discussions were my sources and motivators. I also learned to appreciate the importance of offering courses on behavior analysis to undergraduates.

The Importance of Knowledgeable and Good Teachers and Excellent Mentors

During my masters studies I had superb teachers and models who shaped my behavior in so many important and valuable ways (also see Chapters 5 and 6). It was not an easy task to move to the United States with a five-year-old child, overcome an insect phobia with constant exposure, learn new ways to relate to people in English, and assimilate to a new culture and a new climate. My first year was extremely stressful but I learned so much, adapted, and changed. I was trained for two years as a therapist to families under supervision due to child abuse and neglect. The training program was Project 12-Ways, an eco-behavioral approach to child abuse and neglect (Lutzker et al., 1982; Lutzker & Rice, 1984; Lutzker et al., 1984). Older and more experienced students trained me on the job, and later I did the same with younger students. Weekly, many-hours long, team meetings with a Project 12-Ways Clinical Supervisor, almost throughout the whole two years, was a valuable shaping experience. What I learned in this eco-behavioral treatment program has stayed with me till the present day. Moreover, in my many classes at SIUC, in practica, and internship I became familiar with behavior analysis in several contexts, e.g., behavioral medicine (thanks to Dr. Roger Poppen), head-injury rehabilitation, and, what became my choice for my thesis and PhD research, i.e., stimulus equivalence (Dr. Gina Green became my mentor in this field). I also became familiar with applied behavior analysis in other contexts through my fellow students' projects, theses, and professors' research, for example in developmental disabilities, prevention and treatment of sexual (criminal) behavior, community applications and Organizational Behavior Management (OBM), and HIV prevention.

Pro-seminars were offered regularly where invited lecturers from other universities who were pioneers in behavior analysis in various fields gave talks. Their presentations were informative; they were excellent models of professional and scientific behavior. The program coordinator, Dr. Brandon Greene, or another faculty member, usually held potlucks for the faculty and students with the invited lecturer as the guest of honor. Students could have informal interactions with them on those occasions. I very much remember advice given to me by Dr. Iwata, Dr. Sidman, and other pioneers of behavior analysis in such gatherings. This advice I followed later and it turned out to be very useful.

Last but not least were all the opportunities, support, and encouragement given to students to attend conferences and present posters about our program or our own research. In just my first term I attended two conferences, including a small BASIL (Behavior Analysis Society of Illinois) conference where Professor Rubin introduced me to B. F. Skinner. I disclosed to Dr. Skinner that I was going to establish behavior analysis in Iceland and I wholeheartedly meant it; he was surprised, smiled and wished me good luck (I can still hear him and see him saying this to me). At that time, there was very little behavior analysis in Europe but it was underway. As I was finishing my first year of graduate school, I attended my first Association for Behavior Analysis-International (ABAI) conference. I consider myself fortunate enough to not only get to see, observe, listen to, and learn from B. F. Skinner directly, but also from so many other pioneers of behavior analysis and even interact informally with some of them. I remember how overwhelmed I felt after attending each conference; I was impressed by everything and everyone.

All these experiences shaped me, gave me new perspectives, new rules to follow, new knowledge, lots of new skills, and showed me that with collective effort the world could be saved with behavior analysis, slowly but steadily, one step at a time. I developed a strong sense of belonging to a professional group and established long-term bonds with fellow students that turned out to be stronger and deeper than I ever imagined then, as life showed me later.

The last graduate training years were especially influential. In my last year at SIUC, I ran the stimulus equivalence lab for Dr. Gina Green and did more experiments and taught other students to use the equipment and software. Gina and I then went to Boston. I was accepted into the PhD program at Northeastern University with Dr. Harry Mackay, and Gina went to do exciting research at the E. K. Shriver Center. I left SIUC well equipped and prepared to continue to learn more about the experimental analysis of human behavior, or more specifically stimulus control and stimulus equivalence. During my three years at Northeastern University, I was trained to do research by some of the best scientists in the area of stimulus equivalence. Their research inspired me to ask new research questions. At Northeastern, I also learned to teach and grade. The PhD program was in experimental psychology. Having fellow students and friends in various areas of experimental psychology and having to take courses in those areas made me relate my research area to and analyze it from many different perspectives, e.g., social psychology, cognitive psychology, psycholinguistics, developmental psychology, etc. I had to find ways to explain the value of my research to others, and build "bridges" between our fields of study. I had excellent mentors who helped me do that. I searched and discovered a vast literature that related to my research, both in behavior analysis and in other fields that taught me the similarities and differences between my field of research and others.

Those were indeed learning years that widened my horizon but also gave me even more depth in behavior analysis. I was so fortunate to get to know Murray and Rita Sidman during my years in Boston; they became my family. I enjoyed their support, encouragement, guidance, and company. I always had a home in their home, even after I returned to Iceland. In Boston, I established lifelong friendships that I still enjoy both with my colleagues and mentors. I have often been able to turn to these friends and colleagues for advice, help, and support.

The Importance of Having Vision and Grabbing Opportunities

Back in Iceland. Mission Begins

I headed back home to Iceland after I finished my PhD; I had a mission to accomplish. I had just turned 30 years old. There was no job waiting for me. I decided to grab anything that would come along just to be able to make a living with my son. Salaries were absurdly low and it felt like a puzzle to find a way to make a living here. I soon became licenced to practice as a psychologist in Iceland. I ended up having two part-time jobs, one as a counselor for the Women's Shelter in Reykjavík where a preschool teacher was setting up support services and shelter for child victims of family violence. A few months after I became a contractor for the Shelter; a political activist administrator asked me to write scientifically about family violence, specifically on the battering of women. The aim was to publish an article in the biggest newspaper in the nation to increase awareness of this problem. This was to commemorate the ten-year anniversary of the Women's Shelter. I gladly wrote articles for the public, published on three consecutive weekends. They received a lot of attention. Soon I was giving interviews to magazines, and the national radio station invited me on numerous occasions.

I welcomed and seized any opportunity to inform and educate the public. At that time there were almost no PhD-level practicing clinicians in Iceland. I approached each topic discussed from a scientific perspective; that was unusual at that time. I was clearly bringing something new to this society and a lot of people were curious, noticing, and listening. Soon I learned, to my surprise, that my newspaper articles were being used in courses on family violence at the university. Two years later, I advocated for the treatment of perpetrators of family violence. Even though my work in the Women's Shelter did not offer me a lot of opportunities to engage in behavior analysis, it did offer me the opportunity to disseminate research and to educate whoever would listen and embrace the importance of practice and policy built on scientific research. This was a novelty.

My other part-time job had turned to full time soon afterward. I worked at the Regional office for the affairs of the disabled in the capital city, Reykjavík. There were eight such regional offices in the country, all state-run. The one in the capital was a model to the rest of them because it was the largest. I had many responsibilities there. Initially, I was hired to be the director of a group home in preparation for five adults with developmental disabilities, including three young adults with Down syndrome. I soon learned that the system of services placed a large emphasis on financial matters and their supervision but none at all on quality of services. I had to rationalize every expense and keep tabs on them. However, nobody asked how I was going to train the staff, how I planned to create a home environment for the residents, how I would deal with behavior problems or other kinds of challenges, etc. My superiors assumed that I knew what I was doing but nobody assessed if that was correct. I was a bit shocked but as time passed I realized that this was true for many human services, even in education. I realized that there was a lot of room for change and I was going to do my best to occasion change.

The director of the Regional office turned my half-time job into a full-time job within three months of hiring me as some problems with the government office responsible for building the group home surged. The reasons for increasing my work time were that I provided reinforcers to the director, as Dr. Iwata had suggested to me during a short conversation at a pot-luck many years earlier in Carbondale, i.e., I solved the director's problems. The director said that she needed me at the main office, not as the director of the group home because I had solved the problems that surged so effectively. We found people to take over the group home project. I settled into this new position. My main responsibility was to develop services for our clients who chose independent living arrangements instead of a group home living arrangement. A law had recently been passed that allowed for provision of such services but there was no national model to follow as a basis. Two staff members had started something; progress had been slow and not systematic. My experience of the organization of Project 12-Ways came in handy in solving this task. I set up the service system in a similar way as Project 12-Ways was organized with regard to teams servicing specific areas, weekly service time, goal setting for each client, regular data collection for evaluation of services and skill acquisition of the clients, regular updating of service goals, regular documentation of services provided, and weekly meetings for supervision and feedback to staff and updates of matters. I also requested development of new services in society in collaboration with banks, Community Service Centers that provided home nursing, home makers, and aids for clients' leisure activities.

In the next four years the number of clients serviced and able to live independently regardless of disability went from five to 50. The staff efficiency, their skills, and the service model raised many eyebrows during conferences and meetings. I organized the staff of the independent living services to give a presentation at a conference offered by the government on efficiency and quality in human services. The service model was noted and adopted to some extent by many other regional offices; some asked for guidance, others did not. My responsibilities grew steadily at the regional office the four years I worked there. Parallel to developing independent living services, I became a consultant to directors of group homes with regard to behavior problems of both staff and residents. I visited the group homes regularly and worked with all the staff in each one. Some directors of group homes were very skeptical and never sought my services. I thought that the best way to handle this was to do my job; sometimes actions speak louder than words. The majority did at some point seek my help and I always reinforced such behavior.

I was also a counselor to parents of our clients, usually due to behavior or interaction problems—a behavior therapist for some clients, and director of employee education. I was disseminating behavior analysis in one way or the other, throughout my work. In other words, I was applying it, showing it, talking about it, explaining it, educating about misconceptions of it, teaching parents and staff to use procedures and techniques, observing them, and following them up. Sometimes I did not mention behavior analysis, I just described what I did or needed to be done and reinforced others for following through, all depending on the audience.

Flirting with Academia

Two years into my two aforementioned jobs and thus two years after moving back home, I was asked to teach at the University of Iceland. First I was asked to teach an elective undergraduate course in psychology on methods in applied behavior analysis. The temporary teacher of that course, a graduate of West Virginia University and associate professor of methodology, who was a behavior analyst, asked me to teach with him. We had seven students in our class, five of them ended up some years later in behavior analysis, two of them are very recognized scientists in behavior analysis today and live in the United States, three others from that student group practice in Iceland in various areas, two of them also went to the United States to study and get their degrees. My colleague asked me to take over the course and I accepted gladly. It had been taught every two years and continued at that pace until the psychology department chair requested that I teach it yearly; I am still responsible for the teaching of that course.

After I started teaching this course, I grabbed the opportunity to arrange meetings with various behavior analysts that I knew were on their way to Iceland. I invited students to meet with them at the university and hear about studies in behavior analysis, sometimes they also gave presentations about their research to the psychology department. I began doing this very systematically in 1996. Those meetings motivated many psychology students to seek more information about studies in behavior analysis, and many went all the way and are behavior analysts today. My colleagues in the department of psychology noticed this and were very fond of what I was doing. Many behavior analysts have visited Iceland in the last decades and most of them have met with my students or given talks at my department. That has been delightful and influential.

The university asked me to teach other courses. The teacher of a course in Education and Work Counseling had to suddenly go on sick leave so I was asked to jump in. I had less than a week to prepare to teach the book by Alberto and Troutman (1990), *Applied Behavior Analysis for Teachers* (third edition). I taught that course yearly for the next seven years. Many of the students in that course were special education teachers in elementary schools, others were regular elementary school teachers, and some had a bachelor's degree in psychology. At some point soon thereafter, the then-existing teachers college contacted me to teach the same course to master's students in special education and in their summer re-education program for teachers. This was one more opportunity given to me to spread the word about behavior analysis. I could always find time even if it meant sacrificing time with my family and friends; I was on the mission of disseminating and establishing behavior analysis in Iceland. I was sure it would pay off in the long run to grab opportunities that came along, and it did.

A Small, Private Practice

Around the time that I started teaching miscellaneous courses at the University of Iceland, I also established a small private practice. I saw clients on Saturdays. My target group was men who abused women. A journalist found out about my treatment, interviewed a client of mine and shortly after, this journalist invited us to appear in a television program about family violence: prevention and remedies. That turned out to be a very influential television broadcast. Relatively shortly after that show, the government of Iceland, in collaboration with the Red Cross, decided to establish a treatment center for male batterers. This is an example of the changes that can take place with systematic education of the public, of officials, and politicians. The effects are not necessarily noticeable immediately after one educates, the effects are cumulative with enough repetition and it takes time for things to develop after exposure to facts and discussions that heat things up slowly but to the point of boiling and changing.

Because I had a private practice, psychologists working in the area of cognitive behavior therapy were interested in getting me to join them in their efforts to establish a strong group of cognitive behavior therapists. I attended a few meetings and was asked to give a presentation. Thereafter, they invited me to teach about behavioral assessment and single-case experimental methodology as part of the two-year reeducation course in cognitive behavior therapy. I taught every two years and my course was rated very practical.

I still have a small private practice with a very narrow clientele group. The 27 years of this practice have made it possible for me to disseminate behavior analysis in many ways. In addition to providing services for family violence, I have given presentations and courses for teachers, parents, and a myriad of professions.

A New Oasis Discovered

After working for almost four years in the Regional Office, teaching part time at the university for two years, and being involved in family violence in various ways, the winds of change spread over Iceland. Due to Iceland joining the European Economic Area, which is affected by the European Union laws and regulations, the political climate also began changing. Many structural changes were being prepared in this society and took place during that time. One of them was the transfer of various services from the state to the communities, including those for the disabled population. These changes took about ten to 12 years but preparations began early, including in Reykjavík. The director of social welfare services in Reykjavík warned us psychologists at the Regional Office that she would not hire any psychologists when the transfer of services would take place. This pushed me to regretfully look for employment elsewhere. However, I had learned how the system in the disability sector worked, what services were provided and what was lacking, who were the key people making decisions about service provisions in the ministry of social welfare, how the special interest groups of the disabled affected the services provided, what groups of people with disabilities were getting what services, and the reasons for that. This was all important information and a valuable experience.

After I told my colleagues at the university that I was looking for a new position and attending some job interviews, I received a phone call which led me to apply for a position as head of the psychology department of the new Reykjavík Education Center. This new service center for all elementary schools in Reykjavík (for children of the ages six to sixteen) provided various services to the schools. These services had been provided by the state in several different offices but, due to the political climate of the time, including new laws, the services were transferred to the communities. In Reykjavík, the new service center was to provide all the services requested by the schools, including psychological services. Psychological services had been provided to the schools since 1960, mainly psychological testing for students who fell behind in their studies and psychological reports to be used by teachers in special education planning or referrals for further psychological testing and evaluation of the student.

Unfortunately, throughout the years, many psychologists working in the school system (there is still no requirement in Iceland to have a degree in school or educational psychology to do so) went beyond their assigned duties. They mostly met with the students and their parents. Some provided children with (psychodynamic) play therapy in their offices, others provided therapy to the students' parents, if they felt that the problem of the child was due to parental negligence (some always did). Many psychologists never worked directly with the schools that they were supposed to serve. I was skeptical about applying for the job because I had never seen myself working in the school system. I had taught a course twice on applied behavior analysis for teachers and read literature on the subject, so I was familiar with the context but mostly from books and articles. I decided, after much encouragement, to apply for the position and see what would happen. I was open to trying something new (also see Chapter 13). The director of the Education Center and politicians in the Education council of the City of Reykjavík called for an interview.

A three-party political coalition to the left from the middle ruled the capital city during those years. They asked me questions about my ideas and vision for services to the schools and I answered as a behavior analyst. They hired me. All of a sudden, I had a new job where I would have to supervise the work of 12 psychologists trained in a psychoanalytic or humanistic tradition. Some of them had worked in the field for many years and believed they had all the answers. Some had applied for my position and were frustrated and disappointed to not get it as many others were. I was a female they did not know, the youngest among them, a behaviorist and behavior analyst, a PhD (which was very rare), and I had not worked in elementary schools before. This was a recipe for conflict and disaster (see also Chapter 21).

Had it not been for the director of the Education Center, a woman who supported me in every way, and for conversations with two behavior analysts, I would not have survived what followed in the next ten months. I had to deal with my staff's constant distrust towards all officials in the new Education Center, partly due to moving the new Center to another building which meant that there was a little chaos as is typical when moving. I met constant resistance to change, opposition to and ridicule of all my ideas and plans for new policies. They justified their behavior in light of their prior experience as psychologists in the school system. Small groups teamed up against me, belittling me during meetings, ignoring me otherwise, complaining and lying about me to the psychological association, and more. There were all kinds of strange stories being told about me. Even school principals were taking part, especially those that did not like the new coalition government of the city and were right wing political party supporters. It was a very messy situation for so many reasons. I was doing my best, I was cordial, I tried to build rapport, I listened to their complaints, I encouraged them to be patient, explained my vision and the director's vision for how services to the schools should be in accordance with the new education act. The work conditions and atmosphere led nowhere. I had to breathe deeply often and try to reinforce appropriate behavior when I was lucky enough to witness it.

After a month in the job I was giving up. A behavior analyst called me many times per week to allow me to vent and encouraged me to not give up. One day I went to meet with my colleague, a professor in methodology and a behavior analyst. He asked me how I was doing in the new job and I described to him how bad the situation had been in the last weeks and started crying. Then he said to me: "Gabriela, you know what is happening, don't you?" I asked back, "What do you mean?" He responded, "All behavior you have described to me seems to me like an extinction burst, they are not getting away with all they have gotten away with throughout the years, they don't have the skills to do what the new law is demanding of them and many did not get the job they wanted." Boy! Was that an eye-opener!! I realized he was absolutely correct. At that moment I stopped suffering, I saw the whole situation in a completely different light and all of a sudden I knew what to do. I felt saved.

I went back to work that day, almost completely emotionally distanced from the situation and I started a differential reinforcement of other behaviors (DRO) procedure for the whole group and for each individual. I prompted them to celebrate when something positive happened that day, for example when the copy machine became available. I also set them a limit: I said, "Do not complain again until the next day for the next thing that needs to be fixed, let us just enjoy the positive event of today for the rest of the day." I gave more clear commands and requests, I praised appropriately extra often, I ignored complaints and criticism and presented my plans and rationale for them, listened to their comments and incorporated changes if their comments or suggestions made sense. I started having team meetings as I had announced. I advised the teams on how to tackle problems according to new policies. My policy was to teach and aid the schools to deal with behavior problems themselves, with guidance and support from the professionals, instead of solely referring children for diagnosis and hoping that the psychologists would fix the problem in their office or would find another placement for them, somewhere far away. Many psychologists started adapting to the new rules and my weekly management routine. Some settled slowly in the next three to four months. Things started to work out. A few of them resigned. One psychologist got ill and died very soon after her diagnosis. These changes led to hiring new psychologists on new terms; they either supported me or were at least neutral and did not take part in occasional extinction bursts. After less than one year on the job, I was accepted by the group. The extinction bursts were over, and people seemed calm and content. I had taken over the most difficult cases in the schools of Reykjavík.

I had a caseload of approximately 25 very heavy cases, including clients with autism or a long history of behavior problems. This gave me an opportunity to demonstrate my skills to the schools to solve problems in collaboration with them, the parents, and the students themselves. Functional assessments, a behavioral consultation model for services, effective behavioral contracts, and intervention programs that did not end until well after the problems were solved were all new experiences for the teachers and principals. Most of them loved the change and asked for more. I was so fortunate to be able to invite Drs. Gina Green and Lynn Brennan to Iceland to do presentations for the staff of the schools who were servicing children with autism and other disabilities. It made such a big difference for me to have specialists to whom I could turn and who were ready to support me and my mission, with all their skills, knowledge, and valuable experience. For this, I am still grateful.

I offered a course for the schools that became very popular very soon. I taught teachers and principals some basics on how to deal with behavior problems in the classroom. The course was two days before schools started in the fall, one half day during the following three months and one day at the end of the course. It included lectures, discussions, and a hands-on project over the time of the course, and a final day with presentations of their projects. This course became very acclaimed and soon I was being asked by school principals in other communities surrounding Reykjavík to teach the course in their schools. I found a way to do that under the hat of my private practice. These courses led to one other course activity—parenting courses. I had seen the SOS-Help for Parents course by Lynn Clark (Clark, 1996) advertised in the ABAI newsletter. I was familiar with other behavior-management books from my Project 12-Ways years. We used Wesley Becker's (1971) *Parents are Teachers*. In 1997, I embarked on the translation of the SOS-Help for Parents course materials with a private company led by a psychologist who was my acquaintance. She contacted Lynn Clark, the author, and we established a contract with him to translate all course materials to Icelandic with the goal to start the first course for parents on behavior management in this society.

I began teaching the courses to parents, but soon, elementary school teachers, preschool teachers, and other staff of schools became a big part of the participants. Behavior management had never been available to them before. This was the first behavior-management course available in Iceland (also see Chapter 19). To me, that was almost incredible.

Throughout the years, teachers were big consumers of these courses, as much as or more than parents. I always wanted materials that would be more appropriate for the school context. I found them later.

During the three years that I worked as the head of psychological services to elementary schools in Reykjavík, I came to realize that the schools were an oasis for behavior analysis. First, I realized that the school setting involves everybody, i.e., administrators, teachers, teacher aids, typically developing children, children with disabilities, children who excel academically, children (and adults) who lack social skills, children who fall academically behind their peers, children (and adults) who have other adaptation problems, their parents (including grandparents, step parents, foster parents), and siblings. I also realized how politics constantly affect the school system. All kinds of interest groups are trying to affect the system—teachers' unions, politicians, parent groups, professionals in education, minority groups, nutritionists, sports advocates, etc. Even international politicians' work, far away from any school, leads to international treaties that trigger a change in national policies that affect the school system and everybody in it. There is a lot of behavior of so many people taking place in the schools and the school system as a whole.

Obviously, schools are places where there is plenty to do for behavior analysts. I am glad to have discovered this sector because my research in academia has mainly taken place there for the last 22 years. The experience of working for the school system as a psychologist and administrator for three years certainly gave me a lot of material to work and focus on when I switched to academia, which is the place where I went next. Remarkably, when I left, the psychologists who had given me so much trouble when I was hired were devastated at the news of my application for the academic position many months before I left the Education Center. They clearly had learned to appreciate me and my work. They did not want me to leave them. Some approached me in the weeks that followed to apologize for their behavior during my first year of work, others came to express their emotions about me leaving. As my last day of work approached, many came with heartwarming gifts, others with best wishes for continuing collaboration. In my mind, I was not going very far and would continue working in the school system. However, in a different way, I knew I would miss "my psychologists," but I also knew that I was ready to return to doing research and to teaching. What I had not yet realized then was how much impact I could have on society by teaching and doing research.

Building Momentum for a Future Generation of Behavior Analysts in Iceland

During my practicing years as a clinician and administrator, there were a few students who had taken the classes I taught at the university or had been working with children with autism in preschools or elementary schools, many under my supervision while I was providing consultation, who decided to go for further studies in behavior analysis in the United States. They came to me for information, advice, and recommendation letters. I met with them, of course, and lighted their path. I was impressed every time somebody contacted me with this purpose, and I felt so proud that I had motivated them to enter the world of behavior analysis. After this development began, and I realized that these students usually came home to Iceland for the summer and Christmas vacations, I saw the opportunity to gather with them and with students at the University of Iceland who had shown interest in behavior analysis. I started organizing potlucks at my home twice per year to have all these students meet regularly, the ones already studying and those who were interested in further studies. They enjoyed meeting those who were already in the United States studying behavior analysis, learned from them, and received further encouragement to follow this path. At some point, an award ceremony began to recognize students who had been accepted to a behavior analysis program or who were about to leave to the United States to study. A custom-made T-shirt with an artist's caricature of B. F. Skinner and the text "Pioneer in behavior analysis" in Icelandic was the prize. I am told that students who witnessed these fun ceremonies during the twice-yearly pot-lucks at my house looked at these T-shirts as something desirable. These regular meetings were held from approximately 1998 to 2005, i.e., before and after I entered academia. They built momentum and the number of students applying for studies in behavior analysis in the United States grew steadily and rapidly during those years. In 2004, the Iceland-ABA (Ice-ABA) was founded. This led to these meetings fading out slowly as more formal meetings and other activities were offered by the association. The last of these meetings was held at my home in 2005.

During these years of motivating students to go for graduate studies in behavior analysis, I applied and was awarded the ABAI-International Development Grant in the year 2000. The grant was awarded so that I could prepare a website to provide more students with information about all the steps involved in moving to the United States to study behavior analysis. The student I hired to build the website later ended up in a master's program in behavior analysis. Sadly, the number of psychology students who went to the United States to study behavior analysis began to decrease after the attack on the Twin Towers of the World Trade Center in 2001—only four students went after that. They are all back in Iceland now, two of them have PhDs and BACB certification, the other two are also certified. However, in the last ten years, four students with an education background, whom I had never met, did go to study behavior analysis with an emphasis on acquiring certification. They are also back in Iceland and practice here. A few students have gone to study in Norway at Oslo Met; I also guided them to apply for studies with Dr. Erik Arntzen, my dear colleague and friend. Many found jobs after they got their master's degrees at Oslo Met and have settled down in Norway. Two are working towards their PhD, one of them is now teaching part time at the University of Iceland. One PhD, who graduated recently from Oslo Met, is back in Iceland and is now teaching behavior analysis here at University of Reykjavík (the private one). Many of these new behavior analysts are very active in the Ice-ABA association. It is no longer only me who is encouraging students to study behavior analysis, now there are new role models doing that. PhD behavior analysts teach in all three universities in Iceland, more than one in two universities. Clearly, motivating students systematically to study behavior analysis around the turn of the millennium paid off. Some worked with me in the school system, others did research with me, took my courses, attended meetings with visiting behavior analysts, or with students already studying in the USA.

The Importance of Joining Academia

When I returned to Iceland after my studies in the USA, I never thought I would end up in academia, I felt I did not want to lock myself in an ivory tower. I thought that what was necessary to establish behavior analysis in Iceland and disseminate our science was to serve as a role model, practice behavior analysis, and show good results. I also planned to write scientific articles based on my dissertation, but my main goal was not to work as a scientist. I wanted to make an impact on society on a large scale that would lead to behavior analysis being visible and salient in as many realms as possible. I did not realize in my early 30s how necessary and important academia was in reaching this goal. Fortunately, wiser people than myself knew this when I did not and they helped me and pushed me, probably because they thought that I was offering something worthwhile that this society needed.

My entrance to a full-time academic job was through part-time teaching. I enjoyed teaching very much as well as working with students. I felt I was really able to motivate them and I received a lot of positive feedback from them. Psychology studies at the University of Iceland, which is still the largest university in the country, had up to that point in time mainly been at the undergraduate level. The first graduate program in psychology began in 1999. That is when I was encouraged to apply for a position in what my colleagues called "behavior modification." As I have explained elsewhere (Roll-Pettersson et al., 2020), the psychology department had throughout the years emphasized the importance of behavior modification and evidence-based practice. This was also the emphasis in the new master's program. However, this emphasis was presented as pertaining mostly to work with children and individuals with disabilities, and with a particular set of tools, e.g., a token economy. Behavior analysis had not yet been taught as a scientific field of inquiry, so there was space to expand.

Only male professors taught in the psychology department and that had been a fact from the beginning. Two of them had been my professors during my undergraduate years. Shortly after I started working in academia, three new male teachers were hired. Hence, I was the only woman working with nine male colleagues. I was always treated well and I felt the support of most. They encouraged me and guided me despite the competition that I could feel. It was sometimes intimidating and uncomfortable, sometimes lonely, to teach in an all-male department. The change towards including a woman in the faculty was so radical that it was much celebrated by women in the faculty of Social Science, where the psychology department was situated at the time. My female colleagues in various departments within the faculty of Social Science stopped me in the halls and expressed how joyous they were with this shift in policy of the faculty of psychology. They could hardly believe that this change had at last taken place after 23 years. When I heard these comments, I was of course thankful and glad, but in my mind I was mainly happy for my position as a behavior analyst within the psychology department. I felt that the real progress was in that regard. Today, almost 22 years later, I can see that my hiring gave way to other women, although that took eight years. There were women teaching on a part-time basis for many years. After the second woman joined the faculty, many others followed. Today, female faculty staff has soared to 50%. Unfortunately, I am still the only behavior analyst in the faculty, but nobody knows what the future holds. Most growth has been, not surprisingly, in the area of clinical psychology, and all those colleagues emphasize cognitive behavior therapy. The competition with the statisticians, psychometricians, mostly group-design colleagues, e.g., the cognitive behavior therapists, social and developmental psychologists, and the neuro- and cognitive scientists can be demoralizing at times.

Shifting from Mainly Teaching to Doing Research and Teaching

In the beginning of my academic career, around the millennium, I had a very heavy course load. I enjoyed teaching and was still teaching three of the courses I had taught during my part-time teaching years. In addition, I had to teach two and a half new courses in the new master's program in psychology and took over the undergraduate course on behavior principles. The University of Iceland, at that time, did not place much emphasis on research and the research grants available in Iceland were small and few. The university was in its beginning stages of increasing its emphasis on research. The number of master's programs were increasing but doctoral programs were scarce. The number of students attending the university was around 6,000. There has been a complete change. Today, research is the number one preferred activity. The number of graduate students, including doctoral students, has increased enormously in all departments as well as the number of graduates. The number of students is over 16,000. Research grants have multiplied and the amount of support available for each funded research project has increased considerably. Teaching is still considered important, of course, but there are many more programmed reinforcers associated with research activities. The pressure to apply for grants and to publish increases every year. Demands have also been raised on applicants for academic positions in this regard.

Soon after I was hired full time, my colleagues encouraged me to give up the courses that I had taught when I taught on a part-time basis and to decrease my private practice activities. They encouraged me to instead engage in research. I took the advice, except I kept teaching the single-case experimental-methodology course. I soon applied for and received a grant to do research in stimulus equivalence. I was also doing demonstration research in applied behavior analysis with an increasing number of students. Undergraduates in psychology always have had to complete a research thesis to fulfill the requirements for a bachelor's degree. My supervision responsibilities of student research increased constantly after I became a full-time faculty member. I also had to supervise master's theses. For several years, I was the only faculty member who had many years' experience of clinical practice. Most of the research projects I offered were out in the field, mostly in schools but also in the National Hospital, and National Diagnostic Center. They were mainly interventions for behavior problems, or children with autism, or clients with other disabilities. I was still in contact with my colleagues in the area of services to the disabled and with colleagues in the school system, and they welcomed the students. Occasionally, students who were interested in other realms of behavior analysis, like OBM, safety, head-injury interventions, stimulus equivalence, behavioral economics, parent or staff training, reading or math problems, and interventions with children with autism, asked me to supervise their undergraduate research projects. I did because I considered it important to teach about behavior analysis in all these areas and beyond. It also kept me updated on the literature. More importantly, I saw their projects as demonstration research that had the goal of disseminating behavior analysis in Iceland. Some of the research has also been analytic. Many of these research projects have been published in international journals (e.g., Pétursdóttir & Sigurðardóttir, 2006; Sigurðardóttir & Sighvatsson, 2006; Sigurðardóttir & Sighvatsson, 2011; Valdimarsdóttir et al., 2010; Þorsteinsson & Sigurðardóttir, 2007). Others in Icelandic journals. As my research grew, I began involving students in specific research projects of mine for their theses. My research in stimulus equivalence unfortunately had to give in to research in applied behavior analysis, for which there was more demand. One of the reasons was that I was not well equipped—I did not have the necessary software for computerized experiments or resources to have one made for me, as research grants at that time were very small. I regret not having had the means to continue doing stimulus equivalence research and teach about it. However, the research I did in this area gave me such a strong basis in the area of stimulus control of behavior. I am still a big fan of research in the area.

One early development in my academic career was when the psychology department purchased the copyright of all the SOS-Help for Parents materials in Icelandic from the private company that had originally translated the materials and had worked with me to offer those parenting courses in collaboration with Lynn Clark, the author. The department also took over the contract with him. The idea behind this was to teach our graduate students to use this tool in their future work with parents. I developed a course for our graduate students that was compulsory for many years. I also organized courses for psychologists who wanted to become instructors. This step was a big step in disseminating behavior-management techniques in Iceland. Those who took the course and met the requirements were granted permission to offer the courses and become instructors. They had to adhere to the frame I developed for the course offerings. That worked very well. This development continued until 2010 and faded out slowly after that as a result of the bank crisis in 2008. Thousands of families benefitted. The financial depression that followed after the bank crisis ended in approximately 2016–2017. The SOS-Help for Parents course has had to compete with many other evidence-based behavior-management courses available to both parents and teachers. This I find a very pleasant new reality because when I began offering the course almost 20 years earlier, it was the first and only one available. During the golden years of the SOS-Help for Parents courses, after I entered academia, many students collected or analyzed available data in order to evaluate the impact of these parenting courses. Approximately ten theses were written and they all showed the courses to be a success.

One other development, related to behavior management, took place in 2003 and thereafter led to a six-year research project in the schools. A graduate of ours, who was working as a psychologist in the schools and had done her master's thesis with me, called me looking for advice on how to better serve the schools when it came to behavior problems. She felt the need for better tools to work with the schools as a whole. I put her in contact with a psychologist who had been offered participation in a summer course on School Wide Positive Behavior Support (SW-PBS) in the Oregon Social Learning Center. She was not going to go; therefore, my former student and a thesis student of mine at that time who could go to take the course in Oregon went. When they came back from that course, and with the support and guidance of colleagues at the University of Oregon, they began installing SW-PBS in schools in two communities, Reykjavík and Hafnarfjörður. The book *Best Behavior: Building Positive Behavior Support in Schools* (Sprague & Golly, 2004) was translated to Icelandic shortly after by a group of psychologists working in the schools. Three years later, I was able to convince a colleague in a third community, who had systematically held SOS-Help for Parents courses in the school system, to instead adopt a SW-PBS system in the schools. He then attended workshops and worked with the SW-PBS psychologists in Reykjavik to install SW-PBS in collaboration with me and them in his community. We began a research project in his community where my students and I measured the procedural integrity of the adoption and installment of a SW-PBS system in three elementary schools. We used direct observation of teachers' and students' behavior over a six-year period. A total of 38 undergraduate theses, three master's theses, and one research article were the result of that research project. It also resulted in a new research project where we looked at procedural integrity in preschools where SW-PBS was being adopted and installed, also with direct observation. Several more theses were written.

Other research of mine has been in the area of academic problems, i.e., reading and math. I started this research in 2004 when a student, who is today a behavior analyst in the US, wanted to try using Direct Instruction and precision teaching with a student in the seventh grade who was behind in math. When we saw the encouraging results I wanted to do more of this. So a few years later I started offering students the possibility of doing their thesis in this area. After approximately 50 children participated in various single-subject experimental studies in the schools over the course of a few years, both in reading and math, I applied for a research grant to do a group study. The aim was to assess the effects of Direct Instruction and precision teaching applied by trained teachers compared to the effects of teaching as usual. Unfortunately, most policymakers are still more familiar with group designs. This is the project of my doctoral student, who had also worked in this area for her master's thesis. Manuscripts are being written about the results of this funded group study.

During the preparation of that research project I contacted two SIU-Carbondale graduates because I knew of their research in Direct Instruction, i.e., Drs. Nancy Marchand-Martella and Ron Martella. We had seen each other at ABAI conferences and always chatted briefly. They turned out to be such unbelievable supporters of my research that I consider their contributions as a grant. They came to Iceland to train the elementary school teachers, meet with government officials to introduce research in the area, and to train my students. They have provided their personal support for this project over the last years. I never imagined that former fellow students could turn out to be so extremely supportive. They made all the difference. In addition, Dr. Kent Johnson and Morningside Academy provided a scholarship for two doctoral students for a one-week training in precision teaching at Morningside. That was an immense support also. This research project is the second doctoral research project in behavior analysis in Iceland that has been funded by Iceland's Research Center. The first research project ended in 2018 with the defense by the student who was already a behavior analyst with an MA from the University of North Texas. The PhD project was supervised by Dr. Shahla Ala'i-Rosales and myself. Our student looked at the effects of parent training via telehealth with children with autism in a rural setting in Iceland (Guðmundsdóttir, Ala'i-Rosales et al., 2019; Guðmundsdóttir, Sigurðardóttir et al., 2017). This doctoral defense was the first one, and the only one yet, in behavior analysis in Iceland; I expect many more in the future.

Last but not least, I want to mention a study I conducted with my students that has received sporadic attention from the media, and was funded by the University of Iceland several times and by an insurance company. It is in the area of safety. I wanted to increase toddlers' safety in supermarkets by changing the behavior of caretakers putting children at risk by placing them inside supermarket carts, not on the seat but inside the cart itself. The intervention was a total success. When I presented this study at an ABAI conference some years ago, a colleague encouraged me to publish the data in a non-behavioral journal. I followed his advice and the study was published in the journal *Safety Science* (Eiríksson & Sigurðardóttir, 2020). More is on the way.

Teaching About Functional Assessment to Future Psychologists

When I started teaching in the first psychology master's program in Iceland, I taught three courses that later became two. In the first fall term I taught a behavioral and functional assessment class with an introduction to single-case experimental methodology. This course is still taught and is compulsory for master's students in clinical psychology. In the second term I taught a course that focused on behavior analysis in the school system. I also taught half of the third course and there I concentrated on interventions for academic problems, emphasizing Direct Instruction and precision teaching. Later I changed the second-term course to include both behavior and academic problems. That course is still taught in clinical psychology. In addition to these two compulsory classes, students had to take the SOS-Help for Parents course. Moreover, some students did their internship in schools and worked on their thesis under my supervision; usually they did an experiment in applied behavior analysis. Many of my former students have gone on to work in schools and are able to apply what I taught them; they have been great supporters of my work. Some have gone to work in the pediatric unit of the National Hospital or in private clinics; others work with adults. Many apply the principles of behavior in their work and have become good colleagues. Some have kept in contact with me and I have supported their efforts in every way I have been able. A few of them have gone on to get PhDs abroad and have come back to Iceland to support the establishment and dissemination of behavior analysis. For that I am always grateful. In addition to students who have studied to become psychologists, I have taught and mentored a dozen larger research projects of master's students who have also ended up working in the school system and have skills in behavior analysis. Around 2006, the National Hospital began including the requirement to be familiar with applied behavior analysis when they advertised for psychologists.

From Psychology to Behavior Analysis

Psychologists working in schools are under great pressure from the school system to do psychological testing because that has been the foundation for provision of psychological services. I tried changing that process and those attitudes when I was in the school system. That part of psychological services for schools is unfortunately still strongly ingrained in the system. Sometimes, there have been signs that this may be changing. Only a few psychologists in the schools have made demands to get to spend more of their working time helping schools to self-help with behavior analysis. Psychologists working with adults mostly rely on cognitive behavior therapy. That is the golden standard. I have wanted to see people working within the realm of behavior analysis full time, not part time, and not only when possible or when they are allowed by their superiors. I often felt that my efforts in teaching behavior analysis in a psychology department were not resulting in creating the behavior analysts that I aimed for when I began teaching in the psychology department. Nevertheless, I must mention the fact that many psychologists have supported my research in schools throughout the years and their support has often been crucial. Obviously, my teaching in the psychology department has proved fruitful in opening doors.

In 2011 and 2012, a former student, Dr. Anna-Lind Pétursdóttir, and I began to plan a master's program in behavior analysis. She had recently become a member of the faculty of the School of Education (as we had planned for over a decade), with a PhD from the University of Minnesota in Special Education. We had worked closely for many years, both while she was practicing as a psychologist and after she became assistant professor. She had been my assistant in the school system when she only had a bachelor's degree in psychology. I pushed her to go for further studies in behavior analysis and get a PhD. She entered the master's program in psychology at the University of Iceland when it began. I became her teacher and later her thesis supervisor. We wanted the master's program to be in the education department but in collaboration with the psychology department. We acquired letters of support from different institutions and individuals, for example, the pediatric unit of the University/National Hospital, from the Director of Education of the City of Reykjavík, and from the National Diagnostic Center. Our first plan to establish a master's program in behavior analysis came to light two years later. Colleagues in the National Diagnostic Center, where early intensive behavioral interventions for children with autism and other developmental disabilities had been formally encouraged for at least one decade (and informally much longer), tried pressuring the School of Education to consider the possibility of a master's degree in behavior analysis. The Diagnostic Center had originally sent a request to the University of Iceland in 2010. They were following up their request in 2014, after a committee had evaluated the needs and ways to establish such a program, and how to make it happen (my colleague and I were in that committee). This committee's report (which I prepared) had been sent to the University in 2013. By coincidence and very luckily, Anna-Lind involved another colleague, a psychologist, also a part of the faculty staff in the School of Education, to be with us in meetings that were held in 2014 to discuss the request from the National Diagnostic Center.

Professors in education who were chairs of departments, and the dean of the School of Education attended those meetings. This psychologist colleague has strong ties to behavior analysis through her husband who is also a behavior analyst. She was appalled at the attitude and rejection by her colleagues in the School of Education. The dean of the School of Education supported the suggestion of establishing a program in behavior analysis, but others did not. This colleague who witnessed what happened became instrumental, a couple of years later when she became an administrator for the university, in starting a master's program in behavior analysis. She received news that the private University of Reykjavík was preparing to offer such a program. Early in 2018, she contacted my psychology department to announce that she would create a committee that would assess the possibility of establishing a master's program in behavior analysis. I was on sabbatical during that time; the committee did not start to work until the fall of 2018 when I had returned. By that time I had been promoted to full professor. So had Anna-Lind in the faculty of Education. The plan was for a master's program in behavior analysis to start its course in the fall of 2019, i.e., at the same time as the one in the University of Reykjavík. However, the committee preparing the master's program for the University of Iceland found it wise to spend more time in preparation. Therefore, our program did not start until the fall of 2020. Having good preparation time did pay off in every aspect.

The program is an interdisciplinary program, situated in the School of Education, in the department of Sports, Nutrition and Leisure, but financially supported and directed by the faculty of psychology as well. Psychology is now situated in the School of Health Sciences. The program offers a one-year graduate diploma and a two-year master's program. The focus of the program was dictated to the preparation committee in the beginning: it is on children with special needs. Within that frame we teach about developmental disabilities, behavior problems, and academic problems. We planned our program to meet the requirements for accreditation by ABAI. Our courses are based on many of the courses that I have taught before in psychology and those of Anna-Lind. In fact, some of those courses are taught in our program, but we also had to create new ones. We are the two main professors but we also have had part-time teachers, including a very dear colleague from the United States, who trained me during my Project 12-Ways years, Dr. Dave Wesch. He has retired, and came to the rescue by teaching in our program, as we needed a teacher.

The Importance of Lessons Learned

It's too late to change what I have done. Luckily I do not regret any of it. These accomplishments have been made possible with a little help from my friends, both in Iceland and abroad. They have made all my efforts better and more fruitful. To them I am enormously grateful as much as I am to all my former students who are now shaping and developing the field of behavior analysis in Iceland. They joined my mission and I see the effects multiplying. Sometimes I feel I could have done more. There is still so much left to do, so many unwritten manuscripts, so much left to teach, so much more research that needs to be done, so many bridges left to build. Academia has given me countless opportunities to learn and grow, to develop further as no other occupation has. I have been able to join editorial and review boards of journals, committees of agencies that evaluate grant applications, and be an examiner of PhD theses. I have established new international relations and have had the opportunity to help disseminate behavior analysis in Europe. In almost three decades, I have taught a few thousand students. The effects are cumulative and widespread. Every research project of mine results in an increasing number of students requesting to participate. Now they are applying to our master's program in behavior analysis, and that too is very gratifying. The ball can continue to roll. It is also enormously gratifying to see so many former students who have become first-class behavior analysts. Some are in the United States, some in Norway, and others in Iceland. They are all role models. Some are in academia doing exemplary analytical work that is developing our field further. Without behavior analysts who are willing to join academia, our field runs the danger of becoming stagnant and then decaying slowly until we become obsolete. Practitioners are necessary, but academicians are essential to keep our field scientific, growing, alive, creative, and strong.

References

Alberto, P. A., & Troutman, A. C. (1990). *Behavior analysis for teachers* (3rd ed.). Merrill.

Becker, W. C. (1971). *Parents are teachers: A child management program*. Research Press.

Clark, L. (1996). *Sos—help for parents*. Parents press.

Eiríksson, Á., & Sigurðardóttir, Z. G. (2020). Decreasing falls from shopping-carts: An effective pro-active intervention. *Safety Science, 127*. https://doi.org/10.1016/j.ssci.2020.104685

Ferster, C. B., Culbertson, S., & Boren, M. C. P. (1975). *Behavior principles*. Prentice Hall.

Guðmundsdóttir, K., Ala'i-Rosales, S., & Sigurðardóttir, Z. G. (2019). Extending caregiver training via telecommunication for rural Icelandic children with autism. *Rural Special Education Quarterly, 38*(1), 26–42.

Guðmundsdóttir, K., Sigurðardóttir, Z. G., & Ala'i-Rosales, S. (2017). Evaluation of caregiver training via telecommunication for rural Icelandic children with autism. *Behavior Development Bulletin, 22*(1), 215–229.

Lutzker, J. R., Frame, R. E., & Rice, J. M. (1982). Project 12-Ways: An ecobehavioral approach to the treatment and prevention of child abuse and neglect. *Education and Treatment of Children, 5*(2), 141–155.

Lutzker, J. R., & Rice, J. M. (1984). Project 12-ways: Measuring outcome of a large in-home service for treatment and prevention of child abuse and neglect. *Child Abuse & Neglect, 8*(4), 519–524. https://doi.org/10.1016/0145-2134(84)90034-6

Lutzker, J. R., Wesch, D., & Rice, J. M. (1984). A review of project "12-Ways": An ecobehavioral approach to the treatment and prevention of child abuse and neglect. *Advances in Behaviour Research and Therapy, 6*, 63–73. https://doi.org/10.1016/0146-6402(84)90013-4

Pétursdóttir, A. L., & Sigurðardóttir, Z. G. (2006). Increasing the skills of children with developmental disabilities through staff training in behavioral teaching techniques. *Education and Training in Developmental Disabilities, 41*, 264–279.

Þorsteinsson, H., & Sigurðardóttir, Z. G. (2007). Backward chaining used to teach a woman with aphasia to read long words: A single case study. *Journal of Speech-Language Pathology and Applied Behavior Analysis, 2*, 81–90. https://doi.org/10.1037/h0100226

Roll-Pettersson, L., Gena. A., Eldevik, S., Moderato, P., Sigurðardóttir, Z. G., Dillenburger, K., Keenan, M., & Ala'i-Rosales, S. (2020). Higher education and behavior analysis in Europe: Creating a unified approach for the training of autism professionals. *European Journal of Behavior Analysis, 21*(1), 158–184. https://doi.org/10.1080/15021149.2020.1758990

Sidman, M. (1960). *Tactics of scientific research, evaluating experimental data in psychology*. Authors Cooperative, Inc.

Sigurðardóttir, Z. G., & Sighvatsson, M. B. (2006). Operant conditioning and errorless learning procedures in the treatment of chronic aphasia. *International Journal of Psychology, 41*, 527–540.

Sigurðardóttir, Z. G., & Sighvatsson, M. B. (2011). Treatment of chronic aphasia with errorless learning procedures: A direct replication. *Journal of Speech-Language Pathology and Applied Behavior Analysis, 5*, 47–58.

Skinner, B. F. (1976). *About behaviorism*. Vintage books, Random House.

Sprague, J., & Golly, A. (2004). *Best behavior: Building positive behavior support in schools.* Sopris West.

Valdimarsdóttir, H., Halldórsdóttir, L. Ý., & Sigurðardóttir, Z. G. (2010). Increasing the variety of foods consumed by a picky eater: Generalization of effects across caregivers and settings. *Journal of Applied Behavior Analysis, 43*, 101–105. https://doi.org/10.1901/jaba.2010.43-101

17 Expanding

Traci M. Cihon

Expanding

We live in a world in which the cultural contingencies often suppress variability and expansion in favor of specialization. This is evident in at least three areas: the US educational (K-12) system, health care, and higher education systems. The contingencies that tie school funding to state and district assessments in public education, for example, strengthen the probability that instruction will be tied to the test, leading teachers to emphasize students' restating information verbatim in lieu of synthesis. When students perform well on state and district assessments, the schools sustain their funding streams (Every Student Succeeds Act, 2015). In health care, there is a shortage of primary care physicians (e.g., family physicians; Jacob, 2012). Specialists (e.g., cardiology) and sub-specialists (e.g., interventional cardiology) secure incomes that are two to three times that which could be earned as a primary care physician; fewer individuals are choosing to enter family medicine, general internal medicine, and pediatrics, all of which are vitally important to meet primary care health needs of the US population. Universities set up contingencies for promotion and tenure that support specialized scholarship and other outputs like research grants, rather than diversity of thought and generalized repertoires. Undergraduate students are asked often to select majors in their first year, before many have been exposed to less common discipline areas and potential career paths.

Behavior analysis and behavior science, especially applied behavior analysis, are no exception to the cultural contingencies that emphasize specialization. Applications of behavior analysis to autism intervention have become more widespread (BACB, 2021a). A growing interest in behavior analysis from consumers and families impacted by autism, the increasing prevalence of autism, and insurance mandates for programs have collectively increased employment opportunities for behavior analysts in autism services (BACB, 2021b; Burning Glass Technologies, 2015). An aspiring behavior analyst might find a graduate training program that provides opportunities to explore multiple applications of behavior analysis, but finding a job in a diverse application after graduation is less probable. Thus, despite the great achievements of behavior analysts, especially in the field of autism services, the contingencies have not supported the promise of behavior science to ameliorate human suffering in its broadest applications. The diversity of applications of behavior science, once apparent in the early work of applied behavior analysts, has not been actualized (e.g., Dixon et al., 2018; Friman, 2010; Skinner, 1987).

Author's note: I would like to thank my friends and colleagues Drs. John Eshleman, Shahla Ala'I, and Katie Hine, and Rita Olla, who provided insight and comments on versions of this chapter. I would also like to thank Alex Love who created the graphics I needed to actualize the metaphor that serves to illustrate the ideas put forth in this chapter.

DOI: 10.4324/9781003216773-21

Given the confluence of these variables, I am not surprised when students and aspiring behavior analysts ask for guidance regarding how they can diversify and expand their work in behavior science. They ask me about how to work in areas other than autism intervention, because I have worked outside of autism intervention. I have conducted research on establishing intraverbal relations (Cihon, 2007; Cihon et al., 2017; Emmick et al., 2010) and on the scholarship of teaching and learning (Adams et al., 2017; Ala'i-Rosales et al., 2010; Armshaw et al., 2021; Cihon, Sturtz, et al., 2012; Cihon et al., 2017; Goodhue et al., 2019; Lovitz et al., 2020; Neef et al., 2007; Urbina et al., 2021). I have taught textual relations to children who are at risk of school failure (Cihon et al., 2008; Gardner et al., 2013) and to adults learning another language (Cihon & Stephens, 2011; Cihon, Stephens et al., 2012; Cihon et al., 2013). I explore areas less frequently addressed by behavior analysts such as quantifying the changes in behavior as a function of studying abroad (Cihon & Stephens, 2011; Cihon, Stephens, et al., 2012; Stephens et al., 2018). Most recently, I have found a home in an emerging specialization in behavior science—Culturo Behavior Science (CBS; cf. Cihon & Mattaini, 2019, 2020).

For some students and aspiring behavior analysts, the advice is simple; many have already provided such guidance and tangible recommendations (Alligood & Gravina, 2021; BACB, 2020; Friman, 2010; LeBlanc et al., 2012). Their advice ranges from high-effort responses such as obtaining a degree in the content area or discipline in which one wants to work to potentially lower-effort responses such as finding a mentor or engaging in volunteer work. Obtaining a credential recognized by other disciplines certainly eases one's transition into *one* new area. Behavior scientists with a teaching certificate are more likely to find positions in the education sector just as those with a master's in business administration are more likely to gain employment in organizational behavior management (OBM). Similarly, finding a mentor who has experience with a particular group of individuals (e.g., veterans, seniors, etc.) or content area (e.g., smoking cessation, juvenile justice) often potentiates similar outcomes, even if it may prove more challenging depending on the content area or population of interest. These recommendations are sage advice, especially if one is positioned to engage in these responses and the contingencies support such individual actions (e.g., increased costs, potentially lower salaries, etc.). If one can navigate the challenges associated with more schooling and can accept a potentially lower salary than those working in the autism profession, it is probable that one will succeed in such endeavors, securing employment as a behavior scientist while meeting the credentialing requirements in another discipline. Many have followed this advice and are addressing the troubles and issues that are of concern to that discipline or working with one's population of interest. My cross-disciplinary training in behavior analysis, psychology, education (and more recently public health), has certainly proved advantageous in potentiating my work in areas other than behavioral interventions for autistic individuals/individuals with autism.

Students and aspiring behavior analysts also approach me seeking advice on how to forge new pathways for behavior scientists or how to prepare in ways that support the application of behavior analysis to *multiple* areas of human suffering. For these students and aspiring behavior scientists, the advice is more nuanced. The systemic contingencies that support specialization rather than variability and expansion have affected both the practice and the training of behavior scientists. Finding a graduate training program that provides experiences in diverse areas of the application in behavior analysis may prove just as difficult as finding a faculty member who does not subscribe to only one lineage of thought within behavior science (e.g., relational frame theory, verbal behavior, precision teaching, etc.) or who works with more than one population or in more than one setting (e.g., autism, adults with intellectual disabilities, nonhuman organisms, organizations). These students and aspiring behavior scientists are rarely satisfied when I respond that I work in multiple areas and diverse applications of behavior science because I like challenges or because I pursue research questions that interest me the most. Instead, they want to know how I have cultivated and capitalized on opportunities to work in multiple and diverse areas, often recombining distinct areas within behavior analysis (e.g., verbal behavior and precision teaching) as well as working inter- and transdisciplinarily (e.g., in behavior analysis and education or theatre). It is not specific or tangible enough to share that when presented with an opportunity to collaborate on an interdisciplinary project or to consider how behavior analysts might apply their perspectives (either theoretical or methodological) to a new content area, trouble, or issue, if I am curious about it, I simply find a way or carve a path to pursue it.

Given we live in a world that increasingly focuses on developing specialists rather than generalists, there may be fewer behavior scientists than there once were who serve as exemplars in broad applications of behavior science. Perhaps there are even fewer who have offered strategies and tactics for behavior scientists who seek to develop a generalist repertoire in behavior science that is broadly applicable. Yet students and aspiring behavior scientists still ask me how to do so; and they are asking me at an increasing frequency. Students and aspiring behavior scientists see that many of the current and future challenges facing humanity are caused by human behavior, and the natural science of behavior is perhaps the best chance we have in ameliorating the intense human suffering that is rapidly increasing due to our own actions (e.g., climate change). They ask me these questions because I am a rare generalist in a larger community of specialists and because they too see the promise of behavior science in addressing some of the most challenging issues facing humanity now and in the future.

In reflecting on my own experiences and path toward this seemingly less common outcome, I have come to wonder how I might better advise and support students and aspiring behavior scientists to cultivate their own training and experiences and develop a repertoire that prepares them to work in multiple and diverse applications of behavior science. How is it that one can become a generalist in a world that reinforces and selects specialization? How might one be prepared to work in diverse areas, in areas that are less explored by behavior analysts, or in areas in which one has not had and cannot find a direct training experience?

Recombinative Repertoires

Early in my career, I was introduced to Alessi (1987), a paper to which I return frequently. Alessi introduces the concept of generative instruction, explaining that generative instruction is actualized through the explicit instruction of a minimum set of discrete stimulus-response relations. These repertoires are recombinative in that they "generate a *maximum* novel repertoire after teaching only a *minimum* number of discrete stimulus-response relationships (emphasis original, Alessi, 1987, p. 15). Skinner's (1957) discussion of the echoic (e.g., hearing a speech sound and repeating it) and textual (as in decoding, seeing a letter and saying the corresponding sound) provide two examples of how generative instruction can result in minimal recombinative repertoires that transform into novel responses. Skinner (1957) explains that once an individual has acquired a minimal echoic or textual repertoire, these repertoires can recombine into novel response forms such as repeating or decoding words one has never heard or seen before in the language in which one has acquired a minimal echoic or textual repertoire (see also Cihon, Becker et al., 2020).

Behavior analysts run into "new words" all the time, such as when they are working with a child who needs to learn a skill that the behavior analyst has never taught before. Perhaps they are tasked with arranging support for six caregivers who interact with a child in any given week but are given only two hours by the insurance company to support them. They may be called upon to do a behavioral systems analysis for an organization for which they have no experience with the product or market. Or maybe they need to teach and measure problem solving or teach study skills in subjects they have never encountered or studied. Sometimes, to tackle these challenges, the behavior analyst can fall back on a specific training experience they have had, or they might find a mentor who has experience in these areas, replicate a study that has tackled a similar problem, and so forth. Oftentimes, however, the situations facing behavior analysts do not have a one-to-one correspondence between something they have previously experienced and the problem they are currently facing, or enough overlap between experiences for generalization to readily occur. This is especially common when behavior scientists start to work in areas less commonly explored. In these instances, the behavior scientist must rely on their minimal repertoires to recombine and produce a response to a novel situation or problem. The behavior scientist working in public health, for example, may have a strong understanding of the motivating contexts and discriminative stimuli that are immediately temporally related to the behavior of interest for the individual. However, they may be less familiar with how policy (Mattaini et al., 2020) or socio-ecological variables (Bronfenbrenner, 1979, 2005) more temporally distant affect the behavior of interest (see also Cihon, 2022). Such considerations can prove challenging to the behavior scientist who finds themselves working at the population level to promote widespread behavior change.

Those who are in the practice of teaching students of behavior analysis, or those in supervisory roles, recognize the benefit of developing a minimal recombinative repertoire. Moreover, as one gains more experience in a particular application of behavior analysis, the necessary minimal recombinative repertoires become more apparent. But what is the minimal recombinative repertoire for students and aspiring behavior analysts who want to be prepared to forge new pathways for behavior scientists or to be prepared to apply behavior analysis to *multiple* areas? The next section provides a metaphor and examples based on the work of a lesser-known classical sociologist that can be applied to contemporary issues.

Trees as Metaphor for Minimal Recombinative Repertoires in Behavior Science

Henry Carey, a physical science applied sociologist, used a tree as a metaphor to show the close proximity of the social and physical sciences, illustrating the exchange of ideas between them (McKean, 1874; see Figure 17.1). This exchange of ideas, or the unique re-combinations of different streams of knowledge, parallel the ideas put forth by Alessi (1987) and others (e.g., Johnson & Street, 2004, 2012, 2020). This metaphor is consistent with a natural science of behavior and its conceptually systematic basis that creates the potential for its application to problems of social significance as evidenced in the vast array of work in applied behavior analysis (Heward et al., 2022). In fact, a similar metaphor might be helpful in pinpointing the minimal recombinative repertoire (or the exchange and recombination of ideas) for a behavior scientist who is successful in expanding. The basic principles of behavior science after all are not organism- or setting-specific (Skinner, 1953). They have broad generality, and many have commented on the importance of the intersections between basic and applied behavior analysis (e.g., Mace & Critchfield, 2010; Marr, 1991, 2017), especially evidenced in early applications of behavior science (e.g., Baer, 1981; Normand & Kohn, 2013).

Returning to the tree metaphor Carey (1858, 1859) has applied to understand the intersection between social and physical or natural sciences, a tree has five major parts: roots, a trunk, rings, branches, and leaves. Extending this metaphor to the developing repertoire of a behavior analyst, each component of the tree might represent a particular aspect of one's unique training and experience, in other words one's minimal recombinative repertoires, how they might recombine, and what novel responses and outcomes may result.

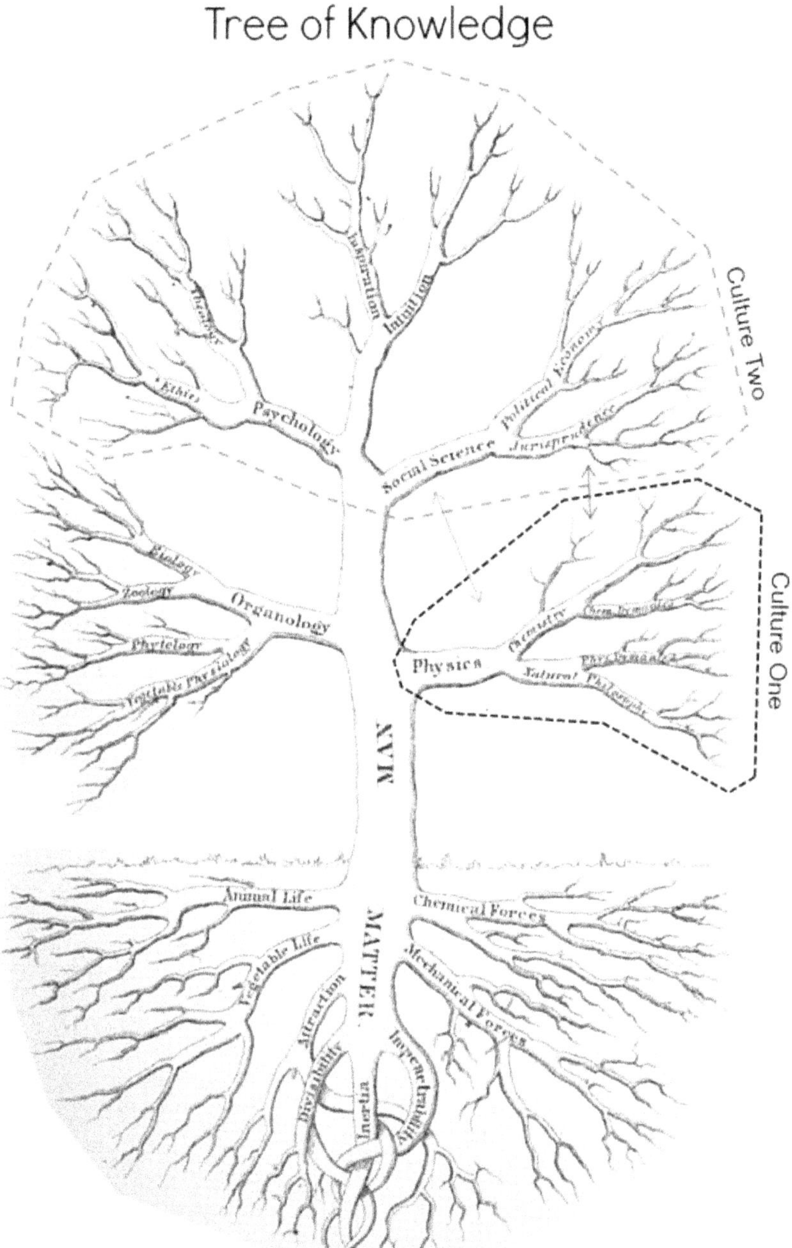

Figure 17.1 Carey (1858, 1859) Tree of Knowledge ("tree of knowledge" diagram, Vol 1, pgs. 20–21)

As behavior scientists, one's roots are grounded in the philosophy of science, which is upheld by certain assumptions (e.g., parsimony, empiricism, determinism, etc.; Chiesa, 1994). The specific philosophy of science is radical behaviorism—in which behavior analysts accept private events as observable and measurable while continuing to find the controls for behavior in the organism's environment (Lee, 1988). Many might also add dimensions of the experimental analysis of behavior (EAB; Skinner, 1966) and/or applied behavior analysis

(ABA; e.g., applied, behavioral, conceptually systematic, analytical, etc.; Baer et al., 1968, 1987) to their roots.

The roots keep behavior scientists grounded in the conceptualization of a problem and its solution; they provide the basis from which behavior scientists grow into the specific domains of their work. They give behavior scientists the very foundation from which the rest of the tree grows. The roots allow behavior scientists to tackle problems from a specific conceptual framework; solutions are found by examining the organism's natural functional history rather than seeking explanations in the control by inner agencies. The roots ground behavior scientists in the natural science of behavior; the principles and the techniques of behavior analysis are extended from these roots. Strong roots are crucial to grow a strong tree (see Figure 17.2).

Figure 17.2 "Tree" of the Author, Depicting the Roots, Trunk, Branches, and Leaves of Her Work in Multiple and Diverse Applications of Behavior Science; original artwork created by Alex Love

The trunk grows from the roots. However, the trunk is also made up of several other minimal repertoires, represented by the rings. The trunk is constantly growing; to use Alessi's (1987) term, it is generative. The rings collectively make up the trunk, each representing a different year of growth (see Figure 17.3). The rings of a tree show evidence of years of drought, heavy rains, indications of trauma, etc. Each year the ring also has a larger circumference than the prior year(s). If one considers each ring of the trunk as a year in one's studies or career as a behavior scientist, early in one's career the rings may be small in circumference; they may also be of great or narrow width depending on the scope of one's experiences and training. As one's career develops, the rings grow larger in circumference; however, they may be wider or narrower depending on the depth and breadth of one's experiences or they might be injured or scarred depending on one's interactions with the world around them.

Figure 17.3 shows some of the rings from my tree. Within each ring are several different minimal sets and experiences that have recombined and continue to recombine. Each ring is also influenced by the minimal sets in the roots and rings of those with whom I interact each year (e.g., students, clients, colleagues, or other collaborators and stakeholders). In addition, they are inextricably linked with all prior and forthcoming rings. Later I will describe in more detail some examples of the experiences, persons, settings, focus areas, and the like, that have recombined in novel ways to produce the work I do in multiple and diverse applications of behavior science (see also Chapter 22). First, however, I want to emphasize the importance of these rings; they represent how much one's lived experiences matter in

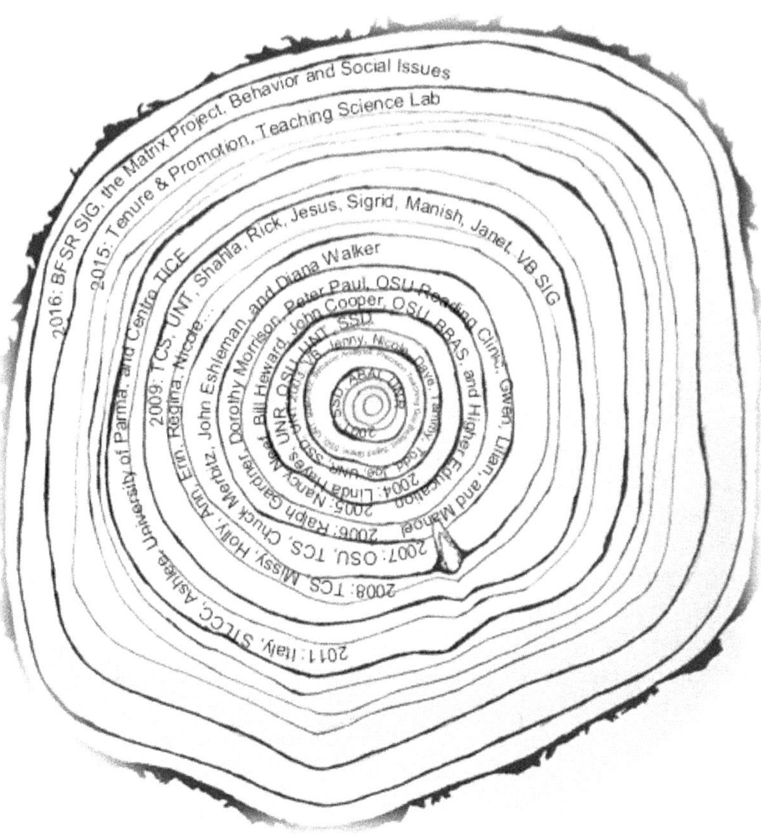

Figure 17.3 My Tree Rings; original artwork created by Alex Love

the expansion of one's work. The trunk is formed from the combination of these rings. From a component-composite perspective (Binder, 1996), the trunk might be thought of as representing the major area(s) of one's work. The major areas of my work, for instance, are broadly grounded in behavior analysis and education. The trunk of the tree, comprised of all of one's minimal sets and experiences, allows the growth of the tree's branches.

Metaphorically, the branches of the tree represent the specific domains in which a behavior scientist works. The tree depicted in Figure 17.2, for example, has several different branches—each representing one or more of the domains in which I currently work or have previously worked. Even though each branch may grow independent of another branch, there may be and often are branches that overlap or extend or grow from another. Each branch has leaves. A leaf might represent a study, publication, project, outcome, impact, or accomplishment that has grown from the branch. When one works in multiple and diverse applications of behavior science, a tree may have many branches. Some branches may have more leaves than others, and each behavior scientist's tree will look a little different—scientists' trees may be shaped like a palm tree, an evergreen tree, or even a bonsai tree.

Conceptualizing the behavior scientist's potential for generality of applications of the science as a tree helps to illustrate the idea that diverse sets of in-depth experiences increase the probability of the recombinative nature of different behavior analytic skill sets. Each in-depth experience can generate a new minimum set of responses that provide more opportunities for different recombinative repertoires to emerge. Next, I will illustrate this idea with a few examples from my own tree, looking both at some of the clinical and research areas I have explored, as well as what repertoires may have recombined to occasion it.

Precision Teaching and Verbal Behavior

In the first example, the minimal recombinative repertoires developed from two, seemingly distinct lines of inquiry from within behavior science. Later examples will show the integration of multiple domains within and outside of behavior science. The two minimum sets from within behavior science in the first example are indicative of my early-career experiences with precision teaching (PT; Lindsley, 1990, 1992) and verbal behavior (VB; Skinner, 1957). My interests in each of these areas were initially separate lines of inquiry that I explored in-depth and intentionally. The recombination of the repertoires was strengthened when I was faced with the practical challenge of establishing intraverbal repertoires with autistic individuals/individuals with autism.[1] In Cihon (2007), I presented an argument for conducting research that combined the work of behavior scientists in PT and in VB. The minimal response repertoires I had acquired in each area, grounded in and extrapolated from the existing research base, recombined to generate new lines of inquiry that served to promote unique instructional arrangements that might further enhance the development of intraverbal repertoires in children with autism.

For example, Emmick et al. (2010) began the process of actualizing that which was proposed in Cihon (2007). Emmick et al. was the result of another set of minimal response repertoires that recombined. The two repertoires that recombined to produce Cihon (2007) were at play in addition to the skill sets I had developed with respect to fluency-based instruction. The recombination of these minimal repertoires was occasioned by other salient environmental events, such as working with children with autism and developmental disabilities who presented with a limited intraverbal repertoire, my roots, co-authors' trees, and a very bright and motivated graduate student Jill (née Meiste) Emmick, and my colleague Dr. John Eshleman. A community of practice formed as each of us brought different individual and recombinative repertoires like those from our roots in radical behaviorism, research design, and applied behavior analysis. These individual repertoires further recombined *across* the members of the research team to produce Emmick et al., in which we explored the effects of fluency-based instruction for textual responses on the rate of acquisition of intraverbal relations established using transfer of stimulus control from text to social questions.

Cihon, White et al. (2017) extended this line of inquiry, addressing some of the limitations and potential extensions noted by Emmick et al. (2010). In the first of two studies, we replicated and investigated further the relation between fluency-based instruction for textual responses to the rate of acquisition of intraverbal relations. In the second study, we extended the work with tact relations. Interestingly, the two studies show an explicit investigation of minimal recombinative repertoires with the research participants; once tact or textual relations are taught to fluent levels, the corresponding intraverbal relations were more likely to be emitted. In addition, the work exemplifies how one researcher's minimal sets can recombine to generate novel responses in setting up a unique line of inquiry (Cihon, 2007) as well as how multiple individuals' minimal sets can recombine to produce novel responses that serve to address the scholarly and clinical challenges we were facing in developing intraverbal responding for those with limited verbal repertoires.

Scholarship of Teaching and Learning

A second example of how repertoires might recombine is found on a different branch of my tree. In my doctoral training program, I was advised by Dr. Nancy Neef, a brilliant scholar and researcher with an extensive history in translational research (e.g., Neef et al., 1992, 1994) and in applying behavioral principles in educational settings, including university settings (e.g., Neef et al., 2006; Saville et al., 2006). The rings on my tree that developed during the years I worked with Nancy, combined with my earlier experiences in instructional design, developed the basis for my subsequent work in behavioral education. For example, Neef et al. (2007) arranged two variations of study sessions: traditional question and answer and game show-based, and evaluated their comparative effects on graduate students' quiz scores. Working on this study, three minimum sets were established: 1) teaching at the university level, 2) conducting research on my teaching, and 3) using research to inform teaching. These minimum sets then entered recombinative relations with other minimum sets, growing the branch of my tree that represents behaviorally based instruction in higher education.

These repertoires later recombined with my minimal response repertoires in PT, VB, and active student responding (Heward, 1994), yielding a line of research (and ultimately a strong pillar of the Teaching Science Lab; see Cihon, Kieta et al., 2017) focused on the identification of instructional strategies to establish technical vocabulary repertoires for undergraduate and graduate students of behavior analysis. In Cihon, Sturtz et al. (2012), for example, each of these component or minimal repertoires worked in tandem with my ongoing interest in helping graduate and undergraduate students develop the technical vocabulary of behavior analysis. Cihon, Sturtz et al. was also the product of the repertoire of yet another motivated graduate student, Ann (née Sturtz) Nuss, who was brave enough to collect hundreds of data points from nearly a hundred participants for her master's thesis. With the support of Dr. John Eshleman, we explored the comparative effects of instructor-provided or student-created Say All Fast Minute Each Day Shuffled (SAFMEDS) on students' quiz scores. The results suggested some benefit to the combination of alternating instructor-provided SAFMEDS and student-developed SAFMEDS practiced through weekly, one-minute timings on students' quiz scores.

Access to the Teaching Science Lab (TSL) at the University of North Texas (UNT) created another opportunity for me to revisit my work with SAFMEDS. The research questions the TSL asked were driven by my own history and repertoire as well as the histories and repertoires of the graduate and undergraduate students in the lab and the classes. In Adams et al. (2017), for example, we evaluated the differential effects of cumulative and unitary SAFMEDS deck presentations on undergraduate students: correct, incorrect, and skipped terms during midterm and/or final SAFMEDS timings. Our findings from this research showed that cumulative deck presentations positively influenced student responding. In addition, it served to strengthen and grow these branches. Each branch grew flush with leaves from each published study focused on both improving undergraduate students' repertoires related to the course material and the exploration of research questions related to fluency-based instruction and its reported benefits (Lovitz et al., 2020; Urbina et al., 2021).

The previously described branches and leaves and the recombinative repertoires they illustrate are not necessarily examples of forging a path in new or diverse areas in behavior analysis. Others have conducted work that combines the analyses of both Skinner's (1957) VB and Lindsley and others' work in PT (e.g., Bulla et al., 2021). However, the examples pertaining to VB and PT and the scholarship of teaching and learning provide a straightforward illustration as to how generative instruction and recombinative repertoires can be extrapolated to consider one's own training and experience in behavior analysis. Without one or more of the minimal sets that entered the PT and VB and college teaching research, I might still be exploring questions related to only PT, only VB, or only college teaching. Without the minimal sets described; the mentors, colleagues, and graduate students who were involved; and the opportunity to develop the TSL, the associated lines of research may not have come to fruition. Further, the minimal sets I have acquired with respect to the work I do in higher education were critical in establishing the generative sets that served as the foundation on which I have relied while indulging my interest in the application of behavior analysis to individuals participating in study-abroad programs, an underrepresented, and basically nonexistent area of exploration for behavior analysts.

Measuring Student Learning Outcomes in Short-Term Study-Abroad Programs

My work applying behavior science to study-abroad programs started as a function of a unique combination of variables that are beyond the scope of what can be conveyed fully in this chapter (interested readers are encouraged to read Cihon & Stephens, 2011; Cihon, Stephens et al., 2012; Stephens et al., 2018). What I want to emphasize are the repertoires that I relied on to venture into work with students participating in study-abroad programs, a relatively unexplored area (in behavior analytic circles at least), illustrating how minimal sets can recombine to set the occasion to forge new pathways.

Several generative sets worked in tandem to facilitate the work that explored how to measure the impact of a short-term study-abroad program (i.e., shorter than one semester), supported by an interdisciplinary learning community, on participating undergraduate students' repertoires. The first of which, working in interdisciplinary settings, likely started when I worked as a behavior analyst in a public school system. This experience highlighted the ways in which behavior analysis and education were informed by distinct philosophies but related by their common goals—to produce new repertoires for the students and to create environments to support these repertoires. My interdisciplinary work was further developed in my formal coursework and degree programs that span three (now four) discipline areas as well as my interdisciplinary work on reading instruction at The Ohio State University (see for example, Cihon et al., 2008; Gardner et al., 2013). Recall that when I started working in the public schools, I also gained a history with instructional design and later with research in college teaching, both of which are also relevant to my work with short-term study-abroad programs.

At the base of my tree were my roots that grounded me in the philosophy of science, preventing me from accepting the common responses from students who returned from study abroad and expressed that their experience was "life changing." My roots in the philosophy of science and in behavior science more specifically prevented me from accepting this reported outcome as descriptive enough to allow us to develop more effective programs as the student learning outcomes related to "life changing" were not readily quantifiable. The learning community and students who provided the opportunity for this line of work were also open to my expertise in instructional design and the development of new verbal repertoires (i.e., teaching Italian to native English speakers). Finally, as it seems to be the case in much of my work, there were some extremely motivated and talented graduate students in behavior analysis whose repertoires also supported this work.

Cihon and Stephens (2011) relied on an exploratory research methodology to get a better understanding of the settings and experiences students participating in short-term study-abroad programs were having and to develop a better understanding of what would come to be the dependent variables of interest. Coming back to the recombinative nature of the minimal repertoires I brought from my training in behavior analysis and education, a sampling of the references cited in our first exploratory study is perhaps a better indicator than what I can describe otherwise with words (e.g., Baer et al., 1968, 1987; Barlow & Hayes, 1979, Binder, 1996; Goldiamond, 2002; Mechner, 1959, Skinner, 1953, 1957). In Cihon, Stephens et al. (2012) we piloted our data collection system, developed our coding system, and conducted replications across study-abroad programs (see also Stephens et al., 2018). I have left out the details of the language-acquisition studies, teaching Italian to native English speakers, even though this work is interesting. It does, however, deserve a brief mention, as it illustrates nicely when one might need to develop a new repertoire to work in a less common area for behavior analysts. Notably, to engage in this work, I had to develop a basic fluency in reading, speaking, and listening in Italian (see Cihon, Stephens et al., 2012), which further recombined with my work in See the Sound/Visual Phonics, a tactic with its roots in reading instruction for individuals who are deaf and hard of hearing (Cihon et al., 2008; Gardner et al., 2013).

The final example of work from this branch of my tree did not result in a publication but is still important to mention. This work consisted of service to the university and intervening at the systems and individual levels of behavioral influence. It also serves an example of how one might take behavior analysis to scale. Additionally, this work set the occasion for me to acquire a few new minimal sets. Building from my work in study abroad, I connected with other faculty and staff at UNT who were similarly interested in getting college students engaged globally. The result was a proposal, Engaging the Global Generations, for the UNT Quality Enhancement Plan (QEP) developed by over 40 collaborators that was selected as one of the four UNT QEP finalists. Even though our proposal was not selected as the final QEP proposal, components of our measurement system (grounded in behavior analysis) and use of within subject evaluation of student learning outcomes were incorporated into the QEP that was selected at a later phase of implementation, Career Connect. This project further connected me to other members of the university and raised awareness across the university of the potential for diverse applications of behavior analysis, harmonizing with many different discipline areas with which behavior analysis may not have otherwise had the opportunity to connect.

Culturo-Behavior Science

The final example of recombining repertoires comes from my work in culturo-behavior science and behavioral systems analysis. Early in my tenure at UNT, Dr. Sigrid Glenn maintained the Culture Lab but was no longer chairing student thesis projects. One graduate student, Zachary Morford, wanted to do his thesis in the Culture Lab but needed a chair. Since early in my career, I had been interested in Sigrid's work with culture and the metacontingency, but I hadn't had the opportunity to study deeply in this area. Zach's interest in the area and Sigrid's willingness to mentor me allowed me to develop a new minimal set. Morford and Cihon (2013) evaluated how fines, imposed on other players by players, affected cooperation in an experimental analysis of the metacontingency using an iterated prisoner's dilemma game (IPDG). This work set the occasion for me to become more involved in CBS, both as an active member of the Behaviorists for Social Responsibility Special Interest Group (BFSR SIG) of the Association for Behavior Analysis International (ABAI) and with the editorial board for *Behavior and Social Issues*.

BFSR SIG & the Matrix Project

Following the publication of Morford and Cihon (2013) and during the changing political climate in the US leading up to and following the 2016 presidential election, my interest in working in diverse areas of behavior science, metacontingencies, CBS, and behavioral systems analysis took on a new sense of urgency. The BFSR SIG's Matrix Project (Mattaini & Luke, 2014) offered a unique opportunity to get more involved in this emerging specialization in behavior science. The Matrix Project seeks to improve preparation of and opportunities for behavior scientists working to address impending social issues. Through the identification of 28 societal sectors, those involved in the Matrix Project identified the key behaviors and practices, the motivating contexts and consequences that strengthen and support the target practices, and the interdependencies among the sectors that can support and oppose the adoption of behavior science and CBS to address significant social issues. The initial phase of the Matrix Project involved "conceptual work and literature reviews of cultural-level, systemic practice and research areas" that resulted in the development of "contingency networks that could support and oppose adoption of those practices" (Matrix Project, n.d., para. 1) that have since been actualized through the implementation of some of the immediately feasible practices that had been identified. The Matrix Project continues to grow and develop with numerous volunteers working to develop content, change contingencies (and thereby the behaviors and practices of key actors and sectors), and engage in continual evaluation, revision, and expansion of activities that support the goals of the Matrix Project.

Many of my recent accomplishments and current work are inextricably linked with these early opportunities (see for example Cihon & Mattaini, 2019, 2020). This work occasioned my development of new repertoires, opportunities for these new repertoires to recombine with the minimal sets previously described as well as those of other behavior scientists who participate in unique and ambitious learning communities of CBS, and social, economic, and environmental justice. The development and implementation of the new ABAI verified course sequence and certificate program in CBS and work with students and colleagues in faculty-advised teaching and research laboratories at UNT (the CBS Lab and the Community Lab) illustrates what might transpire from the development of a minimal recombinative repertoire in behavior science. My work in CBS might be summarized across four categories: 1) philosophical, theoretical, and conceptual considerations, 2) basic research, 3) cultural and community applications, and 4) education and training of behavior scientists.

Past and Present Masters

There are numerous examples of behavior scientists who have worked in diverse areas. Their work provides a starting point from which one can attempt to derive the minimal response repertoires that may have recombined to create their novel contributions to the discipline or the unique paths they have taken, an exercise that I strongly recommend students and aspiring behavior scientists seeking to expand the scope and reach of behavior science and their own contributions conduct. Perhaps the development of a minimal recombinative repertoire is a natural outcome of those whose work is grounded firmly in the assumptions of science and a principles-based natural science of behavior. Two well-known examples are evidenced in the work of Skinner and Sidman. Skinner's work pushed the boundaries of traditional psychology, moving behaviorism beyond its methodological behaviorism roots into radical behaviorism, providing the very foundation by which many of us think about and study behavior. As another example, Sidman's (2011) reflections on his own training and experiences in the experimental analysis of behavior prepared him for his work in applied behavior analysis and led to his groundbreaking work in stimulus equivalence (Sidman, 1994). A third exemplar who has been particularly influential to my work, for instance, is Lindsley (1990, 1992), who extended his experiences in the experimental laboratory with response-rate measures to education and classroom-based settings, and then to the development of PT.

Nonetheless, the previously mentioned contingencies that favor specialization over variability and expansion may mask or overshadow the work of many who have forged new pathways in behavior science or who have worked across diverse areas of application. Concurrent cultural-level contingencies do not always recognize the contributions of diverse groups of scientists—BIPOC, LGBTQIA+, and women for example. Those who have made important contributions and who show clear examples of recombinative repertoires may have been overlooked in the history and status of behavior science. Systemic contingencies diminish the contributions made by those whose very intersectionality *requires* them to work on the margins, if not outside of the mainstream, many of whom are contributors to this very volume. Even if the discipline has benefited from the contributions of these scholars, their work has been less recognized and is therefore potentially less familiar to some readers. Perhaps, intersectionality functions as another minimal set that leads to opportunities for expansion of one's interests and the science itself.

Dr. Beth Sulzer-Azaroff's early experiences, for instance, were in education before she shifted her work toward business and organizational leadership (Sulzer-Azaroff, 2016). Dr. Florence DiGennaro Reed completed her graduate training in experimental psychology and school psychology. Her work, while grounded in OBM, spans across several different settings from the classroom to animal shelters to senior centers and more (DiGennaro Reed, n.d.). Dr. Jomella Watson-Thompson completed her academic training in urban studies, urban planning, behavior analysis, public health, and prevention science. She now works to bring behavioral science research and interventions to address issues in community health and development (Watson-Thompson, n.d.). Dr. August Stockwell started their academic career in social work and then studied clinical psychology and behavior analysis in graduate school. They are the former director of research and programs at Upswing Advocates—whose work at the time was in using precise measurement and an individualized approach in working to strengthen the LGBTQIA+ community (Stockwell, n.d.). Many other notable examples are provided in Table 17.1, a list that resulted from a series of 30-second to 1-minute think-write exercises I completed in preparation for writing this chapter. I encourage you to do your own think-write exercises and add to the table; it is far from complete!

Minimal Recombinative Repertoires for Expanding Behavior Science

Each of the exemplars presented in this chapter illustrates how one's training and experiences yield what some might call novel or diverse applications or expansions of behavior

Table 17.1 List of Women Expanding Behavior Science and Its Applications to Multiple and Diverse Areas

Shahla Ala'I	Ramona Houmanfar	Ruth Anne Rehfeldt
Maria Amalia Andery	Veronica Howard	Sarah M. Richling
Natalia Baires	Martha Hübner	Lise Roll-Peterson
Bea Barrett	Corina Jimenez-Gomez	Ellie Reese
April Becker	Ellie Kazemi	Joanne Robbins
Marlesha Bell	Karen Kate Kellum	Kathryn M. Roose
Veronica Bender-Haydu	Camille Kolu	Denise Ross
Molly Benson	Darnell Lattal	Maria Ruiz
Kim Berens	Linda Leblanc	Ingunn Sandaker
Martha E. Bernal	Sarah Lechago	Emily K. Sandoz
Sarah Bloom	Vicki Lee	Angela Sanguinetti
Gwendolyn Cartlidge	Roberta Lemos	Kate Saunders
Abigail Calkin	Dorthea Lerman	Susan Schnieder
Francesca Cavallini	Molli Luke	Tyra Sellers
Nasaih Crincione-Ulezi	Maria Malott	Holly Seniuk
Berenice de la Cruz	Heather McGee	Jan Sheldon
Karloa Dillenberger	Louise McHugh	Zuilma Gabriela Sigurðardóttir
Jovonnie Esquierdo-Leal	Fran McSweeny	Carsta Simon
Barbara Etzel	Camila de Melo	Devon Sundberg
Judy Favell	Megan Miller	Janet Twyman
Julia Fiebig	Debbi Napolitano	Julie Vargas
Elizabeth Fong	Nancy Neef	Diana Walker
Angeliki Gena	Amy L. Odum	Wendy Donlin Washington
Marilyn Gilbert	Martha Paleaz	Jomella Watson-Thompson
Denisha Gingles	Dana Paliliunas	Mary Jane Weiss
Sigrid Glenn	Stephanie M. Peterson	Chris Wilhite
Nicole Gravina	Cynthia Pietras	Patricia Wright
Gina Green	Carol Pilgrim	Jenn Yoon-Fritz
Landria Seals Green	Elsie Pinkston	
Linda Hayes	Erin B. Rasmussen	

science. Yet the individual and cultural- and systems-level contingencies tend to promote specialization and even replication of our mentor(s)' repertoires. Consider, however, if Skinner had simply replicated Pavlov's or Watson's trees, we might still be working solely within the framework of respondent conditioning or methodological behaviorism. Had Dr. Nancy Neef conducted work only in the functional analysis of problem behavior or in the analysis of verbal behavior, behavior scientists might not be as informed about how the dimensions of reinforcement can be altered in lieu of pharmacological interventions for individuals with attention deficit hyperactive disorders. And if Dr. Linda (née Parrot) Hayes did not combine her experiences in radical behaviorism with the philosophy of science put forth by Kantor, we would not know Interbehaviorism (e.g., Hayes & Fryling, 2018; Parrott, 1983).

In essence, those seeking to expand and work in diverse areas of application of behavior science may not be able to simply replicate someone else's tree. If one wants to work in diverse areas, one might need to replicate some components of others' trees, but the tree that grows is different; it has its own roots, trunk, branches, and leaves. I do not have the same tree as Nancy or Linda, nor do they share the same tree, even if they attended and overlapped at the same doctoral training program. Each person with whom one studies; each mentored experience; each course in and outside of behavior science; each project, study, or application of behavior science, and so on will contribute to the roots, rings, and trunk of one's tree. Some experiences will support the growth of the branches, many that will be populated with leaves. The confluence of these experiences generates several minimum sets which will provide the possibility for recombinative or generative repertoires moving forward.

Growing Your Tree

But what is the minimal recombinative repertoire for students and aspiring behavior analysts who want to be prepared to forge new pathways for behavior scientists or to be prepared to apply behavior analysis to *multiple* areas? To be honest, I really do not know all the intricacies of what makes the minimal recombinative repertoire for a behavior analyst. In fact, I think they could be infinite. I hope the metaphor and examples presented in this chapter can help one to reflect on their own tree and its various components and to give one a way to think about what additional in-depth teaching and learning experiences they still need to cultivate their tree. One's roots and rings or experiences can be thought to comprise several minimal sets that under the right conditions can recombine and produce universal sets—or those novel responses each of you who want to work in diverse areas are seeking.

> Teaching involves much more than enumerating lists of behavioral objectives and teaching these, and hoping for "generalization." Teaching for generalization begins with an analysis of the structure of the subject matter for stimulus-response patterns having great generality of application, and then selecting teaching approaches that establish patterns to capitalize on these regularities. Possibilities for use of minimal recombinative repertoires and transformation of available repertoire patterns are carefully explored. . . . Although it is not completely clear how basic behavioral principles interact to produce the effects, instructional planners can currently make use of recombinative or generative repertoires to ensure a maximum amount of learning with a minimum amount of instruction. This is "smart teaching" or "strategic teaching."
>
> (Alessi, 1987, p. 26)

In this moment, each of you reading this chapter is establishing your roots and acquiring your minimum sets of responses. No one can teach you everything you will need to know moving forward, whether you end up working in an area that is more frequently explored by behavior scientists or in an area that is rarely, if ever, explored by behavior scientists.

Nevertheless, I think there are three general pieces of advice for current and aspiring behavior scientists leaning toward expansion. First, generative sets are not all that one needs to work in diverse areas. Another very important contributing factor to the work that we do is the verbal and learning communities of which we are a part. Not a single study or project that I presented here was done in the absence of a community. Often, the minimum sets from each member of those communities were necessary for the resulting products, like the assumption of holism in systems science (Mobus & Kalton, 2015) that reminds us the whole is greater than the sum of its parts. Second, one must stay intensely curious and, at times, dissatisfied with what we know or have discovered about behavior science and its applications. Third, working in diverse areas is a product of more than just a scattering of experiences. Developing a generative set that prepares one to work in diverse settings requires strategic teaching or when it is not available, it requires strategic learning. Make your roots strong and grounded in the science of behavior. Create a good verbal community. Seek varied, in-depth experiences. Reach out to others who may be informative on new areas you might wish to expand into. And stay curious.

Note

1. Extinction, often experienced when encountering a problem for which no readily apparent solution presents itself, tends to be a condition that sets the occasion for the recombination of repertoires described here within.

References

Adams, O., Cihon, T. M., Urbina, T., & Goodhue, R. J. (2017). Comparative effects of cumulative and unitary SAFMEDS terms in an introductory undergraduate behavior analysis course. *European Journal of Behavior Analysis, 19*(2), 176–194. https://doi.org/10.1080/15021149.2017.1404394

Ala'i-Rosales, S., Roll-Pettersson, L., Pinkelman, S., & Cihon, T. M. (2010). Emerging opportunities in higher education: Applied behavior analysis and autism. *European Journal of Behavior Analysis, 11*, 207–216. https://doi.org.10.1080/15021149.2010.11434344

Alessi, G. (1987). Generative strategies and teaching for generalization. *The Analysis of Verbal Behavior, 5*, 15–27. https://doi:10.1007/BF03392816

Alligood, C. A., & Gravina, N. E. (2021). Branching out: Finding success in new areas of practice. *Behavior Analysis in Practice, 14*, 283–289. https://doi.org/10.1007/s40617-020-00483-2

Armshaw, B., Cihon, T. M., & Lopez, C. (2021). The effects of exploratory logs and instructor feedback on student identification of functional relations in undergraduate behavior analysis courses. *Behavior Analysis in Practice*. https://doi.org/10.1007/s40617-021-00608-1

Baer, D. M., Wolf, M. M., & Risley, T. R. (1968). Some current dimensions of applied behavior analysis. *Journal of Applied Behavior Analysis, 1*(1), 91–97. https://doi:10.1901/jaba.1968.1-91

Baer, D. M., Wolf, M. M., & Risley, T. R. (1987). Some still-current dimensions of applied behavior analysis. *Journal of Applied Behavior Analysis, 20*(4), 313–327. https://doi.org/10.1901/jaba.1987.20-313

Barlow, D. H., & Hayes, S. C. (1979). Alternating treatments design: One strategy for comparing the effects of two treatments in a single subject. *Journal of Applied Behavior Analysis, 12*(2), 199–210. https://doi.org/10.1901/jaba.1979.12-199

Behavior Analyst Certification Board (BACB). (2021a). *Certificant data*. www.bacb.com/bacb-certificant-data/

Behavior Analyst Certification Board. (2021b). *US employment demand for behavior analysts: 2010–2020*. Author.

Binder, C. (1996). Behavioral fluency: Evolution of a new paradigm. *The Behavior Analyst, 19*(2), 163–197. https://doi.org/10.1007/BF03393163.

Bronfenbrenner, U. (1979). *The ecology of human development: Experiments in nature and design*. Harvard University Press.

Bronfenbrenner, U. (Ed.). (2005). *Making human beings human: Bioecological perspectives on human development*. Sage.

Bulla, A. J., Calkin, A., & Sawyer, M. (2021). Introduction to the special section: Precision Teaching: Discoveries and applications. *Behavior Analysis and Practice, 14*, 555–558. https://doi.org/10.1007/s40617-021-00624-1

Burning Glass Technologies. (2015). *US behavior analyst workforce: Understanding the national demand for behavior analysts*. www.simmons.edu/sites/default/files/201903/Behavior%20Analysis%20Ca reers.pdf

Carey, H. C. (1858, 1859). *The principles of social science* (Vol. I). J.B. Lippincott & Co.

Chiesa, M. (1994). *Radical behaviorism: The philosophy and the science*. Authors Cooperative.

Cihon, T. M. (2007). A review of training intraverbal repertoires: Can precision teaching help? *The Analysis of Verbal Behavior, 23*, 123–133. https://doi.org/10.1007/bf03393052

Cihon, T. M. (2022). Editorial: Expanding our scientific lens in the search for humility and advancing culturo-behaviorscience. *Behavior and Social Issues, 31*, 1–10. https://doi.org/10.1007/s42822-022-00112-3

Cihon, T. M., Becker, A., Ortu, D., & Glenn, S. S. (2020). Multiple perspectives on establishing a research lab for culturo-behavior science. In T. M. Cihon & M. A. Mattaini (Eds.), *Behavior science perspectives on culture and community*. Association for Behavior Analysis International book series: Behavior Science: Theory, Research, and Practice. Springer.

Cihon, T. M., Gardner, R., Morrison, D., & Paul, P. V. (2008). Using visual phonics as a strategic intervention to increase literacy behaviors for kindergarten students at-risk for reading failure. *Journal of Early Intensive Behavior Interventions, 5*(3), 138–155. https://doi.org/10.1037/h0100428

Cihon, T. M., Kieta, A., & Glenn, S. (2017). Teaching behavior analysis with behavior analysis: 30 years of a work in progress. *European Journal of Behavior Analysis, 19*(2), 150–175. https://doi.org/10.1080/15021149.2017.1404393.

Cihon, T. M., & Mattaini, M. A. (2019). Editorial: Emerging cultural and behavioral systems science. *Perspectives on Behavior Science, 42*(4), 699–711. https://doi.org/10.1007/s40614-019-00237-8

Cihon, T. M., & Mattaini, M. A. (Eds.). (2020). *Behavior science perspectives on culture and community*. Association for Behavior Analysis International book series: Behavior Science: Theory, Research, and Practice. Springer.

Cihon, T. M., Morford, Z., Stephens, C. J., Morrison, D., Shrontz, R., & Kelly, K. L. (2013). The effects of large-group instruction, modeling, or see the sound/visual phonics on undergraduate students learning to read Italian. *Teaching Reading in a Foreign Language* (Special Issue), *25*(1), 26–51.

Cihon, T. M., Stephens, C. J., & Dean, B. (2012). Global understanding through theatre: Enhancing second language acquisition and cultural competence with interdisciplinary research bridging theatre arts and behavior analysis. *Journal of the Speech and Theatre Association of Missouri*, *41*, 65–82.

Cihon, T. M., & Stephens, C. J. (2011). Integrating teaching and interdisciplinary scholarship to enhance student learning outcomes. *Journal of the Speech and Theatre Association of Missouri*, *41*, 65–82.

Cihon, T. M., Sturtz, A., & Eshleman, J. (2012). The effects of instructor-provided or student- created flashcards with weekly, one-minute timings on unit quiz scores in Introduction to Applied Behavior Analysis courses. *The European Journal of Behavior Analysis*, *13*(1), 47–57. https://doi.org/10.1080/15021149.2012.11434404

Cihon, T. M., White, R., Zimmerman, V. L., Stordahl, S., Geick, J., & Eshelman, J. (2017). The effects of precision teaching with textual or tact relations on intraverbal relations. *Behavior Development Bulletin* (Special Issue), *22*(1), 129–146. https://doi.org/10.1037/bdb0000056

DiGennaro Reed, F. (n.d.). *KU life span institute center for community health and development: Florence DiGennaro reed, Ph.D, BCBA-D.* https://communityhealth.ku.edu/people/florence-d-digennaro-reed-phd-bcba-d

Dixon, M. R., Belisle, J., Rehfeldt, R. A., & Root, W. B. (2018). Why we are still not acting to save the world: The upward challenge of a post-Skinnerian behavior science. *Perspectives on Behavior Science*, *41*, 241–267. https://doi.org/10.1007/s40614-018-0162-9

Emmick, J., Cihon, T. M., & Eshleman, J. (2010). An analysis of the effectiveness of transfer of stimulus control from text to verbal cues with an added fluency-based component on the acquisition of intraverbal behavior with individuals with developmental disabilities. *The Analysis of Verbal Behavior*, *26*, 31–40. https://doi.org/10.1007/bf03393080

Every Student Succeeds Act, 20 U.S.C. § 6301 (2015). www.congress.gov/114/plaws/publ95/PLAW-114publ95.pdf

Friman, P. C. (2010). Come on in, the water is fine: Achieving mainstream relevance through integration with primary medical care. *The Behavior Analyst*, *33*(1), 19–36. https://doi.org/10.1007/BF03392201

Gardner, R., Cihon, T. M., Morrison, D., & Paul, P. V. (2013). Implementing visual phonics with hearing kindergarteners at risk for reading failure. *Preventing School Failure*, *57*(1), 30–42. https://doi.org/10.1080/1045988x.2011.654365

Goldiamond, I. (2002). Toward a constructional approach to social problems: Ethical and constitutional issues raised by applied behavior analysis. *Behavior and Social Issues*, *11*(2), 108–197. https://doi.org/10.5210/bsi.v11i2.92

Goodhue, R. J., Liu, S. C., & Cihon, T. M. (2019). An alternative to non-human laboratory experiences for students of behavior analysis: The portable operant research and teaching laboratory (PORTL). *Journal of Behavioral Education*, *28*(4), 517–541. https://doi.org/10.1007/s10864-019-09323-y

Hayes, L. J., & Fryling, M. J. (2018). Psychological events as integrated fields. *Psychological Record*, *68*, 273–277. https://doi.org/10.1007/s40732-018-0274-3

Heward, W. L. (1994). Three "low-tech" strategies for increasing the frequency of active student response during group instruction. In R. Gardner III, D. M. Sainato, J. O. Cooper, T. E. Heron, W. L. Heward, J. W. Eshleman, & T. A. Grossi (Eds.), *Behavior analysis in education: Focus on measurably superior instruction* (pp. 283–320). Thomson Brooks/Cole Publishing Co.

Heward, W. L., Critchfield, T. S., Reed, D. D., Detrich, R., & Kimball, J. W. (2022). ABA from A to Z: Behavior science applied to 350 domains of socially significant behavior. *Perspectives on Behavior Science*, *45*, 327–359. https://doi.org/10.1007/s40614-022-00336-z

Jacob, S. (2012). *Health Care in 2020: Where uncertain reform, bad habits, too few doctors, and skyrocketing costs are taking us.* Dorsam Publishing.

Johnson, K., & Street, E. M. (2004). *The morningside model of generative instruction: What it means to leave no child behind.* The Cambridge Center for Behavioral Studies.

Johnson, K., & Street, E. M. (2012). From the laboratory to the field and back again: Morningside academy's 32 years of improving student performance. *The Behavior Analyst Today*, *13*(1), 20–40. https://doi.org/10.1037/h0100 715.

Johnson, K., & Street, E. M. (2020). Generative responding through contingency adduction. In R. A. Rehfeldt, J. Tarbox, M. Fryling, & L. Hayes (Eds.), *Applied behavior analysis of language and cognition.* New Harbinger.

Leblanc, L. A., Heinicke, M. R., & Baker, J. C. (2012). Expanding the consumer base for behavior-analytic services: Meeting the needs of consumers in the 21st century. *Behavior Analysis in Practice, 5*(1), 4–14. https://doi.org/10.1007/BF03391813

Lee, V. L. (1988). *Beyond behaviorism.* Routledge

Lindsley, O. R. (1990). Precision teaching: By teachers for children. *Teaching Exceptional Children, 22*(3), 10–15. https://doi.org/10.1177/004005999002200302.

Lindsley, O. R. (1992). Precision teaching: Discoveries and effects. *Journal of Applied Behavior Analysis, 25,* 51–57. https://doi.org/10.1901/jaba.1992.25-51.

Lovitz, E. D., Cihon, T. M., & Eshleman, J. W. (2020). Exploring the effects of daily, timed, and typed technical term definition practice on indicators of fluency. *Behavior Analysis in Practice* (Special Section). https://doi.org/10.1007/s40617-020-00481-4

Mace, F. C., & Critchfield, T. S. (2010). Translational research in behavior analysis: Historical traditions and imperative for the future. *Journal of the Experimental Analysis of Behavior, 93*(3), 293–312. https://doi.org/10.1901/jeab.2010.93-293

Marr, M. J. (1991). The speciation of behavior analysis: The unnatural selection of foxes and hedgehogs. *The Behavior Analyst, 14,* 183–186. https://doi.org/10.1007/BF03392568

Marr, M. J. (2017). The future of behavior analysis: Foxes and hedgehogs revisited. *The Behavior Analyst, 40*(1), 197–207. https://doi.org/10.1007/s40614-017-0107-8

Matrix Project. (n.d.). https://bfsr.abainternational.org/the-matrix-project/

Mattaini, M. A., Esquierdo-Leal, J., Ardila Sánchez, J. G., & Richling, S. (2020). Public policy advocacy in culturo-behavior science. In T. M. Cihon & M. A. Mattaini (Eds.), *Behavior science perspectives in culture and community* (pp. 385–412). Springer.

Mattaini, M. A., & Luke, M. (2014). Editorial: "Saving the World" with a matrix. *Behavior and Social Issues, 23,* 1–4. https://doi.org/10.5210/bsi.v23i0.5860

McKean, K. (1874). *Manual of social science; Being a condensation of the "principles of social science" of H. C. Carey, LLD.* Harry Carey Baird.

Mechner, F. (1959). A notation system for the description of behavioral procedures. *Journal of the Experimental Analysis of Behavior, 2*(2), 133–150. https://doi.org/10.1901/jeab.1959.2-133

Mobus, G. E., & Kalton, M. C. (2015). *Principles of systems science.* Springer.

Morford, Z. H., & Cihon, T. M. (2013). The effects of fines on cooperation in a four-person prisoner's dilemma game. *Behavior & Social Issues, 22,* 5–20. https://doi.org/10.5210/bsi.v22i0.4207

Neef, N. A., Cihon, T. M., Kettering, T., Guld, A., Axe, J., Itoi, M., & DeBar, R. (2007). A comparison of study session formats on attendance and quiz performance in a college course. *Journal of Behavioral Education, 16,* 235–249. https://doi.org/10.1007/s10864-006-9037-3

Neef, N. A., Mace, F. C., Shea, M. C., & Shade, D. (1992). Effects of reinforcer rate and reinforcer quality on time allocation: Extensions of matching theory to educational settings. *Journal of Applied Behavior Analysis, 25*(3), 691–699. https://doi:10.1901/jaba.1992.25-691

Neef, N. A., McCord, B. E., & Ferreri, S. J. (2006). Effects of guided notes versus completed notes during lectures on college students' quiz performance. *Journal of Applied Behavior Analysis, 39*(1), 123–130. https://doi.org/10.1901/jaba.2006.94-04

Neef, N. A., Shade, D., & Miller, M. S. (1994). Assessing influential dimensions of reinforcers on choice in students with serious emotional disturbance. *Journal of Applied Behavior Analysis, 27*(4), 575–583. https://doi.org/10.1901/jaba.1994.27-575.

Normand, M. P., & Kohn, C. S. (2013). Don't wag the dog: Extending the reach of applied behavior analysis. *The Behavior Analyst, 36*(1), 109–122. https://doi.org/10.1007/BF03392294

Parrott, L. J. (1983). On the differences between Skinner's radical behaviorism and Kantor's interbehaviorism. *Mexican Journal of Behavior Analysis, 9,* 95–115.

Saville, B. K., Zinn, T. E., Neef, N. A., Van Norman, R., & Ferreri, S. J. (2006). A comparison of interteaching and lecture in the college classroom. *Journal of Applied Behavior Analysis, 39*(1), 49–61. https://doi.org/10.1901/jaba.2006.42-05

Sidman, M. (1994). *Equivalence relations and behavior: A research story.* Authors Cooperative.

Sidman, M. (2011). Can an understanding of basic research facilitate the effectiveness of practitioners? Reflections and personal perspectives. *Journal of Applied Behavior Analysis, 44*(4), 973–991. https://doi.org/10.1901/jaba.2011.44-973

Skinner, B. F. (1953). *Science and human behavior*. Free Press.

Skinner, B. F. (1957). *Verbal Behavior*. Prentice Hall.

Skinner, B. F. (1966). What is the experimental analysis of behavior? *Journal of the Experimental Analysis of Behavior, 9*(3), 213–218. https://doi.org/10.1901/jeab.1966.9-213

Skinner, B. F. (1987). Why we are not acting to save the world. In B. F Skinner (Ed.), *Upon further reflection* (pp. 1–14). Prentice Hall.

Stephens, C. J., Morford, Z. H., Cihon, T. M., Forand, E. H., & Neri-Hernandez, L. (2018). Exploring the impact of global studies experiences on undergraduate student development: Some curricular considerations. *Frontiers: The Interdisciplinary Journal of Study Abroad, XXX*(2), 63–76. https://doi.org/10.36366/frontiers.v30i2.412

Stockwell, A. (n.d.). *Upswing advocates: August stockwell, BCBA-D, executive director, researcher and educator*. www.upswingadvocates.org/crew

Sulzer-Azaroff, B. (2016). The journey of a pioneer woman applied behavior analyst. In R. Holdsambeck & H. S. Pennypacker (Eds.), *Behavioral science: Tales of inspiration, discovery, and service* (pp. 139–166). The Cambridge Center for Behavioral Studies.

Urbina, T., Cihon, T. M., & Baltazar, M. (2021). Exploring procedural manipulations to enhance student performance on SAFMEDS in undergraduate introduction to behavior analysis courses. *Journal of Behavioral Education, 30*, 130–148. https://doi.org/10.1007/s10864-019-09359-0

Watson-Thompson, J. (n.d.). *KU life span institute center for community health and development: Jomella Watson-Thompson, Ph.D.* https://communityhealth.ku.edu/people/jomella-watson-thompson-phd

18 Staying Motivated

An Intermezzo

Ruth Anne Rehfeldt

Why This Chapter?

When we consider what it means to be motivated in one's life inside and outside of the academy, most behavior analysts probably regard behaving at a high rate and deriving enjoyment from what one is doing as a colloquial definition of what it means to be motivated. Why, from the perspective of mid- to late-career women, is the topic of staying motivated important to consider? Any number of variables may negatively impact one's motivation, both within and outside the workplace. Within the academy, an unsupportive department and an institution with ideals that are different from one's own may affect one's psychological comfort with their place of work. A woman's working conditions have been shown to be an important contributor to stress and job burn-out (Nascimento et al., 2018), and an individual's own private psychological experience no doubt affects their motivation. Hyde and Kling (2001) found that high-achieving women frequently reported fearing career success because of the challenges associated with advancement, including their own self-doubt, and avoided opportunities for that reason. Variables outside of work, including those associated with work-family balance and health and well-being no doubt also affect response allocation and the joy that life as a faculty member should ultimately deliver. Indeed, Schenk (2003) found that research and teaching were reported to be the most motivating aspects of the job for female academicians living in Germany and Sweden.

The purpose of this chapter is to share insights that I have developed over the course of a 20+-year career in academia as to how one might stay motivated as interests, goals, responsibilities, and phases in life change. Careers in academia can last for many years—in some cases, comprising the majority of adult life. It is reasonable to expect that one's motivation may wax and wane as contextual variables change. I first begin by providing a behavior analytic conceptualization of motivation, which will set the stage for the chapter here forward.

Conceptualizing Motivation

Motivating Operations

In traditional psychology, a distinction has been drawn between intrinsic and extrinsic motivation. Intrinsic motivation refers to satisfaction that comes from an activity itself that is not contingent upon the delivery of some outcome separable from the behavior, whereas extrinsic motivation refers to the engagement in an activity that produces a reinforcer following its completion other than the activity itself (Legault, 2016). This distinction is not too disparate from how behavior analysts might similarly conceptualize the term. Behavior analysts have conceptualized motivation in terms of the contingent relations between behavior and the

DOI: 10.4324/9781003216773-22

environmental variables of which behavior is a function. Motivating operations (MOs), as explained by Laraway and colleagues (2003), is a behavioral process that 1) establishes the effectiveness of both reinforcers or punishers to affect the probability of behavior, and 2) changes the current strength of behavior that is under the control of specific consequences. This first effect is known as the value-altering effect, and the second effect is known as the behavior-altering effect. The value-altering effect of MOs is important for the discussion in this chapter as it speaks to the potency of behavioral consequences, including both reinforcers and punishers, over lengthy time periods, during which satiation and deprivation levels may shift as the contingencies in a given context change. I will discuss how contact with reinforcers and punishers alike have affected my own motivation inside and outside of my places of work over the various phases of my career. Edwards et al. (2019) expanded the definition of MOs to include control over behavior by discriminative stimuli that are historically relevant to behavioral consequences. I will also explore strategies that I have learned (but not necessarily mastered) for arranging stimuli to occasion behaviors that are likely to be strengthened by specific appetitive consequences in specific contexts.

Values as Verbal Motivating Operations

Several chapters in this book have focused upon the importance of values clarification in sustaining a meaningful life inside and outside of the academy (see Chapters 4 and 20). Values are colloquially viewed as those that give life purpose. For verbal organisms, a verbal "life's purpose" is constructed as a form of relational responding, in which we consider the outcomes of our behavior in a verbally constructed future, where the consequences are temporally distant and probabilistic (see Plumb et al., 2009). Within the community of Acceptance and Commitment Therapy, values are defined as "freely chosen and verbally constructed consequences for ongoing and evolving patterns of activity that are intrinsic of and inherent in the valued behavioral pattern itself" (Wilson & Dufrene, 2009, p. 64). For verbal humans, values can be conceptualized as verbal MOs—a verbal rule known as an augmental, which, consistent with the definition of MOs, establishes the reinforcing or punishing effectiveness of some consequence. Values statements often take the form of motivative augmentals, which temporarily increase the value of an already established reinforcer (Plumb et al.). For example, the value statement, "My door is always open for students" makes salient an already established reinforcer in one's work (mentoring or interacting with students), thus making it likely that the instructor will be accessible to students, at least on some temporary basis. Plumb et al. (2009) describe this MO as verbal because the values statement includes verbal descriptions of the valued phenomenon itself (keeping one's office door open), which is in a relational frame with the valued phenomenon itself. This thus increases the motivational power of the valued phenomenon, keeping one's office door open and being available to one's students on a frequent basis. To wit, Sandoz et al. (2021) demonstrated that written values statements influenced the likelihood with which participants engaged in subsequent behaviors that were consistent with their written values statements.

Although values are related to goals, values can never be fulfilled, satisfied, or completed. Rather, values may set the occasion for concrete goals. Committed actions, Plumb et al. (2009) contend, are the logical extension of values, where an individual pursues patterns of values-directed behavior and contacts the reinforcers that result. While an academician may have the goal of obtaining three publications a year, they may value high-quality research that contributes to the knowledge base on Acceptance and Commitment Training (ACT). This value may set the occasion for such values-consistent behaviors as reading the literature on ACT on the train to work every day. Although a favorable peer review and eventual publication are obvious reinforcers, one would hope that the values-consistent behaviors themselves provide reinforcement for the individual because of their interest in and passion for ACT and applied behavior analysis, and therefore sustain moderate-to-high rates of behavior.

An entire subdomain within ACT focuses upon helping people identify their values in the work-place, and in so doing re-establish contact with important reinforcers with which one may have lost contact over the course of time spent in their job (Flaxman et al., 2013). Values clarification has been shown to be successful in preventing job stress and burnout for people in a variety of occupations (e.g., Flaxman & Bond, 2010)

On Contexts

It is important to acknowledge that the contingencies influencing behavior, including one's own covert experience, enact their influence in rich, multilayered contexts in which the functions of numerous stimuli interact. For this reason, it seems illogical to discuss how to best stay motivated separately inside and outside of work given that the contingencies in the different contexts intersect. Any dimension of life that is rich or scarce with reinforcers will no doubt impact one's behavior in another area of life. The same is true for compartmentalizing motivation into different domains of one's work, such as teaching, research and service. Thus, any discussion of staying motivated by necessity should treat how one cultivates happiness and high performance in all facets of life intertwined. For the sake of organization, however, I am treating the two contexts—work and not work—separately in this chapter simply for ease of communication. One's values at work aren't necessarily different from one's values outside of work, although the contexts may differ in terms of how they support values-consistent behavior. The same is true for the different domains of work in which most academicians typically invest their time. Thus, I acknowledge at the outset that the contexts in which women engage in work and non-work-related behavior are rich, multilayered, and interconnected.

Scholarly Activity

The Contingencies

Institutions of higher education vary in terms of how contingencies for scholarly activity are arranged (also see Chapter 7). For some institutions, research publications, conference presentations, and grantsmanship figure prominently in promotion and tenure decisions, whereas other institutions may place a greater emphasis on teaching proficiency and service. Regardless, some degree of scholarly activity and engagement in one's professional discipline is expected at nearly every type of institution. Greenspoon (1991) provided a cogent analysis of the different levels of contingencies operating at institutions of higher learning, which may at times conflict. Administrators are faced with the challenges of declining enrollment, shrinking operating budgets, and the changing job market, along with the goal of maintaining the institution's prestige. Greenspoon noted that some academicians feel as though the majority of published studies will "soon be forgotten by all but their authors" (p. 151), and with contingencies to publish or perish, some will "publish anything that might be accepted" (p. 151). Further contributing to such complex contingencies is the notion that "deans don't read them; they just count them" (Greenspoon, 1991, p. 151).

In light of this, the key to staying motivated would seem to be ensuring that dense schedules of reinforcement maintain one's performance in scholarly activity. Unfortunately, most institutions themselves do not operate in such a way that faculty regularly contact external reinforcers delivered by the institution itself. For this reason, ideally one's work, or certain aspects thereof, should provide reinforcers that are sufficient to sustain performance and provide enjoyment and satisfaction. Identifying reinforcers through one's scholarly activity and identifying the behaviors that will reliably produce them may be easier said than done, particularly as schedules become busy and routines are established. Years may go by and over time a person may lose sight of what was originally important to them about their career in the first place, at which point in time the values clarification described by Chapters 4 and 20 becomes necessary.

Discovering What You Have to Say[1]

Ideally, the best position to be in with regards to contacting reinforcers for scholarly work is one where the science itself is reinforcing because it is so stimulating and interesting to you. I fell in love with behavior analysis over the course of an undergraduate class in the experimental analysis of behavior. I vividly recall the hours I spent laboring over Catania's (1992) *Learning* text, having found a true passion for the content. Mastering the vernacular was hard work; but because I was so stimulated by the material, it was not a chore. In graduate school at the University of Nevada-Reno, my interests in behavior analytic conceptualizations of language and cognition intensified, and although the types of applications I have focused on have shifted over the course of 20+ years in academia, my passion for this topic area hasn't wavered. Contingencies within the contexts of my life may have allowed me to be more productive—and satisfied—during different phases of my career nonetheless.

I have found that research or writing collaborations can have a huge impact on one's enjoyment when they are completed with a partner. For me, many of those collaborators have been outside of my own places of employment, and instead were people elsewhere who shared my interests, many of whom are European. Seemingly trivial social reinforcers, such as opening one's email and finding correspondence from a collaborator, exchanging a manuscript back and forth, or simply sharing news of interesting new publications or conference publications, can have an enormous impact on one's enjoyment and hence productivity. Social media no doubt provides the same form of social support (see Chapter 14). Given the size of most university departments, it seems unlikely that one might find collaborators in one's institution who share the same exact research niche, so I have strongly come to value relationships with colleagues elsewhere. Given the sophistication of technology today, there are virtually no geographic limits with whom one can collaborate (Chapter 14). Collaborators can help share the workload, but the additional social reinforcers inherent in working with people from other places who may have trained elsewhere and have grown up with different cultural perspectives is rich and life enhancing. For me such collaborations have been very effective in sustaining excitement, particularly during times that I may have strayed off course from my values. Collaborators are great at reminding a person of what excited them about the discipline in the first place.

Other elicitors of excitement over behavior science may come from reviewing articles, reading journal articles, and attending conference presentations. Many faculty struggle to find time for editorial work but turning down opportunities to review the work of others may be a missed opportunity for some really engaging concept or idea. I also always urge newer academicians to sign up for journal alerts so that they know when the new issues are out, and so that they never stop reading and growing. The same is true about attending conference presentations. One can never predict which presentation may inspire the next study. I can easily count on one hand the articles and accompanying presentations, some long ago and others more recent, that were career-changing in this regard (Barnes-Holmes et al., 2000; Greer et al., 2005).

It is a great idea to try to make writing itself a reinforcing activity if it isn't already. I have always loved writing and found the process and products to be equally reinforcing. I did nonetheless experiment with some amusing strategies in graduate school to establish even more conditioned reinforcing properties to writing as an activity, including pairing the activity with incense and my favorite music. Skinner (1981) offered numerous suggestions for enhancing one's writing productivity, including identifying a regular, convenient place to establish effective stimulus control over writing, writing at the same time of day, writing in small steps, and avoiding an attempt to accomplish too much in one sitting. In keeping with the contextual approach of this chapter, Skinner (1981) further advised that "there is usually some leisure time, and a fundamental rule is not to try to do more writing" (p. 3). If so, he claimed, you will pay the price during the next writing session and experience ineffectiveness. Although verbal behavior may occur at other times of the day, Skinner (1981) encouraged putting it down in lasting form in a notepad or notebook. Phones are great for this purpose today. With regards to finding something to say, Skinner (1981) contended that, also consistent with the contextual approach of this chapter, the easiest way to do this is to collect life experiences—"moving about in the world and by reading and listening to what others have to say" (p. 2).

Punishers and Paradigm Shifts

There are a few things that I have learned within the world of academia that can have a punitive effect on one's motivation, including on one's productivity, how one allocates their time, and the joy that one receives out of their scholarly work. It is conceivable that one may simply burn out on a particular topic. Skinner (1981) explained with regards to writing specifically that people often get to a point where they stop writing or find it difficult to go on, as extinction may set in and aversive consequences may take over. Not only does Skinner's point serve as a reminder for pursuing values in all of the different contexts described in this chapter, it also reinforces the notion that one may simply grow tired of conducting research on a particular topic. I have always been interested in behavioral analyses of language and cognition, broadly defined, which encompassed a variety of topics and theoretical orientations at different stages of my career. Earlier in my career I devoted a lot of time and energy to applied, educationally relevant studies on stimulus equivalence. 20 years is a very long time to continue studying one behavioral phenomena, so my interests shifted to relational operants, multiple-exemplar instruction, and ACT as time went on. It is thus natural to expand one's interests over the course of one's career; doing so simply creates opportunities for stimulation by new material, ideas, projects, and collaborations (see also Chapter 17).

It is also important to recognize that the paradigms of a scientific community also change as research findings accumulate, and as a scholar you will want to move with the changing times.

Thomas Kuhn (1962/1996) defined a paradigm as a worldview, or a universally recognizable scientific achievement that for some period of time provides a framework for solving problems for a community of practitioners. In his book *The Structure of Scientific Revolutions* (1962/1996), Kuhn elaborated upon the period of time during which scientists engage in "normal" science, which for Kuhn is akin to puzzle-solving. When a revolutionary discovery occurs, a new paradigm is ushered in. To some extent Kuhn's conceptualization mirrors my own abandonment of studies on stimulus equivalence to that of relational responding and behavioral flexibility. Barnes-Holmes et al. (2001) wrote over 20 years ago about the need to discontinue investigations of stimulus equivalence in favor of newer studies of language and cognition, acknowledging that "stimulus equivalence is simply too narrow and too limited to carry the weight some have put on it. It is a research preparation that shows every sign of exhaustion" (p. 36). The authors' comments could easily apply to any area of research investigation that perhaps gets to a point of advancing the field only incrementally, if at all. The authors further contend that "it (stimulus equivalence) has already been studied for 30 years, and the field could spend another 30 years in research primarily characterized by its precise irrelevancy. Behavior analysis does not have that time to waste" (Barnes-Holmes et al., 2001, p. 36). I think the lesson in these remarks is that one needs to continue evolving their own world view with that of the changing paradigms of their scientific community. This may mean updating one's perspective and taking time to master new literature that may challenge or contradict a prior worldview. Becoming stagnant is a certain way to cut off intellectual reinforcers.

Kuhn (1962/1996) observed that resistance to changes in paradigms is common. Unfortunately, I have observed much behavior on the part of a very small number of people in our field who have been resistant to the progression of Skinner's (1957) now 70-year-old analysis to Relational Frame Theory. Sometimes such resistance appears in peer review, and other times it appears in unbecoming, interpersonal, and unprofessional ways. Whether such behavior is more commonly exhibited by male colleagues we can only speculate, and I only have my own observations to inform. The best thing one can do is ensure that they are behaving in ways that are consistent with their own values (also see Chapters 4 and 19), and surround oneself with supportive colleagues who share those values, even if they are not located in the same physical space (see Chapter 14).

At some point during a female academician's career, particularly one who is organized and reliable, it is likely that they will be recruited for an administrative position or at least administrative work. University administration tends to come with drama in most any institution, so it is probably worth considering whether one wants to shift focus from teaching and mentoring to what may often seem like putting out fires. Administrators often have less flexible schedules than do faculty members, so the decision to change course in that direction should not be made lightly and should be done so with consideration of all of the contextual variables described in this chapter. During one phase of university life I believe I was recruited for administration before I was ready to shift attention from scholarly work, and the experience at that time did not work well for me. At that point in time I found comfort in the words of a close friend and mentor, Dr. Douglas Greer, who said, "I prefer plain vanilla researchers like B. F. Skinner. Let someone else take out the garbage" (Greer, personal communication, sometime). Later in my career I felt more prepared, confident and comfortable with shifting my time allocation from student mentorship to administrative work.

Teaching: Affecting Eternity[2]

Although different institutions place different levels of emphasis on the amount that one teaches as well as the quality that is expected from teaching, all institutions of higher education require teaching, and most academicians in behavior analysis, save for those who may have ongoing research funding or administrative responsibilities, do teach. At some institutions it may seem as though teaching is valued second to research and scholarly activity, and an individual can decide on the extent to which high-quality teaching fits into their own values framework. I have never forgotten my own college instructors who inspired not only the direction my career would take, but my critical thinking and citizenship skills as well. I have thus always valued teaching as much as my commitment to scholarly work even in situations in which the contingencies at a particular institution did not. With regards to staying motivated, one should never underestimate the role that students may play in sustaining one's excitement and energy for their subject matter. I have taught many doctoral seminars over the course of long weekends and will never forget some of the lengthy philosophical discussions we held. I had as much to learn from them as they did me, and often found that their way of looking at a topic could spark a new idea or simply stimulate the imagination. The same is true for lower-division classes. I have found that sometimes simply preparing for a class or considering a unique point that a student raises in class can generate contemplation and excitement on my part as instructor.

New faculty often lament about the amount of time they devote to preparing new courses and look forward to the day that their classes require little to no prep work in advance of a class session. Of course, at some institutions courses are completely prepared and essentially handed to a faculty member to teach with little expectation for the faculty member's own creative development. I think it is very unfortunate that some degree fields in higher education have gone in this direction. It removes a very important element from teaching, an element that I believe *defines* teaching. I hope that most academicians today truly have the chance to contribute creatively to the courses that they teach. If they do, I would not eagerly await the day that the prepping is over. To stay up to date in one's field one must constantly explore content so that their courses are contemporary (another element that defines teaching); so it is not only important for one's students and the discipline to constantly revise courses, but it may help the instructor come into contact with new content as well. In addition, I know a number of mid-career faculty who have expressed being bored or burned out on the classes that they have taught for a while. Constantly revising and inserting new content to remain up to date is one way to prevent that boredom, as is pursuing opportunities to develop new courses. I was lucky to have been afforded opportunities to develop a number of new and intriguing graduate and undergraduate courses, including on topics such as Philosophy of Science, ACT, Relational Frame Theory, Verbal Behavior, and even a seminar in Chaos Theory. Although the courses affected my time allocation during the week, I honestly found that preparing new courses in content that was stimulating to me and a little bit outside of the box piqued my interests and got me excited.

Teaching can be one of the most rewarding parts of an academician's job, even through to retirement. I once heard an individual who was close to retiring comment on how many times they had walked into the same classroom during the duration of their employment. Years of teaching can be rewarding if one remains open to being in the present moment and available for contacting the reinforcers that teaching may bring. This may mean engaging one's acceptance repertoire when it comes to the unpleasant aspects of teaching, including dealing with student complaints, uninterested students, and the like.

Online courses may make it challenging to contact reinforcers that come from interacting with students if one does not have plenty of opportunities for interactions with students built into their courses. Indeed, best practices in online teaching advise plenty of techniques for building community and fostering interactions between students, instructors, and other students in their courses (see O'Malley, 2017). I would strongly encourage those who teach online to contact resources from the Online Learning Consortium to ensure that their courses incorporate such opportunities. Otherwise, not only may a course risk failing to adhere to what is today recognized as common expectations for an online course, but one may miss out completely on some of the most pleasurable aspects of teaching.

A Cautionary Note about Service

Guarino and Borden (2017) report that women are disproportionately assigned university service opportunities relative to their male colleagues, which is ironic given that there are still far fewer women in higher-level administrative leadership positions in higher education today than men (see Blackmore, 2017), and even fewer who are black (Jean-Marie, 2017). I was recruited for many university service obligations over the years (i.e., chairing this or that provost-appointed task force, coordinating university accreditation efforts as a faculty member, etc.). Unless such obligations open the door to other desired leadership opportunities or one truly finds the work interesting, I believe that such service work provides few reinforcers in and of itself unless one finds helping a university administrator reinforcing (also see Chapter 8). In light of Guarrino and Bowden's (2017) findings, I hope other women will be wary of saying yes to too many university service obligations. I can't imagine anyone looking back on their academic career as one approaches retirement and lamenting "if only I had engaged in more university service to help out the provost." I think as women faculty we need to be cautious about such opportunities and ensure that those that require substantial time and effort come with release time and a title or advancement to go along with it.

I feel differently about allocating one's professional time toward community service. Greenspoon (1991) contended that academicians tend to consider a higher education institution to be a vehicle for change, which may encourage some to get involved in their local community. Not every discipline may afford opportunities for community service. Some may not wish to participate because it removes time that could otherwise be granted toward scholarly activity. For faculty members in applied behavior analysis, there may be opportunities to serve on community agency boards or to provide trainings at community agencies or schools every now and again. Not only have I found that such community relationships shape one's perspective for research and teaching, but they provide a great opportunity to socially connect with people outside of the work-place and learn the "real" status of the discipline from the people doing the work every day. Everyone gets tired of sitting in their office day after day, so I encourage people to take advantage of community partnerships whenever they can to learn new viewpoints, new ways of looking at things, and in actuality, just connect socially with those outside of the university setting. Interacting with one's community, if it makes sense to do so within the context of one's position, is just another opportunity for social reinforcers from meeting and engaging with other human beings that is so important for our health and well-being. It would be great if there were more contingencies in higher education to support such community outreach. I found that such experiences were consistent with Skinner's (1981) notion of finding what you have to say by "moving about the world" (p. 2).

Leisure: The Time for Doing Something Useful[3]

ACT emphasizes living a life that is characterized by purpose and vitality—in other words, living life to the fullest. For years I was recognized as one of the first to arrive at work in the morning and the last to leave. After experiencing the untimely passing of colleagues who may have similarly devoted the preponderance of their waking hours to working and reading the likes of Russ Harris (see also Chapter 20), I realized that there is a life to be led outside of the workplace, and one doesn't want to realize that before it is too late. I know of several colleagues who had glorious plans for their retirement, and then an unexpected disaster hit. Indeed, the eulogy exercise referenced by Adel C. Najdowski (Chapter 20) is a powerful tool for bringing one's values into unavoidable focus and influencing how one allocates their time and energy. Having passions outside of work is an obvious way to ensure motivation and stimulation in all of the interwoven contexts in one's life. Indeed Skinner (1981) observed that writing may be ineffective if one does not make time for leisure (see also Chapter 15).

Although I have worked a lot, I have always been an avid lover of classical music from even a very young age. In fact, given my deep passion for music, I have often regretted that I did not pursue a career of some sort in music instead. Nonetheless, I began playing viola at a young age and have spent most of my life playing in a variety of community orchestras, some professional, some semi, and some purely volunteer, depending on where I lived. For me, playing in orchestras and learning about the repertoire each orchestra performed has granted a great deal of meaning to my life. Some of the most interesting memories stem from my experience playing in the Reno Philharmonic while a graduate student at the University of Nevada. The Philharmonic had a somewhat unconventional performance schedule given the nature of the casino industry. I'll never forget the opportunity to accompany Luciano Pavarotti on a very late career tour, or the Moody Blues outside of the Reno Hilton. As evidence of how contexts intertwine, I finally found a way to work my love for classical music into my conceptual work in behavior analysis and wrote about the relational properties of music and its role in enacting social change during the COVID-19 pandemic—a time during which attending concerts or making music with others in an organized fashion was not possible. Interestingly, Fink et al. (2021) report that many people around the world sought comfort and entertainment from listening to music or engaging in music during lockdown conditions during the pandemic. My experience was similar except that I wrote about it.

Hopefully my recommendation is clear. I strongly encourage readers to find one's passions in life as early in one's career as possible, potentially with the help of values clarification exercises popular in the ACT community (also see Chapters 4 and 20) and allocating time for them. As previously mentioned, work and leisure are not separate compartments. How you behave in one context and the consequences you contact will affect your behavior and well-being in another context.

Social Relationships and Community

The pandemic was a particularly challenging time for me and my family, as we had just relocated to Chicagoland from Carbondale, IL, where we had lived for a number of years. We lived in Chicagoland for only a few short months so we had not established social connections in our neighborhood or community before the pandemic hit. Given this, the many months of the pandemic taught me the value of connecting with other humans. Although like many I engaged in numerous meetings with students and colleagues via Zoom, after so many months the limited amount of face-to-face interaction took its toll. I'm grateful to have sustained relationships with two very close friends, one from graduate school and one from early in my academic career, so that I at least had the benefit of regular texts and phone calls with close friends. Their presence in my life was a huge source of support during so many months of limited social connections. I think it is easy for a person to bury oneself in work and lose out on chances to get to know others, share a few laughs, and form connections, and I learned this lesson later in life. I felt lucky to have had relationships with parents of other children as my daughters grew. Even though not all moms work or share the same lifelong goals, it can be rewarding to get to know individuals in other phases of life who may have different perspectives to bring to the present moment. I encourage you to not miss out on these human connections—don't let work take a priority. Hayes (2005) reminds us that humans don't come with owner manuals. A terrifying reality may be looking back on one's life in later years and realizing that one devoted so much time to work and missed out on other relationships, perhaps as a form of avoidance. As Hayes (2005) warns, "Opportunities may have been spoiled forever. Sometimes it is not even possible to apologize. People have died or are no longer interested" (p. 193). Thinking back again to the eulogy exercise presented in Chapter 20, I urge you to ensure that social relationships with others are always a priority (see also Chapters 6, 10, 15, and 19).

Related to this is the importance of engaging with one's community, something else that I came to value during the pandemic, and similarly regret to say was a later-in-life recognition. Doing volunteer work in one's community may refine one's values and identify new possibilities for committed actions. Engaging with one's community is another example of realizing what one "has to say" from accruing life experiences (Skinner, 1981). Participating in an engaged community seems to be correlated with better health outcomes as well (see Strom & Egede, 2012). As elaborated upon by Rehfeldt and Tyndall (2021), research shows that people living in communities in which caring for others is prioritized report significantly less stress and greater life satisfaction than others (Grinde et al., 2018), leading Wilson (2016) to propose an evolutionary basis for caring for others as an engaged community member. I myself have derived satisfaction from raising funds for women's cancer organizations via online ACT workshops and making supply bags for women undergoing cancer treatment.

Health: The Real Wealth[4]

Those who have contributed to the scholarly work on motivating operations have suggested that physiological states can serve as motivating operations (Cautilli & Dziewolska, 2004). This would presumably include a health condition or illness, which undeniably affects one's response allocation (see Chapter 14). Importantly, illness may also serve as a form of values clarification. I had a surprise diagnosis that was neither expected nor predicted on the basis of available evidence, and although at an early stage with a favorable prognosis, aggressive frontline treatment was prescribed. Looking back I wish it had been possible to have a mentor (see Chapters 5 and 6) during that time period who could have advised me on how to manage the requirements of all of the contexts of my life during a lengthy period of difficult treatment with challenging side effects, including continuous and extreme fatigue. Some health conditions and the treatments thereof make it impossible to allocate one's responding as one might wish, at which point in time one's committed actions must shift almost in their entirety to the domains of wellness, healing, and self-care. Physical health must take precedent, as many forms of academic work may be simply incompatible with managing treatment and its potentially grueling side effects. Managing a long-term health condition is the time to say "no" with no questions asked and ask for and expect grace when it comes to deadlines or extensions. Or, better yet, be open and transparent about what is do-able and not do-able at the time. Although one will certainly work with their chair or other supervisor during periods of illness to adjust one's workload, colleagues in the professional discipline will have no idea what is going on unless you disclose. I myself was, and have remained, very private, which had its drawbacks. If the situation were known to others, it may have been easier to arrange the contingencies in the way that mattered. Social media, for those who do not have a "health mentor" at their disposal, may provide an opportunity for connecting with others around the world who are enduring something similar.

Chapter 14 provides a wealth of insights on how chronic health conditions fit into the milieu of one's life for much longer durations. Many have observed that once they are rested and in some form of remission or recovery, values such as family, time with others, and time engaging with life became priorities (see Feros, Lane, Ciarrochi, & Blackledge, 2013). I agree wholeheartedly.

Conclusion

The purpose of this chapter was to offer insights as to how one can do their best to sustain motivation over the course of a career in academia. Much of my discussion focused upon how one might identify important and powerful reinforcers both within and outside of one's work, and clarify values that are likely to occasion behaviors that will contact those reinforcers. It is clear that a large part of ensuring motivation in one's job has to do with the presence of freely available reinforcers in other contexts of life. Challenges may result when research paradigms shift and interpersonal dynamics unnecessarily detract from interesting work. Likewise, administrative responsibilities may creep into the agenda, and may or may not be a welcome diversion. Finally, friendships, engagement with one's community, and one's health status may all affect one's priorities and well-being.

The climate towards women and non-binary individuals (see Chapters 4 and 11) has changed since I first began working in an academic setting. It seems that the voices of women are not only valued but even celebrated more today than might have been the case 20+ years ago. Subtle biases and pressures may nonetheless still exert influence. I hope that this chapter will offer assurance to others that they can perform the duties of an academic position in an exemplary manner—and enjoy their responsibilities—yet also experience a rich, meaningful life in all of the contexts of their being.

Notes

1. Skinner, B. F. (1981). How to discover what you have to say—A talk to students. *The Behavior Analyst*, *4*(1), 1–7. Foundational questions in science). Yale University Press.
2. From a quote by Henry Brooks Adams.
3. Based on a quote by Benjamin Franklin.
4. Based on a quote by Mahatma Gandhi.

References

Barnes-Holmes, D., Barnes-Holmes, Y., & Cullinan, V. (2000). Relational frame theory and skinner's *verbal behavior*: A possible synthesis. *The Behavior Analyst*, *23*(1), 69–84. https://doi.org/10.1007/bf03392000

Barnes-Holmes, D., Hayes, S. C., & Roche, B. (2001). The (not so) strange death of stimulus equivalence. *European Journal of Behavior Analysis*, *2*(1), 35–41. https://doi.org/10.1080/15021149.2001.11434166

Blackmore, J. (2017). 'In the shadow of men': The historical construction of educational administration as a 'masculinist' enterprise. In *Gender matters in educational administration and policy* (pp. 27–48). Routledge.

Catania, A. C. (1992). *Learning and behavior*. Prentice-Hall, Inc.

Cautilli, J., & Dziewolska, H. (2004). A brief report: The neutralizing effects of stimulus control intervention for sleep on escape behavior and token performance of a nine-year-old child with oppositional defiant disorder. *Journal of Early and Intensive Behavior Intervention*, *1*(2), 232–238. https://doi.org/10.1037/h0100291

Edwards, T. L., Lotfizadeh, A. D., & Poling, A. (2019). Motivating operations and stimulus control. *Journal of the Experimental Analysis of Behavior*, *112*(1), 1–9. https://doi.org/10.1002/jeab.516

Feros, D. L., Lane, L., Ciarrochi, J., & Blackledge, J. T. (2013). Acceptance and commitment therapy (ACT) for improving the lives of cancer patients: A preliminary study. *Psycho-oncology*, *22*(2), 459–464. https://doi.org/10.1002/pon.2083

Fink, L. K., Warrenburg, L. A., Howlin, C., Randall, W. M., Hansen, N. C., & Wald-Fuhrmann, M. (2021). Viral tunes: Changes in musical behaviours and interest in coronamusic predict socio-emotional coping during COVID-19 lockdown. *Humanities and Social Sciences Communications*, *8*(1), 1–11. https://doi.org/10.31234/osf.io/7mg2v

Flaxman, P. E., & Bond, F. W. (2010). A randomised worksite comparison of acceptance and commitment therapy and stress inoculation training. *Behaviour Research and Therapy*, *48*(8), 816–820. https://doi.org/10.1016/j.brat.2010.05.004

Flaxman, P. E., Bond, F. W., & Livheim, F. (2013). *The mindful and effective employee: An acceptance and commitment therapy training manual for improving well-being and performance*. New Harbinger Publications.

Greenspoon, J. (1991). Behavioral analysis in higher education. In P. A. Lamal (Ed.), *Behavioral analysis of societies and cultural practices* (pp. 141–164). Hemisphere Publishing Corporation.

Greer, R. D., Stolfi, L., Chavez-Brown, M., & Rivera-Valdes, C. (2005). The emergence of the listener to speaker component of naming in children as a function of multiple exemplar instruction. *The Analysis of Verbal Behavior*, *21*(1), 123–134. https://doi.org/10.1007/bf03393014

Grinde, B., Nes, R. B., MacDonald, I. F., & Wilson, D. S. (2018). Quality of life in intentional communities. *Social Indicators Research: An International and Interdisciplinary Journal for Quality-Of-Life Measurement*, *137*(2), 625–640. https://doi.org/10.1007/s11205-017-1615-3

Guarino, C. M., & Borden, V. M. (2017). Faculty service loads and gender: Are women taking care of the academic family? *Research in Higher Education, 58*(6), 672–694. https://doi.org/10.1007/s11162-017-9454-2

Hayes, S. C. (2005). *Get out of your mind and into your life: The new acceptance and commitment therapy*. New Harbinger Publications.

Hyde, J. S., & Kling, K. C. (2001). Women, motivation, and achievement. *Psychology of Women Quarterly, 25*(4), 364–378. https://doi.org/10.1111/1471-6402.00035

Jean-Marie, G. (2017). Black women at the helm in HBCUs: Paradox of gender and leadership. In M. Christopher Brown II and T. Elon Dancy II (Eds.), *Black colleges across the diaspora: Global perspectives on race and stratification in postsecondary education* (pp. 101–124). Emerald Publishing Limited.

Kuhn, T. S. (1962, 1996). *The structure of scientific revolutions* (3rd ed.). University of Chicago Press.

Laraway, S., Snycerski, S., Michael, J., & Poling, A. (2003). Motivating operations and terms to describe them: Some further refinements. *Journal of Applied Behavior Analysis, 36*(3), 407–414. https://doi.org/10.1901/jaba.2003.36-407

Legault, L. (2016). Intrinsic and extrinsic motivation. In *Encyclopedia of personality and individual differences* (pp. 1–4). https://doi.org/10.1007/978-3-319-28099-8_1139-1

Nascimento, V. L., Revorêdo, S. F., Nascimento, E. H. L., Brasil, D. M., Freitas, D. Q., & Lima, G. A. (2018). Burnout syndrome among dental professors: A cross-sectional study. *Revista Da ABENO, 18*(2), 62–71. https://doi.org/10.30979/rev.abeno.v18i2.557

O'Malley, S. (2017, July 26). Professors share ideas for building community in online courses. *Inside Higher Ed*. www.insidehighered.com/digital-learning/article/2017/07/26/ideas-building-online-community

Plumb, J. C., Stewart, I., Dahl, J., & Lundgren, T. (2009). In search of meaning: Values in modern clinical behavior analysis. *The Behavior Analyst, 32*(1), 85–103. https://doi.org/10.1007/bf03392177

Rehfeldt, R. A., & Tyndall, I. (2021). Why we are not acting to save ourselves: ACT, health, and culture. *Behavior Analysis Practice*. https://doi.org/10.1007/s40617-021-00592-6

Sandoz, E. K., Bordieri, M. J., Boullion, G. Q., & Tyndall, I. (2021). An examination of transformation of evaluative and consequential functions through derived relations with participant-generated values-relevant stimuli. *Journal of Contextual Behavioral Science, 21*, 144–157. https://doi.org/10.1016/j.jcbs.2021.07.002

Schenk, A. (2003). *Female professors in Sweden and Germany*. (Training Papers; Vol. TP 03/03). Research Training Network "Women in European Universities"

Skinner, B. F. (1957). *Verbal behavior*. Appleton-Century-Crofts.

Skinner, B. F. (1981). How to discover what you have to say—A talk to students. *The Behavior Analyst, 4*(1), 1–7. Foundational questions in science). Yale University Press.

Strom, J. L., & Egede, L. E. (2012). The impact of social support on outcomes in adult patients with type 2 diabetes: A systematic review. *Current Diabetes Reports, 12*(6), 769–781. https://doi.org/10.1007/s11892-012-0317-0

Wilson, D. S. (2016). Quality of life from an evolutionary perspective. *Applied Research in Quality of Life: The Official Journal of the International Society for Quality-of-Life Studies, 11*(2), 331–342. https://doi.org/10.1007/s11482-014-9341-3

Wilson, K. G., & Dufrene, T. (2009). *Mindfulness for two: An acceptance and commitment Therapy approach to mindfulness in psychotherapy*. New Harbinger Publications.

19 A Cross-Continental Journey Through Academia; Life Partners, Tensions, and the People Who Influenced My Path

Lise Roll-Pettersson

A Cross-Continental Journey Through Academia; Life Partners, Tensions, and the People Who Influenced My Path

The Beginning of My Story

I was born in the United Kingdom (UK) and I grew up in North Carolina in a multicultural family. My father was a first-generation Danish-Norwegian who had, in the early 1960s, obtained a research position at Duke university; my mother came from a "Russian Jewish" family that had immigrated from Ukraine and Lithuania to New York City in the 1920s. Due to oppressions encountered in her family, she was adamant that we hide our Jewish roots to avoid encountering anti-Semitism in school, our neighborhood, or worse, by the KKK. This entailed that I avoided talking openly about my background, yet I yearned to learn more about it. At 15 years of age I was sent back to the UK to an all-girl boarding school to get a "decent" education. Though the school was extremely strict, I made a number of friends mainly from the Middle East, who on a cultural basis had different ways of reasoning and behaving than I had previously encountered. During a school vacation, when visiting family in Denmark, I met a Swedish man and eventually moved to Sweden, which was also different from the other cultural contexts which I had experienced. People were more reserved, societal norms were not apparent for non-Swedes, and there was more interaction between societal classes. In hindsight I realize that through my multi-cultural encounters, I learned to be cautious, and to be a swayer, re-adjusting and compromising when moving between cultures, a trait, which for better or worse, I brought with me to academia.

A Bit of History: The Swedish "Folkhem" Ideology and Gender Issues

Comparing the Nordic societies to the rest of Europe, Parker (2002) described the Nordics as "small non-aggressive states, built on consensus politics, welfare and a search for security" (p. 357), noting that "rural classes and purportedly rural values (of community and independence) remained politically prominent until . . . late in the 20th century" (p. 357). Indeed, during this period the majority of adult citizens in Sweden had a vocational high school degree (i.e., not a university degree), which prepared them for some kind of trade (e.g., child caretaker, car or airplane mechanic, horse caretaker, or "high school" engineer). Also within this timeframe, the Swedish "Folkhemmet" (The People's Home) ideology was flourishing, in which the ideal society was likened to a "good home" consisting of kindness, social solidarity, humane political values, equality between women and men, as well as between wealthy and poor (Götz, 2004; Wikipedia, 2021). This movement laid

DOI: 10.4324/9781003216773-23

the foundation for the Swedish welfare system which involved numerous societal reforms, including paid parental leave which started in the 1970s with six months paid leave per child, which has since increased, and is at present at 480 days. The governmental hope was that parental leave would be shared between mothers and fathers, enhancing equality between sexes. In 1974 approximately 0.5% of the allotted time was used by fathers, while in 2020 about 30% of the allotted time was used, with highly educated men working within the public sector using this opportunity to a higher degree than lower-income fathers and/or fathers with non-Swedish backgrounds (Försäkringskassa, n.d.).

Another part of the Folkhem movement was to provide the incentives for both parents to work through the creation of a high-quality preschool (daycare) for all children over one year of age, consisting of small groups and well-educated staff, with spacious and designated indoor and outdoor areas. The National Curriculum for Preschool (Lpfö, 98) highlights fundamental democratic values such as: the right of every child to express themselves, make choices, that preschool be enjoyable, safe, and provide a rich learning environment free of discriminatory influences. It is estimated that approximately 94% of two- to five-year-old children in Sweden attend a public funded municipality-based or independent preschool, both of which are funded through taxpayer monies (Skolverket, 2021). The monthly fee is subsidized based on parents' salaries, ranging from $0 to approximately $175 (Stockholms Stad, 2021). Thus, a single parent studying at a university without a salary would not pay a monthly fee while a two-parent high-income couple would pay the max fee. There is also a unitarian child-benefit monthly allowance for each child that is paid to all parents regardless of income to avoid stigmatization for those who have lower economical means; meals at preschool and school are also free of charge for the same reason. According to UNICEF (2008), in a comparison among Organisation for Economic Co-operation and Development (OECD) countries, Sweden is the only country meeting all benchmark standards concerning early-childhood services.

There is no tuition for higher education studies; an aim of the 1977 higher education reform (see UKÄ, 2017) was to encourage more females to obtain a university/higher education degree and to pursue an academic career. Numerous steps have been taken on a national level since to recruit women professors. A national goal is that by 2030 half of newly recruited professors should be women (UKÄ, 2020).

In Sweden there are two ways of obtaining a permanent position as professor: one is by applying for an open advertised position at a university or college in competition with others, the other is to apply for promotion within one's own department; both types of positions are externally evaluated. Statistics from the national follow-up in 2019 reveal that approximately 29% of professors were women while the percentage of women assistant professors was 48% (UKÄ, 2020). The percentage of newly recruited women professors between 2017 and 2019 varied between faculties, with social sciences reporting 44%, medical 49%, and agriculture 14% (UKÄ).

On the one hand, the gender differences may appear considerable in regard to fathers' v. mothers' usage of child care leave and the total percentage of women professors. Nevertheless, Sweden is an egalitarian society—couples share responsibilities within the home, regardless of gender. Students refer to all university staff by first name and not by title or marital status (i.e., Dr./Professor/Ms./Miss/Mister). On the surface level, societal contingencies are in place for promoting women to choose an academic career. However, one can wonder why there is low representation of women professors within specific faculties (i.e., agriculture) and no overrepresentation of women within any of the other faculties (i.e., social sciences or medical), thereby raising the question if there might be other distal-level and/or structural issues in place affecting women's possibilities or choices.

Tensions Within Higher Education Affecting Behavior Analysis

At some point, learning psychology as a subject matter was ousted by influential mainstream educational scholars. This was possibly a reaction to the accomplishments of Torsten Husen, one of the most internationally recognized Swedish professors in education, who in 1969 wrote the preface to the Swedish translation of Skinner's (1968) *Technology of Teaching*. The predominant theoretical and ideological framework in educational academia (of which special education was a part) in the 1980s to the early 2000s was post-modernism (Fischbein & Allodi Westling, in press) (spiced with a touch of psychoanalytic interpretation – author's personal reflection). According to Rikowski and McLaren (2002), post-modernism evolved as a reaction to "decades of research dominated by structural, functionalist, and empirical approaches within the human sciences" (p. 3). Within the postmodern paradigm, objectivity is perceived as erroneous, the focus being subjective meaning, entailing that data-based quantitative research methodologies including single-case research designs have no true value—mirroring the situation in Sweden stated by Fischbein and Allodi Westling: "the critique of modernism and ideals of enlightenment leading to a refusal of scientific standpoints, accused of being positivistic. The objectivity of science was questioned . . . virtually being impossible for anyone with another perspective to break through" (p. 2). Echoing this perception, an article in *Pedagogiska Magasinet*, a teacher-union magazine with approximately 200,000 subscribers, by Englund and Engström (2011), warned against the "Return of Behaviorism," stating that behaviorism is mainly based on simple stimulus-response mechanisms, which may have a place in psychotherapies for phobias but not within current pedagogical practice where there is an emphasis on empathy, dialogue, and mutual respect between educator and student/child. The article presents an illustration of children as marionettes helplessly hanging from strings, merely puppets, controlled by a "behavior modifier." In hindsight I can see how this false dichotomy within Swedish post-modernism not only closed the door to empirically supported behavioral interventions, but also opened the door for the acceptance and usage of non-evidence-based interventions and possibly harmful pseudo-psychoanalytic-based methods such as "holding" (Bökstedt, 1983) and "facilitated communication" (Dagens Nyheter, 2014).

My Story Continued

Extending Perspectives

By the late 1980s I was married to a middle school teacher and had two children; we shared all responsibilities for the home and caretaking of the children. Together with a group of acquaintances who also had preschool-aged children, we started a Maria Montessori preschool in an old manor house, and in accordance with the previously mentioned Swedish welfare model, costs were subsidized. We put together a parental board of directors, and through this common endeavor, developed close friendships with other parents. A number of the families lived in the countryside, close to nature. Through the close and supportive friendships I made with several of the mothers, I learned to appreciate the gift of nature, taking long weekend walks, in the winter cross-country skiing, and talking with the other mothers about everything.

Within this period, I had obtained Swedish degrees in early childhood and special education and a teaching position in a special school for pupils with intellectual disabilities with classrooms mainstreamed in a regular school. Though I loved my work, I realized that when it came to understanding how to enhance a pupil's communication skills and deal with aggressive and self-injurious behaviors, the lack of theoretical and practical knowledge of "how to" provide high-quality hands-on support and supervision in my special education degree program stifled the well-being and development of the pupils I worked with. This was a very disturbing and aggravating realization.

Also, in the late 1980s, after I had completed my special education degree and before our children started school, my husband and I decided to test out living in North Carolina for a year. During this period, he taught in a middle school, our eldest child began first grade, and our youngest went to a Montessori preschool (where I also worked). I began taking graduate courses at the University of North Carolina-Chapel Hill (UNC-CH), Department of Special Education in early-childhood education. The coursework had an interdisciplinary, family-centered focus in which Bronfenbrenner's (1979) ecological-systems theory was used to conceive the interrelatedness of various proximal and distal contexts on families, underscoring the importance of a needs-based approach, of coordinated enabling help-giving practices, and individualized culturally sensitive services (see Winton, 1992). The transactional theory of child development within an ecological-systems framework (entailing that influences within the ecological system can be non-linear as well as bidirectional) was also a central theme (see Winton). I also had contact with professor Rune Simeonsson at UNC-CH and the Frank Porter Graham Child Development Institute (FPG) regarding possible future projects involving Sweden and concerning parental needs. Rune also introduced me to "peer mediation" through the work of Sam Odom (Roll-Pettersson, 1992). This year turned out to be a turning point in my life, inspiring me to pursue an academic career in special education.

After the year was over, however, we decided to move back to Sweden. My husband felt that he would never be able to adjust to the American lifestyle; he missed the seasonal closeness to nature. I resumed my position as special education teacher and contacted Mats Granlund, a research director at the Anpassning till Liv och Arbete (Adjusting to Life and Work [ALA]) research institute in Stockholm to initiate a project using instruments like the Family Needs Survey (Bailey & Simeonsson, 1988) and the ABILITIES index (Simeonsson & Bailey, 1991), both developed at FPG. ALA was a small research institute founded in the 1960s which conducted mainly applied research and outreach projects that were supported through the national parental organization for children with intellectual disabilities. Researchers also applied for grants from a number of charities within the country. At this time there were two research directors at ALA, representing male and female sexes. Both had degrees in psychology and there was a board of directors consisting of members of the parental organization and university staff. ALA also had close collaborations with practitioners. We applied for funding to investigate the needs of parents of preschool children with intellectual disabilities (ID) and were successful in obtaining a grant. The staff at ALA were young, dynamic, and had differing perspectives, which included behavioral psychology. They accepted and used both qualitative and quantitative methods. Numerous reports, published peer-reviewed articles, and research were produced from ALA (e.g., Kylén, 1979, 1985; Göransson, 1982; Göransson et al., 2000; Granlund, 1984; Granlund et al., 1999). The climate was open and supportive, lacking the coerciveness found in some university-based academic environments. We had regular seminars on topics pertaining to IDs, and we read and provided feedback on each other's manuscripts and research applications. It was through this supportive climate that I was able to build the self-confidence needed to pursue a university career. Yet I also came to the realization that I am not a self-sufficient loner; rather, I am a person who prefers to work collaboratively in teams, and I need input from supportive colleagues with complementary knowledge and experience.

First Life Partner in Academia

Though the term "life partners" is usually used in reference to intimate partners such as a spouse, I am also using it in this chapter more broadly to describe decisive roles specific persons have played for me within my academic career. In the early 90s I began applying for doctoral positions at the Department of Special Education, Stockholm Institute of Education. In keeping with the Swedish post-modernist movement, reviewers of my first application rejected it based on content being of a "positivistic tradition." However, in 1993 I finally obtained a doctoral position, continued to conduct research at the ALA institute, and a collaboration between Rune Simeonsson, the department, and ALA evolved. Siv Fischbein, who was now my supervisor and also my first life partner in academia, obtained professorship in 1995 after substituting five years for a male professor who had moved to another university. Siv was the 142nd woman professor in Sweden and the first in special education at a time when only 7% of professors were female (Heimdahl Mattsson et al., 2005). Differing from most contemporary educational researchers, her background had been in twin studies from which she developed a transactional model involving a nature v. nurture stance, postulating that if you change the learning environment (educational practices) you change the strength of genetic influences. According to her work there was "no one size fits all" entailing that if you do not plan and structure learning situations (i.e., the predominant "laissez-faire" stance), Darwinism's survival of the fittest will take over, and there will be no positive changes in learning and development for children who have learning disabilities or who are not self-reliant (personal communication, Siv Fischbein December 7, 2021). Through her supportive guidance and supervision, we conducted both quantitative and qualitative studies concerning the perspectives and needs of parents who have a child with an ID, as well as investigated teacher's needs, perceived efficacy, and attitudes toward inclusion of pupils with disabilities.

It was during this period, when desperately in need of course credits in order to defend my doctoral thesis, that I accidently came in contact with Applied Behavior Analysis (ABA). The only summer school courses that fit in with my tight schedule were in "behavior modification" and "positive behavior support," taught at Muskingham College, Ohio by professors in Special Education from Penn State. While taking these courses I realized that the total exclusion of this field in Swedish special education was having a devastating effect on the learning development and participation of children with disabilities. I felt a deep frustration, sadness, and bitterness that my own pupils and others had not been given the opportunity to learn and develop to their own potential, i.e., obtain an appropriate education. I could see that the pragmatic, socially valid, and data-based approaches within ABA were the missing link to Bronfenbrenner's (1979) ecological model and transactional theories of development.

After defending my doctoral thesis in 2001, "Between open systems and closed doors," representatives from the Stockholm Autism Parental Organization met Siv and I to advocate for the inclusion of ABA in special education degree coursework. They brought up that the lack of knowledge of ABA evidence-based teaching practices and ineffective supervision provided by special educators was leading to adverse effects on the learning, well-being, and development of children with autism (Roll-Pettersson, 2003; Roll-Pettersson et al., 2020b). Siv and I were well aware that due to prevailing ontological beliefs it would be impossible to incorporate ABA evidence-based interventions with a focus on children with autism in the prevailing special education/pedagogy degree programs. Through the support and encouragement of Siv and the Special Education Forum (an interdisciplinary forum that Siv initiated) involving collaboration between the Karolinska Institute (KI), Mälardalen

University College, and Department of Special Education Stockholm Institute of Education, we decided the course sequence should be at the graduate level, interdisciplinary, and students would be professionals holding degrees as educators, speech language pathologists, psychologists, special educators, and physiotherapists. We decided also they would be given through KI beginning in 2004 (with financial support from the city of Stockholm and private charities). While developing the course sequence at KI, I was in contact with Jerry Shook (then director of the Behavior Analytic Certification Board [BACB]) who was supportive of my efforts to establish the field within higher education in Sweden.

In 2006 the course sequence was verified and moved to the School of Education (see Hughes & Shook, 2007); and since 2010 it has been given jointly by the Department of Special Education and Department of Psychology at Stockholm University (Roll-Pettersson et al., 2010). Since 2017 the joint verified course sequence (VCS) is offered as a master's program in special education with a focus on autism and approved by ABAI, and is the only master's program in the country that has a focus on the practice and science of behavior analysis.

Next Life Partner in Academia

In 2005, at the annual Penn State summer conference, as a means to support my effort in establishing the field of ABA in Sweden, Jerry Shook put me in contact with Shahla Ala'i-Rosales from the University of North Texas (UNT), whom he correctly presumed would be a supportive collaborative partner, and he believed that we would make an excellent and productive team. Shahla and I have collaborated in different formats since this first meeting. Her guidance, wisdom, and support have been paramount for me as a person, researcher, and professional, as well as for the development and evolution of the field within Sweden. Our differing academic backgrounds complemented each other's, and she showed me that personal friendship can be intertwined with work and that colleagues in academia can support one another emotionally and spiritually. This socially supportive and collaborative relationship empowered me emotionally, and gave me the courage to take decisive steps such as accepting a 20% associate professor position between 2008–2011 at the Department of Behavior Analysis, Akershus University College in Norway where I came in contact with a community of scholars for whom the field of behavior analysis is the central theme. Through the encouragement and constructive collaboration with Shahla as well as experiences from Akershus (now Oslo-Met), I came to the realization that it was possible to follow my core instincts concerning the importance of both contributing to formally establishing the field in Sweden and of humane relationships in academia. This lessened the emotional toll of working within an academic environment, where pulling rank, lack of warm social relationships, and tendencies of bullying among staff, regardless of gender, were engrained (also see Chapters 4 and 21).

Shahla and I have organized two summits and edited two adjoining special issues in the *European Journal of Behavior Analysis* (see also Arntzen & Pellón, 2021). The first summit was held in Texas (Ala i-Rosales et al., 2010) and the second in Stockholm (Roll-Pettersson, Dillenburger et al., 2020a), followed by our leadership and in collaboration with Karola Dillenburger (Chapter 21), Mickey Keenan, and Zuilma Gabriela Sigurðardóttir (Chapter 16); these summits and scholarly works focused on the specific needs, tensions, and possibilities from international perspectives within higher education, ABA, and autism. An additional focus of the Stockholm summit was consolidating behavioral and non-behavioral approaches. To this end we also invited keynote speakers with non-behavior analytic backgrounds to present research on topics of joint interest such as participation, engagement, and inclusion. Several of the articles from the Stockholm summit highlight broadening perspectives. For example, Todd (2020) discussed narrowness, warned of isolation within the field of behavior analysis, and recommended students expanding their knowledge repertoire in other areas. From an implementation science and Organizational Behavior Management (OBM) perspective, Odom et al. (2020) made the case that if behavior analysis is to move forward as a discipline addressing "socially and globally important problems," it will require behavior analysts having knowledge of inter- and intra- organizational factors and metacontingencies affecting implementation of evidence-based behavioral interventions. Also, in order to induce national recognition of ABA among decision makers, the organizing committee arranged a half-day summary of the summit in which key governmental policy makers, as well as representatives of parental groups, were invited.

Tensions and Partners within Academia, Con't

Contradictive to international research findings on the positive effects of Early Intensive Behavioral Intervention (EIBI), a prospective naturalistic longitudinal study in community-based preschools between 2005 and 2008 by Fernell et al. (2011) found no statistical pre-post effects in child outcome measures between children in the high and low EIBI intensity groups. These findings inspired us to further examine institutional and organizational barriers and supports within the Swedish support system concerning the implementation of EIBI. Through collaboration with Autism habilitation centers and using an ethnographic approach in two preschool settings considered high quality, we (Roll-Pettersson et al., 2016) found that children with autism and paraeducators were often isolated from the group. In addition, interviewees reported low levels of competence among pre-school staff and special educators. Also noted were differing theoretical frameworks and guidelines between the preschool (education) and habilitation center (medical affiliation), the organization that provides supervision to parents and paraeducators. These factors, combined with inadequacies in the learning environment, impeded both the quality and implementation of EIBI as well as the social inclusion of the child. Findings from this study, and the pioneering work of Odom, Cox, and the National Professional Development Center for ASD (2013), highlighting the importance of a high-quality learning environment, led to initiating a collaboration with Professor Sven Bölte at Karolinska Institute Neurodevelopmental Disorders (KIND).

We jointly applied for a research grant from the Swedish Research Council (obtained 2016) to translate and culturally adapt the Autism Program Environmental Rating Scale (APERS; Odom, Cox et al., 2013) to the Swedish preschool context, and test it in an experimental design study. In this study all participating preschools had a child on the autism spectrum obtaining EIBI. In the experimental group, supervisors were trained to provide onsite coaching, and together with preschool staff jointly formulated individualized inclusive evidence-based practice learning goals embedded in the EIBI program (Bejnö, Bölte et al., 2021a; Bejnö, Roll-Pettersson et al., 2021b). Parallel and through support of a new department head who actively strove to create a non-power-centric institutional culture conducive to collaboration, and supportive colleagues, Sam Odom was offered and accepted a 20% position in 2017 as guest professor in Special Education. The collaboration between myself, Sven Bölte, and Sam Odom, both of whom are knowledgeable, dedicated and humane scientists, has continued and evolved. We have recently obtained a four-year grant from the Swedish Research Council to extend the previously mentioned learning-environment preschool project to kindergarten and elementary schools with an overall aim to improve the learning situation for children on the autism spectrum as well as for all children in participating classrooms.

Reflections and Concluding Remarks

Reflections on My Story and Life Partners

I came to Sweden as a foreigner with a mixed cultural background, married a Swedish man and was unknowingly at the time nurtured into the Swedish "Folkhemmet" which strove to create a society likened to a "good home," with kindness, equality between men and women, and between wealthy and poor. My husband and I had an egalitarian relationship. We shared parental leave, each taking six-months leave per child. Together with a group of other parents who later became close friends, we started a Montessori preschool. Having close friends outside of academia with whom I could discuss both personal matters as well as pressures, feelings of insecurities, and tensions of working within academia, provided a source of reflection and emotional support. In hindsight, it is my conviction that living in an egalitarian relationship was a decisive factor regarding my choice to pursue a career in academia—this combined with the deep sense of purpose and urgency I felt concerning disseminating and developing competence of ABA among professionals and stakeholders. Nevertheless, the outer-level contingencies (i.e., high-quality preschool for my children coupled with the fact that there is no higher education tuition) enabled me to pursue an academic career—a career I might have not prioritized, nor had the opportunity to choose, in another society.

Life Partners in Academia and Tensions

Over time the predominant post-modernistic laissez-faire stance in education and special education has modified itself and changed. However, in some ways old biases still prevail (i.e., establishment of nonevidence-based school practices by change agents advocating their own methods and philosophies). Yet there is a general trend concerning a recognition of empirically based practices, noted first in 2010 in the Education Act that "education should be based on empirical evidence and practitioner expertise" (Skollag, 2010). In 2017, Ulrika Långh completed her doctoral thesis at KIND which focused on improving implementation of EIBI in community-based preschools through enriched supervision using video feedback, and has since continued to produce research within this area as well as on improving the prerequisites for implementing EIBI in general.

In addition, there are now a number of externally funded projects implementing culturally adapted Swedish versions of Schoolwide Positive Behavior Support, e.g., *Inclusive Behavioral Support In School* (IBIS), and PAX GBG, both of which have broad international networks. The Department of Education, Uppsala University initiated in 2017 an IBIS pilot project involving a substantial number of classrooms and schools; the project has recently received a furthering research grant from the Swedish Research Council and will over the next few years recruit around 100 schools for a comparative study to evaluate the impact of the program. Using the Swedish cultural adaptation of PAX GBG (Ghaderi et al., 2017), Linnaeus University has also obtained funding from the Swedish Research Council and other sources for conducting a cluster-randomized trial to evaluate the effects on the classroom study environment, pupils' well-being and academic performance, and teachers' experiences and work-related stress when PAX GBGs are implemented in Swedish schools and compared to a control intervention. One doctoral student at Linnaeus University is currently coordinating the RCT, and an additional doctoral student at Stockholm University is affiliated with another study of PAX GBG focusing on effects of PAX GBG in relation to students with special educational needs. In 2021, a doctoral position funded by the Department of Special Education was approved which will focus on supporting the development of social responding in naturalistic settings among preschool children with autism. Taken together, the magnitude of externally funded projects with a basis in behavior analysis, as well as departmental support, clearly witnesses recognition of the field, at least to some degree on the macro system level.

A question not yet answered is: why aren't there more women professors in Sweden? Wennerås and Wold (1997) investigated gender bias in the peer review system for postdoctoral scholarships in the Swedish Medical Research Council between 1986–1995, with a focus on 1994 and reported clear bias against women. The follow-up of this paper contributed to general awareness of gender bias within academic systems previously assumed to be gender neutral, and to substantial changes therein. However, to date there is no evidence (as far as I am aware) that women are in fact being discriminated against. With a basis in male power-system theory, Madison and Fahlman (2020) predicted that females who reach the rank of professor would need to have more publications than males; however, when they examined promotion or hired rank professors they did not find evidence to support this hypothesis. Could it be that women, due to life situations combined with unsurmountable demands (i.e., expected to work six days a week, extreme competition) purposefully chose not to further pursue professorship? This is an area that needs to be studied in further detail as several women in Sweden have PhDs focused on ABA, autism, and early intervention, yet have chosen not to pursue academic careers. The result of these decisions is a shortage of talented women in a clinical field that badly needs their expertise and clearly would prosper if it did in fact find a way to recruit these women into academia.

Within Swedish academia there is still a prevailing tension between "mainstream" pedagogies and ABA, and the rightful place of ABA in higher education as subject matter is still lacking. Most likely this lack of recognition is the greatest threat to the field. As we all know, low levels of competence among practitioners on all levels can inflict harm both on an individual level as well as to the reputation of the field. As previously mentioned, I accidently discovered ABA while taking doctoral courses in the USA, and came to the realization that this field was overridden by the more dominant and powerful post-modernistic educational theory. Possibly in line with my multi-cultural background, I have taken care to avoid outright conflict. My posture has been rather a discrete form of interdependence, highlighting aspects of ABA which are congruent with basic Swedish ideology, a sort of "cultural cautiousness," negotiating and compromising, being persistent yet diplomatic, weighing words with gold, and avoiding confrontation, possibly shaping systemic acceptance. The science and practice of ABA is dynamic, and continually evolving. However, the dissolvement of international certification through BACB by 2022 has created a need for other forms of consumer protection and quality assurance; maybe the next step is development of regional qualification standards, e.g., European- or Nordic-developed, in close collaboration with ABAI.

In keeping with the mission of the science and practice of behavior analysis to improve society, the well-being of the families, children, professionals, and those we serve, combined with the recent magnitude of governmental-funded evidence-based behavioral research projects, it may be time to take a cleave forward, and be more articulate on a socio-political level concerning the imperative role of behavior analysis. According to Morris et al. (2011), it takes on average 17 years for health-related research findings to translate into clinical guidelines and practice, especially when linked to policy changes and measures that will need to be taken to protect clients and guarantee efficacy of implementation. With a basis in the first course sequence which started in 2004, we have just reached the 17-year threshold.

In sum, supportive leadership and colleagues within academia have been paramount for myself as a woman professor. In hindsight it is doubtful that without the early support of Profs. Siv Fischbein and Shahla Ala'í-Rosales that there ever would have been a VCS or master's program, underscoring the importance of supportive and collaborative partnerships. And without the Folkhemmet and my egalitarian personal partnership, it would have been significantly harder for me to accomplish these efforts.

References

Ala i-Rosales, S., Roll-Pettersson, L., Pinkelman, S., & Cihon, T. M. (2010). Emerging opportunities in higher education: Applied Behavior Analysis and autism. *European Journal of Behavior Analysis, 11*(2), 207–216. https://doi.org/10.1080/15021149.2020.1760472

Arntzen, E., & Pellón, R. (2021). A view on the development and current situation of behavior analysis in Europe. *Behavior and Social Issues*, 1–15. Advance online publication. https://doi.org/10.1007/s42822-021-00068-w

Bailey, D. B., & Simeonsson, R. J. (1988). Assessing needs of families with handicapped infants. *The Journal of Special Education, 22*(1), 117–127. https://doi.org/10.1177/002246698802200113

Bejnö, H., Bölte, S., Linder, N., Långh, U., Odom, S. L., & Roll-Pettersson, L. (2021a). From someone who may cause trouble to someone you can play with: Stakeholders' perspectives on preschool program quality for autistic children. *Jouranl of Autism and Developmental Disorders*. https://doi-org.ezp.sub.su.se/10.1007/s10803-021-05268-2

Bejnö, H., Roll-Pettersson, L., Klintwall, L., Långh, U., Odom, S. L., & Bölte, S. (2021b). Adapting the preschool environment to the needs of children on the autism spectrum in Sweden: A quasi-experimental study. *Scandinavian Journal of Occupational Therapy*, 1–20. https://doi-org.ezp.sub.su.se/10.1080/11038128.2021.1993330

Bökstedt, H. (1983). Autistiska barn kan botas: Behandlingen för autism barnsligt enkelt [Autistic children can be cured; Treatment is very simple]. *Vetenskap [Science], Svenska Dagbladet [The Swedish Daily Newspaper], 33.*

Bronfenbrenner, U. (1979). *The ecology of human development: Experiments by nature and design*. Harvard University Press.

Dagens Nyheter. (2014, July 20). *Skolor använder omstridd metod för autistiska barn [Schools use controversial method for autistic children]*. www.dn.se/nyheter/sverige/skolor-anvander-omstridd-metod-for-autistiska-barn/

Englund, T., & Engström, I. (2011, October 5). Behaviorisms återkomst i Svenskskola [The return ofbehaviorism in the Swedish school]. *Pedagogiska Magasinet*. www.lararnasnyheter.se/pedagogiska-magasinet/2011/05/10/behaviorismens-aterkomst-svensk-skola

Fernell, E., Hedvall, Å., Westerlund, J., Höglund Carlsson, L., Eriksson, M., Barnevik Olsson, M., Holm, A., Norrelgen, F., Kjellmer, L., & Gillberg, C. (2011). Early intervention in 208 Swedish preschoolers with autism spectrum disorder. A prospective naturalistic study. *Research in Developmental Disabilities, 32*, 2092–2101. https://DOI:10.1016/j.ridd.2011.08.002

Fischbein, S., & Westling, A. (in press). Postmodernism and the negligence of facts: An example from teacher education in Sweden (permission provided to cite). In *Confronting Anti-Semitism on campus*. Peter Langs publisher.

Försäkringskassa. (n.d.). *Det som är bra delar man lika på [What is good you share equally]*. Retrieved October 16, 2021, from www.forsakringskassan.se/privatpers/foralder/dela-lika

Ghaderi, A., Johansson, M., & Enebrink, P. (2017). *Pilotstudie av PAX i skolan; En kulturanpassad version av PAX good behavior game [pilot study of PAX in school; A culturally adapted version of PAX, good behavior game]*. Forskningsrapport, uppdrag av Folkhälsomyndigheten, Karolinska Institutet.

Göransson, K. (1982). *Hur vår förståelsen av verkligheten utvecklas [How our understanding of reality develops]*. Stockholm, Stiftelsen ALA.

Göransson, K., Stéenson, A-L., Roll-Pettersson, L., Stenhammar, A-M., & Thorsson, L. (2000). *Om alla är lika skulle det inte vara lika roligt: Att bygga en skola, samverkan mellan särskola och grundskola [If everyone was exactly alike it wouldn't be as fun: Constructing a school, collaboration between the special school and regular school]*. Stiftelsen ALA.

Götz, N. (2004). The modern home sweet home. In K. Almqvist & K. Glans (Eds.), *The Swedish success story?*, (pp. 97–107). Axel and Margaret Axson Johnson foundation.

Granlund, M. (1984). *Kommunicera Mera; Ett kursmaterial, teoribok [Communicate more: Course material, theoretical book*]. Stiftelsen ALA.

Granlund, M., Steenson, A-L., Roll-Pettersson, L., Björck-Åkesson, E., Sundin, M., & Kylen, A. (1999). *Elever med flera funktionsnedsättningar i särskolan; utbildningens effecter och effektivitet [Pupils with several disabilities in special education schools: The effect and effectiveness of education]*. Stiftelsen ALA.

Heimdahl Mattsson, E., Lange, A-L., Roll-Pettersson, L., & Westling Allodi, M. (2005). *Mångsidigt Samspel: En vän bok till Siv Fischbein [Many-sided Interactions: A friendship book to Siv Fischbein]*. HLS Förlag.

Hughes, C. J., & Shook, G. L. (2007). Training and certification of behaviour analysts in Europe: Past, present, and future challenges *European Journal of Behavior Analysis, 8*(2), 239–249. www.tandfonline.com/doi/abs/10.1080/15021149.2007.11434285

Kylén, G. (1979). *Helhetssyn på människan [A wholistic perspective of humanbeings]*. Stiftelsen ALA.

Kylén, G. (1985). *En Begåvningsteori [A theory of intelligence]*. Stiftelsen ALA.

Madison, G., & Fahlman, P. (2020). Sex differences in the number of scientific publications and citations when attaining the rank of professor in Sweden. *Studies in Higher Education*, 1–22. https://doi-org.ezp.sub.su.se/10.1080/03075079.2020.1723533

Morris, Z. S., Wooding, S., & Grant, J. (2011). The answer is 17 years, what is the question: Understanding time lags in translational research. *Journal of the Royal Society of Medicine, 104*(12), 510–520. https://doi-org.ezp.sub.su.se/10.1258/jrsm.2011.110180

The National Curriculum for the Preschool. (Lpfö 98). *Swedish national agency for education*. Fritzes.

Odom, S. L., Cox, A., Brock, National Professional Development Center on ASD. (2013). Implementation science, professional development, and autism spectrum disorders. *Exceptional Children, 79*(2), 233–251. https://doi.org/10.1177/001440291307900207

Odom, S. L., Hall, L. J., & Suhrheinrich, J. (2020). Implementation science, behavior analysis, and supporting evidence-based practices for individuals with autism. *European Journal of Behavior Analysis, 21*(1), 55–73. https://DOI:10.1080/15021149.2019.1641952

Parker, N. (2002). Differentiating, collaborating, outdoing: Nordic identity and marginality in the contemporary world. *Identities: Global Studies in Culture and Power, 9*(3), 355–381. https://doi.org/10.1080/10702890213973

Rikowski, G., & McLaren, P. (2002). Postmodernism in educational theory, introduction. In D. Hill, P. McLaren, M. Cole, & G. Rikowski (Eds.), *Marxism against postmodernism in educational theory* (pp. 1–12). Lexington Books.

Roll-Pettersson, L. (1992). En särskollärare berättar; Vanliga elever undervisar förstånds handikappade- en ny modell för integration [A special educator talks; Typical students teach intellectually disabled- a new model for integration], *Specialpedagogen, 3*, 18–20 (written under pseudo-name Gudrun Agerholm).

Roll-Pettersson, L. (2003). *Ansökan om stöd för utvecklingen av en ny utbildning inom Området autism. Till Kempe Carlgrenska minnesfond [Application to support the development of a new degree in field of autism.* To Kempe Carlgrenska memorial fund-application approved].

Roll-Pettersson, L., Dillenburger, K., Keenan, M., Alai-Rosales, S., & Sigurdardottir, G. (2020a). Higher education, behaviour analysis, and autism: Time for coalescence. *European Journal of Behavior Analysis, 21*(1), 1–8. https://doi-org.ezp.sub.su.se/10.1080/15021149.2020.1760472

Roll-Pettersson, L., Ek, U., & Ramnerö, J. (2010). Benefits of BACB certification for universities in Europe: A case study from Sweden. *Association of Professional Behavior Analysts, 17*.

Roll-Pettersson, L., Gena, A., Eldevik, S., Moderato, P., Sigurdardottir, Z. G., Dillenburger, K., Keenan, M., & Ala'i-Rosales, S. (2020b). Higher education and behavior analysis in Europe: Creating a unified approach for the training of autism professionals. *European Journal of Behavior Analysis, 21*(1), 158–184. https://doi-org.ezp.sub.su.se/10.1080/15021149.2020.1758990

Roll-Pettersson, L., Olsson, I., & Ala i-Rosales, S. (2016). Bridging the research to practice gap: A case study approach to understanding EIBI supports and barriers in Swedish preschools. *International Electronic Journal of Elementary Education, 9*(2), 317–336.

Simeonsson, R. J., & Bailey, D. B. (1991). *The abilities index*. Frank Porter Graham Child Development Institute, University of North Carolina in Chapel Hill.

Skinner, B. F. (1968). *The technology of teaching*. Meredith Corporation.

Skollag. (2010). *Sveriges riksdagen, skollag 2010:800, Utbildningsdepartementet [Swedish parliament, education act 2010:800, department of education]*. www.riksdagen.se/sv/dokument-lagar/dokument/svensk-forfattningssamling/skollag-2010800_sfs-2010-800

Skolverket. (2021). *Sveriges officiella statistik, statistik på riksivå [Swedish official statistics, statistics national level].* Swedish National Agency for Education. www.skolverket.se/skolutveckling/statistik/sok-statistik-om-forskola-skola-och-vuxenutbildning?sok=SokC&verkform=F%C3%B6rskola&omrade=Barn%20och%20grupper&lasar=2020&run=1

Stockholms Stad. (2021). *Beräkna avgift för förskola i Stockholm, [Calulate fee for preschool].* https://forskola.stockholm/avgifter/berakna-avgift-for-forskola/

Todd, J. T. (2020). Some things you need to know to be a behavior analyst and other considerations: An informal recollection with examples. *European Journal of Behavior Analysis, 21*(1), 110–132. https://DOI:10.1080/15021149.2019.1673622

UKÄ, Swedish Higher Education Authority. (2017). *Fakta om högskolan/dem Svenska Högskolans historia [Facts about the history of Swedish higher education].* www.uka.se/fakta-om-hogskolan/den-svenska-hogskolans-historia/aren-1900-2000.html

UKÄ, Swedish Higher Education Authority. (2020). *Uppföljning av rekryteringsmål för professorer 2017–2019 [Follow-up of recruiting goals for professors 2017–2019].* No. 111–263–20. Stockholm.

UNICEF. (2008). *The child care transition. A league table of early childhood and care in economically advanced countries.* UNICEF Innicenti Research Centre.

Wennerås, C., & Wold, A. (1997). Nepotism and sexism in peer-review. *Nature* 387, 341–343. https://doi-org.ezp.sub.su.se/10.1038/387341a0

Wikipedia. (2021). *Folkhemmet [The peoples home].* Retrieved October 16, from https://en.wikipedia.org/wiki/Folkhemmet

Winton, P. (1992). *Working with families in early intervention: An interdisciplinary preservice curriculum* (2nd ed.). Frank Porter Graham, University of North Carolina in Chapel-Hill.

20 A Northeast Journey Toward Values-Based Living

Adel C. Najdowski

A Northeast Journey Toward Values-Based Living

Thank you! Thank you for seeing something in me that might potentially be worth taking your valuable time to read my story. I know you have many options of readings, podcasts, and other material that might be more exciting than hearing what I have to say, and therefore, I sincerely thank you for investing your time in me.

You might be wondering how a woman in academia who holds many other identities can go about living a values-based life. You might even be looking for a task analysis for how to go about making this happen. If that is the case, I cannot promise that reading this chapter is going to provide the solutions you are seeking, but I hope it may, at the least, be a fun journey in the Northeast direction with a middle-aged woman who has been through some stuff. Why Northeast, you ask? This will be uncovered later. I cannot promise you that after reading this chapter, you will have all the answers to living a values-based life, because I surely do not have these answers myself. We are all human and we all make mistakes, and I too, have made plenty. I am still learning every day how to live a values-based life, as it surely is not a destination but only a journey.

I was born in 1976 in Santa Barbara, California, to a 16-year-old White mother and 17-year-old Latino father. Believe it or not, my parents were married before my mother became pregnant (at ages 15 and 16)! Yes, that is possible, as they ran away to Mexico to get married in Tijuana. My mother had convinced my father to marry her so that she could move in with my father's family in order to avoid having to go home to her family. My mother experienced a great deal of trauma during her adolescent and teenage years that led to this rebellious behavior.

When I was two years old, my mother left my father and moved with me to Las Vegas, Nevada to find her biological father, whom she had never met. That is when my upbringing in a fast-paced lifestyle with a single high school-drop-out mother who would soon become an addict began. Although my mother worked full time as an administrative assistant, we lived on food stamps and in low-income housing. I was a latch-key kid who had to learn to take care of and entertain myself a lot of the time. Given my environment, I was on my way to becoming a delinquent, and I escaped a few close calls. In one of these close calls, I survived a horrific car accident wherein my uncle was driving drunk, and I was put through the windshield head first due to not wearing a seatbelt, landing 50 feet away from the car. It was this pivotal event that changed my trajectory in life. This tragic event triggered my mother to realize that she needed to discontinue her drug use, so she made a huge values-based decision to become clean and sober and to move us to Reno, Nevada for a fresh start (this is where the "Leaving Las Vegas" song begins playing in the background).

Upon moving, my mother asked a friend who lived in Reno which middle school and high school were the best and then made sure we moved into an apartment complex that

DOI: 10.4324/9781003216773-24

would get me into those schools. My new environment painted an entirely new picture for me that I did not know existed prior. As I met friends in Reno and visited their homes and their families, I became aware that my peers were college-bound and had goals to have careers. It was the first time in my life that I realized I was living a life that many people looked down upon. It was embarrassing to me, so I avoided having peers come to my house so that they would not see the environment in which I lived and judge me. I soon equated the idea of being college-bound to not having to live in poverty, and I could pursue things that I cared about. So, I made a decision during high school to attend college and to live the American dream. I suppose this was the first major values-based decision I made.

I began attending the University of Nevada, Reno in 1994 on financial aid and majored in psychology simply because it was the only subject I had taken that kept my interest. I had no idea what I was doing at the time. I was simply responding naively to stimuli placed in front of me, and this is how I fell into behavior analysis. One day in my undergraduate Applied Behavior Analysis (ABA) course, some graduate students came to recruit undergraduates who wanted to learn to work with children with autism. I signed up, was hooked on the power of ABA immediately, and never turned back. I was in awe watching what ABA-based intervention could do for a young learner in only a two-hour session, and I realized that I wanted to help children like this learner more than anything else going on in my life. This is how I came to the field of ABA and ultimately ended up receiving my doctorate degree in behavior analysis in 2004. This was the second most significant values-based decision I made.

While I was in graduate school, one of my dear friends got married and became pregnant. At the time, she was an elementary school teacher, and she informed me that she would have to go back to work only three months after her baby was born. I was in shock. I told you I was naive when I was young, and I am not lying. I have always been a late bloomer. I think because I spent so much of my childhood simply trying to stay alive, I did not think too deeply about much. I had no idea that the Family and Medical Leave Act only allowed for three months with one's newborn. That just seemed insane to me. I knew I wanted to have children someday (not right then; I was definitely not ready then!), but I was terrified by the idea of putting my infant in daycare at the age of three months with someone I did not even know. So, I suggested to my husband that maybe we should have a baby while I was in graduate school, with the baby being born around the time that I would graduate so that I could stay home with our baby for as long as felt right before applying for a post-graduate school position. You are not going to believe this, because even I cannot believe it, but I defended my dissertation on October 1, 2004 and my son was born on October 17, 2004! This was the third largest values-based decision I ever made.

That decision was soon followed by another values-based decision for me to accept my first postdoctoral position when my son was nine months old and for my husband to quit his job (at the time he had not yet found his career calling) and become a stay-at-home father until we were ready for our son to go to preschool, which ended up happening when my son turned two. We knew that having a child while one of us was not employed meant we would not be able to purchase a home, but what seemed to matter more to us at the time was being with our son, not where we lived or how much money we had to live.

These types of values-based decisions are different for everyone. There is no right or wrong way to view what matters to you. For some people, it is more important to be financially stable prior to having children, and they may prefer to do things in that order. However, that was not for us. The beauty of values-based living is you get to decide what is important to you. There is no universally right or wrong set of values; rather, they are a personal choice.

At this point in my life, I can say I did okay at making life's larger decisions based on values. I think many of us are pretty good at that—these are the types of decisions such as whether to go to college, who and when to marry, whether and when to have children, and so on. However, it was the little things that I was not so good at. I was lacking in my relationships with people. I lacked good listening and perspective-taking skills and tended to be hot-headed when things did not go my way. Let me just say I had some personal-development issues to work on, and sadly, I was not even aware of this.

It was not until I participated in a week-long Acceptance and Commitment Therapy (ACT) workshop that this deficit became clear to me. We read Russ Harris's (2009) book *ACT Made Simple* and did many ACT exercises over that week, but the two I will never forget and that impacted me the most were the Bullseye exercise (Lundgren et al., 2012) and the Eulogy Speech (Hayes et al., 1999). These two exercises were pivotal in making me aware of my deficits.

Bullseye

The workshop facilitators gave me a picture of a bullseye (Lundgren et al., 2012) that was divided into four quadrants containing the titles: (1) work/education, (2) health/personal development, (3) relationships, and (4) leisure. I was asked to write what my personal values were in each quadrant (see Figure 20.1 for an example of a blank bullseye). For example, in the "relationships" quadrant, I wrote, "Quality time with my husband," "Quality time with

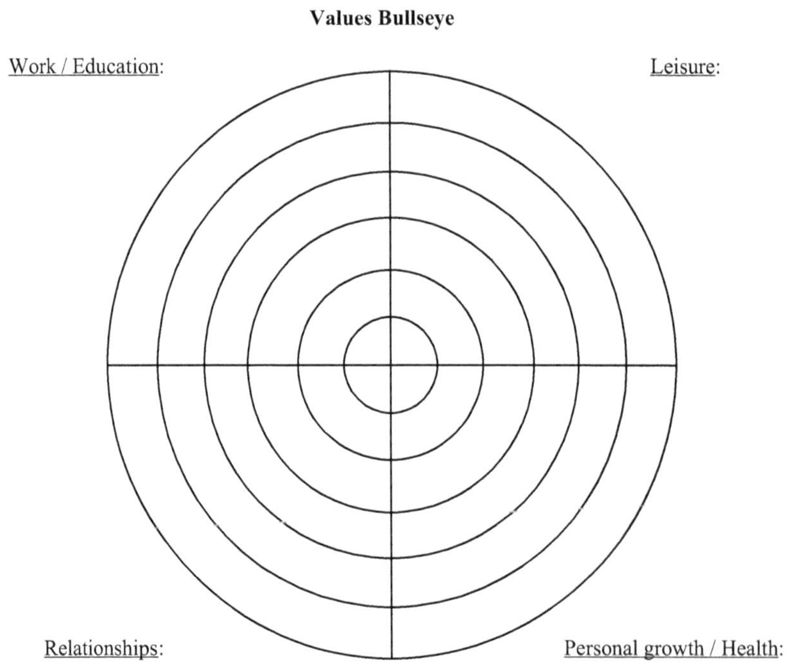

Committed Actions:

1. Work/Education:
2. Leisure:
3. Relationships
4. Personal growth/health:

Figure 20.1 Blank Bullseye

Values Bullseye

Work / Education:

Preparing students for purpose, service, and leadership

Creating a culture that exudes diversity, equity, and inclusion (DEI)

Leisure:

Traveling
Cooking
Boating

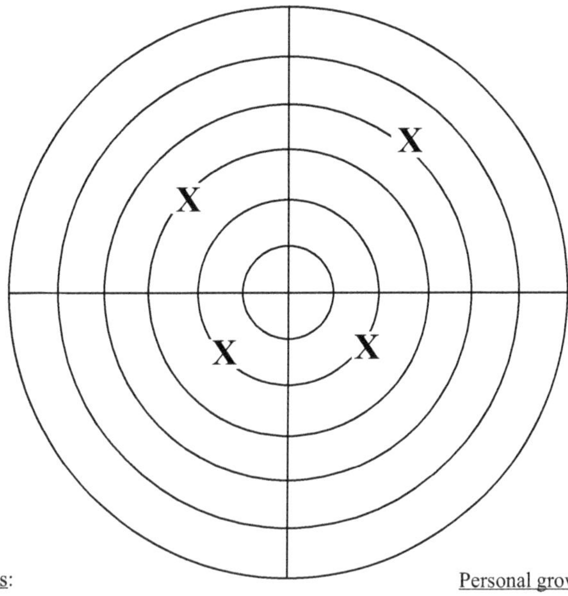

Relationships:

Quality time with husband

Quality time with kids

Being authentic and connecting with people

Personal growth / Health:

Life-long learning
Working out regularly
Eating foods with nutritional value

Committed Actions:

1. Work/Education: Set up a meeting with MSABA program leadership to discuss a strategic plan for rolling out more DEI initiatives.
2. Leisure: Talk to husband about our next family trip.
3. Relationships: Take time for chit chat with other faculty and staff when I see them.
4. Personal growth/health: Order more plant-based foods when eating out at restaurants.

Figure 20.2 Example of Bullseye Filled Out

my children," and so on (see Figure 20.2 for an example of a bullseye that has been completed). After writing my values in each quadrant, I was asked to put an X on the target that represented how close I was living my current life in line with my values listed. If I was living my life completely in line with my values, I was to draw the X on the bullseye, but if I was not living my life in line with my values, I was to draw the X on one of the outer circles of the target board (the furthest ring represented being completely out of line with my values). After drawing the Xs, I was to identify what committed action(s) I could take to move the Xs closer to the bullseye, and finally, I was asked to make the commitment to fulfill even one small behavior that would move me closer to what I valued. This was an enlightening experience for me, because prior to this exercise, I do not think I thought much about my values—not what they were, whether I was living in line with them, or much of anything at all. This exercise made me want to do better and to be a better person.

Eulogy Speech

The next exercise turned my world upside down. In this exercise, the workshop facilitators told me to think about what my friends and family would say about me during a eulogy speech at my funeral. Would they say I never missed a day of work and traveled all the time to conferences and gave the best speeches, or would they say I was kind, compassionate, loving, and there for them? This exercise brought me and many of the other workshop attendees to tears. It was such an eye-opening experience that helped me to realize that the things I thought I cared so much about were not necessarily what I truly cared about in my heart. In fact, I realized that many of the things I was putting so much of my time and energy into on a daily basis were not the things that I really cared that much about at all.

Values Clarification and Committed Action

From that week forward, I began to use values clarification over the course of my life so that my behavior both inside and outside the context of my career were consistent with what was important to me. After ten years working for an ABA-based agency, I discovered that what I wanted more than anything for the future of my career was to be able to excite others to learn about behavior analysis. At the time, I was living in North Los Angeles and none of the local universities with graduate training programs in behavior analysis were hiring full-time faculty.

Given those circumstances, I made the decision that I was going to start a new master's program at a local university. I was told by some that this would not be possible and that I should not bother trying, but there was no way I was going to take no for an answer. After talking to anyone and everyone I knew about my plan, a friend of mine was able to get the Senior Vice President of Advancement and Public Affairs at Pepperdine University to meet with me so I could pitch the idea of starting a master's program in ABA. Many meetings and two years later, the Master of Science in Applied Behavior Analysis at Pepperdine University was launched in Fall of 2016! From this experience, I learned that if you have a dream, you need to go for it. Even if some may try to stop you, or you may be told no a few times (as I was from some universities before Pepperdine), you need to continue as if it is going to happen and it will happen. Had I believed the warnings that it would not be possible, Pepperdine's program may not exist today. You may wonder why I did not apply for a faculty position outside Los Angeles, and that also goes back to values. At the time, my husband was established in his career and my kids were established in their schools and friend circles. I felt keeping them in that environment was what was best for the family.

Once I was at Pepperdine, I continued my interest and personal learning in ACT. I attended more ACT workshops and eventually also participated in facilitating a few ACTraining workshops. Through these experiences, I learned about another ACT tool called the Matrix (Polk et al., 2016).

Matrix

The Matrix is composed of four quadrants (see Figure 20.3) wherein the top two quadrants represent overt behavior and the bottom two quadrants represent covert behavior. The left two quadrants represent overt (top) and covert (bottom) behaviors that move you away from what you care about, and the right two quadrants represent overt (top) and covert (bottom) behaviors that move you toward what you care about. The Matrix can be used to help you engage in overt behaviors that move you toward what you care about. Dr. Stuart Libman introduced me to the Matrix and taught me the expression of "living life in the Northeast

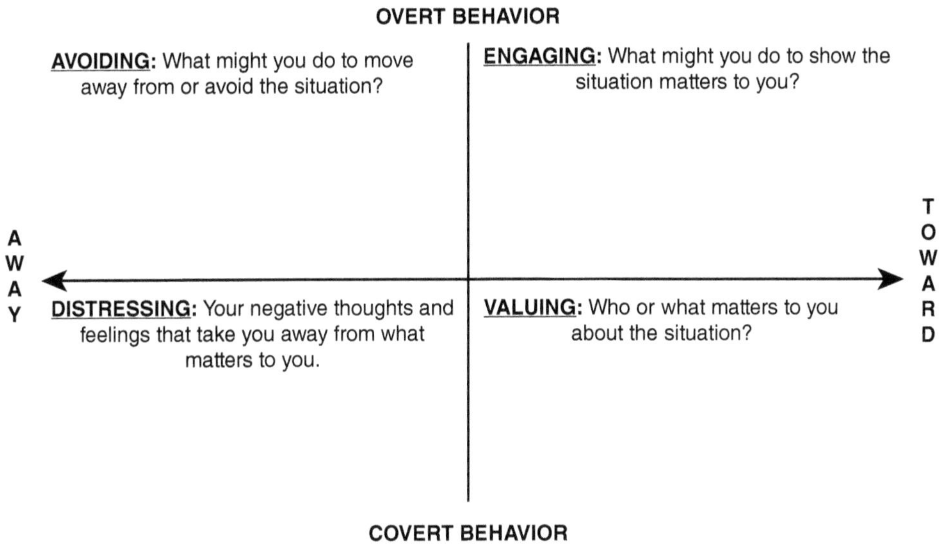

Figure 20.3 Blank Matrix

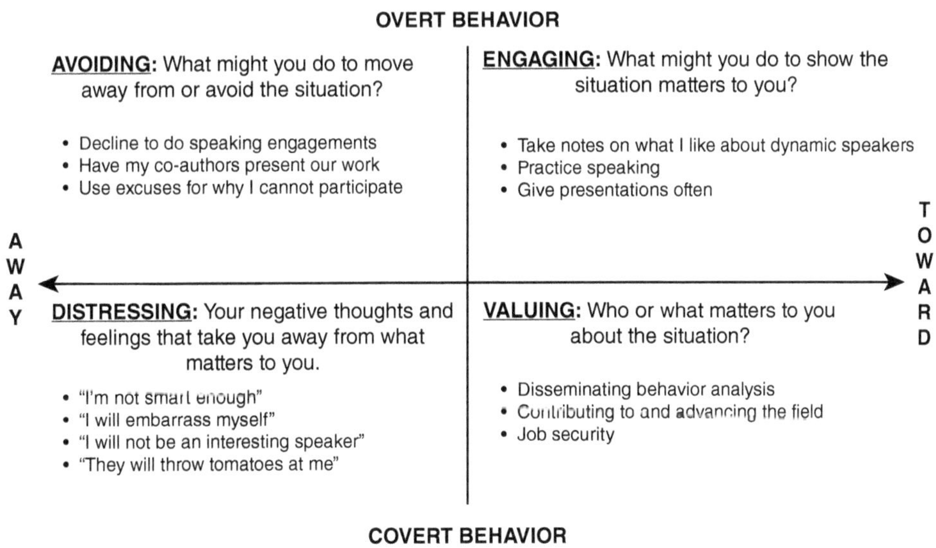

Figure 20.4 Example of Matrix Filled Out for Public Speaking Scenario

direction" to refer to engaging in overt behaviors related to the top-right quadrant of the Matrix.

When using the Matrix, the first step is to start in the bottom-right quadrant by listing out what matters to you about a given situation. For example, let's say the situation of interest is public speaking. Like many people, I used to be deathly afraid of public speaking (see Figure 20.4 for a Matrix filled out for the situation of public speaking). Starting in the bottom-right quadrant, I would write what matters to me about public speaking. This is a values-clarification exercise. I might list "disseminating behavior analysis," "contributing to and advancing the field," and "job security." Then, I would move to the bottom-left quadrant and identify the negative thoughts and feelings that take me away from what I really care about. These might be things like "I'm not smart enough," "I will embarrass myself," "I will not be an interesting speaker," and "They will throw tomatoes at me." I would then move up to the top-left quadrant and identify what overt behaviors I engage in when these negative thoughts and feelings show up. I might identify "Decline to do speaking engagements," "Have my co-authors present our work," and "Use excuses for why I cannot participate." Finally, I would move up to the top-right quadrant to identify the overt behaviors that would move me closer to the things that I care about and help me to be the person I really want to be. In this quadrant I might list "Take notes on what I like about dynamic speakers and try to emulate those behaviors," "Practice speaking," and "Give presentations often." After this, I would come up with small goals or committed actions that I could perform in the near future, and I would hold myself to them.

The ACT exercises I have outlined so far are ones that I do at least annually to identify if I am living my life in a Northeast direction.

Mindfulness and Meditation

Meditation has helped me in many ways. When I first started meditation, I admittedly did not see how it could be helpful. Whenever I tried to do it, I felt I was doing it wrong, and I noticed that I had more anxiety. Having to focus on my breath and bodily sensations during meditation initially made me feel like I could not breathe and like I was going to have a panic attack. However, after a while, I suppose habituation kicked in. After practice, I learned to do it like any other skill one has to learn. Nowadays, it is one of my best things. It makes me feel so grounded and calm. I have found it to be helpful in daily life too. For example, when I find myself feeling angry or impatient, or when I begin thinking about unhelpful past experiences or what I wish could happen for me, I try to bring my attention toward the present experience, and commit to accepting the negative feelings while still moving Northeast toward what I care about.

My favorite meditation application is Headspace, but I have also learned to do meditation on my own. An easy exercise you can try when you feel yourself engaging in unhelpful thoughts or emotions is called Notice Five Things (Harris, 2007). This activity involves noticing something you can hear, something you can smell, and so on, until you have noticed something for all five senses. This activity brings one back to the present moment so that they can refocus their attention toward committed actions that are values-based.

Vulnerability

In addition to the components of ACT, author and Ted Talk speaker Brené Brown (2010) has had a significant impact on my values clarification and has helped me to be more authentic and vulnerable. Her books *Daring Greatly* (2015) and *Dare to Lead* (2018) have been influential for me. One of the things that really resonated with me and has become a huge value for me is being courageous. The value of being courageous shows up for me in all four quadrants of the bullseye. Another way I like to think about it is like this: whenever I am afraid to do something, this is the clue for me that I *have* to do it. Now of course, I am not talking about things like skydiving and bungee jumping. I am talking about things that bring me anxiety, such as public speaking, doing a task that I think is above me or that I am not good enough or smart enough to achieve, and having difficult conversations. I heard a wonderful thing said by Veronique Stokes during the Juneteenth conference held by Black

Applied Behavior Analysts, Inc. (BABA) recently which went something like, "You are going to have to get uncomfortable so you can do better. You don't grow when you're comfortable." I wholeheartedly agree with this, as this is how I try to live my life.

More Examples of the Application of Values-Clarification to My Life

The purpose of this chapter is not for me to list out all the values clarification I have done in my life inside and outside of my career, because as previously mentioned, everyone has different values. There is no special set of rules to live by; rather, they are deeply personal. However, I feel that I might be selling you short if I do not at least address some examples of values-based living experiences or decisions I have made, so I will leave you with a short list of what comes immediately to mind for me. This includes:

- Putting my family's needs before my career's needs. At a certain point, I noticed my family engages in challenging behavior (ha!) whenever I travel more than once per month for a speaking engagement, so now I only agree to one speaking engagement per month. Now that we are coming out of the pandemic and I have not been traveling at all, I am considering reducing my traveling more.
- Doing my part to contribute to social justice. For example, I participate in a group of faculty at Pepperdine as well as with a group of women faculty from many other universities to identify how to drive anti-racist policies in our institutions. I also do a lot of self-education on this topic. As another example, once I was offered pay at half the amount that was offered to a male colleague for doing the same job. I refused the job and explained that I knew the pay was twice as much for the colleague. The job offer was re-presented with equal pay, and I accepted.
- Being a lifelong learner and engaging in self-awareness. I realize that I can always improve myself in many ways and that there are endless opportunities to learn. I enjoy learning as a regular part of my life and value it highly. I want to be the best version of myself that I can be. This includes becoming self-aware of my biases and weaknesses and working to improve.
- Keeping work boundaries. I use a structured work schedule that allows me to be productive, but also responsive to needs for meetings and emails, by having days and/or timeframes set aside for research/writing, class preparation, and meetings. I try to have separate reserved time for deep work versus emails, and I try to avoid emailing others after work hours/weekends. If I do write an email after work hours, I use a timed delivery so that it arrives in the person's inbox during work hours the next work day. I avoid working on evenings and weekends as much as possible and try to reserve that as family time.
- Focusing my time on projects and opportunities that are most in line with my values and priorities, and saying no to other opportunities that will delay or distract me from achieving what is most important to me. I do not want to be spread so thin that I perform poorly on commitments. When I commit to something, I want to provide my best effort. Prioritization of commitments also involves thinking about how projects will impact my family's needs.
- Being realistic about when I can make a deadline and letting folks know when I have too much on my plate, need help, or need to request priority be given to a task but not all tasks. When you do not do this, it is possible for more tasks to be assigned to you than you can handle or you may become overworked and burnt out trying to do it all. Sometimes the only way for your supervisor to realize this is for you to be honest with yourself and them. In my experience, being transparent about this with supervisors has led to being able to hire more staff.

- Doing my best and trying to avoid getting caught up in caring too much about getting tenure. I am not willing to fight for resources or to step on others to get what I want.
- Putting health as a priority, which includes working out regularly, eating mostly clean, and trying to do my part for sustainability of the environment.
- Putting my students' and supervisors' needs above all else at work.
- Putting service as priority, which involves volunteering hours with my kids for several community organizations.
- Doing the right thing by trying to make decisions that are the best for others (not for me) and being honest, kind, open, nonjudgmental, and curious to different perspectives.
- Treating others with compassion. All of us are a product of our very unique learning histories and are usually doing the best we can.

Thank you again for taking this journey with me. It has been a fun and enjoyable experience for me to be able to be vulnerable and share with you. I hope it has been helpful.

References

Brown, B. (2015). *Daring greatly: How the courage to be vulnerable transforms the way we live, love, parent, and lead*. Penguin.

Brown, B. (2018). *Dare to lead: Brave work. Tough conversations. Whole hearts*. Random House.

Harris, R. (2007). *Acceptance and commitment therapy (ACT) introductory workshop handout*. Psych Med.

Harris, R. (2009). *ACT made simple: An easy-to-read primer on acceptance and commitment therapy*. New Harbinger Publications.

Harris, R. (2013). *The happiness trap: Stop struggling, start living*. Exisle Publishing (Trumpeter).

Hayes, S. C., Strosahl, K., & Wilson, K. G. (1999). *Acceptance and commitment therapy: An experiential approach to behavior change*. Guilford Press.

Lundgren, T., Luoma, J. B., Dahl, J., Strosahl, K., & Melin, L. (2012). The bull's-eye values survey: A psychometric evaluation. *Cognitive and Behavioral Practice*, *19*(4), 518–526. https://doi.org/10.1016/j.cbpra.2012.01.004

Polk, K. L., Schoendorff, B., Webster, M., & Olaz, F. O. (2016). *The essential guide to the ACT matrix: A step-by-step approach to using the ACT matrix model in clinical practice*. New Harbinger Publications.

TED. (2010, June). *Brené Brown: The power of vulnerability* [Video]. YouTube. www.ted.com/talks/brene_brown_the_power_of_vulnerability

21 Promoting Prosociality and Compassion in Competitive Environments

Karola Dillenburger

Promoting Prosociality and Compassion in Competitive Environments

It was a woman professor in the early 1990s who was my first role model for prosociality and compassion in academia. She had been appointed to rescue a relatively small department that was in danger of being shut down. Her enthusiasm and love for the staff and students turned around the department. In meetings, she would introduce junior appointments or graduates using their full title, "Dr. xxx" (emphasis on "Doctor . . ."), and describe their area of expertise in glowing terms. When she was asked to contribute a chapter to a book or review a paper or funding application, she frequently offered the contract to early-career colleagues to allow them to gain experience and enhance their chances of promotion. She invited junior staff to co-author invited papers. She delegated important responsibilities to trusted colleagues and relished in their subsequent achievements. The secret to her success was her skill to arrange contingencies to ensure individual and team achievements (Agnew & Uhl, 2021). She identified effective reinforcers, which led to everyone doing their best for the department and the students. After her retirement, we meet occasionally to reminisce about the good old days.

To be honest, though, apart from some shining examples like her, the "good old days" were not really so very good at all in higher education institutions (HEI). At staff induction, new staff were informed that only 3.2% of professors were female, while about 60–70% of all staff (academics, secretaries, cleaners, porters, and others) were women. Female professors earned 14.5% less than their male counterparts and women rarely got leadership positions; most heads of schools and deans and all vice-chancellors were male.

The Terms

Before we delve more deeply into the topic, a quick word about terms. In this chapter, the term "behavior" is defined as the interaction of an organism with their environment. This includes publicly observable as well as private, inner behavior, such as thoughts (cognitions) or feelings (emotions) (Cooper et al., 2020; Keenan & Dillenburger, 2020; Skinner, 1938).

The term "professor" is used quite flexibly in some places, like in France, where secondary/high school teachers are called "le professeur," or in some German colleges where all teaching staff are called "Professor" regardless of their seniority. In the USA, the term "professor" is used widely but modified by prefixes such as "assistant" or "associate" or "full." In the United Kingdom the term "Professor" is used only for full professors who work at universities.

The term "compassion" is defined as the feelings that arise when someone is aware of another person's suffering and is motivated to help or relieve that suffering (Keltner, 2012;

DOI: 10.4324/9781003216773-25

Strauss et al., 2016). Translated into behavioral terms, this means that the term compassion is used as a summary label for public and private behaviors that are determined by the other person(s)' verbal and nonverbal behavior (Slim & Reuter-Yuill, 2021) within contingencies that indicate some level of privation. The term "prosociality" refers to behaviors that are "intended to benefit others" (Jensen, 2016), not necessarily only those who need help. In a sense, prosocial behaviors are reinforced vicariously, via observation of the positive consequences for the person on the receiving end of the prosocial behavior.

Prevailing Contingencies in Academia

The Higher Education Statistics Agency (HESA, 2021) reported that in 2021 in the UK there were 223,525 academics employed within universities, with 28% of the professors being female and 11% of the professors being ethnically diverse. Of all academic staff, 31% were non-UK nationals and 33% were employed on fixed-term contracts (2% on zero-hours contracts).

Most academics in the UK are appointed initially as "lecturers" (in US terms assistant professor), and after some 6–12 years of meeting rather stringent performance criteria, a lecturer may be promoted to become a "senior lecturer" (in US terms associate professor), but this is by no means guaranteed. A further 6–12 years later, she may be promoted to "Reader",[1] but only after meeting even more stringent performance criteria that include excellent teaching evaluations, successful supervision of numerous PhD students, significant research income, and many very high-level internationally recognized peer-reviewed publications. A reader is on the same pay-scale as a senior lecturer, but, with more focus on research, this title carries a bit more prestige.

Only after another five or more years, she might be promoted to a professorship, if she has not retired before that; again, only after meeting very high standards and being of international renown. While very occasionally someone under 40 years of age is promoted or even appointed directly to a professorship, most woman professors in the UK are in their mid to late 50s or 60s. None of these academic promotions are guaranteed and the dial is reset after each promotion; all performance targets have to be met again. Consequently, in a male-dominated relatively non-diverse population, those with successful competitive learning histories dominate, while others are left behind.

Competitive Environments

Academics are either envied or made fun of for living in the "ivory tower" or revered for their expertise and admired for their authority on a topic. They are interviewed for sound bites on the radio or TV but, secretly, everyone thinks they play on the computer all day and have long summer holidays. In reality, academics are exposed to a very peculiar set of contingencies and experience very specific mental and physical stresses. The pressures to "publish or perish" are ever present. In the UK, the Research Excellent Framework (REF) is a country-wide assessment framework that is carried out every five to six years. Performance of a department and thus a university is assessed via quality of publications, research income, student feedback, the general research environment, impact, and supports available. The public funding for universities is allocated depending on the REF scores and consequently the pressure to perform well is huge. This is felt most keenly by the individual academic who is expected to publish highly rated peer-reviewed research papers, earn significant research funding, and supervise relatively large numbers of doctoral students. New academic appointments are targeting individuals who already meet the REF criteria, including having a doctorate and at least two good-quality publications.

Good-quality publications in the field of behavior analysis, such as those published in journals like the *Journal of Applied Behavior Analysis* (*JABA*), generally are not highly regarded in the terms of the REF, because their circulation mainly targets a relatively limited readership and thus they do not have high impact factors. Behavior analytic research that is based on single-system design (with small n)[2] generally is not funded by UK research councils who prefer large surveys or randomized controlled trials (Keenan & Dillenburger, 2011). While behavior analysis usually attracts high-caliber PhD students, the sheer teaching loads in undergraduate or postgraduate courses often prevent the academic from taking on many of these candidates.

These competitive contingencies lead to a number of other issues that either help or hinder the work and/or progression of academics. In the following section of this chapter, I describe a number of human interactions I have experienced over the years and outline how I responded. These are general examples that reflect contingencies that prevail at many universities, not at one specific university. I hope they will be useful to others who find themselves in similar situations.

Bullying and Harassment Within Academia: Flight or Fight?

Contingencies that prevail in academic institutions can lead to outcomes best described by the "Peter Principle" (Peter & Hull, 1969). The Peter Principle refers to the observation that in a hierarchical system, individuals tend to be promoted until they reach their personal level of incompetence. Once someone is found to be incompetent in their new role, they tend to remain in post. They usually are neither demoted back to their level of competence nor are they promoted further up the hierarchy. This leads to the corollary that, eventually, every position is occupied by someone who actually is incompetent for the job (Peter & Hull, 1969). When someone has been promoted beyond their level of competence, of course, staff training may help, such as leadership or management training. But in cases where the person does not reach the required level of competence, they tend to cover up their incompetence with well-known tactics that can involve misinformation, bullying, and harassment (Gambrill, 2012; Keenan & Dillenburger, 2018).

Promotion above the level of competence and the use of tactics to cover up does not depend on gender. A bully is a bully, irrespective of gender, age, or ethnicity. The idea that women are more emotionally attuned or sympathetic simply does not hold up. There are many examples of women as well as men bullying and harassing staff who are lower in the hierarchy. The professor in the next example amplifies this case. One of her bullying tactics was to arrange contingencies that ensured failure of others. She frequently did not share information about jobs that needed to be done, until very close to the deadline and then staff were punished for not meeting the expectations. For example, if a report was needed for a certain date, she informed staff two or three days before the deadline, despite the fact that she had known about the deadline weeks earlier. If something went wrong, she blamed the staff, never herself. On one occasion she changed the teaching schedule without telling me. I was working from home that day, when I got a phone call from the secretary to say that a class of students were sitting in the lecture hall waiting for me to teach. I had a two-hour commute. There was no way I could be there in time to give that lecture. I was horrified: a total nightmare for someone who never was late for a meeting nor missed a lecture.

At that time, I was running a very successful professional master's degree course, including all administrative tasks, marketing and advertisement, student selection and admissions, timetabling and room-booking, teaching and marking, and any other responsibilities that come with managing such a demanding course. When I was on sabbatical, there was no permanent faculty member who could cover my absence. I was asked to find an alternative and it was agreed that a very experienced part-time tutor would get the contract to lead the course temporarily during my absence. I started my sabbatical having provided the temporary course leader with everything they needed to run the course successfully. Shortly afterwards, I got a message directing me to report back immediately. A meeting with the dean of faculty had been scheduled to reprimand me for leaving the course unattended. What had happened was that the temporary course leader had been exposed to such unsupportive contingencies that she had become unable to run the course. Students were complaining. Thankfully the dean grasped the situation very quickly and was sympathetic. On my eventual return from sabbatical a few months later, I pointed out the significant risk to the university of having only one member of staff responsible for a whole master's course. Support was refused and I was told that I alone was responsible for "ALL" (their emphasis) of the work related to the course. Additional contingencies were arranged to prevent me from doing my job responsibly and competently, such as attempts at preventing me from gaining the necessary continuing education units (CEUs) for my first Board Certified Behavior Analyst (BCBA) renewal. I was told that I did not need this certification for my present job. I was quite proud of being the first BCBA in my local area at that time and I was not going to let it lapse.

Unable to combat the obstacles that had been put before me, I accepted a job in a different department. At a meeting that had been scheduled to allocate more work for the coming term, I will never forget the faces when I told them that I would not be able to do the work. They asked "Why?" My response: "because I won't be here. I have accepted a job in another department." The meeting was terminated. I got up and left. That was the last time I saw them. I had worked in that department for 15 years. There was no farewell event, no card, no present, no hand shake, no "thank you." Nothing.

I had accepted my new job despite the fact that it was at a lower level in the hierarchical ladder. My strategy had been simply to "get out," to run, to get away from all the bullies in that old department. The options were very basic, "fight or flight." I had exhausted the rather limited "fight" options that were available at the time, and "flight" was the only option left to me under the prevailing contingencies (also see Chapter 13).

A month after I had started the new job, attempts at bullying me continued. I received an email from my old department asking me to grade assignments for the course I used to run. They were surprised when I said that I was not in a position to do this work, as I no longer worked for them. When my new department was informed about the request, they handled the situation remarkably well. With the understanding that a certain level of pro-social behavior was expected across departments of the university, they asked me very nicely if I would grade these assignments for the old department in the spirit of collegiality. I agreed and my workload in the new department was reduced accordingly. Once the marking was done, my new department submitted the work to the old department. I was not contacted by the old department again.

In my new department, there were quite a few woman professors, a very unusual situation in the 2000s (HESA, 2021). The issue of female academic promotions (also see Chapter 8) had become crystalized nationally as something that needed to be addressed urgently. My university responded by setting up a Gender Initiative with a very successful mentoring scheme (QGI, 2021; also see Chapters 5 and 6). I remember mentoring a junior colleague some years later. She described contingencies that were very similar to those I had experienced in my previous department. I told her that at times getting out, a.k.a. flight, is an acceptable option. I supported her to apply successfully for a more senior position elsewhere. She got the job, where she was appreciated for her talents and skills. In hindsight, "flight" can be one way to deal with aversive contingencies maintained by people who have no understanding of the power of positive reinforcement (Daniels, 2000).

Work-Life Balance: Timing is Important

Much is made of work-life balance, but it can be difficult to achieve when life or work throws you curveballs (also see Chapter 15). I started my academic career in my mid-30s with a one-year old infant at home (also see Chapters 5 and 10). A couple of years later, I was on maternity leave for our second child. In those days, maternity leave was approximately 12 weeks (six weeks before and six weeks after the birth), paternity leave was three days after the birth. Thanks in no small part to the Gender Initiative, since then colleagues can take up to one year off work and return to a teaching-free semester that allows them to re-establish their research momentum and publication trajectory.

Before I went off on maternity leave, I was teaching a course to master's-level students. The course was going great. For the assignment, I asked my students to plan and carry out a small-scale behavior-change program targeting non-clinical behavior with non-vulnerable adults; examples they came up with included teaching their grandmother/father to write emails, teaching their dad to play a tune on the tin whistle, or teaching their partners to cook a favorite dish. The students had to operationally define the behavior, take a stable baseline, collect socially valid intervention and follow-up data; they had to submit a one-minute video to prove that they did the "project" themselves and to learn about the usefulness of video recording behavioral interventions, and they had to include a simple single-system design graph into their brief project report. It was a fun project that yielded some interesting results, some of which got published (Dillenburger et al., 1997). My students on different courses did similar projects (Iwaniec et al., 1998). The students loved the practical applications of the theoretical content they had been taught.

When I returned from my 12-week maternity leave, I was told that the project assignment had been scrapped in favor of a generic 3,000-word essay. Evidently, the non-behavioral faculty who covered the class during my maternity leave had been unable to teach the students how to conduct the project. An essay was much easier to teach to and assess. I tried to return to the project idea, but to no avail. I was a junior faculty member with two small children at home. I neither had enough energy nor clout to win this fight, so I chose to let it go for now and fight for it another day.

Years later, I reintroduced the project assignment idea in a new master's course, where it has been used very successfully ever since. What can we learn from this episode? Sometimes, when something does not work out early on, it is worth waiting or pausing for. Timing is important. Use the energy for causes that can be won. Pick your battles. As the old Indian saying goes: "All things end well. If they are not well, it's not the end yet." A behavior analyst might say, "the right time for a good idea will come when the contingencies align."

Research Impact in the Community: A Cause that's Worth Fighting For

In the UK, academics are expected to produce evidence that their work has an impact directly in the community or with policy-makers. Early on in my career and based on ample evidence, I got involved in promoting Applied Behavior Analysis (ABA)-based interventions for children and adults on the autism spectrum (e.g., Keenan et al., 2000). The impact of this work was significant (Dillenburger, 2015). However, just as Schoppenhauer (1788–1860) outlined, new ideas first are ridiculed, then laughed at, before they are considered obvious (Dillenburger, 2014). In the UK, ABA went through this process, and while most schools and parents use behavioral principles, many still misinterpret and ridicule the application of the science of behavior analysis (Keenan et al., 2014; Kelly et al., 2018).

As it happened, I secured a major government grant to conduct a number of studies related to people affected by autism, including a thorough literature review regarding available policies and supports (Dillenburger et al., 2014), a large-scale general-population survey about autism awareness (Dillenburger et al., 2013; Dillenburger et al., 2017; Dillenburger et al., 2015), a number of secondary data analyses, including a secondary analysis of the Millennium Cohort study (Dillenburger et al., 2015; Fitzsimmons, 2000), a staff survey (Dillenburger et al., 2016), and interviews with adults with an autism diagnosis and parents of young children on the spectrum (Dillenburger et al., 2016). The study took over three years and yielded eight high-impact publications and five lengthy reports (BASE Project, 2016). We left no stone unturned to discover everything that was known about autism in our country. Amongst many other findings, the research confirmed that, internationally, ABA was considered the basis of evidence-based practice, but that children with autism in our community were not able to benefit from ABA-based interventions. The final report was published on the government website (Dillenburger et al., 2015) and results were reported widely (Dillenburger, 2015).

What happened next is a bit difficult to believe. During the process of the research, we had consulted regularly (every six months) with the government funders and departments. We had addressed any issues that arose during the study and experienced no major problems or critiques. However, after completion of the work we got serious opposition from one of the departments and a local autism charity that was closely associated with that department. They did not like that the findings were critical of their practices. For example, on the basis of data provided by the government, we reported a severe lack of educational provision for children on the autism spectrum, with one-third of these children not receiving a needs assessment within the legal timeframe of 26 weeks. The department claimed that we got it wrong and that, on the contrary, all children with special needs were fully assessed within the required timeframe. We went back to check all available government data and reports and found that the government had commissioned a new report, specifically on the needs assessment of all school children with special needs. This report found that nearly two-thirds (59%) of the children were not assessed within the legal time frame (Perry, 2015). We amended our report to include these much higher government figures. The department that had made the complaint did not respond.

After the publication of our reports, the autism charity employed two well-known individuals to supply a lengthy report criticizing our work. They sent this report directly to the vice-chancellor of my university to try to have my work discredited. The university responded by confirming that my work had been approved by the ethics board and that the findings had been thoroughly reviewed and accepted by the government funder. No further action was taken by the charity.

Impact is best achieved by communication. Universities have an "Expert Directory." Those registered in this directory get frequent media requests from newspapers, television, radio, and/or online to talk about the topic of their expertise. I am always happy to talk about autism and ABA. It is important to reinforce behavior that opens channels of communication (Daniels, 2000). Obviously, communication and exchange also are the best way to win friends and influence people (Carnegie, 2006).

Students: Another Cause Worth Fighting For

As if academic work were not stressful enough with pressures of high teaching loads, demanding publication schedules, and funders breathing down your neck, the Dunning-Kruger effect (Dunning, 2011; Kruger & Dunning, 1999) can cause untold additional damage and stress. For example, junior colleagues with limited experience who overestimate their knowledge can cause a major problem. The victim in this case was a doctoral student.

The student was a well-respected behavior analyst and an accomplished author of multiple papers in their area of expertise. The doctoral training had covered a number of different research methodologies and yielded three further high-impact publications: quite an overachievement for any doctoral student (to maintain anonymity, the publications are not referenced here). The student submitted their thesis for examination, meeting all deadlines and university requirements.

A junior colleague had been nominated as internal examiner mainly to give them the experience of examining a particularly good student. While some written guidance was provided, additional training for the role as doctoral examiner was not available. Days before the viva voce, an allegation of serious research misconduct was made against the student and the supervisor. Rather than viewing this as an educational opportunity for a new examiner, the decision was taken to postpone the student's viva voce and proceed with the investigation using the full force of the relevant university disciplinary procedures. This included a number of hearings with the student and the supervisor separately in front of senior representatives of the university, and the submission of a mountain of evidence of every supervision session, every email exchange, every communication related to many years of study. The exact details of the allegations are not important here, the point is that contingencies had been arranged that allowed an inexperienced examiner to fall prey to the Dunning-Kruger effect by overestimating their own competence without any checks or balances. This led to months of extreme stress for the doctoral student. In order to identify evidence, the supervisor consulted with people high up in the university hierarchy who were authorities regarding the issues raised and who confirmed that neither the student nor the supervisor had done anything wrong. Ultimately, the disciplinary panel concluded that the allegations were unsubstantiated and recommended that better and clearer guidance and staff training were necessary and should be developed regarding the issues raised.

Summary

In this chapter I have described a number of different ways a behavior analyst can deal with conflict, harassment, bullying, and coercion (Sidman, 2000). These processes fall into three main categories: flight, pause, or fight. The challenge for the behavior analyst is to arrange contingencies so as to avoid future conflicts and ensure prosociality and compassion. There are times, though, when we are powerless to do this and "flight" seems the only way out. This means a 100% change of contingencies, for example, a move to a different department or university. This can be a scary process as the contingencies operating in the new place may not be better than those that operated before. However, a change combined with experience can be a useful strategy and the decision can be reinforced by supportive contingencies arranged by compassionate and prosocial colleagues (also see Chapter 13). It is important to remember that the decision to leave a situation that cannot be changed is not a failure. It takes courage and determination and can lead to success.

At other times, it may be necessary to pause, to wait until better contingencies are in place. Of course, as behavior analysts, we should try and arrange these contingencies, we do not have to wait without action. We can use the time constructively by developing new skills or establishing new, supportive, and compassionate networks (also see Chapter 17). If the idea and the behavior are good and worthwhile, their time will come.

Finally, there are some causes worth fighting for. When it comes to community impact or the rights of students, compassion becomes the leading motivator and "flight or pause" are not options. In these situations, remember your behavior analytic training. It will help you prepare and manage conflict. Try to find good allies and do not hesitate to contact those in "high places" in the echelons of the university for advice and support. In the fight for the rights of your students or service users, leave no stone unturned. Make sure that you arrange contingencies that promote prosociality and compassion in the long run.

During times when bullying and harassment are ongoing, the problems they create may seem nearly insurmountable. However, in hindsight you will either have learned something (e.g., the event was not as important as it seemed at the time), or it will have led to change and eventually a good outcome. In order to achieve a good outcome, it is important to protect yourself and others. When it seems that a situation may start to get out of hand, keep all potential evidence on file with dates and times, copies of emails and other correspondence, and records of phone calls and in-person discussions or encounters. These records are the evidence you may need to argue your case when you have to fight the system or have to defend yourself against those who use contingencies of coercion (Sidman, 2000), or those who have fallen prey to the Peter Principle or the Dunning-Kruger effect.

Of course, in a highly competitive environment, it is not only important to protect yourself, it also is important to protect others around you, especially those more vulnerable than yourself. There are a number of strategies that can be employed to promote collegiality and compassion in competitive settings: for example, setting up fora, such as a Gender Initiative or a mentoring scheme for junior faculty. Mentors are senior faculty who volunteer their time and expertise. They meet with mentees to support them in their career plans (also see Chapters 5 and 6). Appraisals and personal support also can be utilized to establish collegiality and gain support if necessary. As academics we also have the avenue of publications. Depending on the situation, you can use examples of how to deal with conflict and build compassion for a journal paper (e.g., Dillenburger, 2007; Keenan & Dillenburger, 2018), a presentation (e.g., Dillenburger, 2014), by developing online content (e.g., Keenan & Dillenburger, 2020, 2021), or in a book chapter, as I have done here. This is educational for the reader and can be quite cathartic for the author.

Conclusion

A lot of water has gone under the bridge since I was first appointed to my university. When I was asked to reflect upon my 30 years of academic experiences, I was not sure what I could contribute. Now that I read over the pages, for the last time before they go off to press, I reckon that some of the ideas and experiences described in this chapter may make it a little bit easier for others to understand the effects of exposing good people to damaging and competitive contingencies, and help them forge their own path to promote prosociality and compassion.

Notes

1. The term "she/her" is used throughout this chapter, rather than more inclusive term "they/them," because this book is specifically focussed on women in behavior analysis.
2. The term single-system is used here, rather than the more common term single-subject, to include research regarding whole-system behavior change, for example, organizational or community change.

References

Agnew, J., & Uhl, D. (2021). *Safe by design. A behavioral systems approach to human performance improvement.* Aubrey Daniels International.

BASE Project. (2016). *BASE reports (full copies; free download).* www.qub.ac.uk/research-centres/CentreforBehaviourAnalysis/Research/BenchmarkingAutismServiceEfficacyBASE/

Carnegie, D. (2006). *How to win friends and influence people*. Vermilion.

Cooper, J., Heron, T., & Heward, W. (2020). *Applied behaviour analysis* (3rd ed.). Pearson Prentice Hall.

Daniels, A. C. (2000). *Bringing out the best in people* (2nd ed.). McGraw-Hill Education.

Dillenburger, K. (2007). A behavior analytic perspective on victimology. *International Journal of Behavioral Consultation and Therapy*, *3*(3), 433–448. https://psycnet.apa.org/fulltext/2008-06145-010.html

Dillenburger, K. (2014). *Behavioural insights into autism: Lost in translation?* https://mediasite.qub.ac.uk/Mediasite/Play/5af4e8fd06604922a106aca2f0fed0761d

Dillenburger, K. (2015). *Early intervention for autism spectrum disorder: KESS Presentation*. www.niassembly.gov.uk/assembly-business/research-and-information-service-raise/knowledge-exchange/knowledge-exchange-seminar-series-4–2014–2015/early-intervention-for-autism-spectrum-disorder/

Dillenburger, K., Godina, L., & Burton, M. (1997). Training in behavioral social work: A pilot study. *Research on Social Work Practice*, 7(1), 70–78. https://doi.org/10.1177/104973159700700104

Dillenburger, K., Jordan, J.-A., & McKerr, L. (2016). School's out forever: Postsecondary educational trajectories of students with autism. *Australian Psychologist* (4), 304–315d. https://doi.org/10.1111/ap.12228

Dillenburger, K., Jordan, J.-A., McKerr, L., Devine, P., & Keenan, M. (2013). Awareness and knowledge of autism and autism interventions: A general population survey. *Research in Autism Spectrum Disorders*, 7(12). https://doi.org/10.1016/j.rasd.2013.09.004

Dillenburger, K., Jordan, J.-A., McKerr, L., & Keenan, M. (2015). The Millennium child with autism: Early childhood trajectories for health, education and economic wellbeing. *Developmental Neurorehabilitation*, *18*, 37–46. https://doi.org/10.3109/17518423.2014.964378

Dillenburger, K., Jordan, J.-A., McKerr, L., Lloyd, K., & Schubotz, D. (2017). Autism awareness in children and young people: Surveys of two populations. *Journal of Intellectual Disability Research*, *61*(8), 766–777. https://doi.org/10.1111/jir.12389

Dillenburger, K., McKerr, L., & Jordan, J.-A. (2015). *BASE project (Vol. 5): Final report*. www.executiveoffice-ni.gov.uk/publications/helping-most-vulnerable-out-poverty-trap-and-reducing-inequality-policies-strategies-and-services

Dillenburger, K., McKerr, L., & Jordan, J.-A. (2017). *Preventing poverty and social exclusion for those affected by autism and their families: KESS presentation*. Knowledge Exchange Seminar Series: Northern Ireland Assembly. https://niassembly.tv/preventing-poverty-social-exclusion-affected-autism-families/

Dillenburger, K., McKerr, L., Jordan, J.-A., Devine, P., & Keenan, M. (2015). Creating an inclusive society . . . How close are we in relation to autism spectrum disorder? A general population survey. *Journal of Applied Research in Intellectual Disabilities*, *28*(4), 330–340. https://doi.org/10.1111/jar.12144

Dillenburger, K., McKerr, L., Jordan, J.-A., & Keenan, M. (2016). Staff training in autism: The one-eyed wo/man . . .. *International Journal of Environmental Research and Public Health*, *13*(7), 716. https://doi.org/10.3390/ijerph13070716

Dillenburger, K., McKerr, L., & Jordan, J.-A. (2014). Lost in translation: Public policies, evidence-based practice, and autism spectrum disorder. *International Journal of Disability, Development and Education*, *61*(2), 134–151. https://doi.org/10.1080/1034912X.2014.905059

Dunning, D. (2011). *The Dunning–Kruger effect. Being ignorant of one's own ignorance*. https://books.google.co.uk/books?hl=en&lr=&id=KlaWDbvRY1UC&oi=fnd&pg=PA247&dq=The+Dunning–Kruger+effect+&ots=OwMM4ih31w&sig=DfILaJHZAT1IOmGQPoeC78JD0R4#v=onepage&q=The Dunning–Kruger effect&f=false

Fitzsimmons, E. (2000). *Millennium cohort study*. www.cls.ioe.ac.uk/page.aspx?sitesectionid=851

Gambrill, E. D. (2012). *Propaganda in the helping professions*. Oxford University Press.

HESA. (2021). *Age and gender statistics for HE staff*. www.hesa.ac.uk/news/26-02-2015/age-and-gender-of-staff

Iwaniec, D., McAuley, R., & Dillenburger, K. (1998). Multi-disciplinary Diploma in applied social learning theory in child care. *Multi-Disciplinary Journal, Child Care in Practice*, *1*, 30–37. https://doi.org/10.1080/13575279608410455

Jensen, K. (2016). *Prosociality*. https://doi.org/10.1016/j.cub.2016.07.025

Keenan, M., & Dillenburger, K. (2011). When all you have is a hammer . . .: RCTs and hegemony in science. *Research in Autism Spectrum Disorders*, *5*(1), 1–13. https://doi.org/10.1016/j.rasd.2010.02.003

Keenan, M., & Dillenburger, K. (2018). How "fake news" affect autism policies. *Societies*, *2018030238*. https://doi.org/10.20944/preprints201803.0238.v1

Keenan, M., & Dillenburger, K. (2020). *Behaviour analysis: A primer*. www.behaviouranalysis.eu.com

Keenan, M., & Dillenburger, K. (2021). *Nurturing project*. www.youtube.com/watch?v=xfDRf2tHCyU
Keenan, M., Dillenburger, K., Röttgers, H.-R., Dounavi, K., Jónsdóttir, S. L., Moderato, P., Schenk, J. J. A. M., Virués-Ortega, J., Roll-Pettersson, L., & Martin, N. (2014). Autism and ABA: The gulf between North America and Europe. *Review Journal of Autism and Developmental Disorders*, *2*(2), 167–183. https://doi.org/10.1007/s40489-014-0045-2
Keenan, M., Kerr, K. P., & Dillenburger, K. (2000). *Parents education as autism therapists*. Jessica Kingsley Publishers.
Kelly, M., Martin, N., Dillenburger, K., Kelly, A., & Miller, M. M. (2018). Spreading the news: History, successes, challenges and the ethics of effective dissemination. *Behavior Analysis in Practice*. https://doi.org/10.1007/s40617-018-0238-8
Keltner, D. (2012). *What is compassion?* https://greatergood.berkeley.edu/topic/compassion/definition
Kruger, J., & Dunning, D. (1999). Unskilled and unaware of it: How difficulties in recognizing one's own incompetence lead to inflated self-assessments. *Journal of Personality and Social Psychology*, 77(6), 1121–1134. https://doi.org/10.1037/0022-3514.77.6.1121
Perry, C. (2015). *SEN legislation and policy in Northern Ireland*. Northern Ireland Assembly: Research and Information Service Research Paper. www.niassembly.gov.uk/globalassets/documents/raise/publications/2015/ed u
Peter, L. J., & Hull, R. (1969). *The Peter principle*. Pan Books.
QGI. (2021). *Queens university Belfast gender initiative*. www.qub.ac.uk/sites/QueensGenderInitiative/
Schoppenhauer, A. (1788–1860). *Arthur Schoppenhauer*. http://en.wikipedia.org/wiki/Arthur_Schopenhauer
Sidman, M. (2000). *Coersion and its fallout*. Authors Cooperative.
Skinner, B. F. (1938). *Behavior of organisms*. D. Appleton-Century Company, Inc.
Slim, L., & Reuter-Yuill, L. M. (2021). A behavior-analytic perspective on interprofessional collaboration. *Behavior Analysis in Practice*. https://doi.org/10.1007/s40617-021-00602-7
Strauss, C., Taylor, B. L., Gu, J., Kuyken, W., Baer, R., Jones, F., & Cavanagh, K. (2016). What is compassion and how can we measure it? A review of definitions and measures. *Clinical Psychology Review*. https://doi.org/10.1016/j.cpr.2016.05.004

22 Reflections on Loss and Grief

Traci M. Cihon

Positionality/Reflexivity Statement*

I am a white, cisgender, straight, female. I was born outside of Chicago in Hammond, Indiana. My first experience with loss was my parents' divorce. I was seven and my brother was three. My father remarried first and had my sister who was born when I was 12. Shortly thereafter, my mother remarried. She and my stepfather bought a house in a small town in southern Illinois about 40 miles south of St. Louis, Missouri where I lived with my mom, my brother, my stepfather, and his three children. My brother and I would spend every other weekend with our dad and eventually my sister. Later, after my dad had divorced his second wife, those weekends included the company of the woman who would become his third wife (then ex-wife) and her three sons.

We were a working-class family and I honestly have no idea how my parents managed financially. I remember that we would bring our own cheese slices when we went to McDonald's (but we were fortunate that we got to go to McDonald's); my mom and my stepfather could not afford the extra ten cents for a slice of cheese. While my birth parents were married, my mother was a stay-at-home mom, and my father was a draftsman. After my parents divorced, my mom went back to work as a secretary; she later retired as a trustee for the federal government. My father worked his way into information technology and worked as a systems analyst until his recent retirement. My stepfather is a mechanic, also recently retired.

I went to high school in New Athens, Illinois, a small town with a population of only 2,000. Most of my friends' parents worked as farmers, coal miners, or in other trades; many belonged to labor unions. The mines closed at some point when I was in high school, causing a reasonable amount of financial instability for my friends and the community. When I was 14, I started working as a server at a pizza place in town; I also babysat and tutored the owners' children. When I was 16, I started working at

* Positionality/responsivity statements provide authors with an opportunity to share aspects of their individual learning history with the reader. In doing so, the reader may be more acquainted with some of the intimate details of the author(s)' history and their own intersectionality, establishing an opportunity for the reader to contextualize later content. Positionality/responsivity statements are not yet common in behavior analytic circles. Recent experiences for both myself and many of my colleagues' positionality statements have varied. Some audiences have been incredibly kind, compassionate, and supportive; others have been less so and sometimes even cruel. Sharing the intimate details of one's learning history, particularly as related to loss and grief, leaves the author in a precariously vulnerable position. Moreover, some details are not mine to share, as I hold only one perspective of many who shared in these experiences with me. Given the still varied and not always supportive response from the larger communities of which I am now a member, I have carefully selected which details to share and which to omit. I do this intentionally, as an action that offers some protection from the systems-level contingencies that do not support such candidness and vulnerability, and from those controlling agents and agencies who arrange and sustain contingencies that prevent some from moving forward with the same opportunities as others simply because of a learning history that may be different from their own.

DOI: 10.4324/9781003216773-26

Steak-n-Shake, which enabled me to move out my senior year of high school (I was 17). I remember my first apartment, also in New Athens. I would lie awake at night listening to the squirrels (or rats?) running through the ceiling rafters.

Unlike many of my friends who had been born and raised in New Athens, I couldn't wait to get out. I graduated second in my class and started my journey as a first-generation college student at Washington University in St. Louis. My first semester was rough. I was living off-campus, working close to full time as a server and bartender, and I was taking 21 credit hours. I ended my first semester with a 1.7 GPA, earning my way to academic probation. At risk of losing my scholarship, I changed majors and career plans, declaring a major in Psychology with hopes of becoming a clinical psychologist.

While serving one night during my sophomore year, one of my customers asked me what I was doing that summer. I had no idea so I responded vaguely that I would be taking a couple of classes and working as much as I could. She happened to the be director for the Illinois Center for Autism, and she suggested that I spend some time volunteering there. As a first-generation college student from a working-class family, I knew volunteer work didn't pay the bills, but I knew the experience would prove beneficial in the long-term. I found a way to get course credit through independent study, and not knowing anything about autism, I read as many books on the subject as I could find. When it came time to consider the goals of my independent study, I opted to evaluate the comparative effectiveness of the teaching strategies the center was using and a new strategy that was showing promise in autism intervention—discrete trial instruction (DTI). This experience later transpired into a paid position working as an in-home behavior therapist for children with autism, a position I learned about from Dr. Leonard Green. The positions were paid through the local public school district who had contracted with the Center for Autism and Related Disorders (CARD) to provide in-home behavior therapy because of a class-action lawsuit. I continued working as a server and bartender as well as an in-home behavior therapist until I graduated with a very expensive psychology degree.

I hadn't gotten into any of the Ph.D. programs to which I had applied, nor was I willing to sign a non-compete clause to advance in position. Not knowing that behavior analysis was something I could study, and with student loan payments coming due quickly, I took a position as Psychosocial Educator and Case Manager working with adults with chronic mental illness and development disabilities with a community-based human support services agency in southern Illinois. I found myself referencing my textbook from my Behavior Modification class, developing token economies and contingency contracts to support the clients in achieving their goals. Even though my clients were making progress, my colleagues referred to them as "lifers" which implied that they would be continually dependent on our support, regardless of intervention. After a few months, I answered an advertisement for a position with the public school system where I had worked previously. The position was for an associate behavior analyst working with children with autism. I wasn't any more qualified than the next person and I remember fumbling through one of the interview questions asking what the four functions of behavior were. I'm still grateful to Tami Galensky-Pentz who, perhaps unknowingly, let me know when my responses were on the right track by nodding enthusiastically when I was getting closer to the right answers. I remember my response . . . kids do things to get out of stuff or to get stuff; they do things to get attention, and they do things because they want to. It wasn't until much later that I learned that these were different ways to describe the escape, attention, access to tangible, and automatic functions of behavior.

In the fall of 2001, with a caseload of 20 students with autism receiving in-home and school-based services and about 50 staff under my supervision, I started my master's in psychology and behavior analysis through a satellite program offered through the University of Nevada-Reno (UNR), which had partnered with the Judevine Center for Autism and Special School District of St. Louis County (SSD). I had amazing on-site supervisors who introduced me to Precision Teaching, Skinner's (1957) Verbal Behavior, naturalistic teaching strategies, and Glenn's (1988, 2004) metacontingency. I attended my first Association for Behavior Analysis convention in New Orleans and met Dr. Glenn in Toronto the following year when I was contemplating transferring to the master's program at the University of

North Texas (UNT). She advised me to finish the master's degree I was currently working on and then to attend the PhD program in Special Education and Applied Behavior Analysis at The Ohio State University (OSU)—I was struggling to understand why the classroom teachers and behavior analysts were sometimes at odds with one another when both seemed to be working toward the same goals. In 2004, I moved to Columbus, Ohio with my fiancé, Guy Bedient, a behavior analyst, and alumnus of UNT's master's program who planned to start the PhD program the following year.

I graduated with my K-12 moderate to intensive teacher certification and PhD in 2007, a year that I will later describe in more detail, and I took a position as an assistant professor at the Chicago School of Professional Psychology where I met some of my closest friends and colleagues. I was teaching seven classes, advising ten thesis students, managing a community-based contract for providing services for children with autism and ultimately running a private caseload of about 20 clients. When Dr. Manish Vaidya told me that UNT was hiring I was surprised; UNT didn't hire often. With Manish's encouragement, I applied; I had always wanted to go to UNT, but I couldn't imagine they would hire me as a faculty member. I was terrified when I walked into the conference room in Chilton Hall, surrounded by those whose work I had studied and admired for years—Drs. Sigrid Glenn, Janet Ellis, Shahla Ala'i-Rosales, Rick Smith, Jesus Rosales-Ruiz, and Manish were all there. At a certain point during the interview, I found myself on a walking tour of the campus with Janet and Sigrid. It was in that moment I realized that it didn't matter if I got the job or not, I was on a tour of UNT with Janet and Sigrid. These were two of the most amazing women and scholars, responsible for founding the first department of behavior analysis, developing the first ABAI accredited master's program in behavior analysis, and I had their undivided attention. I ended up getting the job and later earning tenure, and I recently completed my 13th year as an associate professor at UNT where I taught undergraduate Organizational Behavior Management course, the master's ethics course, and the graduate course in Behavioral Systems Analysis. I co-coordinated the Community Lab with Drs. Shahla Ala'i-Rosales, Alicia Re Cruz, and Malika Pritchett, and I coordinated the Culturo-Behavior Science Lab.

★★★

The great scholar and contemporary writer, Chimamanda Ngozi Adichie advised us: "People mourn differently is easy for the intellectual to absorb, but for the hear it is much harder" (Adichie, 2021, p. 52). This is a story of my journey, as a woman in academia, to merge intellect and heart.

★★★

Many scholars inside and outside of behavior science have studied loss, grief, bereavement, trauma, and violence much more in depth than I have. In preparing for this chapter, I reviewed what behavior scientists have said about these topics (e.g., Averil & Wisocki, 1981; Brasted & Callahan, 1984; Calkin, 1990, 2001; Dillenburger, 2007; Dillenburger & Keenan, 1994, 2001, 2005; Fraley, 2001; Guerin, 2001; Mattaini, 2012; Moynahan, 2001; Rakos, 2001; Sulzer-Azaroff, 1999; Tonneau, 2001), but I will not propose a behavioral analysis of loss, grief, bereavement, or violence. I encourage readers who are interested in a behavior analysis of these topics to review the outstanding work of scholars like Dr. Karola Dillenburger, who has worked extensively in these areas. I am instead writing about my own personal and intimate experiences with loss and grief. Because I also happen to be a behavior scientist and culturo-behavior scientist, the basic concepts and principles from behavior science and culturo-behavior science (CBS) have found their way into my analysis and comments at times. I also read Adichie's (2021) *Notes on Grief*, which served as an opportunity for me to reflect on my experiences with loss and grief. Nonetheless, I am not a scholar or an expert on loss and grief. I am, however, an experienced griever . . . but this wasn't always the case. I had to learn to grieve. I did this through experience and direct contact with the contingencies. I was also fortunate to have had some amazing verbal communities comprised of incredibly supportive friends, family, and colleagues. Thus, the purpose of this chapter is to share those experiences, the contingencies surrounding them (to the best of my recollection), some details regarding the importance of the communities who supported me, and to describe how they have collectively impacted my trajectory and shaped my repertoires as they manifest in my roles as a daughter, sister, aunt, friend, student, colleague, mentor, and professional.

I was fortunate to have not experienced great loss, at least with respect to the loss of the life of a loved one,[1] at an early age. My earliest experience with loss was probably my parents' divorce. In hindsight, I didn't even realize that I should have had the opportunity to grieve; I was too busy assuming new responsibilities, looking after my brother after school when I was just nine years old and helping around the house.[2] Even though my parents were amazing at creating the conditions in which our blended family functioned as one mostly integrated unit—my fiancé Neale and I just attended an event with my mom and stepdad; my dad and his girlfriend; my sister and her boyfriend; two of my stepbrothers from my mom's second marriage, one of my stepbrother's ex-wives, and my three nieces—I was expected to carry on as I had been before the divorce. And like Adichie (2021), I remember asking, "How is it that the world keeps going . . ." (p. 12)? For my immediate and biological family, we have always prioritized and cultivated coming together to support the most vulnerable or oppressed. At the time of my parents' divorce, that wasn't me.

The earliest loss of life I remember was when I was 12 or 13 years old, and my maternal grandfather passed away. I was at the hospital with my great aunt Mabel, who was essentially my surrogate grandmother and the person I looked up to most in the world. She told me not to cry because it wouldn't help anything, and it would upset my mother even more. I wasn't terribly close to my grandpa. I remember going fishing with him and riding my bike to his house with my dad after my parents divorced. Once, while my mom was still at work, he taught me how to make hamburgers on the stove. When my grandpa passed away, I went to school instead of the funeral. At the time I said that I didn't want to see him being put in the ground; I was probably afraid that I would cry. When my mom was five years old, her mother was hospitalized with a brain tumor; she passed away when my mom was ten. For my mother, an only child, the loss of her father marked a significant transition that was lost on me at such a young age. More recently, I've come to better understand why my mom values family and connection so strongly.[3] Generational trauma and grief are not always readily apparent.

The next death I encountered was when the younger of my dad's two older brothers passed away. I was an undergraduate student at Washington University, and I accompanied my dad to the funeral. I listened while he grieved; he was upset because he had not spoken to my uncle for years and was angry at himself for having lost contact with his niece and nephew who no one seemed to know how to reach. I met my other uncle for maybe the second time in my life. His son and I, feeling rather uncomfortable with everything that was happening, volunteered to go get pizzas. We drank Heineken while we were waiting, sharing stories about our dads; he and I had just met at this event. Neither one of us cried . . . but our fathers did.

Through these experiences I learned about loss, but I didn't learn how to grieve.

★★★

Early in the morning on March 1, 2007, in Columbus, Ohio the police rang my doorbell to tell me that my fiancé, Guy, had died. I didn't believe them, so I called his sister and learned the awful news was true. I was 29 years old. We had planned for him to get his PhD. We had planned to open a school for children with autism/autistic children when I graduated later that year. We had plans to finish a book we had started. We had so many plans. These plans didn't happen (see also discussions on "futuring behaviors" in Dillenburger & Keenan, 2005; Keenan, 1996, 1997).

I had just started data collection for my dissertation. I had no idea how to deal with Guy's death, so I didn't. I remember sitting on the couch and occasionally getting up to go to the bathroom. Adichie (2021) counsels us that "grief is a cruel kind of education . . . the pain is not surprising, but its physicality is" (p. 7). I think the landladies at the apartment I was living in tried to get me to eat a bagel. I think my classmate and dear friend Gwen stayed with me. I don't know how long that lasted because the next thing I remember is driving in circles around highway 270. Unable to decide where to go, I must have called my counselor because I ended up in his office. I wanted to quit the PhD and go back home to St. Louis. We called my advisor, Dr. Nancy Neef, to tell her. Nancy insisted that I come to her house to talk it through. I must have agreed to postpone things, because I remember sleeping at her house for a few days.

Then, Nancy did one of the most amazing things anyone has ever done for me to this day. Maybe she had just read Sulzer-Azaroff (1999) because she took my calendar and made a list of had-to's. I had to eat, sleep, see my counselor, attend my classes, run a reading study with which I was heavily involved, and run my dissertation. I protested the latter two.

My dissertation explored two strategies for teaching children with autism mands, tacts, and echoics and most of the sessions were run in-home. The reading study explored the effects of See the Sound/Visual Phonics (STS/VP) on the decoding repertoires of children at risk for school failure. I was unable to take care of myself let alone be responsible for a child for 30 minutes. Nancy must have anticipated my protest because within a few minutes another one of my dear friends and classmates, Lilian, came over and agreed to accompany me for all the sessions until I was more comfortable. My dear friend and colleague, Dr. Dorothy Morrison, would also meet me each morning at the school where we were conducting the reading study. She arrived with an Odwalla™ protein shake and some soup (eating solid food still wasn't going so well). Nancy, Dorothy, and Lilian must have known my reinforcers better than I did because they got me back in contact with them, supporting me in teaching kids to talk and read, and this got me responding again. Maybe they had just read Calkin (1990).[4]

Teaching kids to talk and teaching kids to read are still two of my favorite things to do.

***

Averill and Wisocki (1981) describe four ways in which reinforcement is reduced during bereavement: 1) the reinforcers that were once obtained from interacting with the person you lost are no longer available, 2) some of these reinforcers may still be available but they are no longer effective "as when previously pleasurable activity becomes affectively neutral" (p. 133), 3) responding is too low or not at sufficient strength to contact the reinforcers (e.g., apathy; Kunkel, 1991), or 4) responding contacts aversive stimuli, with memories of the one you lost: "the response might serve as a painful reminder of the deceased or be the source of guilt or social criticism" (p. 133). Brasted and Callahan (1984) note "the resolution of grief occurs because the individual either learns new responses to obtain reinforcers or new reinforcers reward previous behaviors" (p. 533).

Many others have described the role extinction plays in the grieving process (e.g., Averill & Wisocki, 1981; Dillenburger & Keenan, 1994; Guerin, 2001; Moynahan, 2001; Sulzer-Azaroff, 1999) and the disruptions to the setting events, motivating operations, and stimulus controls created by loss (e.g., Dillenburger & Keenan, 2001; Sulzer-Azaroff, 1999). I'm sure I was experiencing a combination of these. Guy's death was like complete system failure for a system on which I was dependent to maintain certain life conditions consistent with my narrative, and for the combinations of stimulus conditions that evoked or sustained (or developed) some of my behavioral repertoire. Although I was managing ok, I was sad and angry, and I needed to learn some new behaviors. I needed a way to bring my sadness and anger under stimulus control. Most importantly, I needed to find a way to stop the memories (i.e., ruminating). But learning new behaviors under extinction schedules is hard and learning new behaviors without contact with all components of your behavioral ecosystem is hard. I started playing a game with myself; I called it the "yellow cup game."

Somewhere in my studies I had discovered the use of "thought stopping" to reduce unwanted recurring thoughts (cf. Massetti & Fabiano, 2005). I must've combined this idea with my understanding of verbal behavior and the role it played in evoking and sustaining the cyclical rumination of memories. Before Guy died, I had been working on a paper on intraverbal behavior and another on stimulus blocking. I was convinced that my keen ability to relate any stimulus, verbal or non-verbal, to a memory of Guy could be interrupted if I could build in enough of a pause to insert a more salient and neutral stimulus. I used a yellow Solo™ cup I had been using with a little water in the bottom as an ashtray. Somehow when I concentrated on that cup, first in its presence and later by recalling the minute details of the cup (e.g., what color the rim of the cup was, how many lines were in each set of ridges) in its absence, I didn't engage in any other covert behavior but describing and visualizing that cup. I carried that "yellow cup" around for a long time.

***

Few people are willing to talk about, much less accompany another through grief; in fact, "we don't know how we will grieve until we grieve" (Adichie, 2021, p. 64). When you experience loss, people send cards or flowers. They say things like, "My condolences,"

"Sorry for your loss," or "They're in a better place." These gestures and statements seem to function as tacts, "What you are going through really sucks," or mands, "Even if I acknowledge that what you are experiencing sucks, please don't draw me into your grief." After a while people don't talk about it at all. I don't think anyone really wants to be good at grieving; this could be why so many people avoid it. I often felt alone with my grief.

I don't think I really learned how to grieve until I moved to Chicago. Michael Fabrizio may have been the catalyst for my initial contact with reinforcement for being in the company of others with my grief. It was the first orientation I was attending at the Chicago School, and the first I was attending as a faculty member. Michael was in town from Seattle and he and I went outside to smoke. He started to talk about the last interaction he had with Guy and what he had come to understand about the exchange since. I began to cry; then I panicked. I knew there was no way that I would be able to regain my composure before the students and my other colleagues saw me. Without missing a beat, Michael jumped in and simply explained to everyone why I was upset. It seemed so uncomplicated when he explained it—I had recently lost someone for whom I cared deeply. No one flinched or acted differently around me.

Prior to that moment, I had been keeping my grief under stimulus control. I would smile and interact with others just as I had before Guy's death, even when it felt like I would never again be the person I had been before Guy died. When I was in situations and environments and I had to be "on," I pretended I was ok. I didn't cry until I was alone. I felt empty and alone.

My colleagues at the Chicago School gave me permission to grieve. They walked with me through my grief and taught me that I didn't have to bear it alone. Dr. Chuck Merbitz, our department chair. Michael and Dr. John Eshleman knew Guy through their work together in Precision Teaching. Drs. Diana Walker, Rachel Taylor, Denise Ross, and Dave Pyles didn't know Guy while he was alive, but they were willing to know him through me. I started to learn how to ride the waves of grief as they came. Instead of bottling up the raw, physical pain of having lost someone for whom I cared so deeply until I was alone, I let the emotions come.

It wasn't until much later that I reflected on why it was that I was so embarrassed and ashamed to let others see me grieve. I didn't respond well to those who were trying to hold me closer, and to support me in my grief. One morning in Chicago, Denise asked me to come into her office. She closed the door, gave me a beautiful journal and Bible, and asked if she could pray with me. I was so uncomfortable with my own vulnerability that I harshly responded that "I don't pray." In hindsight, I realize what a beautiful and profound gesture of kindness and support this was, one that I rejected likely because I had learned it was safer to push others away rather than letting them in and accepting their care. At first, I thought I was so embarrassed and ashamed to let others see me grieve because I didn't want to make anyone else uncomfortable. Later I realized it was also because I didn't want anyone to think I was weak, incompetent, or somehow less than what I was before this loss.

Grief, like any other behavior, takes time. However, academic settings and the associated contingencies leave little time for grief.[5] They are full of strict deadlines. The student doesn't graduate if you don't read the thesis draft before the defense. The publisher doesn't wait if you can't turn the revisions in on time. Your students expect you to provide them with an informative, inspiring, and engaging class. You need to show up. In academia, there is no time for "the symptoms of despair and apathy to run their course without undue interreference, while also providing a timetable for recovery and reintegration into society" (Averill & Wisocki, 1981, p. 135). Together we can change these systemic contingencies and give others the time to grieve.

***

One reason I moved to Texas was that Guy had attended UNT. It made me feel closer to him to see a bound copy of his thesis when I came to the office each morning, to hear stories of the work that he did while he was there, and to have the honor of coordinating a scholarship that Dr. Sigrid Glen was so generous to have established in his memory. It was comforting to be around colleagues who knew him.

Memories, although comforting at times, can also be debilitating. You find yourself missing the best moments. And, you find yourself realizing what "you will never have again" (Adichie, 2021, p. 22). At a certain point you even find yourself missing the worst moments. It feels as the opportunity to spend one last moment with them, even if it was the worst moment you can recollect, is better than the prospect of no future with them whatsoever. You also dream about them, but the dreams are different than the memories because they change the conditions. You dream about the future you would've lived together had they not died, the future you'll never have. You dream that it was some cruel joke and you thought they had died when they didn't, and you will have the future you had planned. You dream about when it happened. You dream that it is happening again. You wake up wishing "that grief was not about the utter impossibility of return" (Adichie, 2021, p. 46). It's hard to rewrite a future that you thought you had already written. It's hard to behave when the expected and actual contingencies don't align. It's hard to narrate a future without a history of behaving under similar conditions.

When I was living in Chicago, John and I started celebrating what we call the "Bedient Effect." When something in our environment triggered a thought or memory of Guy, we texted or called each other to share the experience. We still do this. When I tact an occurrence of the "Bedient Effect" now, I smile. Then, I take a couple of minutes to check in, reflecting on where I've been and where I am now. I do so with gratitude.

★★★

I remember thinking to myself on numerous occasions after Guy died that I really hoped the world was kind enough to give me time to rebuild my strength before I would encounter another significant loss. I wasn't sure I'd live through another one. I tried to convince myself that if I had enough time between losses, the next one wouldn't feel as bad or be as debilitating as when I lost Guy. I was wrong.

In 2013, my great-aunt Mabel passed. She told me once that when she had introduced herself to a four- or five-year-old as his great-great-aunt, he replied, "So how great are you?" She really was great.[6] She was the second youngest of nine children who grew up during the depression. She fought to stay in school past 5th grade, and then 8th grade. As soon as she turned 18, she enlisted in the Women Marine Corps. She liked the uniforms and the mandatory Montezuma Red lipstick;[7] she also saw the Corps as her opportunity to carve a different path than the women in her generation had readily available—getting married or working in a factory. She was the fourth of only six women to achieve the rank of sergeant major, the highest rank for noncommissioned women in the Corps. One of her many accomplishments was the role she played in changing the rule that prevented women from staying in the Corps after it was discovered that they were pregnant. She built her own home (i.e., she didn't hire contractors); she never married (though she maintained a steady relationship with my "uncle" Raymond for 30+ years) nor did she have children. She was a tremendous source of inspiration and strength. She was the person in my family to whom I related most. She guided me with stories of experiences she had had that were relevant to what I was experiencing. When we talked, she made me feel like I could do anything; I could overcome any barrier whether self- or externally imposed because she had already done that very thing or something similar. Further, she had done so when it was much harder for women to do things than anything I was experiencing.

Even though I anticipated that my next loss would be Aunt Mabel, it didn't make it any easier. When she got sick, even though part of me realized it was probably time, I didn't go home immediately. I was busy with work. By the time I got to the hospital, my mom and my cousin were discussing options for hospice care; Aunt Mabel had stopped eating and drinking a few days before and her kidneys were shutting down. The doctor said, within earshot of my aunt, that she had a week at best. My mom and cousin had the decision-making authority, but it was well known in the family that Aunt Mabel and I were close. She had also lived her life in service to the family. I implored them to bring her home to die and promised I would take care of her myself if necessary. It is important to note that I had to be creative with my responsibilities at UNT to create space to be away during this time. Because she was not next-of-kin, her loss did not count as one for which I could exercise the bereavement policy. Eventually, it was arranged. Mom and I took shifts as the primary caregivers with the support of my dad and my sister (this is another example of how my family just does what needs to be done despite my parents' divorce or the lack of a blood relation between my sister and Aunt Mabel). When the ambulance brought my aunt home, I was waiting. She looked at me and, almost accusingly, said, "I knew you'd come." I thought to myself, "Where else would I be?"

Little did I know that providing end-of-life care to someone you love is one of the most challenging things one can do. You are trying to make someone as comfortable as possible, but it is also increasingly clear that you are waiting for them to die. Different people come to pay their respects, and some are lucky enough to have their last interaction be one of the few remaining lucid moments that person will have. I happened to be alone with Aunt Mabel when she had her last lucid moment and she and I had our last conversation. She may have waited for the opportunity; I didn't ask because before I had the chance, she looked at me and, more directly than she's ever asked me anything, said, "What's going to happen next?"

I certainly did not know what happens after you die so I proceeded to explain to her how she would die: that she wouldn't feel pain because of the morphine we were giving her every two hours, that she would soon fall asleep and that she would eventually be in a coma as her organs started to shut down. Then, it would be just a few days more. I explained that we would be right there with her, that she didn't need to be afraid because she would be with her sister who she had been crying out to "come with her" in her sleep since coming home from the hospital. I explained that I would be ok, that the family would be ok (she spent much of her life caring for family, often at great sacrifice to herself), and that when she was ready, she should go. I reassured her that she would be ok and so would we. Somehow, I said all of this without crying (remember that Aunt Mabel often stated that crying didn't help/solve anything). She didn't wake up again, dying exactly one week after the doctor had said as much.

I still long to talk to Aunt Mabel. I find myself reaching for the phone, especially on Sunday mornings (when we often talked). Our conversations grounded me; she gave me a perspective on challenging situations, helped me problem solve, or talked me through hard decisions. There are still questions I wish I had asked her; there are still situations in which I imagine how our conversation would go if I could call her.

***

In the spring of 2012, I had the opportunity to spend some time with my dad and his brother, my Uncle Mike, in Florida. Mike needed surgery. A course release from an internal grant I had been awarded gave me some flexibility, so when Uncle Mike experienced potentially life-threatening complications from the surgery, I was able to go to Florida to support both him and my father. Without the grant, I would not have been able to go and establish a relationship with my uncle and witness how he and my father rekindled their relationship. In 2014, six months after Aunt Mabel passed, so did my Uncle Mike.

If Aunt Mabel was my strongest connection to my mother's extended family and our history, Uncle Mike was the same with respect to my father. Perhaps more impactful to my grieving process, my aunt and my uncle were my parents' last living kin outside of me and my siblings. This dynamic created a new set of intersecting variables that took me by surprise. There were things that needed to be done (e.g., services to be arranged, personal belongings to sift through, estates to be closed). My parents needed support to do these things, and once again it became necessary to experience my grief privately. I needed to maintain an outward showing of strength as my mom grieved the loss of the woman who had stepped into a maternal role, and as my dad came to terms with the loss of his last brother and the recognition that my siblings and I were his closest living relatives.

At times, when I was able to build space to work through my grief, I wasn't sure if I was working through my own grief or my parents' grief. When you share the loss of someone with others, you share the burden of grief. Nevertheless, the form of this shared grief varies. It is influenced by different variables (see also Dillenburger & Keenan, 1994). Was the person older or younger than you? Was the death caused by disease or accident? How often was this individual in your life? How many "life" systems did you share with them? How prepared were you for this death? How many conversations had you shared about it? What was the nature of those conversations? Each of these variables and more affect how you and those who share your loss grieve, how you support each other through that grief, and the roles that each of you take during that journey together. When my aunt and uncle died, my parents began to recognize their own mortality; this realization affected their grieving processes which in turn affected mine. I put my own grief back under stimulus control so that I could write obituaries and help coordinate memorial services. I also began to think more frequently about my parents' mortality, and my own. I'm still working through these thoughts and feelings.

***

I've started to brace myself for the feelings that accompany loss. As Cat Stevens (1974) sang to a generation: "and though you want to last forever/you know you never will . . . and the goodbye makes the journey harder still" (track 2, 1:15). I now anticipate that I will have moments when grief and sadness of the impossibility of recapturing the stimulus conditions and reinforcers I once shared with another occasionally wash over me. These may be connected to Guy, Aunt Mabel, Uncle Mike, or even certain periods in my life (for many years I mourned my pre-PhD self!). I've come to expect loss and the challenging feelings that accompany it, though I'm never truly ready for the loss itself. I've also learned that the feelings that accompany a significant loss hit hard initially and sometimes at unpredictable points years later. They also increase in frequency, duration, and intensity with each subsequent loss. At times it feels as though there is this metaphorical hole in my chest that deepens, with less chance of ever feeling less empty, since losing Guy. I continually remind myself to stay connected and to be vulnerable enough to love deeply. A counselor once told me that when you love deeply, you hurt deeply. After experiencing loss, sometimes it is easier to keep going if you try not to feel; difficult feelings often accompany or follow the euphoria of love.

***

I've come to understand that part of my grieving process involves recapturing myself. I need to work through letting go of the person I was before the loss, and to find ways to accept and love the ways I've changed since and in response to the loss.

When my cat, Anakin, died in August 2020, I wasn't ready. Guy and I found Anakin in 2002; he was scrawny, filthy, and feral, trying to survive a St. Louis winter in the garage under Guy's apartment. Guy was not as keen as I was on "rescuing" this kitten from its inevitable fate. I waited in that garage for several hours each day (and night) with a bowl of tuna. Having recently encountered tactics to establish conditioned reinforcers and to shape new repertoires, I was confident that our bathroom would serve as an operant chamber and that we could pair touch with food and shape approach behavior. Despite Anakin's clear attempts to avoid us initially, it worked. Anakin spent the next 18 years with me—in St. Louis while I completed my master's degree, in Columbus while I lost Guy and completed my PhD, in Chicago when I started my first faculty position, and finally in Denton as I earned tenure and promotion. Losing Anakin felt different than the losses I'd experienced up to this point.

I found Anakin in the hallway between my bedroom and the master bath, and I stayed there until my friends and colleagues, Shahla, and later Kyo,[8] arrived. I heard the vet say to Shahla that I could take Anakin to the pet cemetery. I'd read the Stephen King novel and watched the movie and there was no way I was going to be haunted by dreams of Anakin, decaying yet coming back to "life," so after a couple of tequila shots we had the most interesting, yet beautiful, memorial service in my backyard.

I lost Anakin as the second wave of COVID-19 threatened the US. Racial tensions were escalating, protests were turning violent, an economic crisis was ensuing, and human-driven climate disasters were occurring at a greater frequency and intensity. The certainty of my parents', my own, and really everyone's mortality began to feel imminent. As I watched the number of deaths from COVID-19 increase, my isolation from friends and family also became more pronounced. Once content to live alone in Texas and visit friends and family scattered around the world, I struggled to stay connected. I found myself consumed with thoughts of loved ones I might not have the chance to see again before they died from COVID-19 or the inability to obtain routine medical care from our overburdened healthcare systems. Although I had recently met someone who I cared for deeply, other variables prevented us from acting on our emotions and I found myself feeling very alone. The uncertainty around when I might experience regular contact with other human beings again made my loneliness more acute.

I found comfort in maintaining connections with my friends and colleagues in Italy with a weekly coffee on Zoom, in my weekly trips to the grocery store with Kyo, in increasingly lengthy phone conversations with my dear friends Erin and Suzanne, listening to Motown while gardening, and spending time with my cat(s). Yet, I felt as though I was wrapped in a blanket in grief. Like many others, I was (and am still) grieving pre-pandemic life. I was also exhausted. In the two to three years leading up to the pandemic I had acquired an entirely new teaching load, closed the Teaching Science Lab (Cihon et al., 2017) and started the Culturo-Behavior Science Lab (Cihon et al., 2020; Cihon et al., 2021), supported multiple students through their thesis defenses and served on just as many committees, and had just finished co-editing my first book (Cihon & Mattaini, 2020).

When the spring semester ended, I was grateful. Even though I had been open with my students about the challenges I was facing and was no longer hiding my grief, the nature of our relationships required that I also radiate a sense of hope and optimism that I didn't feel.

I was looking forward to summer; with it came the opportunity to rest and recharge. Shahla and I had plans to teach her granddaughter how to swim, it was possible that a few friends might come to visit, and the conditions that prevented my now life partner and me from being together had changed. As summer unfolded, things seemed to be manageable again, until I lost Anakin.

***

I took the next week off to grieve. I often found Luke, my other cat,[9] sitting in the yard and staring at the marker Shahla and her granddaughter helped me make for Anakin (and for me). I didn't know what to do with the other half of the can of food I usually split between Luke and Anakin each time I fed them; I started to give it to the neighbor cat who had started to visit during the onset of the pandemic. I thought about who I was at each of the parts of my life that Anakin had shared and how I'd changed. I grieved more than Anakin that week; I also grieved the loss of the different "versions" of myself.

***

While contemplating how to close this chapter, I realized that there isn't an ending. The song that plays in my head was crafted by Lennon and McCartney (1965): "There are places I remember/all my life, though some have changed/Some forever, not for better/Some have gone and some remain/All these places have their moments. . . . Though I know I'll never lose affection/For people and things that went before/I know I'll often stop and think about them" (track 10, 0:09). I'm still grieving; I will always be grieving. There isn't a moment at which my love for Guy, my desire to ask Aunt Mabel for her advice, or the longing to feel Anakin nestled up against me will cease. There isn't a way to fill the often-all-consuming void that accompanies the permanency of death that I sometimes feel, especially when the certainty of the next loss is imminent. As I'm writing this chapter, Luke is in the late stages of chronic kidney disease, and I've had to consult with a vet who does in-home euthanasia. We're not there yet, but we will be within a year. I long for the same degrees of freedom (Goldiamond, 1976) I had before each loss. I want to do the things we used to do and the things we planned to do but never did. Aunt Mabel and I were always going to clean her home office together, but she would suggest we sit and visit instead. Perhaps recognizing that the opportunity had passed, I cleaned her office while she was in hospice. In a way, I suppose we did clean the office together.

However, as uncomfortable as my grief is, and even though none of the losses I've experienced have gotten easier, I don't view it as pathological (see also Brasted & Callahan, 1984; Moynahan, 2001). I still don't know if being an experienced griever is a good thing or a bad thing (maybe it simply is). I've learned to own it and to ride the waves of grief as they come. At times I have had to be resilient, to be tough, often at my own expense and manifested in setting my own grief aside to accompany others and to do the tasks that they aren't able to do, that must be done because someone else is depending on me. I've learned to let go of the person I was before the loss; she isn't coming back. I've learned to spend time figuring out who I am again, trying to reconcile and love who I am after I've been changed by the loss. After each loss, the worst (and the best) parts of life have (seemingly) changed forever, yet I've learned to (eventually) find opportunity in loss. I will close, as I opened, with the wisdom of Adichie (2021): "Grief was the celebration of love, those who . . . were lucky to have loved . . . we have been so fortunate" (pp. 46, 51).

Notes

1. Great loss is often experienced, however, even in the absence of death.
2. Grief is a personal and individual process that takes different forms and even functions for the griever. I also believe that the form and function of the behaviors that comprise grieving change over time and as a function of one's experience. It is possible that transitioning into these roles was how my grief manifested.
3. I didn't have the opportunity to know my paternal grandparents. My father's father passed away when my dad was still in high school; his mother passed away when I was only 6 months old.
4. Dorothy also coordinated and planned a memorial service for Guy in Columbus. I still do not have the words to express how grateful I am for the kindness and generosity she offered me during this time and beyond.
5. This is not only restricted to academic settings; it is likely a symptom of modern life in the US as well.
6. It is impossible for me to describe all the ways in which Aunt Mabel was really great, so I have highlighted only a few here. Interested readers can read more about her life and accomplishments here: www.legacy.com/us/obituaries/belleville/name/mabel-otten-obituary?pid=164181340 and here Stremlow, M. V. (2014). *A history of the women marines, 1946–1977* (pp. 184–185). CreateSpace Independent Publishing Platform.
7. www.truthorfiction.com/during-wwii-lipstick-became-a-sign-of-patriotism/
8. Kyo and I became friends after he finished the master's program at The Chicago School. Ten years later he moved to Denton to begin the PhD program at UNT. He often looked after Anakin (and Luke who I'll introduce a bit later) when I would travel.
9. Guy and I adopted Luke, a roughly 10-week-old kitten, four years after we found Anakin. We were living in Ohio, and I went to the shelter to find an older cat no one wanted to adopt, someone who could keep Anakin company while I was at school and Guy was at work. Luke was screeching from a crate when I walked in. Not thinking much about it I picked him up and he immediately nestled into me and started purring. I walked around the shelter with him, looking for that old cat no one wanted. I didn't find it and as I started to put Luke back in his crate, he started that gut-wrenching meow again, so I picked him back up. Again, he nestled and started purring. The woman at the shelter looked at me and said, "should I get the paperwork?"

References

Adichie, C. N. (2021). *Notes on grief*. Knopf.

Averill, R., & Wisocki, P. A. (1981). Some observations on behavioral approaches to the treatment of grief among the elderly. In H. Sobel (Ed.), *Behavior therapy in terminal care: A humanistic approach* (pp. 125–150). Ballinger.

Brasted, W. S., & Callahan, E. J. (1984). A behavioral analysis of the grief process. *Behavior Therapy, 15*(5), 529–543. https://doi.org/10.1016/S0005-7894(84)80054-4

Calkin, A. B. (1990). Changes in behavior as the result of the death of a relative. *Journal of Precision Teaching, 7*(2), 74–78.

Calkin, A. B. (2001). Response to bereavement: A behavioural process. *European Journal of Behavior Analysis, 2*(2), 139–142. https://doi.org/10.1080/15021149.2001.11434188

Cihon, T. M., Becker, A., Ortu, D., & Glenn, S. S. (2020). Multiple perspectives on establishing a research lab for culturo-behavior science. In T. M. Cihon & M. A. Mattaini (Eds.), *Behavior science perspectives on culture and community*. Association for Behavior Analysis International Book Series. Behavior Science: Theory, Research, and Practice. Springer.

Cihon, T. M., Borba, A., Benvenuti, M., & Sandaker, I. (2021). Research and training in culturo-behavior science. *Behavior and Social Issues*. https://doi.org/10.1007/s42822-021-00076-w

Cihon, T. M., Kieta, A., & Glenn, S. (2017). Teaching behavior analysis with behavior analysis: 30 years of a work in progress. *European Journal of Behavior Analysis, 19*(2), 150–175. https://doi.org/10.1080/15021149.2017.1404393

Cihon, T. M., & Mattaini, M. A. (Eds.). (2020). *Behavior science perspectives on culture and community*. Association for Behavior Analysis International Book Series. Behavior Science: Theory, Research, and Practice. Springer.

Dillenburger, K. (2007). A behavior analytic perspective on victimology. *International Journal of Behavioral Consultation and Therapy*, *3*(3), 433–448. https://doi.org/10.1037/h0100817

Dillenburger, K., & Keenan, M. (1994). Bereavement: A behavioural process. *The Irish Journal of Psychology*, *15*(4), 524–539. https://doi.org/10.1080/03033910.1994.10558028

Dillenburger, K., & Keenan, M. (2001). Bereavement: A behavioural process. *European Journal of Behaviour Analysis*, *2*, 129–138. https://doi.org/10.1080/15021149.2001.11434187

Dillenburger, K., & Keenan, M. (2005). Bereavement: A D.I.S.C. analysis. *Behavior and Social Issues*, *14*(2), 92–112. https://doi.org/10.5210/bsi.v14i2.333

Fraley, L. E. (2001). Behaviorological principles for the analysis of bereavement. *European Journal of Behavior Analysis*, *2*(2), 143–153. https://doi.org/10.1080/15021149.2001.11434189

Glenn, S. S. (1988). Contingencies and metacontingencies: Toward a synthesis of behavior analysis and cultural materialism. *The Behavior Analyst*, *11*(2), 161–179. https://doi.org/10.1007/BF03392470

Glenn, S. S. (2004). Individual behavior, culture, and social change. *The Behavior Analyst*, *27*(2), 133–151. https://doi.org/10.1007/bf03393175

Goldiamond, I. (1976). Protection of human subjects and patients: A social contingency analysis of distinctions between research and practice, and its implications. *Behaviorism*, *4*, 1–41.

Guerin, B. (2001). Explanations of bereavement, grief, and trauma: The misuse of both mental and foundational terms. *European Journal of Behavior Analysis*, *2*(2), 154–161. http://doi.org/10.1080/15021149.2001.11434190

Keenan, M. (1996). Teaching about private events in the classroom. *Behavior and Social Issues*, *6*(2), 75–84. https://doi.org/10.5210/bsi.v6i2.283

Keenan, M. (1997). 'W'-ing: Teaching exercises for radical behaviourists. In K. Dillenburger, M. F. O'Reilly, & M. Keenan (Eds.), *Advances in behaviour analysis* (pp. 46–81). University College Dublin Press.

Kunkel, J. H. (1991). Apathy and irresponsibility in social systems. In P. A. Lamal (Ed.), *Behavioral analysis of societies and cultural practices*. Taylor & Francis Group.

Lennon, J., & McCartney, P. (1965). In my life [Recorded by the beatles]. In *Rubber soul* [vinyl]. Parlophone.

Massetti, G., & Fabiano, G. (2005). Thought stopping. In M. Hersen, J. Rosqvist, & A. M. Gross (Eds.), *Encyclopedia of behavior modification and cognitive behavior therapy* (pp. 1067–1068). Sage Publications. https://doi.org/10.4135/9781412950534.n2129

Mattaini, M. A. (2012). Guns: The data tell us . . . . *Behavior and Social Issues*, *21*(1), 1–4. https://doi.org/10.5210/bsi.v21i0.4346

Moynahan, L. (2001). Relatio ergo sum—a suggestive commentary upon Dillenburger and Keenan. *European Journal of Behavior Analysis*, *2*(2), 162–174. https://doi.org/10.1080/15021149.2001.11434191

Rakos, R. F. (2001). Bereavement: Preliminary behavior analytic hypotheses. *European Journal of Behavior Analysis*, *2*(2), 175–182. https://doi.org/10.1080/15021149.2001.11434192

Skinner, B. F. (1957). *Verbal Behavior*. Prentice Hall.

Stevens, C. (1974). Oh very young. In *Buddha and the chocolate box* [vinyl]. A&M.

Sulzer-Azaroff, B. (1999). Meeting life's challenges—strategies and stories: A view from the far side. *Behavior and Social Issues*, *9*(1–2), 55–60. https://doi.org/10.5210/bsi.v9i1.141

Tonneau, F. (2001). The observational analysis of behavior. *European Journal of Behavior Analysis*, *2*, 183–186. https://doi.org/10.1080/15021149.2001.11434193

23 Capitalizing on Applied Behavior Analysis

Within Our Retirement Years

Beth Sulzer-Azaroff

Capitalizing on Applied Behavior Analysis Within Our Retirement Years

To many of us who engage in the field of Applied Behavior Analysis, the concept of *retirement* seems almost irrelevant. Why is that? Because "Once a behavior analyst, always a behavior analyst." Perhaps we no longer are wage earners; nevertheless, generally we have a strong habitual tendency to view behavior through a functional analytic lens. Probably at some level, each of us recognizes the day will come when we no longer officially practice as behavior analysts. Consequently, wisdom suggests we use our knowledge and skills to prepare in advance for a happy, meaningful retirement. But, how can we accomplish that?

Just as we learned to analyze our own clients' behavior scientifically and to implement behavior-management procedures responsibly, we would be wise to recognize that we can apply those same practices to what we ourselves do, say, and think. So, when behavioral challenges arise in our own lives, we who share this perspective would be well advised to remind ourselves how fortunate we are to possess the tools to address those issues. At least that's been my approach. In general, I recognize that we can draw upon the very same behavioral principles we have used to guide our own scientific and professional practice:

- Identify and specifically describe the challenges facing us
- Formulate a set of behavioral objectives to address those challenges
- Choose a system for assessing progress
- Plan the antecedent and consequential events we need to initiate to achieve those objectives
- Implement the plan
- Monitor our progress
- Record the ongoing results
- Analyze the results to determine how effectively those stimulus arrangements generated them

To contextualize this perspective, allow me briefly to review my own history in relation to ABA:

I first learned about this field from my late husband, Edward S. Sulzer. In the 1950s, as a doctoral student of clinical psychology at Columbia University's Teachers College, Ed enrolled in a course taught by Fred Keller. Keller, a disciple, close colleague, and friend of B. F. Skinner, rapidly guided Ed and his fellow students toward the then-novel perspective that behavior, human and otherwise, is lawful and modifiable—that it is a function of individuals' constitutions, their learning histories and the sets of contingencies of reinforcement that affect their thoughts, feelings, and actions. In contrast with what had struck me as the

DOI: 10.4324/9781003216773-27

vague psychoanalytic perspectives of the day, I felt comfortable with the behavior analytic viewpoint, and the scientific methods and the experimental tools the adherents to this perspective developed.

While employed as an elementary school teacher in a racially and culturally diverse neighborhood in Manhattan, I found the lessons Ed shared began to pay off. I learned how to evoke and, especially, to reinforce my students' academic and social progress with attention, praise, preferred assignments, enjoyable activities, and even long-term rewards like opportunities to enjoy small group field trips and larger group celebrations. Applying behavior analysis was magical, in the sense that my students' disciplinary issues and my own related frustrations began to fade, as they increasingly became more accomplished learners.

Fast forward to when, several years later, Ed joined the Medical School faculty of the University of Minnesota, and I, then mother of two young boys, enrolled in its doctoral program in Educational Psychology. There, I had the good fortune to serve as a graduate assistant to Kenneth McCorquodale. Professor McCorquodale, a former colleague and disciple of B. F. Skinner, asked me to help prepare examination questions based on "The Analysis of Behavior," Skinner's programmed instructional text. Along with ongoing conversations with Ed related to his own continuously evolving behavioral perspective, that experience, plus my participation in Robert Orlando's behavior analysis-oriented course in developmental disabilities, solidified the direction of my career.

Just after completing the collection of data for my doctoral dissertation, I became pregnant once again. Simultaneously, Ed was offered, and agreed to assume, the directorship of the Behavior Analysis program at Southern Illinois University, Carbondale. Once settled there, right on the cusp of submitting my doctoral thesis, my daughter Lenore was born. Simultaneously, an opening arose in the Educational Psychology department. The chairman encouraged me to apply, and I agreed, provided I'd be able to maintain a part-time schedule. Fortunately, the administration agreed to the part-time caveat, during which I would teach a course in educational psychology and spend a number of hours counseling in the clinic.

Throughout the next few years, Ed, our children, and I enjoyed a stimulating life full of love and satisfaction. By the time Lenore was three and attending Victoria Azrin's pre-school, I switched to a full-time position. My course offerings expanded to include Educational Psychology, two semesters of Applied Behavior Analysis, a series of related special-topic and research seminars, and an active program of research. Among our joint research projects was a collaborative analysis of the impact of a class-wide computerized quiz feedback system (Sulzer & Sulzer, 1962). Additionally, of course, we enjoyed the stimulation and support of Ed's behaviorally oriented fellow faculty (Guy Renzaglia, Nathan Azrin, Ted Ayllon, Donald Hake, Harris Ruben, Robert Campbell) along with that of the enthusiastic and dedicated students in the Behavior Modification Program, who added to the mix. That continued for several satisfying years, until disaster suddenly struck, in the form of cancer claiming Ed's life at age 39. In the aftermath, our youngsters and I, fortunately, were able to manage, because by then my faculty position had evolved into a tenured associate professorship.

What followed? Again, long story short. Two years later, a colleague/friend, Jacqueline, and I booked a Caribbean cruise over the winter holidays. The second day out, I met Leonid ("Lee") Azaroff, who identified himself as a professor of Materials Science at the University of Connecticut. A week later, while still on the cruise, we tentatively began to plan our future together. Soon thereafter, Lee and the children became acquainted. Scheduled to take his sabbatical leave that spring semester, Lee elected to join us in Carbondale and we married that March, accompanied by his niece, Deanna and her husband William, who were to occupy the role of our additional offspring. With Lee's leave coming to an end in June, our newly amalgamated family moved to Connecticut.

Then my job hunt began. Apparently, in general, the search committees at UConn were not kindly disposed to hiring women at the time. So, despite my fairly strong credentials (a textbook, a good number of publications, positive student ratings, etc.), I broadened my search for a university faculty position. Fortunately, by the following year, thanks to chair Richard Louttit and other members of the search committee, I was invited to join the Department of Psychology at The University of Massachusetts, Amherst.

There, before very long (given a pattern of mentoring a stream of productive graduate students, positive student ratings, multiple textbook authorships and research publications, plus a list of mentored doctoral students) the department promoted me to a full professorship within a comparatively short time period. And I remained there, contentedly, for 19 years. Of course, those years at UMass included numerous other professional events: teaching *educational psychology, applied behavior analysis; research methods* as well as conducting research and publishing over 100, usually collaborative, research and didactic papers, and serving as reviewer of grants in the fields of developmental disabilities and occupational safety. I also was elected to several leadership positions in *The Association for Behavior Analysis International* (e.g., Board Member and President) and of Division 25 (*The Experimental Analysis of Behavior*) and as member and, later, chair of the Board of Scientific Affairs of *The American Psychological Association.*

One especially rewarding feature of my Amherst experience grew out of the collaboration and friendship that Ellen Reese and I established early on. "Ellie," a faculty member of Mount Holyoke College (a co-member of our five-college consortium in the area) had published a text on behavior analysis that I had assigned in some of my classes at SIU (in fact, a few years later, Ellie and I produced a joint text: "Applying Behavior analysis: A Program for Developing Professional Competence").

Meanwhile, my three essentially perfect offspring and a bevy of the talented and highly motivated undergraduate and graduate students I was privileged to mentor progressed toward becoming the fine accomplished scientists and professionals they have. That is where the part about retirement comes in, and how it all came about:

One day, Lee returned home bubbling with excitement after having visited our dentist. Gerry, a friendly, garrulous fellow, had just returned from a professional meeting in Naples, Florida. During the teeth-cleaning process, Gerry entertained Leonid with an enticing tale about Pelican Bay, the community in which the meeting had taken place. Aptly named for its locale as a winter roost for these amazing creatures, Pelican Bay is a planned community, located directly on the southwestern coast of Florida. It contains about three miles of coastal beach, backed by about a third of a mile of mangroves. Further inland, a few square miles are dedicated to multistoried, low-rise and private residences plus commercial properties. Adjoining the Gulf shore, a series of paths (berms) and boardwalks allow passage through the mangroves where wildlife abounds, to the beach and its sparkling Gulf waters, plus a number of other appealing cultural and commercial amenities. In the course of the conversation, Gerry also noted that developers of a modern, creatively designed high-rise residential building had encountered difficulty selling units to its more conservative Mid-western market. So, to promote sales, the developers had decided to offer units at a substantial discount.

Now, given my having fought the cold country elements while living in Minnesota, Connecticut, and Massachusetts, and having traversed the university campuses during many freezing winters, this sounded like heaven to me. "Let's go see," I enthused. So, we booked our flights to Southwest Florida for the following weekend. Alas, I was laid low by a respiratory infection that weekend, but I encouraged Lee to check it out on his own. His phone call on the evening of his arrival was charged with enthusiasm. The place was really enticing, just as Gerry had described.

Another major appeal was that a state university, "Florida Gulf Coast University," was slated to open shortly in the area. As I was not yet prepared to retire fully from my beloved profession, that heightened the appeal. Needless to say, during our joint visit the following weekend, I too fell in love with the place: the following week we purchased an 11th-floor unit at *The Heron*. Yet, neither Lee nor I were prepared to retire from our respective professorships at that time, so we decided to rent out our new property to a retired bachelor for two years. Then, at that point, we cut our academic ties, resumed possession of our Heron unit, and designated it as our winter home.

Again, as luck would have it, another opportunity presented itself the year we moved into our unit. During the spring meeting of the Association for Behavior Analysis, just prior to my UMass retirement, I ran into an old friend, Jack Gewirtz. Jack was currently serving as a member of the Psychology faculty of Florida International University, in Coral Gables—adjacent to Miami. As soon as I mentioned that Lee and I would be spending our winters in South Florida, he responded, "Come join us." I expressed my unwillingness to assume another full-time position, especially one involving a 2+-hour commute each way.

"So, teach part-time," he countered. Ultimately, we did arrange for me to make single trips to Coral Gables for bi-weekly, full days of teaching and student mentoring, spanning a two-year period. Those students, many natives of other countries and willing to share so much about their disparate backgrounds, were a joy to teach. Had it not been for the very difficult commute, especially being blinded by the sun's rays during the westerly return home to Naples, I would gladly have continued in that position.

So, what came next? Apparently, I seem to be programmed to seize fleeting but promising opportunities. And others did come along. The Pelican Bay Community was beginning to become well established. Simultaneously, a group of forward-looking, active ladies assembled and formed an organization to provide their peers with social and educational experiences. Women with their own particular interests and talents would collaborate to form a broad array of interest groups and invite their fellow female residents to attend. My offering, labeled "*Take Charge of Your Life*," comprised a series of workshops in which participants would choose a behavioral goal to pursue for themselves. Each session focused on a fundamental behavior-analytic skill (e.g., using operational language; selecting constructive objectives; planning and implementing and monitoring the effects of behavior analytic applications—primarily positive reinforcement and shaping—and, monitoring, evaluating, and reporting progress). The goals the participants actually chose represented a broad array of interests, from undertaking crafts projects, learning new languages, trying new recipes, to adjusting the way they organized their households or interacted with their spouses. As it turned out, each of the dozen or so members demonstrated progress toward their goals and completed their season's objective to their apparent satisfaction.

Additional opportunities to share my knowledge of applied behavior analysis with others presented themselves along the way. One, in particular, was an invitation to both Lee (Leonid V. Azaroff) and myself to teach senior citizens locally via continuing education. So, while he prepared a series of sessions related to his own specialty area, based upon his recently completed text, *Physics Over Easy: Breakfasts with Beth and Physics* (2010), I assembled and offered material on applying behavior analytic concepts to planning and enjoying a satisfying life in retirement. Each member of my small group chose individually to pursue a goal and to demonstrate progress toward attaining that goal based on that material. Examples included volunteer work, exercise, diet, or other self- or other-management projects (encouraging their recently retired spouses to participate in household activities). They defended their goal selections, including the willingness to participate of any others persons involved. Then we would meet bi-weekly to share and refine such topics as the consent of other participants, measures of performance under baseline and intervention conditions, plus those interventions themselves (I did intentionally help steer them toward selecting what appeared to be somewhat challenging yet achievable goals and manageable procedures).

Surely, I would have repeated that program, but at that point, Charles Hamad (to whom I'd previously provided consulting services, at Southbury Connecticut Training School) dropped an irresistible opportunity in my lap: an invitation to join him in applying for a federally sponsored project which involved designing, implementing, and evaluating a specialized series of *distance learning* courses on the *analysis of behavior, focused on teaching parents of young children on the autism spectrum to work with those youngsters*. Having for a number of years managed a face-to-face graduate training program with that client focus at UMass, my interest was aroused. Would it be feasible to try to meet such a challenge from a distance? Could it function as well as face-to-face instruction?

We proposed a three-year project. In essence, it would include designing and implementing two parallel instructional programs: one a face-to-face sequence; the other strictly internet-based. The content would cover *Applied Behavior Analysis* with a special focus on developmental disabilities. Over a two-year span of time, students would be responsible for mastering both specific didactic material as well as applying a program each developed with actual clients. In addition, to compare the outcome of the two distinct instructional formats, I would use an identical curriculum to teach a face-to-face course at Florida International University. To our delight, the proposal was funded and we constituted our team. Dr. Hamad enticed Dr. Richard Fleming (my former doctoral student from years back, and by then, himself, recently retired from the University of West Virginia faculty) to join us. Richard agreed to teach and analyze the impact of one distance-learning four-course sequence, and I undertook to do the same with two cohorts: one under the distance-learning format and another at the newly operational Florida Gulf Coast University.

When actual clients are involved, we, as supervisors, assume an obligation to monitor the performance of our own students (those involved in learning and applying behavior-management strategies) along with the impact on *their* clientele. Previously, over many years, we had accomplished that purpose by asking students to report their experiences. Then, we could review the data they had collected and physically observe our students' and their own client's or student's progresses. When working from a distance, though, such monitoring formats would not be feasible because the locations of our eventual students would be widely distributed. This having been the very early 2000s, the internet had yet to realize its much broader potential. So, we compromised by requesting that our students video-tape their assigned teaching sessions with their youngsters and mail us the tapes (although a bit awkward for them, they did regularly comply, thereby reassuring us of their adherence to our instructions and the veracity of their reporting).

Our curriculum included a two-year sequence of courses, including the requirements that they complete assigned reading on the specialized topic of behavior analysis as applied to youngsters on the autism spectrum, achieve weekly quiz scores of 85% or above based on those readings (with multiple forms available for retakes, as necessary), provide video-recorded evidence of their completion of assigned field assignments, which included applications of their newly acquired knowledge and skills with actual clients, as well as contribute, at least once, to each of their classes' group discussions.

I, myself, arranged an additional source of quality assurance by undertaking to teach the same curriculum face-to-face, at Florida Gulf Coast University. That class met regularly, replicating the distance learning assignments, including discussing and critiquing the assignments.

The results were heartening. Practically all our students remained throughout, fulfilling their obligations. We assumed that the youngsters with special needs with whom they worked benefitted; to whatever extent, as usual, generally remains a mystery. In one instance, though, a distance learning student has continued to contact me periodically. Early in the course sequence, her son had been diagnosed as "autistic." Age 3+ at the time, he lacked functional communication skills and expressed many typical "autistic behaviors." By the end of the course, his mother had demonstrated star performance academically, and he, in turn, began to display evidence of ongoing progress, which we assumed was a function of her successfully applying behavioral principles with her son.

Several years later, the Association for Behavior Analysis International was scheduled to meet in Chicago. That boy's mother, who lived in a nearby state, contacted me to say she would like to bring her family to meet me. Of course, I was delighted at the prospect. And so, it became my privilege to become personally acquainted with the woman, her husband, her mother, and her then-eight-year-old boy. It was truly amazing to be able to have an actual conversation with the youngster, who, a number of years previously, I had watched on video tape manifesting all the characteristics of autism (even later, just this past summer, both this mother and the young man himself contacted me to announce that he had graduated from college and had been accepted into a highly specialized graduate program).

Around the turn of the century, another fascinating opportunity emerged from my affiliation with The Cambridge Center for Behavioral Studies. While serving as a member of the Center's Board, I had the good fortune to become acquainted with fellow board member Dwight Harshbarger. In a casual discussion of how metacontingencies (configuration of positive and aversive consequences) could affect organizational bottom-line results, Dwight and I hit it off immediately. I told him about my performance-management work with administrators of service and educational organizations. He, having previously served as a consultant to a major sports-shoe organization regarding performance management, enlightened me about his own efforts to treat the related challenges in the commercial sector. The synergy seemed instantaneous, especially because each of us previously had focused on that topic in our university teaching (he at the University of West Virginia, I at the University of Massachusetts.) As a result, we arranged to meet to explore that topic further, eventually arranging for the two of us to visit a Reebok shoe production plant in Bangkok, Thailand.

We then invested a few days observing the interpersonal interactions among and between supervisors and workers at the central Bangkok plant. That led us to conclude that shifting supervisors' emphasis from punishing (scolding, deriding) workers' poor performance, to reinforcing (complimenting, otherwise periodically acknowledging) their meritorious performance promised to improve the situation. So we arranged a series of tutorials directed toward that purpose.

The plant's owner, having studied in the US, was fluent in English, to our good fortune. So, he could translate for the managers a series of our behavior-based lectures we centered on, and the group discussed the following aspects of worker performance:

- What is a good job? (Performance objectives)
- Can I do a good job? (Initial baseline assessment)
- Am I doing a good job? (Extended baseline assessment)
- What happens when I do a good job? (Schedule of social reinforcement)

Naturally, we illustrated and emphasized the value of observing and providing workers with specific, positive feedback. Assisted by a translator, then and during subsequent visits, we toured the plant several times, providing our own feedback to the owner and his managerial staff. To our mutual delight, product quality improved substantially (see Sulzer-Azaroff & Harshbarger, 1995), plus, we noted informally, associated worker and managerial satisfaction seemed to have improved.

As one might imagine, personally I found work of that nature to be extremely rewarding. Yet, it exacted its costs on me too, in terms of time away from Leonid and health-wise (I'd managed to contract some sort of nasty illness during the last Bangkok visit). So, from then on, I limited any further organizational or consulting activities to state-side venues, especially in the areas of performance management.

Fortunately, several opportunities to continue my active participation in the Applied Behavior Analysis field also presented themselves. Especially rewarding among those was the opportunity to serve on the Executive Committee and as president of The Association for Behavior Analysis International (ABAI) and of The Berkshire Association for Behavior Analysis and Therapy, and in related capacities in various other behavior analytic organizations.

As a burgeoning retirement community, Naples, Florida residents involved themselves in promoting an array of opportunities, including among others, theater groups, museums, a zoo, and adult education offerings. Both Leonid and I participated in the latter: he (a retired professor of Materials Science) preparing and accompanying his topic of physics for an adult lay audience with a text he entitled *Physics Over Easy: Breakfasts with Beth and Physics* (2010).

My own offering was a general survey and discussion of applied behavior analysis, peppered with illustrations relevant to the lives of folks in retirement.

Of course, retirement meant greater flexibility to spend time with my family. Gradually, though, the nature of some of my activities has shifted over time. I did indulge in the pleasure of writing a mystery story, *Who Killed My Daddy? A Behavioral Safety Fable* (2009), designed as a vehicle for teaching organizational personnel about behavioral safety systems. I also assisted Andy Bondy, Anne O. Hoffman, and Catherine Horton in preparing the 2009 edition of "The Picture Exchange Communication System (PECS): What Do the Data Say?" And, of course, our team's (e.g., Mayer et al., 2021) periodic revisions of *Behavior Analysis for Lasting Change* have enabled us to remain fairly current with the research literature in our field.

And, for me, at least, each new tidbit of information seems to continue to influence how I address life's challenges and enjoy a satisfying life in retirement. Perhaps, as you yourself contemplate your own retirement, in the near or distant future, some of these examples will inspire you to refer to the applied behavior analytic body of knowledge to guide your direction and to enrich your life.

References

Azároff, L. V. (2010). *Physics over easy: Breakfasts with Beth and physics* (2nd ed.). World Scientific.

Mayer, G. R., Wallace, M., & Sulzer-Azaroff, B. (2021). *Behavior analysis for lasting change* (5th ed.). Sloan Publishing.

Sulzer-Azaroff, B. (2009). *Who killed my daddy? A behavioral safety fable.* Cambridge Center for Behavioral Studies.

Sulzer-Azaroff, B., & Harshbarger, D. (1995). Putting fear to flight: While enhancing quality of performance. *Quality Progress, 28*(12), 61–65.

Sulzer-Azaroff, B., Hoffman, A. O., Horton, C. B., Bondy, A., & Frost, L. (2009). The picture exchange communication system (PECS): What do the data say? *Focus on Autism and Other Developmental Disabilities, 24*(2), 89–103. https://doi.org/10.1177/1088357609332743

Index

Note: Page numbers in *italics* indicate a figure and page numbers in **bold** indicate a table on the corresponding page.

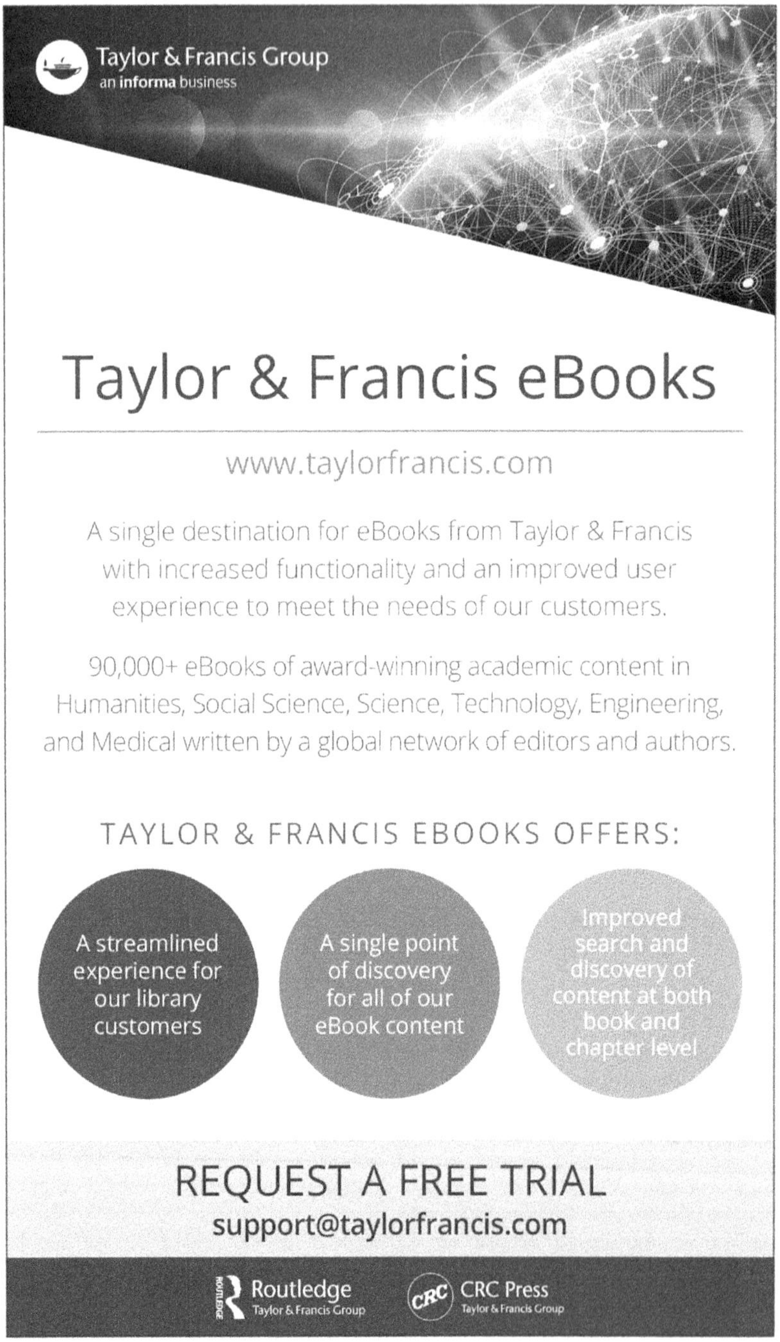
Taylor & Francis Group
an informa business
Taylor & Francis eBooks
www.taylorfrancis.com
A single destination for eBooks from Taylor & Francis with increased functionality and an improved user experience to meet the needs of our customers.
90,000+ eBooks of award-winning academic content in Humanities, Social Science, Science, Technology, Engineering, and Medical written by a global network of editors and authors.
TAYLOR & FRANCIS EBOOKS OFFERS:
A streamlined experience for our library customers
A single point of discovery for all of our eBook content
Improved search and discovery of content at both book and chapter level
REQUEST A FREE TRIAL
support@taylorfrancis.com
Routledge
Taylor & Francis Group
CRC Press
Taylor & Francis Group

For Product Safety Concerns and Information please contact our EU representative GPSR@taylorandfrancis.com
Taylor & Francis Verlag GmbH, Kaufingerstraße 24, 80331 München, Germany

www.ingramcontent.com/pod-product-compliance
Ingram Content Group UK Ltd.
Pitfield, Milton Keynes, MK11 3LW, UK
UKHW050234200926
475702UK00020B/3022
9781032107301